THE ENCYCLOPÆDIA BRITANNICA
A DICTIONARY OF ARTS, SCIENCES, LITERATURE AND GENERAL INFORMATION
ELEVENTH EDITION

VOLUME XII SLICE II

Gloss to Gordon, Charles George

GLOSS, GLOSSARY, &c. The Greek word γλῶσσα (whence our "gloss"), meaning originally a tongue, then a language or dialect, gradually came to denote any obsolete, foreign, provincial, technical or otherwise peculiar word or use of a word (see Arist. *Rhet.* iii. 3. 2). The making of collections and explanations1 of such γλῶσσαι was at a comparatively early date a well-recognized form of literary activity. Even in the 5th century B.C., among the many writings of Abdera was included a treatise entitled Περὶ Ὁμήρου ἤ ὀρθοεπείης καὶ γλωσσέων. It was not, however, until the Alexandrian period that the γλωσσογράφοι, glossographers (writers of glosses), or glossators, became numerous. Of many of these perhaps even the names have perished; but Athenaeus the grammarian alone (*c.* A.D. 250) alludes to no fewer than thirty-five. Among the earliest was Philetas of Cos (d. *c.* 290 B.C.), the elegiac poet, to whom Aristarchus dedicated the treatise Πρὸς Φιλπτᾶν; he was the compiler of a lexicographical work, arranged probably according to subjects, and entitled Ἄτακτα or Γῶσσαι (sometimes Ἄτακτοι γλῶσσαι). Next came his disciple Zenodotus of Ephesus (*c.* 280 B.C.), one of the earliest of the Homeric critics and the compiler of Γλῶσσαι Ὁμηρικαί; Zenodotus in turn was succeeded by his greater pupil Aristophanes of Byzantium (*c.* 200 B.C.), whose great compilation Περὶ λέξεων (still partially preserved in that of Pollux), is known to have included Ἀττικαὶ λέξεις, Λακωνικαὶ γλῶσσαι, and the like. From the school of Aristophanes issued more than one glossographer of name,—Diodorus, Artemidorus (Γλῶσσαι, and a collection of λέξεις ὀψαρτυτικαί), Nicander of Colophon (Γλῶσσαι, of which some twenty-six fragments still survive), and Aristarchus (*c.* 210 B.C.), the famous critic, whose numerous labours included an arrangement of the Homeric vocabulary (λέξεις) in the order of the books. Contemporary with the last named was Crates of Mallus, who, besides making some new contributions to Greek lexicography and dialectology, was the first to create at Rome a taste for similar investigations in connexion with the Latin idioms. From his school proceeded Zenodotus of Mallus, the compiler of Ἐθνικαὶ λέξεις or γλῶσσαι, a work said to have been designed chiefly to support the views of the school of Pergamum as to the allegorical interpretation of Homer.2 Of later date were Didymus (Chalcenterus, *c.* 50 B.C.), who made collections of λέξεις τραγωδουμέναι κωμικαί, &c.; Apollonius Sophista (*c.* 20 B.C.), whose Homeric Lexicon has come down to modern times; and Neoptolemus, known distinctively as ὁ γλωσσογράφος. In the beginning of the 1st century of the Christian era Apion, a grammarian and rhetorician at Rome during the reigns of Tiberius and Claudius, followed up the labours of Aristarchus and other predecessors with Γλῶσσαι Ὁμηρικαί, and a treatise Περὶ τῆς Ῥωμαϊκῆς διαλέκτου; Heliodorus or Herodorus was another almost contemporary glossographer; Erotian also, during the reign of Nero, prepared a special glossary for the writings of Hippocrates, still preserved. To this period also Pamphilus, the author of the Λειμών, from which Diogenian and Julius Vestinus afterwards drew so largely, most probably belonged. In the following century one of the most prominent workers in this department of literature was Aelius Herodianus, whose treatise Περὶ μονήρους λέξεως has been edited in modern times, and whose Ἐπιμερισμοί we still possess in an abridgment; also Pollux, Diogenian (Λέξις παντοδαπή), Julius Vestinus (Ἐπιτομή τῶν Παμφίλου γλωσσῶν) and especially Phrynichus, who flourished towards the close of the 2nd century, and whose *Eclogae nominum et verborum Atticorum* has frequently been edited. To the 4th century belongs Ammonius of Alexandria (*c.* 389), who wrote Περὶ ὁμοίων καὶ διαφόρων λέξεων, a dictionary of words used in senses different from those in which they had 125been employed by older and approved writers. Of somewhat later date is the well-known Hesychius, whose often-edited Λεξικόν superseded all previous works of the kind; Cyril, the celebrated patriarch of Alexandria, also contributed somewhat to the advancement of glossography by hisΣυναγωγὴ τῶν πρὸς διάφορον σημασίαν διαφόρως τονουμένων λέξεων; while Orus, Orion, Philoxenus and the two Philemons also belong to this period. The works of Photius, Suidas and Zonaras, as also the *Etymologicum magnum*, to which might be added the *Lexica Sangermania* and the*Lexica Segueriana*, are referred to in the article DICTIONARY.

To a special category of technical glossaries belongs a large and important class of works relating to the law-compilations of Justinian. Although the emperor forbade under severe penalties all commentaries (ὑπομνήματα) on his legislation (*Const. Deo Auctore*, sec. 12; *Const. Tanta*, sec. 21), yet indices (ἴνδικες) and references (παράτιτλα), as well as translations (ἑρμηνεῖαι κατὰ πόδα) and paraphrases (ἑρμηνεῖαι εἰς πλάτος), were expressly permitted, and lavishly produced. Among the numerous compilers of alphabetically arranged λέξεις Ῥωμαϊκαί or Λατεινικαί, andγλῶσσαι νομικαί (glossae nomicae), Cyril and Philoxenus are particularly noted; but the authors of παραγραφαί, or σημειώσεις, whether ἔξωθενor ἔσωθεν κείμεναι, are too numerous to mention. A collection of these παραγραφαί τῶν παλαιῶν, combined with νέαι παραγραφαί on the revised code called τὰ βασιλικά, was made about the middle of the 12th century by a disciple of Michael Hagiotheodorita. This work is known as the *Glossa ordinaria* τῶν βασιλικῶν.3

In Italy also, during the period of the Byzantine ascendancy, various glossae (glosae) and scholia on the Justinian code were produced4; particularly the Turin gloss (reprinted by Savigny), to which, apart from later additions, a date prior to 1000 is usually assigned. After the total extinction of the Byzantine authority in the West the study of law became one of the free arts, and numerous schools for its cultivation were instituted. Among the earliest of these was that of Bologna, where Pepo (1075) and Irnerius (1100-1118) began to give their expositions. They had a numerous following, who, besides delivering exegetical lectures ("ordinariae" on the *Digest* and *Code*, "extraordinariae" on the rest of the *Corpus juris civilis*), also wrote Glossae, first interlinear, afterwards marginal.5 The series of these glossators was closed by Accursius (*q.v.*) with the compilation known as the *Glossa ordinaria* or *magistralis*, the authority of which soon became very great, so that ultimately it came to be a recognized maxim, "Quod non agnoscit glossa, non agnoscit curia."6 For some account of the glossators on the canon law, see CANON LAW.

In late classical and medieval Latin, *glosa* was the vulgar and romanic (*e.g.* in the early 8th century Corpus Glossary, and the late 8th century Leiden Glossary), *glossa* the learned form (Varro, *De ling. Lat.* vii. 10; Auson. *Epigr.* 127. 2 (86. 2), written in Greek, Quint, i. 1. 34). The diminutive *glossula* occurs in Diom. 426. 26 and elsewhere. The same meaning has *glossarium* (Gell. xviii. 7. 3 *glossaria* = γλωσσάριον), which also occurs in the modern sense of "glossary" (Papias, "unde *glossarium* dictum quod omnium fere partium glossas contineat"), as do the words *glossa, glossae, glossulae, glossemata* (Steinmeyer, *Alth. Gloss.* iv. 408, 410), expressed in later times by *dictionarium, dictionarius, vocabularium, vocabularius* (see DICTIONARY). *Glossa* and *glossema* (Varro vii. 34. 107; Asinius Gallus, ap. Suet. *De gramm.* 22; Fest. 166b. 8, 181a. 18; Quint. i. 8. 15, &c.) are synonyms, signifying (*a*) the word which requires explanation; or (*b*) such a word (called *lemma*) together with the interpretation (*interpretamentum*); or (*c*) the interpretation alone (so first in the *Anecd. Helv.*).

Latin, like Greek glossography, had its origin chiefly in the practical wants of students and teachers, of whose names we only know a few. No doubt even in classical times collections of glosses ("glossaries") were compiled, to which allusion seems to be made by Varro (*De ling. Lat.* vii. 10, "tesca, aiunt sancta esse qui glossas scripserunt") and Verrius-Festus (166b .6, "naucum ... glossematorum ... scriptures fabae grani quod haereat in fabulo"), but it is not known to what extent Varro, for instance, used them, or retained their original forms. The *scriptores glossematorum* were distinguished from the learned glossographers like Aurelius Opilius (cf. his *Musae*, ap. Suet. *De gramm.* 6; Gell. i. 25. 17; Varro vii. 50, 65, 67, 70, 79, 106), Servius Clodius (Varro vii. 70. 106), Aelius Stilo, L. Ateius Philol., whose *liber glossematorum* Festus mentions (181a. 18).

Verrius Flaccus and his epitomists, Festus and Paulus, have preserved many treasures of early glossographers who are now lost to us. He copied Aelius Stilo (Reitzenstein, "Verr. Forsch.," in vol. i. of *Breslauer philol. Abhandl.*, p. 88; Kriegshammer, *Comm. phil. Ien.* vii. 1. 74 sqq.), Aurelius Opilius, Ateius Philol., the treatise *De obscuris Catonis* (Reitzenstein, *ib.* 56. 92). He often made use of Varro (Willers, *De Verrio Flacco*, Halle, 1898), though not of his *ling. lat.* (Kriegshammer, 74 sqq.); and was also acquainted with later glossographers. Perhaps we owe to him the *glossae asbestos* (Goetz, *Corpus*, iv.; *id., Rhein. Mus.* xl. 328). Festus was used by Ps.-Philoxenus (Dammann, "De Festo Ps.-Philoxeni auctore," *Comm. Ien.* v. 26 sqq.), as appears from the *glossae ab absens* (Goetz, "De Astrabae Pl. tragmentis," *Ind. Ien.*, 1893, iii. sqq.). The distinct connexions with Nonius need not be ascribed to borrowing, as Plinius and Caper may have been used (P. Schmidt, *De Non. Marc. auctt. gramm.* 145; Nettleship, *Lect. and Ess. 229*; Fröhde, *De Non. Marc. et Verrio Flacco*, 2; W. M. Lindsay, "Non. Marc.," *Dict. of Repub. Latin*, 100, &c.).

The *bilingual* (Gr.-Lat., Lat.-Gr.) glossaries also point to an early period, and were used by the grammarians (1) to explain the peculiarities (*idiomata*) of the Latin language by comparison with the Greek, and (2) for instruction in the two languages (Charis. 254. 9, 291. 7, 292. 16 sqq.; Marschall, *De Q. Remmii P. libris gramm.* 22; Goetz, *Corp. gloss. lat.* ii. 6).

For the purposes of grammatical instruction (Greek for the Romans, Latin for the Hellenistic world), we have systematic works, a translation of Dositheus and the so-called *Hermeneutica*, parts of which may be dated as early as the 3rd century A.D., and lexica (cf. Schoenemann, *De lexicis ant.* 122; Knaack, in *Phil. Rundsch.*, 1884, 372; Traube, in *Byzant. Ztschr.* iii. 605; David, *Comment. Ien.* v. 197 sqq.).

The most important remains of bilingual glossaries are two well-known lexica; one (Latin-Greek), formerly attributed (but wrongly, see Rudorff, in *Abh.. Akad. Berl.*, 1865, 220 sq.; Loewe, *Prodr.* 183, 190; Mommsen, *C.I.L.* v. 8120; A. Dammann, *De Festo Pseudo-philoxeni auctore*,

2

12 sqq.; Goetz, Corp. ii. 1-212) to Philoxenus (consul A.D. 525), clearly consists of two closely allied glossaries (containing glosses to Latin authors, as Horace, Cicero, Juvenal, Virgil, the Jurists, and excerpts from Festus), worked into one by some Greek grammarian, or a person who worked under Greek influence (his alphabet runs A, B, G, D, E, &c.); the other (Greek-Latin) is ascribed to Cyril (Stephanus says it was found at the end of some of his writings), and is considered to be a compilation of not later than the 6th century (Macrobius is used, and the *Cod. Harl.*, which is the source of all the other MSS., belongs to the 7th century); cf. Goetz, *Corp.* ii. 215-483, 487-506, praef. *ibid.* p. xx. sqq. Furthermore, the bilingual medico-botanic glossaries had their origin in old lists of plants, as Ps.-Apuleius in the treatise *De herbarum virtutibus*, and Ps.-Dioscorides (cf. M. Wellmann, *Hermes*, xxxiii. 360 sqq., who thinks that the latter work is based on Pamphilus, *q.v.*; Goetz, Corp. iii.); the glossary, entitled *Hermeneuma*, printed from the *Cod. Vatic.* reg. Christ. 1260, contains names of diseases.

Just as grammar developed, so we see the original form of the glosses extend. If *massucum edacem* in Placidus indicates the original form, the allied gloss of Festus (*masucium edacem a mandendo scilicet*) shows an etymological addition. Another extension consists in adding special references to the original source, as *e.g.* at the gloss *Ocrem* (Fest. 181a. 17), which is taken from Ateius Philol. In this way collections arose like the *priscorum verborum cum exemplis*, a title given by Fest. (218b. 10) to a particular work. Further the *glossae veterum* (Charis. 242. 10); the *glossae antiquitatum* (*id.* 229. 30); the *idonei vocum antiquarum enarratores* (Gell. xviii. 6. 8); the *libri rerum verborumque veterum* (*id.* xiii. 24. 25). L. 126 Cincius, according to Festus (330b. 2), wrote *De verbis priscis*; Santra, *De antiquitate verborum* (Festus 277a. 2).

Of Latin glossaries of the first four centuries of the Roman emperors few traces are left, if we except Verrius-Festus. Charis, 229. 30, speaks of *glossae antiquitatum* and 242. 10 of *glossae veterum*, but it is not known whether these glosses are identic, or in what relation they stand to the *glossemata per litteras Latinas ordine composita*, which were incorporated with the works of this grammarian according to the index in Keil, p. 6. Latin glosses occur in Ps.-Philoxenus, and Nonius must have used Latin glossaries; there exists a *glossarium Plautinum* (Ritschl, *Op.* ii. 234 sqq.), and the bilingual glossaries have been used by the later grammarian Martyrius; but of this early period we know by name only Fulgentius and Placidus, who is sometimes called Luctatius Placidus, by confusion with the Statius scholiast, with whom the *glossae Placidi* have no connexion. All that we know of him tends to show that he lived in North Africa (like Fulgentius and Nonius and perhaps Charisius) in the 6th century, from whence his glosses came to Spain, and were used by Isidore and the compiler of the *Liber glossarum* (see below). These glosses we know from (1) Codices Romani (15th and 16th century); (2) the *Liber glossarum*; (3) the Cod. Paris. nov. acquis. 1298 (saec. xi.), a collection of glossaries, in which the Placidus-glosses are kept separate from the others, and still retain traces of their original order (cf. the editions published by A. Mai, *Class. auct.* iii. 427-503, and Deuerling, 1875; Goetz, *Corp.* v.; P. Karl, "De Placidi glossis," *Comm. Ien.* vii. 2. 99, 103 sqq.; Loewe, *Gloss. Nom.*86; F. Bücheler, in *Thesaur. gloss. emend.*). His collection includes glosses from Plautus and Lucilius.

(Fabius Planciades) Fulgentius (*c.* A.D. 468-533) wrote *Expositio sermonum antiquorum* (ed. Rud. Helm, Lips. 1898; cf. Wessner, *Comment. Ien.* vi. 2. 135 sqq.) in sixty-two paragraphs, each containing a lemma (sometimes two or three) with an explanation giving quotations and names of authors. Next to him come the *glossae Nonianae*, which arose from the contents of the various paragraphs in Nonius Marcellus' work being written in the margin without the words of the text; these epitomized glosses were alphabetized and afterwards copied for other collections (see Goetz, *Corp.* v. 637 sqq., *id.* v. Praef. xxxv.; Onions and Lindsay, *Harvard Stud.* ix. 67 sqq.; Lindsay, *Nonii praef.* xxi.). In a similar way arose the *glossae Eucherii* or *glossae spiritales secundum Eucherium episcopum* found in many MSS. (cf. K. Wotke, *Sitz. Ber. Akad. Wien*, cxv. 425 sqq.; = the *Corpus Glossary*, first part), which are an alphabetical extract from the *formulae spiritalis intelligentiae* of St Eucherius, bishop of Lyons, *c.* 434-450.7

Other sources were the *Differentiae*, already known to Placidus and much used in the medieval glossaries; and the *Synonyma Ciceronis*; cf. Goetz, "Der Liber glossarum," in *Abhandl. der philol.-hist. Cl. der sächs. Gesellsch. d. Wiss.*, 1893, p. 215; *id.* in *Berl. philol. Wochenschr.*, 1890, p. 195 sqq.; Beck, in *Wochenschr.*, p. 297 sqq., and Sittls, *ibid.* p. 267; *Archiv f. lat. Lex.* vi. 594; W. L. Mahne, (Leid. 1850, 1851); also various collections of *scholia*. By the side of the scholiasts come the grammarians, as Charisius, or an ars similar to that ascribed to him; further, treatises *de dubiis generibus*, the *scriptores orthographici* (especially Caper and Beda), and Priscianus, the chief grammarian of the middle ages (cf. Goetz in *Mélanges Boissier*, 224).

During the 6th, 7th and 8th centuries glossography developed in various ways; old glossaries were worked up into new forms, or amalgamated with more recent ones. It ceased, moreover, to be exclusively Latin-Latin, and interpretations in Germanic (Old High German, Anglo-Saxon) and Romanic dialects took the place of or were used side by side with earlier Latin ones. The origin and development of the late classic and medieval glossaries preserved to us can be traced with certainty. While reading the manuscript texts of classical authors, the Bible or early Christian and profane writers, students and teachers, on meeting with any obscure or out-of-the-way words which they considered difficult to remember or to require elucidation, wrote above them, or in the margins, interpretations or explanations in more easy or better-known words. The interpretations written above the line are called "interlinear," those written in the margins of the MSS. "marginal glosses." Again, MSS. of the Bible or portions of the Bible were often provided with literal translations in the vernacular written above the lines of the Latin version (interlinear versions).

Of such glossed MSS. or translated texts, photographs may be seen in the various palaeographical works published in recent years; cf. *The Palaeogr. Society*, 1st ser. vol. ii. pls. 9 (Terentius MS. of 4th or 5th century, interlinear glosses) and 24 (Augustine's epistles, 6th or 7th century, marginal glosses); see further, plates 10, 12, 33, 40, 50-54, 57, 58, 63, 73, 75, 80; vol. iii. plates 10, 24, 31, 39, 44, 54, 80.

From these glossed or annotated MSS. and interlinear versions glossaries were compiled; that is, the obscure and difficult Latin words, together with the interpretations, were excerpted and collected in separate lists, in the order in which they appeared, one after the other, in the MSS., without any alphabetical arrangement, but with the names of the authors or the titles of the books whence they were taken, placed at the head of each separate collection or chapter. In this arrangement each article by itself is called a gloss; when reference is made only to the word explained it is called the *lemma*, while the explanation is termed the *interpretamentum*. In most cases the form of the lemma was retained just as it stood in its source, and explained by a single word (*tesca: sancta*, Varro vii. 10; *clucidatus: suavis, id.* vii. 107; cf. Isid. *Etym.* i. 30. 1, "quid enim illud sit in uno verbo positum declarat [*scil.* glossa] ut conticescere est tacere"), so that we meet with lemmata in the accusative, dative and genitive, likewise explained by words in the same cases; the forms of verbs being treated in the same way. Of this first stage in the making of glossaries, many traces are preserved, for instance, in the late 8th century Leiden Glossary (Voss. 69, ed. J. H. Hessels), where chapter iii. contains words or glosses excerpted from the *Life of St Martin* by Sulpicius Severus; chs. iv., v. and xxxv. glosses from Rufinus; chs. vi. and xl. from Gildas; chs. vii. to xxv. from books of the Bible (Paralipomenon; Proverbs, &c., &c.); chs. xxvi. to xlviii, from Isidore, the Vita S. *Anthonii*, Cassiodorus, St Jerome, Cassianus, Orosius, St Augustine, St Clement, Eucherius, St Gregory, the grammarians Donatus, Phocas, &c. (See also Goetz, *Corp.* v. 546. 23-547. 6. and i. 5-40 from Ovid's *Metam.*; v. 657 from Apuleius, *De deo Socratis*; cf. Landgraf, in *Arch.* ix. 174).

By a second operation the glosses came to be arranged in *alphabetical* order according to the first letter of the lemma, but still retained in separate chapters under the names of authors or the titles of books. Of this *second* stage the Leiden Glossary contains traces also: ch. i. (*Verba de Canonibus*) and ii. (*Sermones de Regulis*); see Goetz, *Corp.* v. 529 sqq. (from Terentius), iv. 427 sqq. (Virgil).

The third operation collected all the accessible glosses in alphabetical order, in the first instance according to the first letters of the lemmata. In this arrangement the names of the authors or the titles of the books could no longer be preserved, and consequently the sources whence the glosses were excerpted became uncertain, especially if the grammatical forms of the lemmata had been normalized.

A fourth arrangement collected the glosses according to the first two letters of the lemmata, as in the Corpus Glossary and in the still earlier*Cod. Vat.* 3321 (Goetz, *Corp.* iv. 1 sqq.), where even many attempts were made to arrange them according to the first three letters of the alphabet. A peculiar arrangement is seen in the *Glossae affatim* (Goetz, *Corp.* iv. 471 sqq.), where all words are alphabetized, first according to the initial letter of the word (a, b, c, &c.), and then further according to the first *vowel* in the word (a, e, i, o, u).

No date or period can be assigned to any of the above stages or arrangements. For instance, the first and second are both found in the Leiden Glossary, which dates from the end of the 8th century, whereas the Corpus Glossary, written in the beginning of the same century, represents already the fourth stage.

For the purpose of identification titles have of late years been given to the various nameless collections of glosses, derived partly from their first lemma, partly from other characteristics, as glossae *abstrusae*; glossae *abavus major* and *minor*; g. *affatim*; g. *ab absens*; g. *abactor*; g. *Abba Pater*; g. *a, a*; g. *Vergilianae*; g. *nominum* (Goetz, *Corp.* ii. 563, iv.); g. Sangallenses (Warren, *Transact. Amer. Philol. Assoc.* xv., 1885, p. 141 sqq.).

A chief landmark in glossography is represented by the *Origines* (*Etymologiae*) of Isidore (d. 636), an encyclopedia in which he, like Cassiodorus, mixed human and divine subjects together. In many places we can trace his sources, but he also used glossaries. His work became a great

4

mine for later glossographers. In the tenth book he deals with the etymology of many substantives and adjectives arranged alphabetically according to the first letter of the words, perhaps by himself from various sources. His principal source is Servius, then the fathers of the Church (Augustine, Jerome, 127Lactantius) and Donatus the grammarian. This tenth book was also copied and used separately, and mixed up with other works (cf. Loewe, *Prodr.* 167. 21). Isidore's *Differentiae* have also had a great reputation.

Next comes the *Liber glossarum*, chiefly compiled from Isidore, but all articles arranged alphabetically; its author lived in Spain c. A.D. 690-750; he has been called Ansileubus, but not in any of the MSS., some of which belong to the 8th century; hence this name is suspected to be merely that of some owner of a copy of the book (cf. Goetz, "Der Liber Glossarum," in *Abhandl. der philol.-hist. Class, der kön. sächs. Ges.* xiii., 1893; *id., Corp.* v., praef. xx. 161).

Here come, in regard to time, some Latin glossaries already largely mixed with Germanic, more especially Anglo-Saxon interpretations: (1) the Corpus Glossary (ed. J. H. Hessels), written in the beginning of the 8th century, preserved in the library of Corpus Christi College, Cambridge; (2) the Leiden Glossary (end of 8th century, ed. Hessels; another edition by Plac. Glogger), preserved in the Leiden MS. Voss. Qo. 69; (3) the Épinal Glossary, written in the beginning of the 9th century8 and published in facsimile by the London Philol. Society from a MS. in the town library at Épinal; (4) the *Glossae Amplonianae, i.e.* three glossaries preserved in the Amplonian library at Erfurt, known as Erfurt1, Erfurt2 and Erfurt3. The first, published by Goetz (*Corp.* v. 337-401; cf. also Loewe, *Prodr.* 114 sqq.) with the various readings of the kindred Épinal, consists, like the latter, of different collections of glosses (also some from Aldhelm), some arranged alphabetically according to the first letter of the lemma, others according to the first two letters. The title of Erfurt2 (*incipit II. conscriptio glosarum in unam*) shows that it is also a combination of various glossaries; it is arranged alphabetically according to the first two letters of the lemmata, and contains the *affatim* and *abavus maior* glosses, also a collection from Aldhelm; Erfurt3 are the *Glossae nominum*, mixed also with Anglo-Saxon interpretations (Goetz, *Corp.* ii. 563). The form in which the three Erfurt glossaries have come down to us points back to the 8th century.

The first great glossary or collection of various glosses and glossaries is that of Salomon, bishop of Constance, formerly abbot of St Gall, who died A.D. 919. An edition of it in two parts was printed *c.* 1475 at Augsburg, with the headline *Salemonis ecclesie Constantiensis episcopi glosse ex illustrissimis collecte auctoribus.* The oldest MSS. of this work date from the 11th century. Its sources are the *Liber glossarum* (Loewe, Prodr. 234 sqq.), the glossary preserved in the 9th-century MS. *Lat. Monac.* 14429 (Goetz, "Lib. Gloss." 35 sqq.), and the great Abavus Gloss (*id., ibid.*p. 37; *id., Corp.* iv. praef. xxxvii.).

The *Lib. glossarum* has also been the chief source for the important (but not original) glossary of Papias, of A.D. 1053 (cf. Goetz in *Sitz. Ber. Akad. Münch.,* 1903, p. 267 sqq., who enumerates eighty-seven MSS. of the 12th to the 15th centuries), of whom we only know that he lived among clerics and dedicated his work to his two sons. An edition of it was published at Milan "per Dominicum de Vespolate" on the 12th of December 1476; other editions followed in 1485, 1491, 1496 (at Venice). He also wrote a grammar, chiefly compiled from Priscianus (Hagen, *Anecd. Helv.* clxxix. sqq.).

The same *Lib. gloss.* is the source (1) for the *Abba Pater* Glossary (cf. Goetz, *ibid.* p. 39), published by G. M. Thomas (*Sitz. Ber. Akad. Münch.,* 1868, ii. 369 sqq.); (2) the Greek glossary *Absida lucida* (Goetz, *ib.* p. 41); and (3) the Lat.-Arab. glossary in the *Cod. Leid. Scal. Orient.* No. 231 (published by Seybold in *Semit. Studien,* Heft xv.-xvii., Berlin, 1900).

The Paulus-Glossary (cf. Goetz, "Der Liber Glossarum," p. 215) is compiled from the second Salomon-Glossary (*abacti magistratus*), the *Abavus major* and the *Liber glossarum,* with a mixture of Hebraica. Many of his glosses appear again in other compilations, as in the Cod. Vatic. 1469 (cf. Goetz, *Corp.* v. 520 sqq.), mixed up with glosses from Beda, Placidus, &c. (cf. a glossary published by Ellis in *Amer. Journ. of Philol.*vi. 4, vii. 3, containing besides Paulus glosses, also excerpts from Isidore; Cambridge *Journ. of Philol.* viii. 71 sqq., xiv. 81 sqq.).

Osbern of Gloucester (*c.* 1123-1200) compiled the glossary entitled *Panormia* (published by Angelo Mai as *Thesaurus novus Latinitatis,* from Cod. Vatic. reg. Christ. 1392; cf. W. Meyer, *Rhein. Mus.* xxix., 1874; Goetz in *Sitzungsber. sächs. Ges. d. Wiss.,* 1903, p. 133 sqq.; *Berichte üb. die Verhandl. der kön. sächs. Gesellsch. der Wiss.,* Leipzig, 1902); giving derivations, etymologies, testimonia collected from Paulus, Priscianus, Plautus, Horace, Virgil, Ovid, Mart. Capella, Macrobius, Ambrose, Sidonius, Prudentius, Josephus, Jerome, &c., &c. Osbern's material was also used by Hugucio, whose compendium was still more extensively used (cf. Goetz, l.c., p. 121 sqq., who enumerates one hundred and three MSS. of his treatise), and contains many biblical glosses, especially Hebraica, some treatises on Latin numerals, &c. (cf. Hamann, *Weitere Mitteil. aus dem*

Breviloquus Benthemianus, Hamburg, 1882; A. Thomas, "Glosses provençales inéd." in *Romania*, xxxiv. p. 177 sqq; P. Toynbee, *ibid.* xxv. p. 537 sqq.).

The great work of Johannes de Janua, entitled *Summa quae vocatur catholicon*, dates from the year 1286, and treats of (1) accent, (2) etymology, (3) syntax, and (4) so-called prosody, *i.e.* a lexicon, which also deals with quantity. It mostly uses Hugucio and Papias; its classical quotations are limited, except from Horace; it quotes the Vulgate by preference, frequently independently from Hugucio; it excerpts Priscianus, Donatus, Isidore, the fathers of the Church, especially Jerome, Gregory, Augustine, Ambrose; it borrows many Hebrew glosses, mostly from Jerome and the other collections then in use; it mentions the *Graecismus* of Eberhardus Bethuniensis, the works of Hrabanus Maurus, the *Doctrinale* of Alexander de Villa Dei, and the *Aurora* of Petrus de Riga. Many quotations from the *Catholicon* in Du Cange are really from Hugucio, and may be traced to Osbern. There exist many MSS. of this work, and the Mainz edition of 1460 is well known (cf. Goetz in *Berichte üb. die Verhandl. der kön. sächs. Gesellsch. der Wiss.*, Leipzig, 1902).

The gloss MSS. of the 9th and 10th centuries are numerous, but a diminution becomes visible towards the 11th. We then find grammatical treatises arise, for which also glossaries were used. The chief material was (1) the *Liber glossarum*, (2) the Paulus glosses; (3) the *Abavus major*, (4) excerpts from Priscian and glosses to Priscian; (5) Hebrew-biblical collections of proper names (chiefly from Jerome). After these comes medieval material, as the *derivationes* which are found in many MSS. (cf. Goetz in *Sitzungsber. sächs. Ges. d. Wiss.*, 1903, p. 136 sqq.; Traube in *Archiv f. lat. Lex.* vi. 264), containing quotations from Plautus, Ovid, Juvenal, Persius, Terence, occasionally from Priscian, Eutyches, and other grammarians, with etymological explanations. These *derivationes* were the basis for the grammatical works of Osbern, Hugucio and Joannes of Janua.

A peculiar feature of the late middle ages are the medico-botanic glossaries based on the earlier ones (see Goetz, *Corp.* iii.). The additions consisted in Arabic words with Latin explanations, while Greek, Latin, Hebrew and Arabic, interchange with English, French, Italian and German forms. Of glossaries of this kind we have (1) the *Glossae alphita* (published by S. de Renzi in the 3rd vol. of the *Collect. Salernitana*, Naples, 1854, from two Paris MSS. of the 14th and 15th centuries, but some of the glosses occur already in earlier MSS.); (2) *Sinonoma Bartholomei*, collected by John Mirfeld, towards the end of the 14th century, ed. J. L. G. Mowat (*Anecd. Oxon.* i. 1, 1882, cf. Loewe, *Gloss. Nom.* 116 sqq.); it seems to have used the same or some similar source as No. 1; (3) the compilations of Simon de Janua (*Clavis sanationis*, end of 13th century), and of Matthaeus Silvaticus (*Pandectae medicinae*, 14th century; cf. H. Stadler, "Dioscor. Longob." in *Roman. Forsch.* x. 3. 371; Steinmeyer, *Althochd. Gloss.* iii.).

Of biblical glossaries we have a large number, mostly mixed with glosses on other, even profane, subjects, as Hebrew and other biblical proper names, and explanations of the text of the Vulgate in general, and the prologues of Hieronymus. So we have the *Glossae veteris ac novi testamenti* (beginning "Prologus graece latine praelocutio sive praefatio") in numerous MSS. of the 9th to 14th centuries, mostly retaining the various books under separate headings (cf. Arevalo, *Isid.* vii. 407 sqq.; Loewe, *Prodr.* 141; Steinmeyer iv. 459; S. Berger, *De compendiis exegeticis quibusdam medii aevi*, Paris, 1879). Special mention should be made of Guil. Brito, who lived about 1250, and compiled a *Summa* (beginning "difficiles studeo partes quas Biblia gestat Pandere"), contained in many MSS. especially in French libraries. This *Summa* gave rise to the *Mammotrectus* of Joh. Marchesinus, about 1300, of which we have editions printed in 1470, 1476, 1479, &c.

Finally we may mention such compilations as the *Summa Heinrici*; the work of Johannes de Garlandia, which he himself calls *dictionarius* (cf. Scheler in *Jahrb. f. rom. u. engl. Philol.* vi., 1865, p. 142 sqq.); and that of Alexander Neckam (*ib.* vii. p. 60 sqq., cf. R. Ellis, in *Amer. Journ. of Phil.* x. 2); which are, strictly speaking, not glossographic. The *Breviloquus* drew its chief material from Papias, Hugucio, Brito, &c. (K. Hamann, *Mitteil. aus dem Breviloquus Benthemianus*, Hamburg, 1879; *id.*, *Weitere Mitteil.*, &c., Hamburg, 1882); so also the *Vocabularium Ex quo*; the various *Gemmae, Vocabularia rerum* (cf. Diefenbach, *Glossar. Latino-Germanicum*).

After the revival of learning, J. Scaliger (1540-1609) was the first to impart to glossaries that importance which they deserve (cf. Goetz, in *Sitzungsber. sächs. Ger. d. Wiss.*, 1888, p. 219 sqq.), and in his edition of Festus made great use of Ps.-Philoxenus, which enabled O. Müller, the later editor of Festus, to follow in his footsteps. Scaliger also planned the publication of a *Corpus glossarum*, and left behind a collection of glosses known as *glossae Isidori* (Goetz, *Corp.* v. p. 589 sqq.; id. in *Sitzungsber. sächs. Ges.*, 1888, p. 224 sqq.; Loewe, *Prodr.* 23 sqq.), which occurs also in old glossaries, clearly in reference to the tenth book of the *Etymologiae*.

The study of glosses spread through the publication, in 1573, of the bilingual glossaries by H. Stephanus (Estienne), containing, besides the two great glossaries, also the *Hermeneumata*

Stephani, which is a recension of the *Ps.-Dositheana* (republished Goetz, *Corp.* iii. 438-474), and the *glossae Stephani*, excerpted from a collection of the *Hermeneumata* (*ib.* iii. 438-474).

In 1600 Bonav. Vulcanius republished the same glossaries, adding (1) the glossae *Isidori*, which now appeared for the first time; (2) the *Onomasticon*; (3) *notae* and *castigationes*, derived from Scaliger (Loewe, *Prodr.* 183).

In 1606 Carolus and Petrus Labbaeus published, with the effective help of Scaliger, another collection of glossaries, republished, in 1679, by Du Cange, after which the 17th and 18th centuries produced no 128further glossaries (Erasm. Nyerup published extracts from the Leiden Glossary, Voss. 69, in 1787, *Symbolae ad Literat. Teut.*), though glosses were constantly used or referred to by Salmasius, Meursius, Heraldus, Barth, Fabricius and Burman at Leiden, where a rich collection of glossaries had been obtained by the acquisition of the Vossius library (cf. Loewe, *Prodr.* 168). In the 19th century came Osann's *Glossarii Latini specimen* (1826); the glossographic publications of Angelo Mai (*Classici auctores*, vols. iii., vi., vii., viii., Rome, 1831-1836, containing Osbern's *Panormia*, Placidus and various glosses from Vatican MSS.); Fr. Oehler's treatise (1847) on the *Cod. Amplonianus* of Osbern, and his edition of the three Erfurt glossaries, so important for Anglo-Saxon philology; in 1854 G. F. Hildebrand's *Glossarium Latinum* (an extract from *Abavus minor*), preserved in a Cod. Paris. lat. 7690; 1857, Thomas Wright's vol. of Anglo-Saxon glosses, which were republished with others in 1884 by R. Paul Wülcker under the title *Anglo-Saxon and Old English Vocabularies* (London, 2 vols., 1857); L. Diefenbach's supplement to Du Cange, entitled *Glossarium Latino-Germanicum mediae et infimae aetatis*, containing mostly glosses collected from glossaries, vocabularies, &c., enumerated in the preface; Ritschl's treatise (1870) on Placidus, which called forth an edition (1875) of Placidus by Deuerling; G. Loewe's *Prodromus* (1876), and other treatises by him, published after his death by G. Goetz (Leipzig, 1884); 1888, the second volume of Goetz's own great *Corpus glossariorum Latinorum*, of which seven volumes (except the first) had seen the light by 1907, the last two being separately entitled *Thesaurus glossarum emendatarum*, containing many emendations and corrections of earlier glossaries by the author and other scholars; 1900, Arthur S. Napier, *Old English Glosses* (Oxford), collected chiefly from Aldhelm MSS., but also from Augustine, Avianus, Beda, Boethius, Gregory, Isidore, Juvencus, Phocas, Prudentius, &c.

There are a very great number of glossaries still in MS. scattered in various libraries of Europe, especially in the Vatican, at Monte Cassino, Paris, Munich, Bern, the British Museum, Leiden, Oxford, Cambridge, &c. Much has already been done to make the material contained in these MSS. accessible in print, and much may yet be done with what is still unpublished, though we may find that the differences between the glossaries which often present themselves at first sight are mere differences in form introduced by successive more or less qualified copyists.

Some Celtic (Breton, Cornish, Welsh, Irish) glossaries have been preserved to us, the particulars of which may be learnt from the publications of Whitley Stokes, Sir John Rhys, Kuno Meyer, L. C. Stern, G. I. Ascoli, Heinr. Zimmer, Ernst Windisch, Nigra, and many others; these are published separately as books or in Zeuss's *Grammatica Celtica*, A. Kühn's *Beiträge zur vergleich. Sprachforschung, Zeitschr. für celtische Philologie, Archiv für Celtische Lexicographie, the Revue celtique, Transactions of the London Philological Society*, &c.

The first Hebrew author known to have used glosses was R. Gershom of Metz (1000) in his commentaries on the Talmud. But he and other Hebrew writers after him mostly used the Old French language (though sometimes also Italian, Slavonic, German) of which an example has been published by Lambert and Brandin, in their *Glossaire hébreu-français du XIIIe siècle: recueil de mots hébreux bibliques avec traduction française* (Paris, 1905). See further *The Jewish Encyclopedia* (New York and London, 1903), article "Gloss."

AUTHORITIES.—For a great part of what has been said above, the writer is indebted to G. Goetz's article on "Latein. Glossographie" in Pauly's *Realencyklopädie*. By the side of Goetz's *Corpus* stands the great collection of Steinmeyer and Sievers, *Die althochdeutschen Glossen* (in 4 vols., 1879-1898), containing a vast number of (also Anglo-Saxon) glosses culled from Bible MSS. and MSS. of classical Christian authors, enumerated and described in the 4th vol. Besides the works of the editors of, or writers on, glosses, already mentioned, we refer here to a few others, whose writings may be consulted: Hugo Blümner; *Catholicon Anglicum* (ed. Hertage); De-Vit (at end of Forcellini's *Lexicon*); F. Deycks; Du Cange; Funck; J. H. Gallée (*Altsächs. Sprachdenkm.*, 1894); Gröber; K. Gruber (*Hauptquellen des Corpus, Épin. u. Erfurt Gloss.*, Erlangen, 1904); Hattemer; W. Heraeus (*Die Sprache des Petronius und die Glossen*, Leipzig, 1899); Kettner; Kluge; Krumbacher; Lagarde; Landgraf; Marx; W. Meyer-Lubke ("Zu den latein. Glossen" in *Wiener Stud.* xxv. 90 sqq.); Henry Nettleship; Niedermann, *Notes d'étymol. lat.* (Macon, 1902), *Contribut. à la critique des glosses latines* (Neuchâtel, 1905); Pokrowskij; Quicherat; Otto B. Schlutter (many important articles in *Anglia, Englische Studien, Archiv f. latein. Lexicographie*, &c.); Schöll; Schuchardt; Leo Sommer; Stadler; Stowasser; Strachan; H. Sweet; Usener (*Rhein.*

Mus. xxiii. 496, xxiv. 382); A. Way, *Promptorium parvulorum sive clericorum* (3 vols., London, 1843-1865); Weyman; Wilmanns (in *Rhein. Mus.* xxiv. 363); Wölfflin in *Arch. für lat. Lexicogr.*; Zupitza. Cf. further, the various volumes of the following periodicals: *Romania*; *Zeitschr. für deutsches Alterthum*; *Anglia*; *Englische Studien*; *Journal of English and German Philology* (ed. Cook and Karsten); *Archiv für latein. Lexicogr.*, and others treating of philology, lexicography, grammar, &c.

(J. H. H.)

1The history of the literary gloss in its proper sense has given rise to the common English use of the word to mean an interpretation, especially in a disingenuous, sinister or false way; the form "gloze," more particularly associated with explaining away, palliating or talking speciously, is simply an alternative spelling. The word has thus to some extent influenced, or been influenced by, the meaning of the etymologically different "gloss" = lustrous surface (from the same root as "glass"; cf. "glow"), in its extended sense of "outward fair seeming."

2See Matthaei, *Glossaria Graeca* (Moscow, 1774/5).

3See Labbé, *Veteres glossae verborum juris quae passim in Basilicis reperiuntur* (1606); Otto, *Thesaurus juris Romani*, iii. (1697); Stephens, *Thesaurus linguae Graecae*, viii. (1825).

4See Biener, *Geschichte der Novellen*, p. 229 sqq.

5Irnerius himself is with some probability believed to have been the author of the Brachylogus (*q.v.*).

6Thus Fil. Villani (*De origine civitatis Florentiae*, ed. 1847, p. 23), speaking of the Glossator Accursius, says of the Glossae that "tantae auctoritatis gratiaeque fuere, ut omnium consensu publice approbarentur, et reiectis aliis, quibuscumque penitus abolitis, solae juxta textum legum adpositae sunt et ubique terrarum sine controversia pro legibus celebrantur, ita ut nefas sit, non secus quam textui, Glossis Accursii contraire." For similar testimonies see Bayle's *Dictionnaire*, s.v. "Accursius," and Rudorff, *Röm. Rechtsgeschichte*, i. 338 (1857).

7The so-called *Malberg* glosses, found in various texts of the Lex Salica, are not glosses in the ordinary sense of the word, but precious remains of the parent of the present literary Dutch, namely, the Low German dialect spoken by the Salian Franks who conquered Gaul from the Romans at the end of the 5th century. It is supposed that the conquerors brought their Frankish law with them, either written down, or by oral tradition; that they translated it into Latin for the sake of the Romans settled in the country, and that the translators, not always knowing a proper Latin equivalent for certain things or actions, retained in their translations the Frankish technical names or phrases which they had attempted to translate into Latin. E.g. in chapter ii., by the side of *"porcellus lactans"* (a sucking-pig), we find the Frankish *"chramnechaltio,"* lit. a stye-porker. The person who stole such a pig (still kept in an enclosed place, in a stye) was fined three times as much as one who stole a *"porcellus de campo qui sine matre vivere possit,"* as the Latin text has it, for which the Malberg technical expression appears to have been *ingymus*, that is, a one year (winter) old animal, *i.e.* a yearling. Nearly all these glosses are preceded by *"mal"* or *"malb,"* which is thought to be a contraction for *"malberg,"* the Frankish for "forum." The antiquity and importance of these glosses for philology may be realized from the fact that the Latin translation of the Lex Salica probably dates from the latter end of the 5th century. For further information cf. Jac. Grimm's preface to Joh. Merkel's ed. (1850), and H. Kern's notes to J. H. Hessels's ed. (London, 1880) of the Lex Salica.

8Anglo-Saxon scholars ascribe an earlier date to the text of the MS. on account of certain archaisms in its Anglo-Saxon words.

GLOSSOP, a market town and municipal borough, in the High Peak parliamentary division of Derbyshire, England, on the extreme northern border of the county; 13 m. E. by S. of Manchester by the Great Central railway. Pop. (1901) 21,526. It is the chief seat of the cotton manufacture in Derbyshire, and it has also woollen and paper mills, dye and print works, and bleaching greens. The town consists of three main divisions, the Old Town (or Glossop proper), Howard Town (or Glossop Dale) and Mill Town. An older parish church was replaced by that of All Saints in 1830; there is also a very fine Roman Catholic church. In the immediate neighbourhood is Glossop Hall, the seat of Lord Howard, lord of the manor, a picturesque old building with extensive terraced gardens. On a hill near the town is Melandra Castle, the site of a Roman fort guarding Longdendale and the way into the hills of the Peak District. In the neighbourhood also a great railway viaduct spans the Dinting valley with sixteen arches. To the north, in Longdendale, there are five lakes belonging to the water-supply system of Manchester, formed by damming the Etherow, a stream which descends from the high moors north-east of Glossop. The town is governed by a mayor, 6 aldermen and 18 councillors. Area, 3052 acres.

Glossop was granted by Henry I. to William Peverel, on the attainder of whose son it reverted to the crown. In 1157 it was gifted by Henry II. to the abbey of Basingwerk. Henry VIII. bestowed it on the earl of Shrewsbury. It was made a municipal borough in 1866.

GLOUCESTER, EARLS AND DUKES OF. The English earldom of Gloucester was held by several members of the royal family, including Robert, a natural son of Henry I., and John, afterwards king, and others, until 1218, when Gilbert de Clare was recognized as earl of Gloucester. It remained in the family of Clare (*q.v.*) until 1314, when another Earl Gilbert was killed at Bannockburn; and after this date it was claimed by various relatives of the Clares, among them by the younger Hugh le Despenser (d. 1326) and by Hugh Audley (d. 1347), both of whom had married sisters of Earl Gilbert. In 1397 Thomas le Despenser (1373-1400), a descendant of the Clares, was created earl of Gloucester; but in 1399 he was degraded from his earldom and in January 1400 was beheaded.

The dukedom dates from 1385, when Thomas of Woodstock, a younger son of Edward III., was created duke of Gloucester, but his honours were forfeited when he was found guilty of treason in 1397. The next holder of the title was Humphrey, a son of Henry IV., who was created duke of Gloucester in 1414. He died without sons in 1447, and in 1461 the title was revived in favour of Richard, brother of Edward IV., who became king as Richard III. in 1483.

In 1659 Henry (1639-1660), a brother of Charles II., was formally created duke of Gloucester, a title which he had borne since infancy. This prince, sharing the exile of the Stuarts, had incensed his mother, Queen Henrietta Maria, by his firm adherence to the Protestant religion, and had fought among the Spaniards at Dunkirk in 1658. Having returned to England with Charles II., he died unmarried in London on the 13th of September 1660. The next duke was William (1689-1700), son of the princess Anne, who was, after his mother, the heir to the English throne, and who was declared duke of Gloucester by his uncle, William III., in 1689, but no patent for this creation was ever passed. William died on the 30th of July 1700, and again the title became extinct.

Frederick Louis, the eldest son of George II., was known for some time as duke of Gloucester, but when he was raised to the peerage in 1726 it was as duke of Edinburgh only. In 1764 Frederick's third son, William Henry (1743-1805), was created duke of Gloucester and Edinburgh by his brother, George III. This duke's secret marriage with Maria (d. 1807), an illegitimate daughter of Sir Edward Walpole and widow of James, 2nd Earl Waldegrave, in 1766, greatly incensed his royal relatives and led to his banishment from court. Gloucester died on the 25th of August 1805, leaving an only son, William Frederick (1776-1834), who now became duke of Gloucester and Edinburgh. The duke, who served with the British army in Flanders, married his cousin Mary (1776-1857), a daughter of George III. He died on the 30th of November 1834, leaving no children, and his widow, the last survivor of the family of George III., died on the 30th of April 1857.

GLOUCESTER, GILBERT DE CLARE, EARL OF (1243-1295), was a son of Richard de Clare, 7th earl of Gloucester and 8th earl of Clare, and was born at Christchurch, Hampshire, on the 2nd of September 1243. Having married Alice of Angoulême, half-sister of king Henry III., he became earl of Gloucester and Clare on his father's death in July 1262, and almost at once joined the baronial party led by Simon de Montfort, earl of Leicester. With Simon Gloucester was at the battle of Lewes in May 1264, when the king himself surrendered to him, and after this victory he was one of the three persons selected to nominate a council. Soon, however, he quarrelled with Leicester. Leaving London for his lands on the Welsh border he met Prince Edward, afterwards king Edward I., at Ludlow, just after his escape from captivity, and by his skill contributed largely to the prince's victory at Evesham in August 1265. But this alliance was as transitory as the one with Leicester. Gloucester took up the cudgels on behalf of the barons who had surrendered at Kenilworth in November and December 1266, and after putting his demands before the king, secured possession of London. This happened in April 1267, but the earl quickly made his peace with Henry III. and with Prince Edward, and, having evaded an obligation to go on the Crusade, he helped to secure the peaceful accession of Edward I. to the throne in 1272. Gloucester then passed several years in fighting in Wales, or on the Welsh border; in 1289 when the barons were asked for a subsidy he replied on their behalf that they would grant nothing until they saw the king in person (*nisi prius personaliter viderent in Anglia faciem regis*), and in 1291 he was fined and imprisoned on account of his violent quarrel with Humphrey de Bohun, earl of Hereford. Having divorced his wife Alice, he married in 1290 Edward's daughter Joan, or Johanna (d. 1307). Earl Gilbert, who is sometimes called the "Red," died at Monmouth on the 7th of December 1295, leaving in addition to three daughters a son, Gilbert, earl of Gloucester and Clare, who was killed at Bannockburn.

9

See C. Bémont, *Simon de Montfort, comte de Leicester* (1884), and G. W. Prothero, *Simon de Montfort* (1877).

GLOUCESTER, HUMPHREY, DUKE OF (1391-1447), fourth son of Henry IV. by Mary de Bohun, was born in 1391. He was knighted at his father's coronation on the 11th of October 1399, and created duke of Gloucester by Henry V. at Leicester on the 16th of May 1414. He served in the war next year, and was wounded at Agincourt, where he owed his life to his brother's valour. In April 1416 Humphrey received the emperor Sigismund at Dover and, according to a 16th-century story, did not let him land till he had disclaimed all title to imperial authority in England. In the second invasion of France Humphrey commanded the force which during 1418 reduced the Cotentin and captured Cherbourg. Afterwards he joined the main army before Rouen, and took part in subsequent campaigns till January 1420. He then went home to replace Bedford as regent in England, and held office till Henry's own return in February 1421. He was again regent for his brother from May to September 1422.

Henry V. measured Humphrey's capacity, and by his will named him merely deputy for Bedford in England. Humphrey at once claimed the full position of regent, but the parliament and council allowed him only the title of protector during Bedford's absence, with limited powers. His lack of discretion soon justified this caution. In the autumn of 1422 he married Jacqueline of Bavaria, heiress of Holland, to whose lands Philip of Burgundy had claims. Bedford, in the interest of so important an ally, endeavoured vainly to restrain his brother. Finally in October 1424 Humphrey took up arms in his wife's behalf, but after a short campaign in Hainault went home, and left Jacqueline to be overwhelmed by Burgundy. Returning to England in April 1425 he soon entangled himself in a quarrel with the council and his uncle Henry Beaufort, and stirred up a tumult in London. Open war was averted only by Beaufort's prudence, and Bedford's hurried return. Humphrey had charged his uncle with disloyalty to the late and present kings. With some difficulty Bedford effected a formal reconciliation at Leicester in March 1426, and forced Humphrey to accept Beaufort's disavowal. When Bedford left England next year Humphrey renewed his intrigues. But one complication was removed by the annulling in 1428 of his marriage with Jacqueline. His open adultery with his mistress, Eleanor Cobham, also made him unpopular. To check his indiscretion the council, in November 1429, had the king crowned, and so put an end to Humphrey's protectorate. However, when Henry VI. was soon afterwards taken to be crowned in France, Humphrey was made lieutenant and warden of the kingdom, and thus ruled England for nearly two years. His jealousy of Bedford and Beaufort still continued, and when the former died in 1435 there was no one to whom he would defer. The defection of Burgundy roused English feeling, and Humphrey won popularity as leader of the war party. In 1436 he commanded in a short invasion of Flanders. But he had no real power, and his political importance lay in his persistent opposition to Beaufort and the councillors of his party. In 1439 he renewed his charges against his uncle without effect. His position was further damaged by his connexion with Eleanor Cobham, whom he had now married. In 1441 Eleanor was charged with practising sorcery against the king, and Humphrey had to submit to see her condemned, and her accomplices executed. Nevertheless, he continued his political opposition, and endeavoured to thwart Suffolk, who was now taking Beaufort's place in the council, by opposing the king's marriage to Margaret of Anjou. Under Suffolk's influence Henry VI. grew to distrust his uncle altogether. The crisis came in the parliament of Bury St Edmunds in February 1447. Immediately on his arrival there Humphrey was arrested, and four days later, on the 23rd of February, he died. Rumour attributed his death to foul play. But his health had been long undermined by excesses, and his end was probably only hastened by the shock of his arrest.

Humphrey was buried at St Albans Abbey, in a fine tomb, which still exists. He was ambitious and self-seeking, but unstable and unprincipled, and, lacking the fine qualities of his brothers, excelled neither in war nor in peace. Still he was a cultured and courtly prince, who could win popularity. He was long remembered as the good Duke Humphrey, and in his lifetime was a liberal patron of letters. He had been a great collector of books, many of which he presented to the university of Oxford. He contributed also to the building of the Divinity School, and of the room still called Duke Humphrey's library. His books were dispersed at the Reformation and only three volumes of his donation now remain in the Bodleian library. Titus Livius, an Italian in Humphrey's service, wrote a life of Henry V. at his patron's bidding. Other Italian scholars, as Leonardo Aretino, benefited by his patronage. Amongst English men of letters he befriended Reginald Pecock, Whethamstead of St Albans, Capgrave the historian, Lydgate, and Gilbert Kymer, who was his physician and chancellor of Oxford university. A popular error found Humphrey a fictitious tomb in St Paul's Cathedral. The adjoining aisle, called Duke Humphrey's Walk, was frequented by beggars and needy adventurers. Hence the 16th-century proverb "to dine with Duke Humphrey," used of those who loitered there dinnerless.

The most important contemporary sources are Stevenson's *Wars of the English in France*, Whethamstead's *Register*, and Beckington's *Letters*(all in Rolls Ser.), with the various *London Chronicles*, and the works of Waurin and Monstrelet. For his relations with Jacqueline see F. von Löher's *Jacobäa von Bayern und ihre Zeit* (2 vols., Nördlingen, 1869). For other modern authorities consult W. Stubbs's *Constitutional History*; J. H. Ramsay's *Lancaster and York*; *Political History of England*, vol. iv.; R. Pauli, *Pictures of Old England*, pp. 373-401 (1861); and K. H. Viekers, *Humphrey, Duke of Gloucester* (1907). For Humphrey's correspondence with Piero Candido Decembrio see the *English Historical Review*, vols. x., xix., xx.

(C. L. K.)

GLOUCESTER, RICHARD DE CLARE, EARL OF (1222-1262), was a son of Gilbert de Clare, 6th earl of Gloucester and 7th earl of Clare, and was born on the 4th of August 1222, succeeding to his father's earldoms on the death of the latter in October 1230. His first wife was Margaret, daughter of Hubert de Burgh, and after her death in 1237 he married Maud, daughter of John de Lacy, earl of Lincoln, and passed his early years in tournaments and pilgrimages, taking for a time a secondary and undecided part in politics. He refused to help Henry III. on the French expedition of 1250, but was afterwards with the king at Paris; then he went on a diplomatic errand to Scotland, and was sent to Germany to work among the princes for the election of his stepfather, Richard, earl of Cornwall, as king of the Romans. About 1258 Gloucester took up his position as a leader of the barons in their resistance to the king, and he was prominent during the proceedings which followed the Mad Parliament at Oxford in 1258. In 1259, however, he quarrelled with Simon de Montfort, earl of Leicester; the dispute, begun in England, was renewed in France and he was again in the confidence and company of the king. This attitude, too, was only temporary, and in 1261 Gloucester and Leicester were again working in concord. The earl died at his residence near Canterbury on the 15th of July 1262. A large landholder like his son and successor, Gilbert, Gloucester was the most powerful English baron of his time; he was avaricious and extravagant, but educated and able. He left several children in addition to Earl Gilbert.

GLOUCESTER, ROBERT, EARL OF (d. 1147), was a natural son of Henry I. of England. He was born, before his father's accession, at Caen in Normandy; but the exact date of his birth, and his mother's name are unknown. He received from his father the hand of a wealthy heiress, Mabel of Gloucester, daughter of Robert Fitz Hamon, and with her the lordships of Gloucester and Glamorgan. About 1121 the earldom of Gloucester was created for his benefit. His rank and territorial influence made him the natural leader of the western baronage. Hence, at his father's death, he was sedulously courted by the rival parties of his half-sister the empress Matilda and of Stephen. After some hesitation he declared for the latter, but tendered his homage upon strict conditions, the breach of which should be held to invalidate the contract. Robert afterwards alleged that he had merely feigned submission to Stephen with the object of secretly furthering his half-sister's cause among the English barons. The truth appears to be that he was mortified at finding himself excluded from the inner councils of the king, and so resolved to sell his services elsewhere. Robert left England for Normandy in 1137, renewed his relations with the Angevin party, and in 1138 sent a formal defiance to the king. Returning to England in the following year, he raised the standard of rebellion in his own earldom with such success that the greater part of western England and the south Welsh marches were soon in the possession of the empress. By the battle of Lincoln (Feb. 2, 1141), in which Stephen was taken prisoner, the earl made good Matilda's claim to the whole kingdom. He accompanied her triumphal progress to Winchester and London; but was unable to moderate the arrogance of her behaviour. Consequently she was soon expelled from London and deserted by the bishop Henry of Winchester who, as legate, controlled the policy of the English church. With Matilda the earl besieged the legate at Winchester, but was forced by the royalists to beat a hasty retreat, and in covering Matilda's flight fell into the hands of the pursuers. So great was his importance that his party purchased his freedom by the release of Stephen. The earl renewed the struggle for the crown and continued it until his death (Oct. 31, 1147); but the personal unpopularity of Matilda, and the estrangement of the Church from her cause, made his efforts unavailing. His loyalty to a lost cause must be allowed to weigh in the scale against his earlier double-dealing. But he hardly deserves the extravagant praise which is lavished upon him by William of Malmesbury. The sympathies of the chronicler are too obviously influenced by the earl's munificence towards literary men.

See the *Historia novella* by William of Malmesbury (Rolls edition); the *Historia Anglorum* by Henry of Huntingdon (Rolls edition); J. H. Round's *Geoffrey de Mandeville* (1892); and O. Rössler's *Kaiserin Mathilde* (Berlin, 1897).

GLOUCESTER, THOMAS OF WOODSTOCK, DUKE OF (1355-1397), seventh and youngest son of the English king Edward III., was born at Woodstock on the 7th of January 1355. Having married Eleanor (d. 1399), daughter and co-heiress of Humphrey de Bohun, earl of Hereford, Essex and Northampton (d. 1373), Thomas obtained the office of constable of England, a position previously held by the Bohuns, and was made earl of Buckingham by his nephew, Richard II., at the coronation in July 1377. He took part in defending the English coasts against the attacks of the French and Castilians, after which he led an army through northern and central France, and besieged Nantes, which town, however, he failed to take.

Returning to England early in 1381, Buckingham found that his brother, John of Gaunt, duke of Lancaster, had married his wife's sister, Mary Bohun, to his own son, Henry, afterwards King Henry IV. The relations between the brothers, hitherto somewhat strained, were not improved by this proceeding, as Thomas, doubtless, was hoping to retain possession of Mary's estates. Having taken some part in crushing the rising of the peasants in 1381, Buckingham became more friendly with Lancaster; and while marching with the king into Scotland in 1385 was created duke of Gloucester, a mark of favour, which did not prevent him from taking up an attitude of hostility to Richard. Lancaster having left the country, Gloucester placed himself at the head of the party which disliked the royal advisers, Michael de la Pole, earl of Suffolk and Robert de Vere, earl of Oxford, whose recent elevation to the dignity of duke of Ireland had aroused profound discontent. The moment was propitious for interference, and supported by those who were indignant at the extravagance and incompetence, real or alleged, of the king, Gloucester was soon in a position of authority. He forced on the dismissal and impeachment of Suffolk; was a member of the commission appointed in 1386 to reform the kingdom and the royal household; and took up arms when Richard began proceedings against the commissioners. Having defeated Vere at Radcot in December 1387 the duke and his associates entered London to find the king powerless in their hands. Gloucester, who had previously threatened his uncle with deposition, was only restrained from taking this extreme step by the influence of his colleagues; but, as the leader of the "lords appellant" in the "Merciless Parliament," which met in February 1388 and was packed with his supporters, he took a savage revenge upon his enemies, while not neglecting to add to his own possessions.

He was not seriously punished when Richard regained his power in May 1389, but he remained in the background, although employed occasionally on public business, and accompanying the king to Ireland in 1394. In 1396, however, uncle and nephew were again at variance. Gloucester disliked the peace with France and Richard's second marriage with Isabella, daughter of King Charles VI.; other causes of difference were not wanting, and it has been asserted that the duke was plotting to seize the king. At all events Richard decided to arrest him. By refusing an invitation to dinner the duke frustrated the first attempt, but on the 11th of July 1397 he was arrested by the king himself at his residence, Pleshey castle in Essex. He was taken at once to Calais, and it is probable that he was murdered by order of the king on the 9th of September following. The facts seem to be as follows. At the beginning of September it was reported that he was dead. The rumour, probably a deliberate one, was false, and about the same time a justice, Sir William Rickhill (d. 1407), was sent to Calais with instructions dated the 17th of August to obtain a confession from Gloucester. On the 8th of September the duke confessed that he had been guilty of treason, and his death immediately followed this avowal. Unwilling to meet his parliament so soon after his uncle's death, Richard's purpose was doubtless to antedate this occurrence, and to foster the impression that the duke had died from natural causes in August. When parliament met in September he was declared guilty of treason and his estates forfeited. Gloucester had one son, Humphrey (c. 1381-1399), who died unmarried, and four daughters, the most notable of whom was Anne (c. 1380-1438), who was successively the wife of Thomas, 3rd earl of Stafford, Edmund, 5th earl of Stafford, and William Bourchier, count of Eu. Gloucester is supposed to have written *L'Ordonnance d'Angleterre pour le camp à l'outrance, ou gaige de bataille.*

BIBLIOGRAPHY.—See T. Walsingham, *Historia Anglicana*, edited by H. T. Riley (London, 1863-1864); The Monk of Evesham, *Historia vitae et regni Ricardi II.*, edited by T. Hearne (Oxford, 1729); *Chronique de la traison et mort de Richard II*, edited by B. Williams (London, 1846); J. Froissart, *Chroniques*, edited by S. Luce and G. Raynaud (Paris, 1869-1897); W. Stubbs, *Constitutional History*, vol. ii. (Oxford, 1896); J. Tait in *Owens College Historical Essays* and S. Armitage-Smith, *John of Gaunt* (London, 1904).

GLOUCESTER (abbreviated as pronounced *Glo'ster*), a city, county of a city, municipal and parliamentary borough and port, and the county town of Gloucestershire, England, on the left (east) bank of the river Severn, 114 m. W.N.W. of London. Pop. (1901) 47,955. It is served by the Great Western railway and the west-and-north branch of the Midland railway; while the Berkeley Ship Canal runs S.W. to Sharpness Docks in the Severn estuary (16½ m.). Gloucester is situated on a gentle eminence overlooking the Severn and sheltered by the Cotteswolds on the east, while the Malverns and the hills of the Forest of Dean rise prominently to the west and north-west.

The cathedral, in the north of the city near the river, originates in the foundation of an abbey of St Peter in 681, the foundations of the present church having been laid by Abbot Serlo (1072-1104); and Walter Froucester (d. 1412) its historian, became its first mitred abbot in 1381. Until 1541, Gloucester lay in the see of Worcester, but the separate see was then constituted, with John Wakeman, last abbot of Tewkesbury, for its first bishop. The diocese covers the greater part of Gloucestershire, with small parts of Herefordshire and Wiltshire. The cathedral may be succinctly described as consisting of a Norman nucleus, with additions in every style of Gothic architecture. It is 420 ft. long, and 144 ft. broad, with a beautiful central tower of the 15th century rising to the height of 225 ft. and topped by four graceful pinnacles. The nave is massive Norman with Early English roof; the crypt also, under the choir, aisles and chapels, is Norman, as is the chapter-house. The crypt is one of the four apsidal cathedral crypts in England, the others being at Worcester, Winchester and Canterbury. The south porch is Perpendicular, with fan-tracery roof, as also is the north transept, the south being transitional Decorated. The choir has Perpendicular tracery over Norman work, with an apsidal chapel on each side. The choir-vaulting is particularly rich, and the modern scheme of colouring is judicious. The splendid late Decorated east window is partly filled with ancient glass. Between the apsidal chapels is a cross Lady chapel, and north of the nave are the cloisters, with very early example of fan-tracery, the carols or stalls for the monks' study and writing lying to the south. The finest monument is the canopied shrine of Edward II. who was brought hither from Berkeley. By the visits of pilgrims to this the building and sanctuary were enriched. In a side-chapel, too, is a monument in coloured bog oak of Robert Curthose, a great benefactor to the abbey, the eldest son of the Conqueror, who was interred there; and those of Bishop Warburton and Dr Edward Jenner are also worthy of special mention. A musical festival (the Festival of the Three Choirs) is held annually in this cathedral and those of Worcester and Hereford in turn. Between 1873 and 1890 and in 1897 the cathedral was extensively restored, principally by Sir Gilbert Scott. Attached to the deanery is the Norman prior's chapel. In St Mary's Square outside the Abbey gate, Bishop Hooper suffered martyrdom under Queen Mary in 1555.

Quaint gabled and timbered houses preserve the ancient aspect of the city. At the point of intersection of the four principal streets stood the Tolsey or town hall, replaced by a modern building in 1894. None of the old public buildings, in fact, is left, but the New Inn in Northgate Street is a beautiful timbered house, strong and massive, with external galleries and courtyards, built in 1450 for the pilgrims to Edward II.'s shrine, by Abbot Sebroke, a traditional subterranean passage leading thence to the cathedral. The timber is principally chestnut. There are a large number of churches and dissenting chapels, and it may have been the old proverb, "as sure as God's in Gloucester," which provoked Oliver Cromwell to declare that the city had "more churches than godliness." Of the churches four are of special interest: St Mary de Lode, with a Norman tower and chancel, and a monument of Bishop Hooper, on the site of a Roman temple which became the first Christian church in Britain; St Mary de Crypt, a cruciform structure of the 12th century, with later additions and a beautiful and lofty tower; the church of St Michael, said to have been connected with the ancient abbey of St Peter; and St Nicholas church, originally of Norman erection, and possessing a tower and other portions of later date. In the neighbourhood of St Mary de Crypt are slight remains of Greyfriars and Blackfriars monasteries, and also of the city wall. Early vaulted cellars remain under the Fleece and Saracen's Head inns.

There are three endowed schools: the College school, refounded by Henry VIII. as part of the cathedral establishment; the school of St Mary de Crypt, founded by Dame Joan Cooke in the same reign; and Sir Thomas Rich's Blue Coat hospital for 34 boys (1666). At the Crypt school the famous preacher George Whitefield (1714-1770) was educated, and he preached his first sermon in the church. The first Sunday school was held in Gloucester, being originated by Robert Raikes, in 1780.

The noteworthy modern buildings include the museum and school of art and science, the county gaol (on the site of a Saxon and Norman castle), the Shire Hall and the Whitefield memorial church. A park in the south of the city contains a spa, a chalybeate spring having been discovered in 1814. West of this, across the canal, are the remains (a gateway and some walls) of Llanthony Priory, a cell of the mother abbey in the vale of Ewyas, Monmouthshire, which in the reign of Edward IV. became the secondary establishment.

13

Gloucester possesses match works, foundries, marble and slate works, saw-mills, chemical works, rope works, flour-mills, manufactories of railway wagons, engines and agricultural implements, and boat and ship-building yards. Gloucester was declared a port in 1882. The Berkeley canal was opened in 1827. The Gloucester canal-harbour and that at Sharpness on the Severn are managed by a board. Principal imports are timber and grain; and exports, coal, salt, iron and bricks. The salmon and lamprey fisheries in the Severn are valuable. The tidal bore in the river attains its extreme height just below the city, and sometimes surmounts the weir in the western branch of the river, affecting the stream up to Tewkesbury lock. The parliamentary borough returns one member. The city is governed by a mayor, 10 aldermen and 30 councillors. Area, 2315 acres.

History.—The traditional existence of a British settlement at Gloucester (Cær Glow, Gleawecastre, Gleucestre) is not confirmed by any direct evidence, but Gloucester was the Roman municipality or *colonia* of *Glevum*, founded by Nerva (A.D. 96-98). Parts of the walls can be traced, and many remains and coins have been found, though inscriptions (as is frequently the case in Britain) are somewhat scarce. Its situation on a navigable river, and the foundation in 681 of the abbey of St Peter by Æthelred favoured the growth of the town; and before the Conquest Gloucester was a borough governed by a portreeve, with a castle which was frequently a royal residence, and a mint. The first overlord, Earl Godwine, was succeeded nearly a century later by Robert, earl of Gloucester. Henry II. granted the first charter in 1155 which gave the burgesses the same liberties as the citizens of London and Winchester, and a second charter of Henry II. gave them freedom of passage on the Severn. The first charter was confirmed in 1194 by Richard I. The privileges of the borough were greatly extended by the charter of John (1200) which gave freedom from toll throughout the kingdom and from pleading outside the borough. Subsequent charters were numerous. Gloucester was incorporated by Richard III. in 1483, the town being made a county in itself. This charter was confirmed in 1489 and 1510, and other charters of incorporation were received by Gloucester from Elizabeth in 1560, James I. 132in 1604, Charles I. in 1626 and Charles II. in 1672. The chartered port of Gloucester dates from 1580. Gloucester returned two members to parliament from 1275 to 1885, since when it has been represented by one member. A seven days' fair from the 24th of June was granted by Edward I. in 1302, and James I. licensed fairs on the 25th of March and the 17th of November, and fairs under these grants are still held on the first Saturday in April and July and the last Saturday in November. The fair now held on the 28th of September was granted to the abbey of St Peter in 1227. A market on Wednesday existed in the reign of John, was confirmed by charter in 1227 and is still held. The iron trade of Gloucester dates from before the Conquest, tanning was carried on before the reign of Richard III., pin-making and bell-founding were introduced in the 16th, and the long-existing coal trade became important in the 18th century. The cloth trade flourished from the 12th to the 16th century. The sea-borne trade in corn and wine existed before the reign of Richard I.

See W. H. Stevenson, *Records of the Corporation of Gloucester* (Gloucester, 1893); *Victoria County History, Gloucestershire*.

GLOUCESTER, a city and port of entry of Essex county, Massachusetts, U.S.A., beautifully situated on Cape Ann. Pop. (1890) 24,651; (1900) 26,121, of whom 8768 were foreign-born, including 4388 English Canadians, 800 French Canadians, 665 Irish, 653 Finns and 594 Portuguese; (1910 census) 24,398. Area, 53.6 sq. m. It is served by the Boston & Maine railway and by a steamboat line to Boston. The surface is sterile, naked and rugged, with bold, rocky ledges, and a most picturesque shore, the beauties of which have made it a favourite summer resort, much frequented by artists. Included within the city borders are several villages, of which the principal one, also known as Gloucester, has a deep and commodious harbour. Among the other villages, all summer resorts, are Annisquam, Bay View and Magnolia (so called from the *Magnolia glauca*, which grows wild there, this being probably its most northerly habitat); near Magnolia are Rafe's Chasm (60 ft. deep and 6-10 ft. wide) and Norman's Woe, the scene of the wreck of the "Hesperus" (which has only tradition as a basis), celebrated in Longfellow's poem. There is some slight general commerce—in 1909 the imports were valued at $130,098; the exports at $7853—but the principal business is fishing, and has been since early colonial days. The pursuit of cod, mackerel, herring and halibut fills up, with a winter coasting trade, the round of the year. In this industry Gloucester is the most important place in the United States; and is, indeed, one of the greatest fishing ports of the world. Most of the adult males are engaged in it. The "catch" was valued in 1895 at $3,212,985 and in 1905 at $3,377,330. The organization of the industry has undergone many transformations, but a notable feature is the general practice—especially since modern methods have necessitated larger vessels and more costly gear, and correspondingly greater capital—of profit-sharing; all the crew entering on that basis and not independently. There are some manufactures, chiefly connected with the fisheries. The total factory product in 1905 was valued at $6,920,984, of which the canning and preserving of fish represented $4,068,571, and glue represented $752,003. An industry of considerable importance is the quarrying of the beautiful, dark Cape Ann granite that underlies the city and all the environs.

Gloucester harbour was probably noted by Champlain (as La Beauport), and a temporary settlement was made by English fishermen sent out by the Dorchester Company of "merchant adventurers" in 1623-1625; some of these settlers returned to England in 1625, and others, with Roger Conant, the governor, removed to what is now Salem.1 Permanent settlement ante-dated 1639 at least, and in 1642 the township was incorporated. From Gosnold's voyages onward the extraordinary abundance of cod about Cape Ann was well known, and though the first settlers characteristically enough tried to live by farming, they speedily became perforce a sea-faring folk. The active pursuit of fishing as an industry may be dated as beginning about 1700, for then began voyages beyond Cape Sable. Voyages to the Grand Banks began about 1741. Mackerel was a relatively unimportant catch until about 1821, and since then has been an important but unstable return; halibut fishing has been vigorously pursued since about 1836 and herring since about 1856. At the opening of the War of Independence Gloucester, whose fisheries then employed about 600 men, was second to Marblehead as a fishing-port. The war destroyed the fisheries, which steadily declined, reaching their lowest ebb from 1820 to 1840. Meanwhile foreign commerce had greatly expanded. The cod take had supported in the 18th century an extensive trade with Bilbao, Lisbon and the West Indies, and though changed in nature with the decline of the Bank fisheries after the War of Independence, it continued large through the first quarter of the 19th century. Throughout more than half of the same century also Gloucester carried on a varied and valuable trade with Surinam, hake being the chief article of export and molasses and sugar the principal imports. "India Square" remains, a memento of a bygone day. About 1850 the fisheries revived, especially after 1860, under the influence of better prices, improved methods and the discovery of new grounds, becoming again the chief economic interest; and since that time the village of Gloucester has changed from a picturesque hamlet to a fairly modern, though still quaint and somewhat foreign, settlement. Gasoline boats were introduced in 1900. Shipbuilding is another industry of the past. The first "schooner" was launched at Gloucester in 1713. From 1830 to 1907, 776 vessels and 5242 lives were lost in the fisheries; but the loss of life has been greatly reduced by the use of better vessels and by improved methods of fishing. Gloucester became a city in 1874.

Gloucester life has been celebrated in many books; among others in Elizabeth Stuart Phelps-Ward's *Singular Life* and *Old Maid's Paradise*, in Rudyard Kipling's *Captains Courageous*, and in James B. Connolly's *Out of Gloucester* (1902), *The Deep Sea's Toll* (1905), and *The Crested Seas* (1907).

See J. J. Babson, *History of the Town of Gloucester* (Gloucester, 1860; with *Notes and Additions*, on genealogy, 1876, 1891); and J. R. Pringle,*History of the Town and City of Gloucester* (Gloucester, 1892).

1According to some authorities (*e.g.* Pringle) a few settlers remained on the site of Gloucester, the permanent settlement thus dating from 1623 to 1625; of this, however, there is no proof, and the contrary opinion is the one generally held.

GLOUCESTER CITY, a city of Camden county, New Jersey, U.S.A., on the Delaware river, opposite Philadelphia. Pop. (1890) 6564; (1900) 6840, of whom 1094 were foreign-born; (1905) 8055; (1910) 9462. The city is served by the West Jersey & Seashore and the Atlantic City railways, and by ferry to Philadelphia, of which it is a residential suburb. Among its manufactures are incandescent gas-burners, rugs, cotton yarns, boats and drills. The municipality owns and operates the water works. It was near the site of Gloucester City that the Dutch in 1623 planted the short-lived colony of Fort Nassau, the first European settlement on the Delaware river, but it was not until after the arrival of English Quakers on the Delaware, in 1677, that a permanent settlement, at first called Axwamus, was established on the site of the present city. This was surveyed and laid out as a town in 1689. During the War of Independence the place was frequently occupied by troops, and a number of skirmishes were fought in its vicinity. The most noted of these was a successful attack upon a detachment of Hessians on the 25th of November 1777 by American troops under the command of General Lafayette. In 1868 Gloucester City was chartered as a city. In Camden county there is a township named GLOUCESTER (pop. in 1905, 2300), incorporated in 1798, and originally including the present township of Clementon and parts of the present townships of Waterford, Union and Winslow.

GLOUCESTERSHIRE, a county of the west midlands of England, bounded N. by Worcestershire, N.E. by Warwickshire, E. by Oxfordshire, S.E. by Berkshire and Wiltshire, S. by Somerset, and W. by Monmouth and Herefordshire. Its area is 1243·3 sq. m. The outline is very irregular, but three physical divisions are well marked—the hills, the vale and the forest. (1) The first (the eastern part of the county) lies among the 133uplands of the Cotteswold Hills (*q.v.*), whose westward face is a line of heights of an average elevation of 700 ft., but exceeding 1000 ft. at some points. This line bisects the county from S.W. to N.E. The watershed between the Thames and Severn valleys lies close to it, so that Gloucestershire includes Thames Head itself, in the south-east near Cirencester, and most of the upper feeders of the Thames which join the main stream, from narrow and picturesque valleys on the north. (2) The western Cotteswold line overlooks a rich valley, that of the lower Severn, usually spoken of as "The Vale," or, in two divisions, as the vale of Gloucester and the vale of Berkeley. This great river receives three famous tributaries during its course through Gloucestershire. Near Tewkesbury, on the northern border, the Avon joins it on the left and forms the county boundary for 4 m. This is the river known variously as the Upper, Worcestershire, Warwickshire, Stratford or Shakespeare's Avon, which descends a lovely pastoral valley through the counties named. It is to be distinguished from the Bristol Avon, which rises as an eastward flowing stream of the Cotteswolds, in the south-east of Gloucestershire, sweeps southward and westward through Wiltshire, pierces the hills through a narrow valley which becomes a wooded gorge where the Clifton suspension bridge crosses it below Bristol, and enters the Severn estuary at Avonmouth. For 17 m. from its mouth it forms the boundary between Gloucestershire and Somersetshire, and for 8 m. it is one of the most important commercial waterways in the kingdom, connecting the port of Bristol with the sea. The third great tributary of the Severn is the Wye. From its mouth in the estuary, 8 m. N. of that of the Bristol Avon, it forms the county boundary for 16 m. northward, and above this, over two short reaches of its beautiful winding course, it is again the boundary. (3) Between the Wye and the Severn lies a beautiful and historic tract, the forest of Dean, which, unlike the majority of English forests, maintains its ancient character. Gloucestershire has thus a share in the courses of five of the most famous of English rivers, and covers two of the most interesting physical districts in the country. The minor rivers of the county are never long. The vale is at no point within the county wider than 24 m., and so does not permit the formation of any considerable tributary to the Severn from the Dean Hills on the one hand or the Cotteswolds on the other. The Leadon rises east of Hereford, forms part of the north-western boundary, and joins the Severn near Gloucester, watering the vale of Gloucester, the northern part of the vale. In the southern part, the vale of Berkeley, the Stroudwater traverses a narrow, picturesque and populous valley, and the Little Avon flows past the town of Berkeley, joining the Severn estuary on the left. The Frome runs southward to the Bristol Avon at Bristol. The principal northern feeders of the Thames are the Churn (regarded by some as properly the headwater of the main river) rising in the Seven Springs, in the hills above Cheltenham, and forming the southern county boundary near its junction with the Thames at Cricklade; the Coln, a noteworthy trout-stream, joining above Lechlade, and the Lech (forming part of the eastern county boundary) joining below the same town; while from the east of the county there pass into Oxfordshire the Windrush and the Evenlode, much larger streams, rising among the bare uplands of the northern Cotteswolds.

Geology.—No county in England has a greater variety of geological formations. The pre-Cambrian is represented by the gneissic rocks at the south end of the Malvern Hills and by grits at Huntley. At Damory, Charfield and Woodford is a patch of greenstone, the cause of the upheaval of the Upper Silurian basin of Tortworth, in which are the oldest stratified rocks of the county. Of these the Upper Llandovery is the dominant stratum, exposed near Damory mill, Micklewood chase and Purton passage, wrapping round the base of May and Huntley hills, and reappearing in the vale of Woolhope. The Wenlock limestone is exposed at Falfield mill and Whitfield, and quarried for burning at May hill. The Lower Ludlow shales or mudstones are seen at Berkeley and Purton, where the upper part is probably Aymestry limestone. The series of sandy shales and sandstones which, as Downton sandstones and Ledbury shales, form a transition to the Old Red Sandstone are quarried at Dymock. The "Old Red" itself occurs at Berkeley, Tortworth Green, Thornbury, and several places in the Bristol coal-field, in anticlinal folds forming hills. It forms also the great basin extending from Ross to Monmouth and from Dymock to Mitcheldean, Abenhall, Blakeney, &c., within which is the Carboniferous basin of the forest. It is cut through by the Wye from Monmouth to Woolaston. This formation is over 8000 ft. thick in the forest of Dean. The Bristol and Forest Carboniferous basins lie within the synclinal folds of the Old Red Sandstone; and though the seams of coal have not yet been correlated, they must have been once continuous, as further appears from the existence of an intermediate basin, recently pierced, under the Severn. The lower limestone shales are 500 ft.

16

thick in the Bristol area and only 165 in the forest, richly fossiliferous and famous for their bone bed. The great marine series known as the Mountain Limestone, forming the walls of the grand gorges of the Wye and Avon, is over 2000 ft. thick in the latter district, but only 480 in the former, where it yields the brown hematite in pockets so largely worked for iron even from Roman times. It is much used too for lime and road metal. Above this comes the Millstone Grit, well seen at Brandon hill, where it is 1000 ft. in thickness, though but 455 in the forest. On this rest the Coal Measures, consisting in the Bristol field of two great series, the lower 2000 ft. thick with 36 seams, the upper 3000 ft. with 22 seams, 9 of which reach 2 ft. in thickness. These two series are separated by over 1700 ft. of hard sandstone (Pennant Grit), containing only 5 coal-seams. In the Forest coal-field the whole series is not 3000 ft. thick, with but 15 seams. At Durdham Down a dolomitic conglomerate, of the age known as Keuper or Upper Trias, rests unconformably on the edges of the Palaeozoic rocks, and is evidently a shore deposit, yielding dinosaurian remains. Above the Keuper clays come the Penarth beds, of which classical sections occur at Westbury, Aust, &c. The series consists of grey marls, black paper shales containing much pyrites and a celebrated bone bed, the Cotham landscape marble, and the White Lias limestone, yielding *Ostrea Liassica* and *Cardium Rhaeticum*. The district of Over Severn is mainly of Keuper marls. The whole vale of Gloucester is occupied by the next formation, the Lias, a warm sea deposit of clays and clayey limestones, characterized by ammonites, belemnites and gigantic saurians. At its base is the insect-bearing limestone bed. The pastures producing Gloucester cheese are on the clays of the Lower Lias. The more calcareous Middle Lias or marlstone forms hillocks flanking the Oolite escarpment of the Cotteswolds, as at Wotton-under-Edge and Churchdown. The Cotteswolds consist of the great limestone series of the Lower Oolite. At the base is a transition series of sands, 30 to 40 ft. thick, well developed at Nailsworth and Frocester. Leckhampton hill is a typical section of the Lower Oolite, where the sands are capped by 40 ft. of a remarkable pea grit. Above this are 147 ft. of freestone, 7 ft. of oolite marl, 34 ft. of upper freestone and 38 ft. of ragstone. The Painswick stone belongs to lower freestone. Resting on the Inferior Oolite, and dipping with it to S.E., is the "fuller's earth," a rubbly limestone about 100 ft. thick, throwing out many of the springs which form the head waters of the Thames. Next comes the Great or Bath Oolite, at the base of which are the Stonesfield "slate" beds, quarried for roofing, paling, &c., at Sevenhampton and elsewhere. From the Great Oolite Minchinhampton stone is obtained, and at its top is about 40 ft. of flaggy Oolite with bands of clay known as the Forest Marble. Ripple marks are abundant on the flags; in fact all the Oolites seem to have been near shore or in shallow water, much of the limestone being merely comminuted coral. The highest bed of the Lower Oolite is the Cornbrash, about 40 ft. of rubble, productive in corn, forming a narrow belt from Siddington to Fairford. Near the latter town and Lechlade is a small tract of blue Oxford Clay of the Middle Oolite. The county has no higher Secondary or Tertiary rocks; but the Quaternary series is represented by much northern drift gravel in the vale and Over Severn, by accumulations of Oolitic detritus, including post-Glacial extinct mammalian remains on the flanks of the Cotteswolds, and by submerged forests extending from Sharpness to Gloucester.

Agriculture.—The climate is mild. Between three-quarters and seven-eighths of the total area is under cultivation, and of this some four-sevenths is in permanent pasture. Wheat is the chief grain crop. In the vale the deep rich black and red loamy soil is well adapted for pasturage, and a moist mild climate favours the growth of grasses and root crops. The cattle, save on the frontier of Herefordshire, are mostly shorthorns, of which many are fed for distant markets, and many reared and kept for dairy purposes. The rich grazing tract of the vale of Berkeley produces the famous "double Gloucester" cheeses, and the vale in general has long been celebrated for cheese and butter. The vale of Gloucester is the chief grain-growing district. Turnips, &c., occupy about three-fourths of the green crop acreage, potatoes occupying only about a twelfth. A feature of the county is its apple and pear orchards, chiefly for the manufacture of cider and perry, which are attached to nearly every farm. The Cotteswold district is comparatively barren except in the valleys, but it has been famous since the 15th century for the breed of sheep named after it. Oats and barley are here the chief crops.

Other Industries.—The manufacture of woollen cloth followed upon the early success in sheep-farming among the Cotteswolds. This industry is not confined to the hill country or even to Gloucestershire itself in the west of England. The description of cloth principally manufactured is broadcloth, dressed with teazles to produce a short close nap on the face, and made of all shades of colour, but chiefly black, blue and scarlet. The principal centre of the industry lies in and at the foot of the south-western Cotteswolds. Stroud is the centre for a number of manufacturing villages, and south-west of this are Wotton-under-Edge, North Nibley and others. Machinery and tools, paper, furniture, pottery and glass are also produced. Ironstone, clay, limestone and sandstone are worked, and the coal-fields in the forest of Dean are important.

17

Of less extent is the field in the south of the county, N.E. of Bristol. Strontium sulphate is dug from shallow pits in the red marl of Gloucestershire and Somersetshire.

Communications.—Railway communications are provided principally by the Great Western and Midland companies. Of the Great Western lines, the main line serves Bristol from London. It divides at Bristol, one section serving the south-western counties, another South Wales, crossing beneath the Severn by the Severn Tunnel, 4⅓ m. in length, a remarkable engineering work. A more direct route, by this tunnel, between London and South Wales, is provided by a line from Wootton Bassett on the main line, running north of Bristol by Badminton and Chipping Sodbury. Other Great Western lines are that from Swindon on the main line, by the Stroud valley to Gloucester, crossing the Severn there, and continuing by the right bank of the river into Wales, with branches north-west into Herefordshire; the Oxford and Worcester trunk line, crossing the north-east of the county, connected with Cheltenham and Gloucester by a branch through the Cotteswolds from Chipping Norton junction; and the line from Cheltenham by Broadway to Honeybourne. The west-and-north line of the Midland railway follows the vale from Bristol by Gloucester and Cheltenham with a branch into the forest of Dean by Berkeley, crossing the Severn at Sharpness by a great bridge 1387 yds. in length, with 22 arches. The coal-fields of the forest of Dean are served by several branch lines. In the north, Tewkesbury is served by a Midland branch from Ashchurch to Malvern. The Midland and South-western Junction railway runs east and south from Cheltenham by Cirencester, affording communication with the south of England. The East Gloucester line of the Great Western from Oxford terminates at Fairford. The Thames and Severn canal, rising to a summit level in the tunnel through the Cotteswolds at Sapperton, is continued from Wallbridge (Stroud) by the Stroudwater canal, and gives communication between the two great rivers. The Berkeley Ship Canal (16½ m.) connects the port of Gloucester with its outport of Sharpness on Severn.

Population and Administration.—The area of the ancient county is 795,709 acres, with a population in 1891 of 599,947 and in 1901 of 634,729. The area of the administrative county is 805,482 acres. The county contains 28 hundreds. The municipal boroughs are—Bristol, a city and county borough (pop. 328,945); Cheltenham (49,439); Gloucester, a city and county borough (47,955); Tewkesbury (5419). The other urban districts are—Awre (1096), Charlton Kings (3806), Cirencester (7536), Coleford (2541), Kingswood, on the eastern outskirts of Bristol (11,961), Nailsworth (3028), Newnham (1184), Stow-on-the-Wold (1386), Stroud (9153), Tetbury (1989), Westbury-on-Severn (1866). The number of small ancient market towns is large, especially in the southern part of the vale, on the outskirts of the forest, and among the foot hills of the wolds. Those in the forest district are mostly connected with the coal trade, such as Lydney (3559), besides Awre and Coleford; and, to the north, besides Newnham, Cinderford and Mitcheldean. South from Stroud there are Minchinhampton (3737) and Nailsworth; near the south-eastern boundary Tetbury and Marshfield; Stonehouse (2183), Dursley (2372), Wotton-under-Edge (2992) and Chipping Sodbury along the western line of the hills; and between them and the Severn, Berkeley and Thornbury (2594). Among the uplands of the Cotteswolds there are no towns, and villages are few, but in the east of the county, in the upper Thames basin, there are, besides Cirencester, Fairford on the Coln and Lechlade, close to the head of the navigation on the Thames itself. Far up in the Lech valley, remote from railway communication, is Northleach, once a great posting station on the Oxford and Cheltenham road. In the north-east are Stow-on-the-Wold, standing high, and Moreton-in-the-Marsh near the headwaters of the Evenlode. In a northern prolongation of the county, almost detached, is Chipping Campden. Winchcomb (2699) lies 6 m. N.E. of Cheltenham. In the north-west, Newent (2485) is the only considerable town. Gloucestershire is in the Oxford circuit, and assizes are held at Gloucester. It has one court of quarter sessions, and is divided into 24 petty sessional divisions. The boroughs of Bristol, Gloucester and Tewkesbury have separate commissions of the peace and courts of quarter sessions. There are 359 civil parishes. Gloucestershire is principally in the diocese of Gloucester, but part is in that of Bristol, and small parts in those of Worcester and Oxford. There are 408 ecclesiastical parishes or districts wholly or in part within the county. There are five parliamentary divisions, namely, Tewkesbury or northern, Cirencester or eastern, Stroud or mid, Thornbury or southern, and Forest of Dean, each returning one member. The county also includes the boroughs of Gloucester and Cheltenham, each returning one member; and the greater part of the borough of Bristol, which returns four members.

History.—The English conquest of the Severn valley began in 577 with the victory of Ceawlin at Deorham, followed by the capture of Cirencester, Gloucester and Bath. The Hwiccas who occupied the district were a West Saxon tribe, but their territory had become a dependency of Mercia in the 7th century, and was not brought under West Saxon dominion until the 9th century. No important settlements were made by the Danes in the district. Gloucestershire probably originated as a shire in the 10th century, and is mentioned by name in the Anglo-Saxon

Chronicle in 1016. Towards the close of the 11th century the boundaries were readjusted to include Winchcomb, hitherto a county by itself, and at the same time the forest district between the Wye and the Severn was added to Gloucestershire. The divisions of the county for a long time remained very unsettled, and the thirty-nine hundreds mentioned in the Domesday Survey and the thirty-one hundreds of the Hundred Rolls of 1274 differ very widely in name and extent both from each other and from the twenty-eight hundreds of the present day.

Gloucestershire formed part of Harold's earldom at the time of the Norman invasion, but it offered slight resistance to the Conqueror. In the wars of Stephen's reign the cause of the empress Maud was supported by Robert of Gloucester who had rebuilt the castle at Bristol, and the castles at Gloucester and Cirencester were also garrisoned on her behalf. In the barons' war of the reign of Henry III. Gloucester was garrisoned for Simon de Montfort, but was captured by Prince Edward in 1265, in which year de Montfort was slain at Evesham. Bristol and Gloucester actively supported the Yorkist cause during the Wars of the Roses. In the religious struggles of the 16th century Gloucester showed strong Protestant sympathy, and in the reign of Mary Bishop Hooper was sent to Gloucester to be burnt as a warning to the county, while the same Puritan leanings induced the county to support the Parliamentary cause in the civil war of the 17th century. In 1643 Bristol and Cirencester were captured by the Royalists, but the latter was recovered in the same year and Bristol in 1645. Gloucester was garrisoned for the parliament throughout the struggle.

On the subdivision of the Mercian diocese in 680 the greater part of modern Gloucestershire was included in the diocese of Worcester, and shortly after the Conquest constituted the archdeaconry of Gloucester, which in 1290 comprised the deaneries of Campden, Stow, Cirencester, Fairford, Winchcombe, Stonehouse, Hawkesbury, Bitton, Bristol, Dursley and Gloucester. The district west of the Severn, with the exception of a few parishes in the deaneries of Ross and Staunton, constituted the deanery of the forest within the archdeaconry and diocese of Hereford. In 1535 the deanery of Bitton had been absorbed in that of Hawkesbury. In 1541 the diocese of Gloucester was created, its boundaries being identical with those of the county. On the erection of Bristol to a see in 1542 the deanery of Bristol was transferred from Gloucester to that diocese. In 1836 the sees of Gloucester and Bristol were united; the archdeaconry of Bristol was created out of the deaneries of Bristol, Cirencester, Fairford and Hawkesbury; and the deanery of the forest was transferred to the archdeaconry of Gloucester. In 1882 the archdeaconry of Cirencester was constituted to include the deaneries of Campden, Stow, Northleach north and south, Fairford and Cirencester. In 1897 the diocese of Bristol was recreated, and included the deaneries of Bristol, Stapleton and Bitton.

After the Conquest very extensive lands and privileges in the county were acquired by the church, the abbey of Cirencester alone holding seven hundreds at fee-farm, and the estates of the principal lay-tenants were for the most part outlying parcels of baronies having their "caput" in other counties. The large estates held by William Fitz Osbern, earl of Hereford, escheated to the crown on the rebellion of his son Earl Roger in 1074-1075. The Berkeleys have held lands in Gloucestershire from the time of the Domesday Survey, and the families of Basset, Tracy, Clifton, Dennis and Poyntz have figured prominently in the annals of the county. Gilbert de Clare, earl of Gloucester, and Richard of Cornwall claimed extensive lands and privileges in the shire in the 13th century, and Simon de Montfort owned Minsterworth and Rodley.

135

Bristol was made a county in 1425, and in 1483 Richard III. created Gloucester an independent county, adding to it the hundreds of Dudston and King's Barton. The latter were reunited to Gloucestershire in 1673, but the cities of Bristol and Gloucester continued to rank as independent counties, with separate jurisdiction, county rate and assizes. The chief officer of the forest of Dean was the warden, who was generally also constable of St Briavel Castle. The first justice-seat for the forest was held at Gloucester Castle in 1282, the last in 1635. The hundred of the duchy of Lancaster is within the jurisdiction of the duchy of Lancaster for certain purposes.

The physical characteristics of the three natural divisions of Gloucestershire have given rise in each to a special industry, as already indicated. The forest district, until the development of the Sussex mines in the 16th century, was the chief iron-producing area of the kingdom, the mines having been worked in Roman times, while the abundance of timber gave rise to numerous tanneries and to an important ship-building trade. The hill district, besides fostering agricultural pursuits, gradually absorbed the woollen trade from the big towns, which now devoted themselves almost entirely to foreign commerce. Silk-weaving was introduced in the 17th century, and was especially prosperous in the Stroud valley. The abundance of clay and building-stone in the county gave rise to considerable manufactures of brick, tiles and pottery. Numerous minor industries sprang up in the 17th and 18th centuries, such as flax-growing and the manufacture of pins, buttons, lace, stockings, rope and sailcloth.

Gloucestershire was first represented in parliament in 1290, when it returned two members. Bristol and Gloucester acquired representation in 1295, Cirencester in 1572 and Tewkesbury in 1620. Under the Reform Act of 1832 the county returned four members in two divisions; Bristol, Gloucester, Cirencester, Stroud and Tewkesbury returned two members each, and Cheltenham returned one member. The act of 1868 reduced the representation of Cirencester and Tewkesbury to one member each.

Antiquities.—The cathedrals of Gloucester and Bristol, the magnificent abbey church of Tewkesbury, and the church of Cirencester with its great Perpendicular porch, are described under their separate headings. Of the abbey of Hayles near Winchcomb, founded by Richard, earl of Cornwall, in 1246, little more than the foundations are left, but these have been excavated with great care, and interesting fragments have been brought to light. Most of the old market towns have fine parish churches. At Deerhurst near Tewkesbury, and Cleeve near Cheltenham, there are churches of special interest on account of the pre-Norman work they retain. The Perpendicular church at Lechlade is unusually perfect; and that at Fairford was built (*c.* 1500), according to tradition, to contain the remarkable series of stained-glass windows which are said to have been brought from the Netherlands. These are, however, adjudged to be of English workmanship, and are one of the finest series in the country. The great Decorated Calcot Barn is an interesting relic of the monastery of Kingswood near Tetbury. The castle at Berkeley is a splendid example of a feudal stronghold. Thornbury Castle, in the same district, is a fine Tudor ruin, the pretensions of which evoked the jealousy of Cardinal Wolsey against its builder, Edward Stafford, duke of Buckingham, who was beheaded in 1521. Near Cheltenham is the fine 15th-century mansion of Southam de la Bere, of timber and stone. Memorials of the de la Bere family appear in the church at Cleeve. The mansion contains a tiled floor from Hayles Abbey. Near Winchcomb is Sudeley Castle, dating from the 15th century, but the inhabited portion is chiefly Elizabethan. The chapel is the burial place of Queen Catherine Parr. At Great Badminton is the mansion and vast domain of the Beauforts (formerly of the Botelers and others), on the south-eastern boundary of the county.

See *Victoria County History, Gloucestershire*; Sir R. Atkyns, *The Ancient and Present State of Gloucestershire* (London, 1712; 2nd ed., London, 1768); Samuel Rudder, *A New History of Gloucestershire* (Cirencester, 1779); Ralph Bigland, *Historical, Monumental and Genealogical Collections relative to the County of Gloucester* (2 vols., London, 1791); Thomas Rudge, *The History of the County of Gloucester* (2 vols., Gloucester, 1803); T. D. Fosbroke *Abstract of Records and Manuscripts respecting the County of Gloucestershire formed into a History* (2 vols., Gloucester, 1807); *Legends, Tales and Songs in the Dialect of the Peasantry of Gloucestershire* (London, 1876); J. D. Robertson, *Glossary of Dialect and Archaic Words of Gloucester* (London, 1890); W. Bazeley and F. A. Hyett, *Bibliographers' Manual of Gloucestershire* (3 vols., London, 1895-1897); W. H. Hutton, *By Thames and Cotswold* (London, 1903). See also *Transactions of the Bristol and Gloucestershire Archaeological Society*.

GLOVE (O. Eng. *glof*, perhaps connected with Gothic *lofa*, the palm of the hand), a covering for the hand, commonly with a separate sheath for each finger.

The use of gloves is of high antiquity, and apparently was known even to the pre-historic cave dwellers. In Homer Laërtes is described as wearing gloves (χειρῖδας ἐπὶ χερσί) while walking in his garden (*Od.* xxiv. 230). Herodotus (vi. 72) tells how Leotychides filled a glove (χειρίς) with the money he received as a bribe, and Xenophon (*Cyrop.* viii. 8. 17) records that the Persians wore fur gloves having separate sheaths for the fingers (χειρῖδας δασείας καὶ δακτυλήθρας). Among the Romans also there are occasional references to the use of gloves. According to the younger Pliny (*Ep.* iii. 5. 15) the secretary whom his uncle had with him when ascending Vesuvius wore gloves (*manicae*) so that he might not be impeded in his work by the cold, and Varro (*R.R.* i. 55. 1) remarks that olives gathered with the bare fingers are better than those gathered with gloves (*digitabula* or *digitalia*). In the northern countries the general use of gloves would be more natural than in the south, and it is not without significance that the most common medieval Latin word for glove (*guantus* or *wantus*, Mod. Fr. *gant*) is of Teutonic origin (O. H. Ger. *want*). Thus in the life of Columbanus by Jonas, abbot of Bobbio (d. *c.* 665), gloves for protecting the hands in doing manual labour are spoken of as *tegumenta manuum quae Galli wantos vocant*. Among the Germans and Scandinavians, in the 8th and 9th centuries, the use of gloves, fingerless at first, would seem to have been all but universal; and in the case of kings, prelates and nobles they were often elaborately embroidered and bejewelled. This was more particularly the case with the gloves which formed part of the pontifical vestments (see below). In war and in the chase gloves of leather, or with the backs armoured with articulated iron plates, were early worn; yet in the Bayeux tapestry the warriors on either side fight ungloved. The fact that gloves are not represented by contemporary artists does not prove their non-existence, since this might easily be an omission due to lack of observation or of skill; but, so far as the records go, there is no

20

evidence to prove that gloves were in general use in England until the 13th century. It was in this century that ladies began to wear gloves as ornaments; they were of linen and sometimes reached to the elbow. It was, however, not till the 16th century that they reached their greatest elaboration, when Queen Elizabeth set the fashion for wearing them richly embroidered and jewelled.

The symbolic sense of the middle ages early gave to the use of gloves a special significance. Their liturgical use by the Church is dealt with below (*Pontifical gloves*); this was imitated from the usage of civil life. Embroidered and jewelled gloves formed part of the *insignia* of the emperors, and also, and that quite early, of the kings of England. Thus Matthew of Paris, in recording the burial of Henry II. in 1189, mentions that he was buried in his coronation robes, with a golden crown on his head and gloves on his hands. Gloves were also found on the hands of King John when his tomb was opened in 1797, and on those of King Edward I. when his tomb was opened in 1774.

See W. B. Redfern, *Royal and Historic Gloves and Shoes*, with numerous examples.

Gages.—Of the symbolical uses of the glove one of the most widespread and important during the middle ages was the practice of tendering a folded glove as a gage for waging one's law. The origin of this custom is probably not far to seek. The promise to fulfil a judgment of a court of law, a promise secured by the delivery of a *wed* or gage, is one of the oldest, if not the very oldest, of all enforceable contracts. This gage was originally a chattel of value, which had to be deposited at once by the defendant as security into his adversary's hand; and that the glove became the formal symbol of such deposit is doubtless due to its being the most convenient loose object for the purpose. The custom survived after the contract with the *vadium, wed* or gage had been superseded by the contract with pledges (personal sureties). In the rules of procedure of a baronial court of the 14th century we find: "He shall wage his law with his folded glove (*de son gaunt plyee*) and shall deliver it into the hand of the other, and then take his glove back and find pledges for his law." The delivery of the glove had, in fact, become a mere ceremony, because the defendant had his sureties close at hand.1

Associated with this custom was the use of the glove in the wager of battle (*vadium in duello*). The glove here was thrown down by the defendant in open court as security that he would defend his cause in arms; the accuser by picking it up accepted the challenge (see WAGER). This form is still prescribed for the challenge of the king's champion at the coronation of English sovereigns, and was actually followed at that of George IV. (seeCHAMPION). The phrase "to throw down the gauntlet" is still in common use of any challenge.

Pledges of Service.—The use of the glove as a pledge of fulfilment is exemplified also by the not infrequent practice of enfeoffing vassals by investing them with the glove; similarly the emperors symbolized by the bestowal of a glove the concession of the right to found a town or to establish markets, mints and the like; the "hands" in the armorial bearings of certain German towns are really gloves, reminiscent of this investiture. Conversely, fiefs were held by the render of presenting gloves to the sovereign. Thus the manor of Little Holland in Essex was held in Queen Elizabeth's time by the service of one knight's fee and the rent of a pair of gloves turned up with hare's skin (Blount's *Tenures*, ed. Beckwith, p. 130). The most notable instance in England, however, is the grand serjeanty of finding for the king a glove for his right hand on coronation day, and supporting his right arm as long as he holds the sceptre. The right to perform this "honourable service" was originally granted by William the Conqueror to Bertram de Verdun, together with the manor of Fernham (Farnham Royal) in Buckinghamshire. The male descendants of Bertram performed this serjeanty at the coronations until the death of Theobald de Verdun in 1316, when the right passed, with the manor of Farnham, to Thomas Lord Furnival by his marriage with the heiress Joan. His son William Lord Furnival performed the ceremony at the coronation of Richard II. He died in 1383, and his daughter and heiress Jean de Furnival having married Sir Thomas Nevill, Lord Furnival in her right, the latter performed the ceremony at the coronation of Henry IV. His heiress Maud married Sir John Talbot (1st earl of Shrewsbury) who, as Lord Furnival, presented the glove embroidered with the arms of Verdun at the coronation of Henry V. When in 1541 Francis earl of Shrewsbury exchanged the manor of Farnham with King Henry VIII. for the site and precincts of the priory of Worksop in Nottinghamshire he stipulated that the right to perform this serjeanty should be reserved to him, and the king accordingly transferred the obligation from Farnham to Worksop. On the 3rd of April 1838 the manor of Worksop was sold to the duke of Newcastle and with it the right to perform the service, which had hitherto always been carried out by a descendant of Bertram de Verdun. At the coronation of King Edward VII. the earl of Shrewsbury disputed the duke of Newcastle's right, on the ground that the serjeanty was attached not to the manor but to the priory lands at Worksop, and that the latter had been subdivided by sale so that no single person was entitled to perform the ceremony and the right had therefore lapsed. His petition for a regrant to himself as lineal heir of Bertram de Verdun, however, was disallowed by the court of claims, and the serjeanty was declared to be attached to the manor of Worksop (G. Woods Wollaston, *Coronation Claims*, London, 1903, p. 133).

Presentations.—From the ceremonial and symbolic use of gloves the transition was easy to the custom which grew up of presenting them to persons of distinction on special occasions. When Queen Elizabeth visited Cambridge in 1578 the vice-chancellor offered her a "paire of gloves, perfumed and garnished with embroiderie and goldsmithe's wourke, price 60s.," and at the visit of James I. there in 1615 the mayor and corporation of the town "delivered His Majesty a fair pair of perfumed gloves with gold laces." It was formerly the custom in England for bishops at their consecrations to make presents of gloves to those who came to their consecration dinners and others, but this gift became such a burden to them that by an order in council in 1678 It was commuted for the payment of a sum of £50 towards the rebuilding of St Paul's. Serjeants at law, on their appointment, were given a pair of gloves containing a sum of money which was termed "regards"; this custom is recorded as early as 1495, when according to the *Black Book* of Lincoln's Inn each of the new Serjeants received £6, 13s. 4d. and a pair of gloves costing 4d., and it persisted to a late period. At one time it was the practice for a prisoner who pleaded the king's pardon on his discharge to present the judges with gloves by way of a fee. Glove-silver, according to Jacob's *Law Dictionary*, was a name used of extraordinary rewards formerly given to officers of courts, &c., or of money given by the sheriff of a county in which no offenders were left for execution to the clerk of assize and judge's officers; the explanation of the term is that the glove given as a perquisite or fee was in some cases lined with money to increase its value, and thus came to stand for money ostensibly given in lieu of gloves. It is still the custom in the United Kingdom to present a pair of white gloves to a judge or magistrate who when he takes his seat for criminal business at the appointed time finds no cases for trial. By ancient custom judges are not allowed to wear gloves while actually sitting on the bench, and a witness taking the oath must remove the glove from the hand that holds the book. (See J. W. Norton-Kyshe, *The Law and Customs relating to Gloves*, London, 1901.)

Pontifical gloves (Lat. *chirothecae*) are liturgical ornaments peculiar to the Western Church and proper only to the pope, the cardinals and bishops, though the right to wear them is often granted by the Holy See to abbots, cathedral dignitaries and other prelates, as in the case of the other episcopal insignia. According to the present use the gloves are of silk and of the liturgical colour of the day, the edge of the opening ornamented with a narrow band of embroidery or the like, and the middle of the back with a cross. They may be worn only at the celebration of mass (except masses for the dead). In vesting, the gloves are put on the bishop immediately after the dalmatic, the right hand one by the deacon, the other by the subdeacon. They are worn only until the ablution before the canon of the mass, after which they may not again be put on.

At the consecration of a bishop the consecrating prelate puts the gloves on the new bishop immediately after the mitre, with a prayer that his hands may be kept pure, so that the sacrifice he offers may be as acceptable as the gift of venison which Jacob, his hands wrapped in the skin of kids, brought to Isaac. This symbolism (as in the case of the other vestments) is, however, of late growth. The liturgical use of gloves itself cannot, according to Father Braun, be traced beyond the beginning of the 10th century, and their introduction was due, perhaps to the simple desire to keep the hands clean for the holy mysteries, but more probably merely as part of the increasing pomp with which the Carolingian bishops were surrounding themselves. From the Frankish kingdom the custom spread to Rome, where liturgical gloves are first heard of in the earlier half of the 11th century. The earliest authentic instance of the right to wear them being granted to a non-bishop is a bull of Alexander IV. in 1070, conceding this to the abbot of S. Pietro in Cielo d' Oro.

During the middle ages the occasions on which pontifical gloves (often *wanti, guanti*, and sometimes *manicae* in the inventories) 137were worn were not so carefully defined as now, the use varying in different churches. Nor were the liturgical colours prescribed. The most characteristic feature of the medieval pontifical glove was the ornament (*tasellus, fibula, monile, paratura*) set in the middle of the back of the glove. This was usually a small plaque of metal, enamelled or jewelled, generally round, but sometimes square or irregular in shape. Sometimes embroidery was substituted; still more rarely the whole glove was covered, even to the fingers, with elaborate needlework designs.

Liturgical gloves have not been worn by Anglican bishops since the Reformation, though they are occasionally represented as wearing them on their effigies.

See J. Braun, S.J., *Die liturgische Gewandung* (Freiburg im Breisgau, 1907), pp. 359-382, where many beautiful examples are illustrated.

Manufacture of Gloves.—Three countries, according to an old proverb, contribute to the making of a good glove—Spain dressing the leather, France cutting it and England sewing it. But the manufacture of gloves was not introduced into Great Britain till the 10th or 11th century. The incorporation of glovers of Perth was chartered in 1165, and in 1190 a glove-makers' gild was formed in France, with the object of regulating the trade and ensuring good workmanship. The glovers of London in 1349 framed their ordinances and had them approved by the corporation, the city regulations at that time fixing the price of a pair of common sheepskin gloves at 1d. In 1464, when the gild received armorial bearings, they do not seem to have been very strong, but apparently their position improved subsequently and in 1638 they were incorporated as a new company. In 1580 it is recorded that both French and Spanish gloves were on sale in London shops, and in 1661 a company of glovers was incorporated at Worcester, which still remains an important seat of the English glove industry. In America the manufacture of gloves dates from about 1760, when Sir William Johnson brought over several families of glove makers from Perth; these settled in Fulton county, New York, which is now the largest seat of the glove trade in the United States.

Gloves may be divided into two distinct categories, according as these are made of leather or are woven or knitted from fibres such as silk, wool or cotton. The manufacture of the latter kinds is a branch of the hosiery industry. For leather gloves skins of various animals are employed—deer, calves, sheep and lambs, goats and kids, &c.—but kids have had nothing to do with the production of many of the "kid gloves" of commerce. The skins are prepared and dressed by special processes (see LEATHER) before going to the glove-maker to be cut. Owing to the elastic character of the material the cutting is a delicate operation, and long practice is required before a man becomes expert at it. Formerly it was done by shears, the workmen following an outline marked on the leather, but now steel dies are universally employed not only for the bodies of the gloves but also for the thumb-pieces and fourchettes or sides of the fingers. When hand sewing is employed the pieces to be sewn together are placed between a pair of jaws, the holding edges of which are serrated with fine saw-teeth, and the sewer by passing the needle forwards and backwards between each of these teeth secures neat uniform stitching. But sewing machines are now widely employed on the work. The labour of making a glove is much subdivided, different operators sewing different pieces, and others again embroidering the back, forming the button-holes, attaching the buttons, &c. After the gloves are completed, they undergo the process of "laying off," in which they are drawn over metal forms, shaped like a hand and heated internally by steam; in this way they are finally smoothed and shaped before being wrapped in paper and packed in boxes.

Gloves made of thin india-rubber or of white cotton are worn by some surgeons while performing operations, on account of the ease with which they can be thoroughly sterilized.

1F. W. Maitland and W. P. Baildon, *The Court Baron* (Selden Society, London, 1891), p. 17. Maitland wrongly translates *gaunt plyee* as "twisted" glove, adding "why it should be twisted I cannot say." An earlier instance of the delivery of a folded glove as gage is quoted from the 13th-century Anglo-Norman poem known as *The Song of Dermott and the Earl* (ed. G. H. Orpen, Oxford, 1892) in J. H. Round's *Commune of London*, p. 153.

GLOVER, SIR JOHN HAWLEY (1829-1885), captain in the British navy, entered the service in 1841 and passed his examination as lieutenant in 1849, but did not receive a commission till May 1851. He served on various stations, and was wounded severely in an action with the Burmese at Donabew (4th February 1853). But his reputation was not gained at sea and as a naval officer, but on shore and as an administrative official in the colonies. During his years of service as lieutenant in the navy he had had considerable experience of the coast of Africa, and had taken part in the expedition of Dr W. B. Baikie (1824-1864) up the Niger. On the 21st of April 1863 he was appointed administrator of the government of Lagos, and in that capacity, or as colonial secretary, he remained there till 1872. During this period he had been much employed in repelling the marauding incursions of the Ashantis. When the Ashanti war broke out in 1873, Captain Glover undertook the hazardous and doubtful task of organizing the native tribes, whom hatred of the Ashantis might be expected to make favourable to the British authorities—to the extent at least to which their fears would allow them to act. His services were accepted, and in September of 1873 he landed at Cape Coast, and, after forming a small trustworthy force of Hausa, marched to Accra. His influence sufficed to gather a numerous native force, but neither he nor anybody else could overcome their abject terror of the ferocious Ashantis to the extent of making them fight. In January 1874 Captain Glover was able to render some assistance in the taking of Kumasi, but it was at the head of a Hausa force. His services were acknowledged by the thanks of parliament and by his creation as G.C.M.G. In 1875 he was appointed governor of Newfoundland and held the post till 1881, when he was transferred to the Leeward Islands. He returned to Newfoundland in 1883, and died in London on the 30th September 1885.

23

Lady Glover's *Life* of her husband appeared in 1897.

GLOVER, RICHARD (1712-1785), English poet, son of Richard Glover, a Hamburg merchant, was born in London in 1712. He was educated at Cheam in Surrey. While there he wrote in his sixteenth year a poem to the memory of Sir Isaac Newton, which was prefixed by Dr Pemberton to his *View of Newton's Philosophy*, published in 1728. In 1737 he published an epic poem in praise of liberty, *Leonidas*, which was thought to have a special reference to the politics of the time; and being warmly commended by the prince of Wales and his court, it soon passed through several editions. In 1739 Glover published a poem entitled *London, or the Progress of Commerce*; and in the same year, with a view to exciting the nation against the Spaniards, he wrote a spirited ballad, *Hosier's Ghost*, very popular in its day. He was also the author of two tragedies, *Boadicea* (1753) and *Medea* (1761), written in close imitation of Greek models. The success of Glover's *Leonidas* led him to take considerable interest in politics, and in 1761 he entered parliament as member for Weymouth. He died on the 25th of November 1785. The *Athenaid*, an epic in thirty books, was published in 1787, and his diary, entitled *Memoirs of a distinguished literary and political Character from 1742 to 1757*, appeared in 1813. Glover was one of the reputed authors of *Junius*; but his claims—which were advocated in an *Inquiry concerning the author of the Letters of Junius* (1815), by R. Duppa—rest on very slight grounds.

GLOVERSVILLE, a city of Fulton county, New York, U.S.A., at the foot-hills of the Adirondacks, about 55 m. N.W. of Albany. Pop. (1890) 13,864; (1900) 18,349, of whom 2542 were foreign-born; (1910 census) 20,642. It is served by the Fonda, Johnstown & Gloversville railway (connecting at Fonda, about 9 m. distant, with the New York Central), and by electric lines connecting with Johnstown, Amsterdam and Schenectady. The city has a public library (26,000 volumes in 1908), the Nathan Littauer memorial hospital, a state armoury and a fine government building. Gloversville is the principal glove-manufacturing centre in the United States. In 1900 Fulton county produced more than 57%, and Gloversville 38.8%, of all the leather gloves and mittens made in the United States; in 1905 Gloversville produced 29.9% of the leather gloves and mittens made in the United States, its products being valued at $5,302,196. Gloversville has more than a score of tanneries and leather-finishing factories, and manufactures fur goods. In 1905 the city's total factory product was valued at $9,340,763. The extraordinary localization of the glove-making industry in Gloversville, Johnstown and other parts of Fulton county, is an incident of much interest in the economic history of the United States. The industry seems to have had its origin among a colony of Perthshire families, including many glove-makers, who were settled in this region by Sir William Johnson about 1760. For many years the entire product seems to have been disposed of in the neighbourhood, but about 1809 the goods began to find more distant markets, and by 1825 the industry was firmly established on a prosperous basis, the trade being handed down from father to son. An interesting phase of the development is that, in addition to the factory work, a large amount of the industry is in the hands of "home workers" both in the town and country districts. Gloversville, settled originally about 1770, was known for some time as Stump City, its present name being adopted in 1832. It was incorporated as a village in 1851 and was chartered as a city in 1890.

GLOW-WORM, the popular name of the wingless female of the beetle *Lampyris noctiluca*, whose power of emitting light has been familiar for many centuries. The luminous organs of the glow-worm consist of cells similar to those of the fat-body, grouped into paired masses in the ventral region of the hinder abdominal segments. The light given out by the wingless female insect is believed to serve as an attraction to the flying male, whose luminous organs remain in a rudimentary condition. The common glow-worm is a widespread European and Siberian insect, generally distributed in England and ranging in Scotland northwards to the Tay, but unknown in Ireland. Exotic species of *Lampyris* are similarly luminous, and light-giving organs are present in many genera of the family *Lampyridae* from various parts of the world. Frequently—as in the south European *Luciola italica*—both sexes of the beetle are provided with wings, and both male and female emit light. These luminous, winged Lampyrids are generally known as "fire-flies." In correspondence with their power of emitting light, the insects are nocturnal in habit.

Elongate centipedes of the family *Geophilidae*, certain species of which are luminous, are sometimes mistaken for the true glow-worm.

GLOXINIA, a charming decorative plant, botanically a species of *Sinningia* (*S. speciosa*), a member of the natural order Gesneraceae and a native of Brazil. The species has given rise under cultivation to numerous forms showing a wonderful variety of colour, and hybrid forms have also been obtained between these and other species of *Sinningia*. A good strain of seed will

24

produce many superb and charmingly coloured varieties, and if sown early in spring, in a temperature of 65° at night, they may be shifted on into 6-in. pots, and in these may be flowered during the summer. The bulbs are kept at rest through the winter in dry sand, in a temperature of 50°, and to yield a succession should be started at intervals, say at the end of February and the beginning of April. To prolong the blooming season, use weak manure water when the flower-buds show themselves.

GLUCINUM, an alternative name for Beryllium (*q.v.*). When L. N. Vauquelin in 1798 published in the *Annales de chimie* an account of a new earth obtained by him from beryl he refrained from giving the substance a name, but in a note to his paper the editors suggested glucine, from γλυκύς, sweet, in reference to the taste of its salts, whence the name Glucinum or Glucinium (symbol Gl. or sometimes G). The name beryllium was given to the metal by German chemists and was generally used until recently, when the earlier name was adopted.

GLUCK,1 **CHRISTOPH WILLIBALD** (1714-1787), operatic composer, German by his nationality, French by his place in art, was born at Weidenwang, near Neumarkt, in the upper Palatinate, on the 2nd of July 1714. He belonged to the lower middle class, his father being gamekeeper to Prince Lobkowitz; but the boy's education was not neglected on that account. From his twelfth to his eighteenth year he frequented the Jesuit school of Kommotau in the neighbourhood of Prince Lobkowitz's estate in Bohemia, where he not only received a good general education, but also had lessons in music. At the age of eighteen Gluck went to Prague, where he continued his musical studies under Czernohorsky, and maintained himself by the exercise of his art, sometimes in the very humble capacity of fiddler at village fairs and dances. Through the introductions of Prince Lobkowitz, however, he soon gained access to the best families of the Austrian nobility; and when in 1736 he proceeded to Vienna he was hospitably received at his protector's palace. Here he met Prince Melzi, an ardent lover of music, whom he accompanied to Milan, continuing his education under Giovanni Battista San Martini, a great musical historian and contrapuntist, who was also famous in his own day as a composer of church and chamber music. We soon find Gluck producing operas at the rapid rate necessitated by the omnivorous taste of the Italian public in those days. Nine of these works were produced at various Italian theatres between 1741 and 1745. Although their artistic value was small, they were so favourably received that in 1745 Gluck was invited to London to compose for the Haymarket. The first opera produced there was called *La Caduta dei giganti*; it was followed by a revised version of one of his earlier operas. Gluck also appeared in London as a performer on the musical glasses (see HARMONICA).

The success of his two operas, as well as that of a *pasticcio* (*i.e.* a collection of favourite arias set to a new libretto) entitled *Piramo e Tisbe*, was anything but brilliant, and he accordingly left London. But his stay in England was not without important consequences for his subsequent career. Gluck at this time was rather less than an ordinary producer of Italian opera. Handel's well-known saying that Gluck "knew no more counterpoint than his cook" must be taken in connexion with the less well-known fact that that cook was an excellent bass singer who performed in many of Handel's own operas. But it indicates the musical reason of Gluck's failure, while Gluck himself learnt the dramatic reason through his surprise at finding that arias which in their original setting had been much applauded lost all effect when adapted to new words in the *pasticcio*. Irrelevant as Handel's criticism appears, it was not without bearing on Gluck's difficulties. The use of counterpoint has very little necessary connexion with contrapuntal display; its real and final cause is a certain depth of harmonic expression which Gluck attained only in his most dramatic moments, and for want of which he, even in his finest works, sometimes moved very lamely. And in later years his own mature view of the importance of harmony, which he upheld in long arguments with Grétry, who believed only in melody, shows that he knew that the dramatic expression of music must strike below the surface. At this early period he was simply producing Handelian opera in an amateurish style, suggesting an unsuccessful imitation of Hasse; but the failure of his *pasticcio* is as significant to us as it was to him, since it shows that already the effect of his music depended upon its characteristic treatment of dramatic situations. This characterizing power was as yet not directly evident, and it needed all the influence of the new instrumental resources of the rising sonata-forms before music could pass out of what we may call its architectural and decorative period and enter into dramatic regions at all.

It is highly probable that the chamber music of his master, San Martini, had already indicated to Gluck a new direction which was more or less incompatible with the older art; and there is nothing discreditable either to Gluck or to his contemporaries in the failure of his earlier works. Had the young composer been successful in the ordinary *opera seria*, there is reason to fear that the great dramatic reform, initiated by him, might not have taken place. The critical temper of the London public fortunately averted this calamity. It may also be assumed that the musical atmosphere of the English capital, and especially the great works of Handel, were not without beneficial influence upon the young composer. But of still greater importance in this respect was a short trip to Paris, where Gluck became for the first time acquainted with the classic traditions and the declamatory style of the French opera—a sphere of music in which his own greatest triumphs were to be achieved. Of these great issues little trace, however, is to be found in the works produced by Gluck during the fifteen years after his return from England. In this period Gluck, in a long course of works by no means free from the futile old traditions, gained technical experience and important patronage, though his success was not uniform. His first opera written for Vienna, *La Semiramide riconosciuta*, is again an ordinary *opera seria*, and little more can be said of *Telemacco*, although thirty years later Gluck was able to use most of its overture and an energetic duet in one of his greatest works, *Armide*.

Gluck settled permanently at Vienna in 1756, having two years previously been appointed court chapel-master, with a salary of 2000 florins, by the empress Maria Theresa. He had already received the order of knighthood from the pope in consequence of the successful production of two of his works in Rome. During the long interval from 1756 to 1762 Gluck seems to have matured his plans for the reform of the opera; and, barring a ballet named *Don Giovanni*, and some *airs nouveaux* to French words with pianoforte accompaniment, no compositions of any importance have to be recorded. Several later *pièces d'occasion*, such as *Il Trionfo di Clelia* (1763), are still written in the old manner, though already in 1762 *Orfeo ed Euridice* shows that the composer had entered upon a new career. Gluck had for the first time deserted Metastasio for Raniero Calzabigi, who, as Vernon Lee suggests, was in all probability the immediate cause of the formation of Gluck's new ideas, as he was a hot-headed dramatic theorist with a violent dislike for Metastasio, who had hitherto dominated the whole sphere of operatic libretto.

Quite apart from its significance in the history of dramatic music, *Orpheus* is a work which, by its intrinsic beauty, commands the highest admiration. Orpheus's air, *Che faro*, is known to every one; but still finer is the great scena in which the poet's song softens even the *ombre sdegnose* of Tartarus. The ascending passion of the entries of the solo (*Deh! placatevi; Mille pene; Men tiranne*), interrupted by the harsh but gradually softening exclamations of the Furies, is of the highest dramatic effect. These melodies, moreover, as well as every declamatory passage assigned to Orpheus, are made subservient to the purposes of dramatic characterization; that is, they could not possibly be assigned to any other person in the drama, any more than Hamlet's monologue could be spoken by Polonius. It is in this power of musically realizing a character—a power all but unknown in the serious opera of his day—that Gluck's genius as a dramatic composer is chiefly shown. After a short relapse into his earlier manner, Gluck followed up his *Orpheus* by a second classical music-drama (1767) named *Alceste*. In his dedication of the score to the grand-duke of Tuscany, he fully expressed his aims, as well as the reasons for his total breach with the old traditions. "I shall try," he wrote, "to reduce music to its real function, that of seconding poetry by intensifying the expression of sentiments and the interest of situations without interrupting the action by needless ornament. I have accordingly taken care not to interrupt the singer in the heat of the dialogue, to wait for a tedious *ritornel*, nor do I allow him to stop on a sonorous vowel, in the middle of a phrase, in order to show the nimbleness of a beautiful voice in a long *cadenza*." Such theories, and the stern consistency with which they were carried out, were little to the taste of the pleasure-loving Viennese; and the success of *Alceste*, as well as that of *Paris and Helena*, which followed two years later, was not such as Gluck had desired and expected. He therefore eagerly accepted the chance of finding a home for his art in the centre of intellectual and more especially dramatic life, Paris. Such a chance was opened to him through the *bailli* Le Blanc du Roullet, attaché of the French embassy at Vienna, and a musical amateur who entered into Gluck's ideas with enthusiasm. A classic opera for the Paris stage was accordingly projected, and the friends fixed upon Racine's *Iphigénie en Aulide*. After some difficulties, overcome chiefly by the intervention of Gluck's former pupil the dauphiness Marie Antoinette, the opera was at last accepted and performed at the Académie de Musique, on the 19th of April 1774.

The great importance of the new work was at once perceived by the musical amateurs of the French capital, and a hot controversy on the merits of *Iphigénie* ensued, in which some of the leading literary men of France took part. Amongst the opponents of Gluck were not only the admirers of Italian vocalization and sweetness, but also the adherents of the earlier French school, who refused to see in the new composer the legitimate successor of Lulli and Rameau. Marmontel, Laharpe and D'Alembert were his opponents, the Abbé Arnaud and others his enthusiastic friends. Rousseau took a peculiar position in the struggle. In his early writings he is a violent partisan of Italian music, but when Gluck himself appeared as the French champion Rousseau acknowledged the great composer's genius; although he did not always understand it, as for example when he suggested that in *Alceste*, "Divinités du Styx," perhaps the most majestic of all Gluck's arias, ought to have been set as a rondo. Nevertheless in a letter to Dr Burney, written shortly before his death, Rousseau gives a close and appreciative analysis of *Alceste*, the first Italian version of which Gluck had submitted to him for suggestions; and when, on the first performance of the piece not being received favourably by the Parisian audience, the composer exclaimed, "*Alceste est tombée*," Rousseau is said to have comforted him with the flattering *bonmot*, "*Oui, mais elle est tombée du ciel.*" The contest received a still more personal character when Piccinni, a celebrated and by no means incapable composer, came to Paris as the champion of the Italian party at the invitation of Madame du Barry, who held a rival court to that of the young princess (see OPERA). As a dramatic controversy it suggests a parallel with the Wagnerian and anti-Wagnerian warfare of a later age; but there is no such radical difference between Gluck's and Piccinni's musical methods as the comparison would suggest. Gluck was by far the better musician, but his deficiencies in musical technique were of a kind which contemporaries could perceive as easily as they could perceive Piccinni's. Both composers were remarkable inventors of melody, and both had the gift of making incorrect music sound agreeable. Gluck's indisputable dramatic power might be plausibly dismissed as irrelevant by upholders of music for music's sake, even if Piccinni himself had not chosen, as he did, to assimilate every feature in Gluck's style that he could understand. The rivalry between the two composers was soon developed into a quarrel by the skilful engineering of Gluck's enemies. In 1777 Piccinni was given a libretto by Marmontel on the subject of *Roland*, to Gluck's intense disgust, as he had already begun an opera on that subject himself. This, and the failure of an attempt to show his command of a lighter style by furbishing up some earlier works at the instigation of Marie Antoinette, inspired Gluck to produce his *Armide*, which appeared four months before Piccinni's *Roland* was ready, and raised a storm of controversy, admiration and abuse. Gluck did not anticipate Wagner more clearly in his dramatic reforms than in his caustic temper; and, as in Gluck's own estimation the difference between *Armide* and *Alceste* is that "*l'un (Alceste) doit faire pleurer et l'autre faire éprouver une voluptueuse sensation*," it was extremely annoying for him to be told by Laharpe that he had made Armide a sorceress instead of an enchantress, and that her part was "*une criaillerie monotone et fatiguante.*" He replied to Laharpe in a long public letter worthy of Wagner in its venomous sarcasm and its tremendous value as an advertisement for its recipient.

Gluck's next work was *Iphigénie en Tauride*, the success of which finally disposed of Piccinni, who produced a work on the same subject at the same time and who is said to have acknowledged Gluck's superiority. Gluck's next work was *Écho et Narcisse*, the comparative failure of which greatly disappointed him; and during the composition of another opera, *Les Danaïdes*, an attack of apoplexy compelled him to give up work. He left Paris for Vienna, where he lived for several years in dignified leisure, disturbed only by his declining health. He died on the 15th of November 1787.

(F. H.; D. F. T.)

The great interest of the dramatic aspect of Gluck's reforms is apt to overshadow his merit as a musician, and yet in some ways to idealize it. One is tempted to regard him as condoning for technical musical deficiencies by sheer dramatic power, whereas unprejudiced study of his work shows that where his dramatic power asserts itself there is no lack of musical technique. Indeed only a great musician could so reform opera as to give it scope for dramatic power at all. Where Gluck differs from the greatest musicians is in his absolute dependence on literature for his inspiration. Where his librettist failed him (as in his last complete work, *Écho et Narcisse*), he could hardly write tolerably good music; and, even in the finest works of his French period, the less emotional situations are sometimes set to music which has little interest except as a document in the history of the art. This must not be taken to mean merely that Gluck could not, like Mozart and nearly all the great song-writers, set good music to a bad text. Such inability would prove Gluck's superior literary taste without casting a slur on his musicianship. But it points to a certain weakness as a musician that Gluck could not be inspired except by the more thrilling portions of his libretti. When he was inspired there was no question that he was the first and greatest writer of dramatic music before Mozart. To begin with, he could invent sublime melodies; and his power of producing great musical effects by the simplest means was nothing short of Handelian. Moreover, in his peculiar sphere he deserves the title generally accorded to Haydn of "father of modern orchestration." It is misleading to say that he was the first to use the timbre of instruments with a sense of emotional effect, for Bach and Handel well knew how to give a whole aria or whole chorus peculiar tone by means of a definite scheme of instrumentation. But Gluck did not treat instruments as part of a decorative design, any more than he so treated musical forms. Just as his sense of musical form is that of Philipp Emmanuel Bach and of Mozart, so is his treatment of instrumental tone-colour a thing that changes with every shade of feeling in the dramatic situation, and not in accordance with any purely decorative scheme. To accompany an aria with strings, oboes and flutes, was, for example, a perfectly ordinary procedure; nor was there anything unusual in making the wind instruments play in unison with the strings for the first part of the aria, and writing a passage for one or more of them in the middle section. But it was an unheard-of thing to make this passage consist of long *appoggiaturas* once every two bars in rising sequence on the first oboe, answered by deep *pizzicato* bass notes, while Agamemnon in despair cries: "*J'entends retentir dans mon sein le cri plaintif de la nature*." Some of Gluck's most forcible effects are of great subtlety, as, for instance, in *Iphigénie en Tauride*, where Orestes tries to reassure himself by saying: "*Le calme rentre dans mon cœur*," while the intensely agitated accompaniment of the strings belies him. Again, the sense of orchestral climax shown in the oracle scene in *Alceste* was a thing inconceivable in older music, and unsurpassed in artistic and dramatic spirit by any modern composer. Its influence in Mozart's *Idomeneo* is obvious at a first glance.

The capacity for broad melody always implies a true sense of form, whether that be developed by skill or not; and thus Gluck, in rejecting the convenient formalities of older styles of opera, was not, like some reformers, without something better to substitute for them. Moreover he, in consultation with his librettist, achieved great skill in holding together entire scenes, or even entire acts, by dramatically apposite repetitions of short arias and choruses. And thus in large portions of his finest works the music, in spite of frequent full closes, seems to move *pari passu* with the drama in a manner which for naturalness and continuity is surpassed only by the finales of Mozart and the entire operas of Wagner. This is perhaps most noticeable in the second act of *Orfeo*. In its original Italian version both scenes, that in Hades and that in Elysium, are indivisible wholes, and the division into single movements, though technically obvious, is aesthetically only a natural means of articulating the structure. The unity of the scene in Hades extends, in the original version, even to the key-system. This was damaged when Gluck had to transpose the part of Orpheus from an alto to a tenor in the French version. And here, we have one of many instances in which the improvements his French experience enabled him to make in his great Italian works were not altogether unmixed. Little harm, however, was done to *Orfeo* which has not been easily remedied by transposing Orpheus's part back again; and in a suitable compromise between the two versions *Orfeo* remains Gluck's most perfect and inspired work. The emotional power of the music is such that the inevitable spoiling of the story by a happy ending has not the aspect of mere conventionality which it had in cases where the music produced no more than the normal effect upon 18th-century audiences. Moreover Gluck's genius was of too high an order for him to be less successful in portraying a sufficiently intense happiness than in portraying grief. He failed only in what may be called the business capacities of artistic technique; and there is less "business" in *Orfeo* than in almost any other music-drama. It was Gluck's first great inspiration, and his theories had not had time to take action in paper warfare. *Alceste* contains his grandest music and is also very free from weak pages; but in its original Italian version the third act did not give Gluck scope for an adequate climax. This difficulty so accentuated itself in the French version that after continual retouchings a part for Hercules was, in Gluck's absence, added by Gossec; and three pages of Gluck's music, dealing with the supreme crisis where Alceste is rescued from Hades (either by Apollo or by Hercules) were no longer required in performance and have been lost. The Italian version is so different from the French that it cannot help us to restore this passage, in which Gluck's music now stops short just at the point where we realize the full height of his power. The comparison between the Italian and French *Alceste* is one of the most interesting that can be made in the study of a musician's development. It would have been far easier for Gluck to write a new opera if he had not been so justly attached to his second Italian masterpiece. So radical are the differences that in retranslating the French libretto into Italian for performance with the French music not one line of Calzabigi's original text can be retained.

In *Iphigénie en Aulide* and *Iphigénie en Tauride*, Gluck shows signs that the controversies aroused by his methods began to interfere with his musical spontaneity. He had not, in *Orfeo*, gone out of his way to avoid rondos, or we should have had no "*Che faro senza Euridice*." We read with a respectful smile Gluck's assurance to the bailli Le Blanc du Roullet that "you would not believe *Armide* to be by the same composer" as *Alceste*. But there is no question that *Armide* is a very great work, full of melody, colour and dramatic point; and that Gluck has availed himself of every suggestion that his libretto afforded for orchestral and emotional effects of an entirely different type from any that he had attempted before. And it is hardly relevant to blame him for his inability to write erotic music. In the first place, the libretto is not erotic, though the subject would no doubt become so if treated by a modern poet. In the second place a conflict of passions (as, for instance, where Armide summons the demons of Hate to exorcise love from her heart, and her courage fails her as soon as they begin) has never, even in *Alceste*, been treated with more dramatic musical force. The work as a whole is unequal, partly because there is a little too much action in it to suit Gluck's methods; but it shows, as does no other opera until Mozart's *Don Giovanni*, a sense of the*development* of characters, as distinguished from the mere presentation of them as already fixed.

In *Iphigénie en Aulide* and *Iphigénie en Tauride*, the very subtlety of the finest features indicates a certain self-consciousness which, when inspiration is lacking, becomes mannerism. Moreover, in both cases the libretti, though skilfully managed, tell a rather more complicated story than those which Gluck had hitherto so successfully treated; and, where inspiration fails, the musical technique becomes curiously amateurish without any corresponding naïveté. Still these works are immortal, and their finest passages are equal to anything in *Alceste* and *Orfeo*. *Écho et Narcisse* we must, like Gluck's contemporaries, regard as a failure. As in *Orfeo*, the pathetic story is ruined by a violent happy ending, but here this artistic disaster takes place before the pathos has had time to assert itself. Gluck had no opportunities in this work for any higher qualities, musical or dramatic, than prettiness; and with him beauty, without visible emotion, was indeed skin-deep. It is a pity that the plan of the great Pelletan-Damcke critical *édition de luxe* of Gluck's French operas forbids the inclusion of his Italian *Paride e Elena*, his third opera to Calzabigi's libretto, which was never given in a French version; for there can be no question that, whatever he owed to France, the 141period of his greatness began with his collaboration with Calzabigi.

(D. F. T.)

1Not, as frequently spelt, Glück.

GLÜCKSBURG, a town of Germany, in the Prussian province of Schleswig-Holstein, romantically situated among pine woods on the Flensburg Fjord off the Baltic, 6 m. N.E. from Flensburg by rail. Pop. (1905) 1551. It has a Protestant church and some small manufactures and is a favourite sea-bathing resort. The castle, which occupies the site of a former Cistercian monastery, was, from 1622 to 1779, the residence of the dukes of Holstein-Sonderburg-Glücksburg, passing then to the king of Denmark and in 1866 to Prussia. King Frederick VII. of Denmark died here on the 15th of November 1863.

GLÜCKSTADT, a town of Germany, in the Prussian province of Schleswig-Holstein, on the right bank of the Elbe, at the confluence of the small river Rhin, and 28 m. N.W. of Altona, on the railway from Itzehoe to Elmshorn. Pop. (1905) 6586. It has a Protestant and a Roman Catholic church, a handsome town-hall (restored in 1873-1874), a gymnasium, a provincial prison and a penitentiary. The inhabitants are chiefly engaged in commerce and fishing; but the frequent losses from inundations have greatly retarded the prosperity of the town. Glückstadt was founded by Christian IV. of Denmark in 1617, and fortified in 1620. It soon became an important trading centre. In 1627-28 it was besieged for fifteen weeks by the imperialists under Tilly, without success. In 1814 it was blockaded by the allies and capitulated, whereupon its fortifications were demolished. In 1830 it was made a free port. It came into the possession of Prussia together with the rest of Schleswig-Holstein in 1866.

See Lucht, *Glückstadt. Beiträge zur Geschichte dieser Stadt* (Kiel, 1854).

GLUCOSE (from Gr. γλυκύς, sweet), a carbohydrate of the formula $C_6H_{12}O_6$; it may be regarded as the aldehyde of sorbite. The name is applied in commerce to a complex mixture of carbohydrates obtained by boiling starch with dilute mineral acids; in chemistry, it denotes, with the prefixes d, l and d + l (or i), the dextro-rotatory, laevo-rotatory and inactive forms of the definite chemical compound defined above. The d modification is of the commonest occurrence, the other forms being only known as synthetic products; for this reason it is usually termed glucose, simply; alternative names are dextrose, grape sugar and diabetic sugar, in allusion to its right-handed optical rotation, its occurrence in large quantity in grapes, and in the urine of diabetic patients respectively. In the vegetable kingdom glucose occurs, always in admixture with fructose, in many fruits, especially grapes, cherries, bananas, &c.; and in combination, generally with phenols and aldehydes belonging to the aromatic series, it forms an extensive class of compounds termed glucosides. It appears to be synthesized in the plant tissues from carbon dioxide and water, formaldehyde being an intermediate product; or it may be a hydrolytic product of a glucoside or of a polysaccharose, such as cane sugar, starch, cellulose, &c. In the plant it is freely converted into more complex sugars, poly-saccharoses and also proteids. In the animal kingdom, also, it is very widely distributed, being sometimes a normal and sometimes a pathological constituent of the fluids and tissues; in particular, it is present in large amount in the urine of those suffering from diabetes, and may be present in nearly all the body fluids. It also occurs in honey, the white appearance of candied honey being due to its separation.

Pure *d*-glucose, which may be obtained synthetically (see SUGAR) or by adding crystallized cane sugar to a mixture of 80% alcohol and 1/15 volume of fuming hydrochloric acid so long as it dissolves on shaking, crystallizes from water or alcohol at ordinary temperatures in nodular masses, composed of minute six-sided plates, and containing one molecule of water of crystallization. This product melts at 86° C., and becomes anhydrous when heated to 110° C. The anhydrous compound can also be prepared, as hard crusts melting at 146°, by crystallizing concentrated aqueous solutions at 30° to 35°. It is very soluble in water, but only slightly soluble in strong alcohol. Its taste is somewhat sweet, its sweetening power being estimated at from ½ to 3/5 that of cane sugar. When heated to above 200° it turns brown and produces caramel, a substance possessing a bitter taste, and used, in its aqueous solution or otherwise, under various trade names, for colouring confectionery, spirits, &c. The specific rotation of the plane of polarized light by glucose solutions is characteristic. The specific rotation of a freshly prepared solution is 105°, but this value gradually diminishes to 52.5°, 24 hours sufficing for the transition in the cold, and a few minutes when the solution is boiled. This phenomenon has been called mutarotation by T. M. Lowry. The specific rotation also varies with the concentration; this is due to the dissociation of complex molecules into simpler ones, a view confirmed by cryoscopic measurements.

Glucose may be estimated by means of the polarimeter, *i.e.* by determining the rotation of the plane of polarization of a solution, or, chemically, by taking advantage of its property of reducing alkaline copper solutions. If a glucose solution be added to copper sulphate and much alkali added, a yellowish-red precipitate of cuprous hydrate separates, slowly in the cold, but immediately when the liquid is heated; this precipitate rapidly turns red owing to the formation of cuprous oxide. In 1846 L. C. A. Barreswil found that a strongly alkaline solution of copper sulphate and potassium sodium tartrate (Rochelle salt) remained unchanged on boiling, but yielded an immediate precipitate of red cuprous oxide when a solution of glucose was added. He suggested that the method was applicable for quantitatively estimating glucose, but its acceptance only followed after H. von Fehling's investigation. "Fehling's solution" is prepared by dissolving separately 34.639 grammes of copper sulphate, 173 grammes of Rochelle salt, and 71 grammes of caustic soda in water, mixing and making up to 1000 ccs.; 10 ccs. of this solution is completely reduced by 0.05 grammes of hexose. Volumetric methods are used, but the uncertainty of the end of the reaction has led to the suggestion of special indicators, or of determining the amount of cuprous oxide gravimetrically.

Chemistry.—In its chemical properties glucose is a typical oxyaldehyde or aldose. The aldehyde group reacts with hydrocyanic acid to produce two stereo-isomeric cyanhydrins; this isomerism is due to the conversion of an originally non-asymmetric carbon atom into an asymmetric one. The cyanhydrin is hydrolysable to an acid, the lactone of which may be reduced by sodium amalgam to a glucoheptose, a non-fermentable sugar containing seven carbon atoms. By repeating the process a non-fermentable gluco-octose and a fermentable gluconononose may be prepared. The aldehyde group also reacts with phenyl hydrazine to form two phenylhydrazones; under certain conditions a hydroxyl group adjacent to the aldehyde group is oxidized and glucosazone is produced; this glucosazone is decomposed by hydrochloric acid into phenyl hydrazine and the keto-aldehyde glucosone. These transformations are fully discussed in the article SUGAR. On reduction glucose appears to yield the hexahydric alcohol *d*-sorbite, and on oxidation *d*-gluconic and *d*-saccharic acids. Alkalis partially convert it into *d*-mannose and *d*-fructose. Baryta and lime yield saccharates, *e.g.* $C_6H_{12}O_6 \cdot BaO$, precipitable by alcohol.

The constitution of glucose was established by H. Kiliani in 1885-1887, who showed it to be $CH_2OH \cdot (CH \cdot OH)_4 \cdot CHO$. The subject was taken up by Emil Fischer, who succeeded in synthesizing glucose, and also several of its stereo-isomers, there being 16 according to the Le Bel-van't Hoff theory (see Stereo-Isomerism and Sugar). This open chain structure is challenged in the views put forward by T. M. Lowry and E. F. Armstrong. In 1895 C. Tanret showed that glucose existed in more than one form, and he isolated α, β and γ varieties with specific rotations of 105°, 52.5° and 22°. It is now agreed that the β variety is a mixture of the α and γ. This discovery explained the mutarotation of glucose. In a fresh solution α-glucose only exists, but on standing it is slowly transformed into γ-glucose, equilibrium being reached when the α and γ forms are present in the ratio 0.368 : 0.632 (Tanret, Zeit. physikal. Chem., 1905, 53, p. 692). It is convenient to refer to these two forms as α and β. Lowry and Armstrong represent these compounds by the following spatial formulae which postulate a γ-oxidic structure, and 5 asymmetric carbon atoms, *i.e.* one more than in the Fischer formulae. These formulae are supported by many considerations, especially by the selective 142action of enzymes, which follows similar lines with the α- and β-glucosides, *i.e.* the compounds formed by the interaction of glucose with substances generally containing hydroxyl groups (see GLUCOSIDE).

Fermentation of Glucose.—Glucose is readily fermentable. Of the greatest importance is the alcoholic fermentation brought about by yeast cells (*Saccharomyces cerevisiae seu vini*); this follows the equation C6H12O6 = 2C2H6O + 2CO2, Pasteur considering 94 to 95% of the sugar to be so changed. This character is the base of the plan of adding glucose to wine and beer wort before fermenting, the alcohol content of the liquid after fermentation being increased. Some fusel oil, glycerin and succinic acid appear to be formed simultaneously, but in small amount. Glucose also undergoes fermentation into lactic acid (*q.v.*) in the presence of the lactic acid bacillus, and into butyric acid if the action of the preceding ferment be continued, or by other bacilli. It also yields, by the so-called mucous fermentation, a mucous, gummy mass, mixed with mannitol and lactic acid.

We may here notice the frequent production of glucose by the action of enzymes upon other carbohydrates. Of especial note is the transformation of maltose by maltase into glucose, and of cane sugar by invertase into a mixture of glucose and fructose (invert sugar); other instances are: lactose by lactase into galactose and glucose; trehalose by trehalase into glucose; melibiose by melibiase into galactose and glucose; and of melizitose by melizitase into touranose and glucose, touranose yielding glucose also when acted upon by the enzyme touranase.

Commercial Glucose.—The glucose of commerce, which may be regarded as a mixture of grape sugar, maltose and dextrins, is prepared by hydrolysing starch by boiling with a dilute mineral acid. In Europe, potato starch is generally employed; in America, corn starch. The acid employed may be hydrochloric, which gives the best results, or sulphuric, which is used in Germany; sulphuric acid is more readily separated from the product than hydrochloric, since the addition of powdered chalk precipitates it as calcium sulphate, which may be removed by a filter press. The processes of manufacture have much in common, although varying in detail. The following is an outline of the process when hydrochloric acid is used: Starch ("green" starch in America) is made into a "milk" with water, and the milk pumped into boiling dilute acid contained in a closed "converter," generally made of copper or cast iron; steam is led in at the same time, and the pressure is kept up to about 25 ℔ to the sq. in. When the converter is full the pressure is raised somewhat, and the heating continued until the conversion is complete. The liquid is now run into neutralizing tanks containing sodium carbonate, and, after settling, the supernatant liquid, termed "light liquor," is run through bag filters and then on to bone-char filters, which have been previously used for the "heavy liquor." The colourless or amber-coloured filtrate is concentrated to 27° to 28° B., when it forms the "heavy liquor," just mentioned. This is filtered through fresh bone-char filters, from which it is discharged as a practically colourless liquid. This liquid is concentrated in vacuum pans to a specific gravity of 40° to 44° B., a small quantity of sodium bisulphite solution being added to bleach it, to prevent fermentation, and to inhibit browning. "Syrup glucose" is the commercial name of the product; by continuing the concentration further solid glucose or grape sugar is obtained.

Several brands are recognized: "Mixing glucose" is used by syrup and molasses manufacturers, "jelly glucose" by makers of jellies, "confectioners' glucose" in confectionery, "brewers' glucose" in brewing, &c.

GLUCOSIDE, in chemistry, the generic name of an extensive group of substances characterized by the property of yielding a sugar, more commonly glucose, when hydrolysed by purely chemical means, or decomposed by a ferment or enzyme. The name was originally given to vegetable products of this nature, in which the other part of the molecule was, in the greater number of cases, an aromatic aldehydic or phenolic compound (exceptions are sinigrin and jalapin or scammonin). It has now been extended to include synthetic ethers, such as those obtained by acting on alcoholic glucose solutions with hydrochloric acid, and also the polysaccharoses, *e.g.* cane sugar, which appear to be ethers also. Although glucose is the commonest sugar present in glucosides, many are known which yield rhamnose or iso-dulcite; these may be termed pentosides. Much attention has been given to the non-sugar parts of the molecules; the constitutions of many have been determined, and the compounds synthesized; and in some cases the preparation of the synthetic glucoside effected.

The simplest glucosides are the alkyl esters which E. Fischer (*Ber.*, 28, pp. 1151, 3081) obtained by acting with hydrochloric acid on alcoholic glucose solutions. A better method of preparation is due to E. F. Armstrong and S. L. Courtauld (*Proc. Phys. Soc.*, 1905, July 1), who

31

dissolve solid anhydrous glucose in methyl alcohol containing hydrochloric acid. A mixture of α- and β-glucose result, which are then etherified, and if the solution be neutralized before the β-form isomerizes and the solvent removed, a mixture of the α- and β-methyl ethers is obtained. These may be separated by the action of suitable ferments. Fischer found that these ethers did not reduce Fehling's solution, neither did they combine with phenyl hydrazine at 100°; they appear to be stereo-isomeric γ-oxidic compounds of the formulae I., II.: The difference between the α- and β-forms is best shown by the selective action of enzymes. Fischer found that maltase, an enzyme occurring in yeast cells, hydrolysed α-glucosides but not the β; while emulsin, an enzyme occurring in bitter almonds, hydrolyses the β but not the α. The ethers of non-fermentable sugars are themselves non-fermentable. By acting with these enzymes on the natural glucosides, it is found that the majority are of the β-form; e.g. emulsin hydrolyses salicin, helicin, aesculin, coniferin, syringin, &c.

Classification of the glucosides is a matter of some difficulty. One based on the chemical constitution of the non-glucose part of the molecules has been proposed by Umney, who framed four groups: (1) ethylene derivatives, (2) benzene derivatives, (3) styrolene derivatives, (4) anthracene derivatives. A group may also be made to include the cyanogenetic glucosides, i.e. those containing prussic acid. J. J. L. van Rijn (Die Glykoside, 1900) follows a botanical classification, which has several advantages; in particular, plants of allied genera contain similar compounds. In this article the chemical classification will be followed. Only the more important compounds will be noticed, the reader being referred to van Rijn (loc. cit.) and to Beilstein's Handbuch der organischen Chemie for further details.

1. *Ethylene Derivatives.*—These are generally mustard oils, and are characterized by a burning taste; their principal occurrence is in mustard and *Tropaeolum seeds*. Sinigrin or the potassium salt of myronic acid, $C10H16NS2KO9 \cdot H2O$, occurs in black pepper and in horse-radish root. Hydrolysis with baryta, or decomposition by the ferment myrosin, gives glucose, allyl mustard oil and potassium bisulphate. Sinalbin, $C30H42N2S2O15$, occurs in white pepper; it decomposes to the mustard oil $HO \cdot C6H4 \cdot CH2 \cdot NCS$, glucose and sinapin, a compound of choline and sinapinic acid. Jalapin or scammonin, $C34H56O16$, occurs in scammony; it hydrolyses to glucose and jalapinolic acid. The formulae of sinigrin, sinalbin, sinapin and jalapinolic acid are:—

2. *Benzene Derivatives.*—These are generally oxy and oxyaldehydic compounds. Arbutin, $C12H16O7$, which occurs in bearberry along with methyl arbutin, hydrolyses to hydroquinone and glucose. Pharmacologically it acts as a urinary antiseptic and diuretic; the benzoyl derivative, cellotropin, has been used for tuberculosis. Salicin, also termed "saligenin" and "glucose," $C13H18O7$, occurs in the willow. The enzymes ptyalin and emulsin convert it into glucose and saligenin, ortho-oxybenzylalcohol, $HO \cdot C6H4 \cdot CH2OH$. Oxidation gives the aldehyde helicin. Populin, $C20H22O8$, which occurs in the leaves and bark of *Populus tremula*, is benzoyl salicin.

3. *Styrolene Derivatives.*—This group contains a benzene and also an ethylene group, being derived from styrolene $C6H5 \cdot CH:CH2$. Coniferin, $C16H22O8$, occurs in the cambium of coniferous woods. Emulsin converts it into glucose and coniferyl alcohol, while oxidation gives glycovanillin, which yields with emulsin glucose and vanillin (see EUGENOL and VANILLA). Syringin, which occurs in the bark of *Syringa vulgaris*, is methoxyconiferin. Phloridzin, $C21H24O10$, occurs in the root-bark of various fruit trees; it hydrolyses to glucose and phloretin, which is the phloroglucin ester of para-oxyhydratropic acid. It is related to the pentosides naringin, $C21H26O11$, which hydrolyses to rhamnose and naringenin, the phloroglucin ester of para-oxycinnamic acid, and hesperidin, $C50H60O22$(?), which hydrolyses to rhamnose and hesperetin, $C16H14O6$, the phloroglucin ester of meta-oxy-para-methoxycinnamic acid or isoferulic acid, $C10H10O4$. We may here include various coumarin and benzo-γ-pyrone derivatives. Aesculin, $C15H16O9$, occurring in horse-chestnut, and daphnin, occurring in *Daphne alpina*, are isomeric; the former hydrolyses to glucose and aesculetin (4·5-dioxycoumarin), the latter to glucose and daphnetin (3·4-dioxycoumarin). Fraxin, $C16H18O10$, occurring in *Fraxinus excelsior*, and with aesculin in horse-chestnut, hydrolyses to glucose and fraxetin, the monomethyl ester of a trioxycoumarin. Flavone or benzo-γ-pyrone derivatives are very numerous; in many cases they (or the non-sugar part of the molecule) are vegetable dyestuffs. *Quercitrin*, $C21H22O12$, is a yellow dyestuff found in *Quercus tinctoria*; it hydrolyses to rhamnose and quercetin, a dioxy-β-phenyl-trioxybenzo-γ-pyrone. Rhamnetin, a splitting product of the glucosides of *Rhamnus*, is monomethyl quercetin; fisetin, from *Rhus cotinus*, is monoxyquercetin; chrysin is phenyl-dioxybenzo-γ-pyrone. Saponarin, a glucoside found in *Saponaria officinalis*, is a related compound. Strophanthin is the name given to three different compounds, two obtained from *Strophanthus Kombe* and one from *S. hispidus*.

4. *Anthracene Derivatives.*—These are generally substituted anthraquinones; many have medicinal applications, being used as purgatives, while one, ruberythric acid, yields the valuable dyestuff madder, the base of which is alizarin (*q.v.*). Chrysophanic acid, a dioxymethylanthraquinone, occurs in rhubarb, which also contains emodin, a trioxymethylanthraquinone; this substance occurs in combination with rhamnose in frangula bark.

The most important cyanogenetic glucoside is amygdalin, which occurs in bitter almonds. The enzyme maltase decomposes it into glucose and mandelic nitrile glucoside; the latter is broken down by emulsin into glucose, benzaldehyde and prussic acid. Emulsin also decomposes amygdalin directly into these compounds without the intermediate formation of mandelic nitrile glucoside. Several other glucosides of this nature have been isolated. The saponins are a group of substances characterized by forming a lather with water; they occur in soap-bark (*q.v.*). Mention may also be made of indican, the glucoside of the indigo plant; this is hydrolysed by the indigo ferment, indimulsin, to indoxyl and indiglucin.

GLUE (from the O. Fr. *glu*, bird-lime, from the Late Lat. *glutem*, *glus*, glue), a valuable agglutinant, consisting of impure gelatin and widely used as an adhesive medium for wood, leather, paper and similar substances. Glues and gelatins merge into one another by imperceptible degrees. The difference is conditioned by the degree of purity: the more impure form is termed glue and is only used as an adhesive, the purer forms, termed gelatin, have other applications, especially in culinary operations and confectionery. Referring to the article GELATIN for a general account of this substance, it is only necessary to state here that gelatigenous or glue-forming tissues occur in the bones, skins and intestines of all animals, and that by extraction with hot water these agglutinating materials are removed, and the solution on evaporating and cooling yields a jelly-like substance—gelatin or glue.

Glues may be most conveniently classified according to their sources: bone glue, skin glue and fish glue; these may be regarded severally as impure forms of bone gelatin, skin gelatin and isinglass.

Bone Glue.—For the manufacture of glue the bones are supplied fresh or after having been used for making soups; Indian and South American bones are unsuitable, since, by reason of their previous treatment with steam, both their fatty and glue-forming constituents have been already removed (to a great extent). On the average, fresh bones contain about 50% of mineral matter, mainly calcium and magnesium phosphates, about 12% each of moisture and fat, the remainder being other organic matter. The mineral matter reappears in commerce chiefly as artificial manure; the fat is employed in the candle, soap and glycerin industries, while the other organic matter supplies glue.

The separation of the fat, or "de-greasing of the bones" is effected (1) by boiling the bones with water in open vessels; (2) by treatment with steam under pressure; or (3) by means of solvents. The last process is superseding the first two, which give a poor return of fat—a valuable consideration—and also involve the loss of a certain amount of glue. Many solvents have been proposed; the greatest commercial success appears to attend Scottish shale oil and natural petroleum (Russian or American) boiling at about 100° C. The vessels in which the extraction is carried out consist of upright cylindrical boilers, provided with manholes for charging, a false bottom on which the bones rest, and with two steam coils—one for heating only, the other for leading in "live" steam. There is a pipe from the top of the vessel leading to a condensing plant. The vessels are arranged in batteries. In the actual operation the boiler is charged with bones, solvent is run in, and the mixture gradually heated by means of the dry coil; the spirit distils over, carrying with it the water present in the bones; and after a time the extracted fat is run off from discharge cocks in the bottom of the extractor.1 A fresh charge of solvent is introduced, and the cycle repeated; this is repeated a third and fourth time, after which the bones contain only about 0.2% of fat, and a little of the solvent, which is removed by blowing in live steam under 70 to 80 ℔ pressure. The de-greased bones are now cleansed from all dirt and flesh by rotation in a horizontal cylindrical drum covered with stout wire gauze. The attrition accompanying this motion suffices to remove the loosely adherent matter, which falls through the meshes of the gauze; this meal contains a certain amount of glue-forming matter, and is generally passed through a finer mesh, the residuum being worked up in the glue-house, and the flour which passes through being sold as a bone-meal, or used as a manure.

The bones, which now contain 5 to 6% of glue-forming nitrogen and about 60% of calcium phosphate, are next treated for glue. The most economical process consists in steaming the bones under pressure (15 ℔ to start with, afterwards 5 ℔) in upright cylindrical boilers fitted with false bottoms. The glue-liquors collect beneath the false bottoms, and when of a strength equal to about 20% dry glue they are run off to the clarifiers. The first runnings contain about 65 to 70% of the total glue; a second steaming extracts another 25 to 30%. For clarifying the solutions, ordinary alum is used, one part being used for 200 parts of dry glue. The alum is added to the hot liquors, raised to 100°; it is then allowed to settle, and the surface scum removed by filtering through coarse calico or fine wire filters.

The clear liquors are now concentrated to a strength of about 32% dry glue in winter and 35% in summer. This is invariably effected in vacuum pans—open boiling yields a dark-coloured and inferior product. Many types of vacuum plant are in use; the Yaryan form, invented by H. T. Yaryan, is perhaps the best, and the double effect system is the most efficient. After concentration the liquors are bleached by blowing in sulphur dioxide, manufactured by burning sulphur; by this means the colour can be lightened to any desired degree. The liquors are now run into galvanized sheet-iron troughs, 2 ft. long, 6 in. wide and 5 in. deep, where they congeal to a firm jelly, which is subsequently removed by cutting round the edges, or by warming with hot water, and turning the cake out. The cake is sliced to sheets of convenient thickness, generally by means of a wire knife, *i.e.* a piece of wire placed in a frame. Mechanical slicers acting on this principle are in use. Instead of allowing the solution to congeal in troughs, it may be "cast" on sheets of glass, the bottoms of which are cooled by running water. After congealing, the tremulous jelly is dried; this is an operation of great nicety: the desiccation must be slow and is generally effected by circulating a rapid current of air about the cakes supported on nets set in frames; it occupies from four to five days, and the cake contains on the average from 10 to 13% of water.

Skin Glue.—In the preparation of skin glue the materials used are the parings and cuttings of hides from tan-yards, the ears of oxen and sheep, the skins of rabbits, hares, cats, dogs and other animals, the parings of tawed leather, parchment and old gloves, and many other miscellaneous scraps of animal matter. Much experience is needed in order to prepare a good 144glue from such heterogeneous materials; one blending may be a success and another a failure. The raw material has been divided into three great divisions: (1) sheep pieces and fleshings (ears, &c.); (2) ox fleshings and trimmings; (3) ox hides and pieces; the best glue is obtained from a mixture of the hide, ear and face clippings of the ox and calf. The raw material or "stock" is first steeped for from two to ten weeks, according to its nature, in wooden vats or pits with lime water, and afterwards carefully dried and stored. The object of the lime steeping is to remove any blood and flesh which may be attached to the skin, and to form a lime soap with the fatty matter present. The "scrows" or glue pieces, which may be kept a long time without undergoing change, are washed with a dilute hydrochloric acid to remove all lime, and then very thoroughly with water; they are now allowed to drain and dry. The skins are then placed in hemp nets and introduced into an open boiler which has a false bottom, and a tap by which liquid may be run off. As the boiling proceeds test quantities of liquid are from time to time examined, and when a sample is found on cooling to form a stiff jelly, which happens when it contains about 32% dry glue, it is ready to draw off. The solution is then run to a clarifier, in which a temperature sufficient to keep it fluid is maintained, and in this way any impurity is permitted to subside. The glue solution is then run into wooden troughs or coolers in which it sets to a firm jelly. The cakes are removed as in the case of bone glue (see above), and, having been placed on nets, are, in the Scottish practice, dried by exposure to open air. This primitive method has many disadvantages: on a hot day the cake may become unshapely, or melt and slip through the net, or dry so rapidly as to crack; a frost may produce fissures, while a fog or mist may precipitate moisture on the surface and occasion a mouldy appearance. The surface of the cake, which is generally dull after drying, is polished by washing with water. The practice of boiling, clarification, cooling and drying, which has been already described in the case of bone glue, has been also applied to the separation of skin glue.

Fish Glue.—Whereas isinglass, a very pure gelatin, is yielded by the sounds of a limited number of fish, it is found that all fish offals yield a glue possessing considerable adhesive properties. The manufacture consists in thoroughly washing the offal with water, and then discharging it into extractors with live steam. After digestion, the liquid is run off, allowed to stand, the upper oily layer removed, and the lower gluey solution clarified with alum. The liquid is then filtered, concentrated in open vats, and bleached with sulphur dioxide.2 Fish glue is a light-brown viscous liquid which has a distinctly disagreeable odour and an acrid taste; these disadvantages to its use are avoided if it be boiled with a little water and 1% of sodium phosphate, and 0.025% of saccharine added.

Properties of Glue.—A good quality of glue should be free from all specks and grit, have a uniform, light brownish-yellow, transparent appearance, and should break with a glassy fracture. Steeped for some time in cold water it softens and swells up without dissolving, and when again dried it ought to resume its original properties. Under the influence of heat it entirely dissolves in water, forming a thin syrupy fluid with a not disagreeable smell. The adhesiveness of different qualities of glue varies considerably; the best adhesive is formed by steeping the glue, broken in small pieces, in water until they are quite soft, and then placing them with just sufficient water to effect solution in the glue-pot. The hotter the glue, the better the joint; remelted glue is not so strong as the freshly prepared; and newly manufactured glue is inferior to that which has been long in stock. It is therefore seen that many factors enter into the determination of the cohesive power of glue; a well-prepared joint may, under favourable conditions, withstand a pull of about 700 ℔ per sq. in. The following table, after Kilmarsch, shows the holding power of glued joints with various kinds of woods.

Wood.	℔ per sq. in.	
	With grain.	Across grain.
Beech	852	434.5
Maple	484	346
Oak	704	302
Fir	605	132

Special Kinds of Glues, Cements, &c.—By virtue of the fact that the word "glue" is frequently used to denote many adhesives, which may or may not contain gelatin, there will now be given an account of some special preparations. These may be conveniently divided into: (1) liquid glues, mixtures containing gelatin which do not jelly at ordinary temperatures but still possess adhesive properties; (2) water-proof glues, including mixtures containing gelatin, and also the "marine glues," which contain no glue; (3) glues or cements for special purposes, *e.g.* for cementing glass, pottery, leather, &c., for cementing dissimilar materials, such as paper or leather to iron.

Liquid Glues.—The demand for liquid glues is mainly due to the disadvantages—the necessity of dissolving and using while hot—of ordinary glue. They are generally prepared by adding to a warm glue solution some reagent which destroys the property of gelatinizing. The reagents in common use are acetic acid; magnesium chloride, used for a glue employed by printers; hydrochloric acid and zinc sulphate; nitric acid and lead sulphate; and phosphoric acid and ammonium carbonate.

Water-proof Glues.—Numerous recipes for water-proof glues have been published; glue, having been swollen by soaking in water, dissolved in four-fifths its weight of linseed oil, furnishes a good water-proof adhesive; linseed oil varnish and litharge, added to a glue solution, is also used; resin added to a hot glue solution in water, and afterwards diluted with turpentine, is another recipe; the best glue is said to be obtained by dissolving one part of glue in one and a half parts of water, and then adding one-fiftieth part of potassium bichromate. Alcoholic solutions of various gums, and also tannic acid, confer the same property on glue solutions. The "marine glues" are solutions of india-rubber, shellac or asphaltum, or mixtures of these substances, in benzene or naphtha. Jeffrey's marine glue is formed by dissolving india-rubber in four parts of benzene and adding two parts of shellac; it is extensively used, being easily applied and drying rapidly and hard. Another water-proof glue which contains no gelatin is obtained by heating linseed oil with five parts of quicklime; when cold it forms a hard mass, which melts on heating like ordinary glue.

Special Glues.—There are innumerable recipes for adhesives specially applicable to certain substances and under certain conditions. For repairing glass, ivory, &c. isinglass (*q.v.*), which may be replaced by fine glue, yields valuable cements; bookbinders employ an elastic glue obtained from an ordinary glue solution and glycerin, the water being expelled by heating; an efficient cement for mounting photographs is obtained by dissolving glue in ten parts of alcohol and adding one part of glycerin; portable or mouth glue—so named because it melts in the mouth—is prepared by dissolving one part of sugar in a solution of four parts of glue. An india-rubber substitute is obtained by adding sodium tungstate and hydrochloric acid to a strong glue solution; this preparation may be rolled out when heated to 60°.

For further details see Thomas Lambert, *Glue, Gelatine and their Allied Products* (London, 1905); R. L. Fernbach, *Glues and Gelatine* (1907); H. C. Standage, *Agglutinants of all Kinds for all Purposes* (1907).

1This fat contains a small quantity of solvent, which is removed by heating with steam, when the solvent distils off. Hot water is then run in to melt the fat, which rises to the surface of the water and is floated off. Another boiling with water, and again floating off, frees the fat from dirt and mineral matter, and the product is ready for casking.

2The residue in the extractors is usually dried in steam-heated vessels, and mixed with potassium and magnesium salts; the product is then put on the market as fish-potash guano.

GLUTARIC ACID, or NORMAL PYROTARIC ACID, HO2C·CH2·CH2·CH2·CO2H, an organic acid prepared by the reduction of α-oxyglutaric acid with hydriodic acid, by reducing glutaconic acid, HO2C·CH2·CH:CH·CO2H, with sodium amalgam, by conversion of trimethylene bromide into the cyanide and hydrolysis of this compound, or from acetoacetic ester, which, in the form of its sodium derivative, condenses with β-iodopropionic ester to form acetoglutaric ester, CH3·CO·CH(CO2C2H5)·CH2·CH2·CO2C2H5, from which glutaric acid is obtained by hydrolysis. It is also obtained when sebacic, stearic and oleic acids are oxidized with nitric acid. It crystallizes in large monoclinic prisms which melt at 97.5° C., and distils between 302° and 304° C., practically without decomposition. It is soluble in water, alcohol and ether. By long heating the acid is converted into its anhydride, which, however, is obtained more readily by heating the silver salt of the acid with acetyl chloride. By distillation of the ammonium salt glutarimide, CH2(CH2·CO)2NH, is obtained; it forms small crystals melting at 151° to 152° C. and sublimes unchanged.

On the alkyl glutaric acids, see C. Hell (*Ber.*, 1889, 22, pp. 48, 60), C. A. Bischoff (*Ber.*, 1891, 24, p. 1041), K. Auwers (*Ber.*, 1891, 24, p. 1923) and W. H. Perkin, junr. (*Journ. Chem. Soc.*, 1896, 69, p. 268).

145

GLUTEN, a tough, tenacious, ductile, somewhat elastic, nearly tasteless and greyish-yellow albuminous substance, obtained from the flour of wheat by washing in water, in which it is insoluble. Gluten, when dried, loses about two-thirds of its weight, becoming brittle and semi-transparent; when strongly heated it crackles and swells, and burns like feather or horn. It is soluble in strong acetic acid, and in caustic alkalis, which latter may be used for the purification of starch in which it is present. When treated with .1 to .2% solution of hydrochloric acid it swells up, and at length forms a liquid resembling a solution of albumin, and laevorotatory as regards polarized light. Moistened with water and exposed to the air gluten putrefies, and evolves carbon dioxide, hydrogen and sulphuretted hydrogen, and in the end is almost entirely resolved into a liquid, which contains leucin and ammonium phosphate and acetate. On analysis gluten shows a composition of about 53% of carbon, 7% of hydrogen, and nitrogen 15 to 18%, besides oxygen, and about 1% of sulphur, and a small quantity of inorganic matter. According to H. Ritthausen it is a mixture of *glutencasein* (Liebig's vegetable fibrin),*glutenfibrin*, *gliadin* (Pflanzenleim), *glutin* or vegetable gelatin, and *mucedin*, which are all closely allied to one another in chemical composition. It is the gliadin which confers upon gluten its capacity of cohering to form elastic masses, and of separating readily from associated starch. In the so-called gluten of the flour of barley, rye and maize, this body is absent (H. Ritthausen and U. Kreusler). The gluten yielded by wheat which has undergone fermentation or has begun to sprout is devoid of toughness and elasticity. These qualities can be restored to it by kneading with salt, lime-water or alum. Gluten is employed in the manufacture of gluten bread and biscuits for the diabetic, and of chocolate, and also in the adulteration of tea and coffee. For making bread it must be used fresh, as otherwise it decomposes, and does not knead well. Granulated gluten is a kind of vermicelli, made in some starch manufactories by mixing fresh gluten with twice its weight of flour, and granulating by means of a cylinder and contained stirrer, each armed with spikes, and revolving in opposite directions. The process is completed by the drying and sifting of the granules.

GLUTTON, or WOLVERINE (*Gulo luscus*), a carnivorous mammal belonging to the *Mustelidae*, or weasel family, and the sole representative of its genus. The legs are short and stout, with large feet, the toes of which terminate in strong, sharp claws considerably curved. The mode of progression is semi-plantigrade. In size and form the glutton is something like the badger, measuring from 2 to 3 ft. in length, exclusive of the thick bushy tail, which is about 8 in. long. The head is broad, the eyes are small and the back arched. The fur consists of an undergrowth of short woolly hair, mixed with long straight hairs, to the abundance and length of which on the sides and tail the creature owes its shaggy appearance. The colour of the fur is blackish-brown, with a broad band of chestnut stretching from the shoulders along each side of the body, the two meeting near the root of the tail. Unlike the majority of arctic animals, the fur of the glutton in winter grows darker. Like other *Mustelidae*, the glutton is provided with anal glands, which secrete a yellowish fluid possessing a highly foetid odour. It is a boreal animal, inhabiting the northern regions of both hemispheres, but most abundant in the circumpolar area of the New World, where it occurs throughout the British provinces and Alaska, being specially numerous in the neighbourhood of the Mackenzie river, and extending southwards as far as New York and the Rocky Mountains. The wolverine is a voracious animal, and also one with an inquisitive disposition. It feeds on grouse, the smaller rodents and foxes, which it digs from their burrows during the breeding-season; but want of activity renders it dependent for most of its food on dead carcases, which it frequently obtains by methods that have made it peculiarly obnoxious to the hunter and trapper. Should the hunter, after succeeding in killing his game, leave the carcase insufficiently protected for more than a single night, the glutton, whose fear of snares is sufficient to prevent him from touching it during the first night, will, if possible, get at and devour what he can on the second, hiding the remainder beneath the snow. It annoys the trapper by following up his lines of marten-traps, often extending to a length of 40 to 50 m., each of which it enters from behind, extracting the bait, pulling up the traps, and devouring or concealing the entrapped martens. So persistent is the glutton in this practice, when once it discovers a line of traps, that its extermination along the trapper's route is a necessary preliminary to the success of his business. This is no easy task, as the glutton is too cunning to be caught by the methods successfully employed on the other members of the weasel family. The trap generally used for this purpose is made to resemble a cache, or hidden store of food, such as the Indians and hunters are in the habit of forming, the discovery and rifling of which is one of the glutton's most congenial occupations—the bait, instead of being paraded as in most traps, being carefully concealed, to lull the knowing beast's suspicions. One of the most prominent characteristics of the wolverine is its propensity to steal and hide things, not merely food which it might afterwards need, or traps which it regards as enemies, but articles which cannot possibly have any interest except that of curiosity. The following instance of this is quoted by Dr E. Coues in his work on the *Fur-bearing Animals of North America*: "A hunter and his family having left their lodge unguarded during their absence, on their return found it completely gutted—the walls were there, but nothing else. Blankets, guns, kettles, axes, cans, knives and all the other paraphernalia of a trapper's tent had vanished, and the tracks left by the beast showed who had been the thief. The family set to work, and, by carefully following up all his paths, recovered, with some trifling exceptions, the whole of the lost property." The cunning displayed by the glutton in unravelling the snares set for it forms at once the admiration and despair of every trapper, while its great strength and ferocity render it a dangerous antagonist to animals larger than itself, occasionally including man. The rutting-season occurs in March, and the female, secure in her burrow, produces her young—four or five at a birth—in June or July. In defence of these, she is exceedingly bold, and the Indians, according to Dr Coues, "have been heard to say that they would sooner encounter a she-bear with her cubs than a carcajou (the Indian name of the glutton) under the same circumstances." On catching sight of its enemy, man, the wolverine before finally determining on flight, is said to sit on its haunches, and, in order to get a clearer view of the danger, shade its eyes with one of its fore-paws. When pressed for food it becomes fearless, and has been known to come on board an ice-bound vessel, and in presence of the crew seize a can of meat. The glutton is valuable for its fur, which, when several skins are sewn together, forms elegant hearth and carriage rugs.

(R. L.*)

The Glutton, or Wolverine
(*Gulo luscus*).

GLYCAS, MICHAEL, Byzantine historian (according to some a Sicilian, according to others a Corfiote), flourished during the 12th century A.D. His chief work is his *Chronicle* of events 146from the creation of the world to the death of Alexius I. Comnenus(1118). It is extremely brief and written in a popular style, but too much space is devoted to theological and scientific matters. Glycas was also the author of a theological treatise and a number of letters on theological questions. A poem of some 600 "political" verses, written during his imprisonment on a charge of slandering a neighbour and containing an appeal to the emperor Manuel, is still extant. The exact nature of his offence is not known, but the answer to his appeal was that he was deprived of his eyesight by the emperor's orders.

Editions: "Chronicle and Letters," in J. P. Migne, *Patrologia Graeca*, clviii.; poem in E. Legrand, *Bibliothèque grecque vulgaire*, i.; see also F. Hirsch, *Byzantinische Studien* (1876); C.

Krumbacher in *Sitzungsberichte bayer. Acad.*, 1894; C. F. Bähr in Ersch and Gruber's *Allgemeine Encyklopädie.*

GLYCERIN, GLYCERINE or GLYCEROL (in pharmacy *Glycerinum*) (from Gr. γλυκύς, sweet), a trihydric alcohol, trihydroxypropane, C3H5(OH)3. It is obtainable from most natural fatty bodies by the action of alkalis and similar reagents, whereby the fats are decomposed, water being taken up, and glycerin being formed together with the alkaline salt of some particular acid (varying with the nature of the fat). Owing to their possession of this common property, these natural fatty bodies and various artificial derivatives of glycerin, which behave in the same way when treated with alkalis, are known as glycerides. In the ordinary process of soap-making the glycerin remains dissolved in the aqueous liquors from which the soap is separated.

Glycerin was discovered in 1779 by K. W. Scheele and named *Ölsüss* (*principe doux des huiles*—sweet principle of oils), and more fully investigated subsequently by M. E. Chevreul, who named it glycerin, M. P. E. Berthelot, and many other chemists, from whose researches it results that glycerin is a trihydric alcohol indicated by the formula C3H5(OH)3, the natural fats and oils, and the glycerides generally, being substances of the nature of compound esters formed from glycerin by the replacement of the hydrogen of the OH groups by the radicals of certain acids, called for that reason "fatty acids." The relationship of these glycerides to glycerin is shown by the series of bodies formed from glycerin by replacement of hydrogen by "stearyl" (C18H35O), the radical of stearic acid (C18H35O ∙OH):—

The process of saponification may be viewed as the gradual progressive transformation of tristearin, or some analogously constituted substance, into distearin, monostearin and glycerin, or as the similar transformation of a substance analogous to distearin or to monostearin into glycerin. If the reaction is brought about in presence of an alkali, the acid set free becomes transformed into the corresponding alkaline salt; but if the decomposition is effected without the presence of an alkali (*i.e.* by means of water alone or by an acid), the acid set free and the glycerin are obtained together in a form which usually admits of their ready separation. It is noticeable that with few exceptions the fatty and oily matters occurring in nature are substances analogous to tristearin, *i.e.* they are trebly replaced glycerins. Amongst these glycerides may be mentioned the following:

Tristearin—C3H5(O ∙C18H35O)3. The chief constituent of hard animal fats, such as beef and mutton tallow, &c.; also contained in many vegetable fats in smaller quantity.

Triolein—C3H5(O ∙C18H33O)3. Largely present in olive oil and other saponifiable vegetable oils and soft fats; also present in animal fats, especially hog's lard.

Tripalmitin—C3H5(O ∙C16H31O)3. The chief constituent of palm oil; also contained in greater or less quantities in human fat, olive oil, and other animal and vegetable fats.

Triricinolein—C3H5(O ∙C18H33O2)3. The main constituent of castor oil.

Other analogous glycerides are apparently contained in greater or smaller quantity in certain other oils. Thus in cows' butter, *tributyrin*, C3H5(O ∙C4H7O)3, and the analogous glycerides of other readily volatile acids closely resembling butyric acid, are present in small quantity; the production of these acids on saponification and distillation with dilute sulphuric acid is utilized as a test of a purity of butter as sold. *Triacetin*, C3H5(O ∙C2H3O)3, is apparently contained in cod-liver oil. Some other glycerides isolated from natural sources are analogous in composition to tristearin, but with this difference, that the three radicals which replace hydrogen in glycerin are not all identical; thus kephalin, myelin and lecithin are glycerides in which two hydrogens are replaced by fatty acid radicals, and the third by a complex phosphoric acid derivative.

Glycerin is also a product of certain kinds of fermentation, especially of the alcoholic fermentation of sugar; consequently it is a constituent of many wines and other fermented liquors. According to Louis Pasteur, about 1/30th of the sugar transformed under ordinary conditions in the fermentation of grape juice and similar saccharine liquids into alcohol and other products become converted into glycerin. In certain natural fatty substances, *e.g.* palm oil, it exists in the free state, so that it can be separated by washing with boiling water, which dissolves the glycerin but not the fatty glycerides.

Properties.—Glycerin is a viscid, colourless liquid of sp. gr. 1.265 at 15° C., possessing a somewhat sweet taste; below 0° C. it solidifies to a white crystalline mass, which melts at 17° C. When heated alone it partially volatilizes, but the greater part decomposes; under a pressure of 12 mm. of mercury it boils at 170° C. In an atmosphere of steam it distils without decomposition under ordinary barometric pressure. It dissolves readily in water and alcohol in all proportions, but is insoluble in ether. It possesses considerable solvent powers, whence it is employed for numerous purposes in pharmacy and the arts. Its viscid character, and its non-liability to dry and harden by exposure to air, also fit it for various other uses, such as lubrication, &c., whilst its peculiar physical characters, enabling it to blend with either aqueous or oily matters under certain circumstances, render it a useful ingredient in a large number of products of varied kinds.

Manufacture.—The simplest modes of preparing pure glycerin are based on the saponification of fats, either by alkalis or by superheated steam, and on the circumstance that, although glycerin cannot be distilled by itself under the ordinary pressure without decomposition, it can be readily volatilized in a current of superheated steam. Commercial glycerin is mostly obtained from the "spent lyes" of the soap-maker. In the van Ruymbeke process the spent lyes are allowed to settle, and then treated with "persulphate of iron," the exact composition of which is a trade secret, but it is possibly a mixture of ferric and ferrous sulphates. Ferric hydrate, iron soaps and all insoluble impurities are precipitated. The liquid is filter-pressed, and any excess of iron in the filtrate is precipitated by the careful addition of caustic soda and then removed. The liquid is then evaporated under a vacuum of 27 to 28 in. of mercury, and, when of specific gravity 1.295 (corresponding to about 80% of glycerin), it is distilled under a vacuum of 28 to 29 in. In the Glatz process the lye is treated with a little milk of lime, the liquid then neutralized with hydrochloric acid, and the liquid filtered. Evaporation and subsequent distillation under a high vacuum gives crude glycerin. The impure glycerin obtained as above is purified by redistillation in steam and evaporation in vacuum pans.

Technical Uses.—Besides its use as a starting-point in the production of "nitroglycerin" (*q.v.*) and other chemical products, glycerin is largely employed for a number of purposes in the arts, its application thereto being due to its peculiar physical properties. Thus its non-liability to freeze (when not absolutely anhydrous, which it practically never is when freely exposed to the air) and its non-volatility at ordinary temperatures, combined with its power of always keeping fluid and not drying up and hardening, render it valuable as a lubricating agent for clockwork, watches, &c., as a substitute for water in wet gas-meters, and as an ingredient in cataplasms, plasters, modelling clay, pasty colouring matters, dyeing materials, moist colours for artists, and numerous other analogous substances which are required to be kept in a permanently soft condition. Glycerin acts as a preservative against decomposition, owing to its antiseptic qualities, which also led to its being employed to preserve untanned leather (especially during transit when exported, the hides being, moreover, kept soft and supple); to make solutions of gelatin, albumen, gum, paste, cements, &c. which will keep without decomposition; to preserve meat and other edibles; to mount anatomical preparations; to preserve vaccine lymph unchanged; and for many similar purposes. Its solvent power is also 147utilized in the production of various colouring fluids, where the colouring matter would not dissolve in water alone; thus aniline violet, the tinctorial constituents of madder, and various allied colouring matters dissolve in glycerin, forming liquids which remain coloured even when diluted with water, the colouring matters being either retained in suspension or dissolved by the glycerin present in the diluted fluid. Glycerin is also employed in the manufacture of formic acid (*q.v.*). Certain kinds of copying inks are greatly improved by the substitution of glycerin, in part or entirely, for the sugar or honey usually added.

In its medicinal use glycerin is an excellent solvent for such substances as iodine, alkaloids, alkalis, &c., and is therefore used for applying them to diseased surfaces, especially as it aids in their absorption. It does not evaporate or turn rancid, whilst its marked hygroscopic action ensures the moistness and softness of any surface that it covers. Given by the mouth glycerin produces purging if large doses are administered, and has the same action if only a small quantity be introduced into the rectum. For this purpose it is very largely used either as a suppository or in the fluid form (one or two drachms). The result is prompt, safe and painless. Glycerin is useless as a food and is not in any sense a substitute for cod-liver oil. Very large doses in animals cause lethargy, collapse and death.

GLYCOLS, in organic chemistry, the generic name given to the aliphatic dihydric alcohols. These compounds may be obtained by heating the alkylen iodides or bromides (*e.g.* ethylene dibromide) with silver acetate or with potassium acetate and alcohol, the esters so produced being then hydrolysed with caustic alkalis, thus:

$$C2H4Br2 + 2\ C2H3O2 \cdot Ag \rightarrow C2H4(O \cdot C2H3O)2 \rightarrow C2H4(OH)2 + 2\ K \cdot C2H3O2;$$

by the direct union of water with the alkylen oxides; by oxidation of the olefines with cold potassium permanganate solution (G. Wagner, *Ber.*, 1888, 21, p. 1231), or by the action of nitrous acid on the diamines.

Glycols may be classified as *primary*, containing two −CH2OH groups; *primary-secondary*, containing the grouping −CH(OH)·CH2OH; *secondary*, with the grouping −CH(OH)·CH(OH)−; and *tertiary*, with the grouping >C(OH)·(OH)C<. The secondary glycols are prepared by the action of alcoholic potash on aldehydes, thus:

$$3(CH3)2CH \cdot CHO + KHO = (CH3)2CHCO2K +$$
$$(CH3)2CH \cdot CH(OH) \cdot CH(OH) \cdot CH(CH3)2.$$

The tertiary glycols are known as *pinacones* and are formed on the reduction of ketones with sodium amalgam.

The glycols are somewhat thick liquids, of high boiling point, the pinacones only being crystalline solids; they are readily soluble in water and alcohol, but are insoluble in ether. By the action of dehydrating agents they are converted into aldehydes or ketones. In their general behaviour towards oxidizing agents the primary glycols behave very similarly to the ordinary primary alcohols (*q.v.*), but the secondary and tertiary glycols break down, yielding compounds with a smaller carbon content.

Ethylene glycol, C2H4(OH)2, was first prepared by A. Wurtz (*Ann. chim.*, 1859 [3], 55, p. 400) from ethylene dibromide and silver acetate. It is a somewhat pleasant smelling liquid, boiling at 197° to 197.5° C. and having a specific gravity of 1.125 (0°). On fusion with solid potash at 250° C. it completely decomposes, giving potassium oxalate and hydrogen,
$$C2H6O2 + 2KHO = K2C2O4 + 4H2.$$

Two propylene glycols, C3H8O2, are known, viz. α-propylene glycol, CH3 · CH(OH) · CH2OH, a liquid boiling at 188° to 189°, and obtained by heating glycerin with sodium hydroxide and distilling the mixture; and trimethylene glycol, CH2OH · CH2 · CH2OH, a liquid boiling at 214° C. and prepared by boiling trimethylene bromide with potash solution (A. Zander, *Ann.*, 1882, 214, p. 178).

GLYCONIC (from Glycon, a Greek lyric poet), a form of verse, best known in Catullus and Horace (usually in the catalectic variety), with three feet—a spondee and two dactyls; or four—three trochees and a dactyl, or a dactyl and three chorees. Sir R. Jebb pointed out that the last form might be varied by placing the dactyl second or third, and according to its place this verse was called a First, Second or Third Glyconic.

Cf. J. W. White, in *Classical Quarterly* (Oct. 1909).

GLYPH (from Gr. γλύφειν, to carve), in architecture, a vertical channel in a frieze (see TRIGLYPH).

GLYPTODON (Greek for "fluted-tooth"), a name applied by Sir R. Owen to the typical representative of a group of gigantic, armadillo-like, South American, extinct Edentata, characterized by having the carapace composed of a solid piece (formed by the union of a multitude of bony dermal plates) without any movable rings. The facial portion of the skull is very short; a long process of the maxillary bone descends from the anterior part of the zygomatic arch; and the ascending ramus of the mandible is remarkably high. The teeth, 8⁄8 in the later species, are much alike, having two deep grooves or flutings on each side, so as to divide them into three distinct lobes (fig.). They are very tall and grew throughout life. The vertebral column is almost entirely welded into a solid tube, but there is a complex joint at the base of the neck, to allow the head being retracted within the carapace. The limbs are very strong, and the feet short and broad, resembling externally those of an elephant or tortoise.

Two views of the tooth of a *Glyptodon*; the upper figure showing one side, and the lower the crown.

Glyptodonts constitute a family, the *Glyptodontidae*, whose position is next to the armadillos (*Dasypodidae*); the group being represented by a number of generic types. The Pleistocene forms, whose remains occur abundantly in the silt of the Buenos Aires pampas, are by far the largest, the skull and tail-sheath in some instances having a length of from 12 to 16 ft. In *Glyptodon* (with which *Schistopleurum* is identical) the tail-sheath consists of a series of coronet-like rings, gradually diminishing in diameter from base to tip. *Daedicurus*, in which the tail-sheath is in the form of a huge solid club, is the largest member of the family, in *Panochthus* and *Sclerocalyptus* (*Hoplophorus*) the tail-sheath consists basally of a small number of smooth rings, and terminally of a tube. In some specimens of these genera the horny shields covering the bony scutes of the carapace have been preserved, and since the foramina, which often pierce the latter, stop short of the former, it is evident that these were for the passage of blood-vessels and not receptacles for bristles. In the early Pleistocene epoch, when South America became connected with North America, some of the glyptodonts found their way into the latter continent. Among these northern forms some from Texas and Florida have been referred to *Glyptodon*. One large species from Texas has, however, been made the type of a separate genus, under the name of *Glyptotherium texanum*. In some respects it shows affinity with *Panochthus*, although in the simple structure of the tail-sheath it recalls the undermentioned *Propalaeohoplophorus*. All the above are of Pleistocene and perhaps Pliocene age, but in the Santa Cruz beds of Patagonia there occur the two curious genera *Propalaeohoplophorus* and *Peltephilus*, the former of which is a primitive and generalized type of glyptodont, while the latter seems to come nearer to the armadillos. Both are represented by species of comparatively small size. In *Propalaeohoplophorus* the scutes of the carapace, which are less deeply sculptured than in the larger glyptodonts, are arranged in distinct transverse rows, in three of which they partially overlap near the border of the carapace after the fashion of the armadillos. The skull and limb-bones exhibit several features met with in the latter, and the vertebrae of the back are not welded into a continuous tube. There are eight pairs of teeth, the first four of which are simpler than the rest, and may perhaps therefore be regarded as premolars. More remarkable is *Peltephilus*, on account of the fact that the teeth, which are simple, with a chevron-shaped section, form a continuous series from the front of the jaw backwards, the number of pairs being seven. Accordingly, a modification of the character, even of the true Edentata, as given in the earlier article, is rendered necessary. The head bears a pair of horn-like scutes, and the scutes of the carapace and tail, which are loosely opposed or slightly overlapping, form a number of transverse rows.

LITERATURE.—R. Lydekker, "The Extinct Edentates of Argentina," *An. Mus. La Plata— Pal. Argent.* vol. iii. p. 2 (1904); H. F. Osborn, "'Glyptotherium texanum,' a Glyptodont from the Lower Pleistocene of Texas," *Bull. Amer. Mus.*, vol. xvii. p. 491 (1903); W. B. Scott, "Mammalia of the Santa Cruz Beds—Edentata," *Rep. Princeton Exped. to Patagonia*, vol. v. (1903-1904).

(R. L.*)

GLYPTOTHEK (from Gr. γλυπτός, carved, and θήκη, a place of storage), an architectural term given to a gallery for the exhibition of sculpture, and first employed at Munich, where it was built to exhibit the sculptures from the temple of Aegina.
148

GMELIN, the name of several distinguished German scientists, of a Tübingen family. Johann Georg Gmelin (1674-1728), an apothecary in Tübingen, and an accomplished chemist for the times in which he lived, had three sons. The first, Johann Conrad (1702-1759), was an apothecary and surgeon in Tübingen. The second, Johann Georg (1709-1755), was appointed professor of chemistry and natural history in St Petersburg in 1731, and from 1733 to 1743 was engaged in travelling through Siberia. The fruits of his journey were *Flora Sibirica* (4 vols., 1749-1750) and *Reisen durch Sibirien* (4 vols., 1753). He ended his days as professor of medicine at Tübingen, a post to which he was appointed in 1749. The third son, Philipp Friedrich (1721-1768), was extraordinary professor of medicine at Tübingen in 1750, and in 1755 became ordinary professor of botany and chemistry. In the second generation Samuel Gottlieb (1743-1774), the son of Johann Conrad, was appointed professor of natural history at St Petersburg in 1766, and in the following year started on a journey through south Russia and the regions round the Caspian Sea. On his way back he was captured by Usmey Khan, of the Kaitak tribe, and died from the ill-treatment he suffered, on the 27th of July 1774. One of his nephews, Ferdinand Gottlob von Gmelin (1782-1848), became professor of medicine and natural history at Tübingen in 1805, and another, Christian Gottlob (1792-1860), who in 1828 was one of the first to devise a process for the artificial manufacture of ultramarine, was professor of chemistry and pharmacy in the same university. In the youngest branch of the family, Philipp Friedrich had a son, Johann Friedrich (1748-1804), who was appointed professor of medicine in Tübingen in 1772, and in 1775 accepted the chair of medicine and chemistry at Göttingen. In 1788 he published the 13th edition of Linnaeus' *Systema Naturae* with many additions and alterations. His son Leopold (1788-1853), was the best-known member of the family. He studied medicine and chemistry at Göttingen, Tübingen and Vienna, and in 1813 began to lecture on chemistry at Heidelberg, where in 1814 he was appointed extraordinary, and in 1817 ordinary, professor of chemistry and medicine. He was the discoverer of potassium ferricyanide (1822), and wrote the *Handbuch der Chemie* (1st ed. 1817-1819, 4th ed. 1843-1855), an important work in its day, which was translated into English for the Cavendish Society by H. Watts (1815-1884) in 1848-1859. He resigned his chair in 1852, and died on the 13th of April in the following year at Heidelberg.

41

GMÜND, a town of Germany, in the kingdom of Württemberg,1 in a charming and fruitful valley on the Rems, here spanned by a beautiful bridge, 31 m. E.N.E. of Stuttgart on the railway to Nördlingen. Pop. (1905) 18,699. It is surrounded by old walls, flanked with towers, and has a considerable number of ancient buildings, among which are the fine church of the Holy Cross; St John's church, which dates from the time of the Hohenstaufen; and, situated on a height near the town, partly hewn out of the rock, the pilgrimage church of the Saviour. Among the modern buildings are the gymnasium, the drawing and trade schools, the Roman Catholic seminary, the town hall and the industrial art museum. Clocks and watches are manufactured here and also other articles of silver, while the town has a considerable trade in corn, hops and fruit. The scenery in the neighbourhood is very beautiful, near the town being the district called Little Switzerland.

Gmünd was surrounded by walls in the beginning of the 12th century by Duke Frederick of Swabia. It received town rights from Frederick Barbarossa, and after the extinction of the Hohenstaufen became a free imperial town. It retained its independence till 1803, when it came into the possession of Württemberg. Gmünd is the birth-place of the painter Hans Baldung (1475-1545) and of the architect Heinrich Arler or Parler (fl. 1350). In the middle ages the population was about 10,000.

See Kaiser, *Gmünd und seine Umgebung* (1888).

1There are two places of this name in Austria. (1) Gmünd, a town in Lower Austria, containing a palace belonging to the imperial family, (2) a town in Carinthia, with a beautiful Gothic church and some interesting ruins.

GMUNDEN, a town and summer resort of Austria, in Upper Austria, 40 m. S.S.W. of Linz by rail. Pop. (1900) 7126. It is situated at the efflux of the Traun river from the lake of the same name and is surrounded by high mountains, as the Traunstein (5446 ft.), the Erlakogel (5150 ft.), the Wilde Kogel (6860 ft.) and the Höllen Gebirge. It is much frequented as a health and summer resort, and has a variety of lake, brine, vegetable and pine-cone baths, a hydropathic establishment, inhalation chambers, whey cure, &c. There are a great number of excursions and points of interest round Gmunden, specially worth mentioning being the Traun Fall, 10 m. N. of Gmunden. It is also an important centre of the salt industry in Salzkammergut. Gmunden was a town encircled with walls already in 1186. On the 14th of November 1626, Pappenheim completely defeated here the army of the rebellious peasants.

See F. Krackowizer, *Geschichte der Stadt Gmunden in Oberösterreich* (Gmunden, 1898-1901, 3 vols.).

GNAT (O. Eng. *gnæt*), the common English name for the smaller dipterous flies (see DIPTERA) of the family *Culicidae*, which are now included among "mosquitoes" (see MOSQUITO). The distinctive term has no zoological significance, but in England the "mosquito" has commonly been distinguished from the "gnat" as a variety of larger size and more poisonous bite.

GNATHOPODA, a term in zoological classification, suggested as an alternative name for the group Arthropoda (*q.v.*). The word, which means "jaw-footed," refers to the fact that in the members of the group, some of the lateral appendages or "feet" in the region of the mouth act as jaws.

GNATIA (also EGNATIA or IGNATIA, mod. *Anazzo*, near Fasano), an ancient city of the Peucetii, and their frontier town towards the Sallentini (*i.e.* of Apulia towards Calabria), in Roman times of importance for its trade, lying as it did on the sea, at the point where the Via Traiana joined the coast road,138 m. S.E. of Barium. The ancient city walls have been almost entirely destroyed in recent times to provide building material,2 and the place is famous for the discoveries made in its tombs. A considerable collection of antiquities from Gnatia is preserved at Fasano, though the best are in the museum at Bari. Gnatia was the scene of the prodigy at which Horace mocks (*Sat.* i. 5. 97). Near Fasano are two small subterranean chapels with paintings of the 11th century A.D. (E. Bertaux, *L'Art dans l'Italie méridionale*, Paris, 1904, 135).

(T. AS.)

1There is no authority for calling the latter Via Egnatia.

2H. Swinburne, *Travels in the Two Sicilies* (London, 1790), ii. 15, mentions the walls as being 8 yds. thick and 16 courses high.

GNEISENAU, AUGUST WILHELM ANTON, COUNT NEITHARDT VON (1760-1831), Prussian field marshal, was the son of a Saxon officer named Neithardt. Born in 1760 at Schildau, near Torgau, he was brought up in great poverty there, and subsequently at Würzburg and Erfurt. In 1777 he entered Erfurt university; but two years later joined an Austrian regiment there quartered. In 1782 taking the additional name of Gneisenau from some lost estates of his family in Austria, he entered as an officer the service of the margrave of Baireuth-Anspach. With one of that prince's mercenary regiments in English pay he saw active service and gained valuable experience in the War of American Independence, and returning in 1786, applied for Prussian service. Frederick the Great gave him a commission as first lieutenant in the infantry. Made *Stabskapitän* in 1790, Gneisenau served in Poland, 1793-1794, and, subsequently to this, ten years of quiet garrison life in Jauer enabled him to undertake a wide range of military studies. In 1796 he married Caroline von Kottwitz. In 1806 he was one of Hohenlohe's staff-officers, fought at Jena, and a little later commanded a provisional infantry brigade which fought under Lestocq in the Lithuanian campaign. Early in 1807 Major von Gneisenau was sent as commandant to Colberg, which, small and ill-protected as it was, succeeded in holding out until the peace of Tilsit. The commandant received the much-prized order "pour le mérite," and was promoted lieutenant-colonel.

A wider sphere of work was now opened to him. As chief of 149engineers, and a member of the reorganizing committee, he played a great part, along with Scharnhorst, in the work of reconstructing the Prussian army. A colonel in 1809, he soon drew upon himself, by his energy, the suspicion of the dominant French, and Stein's fall was soon followed by Gneisenau's retirement. But, after visiting Russia, Sweden and England, he returned to Berlin and resumed his place as a leader of the patriotic party. In open military work and secret machinations his energy and patriotism were equally tested, and with the outbreak of the War of Liberation, Major-General Gneisenau became Blücher's quartermaster-general. Thus began the connexion between these two soldiers which has furnished military history with its best example of the harmonious co-operation between the general and his chief-of-staff. With Blücher, Gneisenau served to the capture of Paris; his military character was the exact complement of Blücher's, and under this happy guidance the young troops of Prussia, often defeated but never discouraged, fought their way into the heart of France. The plan of the march on Paris, which led directly to the fall of Napoleon, was specifically the work of the chief-of-staff. In reward for his distinguished service he was in 1814, along with York, Kleist and Bülow, made count at the same time as Blücher became prince of Wahlstatt; an annuity was also assigned to him.

In 1815, once more chief of Blücher's staff, Gneisenau played a very conspicuous part in the Waterloo campaign (*q.v.*). Senior generals, such as York and Kleist, had been set aside in order that the chief-of-staff should have the command in case of need, and when on the field of Ligny the old field marshal was disabled, Gneisenau at once assumed the control of the Prussian army. Even in the light of the evidence that many years' research has collected, the precise part taken by Gneisenau in the events which followed is much debated. It is known that Gneisenau had the deepest distrust of the British commander, who, he considered, had left the Prussians in the lurch at Ligny, and that to the hour of victory he had grave doubts as to whether he ought not to fall back on the Rhine. Blücher, however, soon recovered from his injuries, and, with Grolmann, the quartermaster-general, he managed to convince Gneisenau. The relations of the two may be illustrated by Brigadier-General Hardinge's report. Blücher burst into Hardinge's room at Wavre, saying "*Gneisenau has given way*, and we are to march at once to your chief."

On the field of Waterloo, however, Gneisenau was quick to realize the magnitude of the victory, and he carried out the pursuit with a relentless vigour which has few parallels in history. His reward was further promotion and the insignia of the "Black Eagle" which had been taken in Napoleon's coach. In 1816 he was appointed to command the VIIIth Prussian Corps, but soon retired from the service, both because of ill-health and for political reasons. For two years he lived in retirement on his estate, Erdmannsdorf in Silesia, but in 1818 he was made governor of Berlin in succession to Kalkreuth, and member of the *Staatsrath*. In 1825 he became general field marshal. In 1831 he was appointed to the command of the Army of Observation on the Polish frontier, with Clausewitz as his chief-of-staff. At Posen he was struck down by cholera and died on the 24th of August 1831, soon followed by his chief-of staff, who fell a victim to the same disease in November.

As a soldier, Gneisenau was the greatest Prussian general since Frederick; as a man, his noble character and virtuous life secured him the affection and reverence, not only of his superiors and subordinates in the service, but of the whole Prussian nation. A statue by Rauch was erected in Berlin in 1855, and in memory of the siege of 1807 the Colberg grenadiers received his name in 1889. One of his sons led a brigade of the VIIIth Army Corps in the war of 1870.

See G. H. Pertz, *Das Leben des Feldmarschalls Grafen Neithardt von Gneisenau*, vols. 1-3 (Berlin, 1864-1869); vols. 4 and 5, G. Delbrück (*ib.*1879, 1880), with numerous documents and letters; H. Delbrück, *Das Leben des G. F. M. Grafen von Gneisenau* (2 vols., 2nd ed., Berlin, 1894), based on Pertz's work, but containing much new material; Frau von Beguelin, *Denkwürdigkeiten* (Berlin, 1892); Hormayr, *Lebensbilder aus den Befreiungskriegen* (Jena, 1841); Pick, *Aus dem brieflichen Nachlass Gneisenaus*; also the histories of the campaigns of 1807 and 1813-15.

GNEISS, a term long used by the miners of the Harz Mountains to designate the country rock in which the mineral veins occur; it is believed to be a word of Slavonic origin meaning "rotted" or "decomposed." It has gradually passed into acceptance as a generic term signifying a large and varied series of metamorphic rocks, which mostly consist of quartz and felspar (orthoclase and plagioclase) with muscovite and biotite, hornblende or augite, iron oxides, zircon and apatite. There is also a long list of accessory minerals which are present in gneisses with more or less frequency, but not invariably, as garnet, sillimanite, cordierite, graphite and graphitoid, epidote, calcite, orthite, tourmaline and andalusite. The gneisses all possess a more or less marked parallel structure or foliation, which is the main feature by which many of them are separated from the granites, a group of rocks having nearly the same mineralogical composition and closely allied to many gneisses.

The felspars of the gneisses are predominantly orthoclase (often perthitic), but microcline is common in the more acid types and oligoclase occurs also very frequently, especially in certain sedimentary gneisses, while more basic varieties of plagioclase are rare. Quartz is very seldom absent and may be blue or milky and opalescent. Muscovite and biotite may both occur in the same rock; in other cases only one of them is present. The commonest and most important types of gneiss are the mica-gneisses. Hornblende is green, rarely brownish; augite pale green or nearly colourless; enstatite appears in some granulite-gneisses. Epidote, often with enclosures of orthite, is by no means rare in gneisses from many different parts of the world. Sillimanite and andalusite are not infrequent ingredients of gneiss, and their presence has been accounted for in more than one way. Cordierite-gneisses are a special group of great interest and possessing many peculiarities; they are partly, if not entirely, foliated contact-altered sedimentary rocks. Kyanite and staurolite may also be mentioned as occasionally occurring.

Many varieties of gneiss have received specific names according to the minerals they consist of and the structural peculiarities they exhibit. Muscovite-gneiss, biotite-gneiss and muscovite-biotite-gneiss, more common perhaps than all the others taken together, are grey or pinkish rocks according to the colour of their prevalent felspar, not unlike granites, but on the whole more often fine-grained (though coarse-grained types occur) and possessing a gneissose or foliated structure. The latter consists in the arrangement of the flakes of mica in such a way that their faces are parallel, and hence the rock has the property of splitting more readily in the direction in which the mica plates are disposed. This fissility, though usually marked, is not as great as in the schists or slates, and the split faces are not so smooth as in these latter rocks. The films of mica may be continuous and are usually not flat, but irregularly curved. In some gneisses the parallel flakes of mica are scattered through the quartz and felspar; in others these minerals form discrete bands, the quartz and felspar being grouped into lenticles separated by thin films of mica. When large felspars, of rounded or elliptical form, are visible in the gneiss, it is said to have augen structure (Ger. *Augen* = eyes). It should also be remarked that the essential component minerals of the rocks of this family are practically always determinable by naked eye inspection or with the aid of a simple lens. If the rock is too fine grained for this it is generally relegated to the schists. When the bands of folia are very fine and tortuous the structure is called helizitic.

In mica-gneisses sillimanite, kyanite, andalusite and garnet may occur. The significance of these minerals is variously interpreted; they may indicate that the gneiss consists wholly or in part of sedimentary material which has been contact-altered, but they have also been regarded as having been developed by metamorphic action out of biotite or other primary ingredients of the rock.

150

Hornblende-gneisses are usually darker in colour and less fissile than mica-gneisses; they contain more plagioclase, less orthoclase and microcline, and more sphene and epidote. Many of them are rich in hornblende and thus form transitions to amphibolites. Pyroxene-gneisses are less frequent but occur in many parts of both hemispheres. The "charnockite" series are very closely allied to the pyroxene-gneisses. Hypersthene and scapolite both may occur in these rocks and they are sometimes garnetiferous.

In every country where the lowest and oldest rocks have come to the surface and been exposed by the long continued action of denudation in stripping away the overlying formations, gneisses are found in great abundance and of many different kinds. They are in fact the typical rocks of the Archean (Lewisian, Laurentian, &c.) series. In the Alps, Harz, Scotland, Norway and Sweden, Canada, South America, Peninsular India, Himalayas (to mention only a few localities) they occupy wide areas and exhibit a rich diversity of types. From this it has been inferred that they are of great geological age, and in fact this can be definitely proved in many cases, for the oldest known fossiliferous formations may be seen to rest unconformably on these gneisses and are made up of their débris. It was for a long time believed that they represented the primitive crust of the earth, and while this is no longer generally taught there are still geologists who hold that these gneisses are necessarily of pre-Cambrian age. Others, while admitting the general truth of this hypothesis, consider that there are localities in which typical gneisses can be shown to penetrate into rocks which may be as recent as the Tertiary period, or to pass into these rocks so gradually and in such a way as to make it certain that the gneisses are merely altered states of comparatively recent sedimentary or igneous rocks. Much controversy has arisen on these points; but this is certain, that gneisses are far the most common among Archean rocks, and where their age is not known the presumption is strong that they are at least pre-Cambrian.

Many gneisses are undoubtedly sedimentary rocks that have been brought to their present state by such agents of metamorphism as heat, movement, crushing and recrystallization. This may be demonstrated partly by their mode of occurrence: they accompany limestones, graphitic schists, quartzites and other rocks of sedimentary type; some of them where least altered may even show remains of bedding or of original pebbly character (conglomerate gneisses). More conclusive, however, is the chemical composition of these rocks, which often is such as no igneous masses possess, but resembles that of many impure argillaceous sediments. These sedimentary gneisses (or paragneisses, as they are often called) are often rich in biotite and garnet and may contain kyanite and sillimanite, or less frequently calcite. Some of them, however, are rich in felspar and quartz, with muscovite and biotite; others may even contain hornblende and augite, and all these may bear so close a resemblance to gneisses of igneous origin that by no single character, chemical or mineralogical, can their original nature be definitely established. In these cases, however, a careful study of the relations of the rock in the field and of the different types which occur together will generally lead to some positive conclusion.

Other gneisses are igneous (orthogneisses). These have very much the same composition as acid igneous rocks such as granite, aplite, hornblende granite, or intermediate rocks such as syenite and quartz diorite. Many of these orthogneisses are not equally well foliated throughout, but are massive or granitoid in places. They are sometimes subdivided into granite gneiss, diorite gneiss, syenite gneiss and so on. The sedimentary schists into which these rocks have been intruded may show contact alteration by the development of such minerals as cordierite, andalusite and sillimanite. In many of these orthogneisses the foliation is primitive, being an original character of the rock which was produced either by fluxion movements in a highly viscous, semi-solid mass injected at great pressure into the surrounding strata, or by folding stresses acting immediately after consolidation. That the foliation in other orthogneisses is subsequent or superinduced, having been occasioned by pressure and deformation of the solid mass long after it had consolidated and cooled, admits of no doubt, but it is very difficult to establish criteria by which these types may be differentiated. Those gneisses in which the minerals have been crushed and broken by fluxion or injection movements have been called protoclastic, while those which have attained their gneissose state by crushing long after consolidation are distinguished as cataclastic. There are also many examples of gneisses of mixed or synthetic origin. They may be metamorphosed sediments (granulites and schists) into which tongues and thin veins of granitic character have been intruded, following the more or less parallel foliation planes already present in the country rock. These veinlets produce that alternation in mineral composition and banded structure which are essential in gneisses. This intermixture of igneous and sedimentary material may take place on the finest scale and in the most intricate manner. Often there has been resorption of the older rocks, whether sedimentary or igneous, by those which have invaded them, and movement has gone on both during injection and at a later period, so that the whole complex becomes amalgamated and its elements are so completely confused that the geologist can no longer disentangle them.

When we remember that in the earlier stages of the earth's history, to which most gneisses belong, and in the relatively deep parts of the earth's crust, where they usually occur, there has been most igneous injection and greatest frequency of earth movements, it is not difficult to understand the geological distribution of gneissose rocks. All the factors which are required for their production, heat, movement, plutonic intrusions, contact alteration, interstitial moisture at high temperatures, are found at great depths and have acted most frequently and with greatest power on the older rock masses. But locally, where the conditions were favourable, the same processes may have gone on in comparatively recent times. Hence, though most gneisses are Archean, all gneisses are not necessarily so.

45

GNEIST, HEINRICH RUDOLF HERMANN FRIEDRICH VON (1816-1895), German jurist and politician, was born at Berlin on the 13th of August 1816, the son of a judge attached to the "Kammergericht" (court of appeal) in that city. After receiving his school education at the gymnasium at Eisleben in Prussian Saxony, he entered the university of Berlin in 1833 as a student of jurisprudence, and became a pupil of the famous Roman law teacher von Savigny. Proceeding to the degree of *doctor juris* in 1838, young Gneist immediately established himself as a *Privatdozent* in the faculty of law. He had, however, already chosen the judicial branch of the legal profession as a career, and having while yet a student acted as *Auscultator*, was admitted *Assessor* in 1841. He soon found leisure and opportunity to fulfil a much-cherished wish, and spent the next few years on a lengthened tour in Italy, France and England. He utilized his *Wanderjahre* for the purposes of comparative study, and on his return in 1844 was appointed extraordinary professor of Roman law in Berlin university, and thus began a professorial connexion which ended only with his death. The first-fruits of his activity as a teacher were seen in his brilliant work, *Die formellen Verträge des heutigen römischen Obligationen-Rechtes* (Berlin, 1845). *Pari passu* with his academic labours he continued his judicial career, and became in due course successively assistant judge of the superior court and of the supreme tribunal. But to a mind constituted such as his, the want of elasticity in the procedure of the courts was galling. "Brought up," he tells, in the preface to his *Englische Verfassungsgeschichte*, "in the laborious and rigid school of Prussian judges, at a time when the duty of formulating the matter in litigation was entailed upon the judge who personally conducted the pleadings, I became acquainted both with the advantages possessed by the Prussian bureau system as also with its weak points." Feeling the necessity for fundamental reforms in legal procedure, he published, in 1849, his *Trial by Jury*, in which, after pointing out that the origin of that institution was common to both Germany and England, and showing in a masterly way the benefits which had accrued to the latter country through its more extended application, he pleaded for its freer admission in the tribunals of his own country.

The period of "storm and stress" in 1848 afforded Gneist an opportunity for which he had yearned, and he threw himself with ardour into the constitutional struggles of Prussia. Although his candidature for election to the National Assembly of that year was unsuccessful, he felt that "the die was cast," and deciding for a political career, retired in 1850 from his judicial position. Entering the ranks of the National Liberal party, he began both in writing and speeches actively to champion their cause, now busying himself pre-eminently with the study of constitutional law and history. In 1853 appeared his *Adel und Ritterschaft in England*, and in 1857 the *Geschichte und heutige Gestalt der Ämter in England*, a pamphlet primarily written to combat the Prussian abuses of administration, but for which the author also claimed that it had not been without its effect in modifying certain views that had until then ruled in England itself. In 1858 Gneist was appointed ordinary professor of Roman law, and in the same year commenced his parliamentary career by his election for Stettin to the Abgeordnetenhaus (House of Deputies) of the Prussian Landtag, in which assembly he sat thenceforward uninterruptedly until 1893. [151]Joining the Left, he at once became one of its leading spokesmen. His chief oratorical triumphs are associated with the early period of his membership of the House; two noteworthy occasions being his violent attack (September 1862) upon the government budget in connexion with the reorganization of the Prussian army, and his defence (1864) of the Polish chiefs of the (then) grand-duchy of Posen, who were accused of high treason. In 1857-1863 was published *Das heutige englische Verfassungsund Verwaltungsrecht*, a work which, contrasting English and German constitutional law and administration, aimed at exercising political pressure upon the government of the day. In 1868 Gneist became a member of the North German parliament, and acted as a member of the commission for organizing the federal army, and also of that for the settlement of ecclesiastical controversial questions. On the establishment of German unity his mandate was renewed for the Reichstag, and in this he sat, an active and prominent member of the National Liberal party, until 1884. In the Kulturkampf he sided with the government against the attacks of the Clericals, whom he bitterly denounced, and whose implacable enemy he ever showed himself. In 1879, together with his colleague, von Hänel, he violently attacked the motion for the prosecution of certain Socialist members, which as a result of the vigour of his opposition was almost unanimously rejected. He was parliamentary reporter for the committees on all great financial and administrative questions, and his profound acquaintance with constitutional law caused his advice to be frequently sought, not only in his own but also in other countries. In Prussia he largely influenced legislation, the reform of the judicial and penal systems and the new constitution of the Evangelical Church being largely his work. He was also consulted by the Japanese government when a constitution was being introduced into that country. In 1875 he was appointed a member of the supreme administrative court (*Oberverwaltungsgericht*) of Prussia, but only held office for two years. In 1882 was published his *Englische Verfassungsgeschichte* (trans. *History of the English Constitution*, London, 1886), which may perhaps be described as his *magnum opus*. It placed the author at once on the level of such writers on English constitutional history as Hallam and Stubbs, and supplied English literature with a text-book almost unrivalled in point of historical research. In 1888 one of the first acts of the ill-fated emperor Frederick III., who had always, as crown prince, shown great admiration for him, was to ennoble Gneist, and attach him as instructor in constitutional law to his son, the emperor William II., a charge of which he worthily acquitted himself. The last years of his life were full of energy, and, in the possession of all his faculties, he continued his wonted academic labours until a short time before his death, which occurred at Berlin on the 22nd of July 1895.

As a politician, Gneist's career cannot perhaps be said to have been entirely successful. In a country where parliamentary institutions are the living exponents of the popular will he might have risen to a foremost position in the state; as it was, the party to which he allied himself could never hope to become more than what it remained, a parliamentary faction, and the influence it for a time wielded in the counsels of the state waned as soon as the Social-Democratic party grew to be a force to be reckoned with. It is as a writer and a teacher that Gneist is best known to fame. He was a jurist of a special type. To him law was not mere theory, but living force; and this conception of its power animates all his schemes of practical reform. As a teacher he exercised a magnetic influence, not only by reason of the clearness and cogency of his exposition, but also because of the success with which he developed the talents and guided the aspirations of his pupils. He was a man of noble bearing, religious, and imbued with a stern sense of duty. He was proud of being a "Preussischer Junker" (a member of the Prussian squirearchy), and throughout his writings, despite their liberal tendencies, may be perceived the loyalty and affection with which he clung to monarchical institutions. A great admirer and a true friend of England, to which country he was attached by many personal ties, he surpassed all other Germans in his efforts to make her free institutions, in which he found his ideal, the common heritage of the two great nations of the Teutonic race.

Gneist was a prolific writer, especially on the subject he had made peculiarly his own, that of constitutional law and history, and among his works, other than those above named, may be mentioned the following: *Budget und Gesetz nach dem constitutionellen Staatsrecht Englands*(Berlin, 1867); *Freie Advocatur* (*ib.*, 1867); *Der Rechtsstaat* (*ib.*, 1872, and 2nd edition, 1879); *Zur Verwaltungsreform in Preussen* (Leipzig, 1880); *Das englische Parlament* (Berlin, 1886); in English translation, *The English Parliament* (London, 1886; 3rd edition, 1889); *Die Militär-Vorlage von 1892 und der preussische Verfassungsconflikt von 1862 bis 1866* (Berlin, 1893); *Die nationale Rechtsidee von den Ständen und das preussische Dreiklassenwahlsystem* (*ib.*, 1895); *Die verfassungsmässige Stellung des preussischen Gesamtministeriums* (*ib.*, 1895). See O. Gierke, *Rudolph von Gneist, Gedächtnisrede* (Berlin, 1895), an In Memoriam address delivered in Berlin.

(P. A. A.)

GNESEN (Polish, *Gniezno*), a town of Germany, in the Prussian province of Posen, in an undulating and fertile country, on the Wrzesnia, 30 m. E.N.E. of Posen by the railway to Thorn. Pop. (1905) 23,727. Besides the cathedral, a handsome Gothic edifice with twin towers, which contains the remains of St Adalbert, there are eight Roman Catholic churches, a Protestant church, a synagogue, a clerical seminary and a convent of the Franciscan nuns. Among the industries are cloth and linen weaving, brewing and distilling. A great horse and cattle market is held here annually. Gnesen is one of the oldest towns in the former kingdom of Poland. Its name, *Gniezno*, signifies "nest," and points to early Polish traditions. The cathedral is believed to have been founded towards the close of the 9th century, and, having received the bones of St Adalbert, it was visited in 1000 by the emperor Otto III., who made it the seat of an archbishop. Here, until 1320, the kings of Poland were crowned; and the archbishop, since 1416 primate of Poland, acted as protector pending the appointment of a new king. In 1821 the see of Posen was founded and the archbishop removed his residence thither, though its cathedral chapter still remains at Gnesen. After a long period of decay the town revived after 1815, when it came under the rule of Prussia.

See S. Karwowski, *Gniezno* (Posen, 1892).

GNOME, AND **GNOMIC POETRY.** Sententious maxims, put into verse for the better aid of the memory, were known by the Greeks as gnomes, γνῶμαι, from γνώμη, an opinion. A gnome is defined by the Elizabethan critic Henry Peacham (1576?-1643?) as "a saying pertaining to the manners and common practices of men, which declareth, with an apt brevity, what in this our life ought to be done, or not done." The Gnomic Poets of Greece, who flourished in the 6th century B.C., were those who arranged series of sententious maxims in verse. These were collected in the 4th century, by Lobon of Argos, an orator, but his collection has disappeared. The chief gnomic poets were Theognis, Solon, Phocylides, Simonides of Amorgos, Demodocus, Xenophanes and Euenus. With the exception of Theognis, whose gnomes were fortunately preserved by some schoolmaster about 300 B.C., only fragments of the Gnomic Poets have come down to us. The moral poem attributed to Phocylides, long supposed to be a masterpiece of the school, is now known to have been written by a Jew in Alexandria. Of the gnomic movement typified by the moral works of the poets named above, Prof. Gilbert Murray has remarked that it receives its special expression in the conception of the Seven Wise Men, to whom such proverbs as "Know thyself" and "Nothing too much" were popularly attributed, and whose names differed in different lists. These gnomes or maxims were extended and put into literary shape by the poets. Fragments of Solon, Euenus and Mimnermus have been preserved, in a very confused state, from having been written, for purposes of comparison, on the margins of the MSS. of Theognis, whence they have often slipped into the text of that poet. Theognis enshrines his moral precepts in his elegies, and this was probably the custom of the rest; it is improbable that there ever existed a species of poetry made up entirely of successive gnomes. But the title "gnomic" came to be given to all poetry which dealt in a sententious way with questions 152of ethics. It was, unquestionably, the source from which moral philosophy was directly developed, and theorists upon life and infinity, such as Pythagoras and Xenophanes, seem to have begun their career as gnomic poets. By the very nature of things, gnomes, in their literary sense, belong exclusively to the dawn of literature; their naïveté and their simplicity in moralizing betray it. But it has been observed that many of the ethical reflections of the great dramatists, and in particular of Sophocles and Euripides, are gnomic distiches expanded. It would be an error to suppose that the ancient Greek gnomes are all of a solemn character; some are voluptuous and some chivalrous; those of Demodocus of Leros had the reputation of being droll. In modern times, the gnomic spirit has occasionally been displayed by poets of a homely philosophy, such as Francis Quarles (1592-1644) in England and Gui de Pibrac (1529-1584) in France. The once-celebrated *Quatrains* of the latter, published in 1574, enjoyed an immense success throughout Europe; they were composed in deliberate imitation of the Greek gnomic writers of the 6th century B.C. These modern effusions are rarely literature and perhaps never poetry. With the gnomic writings of Pibrac it was long customary to bind up those of Antoine Favre (or Faber) (1557-1624) and of Pierre Mathieu (1563-1621). Gnomes are frequently to be found in the ancient literatures of Arabia, Persia and India, and in the Icelandic staves. The *priamel*, a brief, sententious kind of poem, which was in favour in Germany from the 12th to the 16th century, belonged to the true gnomic class, and was cultivated with particular success by Hans Rosenblut, the lyrical goldsmith of Nuremberg, in the 15th century.

(E. G.)

GNOMES (Fr. *gnomes*, Ger. *Gnomen*), in folk-lore, the name now commonly given to the earth and mountain spirits who are supposed to watch over veins of precious metals and other hidden treasures. They are usually pictured as bearded dwarfs clad in brown close-fitting garments with hoods. The word "gnome" as applied to these is of comparatively modern and somewhat uncertain origin. By some it is said to have been coined by Paracelsus (so Hatzfeld and Darmesteter, *Dictionnaire*), who uses *Gnomi* as a synonym of *Pygmaei*, from the Greek γνώμη, intelligence. The *New English Dictionary*, however, suggests a derivation from *genomus, i.e.* a Greek type γηνόμος, "earth-dweller," on the analogy of θαλασσονόμος, "dwelling in the sea," adding, however, that though there is no evidence that the term was not used before Paracelsus, it is possibly "a mere arbitrary invention, like so many others found in Paracelsus" (*N.E.D.* s.v.).

GNOMON, the Greek word for the style of a sundial, or any object, commonly a vertical column, the shadow of which was observed in former times in order to learn the altitude of the sun, especially when on the meridian. The art of constructing a sundial is sometimes termed *gnomonics.* In geometry, a gnomon is a plane figure formed by removing a parallelogram from a corner of a larger parallelogram; in the figure ABCDEFA is a gnomon. Gnomonic projection is a projection of a sphere in which the centre of sight is the centre of the sphere.

GNOSTICISM (Gr. γνῶσις, knowledge), the name generally applied to that spiritual movement existing side by side with genuine Christianity, as it gradually crystallized into the old

48

Catholic Church, which may roughly be defined as a distinct religious syncretism bearing the strong impress of Christian influences.

I. The term "Gnosis" first appears in a technical sense in 1 Tim. vi. 20 (ἡ ψευδώνυμος γνῶσις). It seems to have at first been applied exclusively, or at any rate principally, to a particular tendency within the movement as a whole, *i.e.* to those sections of (the Syrian) Gnostics otherwise generally known as Ophites or Naasseni (see Hippolytus, *Philosophumena*, v. 2: Νααsoηνοὶ ... οἱ ἑαυτοὺς Γνωστικοὺς ἀποκαλοῦντες; Irenaeus i. 11. 1; Epiphanius, *Haeres.* xxvi. Cf. also the self-assumed name of the Carpocratiani, Iren. i. 25. 6). But in Irenaeus the term has already come to designate the whole movement. This first came into prominence in the opening decades of the 2nd century A.D., but is certainly older; it reached its height in the second third of the same century, and began to wane about the 3rd century, and from the second half of the 3rd century onwards was replaced by the closely-related and more powerful Manichaean movement. Offshoots of it, however, continued on into the 4th and 5th centuries. Epiphanius still had the opportunity of making personal acquaintance with Gnostic sects.

II. Of the actual writings of the Gnostics, which were extraordinarily numerous,1 very little has survived; they were sacrificed to the destructive zeal of their ecclesiastical opponents. Numerous fragments and extracts from Gnostic writings are to be found in the works of the Fathers who attacked Gnosticism. Most valuable of all are the long extracts in the 5th and 6th books of the *Philosophumena* of Hippolytus. The most accessible and best critical edition of the fragments which have been preserved word for word is to be found in Hilgenfeld's *Ketzergeschichte des Urchristentums*. One of the most important of these fragments is the letter of Ptolemaeus to Flora, preserved in Epiphanius, *Haeres.* xxxiii. 3-7 (see on this point Harnack in the *Sitzungsberichte der Berliner Akademie*, 1902, pp. 507-545). Gnostic fragments are certainly also preserved for us in the *Acts of Thomas*. Here we should especially mention the beautiful and much-discussed *Song of the Pearl*, or *Song of the Soul*, which is generally, though without absolute clear proof, attributed to the Gnostic Bardesanes (till lately it was known only in the Syrian text; edited and translated by Bevan, *Texts and Studies*,2 v. 3, 1897; Hofmann, *Zeitschrift für neutestamentliche Wissenschaft*, iv.; for the newly-found Greek text see *Acta apostolorum*, ed. Bonnet, ii. 2, c. 108, p. 219). Generally also much Gnostic matter is contained in the apocryphal histories of the Apostles. To the school of Bardesanes belongs the "Book of the Laws of the Lands," which does not, however, contribute much to our knowledge of Gnosticism. Finally, we should mention in this connexion the text on which are based the pseudo-Clementine *Homilies* and *Recognitiones* (beginning of the 3rd century). It is, of course, already permeated with the Catholic spirit, but has drawn so largely upon sources of a Judaeo-Christian Gnostic character that it comes to a great extent within the category of sources for Gnosticism. Complete original Gnostic works have unfortunately survived to us only from the period of the decadence of Gnosticism. Of these we should mention the comprehensive work called the *Pistis-Sophia*, probably belonging to the second half of the 3rd century.3 Further, the Coptic-Gnostic texts of the *Codex Brucianus*, both the books of Ieu and an anonymous third work (edited and translated by C. Schmidt, *Texte und Untersuchungen*, vol. viii., 1892; and a new translation by the same in *Koptisch-gnostische Schriften*, i.) which, contrary to the opinion of their editor and translator, the present writer believes to represent, in their existing form, a still later period and a still more advanced stage in the decadence of Gnosticism. For other and older Coptic-Gnostic texts, in one of which is contained the source of Irenaeus's treatises on the Barbelognostics, but which have unfortunately not yet been made completely accessible, see C. Schmidt in *Sitzungsberichte der Berl. Akad.* (1896), p. 839 seq., and "Philotesia," dedicated to Paul Kleinert (1907); p. 315 seq.

On the whole, then, for an exposition of Gnosticism we are thrown back upon the polemical writings of the Fathers in their controversy with heresy. The most ancient of these is Justin, who according to his *Apol.* i. 26 wrote a *Syntagma* against all heresies (*c.* A.D. 150), and also, probably, a special polemic against 153Marcion (fragment in Irenaeus iv. 6. 2). Both these writings are lost. He was followed by Irenaeus, who, especially in the first book of his treatise *Adversus haereses* (ἐλέγχου καὶ ἀνατροπῆς τῆς ψευδωνύμου γνώσεως βιβλία πέντε, *c.* A.D. 180), gives a detailed account of the Gnostic heresies. He founds his work upon that of his master Justin, but adds from his own knowledge among many other things, notably the detailed account of Valentinianism at the beginning of the book. On Irenaeus, and probably also on Justin, Hippolytus drew for his *Syntagma* (beginning of the 3rd century), a work which is also lost, but can, with great certainty, be reconstructed from three recensions of it: in the *Panarion* of Epiphanius (after 374), in Philaster of Brescia, *Adversus haereses*, and the Pseudo-Tertullian, *Liber adversus omnes haereses.* A second work of Hippolytus Κατὰ πασῶν αἱρέσεων ἔλεγχος is preserved in the so-called *Philosophumena* which survives under the name of Origen.

Here Hippolytus gave a second exposition supplemented by fresh Gnostic original sources with which he had become acquainted in the meanwhile. These sources quoted in Hippolytus have lately met with very unfavourable criticisms. The opinion has been advanced that Hippolytus has here fallen a victim to the mystification of a forger. The truth of the matter must be that Hippolytus probably made use of a collection of Gnostic texts, put together by a Gnostic, in which were already represented various secondary developments of the genuine Gnostic schools. It is also possible that the compiler has himself attempted here and there to harmonize to a certain extent the various Gnostic doctrines, yet in no case is this collection of sources given by Hippolytus to be passed over; it should rather be considered as important evidence for the beginnings of the decay of Gnosticism. Very noteworthy references to Gnosticism are also to be found scattered up and down the *Stromateis* of Clement of Alexandria. Especially important are the *Excerpta ex Theodoto*, the author of which is certainly Clement, which are verbally extracted from Gnostic writings, and have almost the value of original sources. The writings of Origen also contain a wealth of material. In the first place should be mentioned the treatise *Contra Celsum*, in which the expositions of Gnosticism by both Origen and Celsus are of interest (see especially v. 61 seq. and vi. 25 seq.). Of Tertullian's works should be mentioned: *De praescriptione haereticorum*, especially *Adversus Marcionem*, *Adversus Hermogenem*, and finally *Adversus Valentinianos* (entirely founded on Irenaeus). Here must also be mentioned the dialogue of Adamantius with the Gnostics, *De recta in deum fide* (beginning of 4th century). Among the followers of Hippolytus, Epiphanius in his *Panarion* gives much independent and valuable information from his own knowledge of contemporary Gnosticism. But Theodoret of Cyrus (d. 455) is already entirely dependent on previous works and has nothing new to add. With the 4th century both Gnosticism and the polemical literature directed against it die out.4

III. If we wish to grasp the peculiar character of the great Gnostic movement, we must take care not to be led astray by the catchword "Gnosis." It is a mistake to regard the Gnostics as pre-eminently the representatives of intellect among Christians, and Gnosticism as an intellectual tendency chiefly concerned with philosophical speculation, the reconciliation of religion with philosophy and theology. It is true that when Gnosticism was at its height it numbered amongst its followers both theologians and men of science, but that is not its main characteristic. Among the majority of the followers of the movement "Gnosis" was understood not as meaning "knowledge" or "understanding," in our sense of the word, but "revelation." These little Gnostic sects and groups all lived in the conviction that they possessed a secret and mysterious knowledge, in no way accessible to those outside, which was not to be proved or propagated, but believed in by the initiated, and anxiously guarded as a secret. This knowledge of theirs was not based on reflection, on scientific inquiry and proof, but on revelation. It was derived directly from the times of primitive Christianity; from the Saviour himself and his disciples and friends, with whom they claimed to be connected by a secret tradition, or else from later prophets, of whom many sects boasted. It was laid down in wonderful mystic writings, which were in the possession of the various circles (Liechtenhahn, *Die Offenbarung im Gnosticismus*, 1901).

In short, Gnosticism, in all its various sections, its form and its character, falls under the great category of mystic religions, which were so characteristic of the religious life of decadent antiquity. In Gnosticism as in the other mystic religions we find the same contrast of the initiated and the uninitiated, the same loose organization, the same kind of petty sectarianism and mystery-mongering. All alike boast a mystic revelation and a deeply-veiled wisdom. As in many mystical religions, so in Gnosticism, the ultimate object is individual salvation, the assurance of a fortunate destiny for the soul after death. As in the others, so in this the central object of worship is a redeemer-deity who has already trodden the difficult way which the faithful have to follow. And finally, as in all mystical religions, so here too, holy rites and formulas, acts of initiation and consecration, all those things which we call sacraments, play a very prominent part. The Gnostic religion is full of such sacraments. In the accounts of the Fathers we find less about them; yet here Irenaeus' account of the Marcosians is of the highest significance (i. 21 seq.). Much more material is to be found in the original Gnostic writings, especially in the *Pistis-Sophia* and the two books of Ieu, and again in the *Excerpta ex Theodoto*, the *Acts of Thomas*, and here and there also in the pseudo-Clementine writings. Above all we can see from the original sources of the Mandaean religion, which also represents a branch of Gnosticism, how great a part the sacraments played in the Gnostic sects (Brandt, *Mandäische Religion*, p. 96 seq.). Everywhere we are met with the most varied forms of holy rites—the various baptisms, by water, by fire, by the spirit, the baptism for protection against demons, anointing with oil, sealing and stigmatizing, piercing the ears, leading into the bridal chamber, partaking of holy food and drink. Finally, sacred formulas, names and symbols are of the highest importance among the Gnostic sects. We constantly meet with the idea that the soul, on leaving the body, finds its path to the highest heaven opposed by the deities and demons of the lower realms of heaven, and only when it is in possession of the names of these demons, and can repeat the proper holy formula, or is prepared with the right symbol, or has been anointed with the holy oil, finds its way unhindered to the heavenly home. Hence the Gnostic must above all things learn the names of the demons, and equip himself with the sacred formulas and symbols, in order to be certain of a good destiny after death. The exposition of the system of the Ophites given by Celsus (in Origen vi. 25 seq.), and, in connexion with Celsus, by Origen, is particularly instructive on this point. The two "Coptic Ieu" books unfold an immense system of names and symbols. This system again was simplified, and as the supreme secret was taught in a single name or a single formula, by means of which the happy possessor was able to penetrate through all the spaces of heaven (cf. the name "Caulacau" among the Basilidians; Irenaeus, *Adv. haer.* i. 24. 5, and among other sects). It was taught that even the redeemer-god, when he once descended on to this earth, to rise from it again, availed himself of these names and formulas on his descent and ascent through the world of demons. Traces of ideas of this kind are to be met with almost everywhere. They have been most carefully collected by Anz (*Ursprung des Gnosticismus, Texte und Untersuchungen* xv. 4 *passim*) who would see in them the central doctrine of Gnosticism.

IV. All these investigations point clearly to the fact that Gnosticism belongs to the group of mystical religions. We must 154now proceed to define more exactly the peculiar and distinctive character of the Gnostic system. The basis of the Gnostic religion and world-philosophy lies in a decided Oriental dualism. In sharp contrast are opposed the two worlds of the good and of the evil, the divine world and the material world ὕλη, the worlds of light and of darkness. In many systems there seems to be no attempt to derive the one world from the other. The true Basilides (*q.v.*), perhaps also Satornil, Marcion and a part of his disciples, Bardesanes and others, were frankly dualists. In the case of other systems, owing to the inexactness of our information, we are unable to decide; the later systems of Mandaeism and Manichaeanism, so closely related to Gnosticism, are also based upon a decided dualism. And even when there is an attempt at reconciliation, it is still quite clear how strong was the original dualism which has to be overcome. Thus the Gnostic systems make great use of the idea of a fall of the Deity himself; by the fall of the Godhead into the world of matter, this matter, previously insensible, is animated into life and activity, and then arise the powers, both partly and wholly hostile, who hold sway over this world. Such figures of fallen divinities, sinking down into the world of matter are those of Sophia (*i.e.* Ahamoth) among the Gnostics (Ophites) in the narrower sense of the word, the Simoniani (the figure of Helena), the Barbelognostics, and in the system of the *Pistis-Sophia* or the Primal Man, among the Naasseni and the sect, related to them, as described by Hippolytus.5 A further weakening of the dualism is indicated when, in the systems of the Valentinian school, the fall of Sophia takes place within the godhead, and Sophia, inflamed with love, plunges into the Bythos, the highest divinity, and when the attempt is thus made genetically to derive the lower world from the sufferings and passions of fallen divinity. Another attempt at reconciliation is set forth in the so-called "system of emanations" in which it is assumed that from the supreme divinity emanated a somewhat lesser world, from this world a second, and so on, until the divine element (of life) became so far weakened and attenuated, that the genesis of a partly, or even wholly, evil world appears both possible and comprehensible. A system of emanations of this kind, in its purest form, is set forth in the expositions coming from the school of Basilides, which are handed down by Irenaeus, while the propositions which are set forth in the *Philosophumena* of Hippolytus as being doctrines of Basilides represent a still closer approach to a monistic philosophy. Occasionally, too, there is an attempt to establish at any rate a threefold division of the world, and to assume between the worlds of light and darkness a middle world connecting the two; this is clearest among the Sethiani mentioned by Hippolytus (and cf. the Gnostics in Irenaeus i. 30. 1). Quite peculiar in this connexion are the accounts in Books xix. and xx. of the Clementine *Homilies*. After a preliminary examination of all possible different attempts at a solution of the problem of evil, the attempt is here made to represent the devil as an instrument of God. Christ and the devil are the two hands of God, Christ the right hand, and the devil the left, the devil having power over this world-epoch and Christ over the next. The devil here assumes very much the characteristics of the punishing and just God of the Old Testament, and the prospect is even held out of his ultimate pardon. All these efforts at reconciliation show how clearly the problem of evil was realized in these Gnostic and half-Gnostic sects, and how deeply they meditated on the subject; it was not altogether without reason that in the ranks of its opponents Gnosticism was judged to have arisen out of the question, πόθεν τὸ κακόν.

This dualism had not its origin in Hellenic soil, neither is it related to that dualism which to a certain extent existed also in late Greek religion. For the lower and imperfect world, which in that system too is conceived and assumed, is the nebulous world of the non-existent and the formless, which is the necessary accompaniment of that which exists, as shadow is of light.

In Gnosticism, on the contrary, the world of evil is full of active energy and hostile powers. It is an Oriental (Iranian) dualism which here finds expression, though in one point, it is true, the mark of Greek influence is quite clear. When Gnosticism recognizes in this corporeal and material world the true seat of evil, consistently treating the bodily existence of mankind as essentially evil and the separation of the spiritual from the corporeal being as the object of salvation, this is an outcome of the contrast in Greek dualism between spirit and matter, soul and body. For in Oriental (Persian) dualism it is within this material world that the good and evil powers are at war, and this world beneath the stars is by no means conceived as entirely subject to the influence of evil. Gnosticism has combined the two, the Greek opposition between spirit and matter, and the sharp Zoroastrian dualism, which, where the Greek mind conceived of a higher and a lower world, saw instead two hostile worlds, standing in contrast to each other like light and darkness. And out of the combination of these two dualisms arose the teaching of Gnosticism, with its thoroughgoing pessimism and fundamental asceticism.

Another characteristic feature of the Gnostic conception of the universe is the rôle played in almost all Gnostic systems by the seven world-creating powers. There are indeed certain exceptions; for instance, in the systems of the Valentinian schools there is the figure of the one Demiurge who takes the place of the Seven. But how widespread was the idea of seven powers, who created this lower material world and rule over it, has been clearly proved, especially by the systematic examination of the subject by Anz (*Ursprung des Gnosticismus*). These Seven, then, are in most systems half-evil, half-hostile powers; they are frequently characterized as "angels," and are reckoned as the last and lowest emanations of the Godhead; below them—and frequently considered as derived from them—comes the world of the actually devilish powers. On the other hand, among the speculations of the Mandaeans, we find a different and perhaps more primitive conception of the Seven, according to which they, together with their mother Namrus (Rūhā) and their father (Ur), belong entirely to the world of darkness. They and their family are looked upon as captives of the god of light (Mandā-d'hayyē, Hibil-Zīvā), who pardons them, sets them on chariots of light, and appoints them as rulers of the world (cf. chiefly Genza, in *Tractat.* 6 and 8; W. Brandt, *Mandäische Schriften*, 125 seq. and 137 seq.; *Mandäische Religion*, 34 seq., &c.). In the Manichaean system it is related how the helper of the Primal Man, the spirit of life, captured the evil *archontes*, and fastened them to the firmament, or according to another account, flayed them, and formed the firmament from their skin (F. C. Baur, *Das manichäische Religionssystem*, v. 65), and this conception is closely related to the other, though in this tradition the number (seven) of the *archontes* is lost. Similarly, the last book of the *Pistis-Sophia* contains the myth of the capture of the rebellious *archontes*, whose leaders here appear as five in number (Schmidt, *Koptisch-gnostische Schriften*, p. 234 seq.).6 There can scarcely be any doubt as to the origin of these seven (five) powers; they are the seven planetary divinities, the sun, moon and five planets.

In the Mandaean speculations the Seven are introduced with the Babylonian names of the planets. The connexion of the Seven with the planets is also clearly established by the expositions of Celsus and Origen (*Contra Celsum*, vi. 22 seq.) and similarly by the above-quoted passage in the *Pistis-Sophia*, where the *archontes*, who are here mentioned as five, are identified with the five planets (excluding the sun and moon). This collective grouping of the seven (five) planetary divinities is derived from the late Babylonian religion, which can definitely be indicated as the home of these ideas (Zimmern, *Keilinschriften in dem alten Testament*, ii. p. 620 seq.; cf. particularly Diodorus ii. 30). And if in the old sources it is only the first beginnings of this development that can be traced, we must assume that at a later 155period the Babylonian religion centred in the adoration of the seven planetary deities. Very instructive in this connexion is the later (Arabian) account of the religion of the Mesopotamian Sabaeans. The religion of the Sabaeans, evidently a later offshoot from the stock of the old Babylonian religion, actually consists in the cult of the seven planets (cf. the great work of Daniel Chwolsohn, *Die Ssabier u. der Ssabismus*). But this reference to Babylonian religion does not solve the problem which is here in question. For in the Babylonian religion the planetary constellations are reckoned as the supreme deities. And here the question arises, how it came about that in the Gnostic systems the Seven appear as subordinate, half-daemonic powers, or even completely as powers of darkness. This can only be explained on the assumption that some religion hostile to, and stronger than the Babylonian, has superimposed itself upon this, and has degraded its principal deities into daemons. Which religion can this have been? We are at first inclined to think of Christianity itself, but it is certainly most improbable that at the time of the rise of Christianity the Babylonian teaching about the seven planet-deities governing the world should have played so great a part throughout all Syria, Asia Minor and Egypt, that the most varying sections of syncretic Christianity should over and over again adopt this doctrine and work it up into their system. It is far more probable that the combination which we meet with in Gnosticism is older than Christianity, and was found already in existence by Christianity and its sects. We must also reject the theory that this degradation of the planetary deities into daemons is due to the influence of Hebrew monotheism, for almost all the Gnostic sects take up a definitely hostile attitude towards the Jewish religion, and almost always the highest divinity among the Seven is actually the creator-God of the Old Testament. There remains, then, only one religion which can be used as an explanation, namely the Persian, which in fact fulfils all the necessary conditions. The Persian religion was at an early period brought into contact with the Babylonian, through the triumphant progress of Persian culture towards the West; at the time of Alexander the Great it was already the prevailing religion in the Babylonian plain (cf. F. Cumont, *Textes et monuments rel. aux mystères de Mithra*, i. 5, 8-10, 14, 223 seq., 233). It was characterized by a main belief, tending towards monotheism, in the Light-deity Ahuramazda and his satellites, who appeared in contrast with him as powers of the nature of angels.

A combination of the Babylonian with the Persian religion could only be effected by the degradation of the Babylonian deities into half-divine, half-daemonic beings, infinitely remote from the supreme God of light and of heaven, or even into powers of darkness. Even the characteristic dualism of Gnosticism has already proved to be in part of Iranian origin; and now it becomes clear how from that mingling of late Greek and Persian dualism the idea could arise that these seven half-daemonic powers are the creators or rulers of this material world, which is separated infinitely from the light-world of the good God. Definite confirmation of this conjecture is afforded us by later sources of the Iranian religion, in which we likewise meet with the characteristic fundamental doctrine of Gnosticism. Thus the *Bundahish* (iii. 25, v. 1) is able to inform us that in the primeval strife of Satan against the light-world, seven hostile powers were captured and set as constellations in the heavens, where they are guarded by good star-powers and prevented from doing harm. Five of the evil powers are the planets, while here the sun and moon are of course not reckoned among the evil powers—for the obvious reason that in the Persian official religion they invariably appear as good divinities (cf. similar ideas in the Arabic treatise on Persian religion *Ulema-i-Islam*, Vullers,*Fragmente über die Religion Zoroasters*, p. 49, and in other later sources for Persian religion, put together in Spiegel, *Eranische Altertumskunde*, Bd. ii. p. 180). These Persian fancies can hardly be borrowed from the Christian Gnostic systems, their definiteness and much more strongly dualistic character recalling the exposition of the Mandaean (and Manichaean) system, are proofs to the contrary. They are derived from the same period in which the underlying idea of the Gnostic systems also originated, namely, the time at which the ideas of the Persian and Babylonian religions came into contact, the remarkable results of which have thus partly found their way into the official documents of Parsiism.

With this fundamental doctrine of Gnosticism is connected, as Anz has shown in his book which we have so often quoted, a side of their religious practices to which we have already alluded. Gnosticism is to a great extent dominated by the idea that it is above all and in the highest degree important for the Gnostic's soul to be enabled to find its way back through the lower worlds and spheres of heaven ruled by the Seven to the kingdom of light of the supreme deity of heaven. Hence, a principal item in their religious practice consisted in communications about the being, nature and names of the Seven (or of any other hostile daemons barring the way to heaven), the formulas with which they must be addressed, and the symbols which must be shown to them. But names, symbols and formulas are not efficacious by themselves: the Gnostic must lead a life having no part in the lower world ruled by these spirits, and by his knowledge he must raise himself above them to the God of the world of light. Throughout this mystic religious world it was above all the influence of the late Greek religion, derived from Plato, that also continued to operate; it is filled with the echo of the song, the first note of which was sounded by the Platonists, about the heavenly home of the soul and the homeward journey of the wise to the higher world of light.

But the form in which the whole is set forth is Oriental, and it must be carefully noted that the Mithras mysteries, so closely connected with the Persian religion, are acquainted with this doctrine of the ascent of the soul through the planetary spheres (Origen, *Contra Celsum*, vi. 22).

V. We cannot here undertake to set forth and explain in detail all the complex varieties of the Gnostic systems; but it will be useful to take a nearer view of certain principal figures which have had an influence upon at least one series of Gnostic systems, and to examine their origins in the history of religion. In almost all systems an important part is played by the Great Mother (μήτηρ) who appears under the most varied forms (cf. GREAT MOTHER OF THE GODS). At an early period, and notably in the older systems of the Ophites (a fairly exact account of which has been preserved for us by Epiphanius and Hippolytus), among the Gnostics in the narrower sense of the word, the Archontici, the Sethites (there are also traces among the Naasseni, cf. the*Philosophumena* of Hippolytus), the μήτηρ is the most prominent figure in the light-world, elevated above the ἑβδομάς, and the great mother of the faithful. The sect of the Barbelognostics takes its name from the female figure of the Barbelo (perhaps a corruption of Παρθένος; cf. the form Βαρθενώς for "virgin" in Epiphanius, *Haer.* xxvi. 1). But Gnostic speculation gives various accounts of the descent or fall of this goddess of heaven. Thus the "Helena" of the Simoniani descends to this world in order by means of her beauty to provoke to sensual passion and mutual strife the angels who rule the world, and thus again to deprive them of the powers of light, stolen from heaven, by means of which they rule over the world. She is then held captive by them in extreme degradation. Similar ideas are to be found among the "Gnostics" of Epiphanius. The kindred idea of the light-maiden, who, by exciting the sensual passions of the rulers (ἄρχοντες), takes from them those powers of light which still remain to them, has also a central place in the Manichaean scheme of salvation (F. C. Baur, *Das manichäische Religionssystem*, pp. 219, 315, 321). The light-maiden also plays a prominent part in the *Pistis-Sophia* (cf. the index to the translation by C. Schmidt). With this figure of the mother-goddess who descends into the lower world seems to be closely connected the idea of the fallen Sophia, which is so widespread among the Gnostic systems. This Sophia then is certainly no longer the dominating figure of the light-world, she is a lower aeon at the extreme limit of the world of light, who sinks down into matter (Barbelognostics, the anonymous Gnostic of Irenaeus, 156Bardesanes, *Pistis-Sophia*), or turns in presumptuous love towards the supreme God (Βυθός), and thus brings the Fall into the world of the *aeons* (Valentinians). This Sophia then appears as the mother of the "seven" gods (see above).

The origin of this figure is not far to seek. It is certainly not derived from the Persian religious system, to the spirit of which it is entirely opposed. Neither would it be correct to identify her entirely with the great goddess Ishtar of the old Babylonian religion. But there can hardly be any doubt that the figure of the great mother-goddess or goddess of heaven, who was worshipped throughout Asia under various forms and names (Astarte, Beltis, Atargatis, Cybele, the Syrian Aphrodite), was the prototype of the μήτηρ of the Gnostics (cf. GREAT MOTHER OF THE GODS). The character of the great goddess of heaven is still in many places fairly exactly preserved in the Gnostic speculations. Hence we are able to understand how the Gnostic μήτηρ, the Sophia, appears as the mother of the Hebdomas (ἑβδομάς). The great goddess of heaven is the mother of the stars. Particularly instructive in this connexion is the fact that in those very sects, in the systems of which the figure of the μήτηρ plays a special part, unbridled prostitution appears as a distinct and essential part of the cult (cf. the accounts of particular branches of the Gnostics, Nicolaitans, Philionites, Borborites, &c. in Epiphanius, *Haer.* xxv., xxvi.). The meaning of this cult is, of course, reinterpreted in the Gnostic sense: by this unbridled prostitution the Gnostic sects desired to prevent the sexual propagation of mankind, the origin of all evil. But the connexion is clear, and hence it also explained the curious Gnostic myth mentioned above, namely that the μήτηρ (the light-maiden) by appearing to the archontes (ἄρχοντες), the lower powers of this world, inflames them to sexual lusts, in order to take from them that share of light which they have stolen from the upper world. This is a Gnostic interpretation of the various myths of the great mother-goddess's many loves and love-adventures with other gods and heroes. And when the pagan legend of the Syrian Astarte tells how she lived for ten years in Tyre as a prostitute, this directly recalls the Gnostic myth of how Simon found Helena in a brothel in Tyre (Epiphanius, *Ancoratus*, c. 104). From the same group of myths must be derived the idea of the goddess who descends to the under-world, and is there taken prisoner against her will by the lower powers; the direct prototype of this myth is to be found, *e.g.* in Ishtar's journey to hell. And finally, just as the mother-goddess of south-western Asia stands in particularly intimate connexion with the youthful god of spring (Tammuz, Adonis, Attis), so we ought perhaps to compare here as a parallel the relation of Sophia with the Soter in certain Gnostic systems (see below).

Another characteristic figure of Gnosticism is that of the Primal Man (πρῶτος ἄνθρωπος). In many systems, certainly, it has already been forced quite into the background. But on closer examination we can clearly see that it has a wide influence on Gnosticism. Thus in the system of the Naasseni (see Hippolytus, *Philosophumena*), and in certain related sects there enumerated, the Primal Man has a central and predominant position. Again, in the text on which are based the pseudo-Clementine writings (*Recognitions*, i. 16, 32, 45-47, 52, ii. 47; and *Homilies*, iii. 17 seq. xviii. 14), as in the closely related system of the Ebionites in Epiphanius (*Haer.* xxx. 3-16; cf. liii. 1), we meet with the man who existed before the world, the prophet who goes through the world in various forms, and finally reveals himself in Christ. Among the Barbelognostics (Irenaeus i. 29. 3), the Primal Man (Adamas, *homo perfectus et verus*) and Gnosis appear as a pair of aeons, occupying a prominent place in the whole series. In the Valentinian systems the pair of aeons, Anthropos and Ekklesia, occupy the third or fourth place within the *Oydoás*, but incidentally we learn that with some representatives of this school the Anthropos took a still more prominent place (first or second; Hilgenfeld, *Ketzergeschichte*, p. 294 seq.). And even in the *Pistis-Sophia* the Primal Man "Ieu" is frequently alluded to as the King of the Luminaries (cf. index to C. Schmidt's translation). We also meet with speculations of this kind about man in the circles of

54

non-Christian Gnosis. Thus in the *Poimandres* of Hermes man is the most prominent figure in the speculation; numerous pagan and half-pagan parallels (the "Gnostics" of Plotinus, Zosimus, Bitys) have been collected by Reitzenstein in his work *Poimandres* (pp. 81-116). Reitzenstein has shown (p. 81 seq.) that very probably the system of the Naasseni described by Hippolytus was originally derived from purely pagan circles, which are probably connected in some way with the mysteries of the Attis cult. The figure in the Mandaean system most closely corresponding to the Primal Man, though this figure also actually occurs in another part of the system (cf. the figure of Adakas Mana; Brandt, *Mandäische Religion*, p. 36 seq.) is that of Mandā d'hayyē (γνῶσις τῆς ζωῆς; cf. the pair of aeons, Adamas and Gnosis, among the Barbelognostics, in Irenaeus i. 29. 3). Finally, in the Manichaean system, as is well known, the Primal Man again assumes the predominant place (*Baur, Manich. Religionssystem*, 49 seq.).

This figure of the Primal Man can particularly be compared with that of the Gnostic Sophia. Wherever this figure has not become quite obscure, it represents that divine power which, whether simply owing to a fall, or as the hero who makes war on, and is partly vanquished by darkness, descends into the darkness of the material world, and with whose descent begins the great drama of the world's development. From this power are derived those portions of light existing and held prisoner in this lower world. And as he has raised himself again out of the material world, or has been set free by higher powers, so shall also the members of the Primal Man, the portions of light still imprisoned in matter, be set free.

The question of the derivation of the myth of the Primal Man is still one of the unsolved problems of religious history. It is worthy of notice that according to the old Persian myth also, the development of the world begins with the slaying of the primal man Gayomart by Angra-Mainyu (Ahriman); further, that the Primal Man ("son of man" = man) also plays a part in Jewish apocalyptic literature (Daniel, Enoch, iv. Ezra), whence this figure passes into the Gospels; and again, that the dogma of Christ's descent into hell is directly connected with this myth. But these parallels do not carry us much further. Even the Persian myth is entirely obscure, and has hitherto defied interpretation. It is certainly true that in some way an essential part in the formation of the myth has been played by the sun-god, who daily descends into darkness, to rise from it again victoriously. But how to explain the combination of the figure of the sun-god with that of the Primal Man is an unsolved riddle. The meaning of this figure in the Gnostic speculations is, however, clear. It answers the question: how did the portions of light to be found in this lower world, among which certainly belong the souls of the Gnostics, enter into it?

A parallel myth to that of the Primal Man are the accounts to be found in most of the Gnostic systems of the creation of the first man. In all these accounts the idea is expressed that so far as his body is concerned man is the work of the angels who created the world. So *e.g.* Satornil relates (Irenaeus i. 24. 1) that a brilliant vision appeared from above to the world-creating angels; they were unable to hold it fast, but formed man after its image. And as the man thus formed was unable to move, but could only crawl like a worm, the supreme Power put into him a spark of life, and man came into existence. Imaginations of the same sort are also to be found, *e.g.* in the genuine fragments of Valentinus (Hilgenfeld, *Ketzergeschichte*, p. 293), the Gnostics of Irenaeus i. 30. 6, the Mandaeans (Brandt, *Religion der Mandäer*, p. 36), and the Manichaeans (Baur, *Religionssystem*, p. 118 seq.). The Naasseni (Hippolytus, *Philosophumena*, v. 7) expressly characterize the myth as Chaldean (cf. the passage from Zosimus, in Reitzenstein's *Poimandres*, p. 104). Clearly then the question which the myth of the Primal Man is intended to answer in relation to the whole universe is answered in relation to the nature of man by this account of the coming into being of the first man, which may, moreover, have been influenced by the account in the Old Testament. That question is: how does it happen that in this 157inferior body of man, fallen a prey to corruption, there dwells a higher spark of the divine Being, or in other words, how are we to explain the double nature of man?

VI. Of all the fundamental ideas of Gnosticism of which we have so far treated, it can with some certainty be assumed that they were in existence before the rise of Christianity and the influence of Christian ideas on the development of Gnosticism. The main question with which we have now to deal is that of whether the dominant figure of the Saviour (Σωτήρ) in Gnosticism is of specifically Christian derivation, or whether this can also be explained apart from the assumption of Christian influence. And here it must be premised that, intimately as the conception of salvation is bound up with the Gnostic religion, the idea of salvation accomplished in a definite historical moment to a certain extent remained foreign to it. Indeed, nearly all the Christian Gnostic systems clearly exhibit the great difficulty with which they had to contend in order to reconcile the idea of an historical redeemer, actually occurring in the form of a definite person, with their conceptions of salvation. In Gnosticism salvation always lies at the root of all existence and all history. The fundamental conception varies greatly. At one time the Primal Man, who sank down into matter, has freed himself and risen out of it again, and like him his members will rise out of darkness into the light (*Poimandres*); at another time the Primal Man who was conquered by the powers of darkness has been saved by the powers of light, and thus too all his race will be saved (Manichaeism); at another time the fallen Sophia is purified by her passions and sorrows and has found her *Syzygos*, the Soter, and wedded him, and thus all the souls of the Gnostics who still languish in matter will become the brides of the angels of the *Soter* (Valentinus). In fact salvation, as conceived in Gnosticism, is always a myth, a history of bygone events, an allegory or figure, but not an historical event. And this decision is not affected by the fact that in certain Gnostic sects figured historical personages such as Simon Magus and Menander. The Gnostic ideas of salvation were in the later schools and sects transferred to these persons whom we must consider as rather obscure charlatans and miracle-mongers, just as in other cases they were transferred to the person of Christ. The "Helena" of the Simonian system was certainly not an historical but a mythical figure. This explains the laborious and artificial way in which the person of Jesus is connected in many Gnostic systems with the original Gnostic conception of redemption. In this patchwork the joins are everywhere still clearly to be recognized. Thus, *e.g.* in the Valentinian system, the myth of the fallen Sophia and the Soter, of their ultimate union, their marriage and their 70 sons (Irenaeus i. 4. 5; Hippolytus,*Philos.* vi. 34), has absolutely nothing to do with the Christian conceptions of salvation. The subject is here that of a high goddess of heaven (she has 70 sons) whose friend and lover finds her in the misery of deepest degradation, frees her, and bears her home as his bride. To this myth the idea of salvation through the earthly Christ can only be attached with difficulty. And it was openly maintained that the Soter only existed for the Gnostic, the Saviour Jesus who appeared on earth only for the "Psychicus" (Irenaeus i. 6. 1).

VII. Thus the essential part of most of the conceptions of what we call Gnosticism was already in existence and fully developed before the rise of Christianity. But the fundamental ideas of Gnosticism and of early Christianity had a kind of magnetic attraction for each other. What drew these two forces together was the energy exerted by the universal idea of salvation in both systems. Christian Gnosticism actually introduced only one new figure into the already existing Gnostic theories, namely that of the historical Saviour Jesus Christ. This figure afforded, as it were, a new point of crystallization for the existing Gnostic ideas, which now grouped themselves round this point in all their manifold diversity. Thus there came into the fluctuating mass a strong movement and formative impulse, and the individual systems and sects sprang up like mushrooms from this soil.

It must now be our task to make plain the position of Gnosticism within the Christian religion, and its significance for the development of the latter. Above all the Gnostics represented and developed the distinctly anti-Jewish tendency in Christianity. Paul was the apostle whom they reverenced, and his spiritual influence on them is quite unmistakable. The Gnostic Marcion has been rightly characterized as a direct disciple of Paul. Paul's battle against the law and the narrow national conception of Christianity found a willing following in a movement, the syncretic origin of which directed it towards a universal religion. St Paul's ideas were here developed to their extremest consequences, and in an entirely one-sided fashion such as was far from being in his intention. In nearly all the Gnostic systems the doctrine of the seven world-creating spirits is given an anti-Jewish tendency, the god of the Jews and of the Old Testament appearing as the highest of the seven. The demiurge of the Valentinians always clearly bears the features of the Old Testament creator-God.

The Old Testament was absolutely rejected by most of the Gnostics. Even the so-called Judaeo-Christian Gnostics (Cerinthus), the Ebionite (Essenian) sect of the Pseudo-Clementine writings (the Elkesaites), take up an inconsistent attitude towards Jewish antiquity and the Old Testament. In this respect the opposition to Gnosticism led to a reactionary movement. If the growing Christian Church, in quite a different fashion from Paul, laid stress on the literal authority of the Old Testament, interpreted, it is true, allegorically; if it took up a much more friendly and definite attitude towards the Old Testament, and gave wider scope to the legal conception of religion, this must be in part ascribed to the involuntary reaction upon it of Gnosticism.

The attitude of Gnosticism to the Old Testament and to the creator-God proclaimed in it had its deeper roots, as we have already seen, in the dualism by which it was dominated. With this dualism and the recognition of the worthlessness and absolutely vicious nature of the material world is combined a decided spiritualism. The conception of a resurrection of the body, of a further existence for the body after death, was unattainable by almost all of the Gnostics, with the possible exception of a few Gnostic sects dominated by Judaeo-Christian tendencies. With the dualistic philosophy is further connected an attitude of absolute indifference towards this lower and material world, and the practice of asceticism. Marriage and sexual propagation are considered either as absolute Evil or as altogether worthless, and carnal pleasure is frequently looked upon as forbidden. Then again asceticism sometimes changes into wild libertinism. Here again Gnosticism has exercised an influence on the development of the Church by way of contrast and opposition. If here a return was made to the old material view of the resurrection (the apostolic ἀνάστασις τῆς σαρκός), entirely abandoning the more spiritual conception which had been arrived at as a compromise by Paul, this is probably the result of a reaction from the views of Gnosticism. It was just at this point, too, that Gnosticism started a development which was followed later by the Catholic Church. In spite of the rejection of the ascetic attitude of the Gnostics, as a blasphemy against the Creator, a part of this ascetic principle became at a later date dominant throughout all Christendom. And it is interesting to observe how, *e.g.*, St Augustine, though desperately combating the dualism of the Manichaeans, yet afterwards introduced a number of dualistic ideas into Christianity, which are distinguishable from those of Manichaeism only by a very keen eye, and even then with difficulty.

The Gnostic religion also anticipated other tendencies. As we have seen, it is above all things a religion of sacraments and mysteries. Through its syncretic origin Gnosticism introduced for the first time into Christianity a whole mass of sacramental, mystical ideas, which had hitherto existed in it only in its earliest phases. But in the long run even genuine Christianity has been unable to free itself from the magic of the sacraments; and the Eastern Church especially has taken the same direction as Gnosticism. Gnosticism was also the pioneer of the Christian Church in the strong emphasis laid on the idea of salvation in [158]religion. And since the Gnostics were compelled to draw the figure of the Saviour into a world of quite alien myths, their Christology became so complicated in character that it frequently recalls the Christology of the later dogmatic of the Greek Fathers.

Finally, it was Gnosticism which gave the most decided impulse to the consolidation of the Christian Church as a church. Gnosticism itself is a free, naturally-growing religion, the religion of isolated minds, of separate little circles and minute sects. The homogeneity of wide circles, the sense of responsibility engendered by it, and continuity with the past are almost entirely lacking in it. It is based upon revelation, which even at the present time is imparted to the individual, upon the more or less convincing force of the religious imagination and speculations of a few leaders, upon the voluntary and unstable grouping of the schools round the master. Its adherents feel themselves to be the isolated, the few, the free and the enlightened, as opposed to the sluggish and inert masses of mankind degraded into matter, or the initiated as opposed to the uninitiated, the Gnostics as opposed to the "Hylici" (ὑλικοί); at most in the later and more moderate schools a middle place was given to the adherents of the Church as Psychici (ψυχικοί).

This freely-growing Gnostic religiosity aroused in the Church an increasingly strong movement towards unity and a firm and inelastic organization, towards authority and tradition. An organized hierarchy, a definitive canon of the Holy Scriptures, a confession of faith and rule of faith, and unbending doctrinal discipline, these were the means employed. A part was also played in this movement by a free theology which arose within the Church, itself a kind of Gnosticism which aimed at holding fast whatever was good in the Gnostic movement, and obtaining its recognition within the limits of the Church (Clement of Alexandria, Origen). But the mightiest forces, to which in the end this theology too had absolutely to give way, were outward organization and tradition.

It must be considered as an unqualified advantage for the further development of Christianity, as a universal religion, that at its very outset it prevailed against the great movement of Gnosticism. In spite of the fact that in a few of its later representatives Gnosticism assumed a more refined and spiritual aspect, and even produced blossoms of a true and beautiful piety, it is fundamentally and essentially an unstable religious syncretism, a religion in which the determining forces were a fantastic oriental imagination and a sacramentalism which degenerated into the wildest superstitions, a weak dualism fluctuating unsteadily between asceticism and libertinism. Indirectly, however, Gnosticism was certainly one of the most powerful factors in the development of Christianity in the 1st century.

VIII. This sketch may be completed by a short review of the various separate sects and their probable connexion with each other. As a point of departure for the history of the development of Gnosticism may be taken the numerous little sects which were apparently first included under the name of "Gnostics" in the narrower sense. Among these probably belong the Ophites of Celsus (in Origen), the many little sects included by Epiphanius under the name of Nicolaitans and Gnostics (*Haer.* 25, 26); the Archontici (Epiphanius, *Haer.* xl.), Sethites (Cainites) should also here be mentioned, and finally the Carpocratians. Common to all these is the dominant position assumed by the "Seven" (headed by Ialdabaoth); the heavenly world lying above the spheres of the Seven is occupied by comparatively few figures, among which the most important part is played by the μήτηρ, who is sometimes enthroned as the supreme goddess in heaven, but in a few systems has already descended from there into matter, been taken prisoner,

&c. Numerous little groups are distinguished from the mass, sometimes by one peculiarity, sometimes by another. On the one hand we have sects with a strongly ascetic tendency, on the other we find some characterized by unbridled libertinism; in some the most abandoned prostitution has come to be the most sacred mystery; in others again appears the worship of serpents, which here appears to be connected in various and often very loose ways with the other ideas of these Gnostics—hence the names of the "Ophites," "Naasseni." To this class also fundamentally belong the Simoniani, who have included the probably historical figure of Simon Magus in a system which seems to be closely connected with those we have mentioned, especially if we look upon the "Helena" of this system as a mythical figure. A particular branch of the "Gnostic" sects is represented by those systems in which the figure of Sophia sinking down into matter already appears. To these belong the Barbelognostics (in the description given by Irenaeus the figure of the Spirit takes the place of that of Sophia), and the Gnostics whom Irenaeus (i. 30) describes (cf. Epiphanius, *Haer.* xxvi.). And here may best be included Bardesanes, a famous leader of a Gnostic school of the end of the 2nd century. Most scholars, it is true, following an old tradition, reckon Bardesanes among the Valentinians. But from the little we know of Bardesanes, his system bears no trace of relationship with the complicated Valentinian system, but is rather completely derived from the ordinary Gnosticism, and is distinguished from it apparently only by its more strongly dualistic character. The systems of Valentinus and his disciples must be considered as a further development of what we have just characterized as the popular Gnosticism, and especially of that branch of it to which the figure of Sophia is already known. In them above all the world of the higher aeons is further extended and filled with a throng of varied figures. They also exhibit a variation from the characteristic dualism of Gnosticism into monism, in their conception of the fall of Sophia and their derivation of matter from the passions of the fallen Sophia. The figures of the Seven have here entirely disappeared, the remembrance of them being merely preserved in the name of the ἑβδομάς. In general, Valentinianism displays a particular resemblance to the dominant ideas of the Church, both in its complicated Christology, its triple division of mankind into πνευματικοί, ψυχικοί and ὑλικοί, and its far-fetched interpretation of texts.7 A quite different position from those mentioned above is taken by Basilides (*q.v.*). From what little we know of him he was an uncompromising dualist. Both the systems which are handed down under his name by Irenaeus and Hippolytus, that of emanations and the monistic-evolutionary system, represent further developments of his ideas with a tendency away from dualism towards monism. Characteristically, in these Basilidian systems the figure of the "Mother" or of Sophia does not appear. This peculiarity the Basilidian system shares with that of Satornil of Antioch, which has only come down to us in a very fragmentary state, and in other respects recalls in many ways the popular Gnosticism. By itself, on the other hand, stands the system preserved for us by Hippolytus in the *Philosophumena* under the name of the Naasseni, with its central figure of "the Man," which, as we have seen, is very closely related with certain specifically pagan Gnostic speculations which have come down to us (in the *Poimandres*, in Zosimus and Plotinus, *Ennead* ii. 9). With the Naasseni, moreover, are related also the other sects of which Hippolytus alone gives us a notice in his *Philosophumena* (Docetae, Perates, Sethiani, the adherents of Justin, the Gnostic of Monoimos). Finally, apart from all other Gnostics stands Marcion. With him, as far as we are able to conclude from the scanty notices of him, the manifold Gnostic speculations are reduced essentially to the one problem of the good and the just God, the God of the Christians and the God of the Old Testament. Between these two powers Marcion affirms a sharp and, as it appears, originally irreconcilable dualism which with him rests moreover on a speculative basis. Thanks to the noble simplicity and specifically religious character of his ideas, Marcion was able to found not only schools, but a community, a church of his own, which gave trouble to the Church longer than any other Gnostic sect. Among his disciples the speculative and fantastic element of Gnosticism again became more apparent. As we have already intimated, Gnosticism had such a power 159of attraction that it now drew within its limits even Judaeo-Christian sects. Among these we must mention the Judaeo-Christian Gnostic Cerinthus, also the Gnostic Ebionites, of whom Epiphanius (*Haer.*) gives us an account, and whose writings are to be found in a recension in the collected works of the Pseudo-Clementine *Recognitions and Homilies*, to the same class belong the Elkesaites with their mystical scripture, the *Elxai*, extracts of which are given by Hippolytus in the *Philos.* (ix. 13). Later evidence of the decadence of Gnosticism occurs in the *Pistis-Sophia* and the Coptic Gnostic writings discovered and edited by Schmidt. In these confused records of human imagination gone mad, we possess a veritable herbarium of all possible Gnostic ideas, which were once active and now rest peacefully side by side. None the less, the stream of the Gnostic religion is not yet dried up, but continues on its way; and it is beyond a doubt that the later Mandaeanism and the great religious movement of Mani are most closely connected with Gnosticism. These manifestations are all the more characteristic since in them we meet with a

Gnosticism which remained essentially more untouched by Christian influences than the Gnostic systems of the 2nd century A.D. Thus these systems throw an important light on the past, and a true perception of the nature and purpose of Gnosticism is not to be obtained without taking them into consideration.

BIBLIOGRAPHY.—A. Neander, *Genetische Entwicklung d. vornehmsten gnostischen Systeme* (Berlin, 1818); F. Chr. Baur, *Die christl. Gnosis in ihrer geschichtl. Entwicklung* (Tübingen, 1835); E. W. Möller, *Gesch. der Kosmologie in der griechischen Kirche bis Origenes* (Halle, 1860); R. A. Lipsius, *Der Gnosticismus* (Leipzig, 1860; originally in Ersch and Gruber's *Encyclopädie*); H. L. Mansel, *The Gnostic Heresies of the 1st and 2nd Centuries* (London, 1875); K. Kepler, *Über Gnosis und altbabylonische Religion*, a lecture delivered at the Congress of Orientalists (Berlin, 1881); A. Hilgenfeld, *Ketzergeschichte des Urchristentums* (Leipzig, 1884); and in *Ztschr. für wissenschaftl. Theol.* 1890, i. "Der Gnosticismus"; A. Harnack, *Dogmengeschichte*, i. 271 seq. (cf. the corresponding sections of the *Dogmengeschichten* of Loofs and Seeberg); W. Anz, "Zur Frage nach dem Ursprung des Gnosticismus," *Texte u. Untersuchungen*, xv. 4 (Leipzig, 1897); R. Liechtenhahn, *Die Offenbarung im Gnosticismus* (Göttingen, 1901); C. Schmidt, "Plotins Stellung zum Gnosticismus u. kirchl. Christentum" *Texte u. Untersuch.* xx. 4 (1902); E. de Faye, *Introduction à l'étude du Gnosticisme* (Paris, 1903); R. Reitzenstein, *Poimandres* (Leipzig, 1904); G. Krüger, article "Gnosticismus" in Herzog-Hauck's *Realencyklopädie* (3rd ed.) vi. 728 ff.; Bousset, "Hauptprobleme der Gnosis," *Forschungen z. Relig. u. Lit. d. alten u. neuen Testaments*, 10 (1907); T. Wendland, *Hellenistisch-römische Kultur in ihren Beziehungen zu Judentum und Christentum* (1907), p. 161 seq. See further among important monographs on the individual Gnostic systems, R. A. Lipsius, "Die ophitischen Systeme," *Ztschr. f. wissensch. Theologie* (1863); G. Heinrici, *Die valentinianische Gnosis u. d. Heilige Schrift* (Berlin, 1871); A. Merx, *Bardesanes von Edessa* (Halle, 1863); A. Hilgenfeld, *Bardesanes, der letzte Gnostiker* (Leipzig, 1864); A. Harnack, "Über das gnostische Buch Pistis-Sophia," *Texte u. Untersuch.* vii. 2; C. Schmidt, "Gnostische Schriften," *Texte u. Untersuch.* viii. 1, 2; and also the works mentioned under § II. of this article.

(W. BO.)

1See the list of their titles in A. Harnack, *Geschichte der altchristlichen Literatur*, Teil I. v. 171; *ib.* Teil II. *Chronologie der altchristl. Literatur*, i. 533 seq.; also Liechtenhahn, *Die Offenbarung im Gnosticismus* (1901).

2For the text see A. Merx, *Bardesanes von Edessa* (1863), and A. Hilgenfeld, *Bardesanes der letzte Gnostiker* (1864).

3Ed. Petermann-Schwartze; newly translated by C. Schmidt, *Koptisch-gnostische Schriften*, i. (1905), in the series *Die griechischen christlichen Schriftsteller der ersten drei Jahrhunderte*; see also A. Harnack, *Texte und Untersuchungen*, Bd. vii. Heft 2 (1891), and *Chronologie der altchristlichen Literatur*, ii. 193-195.

4See R. A. Lipsius, *Die Quellen der ältesten Ketzergeschichte* (1875); A. Harnack, *Zur Quellenkritik der Geschichte des Gnosticismus* (1873); A. Hilgenfeld,*Ketzergeschichte*, pp. 1-83; Harnack, *Geschichte der altchristlich. Literatur*, i. 171 seq., ii. 533 seq., 712 seq.; J. Kunze, *De historiae Gnostic. fontibus* (1894). On the *Philosophumena* of Hippolytus see G. Salmon, the cross-references in the Philosophumena, *Hermathena*, vol. xi. (1885) p. 5389 seq.; H. Staehelin, *Die gnostischen Quellen Hippolyts, Texte und Unters.* Bd. vi. Hft. 3 (1890).

5Cf. the same idea of the fall of mankind in the pagan Gnosticism of "Poimandres"; see Reitzenstein, *Poimandres* (1904); and the position of the Primal Man (*Urmensch*) among the Manichaeans is similar.

6These ideas may possibly be traced still further back, and perhaps even underlie St Paul's exposition in Col. ii. 15.

7For the disciples of Valentinus, especially Marcus, after whom was named a separate sect, the Marcosians, with their Pythagorean theories of numbers and their strong tincture of the mystical, magic, and sacramental, see VALENTINUS AND VALENTINIANS.

GNU, the Hottentot name for the large white-tailed South African antelope (*q.v.*), now nearly extinct, know to the Boers as the black wildebeest, and to naturalists as Connochaetes (or Catoblepas) gnu. A second and larger species is the brindled gnu or blue wildebeest (*C. taurinus* or *Catoblepas gorgon*), also known by the Bechuana name *kokon* or *kokoon*; and there are several East African forms more or less closely related to the latter which have received distinct names.

White-tailed Gnu, or Black Wildebeest
(*Connochaetes gnu*).

GO, or GO-BANG (Jap. *Go-ban,* board for playing *Go*), a popular table game. It is of great antiquity, having been invented in Japan, according to tradition, by the emperor Yao, 2350 B.C., but it is probably of Chinese origin. According to Falkener the first historical mention of it was made about the year 300 B.C., but there is abundant evidence that it was a popular game long before that period. The original Japanese Go is played on a board divided into squares by 19 horizontal and 19 vertical lines, making 361 intersections, upon which the flat round men, 181 white and 181 black, are placed one by one as the game proceeds. The men are placed by the two players on any intersections (*me*) that may seem advantageous, the object being to surround with one's men as many unoccupied intersections as possible, the player enclosing the greater number of vacant points being the winner. Completely surrounded men are captured and removed from the board. This game is played in England upon a board divided into 361 squares, the men being placed upon these instead of upon the intersections.

A much simpler variety of Go, mostly played by foreigners, has for its object to get five men into line. This may have been the earliest form of the game, as the word *go* means five. Except in Japan it is often played on an ordinary draughts-board, and the winner is he who first gets five men into line, either vertically, horizontally or diagonally.

See *Go-Bang,* by A. Howard Cady, in Spalding's Home Library (New York, 1896); *Games Ancient and Oriental,* by Edward Falkener (London, 1892); *Das japan.-chinesische Spiel Go,* by O. Korschelt (Yokohama, 1881); *Das Nationalspiel der Japanesen,* by G. Schurig (Leipzig, 1888).

GOA, the name of the past and present capitals of Portuguese India, and of the surrounding territory more exactly described as Goa settlement, which is situated on the western coast of India, between 15° 44' and 14° 53' N., and between 73° 45' and 74° 26' E. Pop. (1900) 475,513, area 1301 sq. m.

Goa Settlement.—With Damaun (*q.v.*) and Diu (*q.v.*) Goa settlement forms a single administrative province ruled by a governor-general, and a single ecclesiastical province subject to the archbishop of Goa; for judicial purposes the province includes Macao in China, and Timor in the Malay Archipelago. It is bounded on the N. by the river Terakhul or Araundem, which divides it from the Sawantwari state, E. by the Western Ghats, S. by Kanara district, and W. by the Arabian Sea. It comprises the three districts of Ilhas, Bardez and Salsette, conquered early in the 16th century and therefore known as the Velhas Conquistas (Old Conquests), seven districts acquired later and known as the Novas Conquistas, and the island of Anjidiv or Anjadiva. The settlement, which has a coast-line of 62 m., is a hilly region, especially the Novas Conquistas; its distinguishing features are the Western Ghats, though the highest summits nowhere reach an altitude of 4000 ft., and the island of Goa. Numerous short but navigable rivers water the lowlands skirting the coast. The two largest rivers are the Mandavi and the Juari, which together encircle the island of Goa (Ilhas), being connected on the landward side by a creek. The island (native name Tisvādī, Tissuvaddy, Tissuary) is a triangular territory, the apex of which, called the *cabo* or cape, is a rocky headland separating the harbour of Goa into two anchorages— Agoada or Aguada at the mouth of the Mandavi, on the north, and Mormugão or Marmagão at the mouth of the Juari, on the south. The northern haven is exposed to the full force of the south-west monsoon, and is liable to silt up during the rains. The southern, sheltered by the promontory of Salsette, is always open, but is less used, owing to its greater distance from the city of Goa, which is built on the island. A railway connects Mormagão, south of the Juari estuary, with Castle Rock on the Western Ghats. Goa imports textiles and foodstuffs, and exports coco-nuts, areca-nuts, spices, fish, poultry and timber. Its trade is carried on almost entirely with Bombay, Madras, Kathiawar and Portugal. Manganese is mined in large quantities, some iron is obtained, and other products are salt, palm-spirit, betel and bananas.

Cities of Goa.—1. The ancient Hindu city of Goa, of which hardly a fragment survives, was built at the southernmost point of the island, and was famous in early Hindu legend and history for its learning, wealth and beauty. In the Puranas and certain inscriptions its name appears as Gove, Govāpurī, Gomant, &c.; the medieval Arabian geographers knew it as Sindābur or Sandābur, and the Portuguese as Goa Velha. It was ruled by the Kadamba dynasty from the 2nd century A.D. to 1312, and by Mahommedan invaders of the Deccan from 1312 until about 1370, during which period it was visited and described by Ibn Batuta. It was then annexed to the Hindu kingdom of Vijayanagar, of which, according to Ferishta, it still formed part in 1469, when it was conquered by the Bahmani sultan of the Deccan; but two of the best Portuguese chroniclers state that it became independent in 1440, when the second city (Old Goa) was founded.

2. Old Goa is, for the most part, a city of ruins without inhabitants other than ecclesiastics and their dependents. The chief surviving buildings are the cathedral, founded by Albuquerque in 1511 to commemorate his entry into Goa on St Catherine's day 1510, and rebuilt in 1623, and still used for public worship; the convent of St Francis (1517), a converted mosque rebuilt in 1661, with a portal of carved black stone, which is the only relic of Portuguese architecture in India dating from the first quarter of the 16th century; the chapel of St Catherine (1551); the church of Bom Jesus (1594-1603), a superb example of Renaissance architecture as developed by the Jesuits, containing the magnificent shrine and tomb of St Francis Xavier (see XAVIER, FRANCISCO DE); and the 17th-century convents of St Monica and St Cajetan. The college of St Paul (see below) is in ruins.

3. Panjim, Pangim or New Goa, originally a suburb of Old Goa, is, like the parent city, built on the left bank of the Mandavi estuary, in 15° 30′ N. and 73° 33′ E. Pop. (1901) 9500. It is a modern port with few pretensions to architectural beauty. Ships of the largest size can anchor in the river, but only small vessels can load or discharge at the quay. Panjim became the residence of the viceroy in 1759 and the capital of Portuguese India in 1843. It possesses a lyceum, a school for teachers, a seminary, a technical school and an experimental agricultural station.

Political History.—With the subdivision of the Bahmani kingdom, after 1482, Goa passed into the power of Yusuf Adil Shah, king of Bijapur, who was its ruler when the Portuguese first reached India. At this time Goa was important as the starting-point of pilgrims from India to Mecca, as a mart with no rival except Calicut on the west coast, and especially as the centre of the import trade in horses (Gulf Arabs) from Hormuz, the control of which was a vital matter to the kingdoms warring in the Deccan. It was easily defensible by any power with command of the sea, as the encircling rivers could only be forded at one spot, and had been deliberately stocked with crocodiles. It was attacked on the 10th of February 1510 by the Portuguese under Albuquerque. As a Hindu ascetic had foretold its downfall and the garrison of Ottoman mercenaries was outnumbered, the city surrendered without a struggle, and Albuquerque entered it in triumph, while the Hindu townsfolk strewed filagree flowers of gold and silver before his feet. Three months later Yusuf Adil Shah returned with 60,000 troops, forced the passage of the ford, and blockaded the Portuguese in their ships from May to August, when the cessation of the monsoon enabled them to put to sea. In November Albuquerque returned with a larger force, and after overcoming a desperate resistance, recaptured the city, permitted his soldiers to plunder it for three days, and massacred the entire Mahommedan population.

Goa was the first territorial possession of the Portuguese in Asia. Albuquerque intended it to be a colony and a naval base, as distinct from the fortified factories which had been established in certain Indian seaports. He encouraged his men to marry native women, and to settle in Goa as farmers, retail traders or artisans. These married men soon became a privileged caste, and Goa acquired a large Eurasian population. Albuquerque and his successors left almost untouched the customs and constitutions of the 30 village communities on the island, only abolishing the rite of suttee. A register of these customs (*Foral de usos e costumes*) was published in 1526, and is an historical document of much value; an abstract of it is given in R. S. Whiteway's *Rise of the Portuguese Empire in India* (London, 1898).

Goa became the capital of the whole Portuguese empire in the East. It was granted the same civic privileges as Lisbon. Its senate or municipal chamber maintained direct communications with the king and paid a special representative to attend to its interests at court. In 1563 the governor even proposed to make Goa the seat of a parliament, in which all parts of the Portuguese east were to be represented; this was vetoed by the king.

In 1542 St Francis Xavier mentions the architectural splendour of the city; but it reached the climax of its prosperity between 1575 and 1625. *Goa Dourada*, or Golden Goa, was then the wonder of all travellers, and there was a Portuguese proverb, "He who has seen Goa need not see Lisbon." Merchandise from all parts of the East was displayed in its bazaar, and separate streets were set aside for the sale of different classes of goods—Bahrein pearls and coral, Chinese porcelain and silk, Portuguese velvet and piece-goods, drugs and spices from the Malay Archipelago. In the main street slaves were sold by auction. The houses of the rich were surrounded by gardens and palm groves; they were built of stone and painted red or white. Instead of glass, their balconied windows had thin polished oyster-shells set in lattice-work.

The social life of Goa was brilliant, as befitted the headquarters of the viceregal court, the army and navy, and the church; but the luxury and ostentation of all classes had become a byword before the end of the 16th century. Almost all manual labour was done by slaves; common soldiers assumed high-sounding titles, and it was even customary for the poor noblemen who congregated together in boarding-houses to subscribe for a few silken cloaks, a silken umbrella and a common man-servant, so that each could take his turn to promenade the streets, fashionably attired and with a proper escort. There were huge gambling saloons, licensed by the municipality, where determined players lodged for weeks together; and every form of vice, except drunkenness, was practised by both sexes, although European women were forced to lead a kind of zenana life, and never ventured unveiled into the streets; they even attended at church in their palanquins, so as to avoid observation.

The appearance of the Dutch in Indian waters was followed by the gradual ruin of Goa. In 1603 and 1639 the city was blockaded by Dutch fleets, though never captured, and in 1635 it was ravaged by an epidemic. Its trade was gradually monopolized by the Jesuits. Thevenot in 1666, Baldaeus in 1672, Fryer in 1675 describe its ever-increasing poverty and decay. In 1683 only the timely appearance of a Mogul army saved it from capture by a horde of Mahratta raiders, and in 1739 the whole territory was attacked by the same enemies, and only saved by the unexpected arrival of a new viceroy with a fleet. This peril was always imminent until 1759, when a peace with the Mahrattas was concluded. In the same year the proposal to remove the seat of government to Panjim was carried out; it had been discussed as early as 1684. Between 1695 and 1775 the population dwindled from 20,000 to 1600, and in 1835 Goa was only inhabited by a few priests, monks and nuns.

Ecclesiastical History.—Some Dominican friars came out to Goa in 1510, but no large missionary enterprise was undertaken before the arrival of the Franciscans in 1517. From their headquarters in Goa the Franciscan preachers visited many parts of western India, and even journeyed to Ceylon, Pegu and the Malay Archipelago. For nearly twenty-five years they carried on 161the work of evangelization almost alone, with such success that in 1534 Pope Paul III. made Goa a bishopric, with spiritual jurisdiction over all Portuguese possessions between China and the Cape of Good Hope, though itself suffragan to the archbishopric of Funchal in Madeira. A Franciscan friar, João de Albuquerque, came to Goa as its first bishop in 1538. In 1542 St Francis Xavier came to Goa, and took over the Franciscan college of Santa Fé, for the training of native missionaries; this was renamed the College of St Paul, and became the headquarters of all Jesuit missions in the East, where the Jesuits were commonly styled *Paulistas.* By a Bull dated the 4th of February 1557 Goa was made an archbishopric, with jurisdiction over the sees of Malacca and Cochin, to which were added Macao (1575), Japan (1588), Angamale or Cranganore (1600), Meliapur (Mylapur) (1606), Peking and Nanking (1610), together with the bishopric of Mozambique, which included the entire coast of East Africa. In 1606 the archbishop received the title of Primate of the East, and the king of Portugal was named Patron of the Catholic Missions in the East; his right of patronage was limited by the Concordat of 1857 to Goa, Malacca, Macao and certain parts of British India. The Inquisition was introduced into Goa in 1560: a vivid account of its proceedings is given by C. Dellon, *Relation de l'inquisition de Goa* (1688). Five ecclesiastical councils, which dealt with matters of discipline, were held at Goa—in 1567, 1575, 1585, 1592 and 1606; the archbishop of Goa also presided over the more important synod of Diamper (Udayamperur, about 12 m. S.E. of Cochin), which in 1599 condemned as heretical the tenets and liturgy of the Indian Nestorians, or Christians of St Thomas (*q.v.*). In 1675 Fryer described Goa as "a Rome in India, both for absoluteness and fabrics," and Hamilton states that early in the 18th century the number of ecclesiastics in the settlement had reached the extraordinary total of 30,000. But the Jesuits were expelled in 1759, and by 1800 Goa had lost much even of its ecclesiastical importance. The Inquisition was abolished in 1814 and the religious orders were secularized in 1835.

BIBLIOGRAPHY.—J. N. da Fonseca, *An Historical and Archaeological Sketch of Goa* (Bombay, 1878) is a minute study of the city from the earliest times, illustrated. For the early history of Portuguese rule the chief authorities are *The Commentaries ... of Dalboquerque* (Hakluyt Society's translation, London, 1877), the *Cartas* of Albuquerque (Lisbon, 1884), the *Historia ... da India* of F. L. de Castanheda (Lisbon, 1833, written before 1552), the *Lendas da India of G. Correa* (Lisbon, 1860, written 1514-1566), and the *Decadas da India* of João de Barros and D. do Couto (Lisbon, 1778-1788, written about 1530-1616). Couto's *Soldado pratico* (Lisbon, 1790) and S. Botelho's *Cartas and Tombo*, written 1547-1554, published in "Subsidios" of the Lisbon Academy (1868), are valuable studies of military life and administration. The *Archivo Portuguez oriental* (6 parts, New Goa, 1857-1877) is a most useful collection of documents dating from 1515; part 2 contains the privileges, &c. of the city of Goa, and part 4 contains the minutes of the ecclesiastical councils and of the synod of Diamper. The social life of Goa has been graphically described by many writers; see especially the travels of Varthema (*c.* 1505), Linschoten (*c.* 1580), Pyrard (1608) in the Hakluyt Society's translations; J. Mocquet, *Voyages* (Paris, 1830, written 1608-1610); P. Baldaeus, in *Churchill's Voyages*, vol. 3 (London, 1732); J. Fryer, *A New Account of East India and Persia* (London, 1698); A. de Mandelslo, *Voyages* (London, 1669); *Les Voyages de M. de*

Thevenot aux Indes Orientales (Amsterdam, 1779), and A. Hamilton, *A New Account of the East Indies* (London, 1774). For Goa in the 20th century see *The Imperial Gazetteer of India.*

(K. G. J.)

GOAL, originally an object set up as the place where a race ends, the winning-post, and so used figuratively of the end to which any effort is directed. It is thus used to translate the Lat. *meta*, the boundary pillar, set one at each end of the circus to mark the turning-point. The word was quite early used in various games for the two posts, with or without a cross-bar, through or over which the ball has to be driven to score a point towards winning the game. The *New English Dictionary* quotes the use in Richard Stanyhurst's *Description of Ireland* (1577); but the word *gōl* in the sense of a boundary appears as early as the beginning of the 14th century in the religious poems of William de Shoreham (*c.* 1315). The origin of the word is obscure. It is usually taken to be derived from a French word *gaule*, meaning a pole or stick, but this meaning does not appear in the English usage, nor does the usual English meaning appear in the French. There is an O. Eng. *gaélan*, to hinder, which may point to a lost *gál*, barrier, but there is no evidence in other Teutonic languages for such a word.

GOALPARA, a town and district of British India, in the Brahmaputra valley division of eastern Bengal and Assam. The town (pop. 6287) overlooks the Brahmaputra. It was the frontier outpost of the Mahommedan power, and has long been a flourishing seat of river trade. The civil station is built on the summit of a small hill commanding a magnificent view of the valley of the Brahmaputra, bounded on the north by the snowy ranges of the Himalayas and on the south by the Garo hills. The native town is built on the western slope of the hill, and the lower portion is subject to inundation from the marshy land which extends in every direction. It has declined in importance since the district headquarters were removed to Dhubri in 1879, and it suffered severely from the earthquake of the 12th of June 1897.

The DISTRICT comprises an area of 3961 sq. m. It is situated along the Brahmaputra, at the corner where the river takes its southerly course from Assam into Bengal. The scenery is striking. Along the banks of the river grow clumps of cane and reed; farther back stretch fields of rice cultivation, broken only by the fruit trees surrounding the villages, and in the background rise the forest-clad hills overtopped by the white peaks of the Himalayas. The soil of the hills is of a red ochreous earth, with blocks of granite and sandstone interspersed; that of the plains is of alluvial formation. Earthquakes are common and occasionally severe shocks have been experienced. The Brahmaputra annually inundates vast tracts of country. Numerous extensive forests yield valuable timber. Wild animals of all kinds are found. In 1901 the population was 462,083, showing an increase of 2% in the decade. Rice forms the staple crop. Mustard and jute are also largely grown. The manufactures consist of the making of brass and iron utensils and of gold and silver ornaments, weaving of silk cloth, basket-work and pottery. The cultivation of tea has been introduced but does not flourish anywhere in the district. Local trade is in the hands of Marwari merchants, and is carried on at the *bazars*, weekly *hats* or markets and periodical fairs. The chief exports are mustard-seed, jute, cotton, timber, lac, silk cloth, india-rubber and tea; the imports, Bengal rice, European piece goods, salt, hardware, oil and tobacco.

Dhubri (pop. 3737), the administrative headquarters of the district, stands on the Brahmaputra where that river takes its great bend south. It is the termination of the emigration road from North Bengal and of the river steamers that connect with the North Bengal railway. It is also served by the eastern Bengal State railway.

GOAT (a common Teut. word; O. Eng. *gát*, Goth. *gaits*, Mod. Ger. *Geiss*, cognate with Lat. *haedus*, a kid), properly the name of the well-known domesticated European ruminant (*Capra hircus*), which has for all time been regarded as the emblem of everything that is evil, in contradistinction to the sheep, which is the symbol of excellence and purity. Although the more typical goats are markedly distinct from sheep, there is, both as regards wild and domesticated forms, an almost complete gradation from goats to sheep, so that it is exceedingly difficult to define either group. The position of the genus *Capra* (to all the members of which, as well as some allied species, the name "goat" in its wider sense is applicable) in the family *Bovidae* is indicated in the article BOVIDAE, and some of the distinctions between goats and sheep are mentioned in the article SHEEP. Here then it will suffice to mention that goats are characterized by the strong and offensive odour of the males, which are furnished with a beard on the chin; while as a general rule glands are present between the middle toes of the fore feet only.

Goats, in the wild state, are an exclusively old-world group, of which the more typical forms are confined to Europe and south-western and central Asia, although there are two outlying species in northern Africa. The wild goat, or pasang, is represented in Europe in the

63

Cyclades and Crete by rather small races. 162more or less mingled with domesticated breeds, the Cretan animal being distinguished as *Capra hircus creticus*; but the large typical race *C. h. aegagrus* is met with in the mountains of Asia Minor and Persia, whence it extends to Sind, where it is represented by a somewhat different race known as*C. h. blythi*. The horns of the old bucks are of great length and beauty, and characterized by their bold scimitar-like backward sweep and sharp front edge, interrupted at irregular intervals by knots or bosses. Domesticated goats have run wild in many islands, such as the Hebrides, Shetland, Canaries, Azores, Ascension and Juan Fernandez. Some of these reverted breeds have developed horns of considerable size, although not showing that regularity of curve distinctive of the wild race. In the Azores the horns are remarkably upright and straight, whence the name of "antelope-goat" which has been given to these animals. The concretions known as *bezoar-stones*, formerly much used in medicine and as antidotes of poison, are obtained from the stomach of the wild goat.

Although there have in all probability been more or less important local crosses with other wild species, there can be no doubt that domesticated goats generally are descended from the wild goat. It is true that many tame goats show spirally twisted horns recalling those of the under-mentioned Asiatic markhor; but in nearly all such instances it will be found that the spiral twists in the opposite direction. Among the domesticated breeds the following are some of the more important.

Firstly, we have the common or European goats, of which there are several more or less well-marked breeds, differing from each other in length of hair, in colour and slightly in the configuration of the horns. The ears are more or less upright, sometimes horizontal, but never actually pendent, as in some Asiatic breeds. The horns are rather flat at the base and not unfrequently corrugated; they rise vertically from the head, curving to the rear, and are more or less laterally inclined. The colour varies from dirty white to dark-brown, but when pure-bred is never black, which indicates eastern blood. Most European countries possess more than one description of the common goat. In the British Isles there are two distinct types, one short and the other long haired. In the former the hair is thick and close, with frequently an under-coat resembling wool. The horns are large in the male, and of moderate size in the female, flat at the base and inclining outwards. The head is short and tapering, the forehead flat and wide, and the nose small; while the legs are strong, thick and well covered with hair. The colour varies from white or grey to black, but is frequently fawn, with a dark line down the spine and another across the shoulders. The other variety has a shaggy coat, generally reddish-black, though sometimes grey or pied and occasionally white. The head is long, heavy and ugly, the nose coarse and prominent, with the horns situated close together, often continuing parallel almost to the extremities, being also large, corrugated and pointed. The legs are long and the sides flat, the animal itself being generally gaunt and thin. This breed is peculiar to Ireland, the Welsh being of a similar type, but more often white. The short-haired goat is the English goat proper. Both British breeds, as well as those from abroad, are frequently ornamented with two tassel-like appendages, hanging near together under the throat. It has been supposed by many that these are traceable to foreign blood; but although there are foreign breeds that possess them, they appear to pertain quite as much to the English native breeds as to those of distant countries, the peculiarity being mentioned in very old works on the goats of the British Islands. The milk-produce in the common goat as well as other kinds varies greatly with individuals. Irish goats often yield a quantity of milk, but the quality is poor. The goats of France are similar to those of Britain, varying in length of hair, colour and character of horns. The Norway breed is frequently white with long hair; it is rather small in size, with small bones, a short rounded body, head small with a prominent forehead, and short, straight, corrugated horns. The facial line is concave. The horns of the males are very large, and curve round after the manner of the wild goat, with a tuft of hair between and in front.

The Maltese goat has the ears long, wide and hanging down below the jaw. The hair is long and cream-coloured. The breed is usually hornless.

The Syrian goat is met with in various parts of the East, in Lower Egypt, on the shores of the Indian Ocean and in Madagascar. The hair and ears are excessively long, the latter so much so that they are sometimes clipped to prevent their being torn by stones or thorny shrubs. The horns are somewhat erect and spiral, with an outward bend.

The Angora goat is often confounded with the Kashmir, but is in reality quite distinct. The principal feature of this breed, of which there are two or three varieties, is the length and quantity of the hair, which has a particularly soft and silky texture, covering the whole body and a great part of the legs with close matted ringlets. The horns of the male differ from those of the female, being directed vertically and in shape spiral, whilst in the female they have a horizontal tendency, somewhat like those of a ram. The coat is composed of two kinds of hair, the one short and coarse and of the character of hair, which lies close to the skin, the other long and curly and of the nature of wool, forming the outer covering. Both are used by the manufacturer, but the exterior portion, which makes up by far the greater bulk, is much the more valuable. The process of shearing takes place in early spring, the average amount of wool yielded by each animal being about 2½ ℔. The best quality comes from castrated males, females producing the next best.

FIG. 1.—Male
Angora Goat.

The breed was introduced at the Cape about 1864. The Angora is a bad milker and an indifferent mother, but its flesh is better than that of any other breed, and in its native country is preferred to mutton. The kids are born small, but grow fast, and arrive early at maturity. The Kashmir, or rather Tibet, goat has a delicate head, with semi-pendulous ears, which are both long and wide. The hair varies in length, and is coarse and of different colours according to the individual. The horns are very erect, and sometimes slightly spiral, inclining inwards and to such an extent in some cases as to cross. The coat is composed, as in the Angora, of two materials; but in this breed it is the under-coat that partakes of the nature of wool and is valued as an article of commerce. This under-coat, or *pushm*, which is of a uniform greyish-white tint, whatever the colour of the hair may be, is beautifully soft and silky, and of a fluffy description resembling down. It makes its appearance in the autumn, and continues to grow until the following spring, when, if not removed, it falls off naturally; its collection then commences, occupying from eight to ten days. The animal undergoes during that time a process of combing by which all the wool and a portion of the hair, which of necessity comes with it, is removed. The latter is afterwards carefully separated, when the fleece in a good specimen weighs about half a pound. This is the material of which the far-famed and costly shawls are made, which at one time had such a demand that, it is stated, 16,000 looms were kept in constant work at Kashmir in their manufacture. Those goats having a short, neat head, long, thin, ears, a delicate skin, small bones, and a long heavy coat, are for this purpose deemed the best. There are several varieties 163 possessing this valuable quality, but those of Kashmir, Tibet and Mongolia are the most esteemed.

FIG. 2.—
Nubian Goat.

The Nubian goat, which is met with in Nubia, Upper Egypt and Abyssinia, differs greatly in appearance from those previously described. The coat of the female is extremely short, almost like that of a race-horse, and the legs are long. This breed therefore stands considerably higher than the common goat. One of its peculiarities is the convex profile of the face, the forehead being prominent and the nostrils sunk in, the nose itself extremely small, and the lower lip projecting from the upper. The ears are long, broad and thin, and hang down by the side of the head like a lop-eared rabbit. The horns are black, slightly twisted and very short, flat at the base, pointed at the tips, and recumbent on the head. Among goats met with in England a good many show signs of a more or less remote cross with this breed, derived probably from specimens brought from the East on board ships for supplying milk during the voyage.

The Theban goat, of the Sudan, which is hornless, displays the characteristic features of the last in an exaggerated degree, and in the form of the head and skull is very sheep-like.

The Nepal goat appears to be a variety of the Nubian breed, having the same arched facial line, pendulous ears and long legs. The horns, however, are more spiral. The colour of the hair, which is longer than in the Nubian, is black, grey or white, with black blotches.

Lastly the Guinea goat is a dwarf breed originally from the coast whence its name is derived. There are three varieties. Besides the commonest *Capra recurva*, there is a rarer breed, *Capra depressa*, inhabiting the Mauritius and the islands of Bourbon and Madagascar. The other variety is met with along the White Nile, in Lower Egypt, and at various points on the African coast of the Mediterranean.

As regards wild goats other than the representatives of *Capra hircus*, the members of the ibex-group are noticed under IBEX, while another distinctive type receives mention under MARKHOR. The ibex are connected with the wild goat by means of *Capra nubiana*, in which the front edge of the horns is thinner than in either the European *C. ibex* or the Asiatic *C. sibirica*; while the Spanish *C. pyrenaica* shows how the ibex-type of horn may pass into the spirally twisted one distinctive of the markhor, *C. falconeri*. In the article IBEX mention is made of the Caucasus ibex, or tur, *C. caucasica*, as an aberrant member of that group, but beside this animal the Caucasus is the home of another very remarkable goat, or tur, known as *C. pallasi*. In this ruminant, which is of a dark-brown colour, the relatively smooth black horns diverge outwards in a manner resembling those of the bharal among the sheep rather than in goat-fashion; and, in fact, this tur, which has only a very short beard, is so bharal-like that it is commonly called by sportsmen the Caucasian bharal. It is one of the species which render it so difficult to give a precise definition of either sheep or goats.

The short-horned Asiatic goats of the genus *Hemitragus* receive mention in the article TAHR; but it may be added that fossil species of the same genus are known from the Lower Pliocene formations of India, which have also yielded remains of a goat allied to the markhor of the Himalayas. The Rocky Mountain goat (*q.v.*) of America has no claim to be regarded as a member of the goat-group.

For full descriptions of the various wild species, see R. Lydekker, *Wild Oxen, Sheep, and Goats* (London, 1898).

(R. L.*)

GOATSUCKER, a bird from very ancient times absurdly believed to have the habit implied by the common name it bears in many European tongues besides English—as testified by the Gr.αἰγοθήλας, the Lat. *caprimulgus*, Ital. *succiacapre*, Span. *chotacabras*, Fr. *tettechèvre*, and Ger. *Ziegenmelker*. The common goatsucker (*Caprimulgus europaeus*, Linn.), is admittedly the type of a very peculiar and distinct family, *Caprimulgidae*, a group remarkable for the flat head, enormously wide mouth, large eyes, and soft, pencilled plumage of its members, which vary in size from a lark to a crow. Its position has been variously assigned by systematists. Though now judiciously removed from the *Passeres*, in which Linnaeus placed all the species known to him, Huxley considered it to form, with two other families—the swifts (*Cypselidae*) and humming-birds (*Trochilidae*)—the division *Cypselomorphae* of his larger group Aegithognathae, which is equivalent in the main to the Linnaean *Passeres*. There are two ways of regarding the *Caprimulgidae*—one including the genus *Podargus* and its allies, the other recognizing them as a distinct family, *Podargidae*. As a matter of convenience we shall here comprehend these last in the *Caprimulgidae*, which will then contain two subfamilies, *Caprimulginae* and *Podarginae*; for what, according to older authors, constitutes a third, though represented only by *Steatornis*, the singular oil-bird, or guacharo, certainly seems to require separation as an independent family (see GUACHERO).

Common
Goatsucker.

Some of the differences between the *Caprimulginae* and *Podarginae* have been pointed out by Sclater (*Proc. Zool. Soc.*, 1866, p. 123), and are very obvious. In the former, the outer toes have *four* phalanges only, thus presenting a very uncommon character among birds, and the middle claws are pectinated, while in the latter the normal number of *five* phalanges is found, and the claws are smooth, and other distinctions more recondite have also been indicated by him (*tom. cit.* p. 582). The Caprimulginae may be further divided into those having the gape thickly beset by strong bristles, and those in which there are few such bristles or none—the former containing the genera *Caprimulgus*, *Antrostomus*, *Nyctidromus* and others, and the latter *Podargus*, *Chordiles*, *Lyncornis* and a few more.

The common goatsucker of Europe (*C. europaeus*) arrives late in spring from its winter-retreat in Africa, and its presence is soon made known by its habit of chasing its prey, consisting chiefly of moths and cockchafers, in the evening-twilight. As 164the season advances the song of the cock, from its singularity, attracts attention amid all rural sounds. This song seems to be always uttered when the bird is at rest, though the contrary has been asserted, and is the continuous repetition of a single burring note, as of a thin lath fixed at one end and in a state of vibration at the other, and loud enough to reach in still weather a distance of half-a-mile or more. On the wing, while toying with its mate, or performing its rapid evolutions round the trees where it finds its food, it has the habit of occasionally producing another and equally extraordinary sound, sudden and short, but somewhat resembling that made by swinging a thong in the air, though whether this noise proceeds from its mouth is not ascertained. In general its flight is silent, but at times when disturbed from its repose, its wings may be heard to smite together. The goatsucker, or, to use perhaps its commoner English name, nightjar,1 passes the day in slumber, crouching on the ground or perching on a tree—in the latter case sitting not across the branch but lengthways, with its head lower than its body. In hot weather, however, its song may sometimes be heard by day and even at noontide, but it is then uttered, as it were, drowsily, and without the vigour that characterizes its crepuscular or nocturnal performance. Towards evening the bird becomes active, and it seems to pursue its prey throughout the night uninterruptedly, or only occasionally pausing for a few seconds to alight on a bare spot—a pathway or road—and then resuming its career. It is one of the few birds that absolutely make no nest, but lays its pair of beautifully-marbled eggs on the ground, generally where the herbage is short, and often actually on the soil. So light is it that the act of brooding, even where there is some vegetable growth, produces no visible depression of the grass, moss or lichens on which the eggs rest, and the finest sand equally fails to exhibit a trace of the parental act. Yet scarcely any bird shows greater local attachment, and the precise site chosen one year is almost certain to be occupied the next. The young, covered when hatched with dark-spotted down, are not easily found, nor are they more easily discovered on becoming fledged, for their plumage almost entirely resembles that of the adults, being a mixture of reddish-brown, grey and black, blended and mottled in a manner that passes description. They soon attain their full size and power of flight, and then take to the same manner of life as their parents. In autumn all leave their summer haunts for the south, but the exact time of their departure has hardly been ascertained. The habits of the nightjar, as thus described, seem to be more or less essentially those of the whole subfamily—the differences observable being apparently less than are found in other groups of birds of similar extent.

A second species of goatsucker (*C. ruficollis*), which is somewhat larger, and has the neck distinctly marked with rufous, is a summer visitant to the south-western parts of Europe, and especially to Spain and Portugal. The occurrence of a single example of this bird at Killingworth, near Newcastle-on-Tyne, in October 1856, has been recorded by Mr Hancock (*Ibis*, 1862, p. 39); but the season of its appearance argues the probability of its being but a casual straggler from its proper home. Many other species of *Caprimulgus* inhabit Africa, Asia and their islands, while one (*C. macrurus*) is found in Australia. Very nearly allied to this genus is *Antrostomus*, an American group containing many species, of which the chuck-will's-widow (*A. carolinensis*) and the whip-poor-will (*A. vociferus*) of the eastern United States (the latter also reaching Canada) are familiar examples. Both these birds take their common name from the cry they utter, and their habits seem to be almost identical, with those of the old world goatsuckers. Passing over some other forms which need not here be mentioned, the genus *Nyctidromus*, though consisting of only one species (*N. albicollis*) which inhabits Central and part of South America, requires remark, since it has tarsi of sufficient length to enable it to run swiftly on the ground, while the legs of most birds of the family are so short that they can make but a shuffling progress. *Heleothreptes*, with the unique form of wing possessed by the male, needs mention. Notice must also be taken of two African species, referred by some ornithologists to as many genera (*Macrodipteryx* and *Cosmetornis*), though probably one genus would suffice for both. The males of each of them are characterized by the wonderful development of the ninth primary in either wing, which reaches in fully adult specimens the extraordinary length of 17 in. or more. The former of these birds, the *Caprimulgus macrodipterus* of Adam Afzelius, is considered to belong to the west coast of Africa, and the shaft of the elongated remiges is bare for the greater part of its length, retaining the web, in a spatulate form, only near the tip. The latter, to which the specific name of *vexillarius* was given by John Gould, has been found on the east coast of that continent, and is reported to have occurred in Madagascar and Socotra. In this the remigial streamers do not lose their barbs, and as a few of the next quills are also to some extent elongated, the bird, when flying, is said to look as though it had four wings. Specimens of both are rare in collections, and no traveller seems to have had the opportunity of studying the habits of either so as to suggest a reason for this marvellous sexual development.

The second group of *Caprimulginae*, those which are but poorly or not at all furnished with rictal bristles, contains about five genera, of which we may particularize *Lyncornis* of the old world and *Chordiles* of the new. The species of the former are remarkable for the tuft of feathers which springs from each side of the head, above and behind the ears, so as to give the bird an appearance like some of the "horned" owls—those of the genus *Scops*, for example; and remarkable as it is to find certain forms of two families, so distinct as are the *Strigidae* and the *Caprimulgidae*, resembling each other in this singular external feature, it is yet more remarkable to note that in some groups of the latter, as in some of the former, a very curious kind of dimorphism takes place. In either case this has been frequently asserted to be sexual, but on that point doubt may fairly be entertained. Certain it is that in some groups of goatsuckers, as in some groups of owls, individuals of the same species are found in plumage of two entirely different hues—rufous and grey. The only explanation as yet offered of this fact is that the difference is sexual, but evidence to that effect is conflicting. It must not, however, be supposed that this common feature, any more than that of the existence of tufted forms in each group, indicates any close relationship between them. The resemblances may be due to the same causes, concerning which future observers may possibly enlighten us, but at present we must regard them as analogies, not homologies. The species of *Lyncornis* inhabit the Malay Archipelago, one, however, occurring also in China. Of *Chordiles* the best-known species is the night-hawk of North America (*C. virginianus* or *C. popetue*), which has a wide range from Canada to Brazil. Others are found in the Antilles and in South America. The general habits of all these birds agree with those of the typical goatsuckers.

We have next to consider the birds forming the genus *Podargus* and those allied to it, whether they be regarded as a distinct family, or as a subfamily of *Caprimulgidae*. As above stated, they have feet constructed as those of birds normally are, and their sternum seems to present the constant though comparatively trivial difference of having its posterior margin elongated into two pairs of processes, while only one pair is found in the true goatsuckers. *Podargus* includes the bird (*P. cuvieri*) known from its cry as morepork to the Tasmanians,2 and several other species, the number of which is doubtful, from Australia and New Guinea. They have comparatively powerful bills, and it would seem feed to some extent on fruits and berries, though they mainly subsist on insects, chiefly *Cicadae* and *Phasmidae*. They also differ from the true goatsuckers in having the outer toes partially reversible, and they build a flat nest on the horizontal branch of a tree for the reception of their eggs, which are of a spotless white. Apparently allied to *Podargus*, but differing 165among other respects in its mode of nidification, is *Aegotheles*, which belongs also to the Australian sub-region; and farther to the northward, extending throughout the Malay Archipelago and into India, comes *Batrachostomus*, wherein we again meet with species having aural tufts somewhat like *Lyncornis*. The *Podarginae* are thought by some to be represented in the new world by the genus *Nyctibius*, of which several species occur from the Antilles and Central America to Brazil. Finally, it may be stated that none of the *Caprimulgidae* seem to occur in Polynesia or in New Zealand, though there is scarcely any other part of the world suited to their habits in which members of the family are not found.

(A. N.)

1Other English names of the bird are evejar, fern-owl, churn-owl and wheel-bird—the last from the bird's song resembling the noise made by a spinning-wheel in motion.

2In New Zealand, however, this name is given to an owl (*Sceloglaux novae-zelandiae*).

GOBAT, SAMUEL (1799-1879), bishop of Jerusalem, was born at Crémine, Bern, Switzerland, on the 26th of January 1799. After serving in the mission house at Basel from 1823 to 1826, he went to Paris and London, whence, having acquired some knowledge of Arabic and Ethiopic, he went out to Abyssinia under the auspices of the Church Missionary Society. The unsettled state of the country and his own ill health prevented his making much headway; he returned to Europe in 1835 and from 1839 to 1842 lived in Malta, where he supervised an Arabic translation of the Bible. In 1846 he was consecrated Protestant bishop of Jerusalem, under the agreement between the British and Prussian governments (1841) for the establishment of a joint bishopric for Lutherans and Anglicans in the Holy Land. He carried on a vigorous mission as bishop for over thirty years, his diocesan school and orphanage on Mount Zion being specially noteworthy. He died on the 11th of May 1879.

A record of his life, largely autobiographical, was published at Basel in 1884, and an English translation at London in the same year.

GOBEL, JEAN BAPTISTE JOSEPH (1727-1794), French ecclesiastic and politician, was born at Thann, in Alsace, on the 1st of September 1727. He studied theology in the German College at Rome, and then became successively a member of the chapter of Porrentruy, bishop *in partibus* of Lydda, and finally suffragan of Basel for that part of the diocese situated in French territory. His political life began when he was elected deputy to the states-general of 1789 by the clergy of the *bailliage* of Huningue. The turning-point of his life was his action in taking the oath of the civil constitution of the clergy (Jan. 3rd, 1791); in favour of which he had declared himself since the 5th of May 1790. The civil constitution of the clergy gave the appointment of priests to the electoral assemblies, and since taking the oath Gobel had become so popular that he was elected bishop in several dioceses. He chose Paris, and in spite of the difficulties which he had to encounter before he could enter into possession, was consecrated on the 27th of March 1791 by

68

eight bishops, including Talleyrand. On the 8th of November 1792, Gobel was appointed administrator of Paris. He was careful to flatter the politicians by professing anti-clerical opinions, declaring himself, among other things, opposed to the celibacy of the clergy; and on the 17th Brumaire in the year II. (7th November 1793), he came before the bar of the Convention, and, in a famous scene, resigned his episcopal functions, proclaiming that he did so for love of the people, and through respect for their wishes. The followers of Hébert, who were then pursuing their anti-Christian policy, claimed Gobel as one of themselves; while, on the other hand, Robespierre looked upon him as an atheist, though apostasy cannot strictly speaking be laid to the charge of the ex-bishop, nor did he ever make any actual profession of atheism. Robespierre, however, found him an obstacle to his religious schemes, and involved him in the fate of the Hébertists. Gobel was condemned to death, with Chaumette, Hébert and Anacharsis Cloots, and was guillotined on the 12th of April 1794.

See E. Charavay, *Assemblée électorale de Paris* (Paris, 1890); H. Monin, *La Chanson et l'Église sous la Révolution* (Paris, 1892); A. Aulard, "La Culte de la raison" in the review, *La Révolution Française* (1891). For a bibliography of documents relating to his episcopate see "Épiscopat de Gobel" in vol. iii. (1900) of M. Tourneux's *Bibliographie de l'histoire de Paris pendant la Rév. Fr.*

GOBELIN, the name of a family of dyers, who in all probability came originally from Reims, and who in the middle of the 15th century established themselves in the Faubourg Saint Marcel, Paris, on the banks of the Bièvre. The first head of the firm was named Jehan (d. 1476). He discovered a peculiar kind of scarlet dyestuff, and he expended so much money on his establishment that it was named by the common people *la folie Gobelin*. To the dye-works there was added in the 16th century a manufactory of tapestry (*q.v.*). So rapidly did the wealth of the family increase, that in the third or fourth generation some of them forsook their trade and purchased titles of nobility. More than one of their number held offices of state, among others Balthasar, who became successively treasurer general of artillery, treasurer extraordinary of war, councillor secretary of the king, chancellor of the exchequer, councillor of state and president of the chamber of accounts, and who in 1601 received from Henry IV. the lands and lordship of Briecomte-Robert. He died in 1603. The name of the Gobelins as dyers cannot be found later than the end of the 17th century. In 1662 the works in the Faubourg Saint Marcel, with the adjoining grounds, were purchased by Colbert on behalf of Louis XIV., and transformed into a general upholstery manufactory, in which designs both in tapestry and in all kinds of furniture were executed under the superintendence of the royal painter, Le Brun. On account of the pecuniary embarrassments of Louis XIV., the establishment was closed in 1694, but it was reopened in 1697 for the manufacture of tapestry, chiefly for royal use and for presentation. During the Revolution and the reign of Napoleon the manufacture was suspended, but it was revived by the Bourbons, and in 1826 the manufacture of carpets was added to that of tapestry. In 1871 the building was partly burned by the Communists. The manufacture is still carried on under the state.

See Lacordaire, *Notice historique sur les manufactures impériales de tapisserie des Gobelin et de tapis de la Savonnerie, précédée du catalogue des tapisseries qui y sont exposés* (Paris, 1853); Genspach, *Répertoire détaillé des tapisseries exécutées aux Gobelins, 1662-1892* (Paris, 1893); Guiffrey, *Histoire de la tapisserie en France* (Paris, 1878-1885). The two last-named authors were directors of the manufactory.

GOBI (for which alternative Chinese names are SHA-MO, "sand desert," and HAN-HAI, "dry sea"), a term which in its widest significance means the long stretch of desert country that extends from the foot of the Pamirs, in about 77° E., eastward to the Great Khingan Mountains, in 116°-118° E., on the border of Manchuria, and from the foothills of the Altai, the Sayan and the Yablonoi Mountains on the N. to the Astin-tagh or Altyn-tagh and the Nan-shan, the northernmost constituent ranges of the Kuen-lun Mountains, on the south. By conventional usage a relatively small area on the east side of the Great Khingan, between the upper waters of the Sungari and the upper waters of the Liao-ho, is also reckoned to belong to the Gobi. On the other hand, geographers and Asiatic explorers prefer to regard the W. extremity of the Gobi region (as defined above), namely, the basin of the Tarim in E. Turkestan, as forming a separate and independent desert, to which they have given the name of Takla-makan. The latter restriction governs the present article, which accordingly excludes the Takla-makan, leaving it for separate treatment. The desert of Gobi as a whole is only very imperfectly known, information being confined to the observations which individual travellers have made from their respective itineraries across the desert. Amongst the explorers to whom we owe such knowledge as we possess about the Gobi, the most important have been Marco Polo (1273-1275), Gerbillon (1688-1698), Ijsbrand Ides (1692-1694), Lange (1727-1728 and 1736), Fuss and Bunge (1830-1831), Fritsche (1868-1873), Pavlinov and Matusovski (1870), Ney Elias (1872-1873), N. M.

Przhevalsky (1870-1872 and 1876-1877), Zosnovsky (1875), M. V. Pjevtsov (1878), G. N. Potanin (1877 and 1884-1886), Count Széchenyi and L. von Loczy (1879-1880), the brothers Grum-Grzhimailo (1889-1890), P. K. Kozlov (1893-1894 and 1899-1900), V. I. Roborovsky (1894), V. A. Obruchev (1894-1896), Futterer and Holderer (1896); C. E. Bonin (1896 and 1899), Sven Hedin (1897 and 1900-1901), K. Bogdanovich (1898), Ladyghin (1899-1900) and Katsnakov (1899-1900).

Geographically the Gobi (a Mongol word meaning "desert") 166is the deeper part of the gigantic depression which fills the interior of the lower terrace of the vast Mongolian plateau, and measures over 1000 m. from S.W. to N.E. and 450 to 600 m. from N. to S., being widest in the west, along the line joining the Baghrash-kol and the Lop-nor (87°-89° E.). Owing to the immense area covered, and the piecemeal character of the information, no general description can be made applicable to the whole of the Gobi. It will be more convenient, therefore, to describe its principal distinctive sections *seriatim*, beginning in the west.

Ghashiun-Gobi and Kuruk-tagh.—The Yulduz valley or valley of the Khaïdyk-gol (83°-86° E., 43° N.) is enclosed by two prominent members of the Tian-shan system, namely the Chol-tagh and the Kuruk-tagh, running parallel and close to one another. As they proceed eastward they diverge, sweeping back on N. and S. respectively so as to leave room for the Baghrash-kol. These two ranges mark the northern and the southern edges respectively of a great swelling, which extends eastward for nearly twenty degrees of longitude. On its northern side the Chol-tagh descends steeply, and its foot is fringed by a string of deep depressions, ranging from Lukchun (425 ft. *below* the level of the sea) to Hami (2800 ft. above sea-level). To the south of the Kuruk-tagh lie the desert of Lop, the desert of Kum-tagh, and the valley of the Bulunzir-gol. To this great swelling, which arches up between the two border-ranges of the Chol-tagh and Kuruk-tagh, the Mongols give the name of Ghashiun-Gobi or Salt Desert. It is some 80 to 100 m. across from N. to S., and is traversed by a number of minor parallel ranges, ridges and chains of hills, and down its middle runs a broad stony valley, 25 to 50 m. wide, at an elevation of 3000 to 4500 ft. The Chol-tagh, which reaches an average altitude of 6000 ft., is absolutely sterile, and its northern foot rests upon a narrow belt of barren sand, which leads down to the depressions mentioned above.

The Kuruk-tagh is the greatly disintegrated, denuded and wasted relic of a mountain range which formerly was of incomparably greater magnitude. In the west, between Baghrash-kol and the Tarim, it consists of two, possibly or three, principal ranges, which, although broken in continuity, run generally parallel to one another, and embrace between them numerous minor chains of heights. These minor ranges, together with the principal ranges, divide the region into a series of long, narrow valleys, mostly parallel to one another and to the enclosing mountain chains, which descend like terraced steps, on the one side towards the depression of Lukchun and on the other towards the desert of Lop. In many cases these latitudinal valleys are barred transversely by ridges or spurs, generally elevations *en masse* of the bottom of the valley. Where such elevations exist, there is generally found, on the E. side of the transverse ridge, a cauldron-shaped depression, which some time or other has been the bottom of a former lake, but is now nearly a dry salt-basin. The surface configuration is in fact markedly similar to that which occurs in the inter-mont latitudinal valleys of the Kuen-lun. The hydrography of the Ghashiun-Gobi and the Kuruk-tagh is determined by these chequered arrangements of the latitudinal valleys. Most of the principal streams, instead of flowing straight down these valleys, cross them diagonally and only turn west after they have cut their way through one or more of the transverse barrier ranges.1 To the highest range on the great swelling Grum-Grzhimailo gives the name of Tuge-tau, its altitude being 9000 ft. above the level of the sea and some 4000 ft. above the crown of the swelling itself. This range he considers to belong to the Chol-tagh system, whereas Sven Hedin would assign it to the Kuruk-tagh. This last, which is pretty certainly identical with the range of Khara-teken-ula (also known as the Kyzyl-sanghir, Sinir, and Singher Mountains), that overlooks the southern shore of the Baghrash-kol, though parted from it by the drift-sand desert of Ak-bel-kum (White Pass Sands), has at first a W.N.W. to E.S.E. strike, but it gradually curves round like a scimitar towards the E.N.E. and at the same time gradually decreases in elevation. In 91° E., while the principal range of the Kuruk-tagh system wheels to the E.N.E., four of its subsidiary ranges terminate, or rather die away somewhat suddenly, on the brink of a long narrow depression (in which Sven Hedin sees a N.E. bay of the former great Central Asian lake of Lop-nor), having over against them the écheloned terminals of similar subordinate ranges of the Pe-shan (Bey-san) system (see below). The Kuruk-tagh is throughout a relatively low, but almost completely barren range, being entirely destitute of animal life, save for hares, antelopes and wild camels, which frequent its few small, widely scattered oases. The vegetation, which is confined to these same relatively favoured spots, is of the scantiest and is mainly confined to bushes of saxaul (*Anabasis Ammodendron*), reeds (*kamish*), tamarisks, poplars, *Kalidium* and *Ephedra*.

Desert of Lop.—This section of the Gobi extends south-eastward from the foot of the Kuruk-tagh as far as the present terminal basin of the Tarim, namely Kara-koshun (Przhevalsky's Lop-nor), and is an almost perfectly horizontal expanse, for, while the Baghrash-kol in the N. lies at an altitude of 2940 ft., the Kara-koshun, over 200 m. to the S., is only 300 ft. lower. The characteristic features of this almost dead level or but slightly undulating region are: (i.) broad, unbroken expanses of clay intermingled with sand, the clay (*shor*) being indurated and saliferous and often arranged in terraces; (ii.) hard, level, clay expanses, more or less thickly sprinkled with fine gravel (*say*), the clay being mostly of a yellow or yellow-grey colour; (iii.) benches, flattened ridges and tabular masses of consolidated clay (*jardangs*), arranged in distinctly defined *laminae*, three stories being sometimes superimposed one upon the other, and their vertical faces being abraded, and often undercut, by the wind, while the formations themselves are separated by parallel gullies or wind-furrows, 6 to 20 ft. deep, all sculptured in the direction of the prevailing wind, that is, from N.E. to S.W.; and (iv.) the absence of drift-sand and sand-dunes, except in the south, towards the outlying foothills of the Astin-tagh. Perhaps the most striking characteristic, after the jardangs or clay terraces, is the fact that the whole of this region is not only swept bare of sand by the terrific sandstorms (*burans*) of the spring months, the particles of sand with which the wind is laden acting like a sand-blast, but the actual substantive materials of the desert itself are abraded, filed, eroded and carried bodily away into the network of lakes in which the Tarim loses itself, or are even blown across the lower, constantly shifting watercourses of that river and deposited on or among the gigantic dunes which choke the eastern end of the desert of Takla-makan. Numerous indications, such as salt-stained depressions of a lacustrine appearance, traces of former lacustrine shore-lines, more or less parallel and concentric, the presence in places of vast quantities of fresh-water mollusc shells (species of *Limnaea* and *Planorbis*), the existence of belts of dead poplars, patches of dead tamarisks and extensive beds of withered reeds, all these always on top of the jardangs, never in the wind-etched furrows, together with a few scrubby poplars and *Elaeagnus*, still struggling hard not to die, the presence of ripple marks of aqueous origin on the leeward sides of the clay terraces and in other wind-sheltered situations, all testify to the former existence in this region of more or less extensive freshwater lakes, now of course completely desiccated. During the prevalence of the spring storms the atmosphere that overhangs the immediate surface of the desert is so heavily charged with dust as to be a veritable pall of desolation. Except for the wild camel which frequents the reed oases on the N. edge of the desert, animal life is even less abundant than in the Ghashiun-Gobi, and the same is true as regards the vegetation.

Desert of Kum-tagh.—This section lies E.S.E. of the desert of Lop, on the other side of the Kara-koshun and its more or less temporary continuations, and reaches north-eastwards as far as the vicinity of the town of Sa-chow and the lake of Kara-nor or Kala-chi. Its southern rim is marked by a labyrinth of hills, dotted in groups and irregular clusters, but evidently survivals of two parallel ranges which are now worn down as it were to mere fragments of their former skeletal structure. Between these and the Astin-tagh intervenes a broad latitudinal valley, seamed with watercourses which come down from the foothills of the Astin-tagh and beside which scrubby desert plants of the usual character maintain a precarious existence, water reaching them in some instances at intervals of years only. This part of the desert has a general slope N.W. towards the relative depression of the Kara-koshun. A noticeable feature of the Kum-tagh is the presence of large accumulations of drift-sand, especially along the foot of the crumbling desert ranges, where it rises into dunes sometimes as much as 250 ft. in height and climbs half-way up the flanks of ranges themselves. The prevailing winds in this region would appear to blow from the W. and N.W. during the summer, winter and autumn, though in spring, when they certainly are more violent, they no doubt come from the N.E., as in the desert of Lop. Anyway, the arrangement of the sand here "agrees perfectly with the law laid down by Potanin, that in the basins of Central Asia the sand is heaped up in greater mass on the south, all along the bordering mountain ranges where the floor of the depressions lies at the highest level."[2] The country to the north of the desert ranges is thus summarily described by Sven Hedin:[3] "The first zone of drift-sand is succeeded by a region which exhibits proofs of wind-modelling on an extraordinarily energetic and well developed scale, the results corresponding to the jardangs and the wind-eroded gullies of the desert of Lop. Both sets of phenomena lie parallel to one another; from this we may infer that the winds which prevail in the two deserts are the same. Next comes, sharply demarcated from the zone just described, a more or less thin kamish steppe growing on level ground; and this in turn is followed by another very narrow belt of sand, immediately south of Achik-kuduk.... Finally in the extreme north we have the characteristic and sharply defined belt of kamish steppe, stretching from E.N.E. to W.S.W. and bounded on N. and S. by high, sharp-cut clay terraces.... At the points where we measured them the northern terrace was 113 ft. high and the southern 85¼ ft.... Both terraces belong to the same level, and would appear to correspond to the shore lines of a big bay of the last surviving remnant of the Central Asian Mediterranean. At the point where I crossed it the depression was 6 to 7 m. wide, and thus resembled a flat valley or immense river-bed."

Desert of Hami and the Pe-shan Mountains.—This section occupies the space between the Tian-shan system on the N. and the Nan-shan Mountains on the S., and is connected on the W. with the desert of Lop. The classic account is that of Przhevalsky, who crossed the desert from Hami (or Khami) to Su-chow (not Sa-chow) in the summer of 1879. In the middle this desert rises into a vast swelling, 80 m. across, which reaches an average elevation of 5000 ft. and a maximum elevation of 5500 ft. On its northern and southern borders it is overtopped by two divisions of the Bey-san (= Pe-shan) Mountains, neither of which attains any great relative altitude. Between the northern division and the Karlyk-tagh range or E. Tian-shan intervenes a somewhat undulating barren plain, 3900 ft. in altitude and 40 m. from N. to S., sloping downwards from both N. and S. towards the middle, where lies the oasis of Hami (2800 ft.). Similarly from the southern division of the Bey-san a second plain slopes down for 1000 ft. to the valley of the river Bulunzir or Su-lai-ho, which comes out of China, from the south side of the Great Wall, and finally empties itself into the lake of Kala-chi or Kara-nor. From the Bulunzir the same plain continues southwards at a level of 3700 ft. to the foot of the Nan-shan Mountains. The total breadth of the desert from N. to S. is here 200 m. Its general character is that of an undulating plain, dotted over with occasional elevations of clay, which present the appearance of walls, table-topped mounds and broken towers (*jardangs*), the surface of the plain being strewn with gravel and absolutely destitute of vegetation. Generally speaking, the Bey-san ranges consist of isolated hills or groups of hills, of low relative elevation (100 to 300 ft.), scattered without any regard to order over the arch of the swelling. They nowhere rise into well-defined peaks. Their axis runs from W.S.W. to E.N.E. But whereas Przhevalsky and Sven Hedin consider them to be a continuation of the Kuruk-tagh, though the latter regards them as separated from the Kuruk-tagh by a well-marked bay of the former Central Asian Mediterranean (Lop-nor), Futterer declares they are a continuation of the Chol-tagh. The swelling or undulating plain between these two ranges of the Bey-san measures about 70 m. across and is traversed by several stretches of high ground having generally an east-west direction.4 Futterer, who crossed the same desert twenty years after Przhevalsky, agrees generally in his description of it, but supplements the account of the latter explorer with several particulars. He observes that the ranges in this part of the Gobi are much worn down and wasted, like the Kuruk-tagh farther west and the tablelands of S.E. Mongolia farther east, through the effects of century-long insolation, wind erosion, great and sudden changes of temperature, chemical action and occasional water erosion. Vast areas towards the N. consist of expanses of gently sloping (at a mean slope of 3°) clay, intermingled with gravel. He points out also that the greatest accumulations of sand and other products of aerial denudation do not occur in the deepest parts of the depressions but at the outlets of the valleys and glens, and along the foot of the ranges which flank the depressions on the S. Wherever water has been, desert scrub is found, such as tamarisks, *Dodartia orientalis*, *Agriophyllum gobicum*, *Calligonium sinnex*, and *Lycium ruthenicum*, but all with their roots elevated on little mounds in the same way as the tamarisks grow in the Takla-makan and desert of Lop.

Farther east, towards central Mongolia, the relations, says Futterer, are the same as along the Hami-Su-chow route, except that the ranges have lower and broader crests, and the detached hills are more denuded and more disintegrated. Between the ranges occur broad, flat, cauldron-shaped valleys and basins, almost destitute of life except for a few hares and a few birds, such as the crow and the pheasant, and with scanty vegetation, but no great accumulations of drift-sand. The rocks are severely weathered on the surface, a thick layer of the coarser products of denudation covers the flat parts and climbs a good way up the flanks of the mountain ranges, but all the finer material, sand and clay has been blown away partly S.E. into Ordos, partly into the Chinese provinces of Shen-si and Shan-si, where it is deposited as loess, and partly W., where it chokes all the southern parts of the basin of the Tarim. In these central parts of the Gobi, as indeed in all other parts except the desert of Lop and Ordos, the prevailing winds blow from the W. and N.W. These winds are warm in summer, and it is they which in the desert of Hami bring the fierce sandstorms or burans. The wind does blow also from the N.E., but it is then cold and often brings snow, though it speedily clears the air of the everlasting dust haze. In summer great heat is encountered here on the relatively low (3000-4600 ft.), gravelly expanses (*say*) on the N. and on those of the S. (4000-5000 ft.); but on the higher swelling between, which in the Pe-shan ranges ascends to 7550 ft., there is great cold even in summer, and a wide daily range of temperature. Above the broad and deep accumulations of the products of denudation which have been brought down by the rivers from the Tian-shan ranges (*e.g.* the Karlyk-tagh) on the N. and from the Nan-shan on the S., and have filled up the cauldron-shaped valleys, there rises a broad swelling, built up of granitic rocks, crystalline schists and metamorphosed sedimentary rocks of both Archaic and Palaeozoic age, all greatly folded and tilted up, and shot through with numerous irruptions of volcanic rocks, predominantly porphyritic and dioritic. On this swelling rise four more or less parallel mountain ranges of the Pe-shan system, together with a fifth chain of hills farther S., all having a strike from W.N.W. to E.N.E. The range farthest N. rises to 1000 ft. above the desert and 7550 ft. above sea-level, the next two ranges reach 1300 ft. above the general level of the desert, and the range farthest south 1475 ft. or an absolute altitude of 7200 ft., while the fifth chain of hills does not exceed 650 ft. in relative elevation. All these ranges decrease in altitude from W. to E. In the depressions which border the Pe-shan swelling on N. and S. are found the sedimentary deposits of the Tertiary sea of the Han-hai; but no traces of those deposits have been found on the swelling itself at altitudes of 5600 to 5700 ft. Hence, Futterer infers, in recent geological times no large sea has occupied the central part of the Gobi. Beyond an occasional visit from a band of nomad Mongols, this region of the Pe-shan swelling is entirely uninhabited.5 And yet it was from this very region, avers G. E. Grum-Grzhimailo, that the Yue-chi, a nomad race akin to the Tibetans, proceeded when, towards the middle of the 2nd century B.C., they moved westwards and settled near Lake Issyk-kul; and from here proceeded also the Shanshani, or people who some two thousand years ago founded the state of Shanshan or Loû-lan, ruins of the chief town of which Sven Hedin discovered in the desert of Lop in 1901. Here, says the Russian explorer, the Huns gathered strength, as also did the Tukiu (Turks) in the 6th century, and the Uighur tribes and the rulers of the Tangut kingdom. But after Jenghiz Khan in the 12th century drew away the peoples of this region, and no others came to take their place, the country went out of cultivation and eventually became the barren desert it now is.6

   Ala-shan.—This division of the great desert, known also as the Hsi-tau and the Little Gobi, fills the space between the great N. loop of the Hwang-ho or Yellow river on the E., the Edzin-gol on the W., and the Nan-shan Mountains on the S.W., where it is separated from the Chinese province of Kan-suh by the narrow rocky chain of Lung-shan (Ala-shan), 10,500 to 11,600 ft. in altitude. It belongs to the middle basin of the three great depressions into which Potanin divides the Gobi as a whole. "Topographically," says Przhevalsky, "it is a perfectly level plain, which in all probability once formed the bed of a huge lake or inland sea." The data upon which he bases this conclusion are the level area of the region as a whole, the hard saline clay and the sand-strewn surface, and lastly the salt lakes which occupy its lowest parts. For hundreds of miles there is nothing to be seen but bare sands; in some places they continue so far without a break that the Mongols call them Tyngheri (*i.e.* sky). These vast expanses are absolutely waterless, nor do any oases relieve the unbroken stretches of yellow sand which alternate with equally vast areas of saline clay or, nearer the foot of the mountains, with barren shingle. Although on the whole a level country with a general altitude of 3300 to 5000 ft., this section, like most other parts of the Gobi, is crowned by a chequered network of hills and broken ranges going up 1000 ft. higher. The vegetation is confined to a few varieties of bushes and a dozen kinds of grasses, the most conspicuous being saxaul and *Agriophyllum gobicum*7(a grass). The others include prickly convolvulus, field wormwood, acacia, *Inula ammophila, Sophora flavescens, Convolvulus Ammani,Peganum* and *Astragalus*, but all dwarfed, deformed and starved. The fauna consists of little else except antelopes, the wolf, fox, hare, hedgehog, marten, numerous lizards and a few birds, *e.g.* the sand-grouse, lark, stonechat, sparrow, crane, *Podoces Hendersoni, Otocorys albigula* and*Galerita cristata.*8 The only human inhabitants of Ala-shan are the Torgod Mongols.

   Ordos.—East of the desert of Ala-shan, and only separated from it by the Hwang-ho, is the desert of Ordos or Ho-tau, "a level steppe, partly bordered by low hills. The soil is altogether sandy or a mixture of clay and sand, ill adapted for agriculture. The absolute height of this country is between 3000 and 3500 ft., so that Ordos forms an intermediate step in the descent to China from the Gobi, separated from the latter by the mountain ranges lying on the N. and E. of the Hwang-ho or Yellow river."9 Towards the south Ordos rises to an altitude of over 5000 ft., and in the W., along the right bank of the Hwang-ho, the Arbus or Arbiso Mountains, which overtop the steppe by some 3000 ft., serve to link the Ala-shan Mountains with the In-shan. The northern part of the great loop of the river is filled with the sands of Kuzupchi, a succession of dunes, 40 to 50 ft. high. Amongst them in scattered patches grow the shrub *Hedysarum* and the trees *Calligonium Tragopyrum* and *Pugionium cornutum*. In some places these sand-dunes approach close to the great river, in others they are parted from it by a belt of sand, intermingled with clay, which terminates in a steep escarpment, 50 ft. and in some localities 100 ft. above the river. This belt is studded with little mounds (7 to 10 ft. high), mostly overgrown with wormwood (*Artemisia campestris*) and the Siberian pea-tree (*Caragana*); and here too grows one of the most characteristic plants of Ordos, the liquorice root (*Glycyrrhiza uralensis*). Eventually 168the sand-dunes cross over to the left bank of the Hwang-ho, and are threaded by the beds of dry watercourses, while the level spaces amongst them are studded with little mounds (3 to 6 ft. high), on which grow stunted *Nitraria Scoberi* and *Zygophyllum*. Ordos, which was anciently known as Ho-nan ("the country south of the river") and still farther back in time as Ho-tau, was occupied by the Hiong-nu in the 1st and 2nd centuries A.D., but was almost depopulated during and after the Dungan revolt of 1869. North of the big loop of the Hwang-ho Ordos is separated from the central Gobi by a succession of mountain chains, the Kara-naryn-ula, the Sheiten-ula, and the In-shan Mountains, which link on to the south end of the Great Khingan Mountains. The In-shan Mountains, which stretch from 108° to 112° E., have a wild Alpine character and are distinguished from other mountains in the S.E. of Mongolia by an abundance of both water and vegetation. In one of their constituent ranges, the bold Munni-ula, 70 m. long and nearly 20 m. wide, they attain elevations of 7500 to 8500 ft., and have steep flanks, slashed with rugged gorges and narrow glens. Forests begin on them at 5300 ft. and wild flowers grow in great profusion and variety in summer, though with a striking lack of brilliancy in colouring. In this same border range there is also a much greater abundance and variety of animal life, especially amongst the avifauna.

Eastern Gobi.—Here the surface is extremely diversified, although there are no great differences in vertical elevation. Between Urga (48° N. and 107° E.) and the little lake of Iren-dubasu-nor (111° 50′ E. and 43° 45′ N.) the surface is greatly eroded, and consists of broad flat depressions and basins separated by groups of flat-topped mountains of relatively low elevation (500 to 600 ft.), through which archaic rocks crop out as crags and isolated rugged masses. The floors of the depressions lie mostly between 2900 and 3200 ft. above sea-level. Farther south, between Iren-dubasu-nor and the Hwang-ho comes a region of broad tablelands alternating with flat plains, the latter ranging at altitudes of 3300 to 3600 ft. and the former at 3500 to 4000 ft. The slopes of the plateaus are more or less steep, and are sometimes penetrated by "bays" of the lowlands. As the border-range of the Khingan is approached the country steadily rises up to 4500 ft. and then to 5350 ft. Here small lakes frequently fill the depressions, though the water in them is generally salt or brackish. And both here, and for 200 m. south of Urga, streams are frequent, and grass grows more or less abundantly. There is, however, through all the central parts, until the bordering mountains are reached, an utter absence of trees and shrubs. Clay and sand are the predominant formations, the watercourses, especially in the north, being frequently excavated 6 to 8 ft. deep, and in many places in the flat, dry valleys or depressions farther south beds of loess, 15 to 20 ft. thick, are exposed. West of the route from Urga to Kalgan the country presents approximately the same general features, except that the mountains are not so irregularly scattered in groups but have more strongly defined strikes, mostly E. to W., W.N.W. to E.S.E., and W.S.W. to E.N.E. The altitudes too are higher, those of the lowlands ranging from 3300 to 5600 ft., and those of the ranges from 650 to 1650 ft. higher, though in a few cases they reach altitudes of 8000 ft. above sea-level. The elevations do not, however, as a rule form continuous chains, but make up a congeries of short ridges and groups rising from a common base and intersected by a labyrinth of ravines, gullies, glens and basins. But the tablelands, built up of the horizontal red deposits of the Han-hai (Obruchev's Gobi formation) which are characteristic of the southern parts of eastern Mongolia, are absent here or occur only in one locality, near the Shara-muren river, and are then greatly intersected by gullies or dry watercourses.[10] Here there is, however, a great dearth of water, no streams, no lakes, no wells, and precipitation falls but seldom. The prevailing winds blow from the W. and N.W. and the pall of dust overhangs the country as in the Takla-makan and the desert of Lop. Characteristic of the flora are wild garlic, *Kalidium gracile*, wormwood, saxaul, *Nitraria Scoberi*, *Caragana*, *Ephedra*, saltwort and *dirisun* (*Lasiagrostis splendens*).

This great desert country of Gobi is crossed by several trade routes, some of which have been in use for thousands of years. Among the most important are those from Kalgan on the frontier of China to Urga (600 m.), from Su-chow (in Kan-suh) to Hami (420 m.) from Hami to Peking (1300 m.), from Kwei-hwa-cheng (or Kuku-khoto) to Hami and Barkul, and from Lanchow (in Kan-suh) to Hami.

Climate.—The climate of the Gobi is one of great extremes, combined with rapid changes of temperature, not only at all seasons of the year but even within 24 hours (as much as 58° F.). For instance, at Urga (3770 ft.) the annual mean is 27.5° F., the January mean −15.7°, and the July mean 63.5°, the extremes being 100.5° and −44.5°; while at Sivantse (3905 ft.) the annual mean is 37°, the January mean 2.3°, and the July mean 66.3°, the range being from a recorded maximum of 93° to a recorded minimum of −53°. Even in southern Mongolia the thermometer goes down as low as −27°, and in Ala-shan it rises day after day in July as high as 99°. Although the south-east monsoons reach the S.E. parts of the Gobi, the air generally throughout this region is characterized by extreme dryness, especially during the winter. Hence the icy sandstorms and snowstorms of spring and early summer. The rainfall at Urga for the year amounts to only 9.7 in.

74

Sands of the Gobi Deserts.—With regard to the origin of the masses of sand out of which the dunes and chains of dunes (*barkhans*) are built up in the several deserts of the Gobi, opinions differ. While some explorers consider them to be the product of marine, or at any rate lacustrine, denudation (the Central Asian Mediterranean), others—and this is not only the more reasonable view, but it is the view which is gaining most ground—consider that they are the products of the aerial denudation of the border ranges (*e.g.* Nan-shan, Karlyk-tagh, &c.), and more especially of the terribly wasted ranges and chains of hills, which, like the gaunt fragments of montane skeletal remains, lie littered all over the swelling uplands and tablelands of the Gobi, and that they have been transported by the prevailing winds to the localities in which they are now accumulated, the winds obeying similar transportation laws to the rivers and streams which carry down sediment in moister parts of the world. Potanin points out[11] that "there is a certain amount of regularity observable in the distribution of the sandy deserts over the vast uplands of central Asia. Two agencies are represented in the distribution of the sands, though what they really are is not quite clear; and of these two agencies one prevails in the north-west, the other in the south-east, so that the whole of Central Asia may be divided into two regions, the dividing line between them being drawn from north-east to south-west, from Urga via the eastern end of the Tian-shan to the city of Kashgar. North-west of this line the sandy masses are broken up into detached and disconnected areas, and are almost without exception heaped up around the lakes, and consequently in the lowest parts of the several districts in which they exist. Moreover, we find also that these sandy tracts always occur on the western or south-western shores of the lakes; this is the case with the lakes of Balkash, Ala-kul, Ebi-nor, Ayar-nor (or Telli-nor), Orku-nor, Zaisan-nor, Ulungur-nor, Ubsa-nor, Durga-nor and Kara-nor lying E. of Kirghiz-nor. South-east of the line the arrangement of the sand is quite different. In that part of Asia we have three gigantic but disconnected basins. The first, lying farthest east, is embraced on the one side by the ramifications of the Kentei and Khangai Mountains and on the other by the In-shan Mountains. The second or middle division is contained between the Altai of the Gobi and the Ala-shan. The third basin, in the west, lies between the Tian-shan and the border ranges of western Tibet.... The deepest parts of each of these three depressions occur near their northern borders; towards their southern boundaries they are all alike very much higher.... However, the sandy deserts are not found in the low-lying tracts but occur on the higher uplands which foot the southern mountain ranges, the In-shan and the Nan-shan. Our maps show an immense expanse of sand south of the Tarim in the western basin; beginning in the neighbourhood of the city of Yarkent (Yarkand), it extends eastwards past the towns of Khotan, Keriya and Cherchen to Sa-chow. Along this stretch there is only one locality which forms an exception to the rule we have indicated, namely, the region round the lake of Lop-nor. In the middle basin the widest expanse of sand occurs between the Edzin-gol and the range of Ala-shan. On the south it extends nearly as far as a line drawn through the towns of Lian-chow, Kan-chow and Kao-tai at the foot of the Nan-shan; but on the south it does not approach anything like so far as the latitude (42° N.) of the lake of Ghashiun-nor. Still farther east come the sandy deserts of Ordos, extending south-eastward as far as the mountain range which separates Ordos from the (Chinese) provinces of Shan-si and Shen-si. In the eastern basin drift-sand is encountered between the district of Ude in the north (44° 30′ N.) and the foot of the In-shan in the south." In two regions, if not in three, the sands have overwhelmed large tracts of once cultivated country, and even buried the cities in which men formerly dwelt. These regions are the southern parts of the desert of Takla-makan (where Sven Hedin and M. A. Stein[12] have discovered the ruins under the desert sands), along the N. foot of the Nan-shan, and probably in part (other agencies having helped) in the north of the desert of Lop, where Sven Hedin discovered the ruins of Loū-lan and of other towns or villages. For these vast accumulations of sand are constantly in movement; though the movement is slow, it has nevertheless been calculated that in the south of the Takla-makan the sand-dunes travel bodily at the rate of roughly something like 160 ft. in the course of a year. The shape and arrangement of the individual sand-dunes, and of the barkhans, generally indicate from which direction the predominant winds blow. On the windward side of the dune the slope is long and gentle, while the leeward side is steep and in outline concave like a horse-shoe. The dunes vary in height from 30 up to 300 ft., and in some places mount as it were upon one another's shoulders, and in some localities it is even said that a third tier is sometimes superimposed.

AUTHORITIES.—See N. M. Przhevalsky, *Mongolia, the Tangut Country, &c.* (Eng. trans., ed. by Sir H. Yule, London, 1876), and *From Kulja across the Tian Shan to Lob Nor* (Eng. trans, by Delmar Morgan, London, 1879); G. N. Potanin, *Tangutsko-Tibetskaya Okraina Kitaya i Centralnaya Mongoliya, 1884-1886* (1893, &c.); M. V. Pjevtsov, *Sketch of a Journey to Mongolia* (in Russian, Omsk, 1691883); G. E. Grum-Grzhimailo, *Opisanie Puteshestviya v Sapadniy Kitai* (1898-1899); V. A. Obruchev, *Centralnaya Asiya, Severniy Kitai i Nan-schan, 1892-1894*(1900-1901); V. I. Roborovsky and P. K. Kozlov, *Trudy Ekspeditsiy Imp. Russ. Geog. Obshchestva Po Centralnoy Asiy, 1893-*

75

1895 (1900, &c.); Roborovsky, *Trudy Tibetskoi Ekspeditsiy, 1889-1890*; Sven Hedin, *Scientific Results of a Journey in Central Asia, 1899-1902* (6 vols., 1905-1907); Futterer, *Durch Asien* (1901, &c.); K. Bogdanovich, *Geologicheskiya Isledovaniya v Vostochnom Turkestane* and *Trudiy Tibetskoy Ekspeditsiy, 1889-1890*; L. von Loczy, *Die wissenschaftlichen Ergebnisse der Reise des Grafen Széchenyi in Ostasien, 1877-1880* (1883); Ney Elias, in *Journ. Roy. Geog. Soc.* (1873); C. W. Campbell's "Journeys in Mongolia," in *Geographical Journal* (Nov. 1903); Pozdnievym,*Mongolia and the Mongols* (in Russian, St Petersburg, 1897 &c.); Deniker's summary of Kozlov's latest journeys in *La Géographie* (1901, &c.); F. von Richthofen, *China* (1877).

(J. T. BE.)

1Cf. G. E. Grum-Grzhimailo, *Opisaniye Puteshestviya*, i. 381-417.
2Quoted in Sven Hedin, *Scientific Results*, ii. 499.
3*Op. cit.* ii. 499-500.
4Przhevalsky, *Iz Zayana cherez Hami v Tibet na Vershovya Shaltoy Reki*, pp. 84-91.
5Futterer, *Durch Asien*, i. pp. 206-211.
6G. E. Grum-Grzhimailo, *Opisanie Puteshestviya v Sapadniy Kitai*, ii. p. 127.
7Its seeds are pounded by the Mongols to flour and mixed with their tea.
8Przhevalsky, *Mongolia* (Eng. trans. ed. by Sir H. Yule).
9Przhevalsky, *op. cit.* p. 183.
10Obruchev. in *Izvestia* of Russ. Geogr. Soc. (1895).
11In *Tangutsko-Tibetskaya Okraina Kitaya i Centralnaya Mongoliya*, i. pp. 96, &c.
12See *Sand-buried Cities of Khotan* (London, 1902).

GOBLET, RENÉ (1828-1905), French politician, was born at Aire-sur-la-Lys, in the Pas de Calais, on the 26th of November 1828, and was educated for the law. Under the Second Empire, he helped to found a Liberal journal, *Le Progrès de la Somme*, and in July 1871 was sent by the department of the Somme to the National Assembly, where he took his place on the extreme left. He failed to secure election in 1876, but next year was returned for Amiens. He held a minor government office in 1879, and in 1882 became minister of the interior in the Freycinet cabinet. He was minister of education, fine arts and religion in Henri Brisson's first cabinet in 1885, and again under Freycinet in 1886, when he greatly increased his reputation by an able defence of the government's education proposals. Meanwhile his extreme independence and excessive candour had alienated him from many of his party, and all through his life he was frequently in conflict with his political associates, from Gambetta downwards. On the fall of the Freycinet cabinet in December he formed a cabinet in which he reserved for himself the portfolios of the interior and of religion. The Goblet cabinet was unpopular from the outset, and it was with difficulty that anybody could be found to accept the ministry of foreign affairs, which was finally given to M. Flourens. Then came what is known as the Schnaebele incident, the arrest on the German frontier of a French official named Schnaebele, which caused immense excitement in France. For some days Goblet took no definite decision, but left Flourens, who stood for peace, to fight it out with General Boulanger, then minister of war, who was for the despatch of an ultimatum. Although he finally intervened on the side of Flourens, and peace was preserved, his weakness in face of the Boulangist propaganda became a national danger. Defeated on the budget in May 1887, his government resigned; but he returned to office next year as foreign minister in the radical administration of Charles Floquet. He was defeated at the polls by a Boulangist candidate in 1889, and sat in the senate from 1891 to 1893, when he returned to the popular chamber. In association with MM. E. Lockroy, Ferdinand Sarrien and P. L. Peytral he drew up a republican programme which they put forward in the *Petite République française*. At the elections of 1898 he was defeated, and thenceforward took little part in public affairs. He died in Paris on the 13th of September 1905.

GOBLET, a large type of drinking-vessel, particularly one shaped like a cup, without handles, and mounted on a shank with a foot. The word is derived from the O. Fr. *gobelet*, diminutive of *gobel*, *gobeau*, which Skeat takes to be formed from Low Lat. *cupellus*, cup, diminutive of *cupa*, tub, cask (see DRINKING-VESSELS).

GOBY. The gobies (*Gobius*) are small fishes readily recognized by their ventrals (the fins on the lower surface of the chest) being united into one fin, forming a suctorial disk, by which these fishes are enabled to attach themselves in every possible position to a rock or other firm substances. They are essentially coast-fishes, inhabiting nearly all seas, but disappearing towards the Arctic and Antarctic Oceans. Many enter, or live exclusively in, such fresh waters as are at no great distance from the sea. Nearly 500 different kinds are known. The largest British species, *Gobius capito*, occurring in the rock-pools of Cornwall, measures 10 in. *Gobius alcocki*, from brackish and fresh waters of Lower Bengal, is one of the very smallest of fishes, not measuring over 16 millimetres (= 7 lines). The males are usually more brilliantly coloured than the females, and guard the eggs, which are often placed in a sort of nest made of the shell of some bivalve or of the carapace of a crab, with the convexity turned upwards and covered with sand, the eggs being stuck to the inner surface of this roof.

FIG. 1.—*Gobius lentiginosus.*

FIG. 2.— United Ventrals of Goby.

FIG. 3.—*Periophthalmus koelreuteri.*

Close allies of the gobies are the walking fish or jumping fish (*Periophthalmus*), of which various species are found in great numbers on the mud flats at the mouths of rivers in the tropics, skipping about by means of the muscular, scaly base of their pectoral fins, with the head raised and bearing a pair of strongly projecting versatile eyes close together.

GOCH, a town of Germany, in the Prussian Rhine province, on the Niers, 8 m. S. of Cleves at the junction of the railways Cologne-Zevenaar and Boxtel-Wesel. Pop. (1905) 10,232. It has a Protestant and a Roman Catholic church and manufactures of brushes, plush goods, cigars and margarine. In the middle ages it was the seat of a large trade in linen. Goch became a town in 1231 and belonged to the dukes of Gelderland and later to the dukes of Cleves.

GOD, the common Teutonic word for a personal object of religious worship. It is thus, like the Gr. θεός and Lat. *deus*, applied to all those superhuman beings of the heathen mythologies who exercise power over nature and man and are often identified with some particular sphere of activity; and also to the visible material objects, whether an image of the supernatural being or a tree, pillar, &c. used as a symbol, an idol. The word "god," on the conversion of the Teutonic races to Christianity, was adopted as the name of the one Supreme Being, the Creator of the universe, and of the Persons of the Trinity. The *New English Dictionary* points out that whereas the old Teutonic type of the word is neuter, corresponding to the Latin *numen*, in the Christian applications it becomes masculine, and that even where the earlier neuter form is still kept, as in Gothic and Old Norwegian, the construction is masculine. Popular etymology has connected the word with "good"; this is exemplified by the corruption of "God be with you" into "good-bye." "God" is a word common to all Teutonic languages. In Gothic it is *Guth*; Dutch has the same form as English; Danish and Swedish have *Gud*, German *Gott*. According to the *New English Dictionary*, the original may be found in two Aryan roots, both of the form *gheu*, one of which means "to invoke," the other "to pour" (cf. Gr. χέειν; the last is used of sacrificial offerings. The word would thus mean the object either of religious invocation or of religious worship by sacrifice. It has been also suggested that the word might mean a "molten image" from the sense of "pour."

See RELIGION; HEBREW RELIGION; THEISM, &c.

GODALMING, a market-town and municipal borough in the Guildford parliamentary division of Surrey, England, 34 m. S.W. of London by the London & South-Western railway. Pop. (1901) 8748. It is beautifully situated on the right bank of the Wey, 170which is navigable thence to the Thames, and on the high road between London and Portsmouth. Steep hills, finely wooded, enclose the valley. The chief public buildings are the church of SS. Peter and Paul, a cruciform building of mixed architecture, but principally Early English and Perpendicular; the town-hall, Victoria hall, and market-house, and a technical institute and school of science and art. Charterhouse School, one of the principal English public schools, originally founded in 1611, was transferred from Charterhouse Square, London, to Godalming in 1872. It stands within grounds 92 acres in extent, half a mile north of Godalming, and consists of spacious buildings in Gothic style, with a chapel, library and hall, besides boarding-houses, masters' houses and sanatoria.

(SeeCHARTERHOUSE.) Godalming has manufactures of paper, leather, parchment and hosiery, and some trade in corn, malt, bark, hoops and timber; and the Bargate stone, of which the parish church is built, is still quarried. The borough is under a mayor, 6 aldermen and 18 councillors. Area, 812 acres.

Godalming (Godelminge) belonged to King Alfred, and was a royal manor at the time of Domesday. The manor belonged to the see of Salisbury in the middle ages, but reverted to the crown in the time of Henry VIII. Godalming was incorporated by Elizabeth in 1574, when the borough originated. The charter was confirmed by James I. in 1620, and a fresh charter was granted by Charles II. in 1666. The borough was never represented in parliament. The bishop of Salisbury in 1300 received the grant of a weekly market to be held on Mondays: the day was altered to Wednesday by Elizabeth's charter. The bishop's grant included a fair at the feast of St Peter and St Paul (29th of June). Another fair at Candlemas (2nd of February) was granted by Elizabeth. The market is still held. The making of cloth, particularly Hampshire kerseys, was the staple industry of Godalming in the middle ages, but it began to decay early in the 17th century and by 1850 was practically extinct. As in other cases, dyeing was subsidiary to the cloth industry. Tanning, introduced in the 15th century, survives. The present manufacture of fleecy hosiery dates from the end of the 18th century.

GODARD, BENJAMIN LOUIS PAUL (1849-1895); French composer, was born in Paris, on the 18th of August 1849. He studied at the Conservatoire, and competed for the Prix de Rome without success in 1866 and 1867. He began by publishing a number of songs, many of which are charming, such as "Je ne veux pas d'autres choses," "Ninon," "Chanson de Florian," also a quantity of piano pieces, some chamber music, including several violin sonatas, a trio for piano and strings, a quartet for strings, a violin concerto and a second work of the same kind entitled "Concerto Romantique." Godard's chance arrived in the year 1878, when with his dramatic cantata, *Le Tasse,* he shared with M. Théodore Dubois the honour of winning the musical competition instituted by the city of Paris. From that time until his death Godard composed a surprisingly large number of works, including four operas, *Pedro de Zalamea,* produced at Antwerp in 1884; *Jocelyn,* given in Paris at the Théâtre du Château d'Eau, in 1888; *Dante,* played at the Opéra Comique two years later; and *La Vivandière,* left unfinished and partly scored by another hand. This last work was heard at the Opéra Comique in 1895, and has been played in England by the Carl Rosa Opera Company. His other works include the "Symphonie légendaire," "Symphonie gothique," "Diane" and various orchestral works. Godard's productivity was enormous, and his compositions are, for this reason only, decidedly unequal. He was at his best in works of smaller dimensions, and has left many exquisite songs. Among his more ambitious works the "Symphonie légendaire" may be singled out as being one of the most distinctive. He had a decided individuality, and his premature death at Cannes on the 10th of January 1895 was a loss to French art.

GODAVARI, a river of central and western India. It flows across the Deccan from the Western to the Eastern Ghats; its total length is 900 m., the estimated area of its drainage basin, 112,200 sq. m. Its traditional source is on the side of a hill behind the village of Trimbak in Nasik district, Bombay, where the water runs into a reservoir from the lips of an image. But according to popular legend it proceeds from the same ultimate source as the Ganges, though underground. Its course is generally south-easterly. After passing through Nasik district, it crosses into the dominions of the nizam of Hyderabad. When it again strikes British territory it is joined by the Pranhita, with its tributaries the Wardha, the Penganga and Wainganga. For some distance it flows between the nizam's dominions and the Upper Godavari district, and receives the Indravati, the Tal and the Sabari. The stream has here a channel varying from 1 to 2 m. in breadth, occasionally broken by alluvial islands. Parallel to the river stretch long ranges of hills. Below the junction of the Sabari the channel begins to contract. The flanking hills gradually close in on both sides, and the result is a magnificent gorge only 200 yds. wide through which the water flows into the plain of the delta, about 60 m. from the sea. The head of the delta is at the village of Dowlaishweram, where the main stream is crossed by the irrigation anicut. The river has seven mouths, the largest being the Gautami Godavari. The Godavari is regarded as peculiarly sacred, and once every twelve years the great bathing festival called *Pushkaram* is held on its banks at Rajahmundry.

The upper waters of the Godavari are scarcely utilized for irrigation, but the entire delta has been turned into a garden of perennial crops by means of the anicut at Dowlaishweram, constructed by Sir Arthur Cotton, from which three main canals are drawn off. The river channel here is 3½ m. wide. The anicut is a substantial mass of stone, bedded in lime cement, about 2¼ m. long, 130 ft. broad at the base, and 12 ft. high. The stream is thus pent back so as to supply a volume of 3000 cubic ft. of water per second during its low season, and 12,000 cubic ft. at time of flood. The main canals have a total length of 493 m., irrigating 662,000 acres, and all navigable; and there are 1929 m. of distributary channels. In 1864 water-communication was opened between the deltas of the Godavari and Kistna. Rocky barriers and rapids obstruct navigation in the upper portion of the Godavari. Attempts have been made to construct canals round these barriers with little success, and the undertaking has been abandoned.

GODAVARI, a district of British India, in the north-east of the Madras presidency. It was remodelled in 1907-1908, when part of it was transferred to Kistna district. Its present area is 5634 sq. m. Its territory now lies mainly east of the Godavari river, including the entire delta, with a long narrow strip extending up its valley. The apex of the delta is at Dowlaishweram, where a great dam renders the waters available for irrigation. Between this point and the coast there is a vast extent of rice fields. Farther inland, and enclosing the valley of the great river, are low hills, steep and forest-clad. The north-eastern part, known as the Agency tract, is occupied by spurs of the Eastern Ghats. The coast is low, sandy and swampy, the sea very shallow, so that vessels must lie nearly 5 m. from Cocanada, the chief port. The Sabari is the principal tributary of the Godavari within the district. The Godavari often rises in destructive floods. The population of the present area in 1901 was 1,445,961. In the old district the increase during the last decade was 11%. The chief towns are Cocanada and Rajahmundry. The forests are of great value; coal is known, and graphite is worked. The population is principally occupied in agriculture, the principal crops being rice, oil-seeds, tobacco and sugar. The cigars known in England as Lunkas are partly made from tobacco grown on *lankas* or islands in the river Godavari. Sugar (from the juice of the palmyra palm) and rum are made by European processes at Samalkot. The administrative headquarters are now at Cocanada, the chief seaport; but Rajahmundry, at the head of the delta, is the old capital. A large but decreasing trade is conducted at Cocanada, rice being shipped to Mauritius and Ceylon, and cotton and oil-seeds to Europe. Rice-cleaning mills have been established here and at other places. The district is traversed by the main line of the East Coast railway, with a branch to Cocanada; the iron girder bridge of forty-two spans over the 171 Godavari river near Rajahmundry was opened in 1900. There is a government college at Rajahmundry, with a training college attached, and an aided college at Cocanada.

The Godavari district formed part of the Andhra division of Dravida, the north-west portion being subject to the Orissa kings, and the south-western belonging to the Vengi kingdom. For centuries it was the battlefield on which various chiefs fought for independence with varying success till the beginning of the 16th century, when the whole country may be said to have passed under Mahommedan power. At the conclusion of the struggle with the French in the Carnatic, Godavari with the Northern Circars was conquered by the English, and finally ceded by imperial *sanad* in 1765. The district was constituted in 1859, by the redistribution of the territory comprising the former districts of Guntur, Rajahmundry and Masulipatam, into what are now the Kistna and Godavari districts.

See H. Morris, *District Manual* (1878); *District Gazetteer* (1906).

GODEFROY (GOTHOFREDUS), a French noble family, which numbered among its members several distinguished jurists and historians. The family claimed descent from Symon Godefroy, who was born at Mons about 1320 and was lord of Sapigneulx near Berry-au-bac, now in the department of Aisne.

DENIS GODEFROY (Dionysius Gothofredus) (1549-1622), jurist, son of Léon Godefroy, lord of Guignecourt, was born in Paris on the 17th of October 1549. He was educated at the Collège de Navarre, and studied law at Louvain, Cologne and Heidelberg, returning to Paris in 1573. He embraced the reformed religion, and in 1579 left Paris, where his abilities and connexions promised a brilliant career, to establish himself at Geneva. He became professor of law there, received the freedom of the city in 1580; and in 1587 became a member of the Council of the Two Hundred. Henry IV. induced him to return to France by making him *grand bailli* of Gex, but no sooner had he installed himself than the town was sacked and his library burnt by the troops of the duke of Savoy. In 1591 he became professor of Roman law at Strassburg, where he remained until April 1600, when in response to an invitation from Frederick IV., elector palatine, he removed to Heidelberg. The difficulties of his position led to his return to Strassburg for a short time, but in November 1604 he definitely settled at Heidelberg. He was made head of the faculty of law in the university, and was from time to time employed on missions to the French court. His repeated refusal of offers of advancement in his own country was due to his Calvinism. He died at Strassburg on the 7th of September 1622, having left Heidelberg before the city was sacked by the imperial troops in 1621. His most important work was the *Corpus juris civilis*, originally published at Geneva in 1583, which went through some twenty editions, the most valuable of them being that printed by the Elzevirs at Amsterdam in 1633 and the Leipzig edition of 1740.

Lists of his other learned works may be found in Senebier's *Hist. litt. de Genève*, vol. ii., and in Nicéron's *Mémoires*, vol. xvii. Some of his correspondence with his learned friends, with his kinsman President de Thou, Isaac Casaubon, Jean Jacques Grynaeus and others, is preserved in the libraries of the British Museum, of Basel and Paris.

His eldest son, THEODORE GODEFROY (1580-1649), was born at Geneva on the 14th of July 1580. He abjured Calvinism, and was called to the bar in Paris. He became historiographer of France in 1613, and was employed from time to time on diplomatic missions. He was employed at the congress of Münster, where he remained after the signing of peace in 1648 as chargé d'affaires until his death on the 5th of October of the next year. His most important work is *Le Cérémonial de France* ... (1619), a work which became a classic on the subject of royal ceremonial, and was re-edited by his son in an enlarged edition in 1649.

Besides his printed works he made vast collections of historical material which remains in MS. and fills the greater part of the Godefroy collection of over five hundred portfolios in the Library of the Institute in Paris. These were catalogued by Ludovic Lalanne in the *Annuaire Bulletin* (1865-1866 and 1892) of the *Société de l'histoire de France*.

The second son of Denis, JACQUES GODEFROY (1587-1652), jurist, was born at Geneva on the 13th of September 1587. He was sent to France in 1611, and studied law and history at Bourges and Paris. He remained faithful to the Calvinist persuasion, and soon returned to Geneva, where he became active in public affairs. He was secretary of state from 1632 to 1636, and syndic or chief magistrate in 1637, 1641, 1645 and 1649. He died on the 23rd of June 1652. In addition to his civic and political work he lectured on law, and produced, after thirty years of labour, his edition of the *Codex Theodosianus*. This code formed the principal, though not the only, source of the legal systems of the countries formed from the Western Empire. Godefroy's edition was enriched with a multitude of important notes and historical comments, and became a standard authority on the decadent period of the Western Empire. It was only printed thirteen years after his death under the care of his friend Antoine Marville at Lyons (4 vols. 1665), and was reprinted at Leipzig (6 vols.) in 1736-1745. Of his numerous other works the most important was the reconstruction of the twelve tables of early Roman law.

See also the dictionary of Moreri, Nicéron's *Mémoires* (vol. 17) and a notice in the *Bibliothèque universelle de Genève* (Dec. 1837).

DENIS GODEFROY (1615-1681), eldest son of Théodore, succeeded his father as historiographer of France, and re-edited various chronicles which had been published by him. He was entrusted by Colbert with the care and investigation of the records concerning the Low Countries preserved at Lille, where great part of his life was spent. He was also the historian of the reigns of Charles VII. and Charles VIII.

Other members of the family who attained distinction in the same branch of learning were the two sons of Denis Godefroy—Denis (1653-1719), also an historian, and Jean, sieur d'Aumont (1656-1732), who edited the letters of Louis XII., the memoirs of Marguerite de Valois, of Castelnau and Pierre de l'Estoile, and left some useful material for the history of the Low Countries; Jean Baptiste Achille Godefroy, sieur de Maillart (1697-1759), and Denis Joseph Godefroy, sieur de Maillart (1740-1819), son and grandson of Jean Godefroy, who were both officials at Lille, and left valuable historical documents which have remained in MS.

For further details see *Les Savants Godefroy* (Paris, 1873) by the marquis de Godefroy-Ménilglaise, son of Denis Joseph Godefroy.

GODESBERG, a spa of Germany, in the Prussian Rhine province, on the left bank of the Rhine, almost opposite Königswinter, and 4 m. S. of Bonn, on the railway to Coblenz. It is a fashionable summer resort, and contains numerous pretty villas, the residences of merchants from Cologne, Elberfeld, Crefeld and other Rhenish manufacturing centres. It has an Evangelical and three Roman Catholic churches, a synagogue and several educational establishments. Its chalybeate springs annually attract a large number of visitors, and the pump-room, baths and public grounds are arranged on a sumptuous scale. On a conical basalt hill, close by, are the ruins, surmounted by a picturesque round tower, of Godesberg castle. Built by Archbishop Dietrich I. of Cologne in the 13th century, it was destroyed by the Bavarians in 1583.

See Dennert, *Godesberg, eine Perle des Rheins* (Godesberg, 1900).

GODET, FRÉDÉRIC LOUIS (1812-1900), Swiss Protestant theologian, was born at Neuchâtel on the 25th of October 1812. After studying theology at Neuchâtel, Bonn and Berlin, he was in 1850 appointed professor of theology at Neuchâtel. From 1851 to 1866 he also held a pastorate. In 1873 he became one of the founders of the free Evangelical Church of Neuchâtel, and professor in its theological faculty. He died there on the 29th of October 1900. A conservative scholar, Godet was the author of some of the most noteworthy French commentaries published in recent times.

His commentaries are on the Gospel of St John (2 vols., 1863-1865; 3rd ed., 1881-1888; Eng. trans. 1886, &c.); St Luke (2 vols., 1871; 3rd ed., 1888; Eng. trans. 1875, &c.); the Epistle to the Romans (2 vols., 1879-1880; 2nd ed., 1883-1890; Eng. trans., 1880, &c.); Corinthians (2 vols., 1886-1887; Eng. trans. 1886, &c.). His other 172works include *Études bibliques* (2 vols., 1873-1874; 4th ed., 1889; Eng. trans. 1875 f.), and*Introduction au Nouveau Testament* (1893 f.; Eng. trans., 1894, &c.); *Lectures in Defence of the Christian Faith* (Eng. trans. 4th ed., 1900).

GODFREY, SIR EDMUND BERRY (1621-1678), English magistrate and politician, younger son of Thomas Godfrey (1586-1664), a member of an old Kentish family, was born on the 23rd of December 1621. He was educated at Westminster school and at Christ Church, Oxford, and after entering Gray's Inn became a dealer in wood. His business prospered. He was made a justice of the peace for the city of Westminster, and in September 1666 was knighted as a reward for his services as magistrate and citizen during the great plague in London; but in 1669 he was imprisoned for a few days for instituting the arrest of the king's physician, Sir Alexander Fraizer (d. 1681), who owed him money. The tragic events in Godfrey's life began in September 1678 when Titus Oates and two other men appeared before him with written information about the *Popish Plot*, and swore to the truth of their statements. During the intense excitement which followed the magistrate expressed a fear that his life was in danger, but took no extra precautions for safety. On the 12th of October he did not return home as usual, and on the 17th his body was found on Primrose Hill, Hampstead. Medical and other evidence made it certain that he had been murdered, and the excited populace regarded the deed as the work of the Roman Catholics. Two committees investigated the occurrence without definite result, but in December 1678 a certain Miles Prance, who had been arrested for conspiracy, confessed that he had shared in the murder. According to Prance the deed was instigated by some Roman Catholic priests, three of whom witnessed the murder, and was committed in the courtyard of Somerset House, where Godfrey was strangled by Robert Green, Lawrence Hill and Henry Berry, the body being afterwards taken to Hampstead. The three men were promptly arrested; the evidence of the informer William Bedloe, although contradictory, was similar on a few points to that of Prance, and in February 1679 they were hanged. Soon afterwards, however, some doubt was cast upon this story; a war of words ensued between Prance and others, and it was freely asserted that Godfrey had committed suicide. Later the falsehood of Prance's confession was proved and Prance pleaded guilty to perjury; but the fact remains that Godfrey was murdered. Godfrey was an excellent magistrate, and was very charitable both in public and in private life. Mr John Pollock, in the *Popish Plot* (London, 1903), confirms the view that the three men, Green, Hill and Berry, were wrongfully executed, and thinks the murder was committed by some Jesuits aided by Prance. Godfrey was feared by the Jesuits because he knew, through Oates, that on the 24th of April 1678 a Jesuit congregation had met at the residence of the duke of York to concert plans for the king's murder. He concludes thus: "The success of Godfrey's murder as a political move is indubitable. The duke of York was the pivot of the Roman Catholic scheme in England, and Godfrey's death saved both from utter ruin." On the other hand Mr Alfred Marks in his *Who killed Sir E. B. Godfrey?* (1905) maintains that suicide was the cause of Godfrey's death.

See the article OATES, TITUS, also R. Tuke, *Memoirs of the Life and Death of Sir Edmondbury Godfrey* (London, 1682); and G. Burnet, *History of my Own Time; The Reign of Charles II.*, edited by O. Airy (Oxford, 1900).

GODFREY OF BOUILLON (*c.* 1060-1100), a leader in the First Crusade, was the second son of Eustace II., count of Boulogne, by his marriage with Ida, daughter of Duke Godfrey II. of Lower Lorraine. He was designated by Duke Godfrey as his successor; but the emperor Henry IV. gave him only the mark of Antwerp, in which the lordship of Bouillon was included (1076). He fought for Henry, however, both on the Elster and in the siege of Rome; and he was invested in 1082 with the duchy of Lower Lorraine. Lorraine had been penetrated by Cluniac influences, and Godfrey would seem to have been a man of notable piety. Accordingly, though he had himself served as an imperialist, and though the Germans in general had little sympathy with the Crusaders (*subsannabant ... quasi delirantes*), Godfrey, nevertheless, when the call came "to follow Christ," almost literally sold all that he had, and followed. Along with his brothers Eustace and Baldwin (the future Baldwin I. of Jerusalem) he led a German contingent, some 40,000 strong, along "Charlemagne's road," through Hungary to Constantinople, starting in August 1096, and arriving at Constantinople, after some difficulties in Hungary, in November. He was the first of the crusading princes to arrive, and on him fell the duty of deciding what the relations of the princes to the eastern emperor Alexius were to be. Eventually, after several disputes and some fighting, he did homage to Alexius in January 1097; and his example was followed by the other princes. From this time until the beginning of 1099 Godfrey appears as one of the minor princes, plodding onwards, and steadily fighting, while men like Bohemund and Raymund, Baldwin and Tancred were determining the course of events.

In 1099 he came once more to the front. The mass of the crusaders became weary of the political factions which divided some of their leaders; and Godfrey, who was more of a pilgrim than a politician, becomes the natural representative of this feeling. He was thus able to force the reluctant Raymund to march southward to Jerusalem; and he took a prominent part in the siege, his division being the first to enter when the city was captured. It was natural therefore that, when Raymund of Provence refused the offered dignity, Godfrey should be elected ruler of Jerusalem (July 22, 1099). He assumed the title not of king, but of "advocate"1 of the Holy Sepulchre. The new dignity proved still more onerous than honourable; and during his short reign of a year Godfrey had to combat the Arabs of Egypt, and the opposition of Raymund and the patriarch Dagobert. He was successful In repelling the Egyptian attack at the battle of Ascalon (August 1099); but he failed, owing to Raymund's obstinacy and greed, to acquire the town of Ascalon after the battle. Left alone, at the end of the autumn, with an army of some 2000 men, Godfrey was yet able, in the spring of 1100, probably with the aid of new pilgrims, to exact tribute from towns like Acre, Ascalon, Arsuf and Caesarea. But already, at the end of 1099 Dagobert, archbishop of Pisa, had been substituted as patriarch for Arnulf (who had been acting as vicar) by the influence of Bohemund; and Dagobert, whose vassal Godfrey had at once piously acknowledged himself, seems to have forced him to an agreement in April 1100, by which he promised Jerusalem and Jaffa to the patriarch, in case he should acquire in their place Cairo or some other town, or should die without issue. Thus were the foundations of a theocracy laid in Jerusalem; and when Godfrey died (July 1100) he left the question to be decided, whether a theocracy or a monarchy should be the government of the Holy Land.

Because he had been the first ruler in Jerusalem Godfrey was idolized in later saga. He was depicted as the leader of the crusades, the king of Jerusalem, the legislator who laid down the assizes of Jerusalem. He was none of these things. Bohemund was the leader of the crusades; Baldwin was first king; the assizes were the result of a gradual development. In still other ways was the figure of Godfrey idealized by the grateful tradition of later days; but in reality he would seem to have been a quiet, pious, hard-fighting knight, who was chosen to rule in Jerusalem because he had no dangerous qualities, and no obvious defects.

LITERATURE.—The narrative of Albert of Aix may be regarded as presenting the Lotharingian point of view, as the *Gesta* presents the Norman, and Raymund of Agiles the Provençal. The career of Godfrey has been discussed in modern times by R. Röhricht, *Die Deutschen im heiligen Lande*, Band ii., and *Geschichte des ersten Kreuzzuges, passim* (Innsbruck, 1901).

(E. BR.)

Romances.—Godfrey was the principal hero of two French *chansons de geste* dealing with the Crusade, the *Chanson d'Antioche* (ed. P. Paris, 2 vols., 1848) and the *Chanson de Jérusalem* (ed. C. Hippeau, 1868), and other poems, containing less historical 173material, were subsequently added. In addition the parentage and early exploits of Godfrey were made the subject of legend. His grandfather was said to be Helias, knight of the Swan, one of the brothers whose adventures are well known, though with some variation, in the familiar fairy tale of "The Seven Swans." Helias, drawn by the swan, one day disembarked at Nijmwegen, and reconquered her territory for the duchess of Bouillon. Marrying her daughter he exacted a promise that his wife should not inquire into his origin. The tale, which is almost identical with the Lohengrin legend, belongs to the class of the Cupid and Psyche narratives. See LOHENGRIN.

See also C. Hippeau, *Le Chevalier au cygne* (Paris, 2 vols., 1874-1877); H. Pigeonneau, *Le Cycle de la croisade et de la famille de Bouillon*(1877); W. Golther, "Lohengrin," in *Roman. Forsch.* (vol. v., 1889); *Hist. litt. de la France*, vol. xxii. pp. 350-402; the English romance of*Helyas, Knyghte of the Swanne* was printed by W. Copland about 1550.

1An "advocate" was a layman who had been invested with part of an ecclesiastic estate, on condition that he defended the rest, and exercised the blood-ban in lieu of the ecclesiastical owner (see ADVOCATE, sec. *Advocatus ecclesiae*).

GODFREY OF VITERBO (*c.* 1120-*c.* 1196), chronicler, was probably an Italian by birth, although some authorities assert that he was a Saxon. He evidently passed some of his early life at Viterbo, where also he spent his concluding days, but he was educated at Bamberg, gaining a good knowledge of Latin. About 1140 he became chaplain to the German king, Conrad III.; but the greater part of his life was spent as secretary (*notarius*) in the service of the emperor

Frederick I., who appears to have thoroughly trusted him, and who employed him on many diplomatic errands. Incessantly occupied, he visited Sicily, France and Spain, in addition to many of the German cities, in the emperor's interests, and was by his side during several of the Italian campaigns. Both before and after Frederick's death in 1190 he enjoyed the favour of his son, the emperor Henry VI., for whom he wrote his *Speculum regum*, a work of very little value. Godfrey also wrote *Memoria seculorum*, or *Liber memorialis*, a chronicle dedicated to Henry VI., which professes to record the history of the world from the creation until 1185. It is written partly in prose and partly in verse. A revision of this work was drawn up by Godfrey himself as *Pantheon*, or *Universitatis libri qui chronici appellantur*. The author borrowed from Otto of Freising, but the earlier part of his chronicle is full of imaginary occurrences. *Pantheon* was first printed in 1559, and extracts from it are published by L. A. Muratori in the *Rerum Italicarum scriptores*, tome vii. (Milan, 1725). The only part of Godfrey's work which is valuable is the *Gesta Friderici I.*, verses relating events in the emperor's career from 1155 to 1180. Concerned mainly with affairs in Italy, the poem tells of the sieges of Milan, of Frederick's flight to Pavia in 1167, of the treaty with Pope Alexander III. at Venice, and of other stirring episodes with which the author was intimately acquainted, and many of which he had witnessed. Attached to the *Gesta Friderici* is the *Gesta Heinrici VI.*, a shorter poem which is often attributed to Godfrey, although W. Wattenbach and other authorities think it was not written by him. The *Memoria seculorum* was very popular during the middle ages, and has been continued by several writers.

Godfrey's works are found in the *Monumenta Germaniae historica*, Band xxii. (Hanover, 1872). The *Gesta Friderici I. et Heinrici VI.* is published separately with an introduction by G. Waitz (Hanover, 1872). See also H. Ulmann, *Gotfried von Viterbo* (Göttingen, 1863), and W. Wattenbach, *Deutschlands Geschichtsquellen*, Band ii. (Berlin, 1894).

(A. W. H.*)

GODHRA, a town of British India, administrative headquarters of the Panch Mahals district of Bombay, and also of the Rewa Kantha political agency; situated 52 m. N.E. of Baroda on the railway from Anand to Ratlam. Pop. (1901) 20,915. It has a trade in timber from the neighbouring forests.

GODIN, JEAN BAPTISTE ANDRÉ (1817-1888), French socialist, was born on the 26th of January 1817 at Esquehéries (Aisne). The son of an artisan, he entered an iron-works at an early age, and at seventeen made a tour of France as journeyman. Returning to Esquehéries in 1837, he started a small factory for the manufacture of castings for heating-stoves. The business increased rapidly, and for the purpose of railway facilities was transferred to Guise in 1846. At the time of Godin's death in 1888 the annual output was over four millions of francs (£160,000), and in 1908 the employees numbered over 2000 and the output was over £280,000. An ardent disciple of Fourier, he advanced a considerable sum of money towards the disastrous Fourierist experiment of V. P. Considérant (*q.v.*) in Texas. He profited, however, by its failure, and in 1859 started the *familistère* or community settlement of Guise on more carefully laid plans. It comprises, in addition to the workshops, three large buildings, four storeys high, capable of housing all the work-people, each family having two or three rooms. Attached to each building is a vast central court, covered with a glass roof, under which the children can play in all weathers. There are also crèches, nurseries, hospital, refreshment rooms and recreation rooms of various kinds, stores for the purchase of groceries, drapery and every necessity, and a large theatre for concerts and dramatic entertainments. In 1880 the whole was turned into a co-operative society, with provision by which it eventually became the property of the workers. In 1871 Godin was elected deputy for Aisne, but retired in 1876 to devote himself to the management of the *familistère*. In 1882 he was created a knight of the legion of honour.

Godin was the author of *Solutions sociales* (1871); *Les Socialistes et les droits du travail* (1874); *Mutualité sociale* (1880); *La République du travail et la réforme parlementaire* (1889). See Bernardot, *Le Familistère de Guise et son fondateur* (Paris, 1887); Fischer, *Die Familistère Godin's* (Berlin, 1890); Lestelle, *Étude sur le familistère de Guise* (Paris, 1904); D. F. P., *Le Familistère illustré, résultats de vingt ans d'association*, 1880-1900 (Eng. trans., *Twenty-eight years of co-partnership at Guise*, by A. Williams, 1908).

GODIVA, a Saxon lady, who, according to the legend, rode naked through the streets of Coventry to gain from her husband a remission of the oppressive toll imposed on his tenants. The story is that she was the beautiful wife of Leofric, earl of Mercia and lord of Coventry. The people of that city suffering grievously under the earl's oppressive taxation, Lady Godiva appealed again and again to her husband, who obstinately refused to remit the tolls. At last, weary of her entreaties, he said he would grant her request if she would ride naked through the streets of the town. Lady Godiva took him at his word, and after issuing a proclamation that all persons should keep within doors or shut their windows, she rode through, clothed only in her long hair. One person disobeyed her proclamation, a tailor, ever afterwards known as Peeping Tom. He bored a hole in his shutters that he might see Godiva pass, and is said to have been struck blind. Her husband kept his word and abolished the obnoxious taxes.

The oldest form of the legend makes Godiva pass through Coventry market from one end to the other when the people were assembled, attended only by two soldiers, her long hair down so that none saw her, "apparentibus cruribus tamen candidissimis." This version is given in *Flores historiarum* by Roger of Wendover, who quoted from an earlier writer. The later story, with its episode of Peeping Tom, has been evolved by later chroniclers. Whether the lady Godiva of this story is the Godiva or Godgifu of history is undecided. That a lady of this name existed in the early part of the 11th century is certain, as evidenced by several ancient documents, such as the Stow charter, the Spalding charter and the Domesday survey, though the spelling of the name varies considerably. It would appear from *Liber Eliensis* (end of 12th century) that she was a widow when Leofric married her in 1040. In or about that year she aided in the founding of a monastery at Stow, Lincolnshire. In 1043 she persuaded her husband to build and endow a Benedictine monastery at Coventry. Her mark, " Ego Godiva Comitissa diu istud desideravi," was found on the charter given by her brother, Thorold of Bucknall—sheriff of Lincolnshire—to the Benedictine monastery of Spalding in 1051; and she is commemorated as benefactress of other monasteries at Leominster, Chester, Wenlock, Worcester and Evesham. She probably died a few years before the Domesday survey (1085-1086), and was buried in one of the porches of the abbey church. Dugdale (1656) says that a window, with representations of Leofric and Godiva, was placed in Trinity Church, Coventry, about the time of Richard II. The Godiva procession, a commemoration of the legendary ride instituted on the 31st of May 1678 as part of Coventry fair, was celebrated at intervals until 1826. From 1848 to 1887 it was revived, and recently further attempts have been made to popularize the pageant. The wooden effigy of Peeping Tom which, since 1812, has looked out on the world from a house at the north-west corner of Hertford Street, Coventry, represents a man in armour, and was probably an image of St George. It was removed from another part of the town to its present position.

GODKIN, EDWIN LAWRENCE (1831-1902), American publicist, was born in Moyne, county Wicklow, Ireland, on the 2nd of October 1831. His father, James Godkin, was a Presbyterian minister and a journalist, and the son, after graduating in 1851 at Queen's College, Belfast, and studying law in London, was in 1853-1855 war correspondent for the London *Daily News* in Turkey and Russia, being present at the capture of Sevastopol, and late in 1856 went to America and wrote letters to the same journal, giving his impressions of a tour of the southern states of the American Union. He studied law in New York City, was admitted to the bar in 1859, travelled in Europe in 1860-1862, wrote for the London *News* and the New York *Times* in 1862-1865, and in 1865 founded in New York City the *Nation*, a weekly projected by him long before, for which Charles Eliot Norton gained friends in Boston and James Miller McKim (1810-1874) in Philadelphia, and which Godkin edited until the end of the year 1899. In 1881 he sold the *Nation* to the New York *Evening Post*, and became an associate editor of the *Post*, of which he was editor-in-chief in 1883-1899, succeeding Carl Schurz. In the 'eighties he engaged in a controversy with Goldwin Smith over the Irish question. Under his leadership the *Post* broke with the Republican party in the presidential campaign of 1884, when Godkin's opposition to Blaine did much to create the so-called Mugwump party (see MUGWUMP), and his organ became thoroughly independent, as was seen when it attacked the Venezuelan policy of President Cleveland, who had in so many ways approximated the ideal of the *Post* and *Nation*. He consistently advocated currency reform, the gold basis, a tariff for revenue only, and civil service reform, rendering the greatest aid to the last cause. His attacks on Tammany Hall were so frequent and so virulent that in 1894 he was sued for libel because of biographical sketches of certain leaders in that organization—cases which never came up for trial. His opposition to the war with Spain and to imperialism was able and forcible. He retired from his editorial duties on the 30th of December 1899, and sketched his career in the *Evening Post* of that date. Although he recovered from a severe apoplectic stroke early in 1900, his health was shattered, and he died in Greenway, Devonshire, England, on the 21st of May 1902. Godkin shaped the lofty and independent policy of the *Post* and the *Nation*, which had a small but influential and intellectual class of readers. But as editor he had none of the personal magnetism of Greeley, for instance, and his superiority to the influence of popular feeling made Charles Dudley Warner style the Nation the "weekly judgment day." He was an economist of the school of Mill, urged the necessity of the abstraction called "economic man," and insisted that socialism put in practice would not improve social and economic conditions in general. In politics he was an enemy of sentimentalism and loose theories in government. He published *A History of Hungary, A.D. 300-1850* (1856), *Government* (1871, in the American Science Series), *Reflections and Comments* (1895), *Problems of Modern Democracy* (1896) and *Unforeseen Tendencies of Democracy* (1898). See *Life and Letters of E. L. Godkin*, edited by Rollo Ogden (2 vols., New York, 1907).

GODMANCHESTER, a municipal borough in the southern, parliamentary division of Huntingdonshire, England, on the right bank of the Ouse, 1 m. S.S.E. of Huntingdon, on a branch of the Great Eastern railway. Pop. (1901) 2017. It has a beautiful Perpendicular church (St Mary's) and an agricultural trade, with flour mills. The town is governed by a mayor, 4 aldermen and 12 councillors. Area, 4907 acres.

A Romano-British village occupied the site of Godmanchester. The town (*Gumencestre, Gomecestre*) belonged to the king before the Conquest and at the time of the Domesday survey. In 1213 King John granted the manor to the men of the town at a fee-farm of £120 yearly, and confirmation charters were granted by several succeeding kings, Richard II. in 1391-1392 adding exemption from toll, pannage, &c. James I. granted an incorporation charter in 1605 under the title of bailiffs, assistants and commonalty, but under the Municipal Reform Act of 1835 the corporation was changed to a mayor, 4 aldermen and 12 councillors. Godmanchester was formerly included for parliamentary purposes in the borough of Huntingdon, which has ceased to be separately represented since 1885. The incorporation charter of 1605 recites that the burgesses are chiefly engaged in agriculture, and grants them a fair, which still continues every year on Tuesday in Easter week.

See *Victoria County History, Huntingdon*; Robert Fox, *The History of Godmanchester* (1831).

GÖDÖLLÖ, a market town of Hungary, in the county of Pest-Pilis-Solt-Kiskun, 23 m. N.E. of Budapest by rail. Pop. (1900) 5875. Gödöllö is the summer residence of the Hungarian royal family, and the royal castle, built in the second half of the 18th century by Prince Anton Grassalkovich, was, with the beautiful domain, presented by the Hungarian nation to King Francis Joseph I. after the coronation in 1867. In its park there are a great number of stags and wild boars. Gödöllö is a favourite summer resort of the inhabitants of Budapest. In its vicinity is the famous place of pilgrimage Mária-Besnyö, with a fine Franciscan monastery, which contains the tombs of the Grassalkovich family.

GODOLPHIN, SIDNEY GODOLPHIN, EARL OF (*c.* 1645-1712), was a cadet of an ancient family of Cornwall. At the Restoration he was introduced into the royal household by Charles II., with whom he had previously become a favourite, and he also at the same period entered the House of Commons as member for Helston. Although he very seldom addressed the House, and, when he did so, only in the briefest manner, he gradually acquired a reputation as its chief if not its only financial authority. In March 1679 he was appointed a member of the privy council, and in the September following he was promoted, along with Viscount Hyde (afterwards earl of Rochester) and the earl of Sunderland, to the chief management of affairs. Though he voted for the Exclusion Bill in 1680, he was continued in office after the dismissal of Sunderland, and in September 1684 he was created Baron Godolphin of Rialton, and succeeded Rochester as first lord of the treasury. After the accession of James II. he was made chamberlain to the queen, and, along with Rochester and Sunderland, enjoyed the king's special confidence. In 1687 he was named commissioner of the treasury. He was one of the council of five appointed by King James to represent him in London, when he went to join the army after the landing of William, prince of Orange, in England, and, along with Halifax and Nottingham, he was afterwards appointed a commissioner to treat with the prince. On the accession of William, though he only obtained the third seat at the treasury board, he had virtually the chief control of affairs. He retired in March 1690, but was recalled on the November following and appointed first lord. While holding this office he for several years continued, in conjunction with Marlborough, a treacherous intercourse with James II., and is said even to have anticipated Marlborough in disclosing to James intelligence regarding the intended expedition against Brest. Godolphin was not only a Tory by inheritance, but had a romantic admiration for the wife of James II. He also wished to be safe whatever happened, and his treachery in this case was mostly due to caution. After Fenwick's confession in 1696 regarding the attempted assassination of William III., Godolphin, who was compromised, was induced to tender his resignation; but when the Tories came into power in 1700, he was again appointed lord treasurer and retained office for about a year. Though not a favourite with Queen Anne, he was, after her accession, appointed to his old office, on the strong recommendation of Marlborough. He also in 1704 received the honour of knighthood, and in December 1751706 he was created Viscount Rialton and earl of Godolphin. Though a Tory he had an active share in the intrigues which gradually led to the predominance of the Whigs in alliance with Marlborough. The influence of the Marlboroughs with the queen was, however, gradually supplanted by that of Mrs Masham and Harley, earl of Oxford, and with the fortunes of the Marlboroughs those of Godolphin were indissolubly united. The services of both were so appreciated by the nation that they were able for a time to regard the loss of the queen's favour with indifference, and even in 1708 to procure the expulsion of Harley from office; but after the Tory reaction which followed the impeachment of Dr Sacheverel, who abused Godolphin under the name of Volpone, the queen made use of the opportunity to take the initiatory step towards delivering herself from the irksome thraldom of Marlborough by abruptly dismissing Godolphin from office on the 7th of August 1710. He died on the 15th of September 1712.

Godolphin owed his rise to power and his continuance in it under four sovereigns chiefly to his exceptional mastery of financial matters; for if latterly he was in some degree indebted for his promotion to the support of Marlborough, he received that support mainly because Marlborough recognized that for the prosecution of England's foreign wars his financial abilities were an indispensable necessity. He was cool, reserved and cautious, but his prudence was less associated with high sagacity than traceable to the weakness of his personal antipathies and prejudices, and his freedom from political predilections. Perhaps it was his unlikeness to Marlborough in that moral characteristic which so tainted Marlborough's greatness that rendered possible between them a friendship so intimate and undisturbed: he was, it would appear, exceptionally devoid of the passion of avarice; and so little advantage did he take of his opportunities of aggrandizement that, though his style of living was unostentatious,—and in connexion with his favourite pastimes of horse-racing, card-playing and cock-fighting he gained perhaps more than he lost,—all that he left behind him did not, according to the duchess of Marlborough, amount to more than £12,000.

Godolphin married Margaret Blagge, the pious lady whose life was written by Evelyn, on the 16th of May 1675, and married again after her death in 1678. His son and successor, Francis (1678-1766), held various offices at court, and was lord privy seal from 1735 to 1740. He married Henrietta Churchill (d. 1733), daughter of the duke of Marlborough, who in 1722 became in her own right duchess of Marlborough. He died without male issue in January 1766, when the earldom became extinct, and the estates passed to Thomas Osborne, 4th duke of Leeds, the husband of the earl's daughter Mary, whose descendant is the present representative of the Godolphins.

A life of Godolphin was published in 1888 in London by the Hon. H. Elliot.

GODOY, ALVAREZ DE FARIA, RIOS SANCHEZ Y ZARZOSA, MANUEL DE (1767-1851), duke of El Alcudia and prince of the Peace, Spanish royal favourite and minister, was born at Badajoz on the 12th of May 1767. His father, Don José de Godoy, was the head of a very ancient but impoverished family of nobles in Estremadura. His mother, whose maiden name was Maria Antonia Alvarez de Faria, belonged to a Portuguese noble family. Manuel boasts in his memoirs that he had the best masters, but it is certain that he received only the very slight education usually given at that time to the sons of provincial nobles. In 1784 he entered the Guardia de Corps, a body of gentlemen who acted as the immediate body-guard of the king. His well-built and stalwart person, his handsome foolish face, together with a certain geniality of character which he must have possessed, earned him the favour of Maria Luisa of Parma, the princess of Asturias, a coarse, passionate woman who was much neglected by her husband, who on his part cared for nothing but hunting.

When King Charles III. died in 1788, Godoy's fortune was soon made. The princess of Asturias, now queen, understood how to manage her husband Charles IV. Godoy says in his memoirs that the king, who had been carefully kept apart from affairs during his father's life, and who disliked his father's favourite minister Floridablanca, wished to have a creature of his own. This statement is no doubt true as far as it goes. But it requires to be completed by the further detail that the queen put her lover in her husband's way, and that the king was guided by them, when he thought he was ruling for himself through a subservient minister. In some respects King Charles was obstinate, and Godoy is probably right in saying that he never was an absolute "viceroy," and that he could not always secure the removal of colleagues whom he knew to be his enemies. He could only rule by obeying. Godoy adopted without scruple this method of pushing his fortunes. When the king was set on a particular course, he followed it; the execution was left to him and the queen. His pliability endeared him to his master, whose lasting affection he earned. In practice he commonly succeeded in inspiring the wishes which he then proceeded to gratify. From the very beginning of the new reign he was promoted in the army with scandalous rapidity, made duke of El Alcudia, and in 1792 minister under the premiership of Aranda, whom he succeeded in displacing by the close of the year.

His official life is fairly divided by himself into three periods. From 1792 to 1798 he was premier. In the latter year his unpopularity and the intrigues of the French government, which had taken a dislike to him, led to his temporary retirement, without, however, any diminution of the king's personal favour. He asserts that he had no wish to return to office, but letters sent by him to the queen show that he begged for employment. They are written in a very unpleasant mixture of gush and vulgar familiarity. In 1801 he returned to office, and until 1807 he was the executant of the disastrous policy of the court. The third period of his public life is the last year, 1807-1808, when he was desperately striving for his place between the aggressive intervention of Napoleon on the one hand, and the growing hatred of the nation, organized behind, and about, the prince of Asturias, Ferdinand. On the 17th of March 1808 a popular outbreak at Aranjuez drove him into hiding. When driven out by hunger and thirst he was recognized and arrested. By Ferdinand's order he was kept in prison, till Napoleon demanded that he should be sent to Bayonne. Here he rejoined his master and mistress. He remained with them till Charles IV. died at Rome in 1819, having survived his queen. The rest of Godoy's life was spent in poverty and obscurity. After the death of Ferdinand VII., in 1833, he returned to Madrid, and endeavoured to secure the restoration of his property confiscated in 1808. Part of it was the estate of the Soto de Roma, granted by the cortes to the duke of Wellington. He failed, and during his last years lived on a small pension granted him by Louis Philippe. He died in Paris on the 4th of October 1851.

As a favourite Godoy is remarkable for the length of his hold on the affection of his sovereigns, and for its completeness. Latterly he was supported rather by the husband than by the wife. He got rid of Aranda by adopting, in order to please the king, a policy which tended to bring on war with France. When the war proved disastrous, he made the peace of Basel, and was created prince of the Peace for his services. Then he helped to make war with England, and the disasters which followed only made him dearer to the king. Indeed it became a main object with Charles IV. to protect "Manuelito" from popular hatred, and if possible secure him a principality. The queen endured his infidelities to her, which were flagrant. The king arranged a marriage for him with Doña Teresa de Bourbon, daughter of the infante Don Luis by a morganatic marriage, though he was probably already married to Doña Josefa Tudó, and certainly continued to live with her. Godoy, in his memoirs, lays claim to have done much for Spanish agriculture and industry, but he did little more than issue proclamations and appoint officers. His intentions may have been good, but the policy of his government was financially ruinous. In his private life he was not only profligate and profuse, but childishly ostentatious. The best that can be said for him is that he was good-natured, and 176did his best to restrain the Inquisition and the purely reactionary parties.

AUTHORITIES.—Godoy's *Memoirs* were published in Spanish, English and French in 1836. A general account of his career will be found in the*Mémoires sur la Révolution d'Espagne*, by the Abbé de Pradt (1816).

GODROON, or GADROON (Fr. *godron*, of unknown etymology), in architecture, a convex decoration (said to be derived from raised work on linen) applied in France to varieties of the bead and reel, in which the bead is often carved with ornament. In England the term is constantly used by auctioneers to describe the raised convex decorations under the bowl of stone or terra-cotta vases. The godroons radiate from the vertical support of the vase and rise half-way up the bowl.

GODWIN, FRANCIS (1562-1633), English divine, son of Thomas Godwin, bishop of Bath and Wells, was born at Hannington, Northamptonshire, in 1562. He was elected student of Christ Church, Oxford, in 1578, took his bachelor's degree in 1580, and that of master in 1583. After holding two Somersetshire livings he was in 1587 appointed subdean of Exeter. In 1590 he accompanied William Camden on an antiquarian tour through Wales. He was created bachelor of divinity in 1593, and doctor in 1595. In 1601 he published his *Catalogue of the Bishops of England since the first planting of the Christian Religion in this Island*, a work which procured him in the same year the bishopric of Llandaff. A second edition appeared in 1615, and in 1616 he published an edition in Latin with a dedication to King James, who in the following year conferred upon him the bishopric of Hereford. The work was republished, with a continuation by William Richardson, in 1743. In 1616 Godwin published *Rerum Anglicarum, Henrico VIII., Edwardo VI. et Maria regnantibus, Annales*, which was afterwards translated and published by his son Morgan under the title *Annales of England* (1630). He is also the author of a somewhat remarkable story, published posthumously in 1638, and entitled *The Man in the Moone, or a Discourse of a Voyage thither, by Domingo Gonsales*, written apparently some time between the years 1599 and 1603. In this production Godwin not only declares himself a believer in the Copernican system, but adopts so far the principles of the law of gravitation as to suppose that the earth's attraction diminishes with the distance. The work, which displays considerable fancy and wit, was translated into French, and was imitated in several important particulars by Cyrano de Bergerac, from whom (if not from Godwin direct) Swift obtained valuable hints in writing of Gulliver's voyage to Laputa. Another work of Godwin's, *Nuncius inanimatus Utopiae*, originally published in 1629 and again in 1657, seems to have been the prototype of John Wilkins's *Mercury, or the Secret and Swift Messenger*, which appeared in 1641. He died, after a lingering illness, in April 1633.

GODWIN, MARY WOLLSTONECRAFT (1759-1797), English miscellaneous writer, was born at Hoxton, on the 27th of April 1759. Her family was of Irish extraction, and Mary's grandfather, who was a respectable manufacturer in Spitalfields, realized the property which his son squandered. Her mother, Elizabeth Dixon, was Irish, and of good family. Her father, Edward John Wollstonecraft, after dissipating the greater part of his patrimony, tried to earn a living by farming, which only plunged him into deeper difficulties, and he led a wandering, shifty life. The family roamed from Hoxton to Edmonton, to Essex, to Beverley in Yorkshire, to Laugharne, Pembrokeshire, and back to London again.

After Mrs Wollstonecraft's death in 1780, soon followed by her husband's second marriage, the three daughters, Mary, Everina and Eliza, sought to earn their own livelihood. The sisters were all clever women—Mary and Eliza far above the average—but their opportunities of culture had been few. Mary, the eldest, went in the first instance to live with her friend Fanny Blood, a girl of her own age, whose father, like Wollstonecraft, was addicted to drink and dissipation. As long as she lived with the Bloods, Mary helped Mrs Blood to earn money by taking in needlework, while Fanny painted in watercolours. Everina went to live with her brother Edward, and Eliza made a hasty and, as it proved, unhappy marriage with a Mr Bishop. A legal separation was afterwards obtained, and the sisters, together with Fanny Blood, took a house, first at Islington, afterwards at Newington Green, and opened a school, which was carried on with indifferent success for nearly two years. During their residence at Newington Green, Mary was introduced to Dr Johnson, who, as Godwin tells us, "treated her with particular kindness and attention."

In 1785 Fanny Blood married Hugh Skeys, a merchant, and went with him to Lisbon, where she died in childbed after sending for Mary to nurse her. "The loss of Fanny," as she said in a letter to Mrs Skeys's brother, George Blood, "was sufficient of itself to have cast a cloud over my brightest days.... I have lost all relish for pleasure, and life seems a burden almost too heavy to be endured." Her first novel, *Mary, a Fiction* (1788), was intended to commemorate her friendship with Fanny. After closing the school at Newington Green, Mary became governess in the family of Lord Kingsborough, in Ireland. Her pupils were much attached to her, especially Margaret King, afterwards Lady Mountcashel; and indeed, Lady Kingsborough gave the reason for dismissing her after one year's service that the children loved their governess better than their mother. Mary now resolved to devote herself to literary work, and she was encouraged by Johnson, the publisher in St Paul's churchyard, for whom she acted as literary adviser. She also undertook translations, chiefly from the French. *The Elements of Morality* (1790) from the German of Salzmann, illustrated by Blake, an old-fashioned book for children, and Lavater's *Physiognomy* were among her translations. Her *Original Stories from Real Life* were published in 1791, and, with illustrations by Blake, in 1796. In 1792 appeared *A Vindication of the Rights of Woman*, the work with which her name is always associated.

It is not among the least oddities of this book that it is dedicated to M. Talleyrand Périgord, late bishop of Autun. Mary Wollstonecraft still believed him to be sincere, and working in the same direction as herself. In the dedication she states the "main argument" of the work, "built on this simple principle that, if woman be not prepared by education to become the companion of man, she will stop the progress of knowledge, for truth must be common to all, or it will be inefficacious with respect to its influence or general practice." In carrying out this argument she used great plainness of speech, and it was this that caused all, or nearly all, the outcry. For she did not attack the institution of marriage, nor assail orthodox religion; her book was really a plea for equality of education, passing into one for state education and for the joint education of the sexes. It was a protest against the assumption that woman was only the plaything of man, and she asserted that intellectual companionship was the chief, as it is the lasting, happiness of marriage. She thus directly opposed the teaching of Rousseau, of whom she was in other respects an ardent disciple.

Mrs Wollstonecraft, as she now styled herself, desired to watch the progress of the Revolution in France, and went to Paris in 1792. Godwin, in his memoir of his wife, considers that the change of residence may have been prompted by the discovery that she was becoming attached to Henry Fuseli, but there is little to confirm this surmise; indeed, it was first proposed that she should go to Paris in company with him and his wife, nor was there any subsequent breach in their friendship. She remained in Paris during the Reign of Terror, when communication with England was difficult or almost impossible. Some time in the spring or summer of 1793 Captain Gilbert Imlay, an American, became acquainted with Mary—an acquaintance which ended in a more intimate connexion. There was no legal ceremony of marriage, and it is doubtful whether such a marriage would have been valid at the time; but she passed as Imlay's wife, and Imlay himself terms her in a legal document, "Mary Imlay, my best friend and wife." In August 1793 Imlay was called to Havre on business, and was absent for some months, during which time most of the letters published after her death by Godwin were written. Towards the end of the year she joined Imlay at Havre, and there in the spring of 1794 she gave birth to a girl, 177who received the name of Fanny, in memory of the dear friend of her youth. In this year she published the first volume of a never completed *Historical and Moral View of the French Revolution.* Imlay became involved in a multitude of speculations, and his affection for Mary and their child was already waning. He left Mary for some months at Havre. In June 1795, after joining him in England, Mary left for Norway on business for Imlay. Her letters from Norway, divested of all personal details, were afterwards published. She returned to England late in 1795, and found letters awaiting her from Imlay, intimating his intention to separate from her, and offering to settle an annuity on her and her child. For herself she rejected this offer with scorn: "From you," she wrote, "I will not receive anything more. I am not sufficiently humbled to depend on your beneficence." They met again, and for a short time lived together, until the discovery that he was carrying on an intrigue under her own roof drove her to despair, and she attempted to drown herself by leaping from Putney bridge, but was rescued by watermen. Imlay now completely deserted her, although she continued to bear his name.

In 1796, when Mary Wollstonecraft was living in London, supporting herself and her child by working, as before, for Mr Johnson, she met William Godwin. A friendship sprang up between them,—a friendship, as he himself says, which "melted into love." Godwin states that "ideas which he is now willing to denominate prejudices made him by no means willing to conform to the ceremony of marriage"; but these prejudices were overcome, and they were married at St Pancras church on the 29th of March 1797. And now Mary had a season of real calm in her stormy existence. Godwin, for once only in his life, was stirred by passion, and his admiration for his wife equalled his affection. But their happiness was of short duration. The birth of her daughter Mary, afterwards the wife of Percy Bysshe Shelley, on the 30th of August 1797, proved fatal, and Mrs Godwin died on the 10th of September following. She was buried in the churchyard of Old St Pancras, but her remains were afterwards removed by Sir Percy Shelley to the churchyard of St Peter's, Bournemouth.

Her principal published works are as follows:—*Thoughts on the Education of Daughters,* ... (1787); *The Female Reader* (selections) (1789);*Original Stories from Real Life* (1791); *An Historical and Moral View of the Origin and Progress of the French Revolution, and the effects it has produced in Europe,* vol. i. (no more published) (1790); *Vindication of the Rights of Woman* (1792); *Vindication of the Rights of Man* (1793);*Mary, a Fiction* (1788); *Letters written during a Short Residence in Sweden, Norway and Denmark* (1796); *Posthumous Works* (4 vols., 1798). It is impossible to trace the many articles contributed by her to periodical literature.

A memoir of her life was published by Godwin in 1798. A large portion of C. Kegan Paul's work, *William Godwin, his Friends and Contemporaries,* was devoted to her, and an edition of the *Letters to Imlay* (1879), of which the first edition was published by Godwin, is prefaced by a somewhat fuller memoir. See also E. Dowden, *The French Revolution and English Literature* (1897) pp. 82 et seq.; E. R. Pennell,*Mary Wollstonecraft Godwin* (1885), in the Eminent Women Series; E. R. Clough, *A Study of Mary Wollstonecraft and the Rights of Woman*(1898); an edition of her *Original Stories* (1906), with William Blake's illustrations and an introduction by E. V. Lucas; and the *Love Letters of Mary Wollstonecraft to Gilbert Imlay* (1908), with an introduction by Roger Ingpen.

GODWIN, WILLIAM, (1756-1836), English political and miscellaneous writer, son of a Nonconformist minister, was born on the 3rd of March 1756, at Wisbeach in Cambridgeshire. His family came on both sides of middle-class people, and it was probably only as a joke that Godwin, a stern political reformer and philosophical radical, attempted to trace his pedigree to a time before the Norman conquest and the great earl Godwine. Both parents were strict Calvinists. The father died young, and never inspired love or much regret in his son; but in spite of wide differences of opinion, tender affection always subsisted between William Godwin and his mother, until her death at an advanced age.

William Godwin was educated for his father's profession at Hoxton Academy, where he was under Andrew Kippis the biographer and Dr Abraham Rees of the *Cyclopaedia,* and was at first more Calvinistic than his teachers, becoming a Sandemanian, or follower of John Glas (*q.v.*), whom he describes as "a celebrated north-country apostle who, after Calvin had damned ninety-nine in a hundred of mankind, has contrived a scheme for damning ninety-nine in a hundred of the followers of Calvin." He then acted as a minister at Ware, Stowmarket and Beaconsfield. At Stowmarket the teachings of the French philosophers were brought before him by a friend, Joseph Fawcet, who held strong republican opinions. He came to London in 1782, still nominally a minister, to regenerate society with his pen—a real enthusiast, who shrank theoretically from no conclusions from the premises which he laid down. He adopted the principles of the Encyclopaedists, and his own aim was the complete overthrow of all existing institutions, political, social and religious. He believed, however, that calm discussion was the only thing needful to carry every change, and from the beginning to the end of his career he deprecated every approach to violence. He was a philosophic radical in the strictest sense of the term.

His first published work was an anonymous *Life of Lord Chatham* (1783). Under the inappropriate title *Sketches of History* (1784) he published under his own name six sermons on the characters of Aaron, Hazael and Jesus, in which, though writing in the character of an orthodox Calvinist, he enunciates the proposition "God Himself has no right to be a tyrant." Introduced by Andrew Kippis, he began to write in 1785 for the *Annual Register* and other periodicals, producing also three novels now forgotten. The "Sketches of English History" written for the *Annual Register* from 1785 onward still deserve study. He joined a club called the "Revolutionists," and associated much with Lord Stanhope, Horne Tooke and Holcroft. His clerical character was now completely dropped.

In 1793 Godwin published his great work on political science, *The Inquiry concerning Political Justice, and its Influence on General Virtue and Happiness*. Although this work is little known and less read now, it marks a phase in English thought. Godwin could never have been himself a worker on the active stage of life. But he was none the less a power behind the workers, and for its political effect, *Political Justice* takes its place with Milton's *Areopagitica*, with Locke's *Essay on Education* and with Rousseau's *Émile*. By the words "political justice" the author meant "the adoption of any principle of morality and truth into the practice of a community," and the work was therefore an inquiry into the principles of society, of government and of morals. For many years Godwin had been "satisfied that monarchy was a species of government unavoidably corrupt," and from desiring a government of the simplest construction, he gradually came to consider that "government by its very nature counteracts the improvement of original mind." Believing in the perfectibility of the race, that there are no innate principles, and therefore no original propensity to evil, he considered that "our virtues and our vices may be traced to the incidents which make the history of our lives, and if these incidents could be divested of every improper tendency, vice would be extirpated from the world." All control of man by man was more or less intolerable, and the day would come when each man, doing what seems right in his own eyes, would also be doing what is in fact best for the community, because all will be guided by principles of pure reason. But all was to be done by discussion, and matured change resulting from discussion. Hence, while Godwin thoroughly approved of the philosophic schemes of the precursors of the Revolution, he was as far removed as Burke himself from agreeing with the way in which they were carried out. So logical and uncompromising a thinker as Godwin could not go far in the discussion of abstract questions without exciting the most lively opposition in matters of detailed opinion. An affectionate son, and ever ready to give of his hard-earned income to more than one ne'er-do-well brother, he maintained that natural relationship had no claim on man, nor was gratitude to parents or benefactors any part of justice or virtue. In a day when the penal code was still extremely severe, he argued gravely against all punishments, not only that of death. Property was to belong to him who most wanted it; 178accumulated property was a monstrous injustice. Hence marriage, which is law, is the worst of all laws, and as property the worst of all properties. A man so passionless as Godwin could venture thus to argue without suspicion that he did so only to gratify his wayward desires. Portions of this treatise, and only portions, found ready acceptance in those minds which were prepared to receive them. Perhaps no one received the whole teaching of the book. But it gave cohesion and voice to philosophic radicalism; it was the manifesto of a school without which liberalism of the present day had not been. Godwin himself in after days modified his communistic views, but his strong feeling for individualism, his hatred of all restrictions on liberty, his trust in man, his faith in the power of reason remained; it was a manifesto which enunciated principles modifying action, even when not wholly ruling it.

In May 1794 Godwin published the novel of *Caleb Williams, or Things as they are*, a book of which the political object is overlooked by many readers in the strong interest of the story. The book was dramatized by the younger Colman as *The Iron Chest*. It is one of the few novels of that time which may be said still to live.1 A theorist who lived mainly in his study, Godwin yet came forward boldly to stand by prisoners arraigned of high treason in that same year—1794. The danger to persons so charged was then great, and he deliberately put himself into this same danger for his friends. But when his own trial was discussed in the privy council, Pitt sensibly held that *Political Justice*, the work on which the charge could best have been founded, was priced at three guineas, and could never do much harm among those who had not three shillings to spare.

From this time Godwin became a notable figure in London society, and there was scarcely an important person in politics, on the Liberal side, in literature, art or science, who does not appear familiarly in the pages of Godwin's singular diary. For forty-eight years, beginning in 1788, and continuing to the very end of his life, Godwin kept a record of every day, of the work he did, the books he read, the friends he saw. Condensed in the highest degree, the diary is yet easy to read when the style is once mastered, and it is a great help to the understanding of his cold, methodical, unimpassioned character. He carried his method into every detail of life, and lived on his earnings with extreme frugality. Until he made a large sum by the publication of *Political Justice*, he lived on an average of £120 a year.

In 1797, the intervening years having been spent in strenuous literary labour, Godwin married Mary Wollstonecraft (see GODWIN, MARY WOLLSTONECRAFT). Since both held the same views regarding the slavery of marriage, and since they only married at all for the sake of possible offspring, the marriage was concealed for some time, and the happiness of the avowed married life was very brief; his wife's death on the 10th of September left Godwin prostrated in affliction, and with a charge for which he was wholly unfit—his infant daughter Mary, and her stepsister, Fanny Imlay, who from that time bore the name of Godwin. His unfitness for the cares of a family, far more than love, led him to contract a second marriage with Mary Jane Clairmont in 1801. She was a widow with two children, one of whom, Clara Mary Jane Clairmont, became the mistress of Lord Byron. The second Mrs Godwin was energetic and painstaking, but a harsh stepmother; and it may be doubted whether the children were not worse off under her care than they would have been under Godwin's neglect.

The second novel which proceeded from Godwin's pen was called *St Leon*, and published in 1799. It is chiefly remarkable for the beautiful portrait of Marguerite, the heroine, drawn from the character of his own wife. His opinions underwent a change in the direction of theism, influenced, he says, by his acquaintance with Coleridge. He also became known to Wordsworth and Lamb. Study of the Elizabethan dramatists led to the production in 1800 of the *Tragedy of Antonio*. Kemble brought it out at Drury Lane, but the failure of this attempt made him refuse *Abbas, King of Persia*, which Godwin offered him in the next year. He was more successful with his *Life of Chaucer*, for which he received £600.

The events of Godwin's life were few. Under the advice of the second Mrs Godwin, and with her active co-operation, he carried on business as a bookseller under the pseudonym of Edward Baldwin, publishing several useful school books and books for children, among them Charles and Mary Lamb's *Tales from Shakespeare*. But the speculation was unsuccessful, and for many years Godwin struggled with constant pecuniary difficulties, for which more than one subscription was raised by the leaders of the Liberal party and by literary men. He became bankrupt in 1822, but during the following years he accomplished one of his best pieces of work, *The History of the Commonwealth*, founded on pamphlets and original documents, which still retains considerable value. In 1833 the government of Earl Grey conferred upon him the office known as yeoman usher of the exchequer, to which were attached apartments in Palace Yard, where he died on the 7th of April 1836.

In his own time, by his writings and by his conversation, Godwin had a great power of influencing men, and especially young men. Though his character would seem, from much which is found in his writings, and from anecdotes told by those who still remember him, to have been unsympathetic, it was not so understood by enthusiastic young people, who hung on his words as those of a prophet. The most remarkable of these was Percy Bysshe Shelley, who in the glowing dawn of his genius turned to Godwin as his teacher and guide. The last of the long series of young men who sat at Godwin's feet was Edward Lytton Bulwer, afterwards Lord Lytton, whose early romances were formed after those of Godwin, and who, in *Eugene Aram*, succeeded to the story as arranged, and the plan to a considerable extent sketched out, by Godwin, whose age and failing health prevented him from completing it. Godwin's character appears in the worst light in connexion with Shelley. His early correspondence with Shelley, which began in 1811, is remarkable for its genuine good sense and kindness; but when Shelley carried out the principles of the author of *Political Justice* in eloping with Mary Godwin, Godwin assumed a hostile attitude that would have been unjustifiable in a man of ordinary views, and was ridiculous in the light of his professions. He was not, moreover, too proud to accept £1000 from his son-in-law, and after the reconciliation following on Shelley's marriage in 1816, he continued to demand money until Shelley's death. His character had no doubt suffered under his long embarrassments and his unhappy marriage.

Godwin's more important works are—*The Inquiry concerning Political Justice, and its Influence on General Virtue and Happiness* (1793);*Things as they are, or the Adventures of Caleb Williams* (1794); *The Inquirer, a series of Essays* (1797); *Memoirs of the Author of the Rights of Woman* (1798); *St Leon, a Tale of the Sixteenth Century* (1799); *Antonio, a Tragedy* (1800); *The Life of Chaucer* (1803); *Fleetwood, a Novel*(1805); *Faulkner, a Tragedy* (1807); *Essay on Sepulchres* (1809); *Lives of Edward and John Philips, the Nephews of Milton* (1815); *Mandeville, a Tale of the Times of Cromwell* (1817); *Of Population, an answer to Malthus* (1820); *History of the Commonwealth* (1824-1828); *Cloudesley, a Novel* (1830); *Thoughts on Man, a series of Essays* (1831); *Lives of the Necromancers* (1834). A volume of essays was also collected from his papers and published in 1873, as left for publication by his daughter Mrs Shelley. Many other short and anonymous works proceeded from his ever busy pen, but many are irrecoverable, and all are forgotten. Godwin's life was published in 1876 in two volumes, under the title *William Godwin, his Friends and Contemporaries*, by C. Kegan Paul. The best estimate of his literary position is that given by Sir Leslie Stephen in his*English Thought in the 18th Century* (ii. 264-281; ed., 1902). See also the article on William Godwin in W. Hazlitt's *The Spirit of the Age* (1825), and "Godwin and Shelley" in Sir L. Stephen's *Hours in a Library* (vol. iii., ed. 1892).

1For an analysis of *Caleb Williams* see the chapter on "Theorists of Revolution" in Professor E. Dowden's *The French Revolution and English Literature*(1897).

GODWIN-AUSTEN, ROBERT ALFRED CLOYNE (1808-1884), English geologist, the eldest son of Sir Henry E. Austen, was born on the 17th of March 1808. He was educated at Oriel College, Oxford, of which he became a fellow in 1830. He afterwards entered Lincoln's Inn. In 1833 he married the only daughter and heiress of General Sir Henry T. Godwin, K.C.B., and he took the additional name of Godwin by Royal licence 179in 1854. At Oxford as a pupil of William Buckland he became deeply interested in geology, and soon afterwards becoming acquainted with De la Beche, he was inspired by that great master, and assisted him by making a geological map of the neighbourhood of Newton Abbot, which was embodied in the Geological Survey map. He also published an elaborate memoir "On the Geology of the South-East of Devonshire" (*Trans. Geol. Soc.* ser. 2, vol. viii.). His attention was next directed to the Cretaceous rocks of Surrey, his home-county, his estates being situated at Chilworth and Shalford near Guildford. Later he dealt with the superficial accumulations bordering the English Channel, and with the erratic boulders of Selsea. In 1855 he brought before the Geological Society of London his celebrated paper "On the possible Extension of the Coal-Measures beneath the South-Eastern part of England," in which he pointed out on well-considered theoretical grounds the likelihood of coal-measures being some day reached in that area. In this article he also advocated the freshwater origin of the Old Red Sandstone, and discussed the relations of that formation, and of the Devonian, to the Silurian and Carboniferous. He was elected F.R.S. in 1849, and in 1862 he was awarded the Wollaston medal by the Geological Society of London, on which occasion he was styled by Sir R. I. Murchison "pre-eminently the physical geographer of bygone periods." He died at Shalford House near Guildford on the 25th of November 1884.

His son, Lieut-Colonel HENRY HAVERSHAM GODWIN-AUSTEN (b. 1834), entered the army in 1851, and served for many years on the Trigonometrical Survey of India, retiring in 1877. He gave much attention to geology, but is more especially distinguished for his researches on the natural history of India and as the author of *The Land and Freshwater Mollusca of India* (1882-1887).

GODWINE (d. 1053), son of Wulfnoth, earl of the West-Saxons, the leading Englishman in the first half of the 11th century. His birth and origin are utterly uncertain; but he rose to power early in Canute's reign and was an earl in 1018. He received in marriage Gytha, a connexion of the king's, and in 1020 became earl of the West-Saxons. On the death of Canute in 1035 he joined with Queen Emma in supporting the claim of Hardicanute, the son of Canute and Emma, to the crown of his father, in opposition to Leofric and the northern party who supported Harold Harefoot (see HARDICANUTE). While together they held Wessex for Hardicanute, the ætheling Ælfred, son of Emma by her former husband Æthelred II., landed in England in the hope of winning back his father's crown; but falling into the hands of Godwine, he and his followers were cruelly done to death. On the death of Hardicanute in 1042 Godwine was foremost in promoting the election of Edward (the Confessor) to the vacant throne. He was now the first man in the kingdom, though his power was still balanced by that of the other great earls, Leofric of Mercia and Siward of Northumberland. His sons Sweyn and Harold were promoted to earldoms; and his daughter Eadgyth was married to the king (1045). His policy was strongly national in opposition to the marked Normanizing tendencies of the king. Between him and Edward's foreign favourites, particularly Robert of Jumièges, there was deadly feud. The appointment of Robert to the archbishopric of Canterbury in 1051 marks the decline of

Godwine's power; and in the same year a series of outrages committed by one of the king's foreign favourites led to a breach between the king and the earl, which culminated in the exile of the latter with all his family (see EDWARD THE CONFESSOR). But next year Godwine returned in triumph; and at a great meeting held outside London he and his family were restored to all their offices and possessions, and the archbishop and many other Normans were banished. In the following year Godwine was smitten with a fit at the king's table, and died three days later on the 15th of April 1053.

Godwine appears to have had seven sons, three of whom—King Harold, Gyrth and Leofwine—were killed at Hastings; two others, Wulfnoth and Ælfgar, are of little importance; another was Earl Tostig (*q.v.*). The eldest son was Sweyn, or Swegen (d. 1052), who was outlawed for seducing Eadgifu abbess of Leominster. After fighting for the king of Denmark he returned to England in 1049, when his murder of his cousin Beorn compelled him to leave England for the second time. In 1050, however, he regained his earldom, and in 1051 he shared his father's exile. To atone for the murder of Beorn, Sweyn went on a pilgrimage to Jerusalem, and on the return journey he died on the 29th of September 1052, meeting his death, according to one account, at the hands of the Saracens.

GODWIT, a word of unknown origin, the name commonly applied to a marsh-bird in great repute, when fattened, for the table, and formerly abundant in the fens of Norfolk, the Isle of Ely and Lincolnshire. In Turner's days (1544) it was worth three times as much as a snipe, and at the same period Belon said of it—"C'est vn Oyseau es delices des François." Casaubon, who Latinized its name "*Dei ingenium*" (*Ephemerides*, 19th September 1611), was told by the "*ornithotrophaeus*" he visited at Wisbech that in London it fetched twenty pence. Its fame as a delicacy is perpetuated by many later writers, Ben Jonson among them, and Pennant says that in his time (1766) it sold for half-a-crown or five shillings. Under the name godwit two perfectly distinct species of British birds were included, but that which seems to have been especially prized is known to modern ornithologists as the black-tailed godwit,*Limosa aegocephala*, formerly called, from its loud cry, a yarwhelp,1 shrieker or barker, in the districts it inhabited. The practice of netting this bird in large numbers during the spring and summer, coupled with the gradual reclamation of the fens, to which it resorted, has now rendered it but a visitor in England; and it probably ceased from breeding regularly in England in 1824 or thereabouts, though under favourable conditions it may have occasionally laid its eggs for some thirty years later or more (Stevenson, *Birds of Norfolk*, ii. 250). This godwit is a species of wide range, reaching Iceland, where it is called *Jardraeka* (= earth-raker), in summer, and occurring numerously in India in winter. Its chief breeding-quarters seem to extend from Holland eastwards to the south of Russia. The second British species is that which is known as the bar-tailed godwit, *L. lapponica*, and this seems to have never been more than a bird of double passage in the United Kingdom, arriving in large flocks on the south coast about the 12th of May, and, after staying a few days, proceeding to the north-eastward. It is known to breed in Lapland, but its eggs are of great rarity. Towards autumn the young visit the English coasts, and a few of them remain, together with some of the other species, in favourable situations throughout the winter. One of the local names by which the bar-tailed godwit is known to the Norfolk gunners is scamell, a word which, in the mouth of Caliban (*Tempest*, II. ii.), has been the cause of much perplexity to Shakespearian critics.

The godwits belong to the group *Limicolae*, and are about as big as a tame pigeon, but possess long legs, and a long bill with a slight upward turn. It is believed that in the genus *Limosa* the female is larger than the male. While the winter plumage is of a sober greyish-brown, the breeding-dress is marked by a predominance of bright bay or chestnut, rendering the wearer a very beautiful object. The black-tailed godwit, though varying a good deal in size, is constantly larger than the bar-tailed, and especially longer in the legs. The species may be further distinguished by the former having the proximal third of the tail-quills pure white, and the distal two-thirds black, with a narrow white margin, while the latter has the same feathers barred with black and white alternately for nearly their whole length.

America possesses two species of the genus, the very large marbled godwit or marlin, *L. fedoa*, easily recognized by its size and the buff colour of its axillaries, and the smaller Hudsonian godwit, *L. hudsonica*, which has its axillaries of a deep black. This last, though less numerous than its congener, seems to range over the whole of the continent, breeding in the extreme north, while it has been obtained also in the Strait of Magellan and the Falkland Islands. The first seems not to go farther southward than the Antilles and the Isthmus of Panama.

180

From Asia, or at least its eastern part, two species have been described. One of them, *L. melanuroides*, differs only from *L. aegocephala* in its smaller size, and is believed to breed in Amurland, wintering in the islands of the Pacific, New Zealand and Australia. The other, *L.

uropygialis, is closely allied to and often mistaken for *L. lapponica*, from which it chiefly differs by having the rump barred like the tail. This was found breeding in the extreme north of Siberia by Dr von Middendorff, and ranges to Australia, whence it was, like the last, first described by Gould.

(A. N.)

1This name seems to have survived in Whelp Moor, near Brandon, in Suffolk.

GOEBEN, AUGUST KARL VON (1816-1880), Prussian general of infantry, came of old Hanoverian stock. Born at Stade on the 10th of December 1816, he aspired from his earliest years to the Prussian service rather than that of his own country, and at the age of seventeen obtained a commission in the 24th regiment of Prussian infantry. But there was little scope there for the activities of a young and energetic subaltern, and, leaving the service in 1836, he entered the Carlist army campaigning in Spain. In the five campaigns which he made in the service of Don Carlos he had many and various vicissitudes of fortune. He had not fought for two months when he fell, severely wounded, into the hands of the Spanish Royal troops. After eight months' detention he escaped, but it was not long before he was captured again. This time his imprisonment was long and painful, and on two occasions he was compelled to draw lots for his life with his fellow-captives. When released, he served till 1840 with distinction. In that year he made his way back, a beggar without means or clothing, to Prussia. The Carlist lieutenant-colonel was glad to be re-admitted into the Prussian service as a second lieutenant, but he was still young, and few subalterns could at the age of twenty-four claim five years' meritorious war service. In a few years we find him serving as captain on the Great General Staff, and in 1848 he had the good fortune to be transferred to the staff of the IV. army corps, his immediate superior being Major von Moltke. The two "coming men" became fast friends, and their mutual esteem was never disturbed. In the Baden insurrection Goeben served with distinction on the staff of Prince William, the future emperor. Staff and regimental duty (as usual in the Prussian service) alternated for some years after this, till in 1863 he became major-general commanding the 26th infantry brigade. In 1860, it should be mentioned, he was present with the Spanish troops in Morocco, and took part in the battle of Tetuan.

In the first of Prussia's great wars (1864) he distinguished himself at the head of his brigade at Rackebüll and Sonderburg. In the war of 1866 Lieutenant-General von Goeben commanded the 13th division, of which his old brigade formed part, and, in this higher sphere, once more displayed the qualities of a born leader and skilful tactician. He held almost independent command with conspicuous success in the actions of Dermbach, Laufach, Kissingen, Aschaffenburg, Gerchsheim, Tauber-Bischofsheim and Würzburg. The mobilization of 1870 placed him at the head of the VIII. (Rhineland) army corps, forming part of the First Army under Steinmetz. It was his resolute and energetic leading that contributed mainly to the victory of Spicheren (6th August), and won the old laurels gained on the Prussian right wing at Gravelotte (18th August). Under Manteuffel the VIII. corps took part in the operations about Amiens and Bapaume, and on the 8th of January 1871 Goeben succeeded that general in the command of the First Army, with which he had served throughout the campaign as a corps commander. A fortnight later he had brought the war in northern France to a brilliant conclusion, by the decisive victory of St Quentin (18th and 19th January 1871). The close of the Franco-German War left Goeben one of the most distinguished men in the victorious army. He was colonel of the 28th infantry, and had the grand cross of the Iron Cross. He commanded the VIII. corps at Coblenz until his death in 1880.

General von Goeben left many writings. His memoirs are to be found in his works *Vier Jahre in Spanien* (Hanover, 1841), *Reise- und Lagerbriefe aus Spanien und vom spanischen Heere in Marokko* (Hanover, 1863) and in the Darmstadt *Allgemeine Militärzeitung*. The former French port (Queuleu) at Metz was renamed Goeben after him, and the 28th infantry bears his name. A statue of Goeben by Schaper was erected at Coblenz in 1884.

See G. Zernin, *Das Leben des Generals August von Goeben* (2 vols., Berlin, 1895-1897); H. Barth, *A. von Goeben* (Berlin, 1906); and, for his share in the war of 1870-71; H. Kunz, *Der Feldzug im N. und N.W. Frankreichs 1870-1871* (Berlin, 1889), and the 14th Monograph of the Great General Staff (1891).

GOEJE, MICHAEL JAN DE (1836-1909), Dutch orientalist, was born in Friesland in 1836. He devoted himself at an early age to the study of oriental languages and became especially proficient in Arabic, under the guidance of Dozy and Juynboll, to whom he was afterwards an intimate friend and colleague. He took his degree of doctor at Leiden in 1860, and then studied for a year in Oxford, where he examined and collated the Bodleian MSS. of Idrīsī (part being published in 1866, in collaboration with R. P. Dozy, as *Description de l'Afrique et de l'Espagne*. About the same time he wrote*Mémoires de l'histoire et de la géographie orientales*, and edited *Expugnatio regionum*. In 1883, on the death of Dozy, he became Arabic professor at Leiden, retiring in 1906. He died on the 17th of May 1909. Though perhaps not a teacher of the first order, he wielded a great influence during his long professoriate not only over his pupils, but over theologians and eastern administrators who attended his lectures, and his many editions of Arabic texts have been of the highest value to scholars, the most important being his great edition of Ṭabarī. Though entirely averse from politics, he took a keen interest in the municipal affairs of Leiden and made a special study of elementary education. He took the leading part in the International Congress of Orientalists at Algiers in 1905. He was a member of the Institut de France, was awarded the German Order of Merit, and received an honorary doctorate of Cambridge University. At his death he was president of the newly formed International Association of Academies of Science. Among his chief works are *Fragmenta historicorum Arabicorum* (1869-1871); *Diwan of Moslim ibn al-Wālid* (1875); *Bibliotheca geographorum Arabicorum* (1870-1894);*Annals of Ṭabari* (1879-1901); edition of Ibn Qutaiba's biographies (1904); of the travels of Ibn Jubaye (1907, 5th vol. of Gibb Memorial). He was also the chief editor of the *Encyclopaedia of Islam* (vols. i.-iii.), and contributed many articles to periodicals. He wrote for the 9th and the present edition of the*Encyclopaedia Britannica*.

GOES, DAMIÃO DE (1502-1574), Portuguese humanist, was born of a patrician family at Alemquer, in February 1502. Under King John III. he was employed abroad for many years from 1523 on diplomatic and commercial missions, and he travelled over the greater part of Europe. He was intimate with the leading scholars of the time, was acquainted with Luther and other Protestant divines, and in 1532 became the pupil and friend of Erasmus. Goes took his degree at Padua in 1538 after a four years' course. In 1537, at the instance of his friend Cardinal Sadoleto, he undertook to mediate between the Church and the Lutherans, but failed through the attitude of the Protestants. He married in Flanders a rich and noble Dutch lady, D. Joanna de Hargen, and settled at Louvain, then the literary centre of the Low Countries, where he was living in 1542 when the French besieged the town. He was given the command of the defending forces, and saved Louvain, but was taken prisoner and confined for nine months in France, till he obtained his freedom by a heavy ransom. He was rewarded, however, by a grant of arms from Charles V. He finally returned to Portugal in 1545, with a view of becoming tutor to the king's son, but he failed to obtain this post, owing to the denunciations of Father Simon Rodriguez, provincial of the Jesuits, who accused Goes of favouring the Lutheran doctrines and of being a disciple of Erasmus. Nevertheless in 1548 he was appointed chief keeper of the archives and royal chronicler, and at once introduced some much-needed reforms into the administration of his office.

In 1558 he was given a commission to write a history of the reign of King Manoel, a task previously confided to João de Barros, but relinquished by him. It was an onerous undertaking for a conscientious historian, since it was necessary to expose 181the miseries as well as relate the glories of the period, and so to offend some of the most powerful families. Goes had already written a *Chronicle* of Prince John (afterwards John II.), and when, after more than eight years' labour, he produced the First Part of his *Chronicle* of King Manoel (1566), a chorus of attacks greeted it, the edition was destroyed, and he was compelled to issue a revised version. He brought out the three other parts in 1566-1567, though chapters 23 to 27 of the Third Part were so mutilated by the censorship that the printed text differs largely from the MS. Hitherto Goes, notwithstanding his Liberalism, had escaped the Inquisition, though in 1540 his *Fides, religio, moresque Aethiopum* had been prohibited by the chief inquisitor, Cardinal D. Henrique; but the denunciation of Father Rodriguez in 1545, which had been vainly renewed in 1550, was now brought into action, and in 1571 he was arrested to stand his trial. There seems to be no doubt that the Inquisition made itself on this occasion, as on others, the instrument of private enmity; for eighteen months Goes lay ill in prison, and then he was condemned, though he had lived for thirty years as a faithful Catholic, and the worst that could be proved against him was that in his youth he had spoken against Indulgences, disbelieved in auricular confession, and consorted with heretics. He was sentenced to a term of reclusion, and his property was confiscated to the crown. After he had abjured his errors in private, he was sent at the end of 1572 to do penance at the monastery of Batalha. Later he was allowed to return home to Alemquer, where he died on the 30th of January 1574. He was buried in the church of Nossa Senhora da Varzea.

Damião de Goes was a man of wide culture and genial and courtly manners, a skilled musician and a good linguist. He wrote both Portuguese and Latin with classic strength and simplicity, and his style is free from affectation and rhetorical ornaments. His portrait by Albrecht Dürer shows an open, intelligent face, and the record of his life proves him to have been upright and fearless. His prosperity doubtless excited ill-will, but above all, his ideas, advanced for Portugal, his foreign ways, outspokenness and honesty contributed to the tragedy of his end, at a time when the forces of ignorant reaction held the ascendant. He had, it may be presumed, given some umbrage to the court by condemning, in the *Chronicle of King Manoel*, the royal ingratitude to distinguished public servants, though he received a pension and other rewards for that work, and he had certainly offended the nobility by his administration of the archive office and by exposing false genealogical claims in his *Nobiliario*. He paid the penalty for telling the truth, as he knew it, in an age when an historian had to choose between flattery of the great and silence. The *Chronicle of King Manoel* was the first official history of a Portuguese reign to be written in a critical spirit, and Damião de Goes has the honour of having been the first Portuguese royal chronicler to deserve the name of an historian.

His Portuguese works include *Chronica do felicissimo rei Dom Emanuel* (parts i. and ii., Lisbon, 1566, parts iii. and iv., *ib.* 1567). Other editions appeared in Lisbon in 1619 and 1749 and in Coimbra in 1790. *Chronica do principe Dom Joam* (Lisbon, 1558), with subsequent editions in 1567 and 1724 in Lisbon and in 1790 in Coimbra. *Livro de Marco Tullio Ciceram chamado Catam Mayor* (Venice, 1538). This is a translation of Cicero's *De senectute*. His Latin works, published separately, comprise: (1) *Legatio magni imperatoris Presbiteri Joannis, &c.*(Antwerp, 1532); (2) *Legatio Davidis Ethiopiae regis, &c.* (Bologna, 1533); (3) *Commentarii rerum gestarum in India* (Louvain, 1539); (4) *Fides, religio, moresque Aethiopum* (Louvain, 1540), incorporating Nos. (1) and (2); (5) *Hispania* (Louvain, 1542); (6) *Aliquot epistolae Sadoleti Bembi et aliorum clarissimorum virorum, &c.* (Louvain, 1544); (7) *Damiani a Goes equitis Lusitani aliquot opuscula* (Louvain, 1544); (8) *Urbis Lovaniensis obsidia* (Lisbon, 1546); (9) *De bello Cambaico ultimo* (Louvain, 1549); (10) *Urbis Olisiponensis descriptio* (Evora, 1554); (11)*Epistola ad Hieronymum Cardosum* (Lisbon, 1556). Most of the above went through several editions, and many were afterwards included with new works in such collections as No. (7), and seven sets of *Opuscula* appeared, all incomplete. Nos. (3), (4) and (5) suffered mutilation in subsequent editions, at the hands of the censors, because they offended against religious orthodoxy or family pride.

AUTHORITIES.—(A) Joaquim de Vasconcellos, *Goesiana* (5 vols.), with the following sub-titles: (1) *O Retrato de Albrecht Dürer* (Porto, 1879); (2) *Bibliographia* (Porto, 1879), which describes 67 numbers of books by Goes; (3) As Variantes das Chronicus Portuguezas (Porto, 1881); (4)*Damião de Goes: Novos Estudos* (Porto, 1897); (5) *As Cartas Latinas*—in the press (1906). Snr. Vasconcellos only printed a very limited number of copies of these studies for distribution among friends, so that they are rare. (B) Guilherme J. C. Henriques, *Ineditos Goesianos*, vol. i. (Lisbon, 1896), vol. ii. (containing the proceedings at the trial by the Inquisition) (Lisbon, 1898). (C) A. P. Lopes de Mendonça, *Damião de Goes e a Inquisição de Portugal* (Lisbon, 1859). (D) Dr Sousa Viterbo, *Damião de Goes e D. Antonio Pinheiro* (Coimbra, 1895). (E) Dr Theophilo Braga,*Historia da Universidade de Coimbra* (Lisbon, 1892), i. 374-380. (F) Menendez y Pelayo, *Historia de los Heter. Españoles*, ii. 129-143.

(E. PR.)

GOES, HUGO VAN DER (d. 1482), a painter of considerable celebrity at Ghent, was known to Vasari, as he is known to us, by a single picture in a Florentine monastery. At a period when the family of the Medici had not yet risen from the rank of a great mercantile firm to that of a reigning dynasty, it employed as an agent at the port of Bruges Tommaso Portinari, a lineal descendant, it was said, of Folco, the father of Dante's Beatrix. Tommaso, at that time patron of a chapel in the hospital of Santa Maria Nuova at Florence, ordered an altar-piece of Hugo van der Goes, and commanded him to illustrate the sacred theme of "Quem genuit adoravit." In the centre of a vast triptych, comprising numerous figures of life size, Hugo represented the Virgin kneeling in adoration before the new-born Christ attended by Shepherds and Angels. On the wings he portrayed Tommaso and his two sons in prayer under the protection of Saint Anthony and St Matthew, and Tommaso's wife and two daughters supported by St Margaret and St Mary Magdalen. The triptych, which has suffered much from decay and restoring, was for over 400 years at Santa Maria Nuova, and is now in the Uffizi Gallery. Imposing because composed of figures of unusual size, the altar-piece is more remarkable for portrait character than for charms of ideal beauty.

There are also small pieces in public galleries which claim to have been executed by Van der Goes. One of these pictures in the National Gallery in London is more nearly allied to the school of Memling than to the triptych of Santa Maria Nuova; another, a small and very beautiful "John the Baptist," at the Pinakothek of Munich, is really by Memling; whilst numerous fragments of an altar-piece in the Belvedere at Vienna, though assigned to Hugo, are by his more gifted countryman of Bruges. Van der Goes, however, was not habitually a painter of easel pieces. He made his reputation at Bruges by producing coloured hangings in distemper. After he settled at Ghent, and became a master of his gild in 1465, he designed cartoons for glass windows. He also made decorations for the wedding of Charles the Bold and Margaret of York in 1468, for the festivals of the Rhetoricians and papal jubilees on repeated occasions, for the solemn entry of Charles the Bold into Ghent in 1470-1471, and for the funeral of Philip the Good in 1474. The labour which he expended on these occasions might well add to his fame without being the less ephemeral. About the year 1475 he retired to the monastery of Rouge Cloître near Ghent, where he took the cowl. There, though he still clung to his profession, he seems to have taken to drinking, and at one time to have shown decided symptoms of insanity. But his superiors gradually cured him of his intemperance, and he died in the odour of sanctity in 1482.

GOES, a town in the province of Zeeland, Holland, on the island of South Beveland, 11½ m. by rail E. of Middelburg. Pop. (1900) 6919. It is connected by a short canal with the East Scheldt, and has a good harbour (1819) defended by a fort. The principal buildings are the interesting Gothic church (1423) and the picturesque old town hall (restored 1771). There are various educational and charitable institutions. Goes has preserved for centuries its prosperous position as the market-town of the island. The chief industries are boat-building, brewing, book-binding and cigar-making. The town had its origin in the castle of Oostende, built here by the noble family of Borssele. It received a charter early in the 15th century from the countess Jacoba of Holland, who frequently stayed at the castle.

182

GOETHE, JOHANN WOLFGANG VON (1749-1832), German poet, dramatist and philosopher, was born at Frankfort-on-Main on the 28th of August 1749. He came, on his father's side, of Thuringian stock, his great-grandfather, Hans Christian Goethe, having been a farrier at Artern-on-the-Unstrut, about the middle of the 17th century. Hans Christian's son, Friedrich Georg, was brought up to the trade of a tailor, and in this capacity settled in Frankfort in 1686. A second marriage, however, brought him into possession of the Frankfort inn, "Zum Weidenhof," and he ended his days as a well-to-do innkeeper. His son, Johann Kaspar, the poet's father (1710-1782), studied law at Leipzig, and, after going through the prescribed courses of practical training at Wetzlar, travelled in Italy. He hoped, on his return to Frankfort, to obtain an official position in the government of the free city, but his personal influence with the authorities was not sufficiently strong. In his disappointment he resolved never again to offer his services to his native town, and retired into private life, a course which his ample means facilitated. In 1742 he acquired, as a consolation for the public career he had missed, the title of *kaiserlicher Rat*, and in 1748 married Katharina Elisabeth (1731-1808), daughter of the *Schultheiss* or *Bürgermeister* of Frankfort, Johann Wolfgang Textor. The poet was the eldest son of this union. Of the later children only one, Cornelia, born in 1750, survived the years of childhood; she died as the wife of Goethe's friend, J. G. Schlosser, in 1777. The best elements in Goethe's genius came from his mother's side; of a lively, impulsive disposition, and gifted with remarkable imaginative power, Frau Rat was the ideal mother of a poet; moreover, being hardly eighteen at the time of her son's birth, she was herself able to be the companion of his childhood. From his father, whose stern, somewhat pedantic nature repelled warmer feelings on the part of the children, Goethe Inherited that "holy earnestness" and stability of character which brought him unscathed through temptations and passions, and held the balance to his all too powerful imagination.

Unforgettable is the picture which the poet subsequently drew of his childhood spent in the large house with its many nooks and crannies, in the Grosse Hirschgraben at Frankfort. Books, pictures, objects of art, antiquities, reminiscences of Rat Goethe's visit to Italy, above all a marionette theatre, kindled the child's quick intellect and imagination. His training was conducted in its early stages by his father, and was later supplemented by tutors. Meanwhile the varied and picturesque life of Frankfort was in itself an education. In 1759, during the Seven Years' War, the French, as Maria Theresa's allies, occupied the town, and, much to the irritation of Goethe's father, who was a stanch partisan of Frederick the Great, a French lieutenant, Count Thoranc, was quartered on the Goethe household. The foreign occupation also led to the establishment of a French troupe of actors, and to their performances the boy, through his grandfather's influence, had free access. Goethe has also recorded his memories of another picturesque event, the coronation of the emperor Joseph II. in the Frankfort Römer or town hall in 1764; but these memories were darkened by being associated in his mind with the tragic dénouement of his first love affair. The object of this passion was a certain Gretchen, who seems to have taken advantage of the boy's interest in her to further the dishonest ends of one of her friends. The discovery of the affair and the investigation that followed cooled Goethe's ardour and caused him to turn his attention seriously to the studies which were to prepare him for the university.

97

Meanwhile the literary instinct had begun to show itself; we hear of a novel in letters—a kind of linguistic exercise, in which the characters carried on the correspondence in different languages—of a prose epic on the subject of Joseph, and various religious poems of which one, *Die Höllenfahrt Christi*, found its way in a revised form into the poet's complete works.

In October 1765, Goethe, then a little over sixteen, left Frankfort for Leipzig, where a wider and, in many respects, less provincial life awaited him. He entered upon his university studies with zeal, but his own education in Frankfort had not been the best preparation for the scholastic methods which still dominated the German universities; of his professors, only Gellert seems to have won his interest, and that interest was soon exhausted. The literary beginnings he had made in Frankfort now seemed to him amateurish and trivial; he felt that he had to turn over a new leaf, and, under the guidance of E. W. Behrisch, a genial, original comrade, he learned the art of writing those light Anacreontic lyrics which harmonized with the tone of polite Leipzig society. Artificial as this poetry is, Goethe was, nevertheless, inspired by a real passion in Leipzig, namely, for Anna Katharina Schönkopf, the daughter of a wine-merchant at whose house he dined. She is the "Annette" after whom the recently discovered collection of lyrics was named, although it must be added that neither these lyrics nor the *Neue Lieder*, published in 1770, express very directly Goethe's feelings for Käthchen Schönkopf. To his Leipzig student-days belong also two small plays in Alexandrines, *Die Laune des Verliebten*, a pastoral comedy in one act, which reflects the lighter side of the poet's love affair, and *Die Mitschuldigen* (published in a revised form, 1769), a more sombre picture, in which comedy is incongruously mingled with tragedy. In Leipzig Goethe also had time for what remained one of the abiding interests of his life, for art; he regarded A. F. Oeser (1717-1799), the director of the academy of painting in the Pleissenburg, who had given him lessons in drawing, as the teacher who in Leipzig had influenced him most. His art studies were also furthered by a short visit to Dresden. His stay in Leipzig came, however, to an abrupt conclusion; the distractions of student life proved too much for his strength; a sudden haemorrhage supervened, and he lay long ill, first in Leipzig, and, after it was possible to remove him, at home in Frankfort. These months of slow recovery were a time of serious introspection for Goethe. He still corresponded with his Leipzig friends, but the tone of his letters changed; life had become graver and more earnest for him. He pored over books on occult philosophy; he busied himself with alchemy and astrology. A friend of his mother's, Susanne Katharina von Klettenberg, who belonged to pietist circles in Frankfort, turned the boy's thoughts to religious mysticism. On his recovery his father resolved that he should complete his legal studies at Strassburg, a city which, although then outside the German empire, was, in respect of language and culture, wholly German. From the first moment Goethe set foot in the narrow streets of the Alsatian capital, in April 1770, the whole current of his thought seemed to change. The Gothic architecture of the Strassburg minster became to him the symbol of a national and German ideal, directly antagonistic to the French tastes and the classical and rationalistic atmosphere that prevailed in Leipzig. The second moment of importance in Goethe's Strassburg period was his meeting with Herder, who spent some weeks in Strassburg undergoing an operation of the eye. In this thinker, who was his senior by five years, Goethe found the master he sought; Herder taught him the significance of Gothic architecture, revealed to him the charm of nature's simplicity, and inspired him with enthusiasm for Shakespeare and the *Volkslied*. Meanwhile Goethe's legal studies were not neglected, and he found time to add to knowledge of other subjects, notably that of medicine. Another factor of importance in Goethe's Strassburg life was his love for Friederike Brion, the daughter of an Alsatian village pastor in Sesenheim. Even more than Herder's precept and example, this passion showed Goethe how trivial and artificial had been the Anacreontic and pastoral poetry with which he had occupied himself in Leipzig; and the lyrics inspired by Friederike, such as *Kleine Blumen, kleine Blätter* and *Wie herrlich leuchtet mir die Natur!* mark the beginning of a new epoch in German lyric poetry. The idyll of Sesenheim, as described in *Dichtung und Wahrheit*, is one of the most beautiful love-stories in the literature of the world. From the first, however, it was clear that Friederike Brion could never become the wife of the Frankfort patrician's son; an unhappy ending to the romance was unavoidable, and, as is to be seen in passionate outpourings like the *Wanderers Sturmlied*, and in the bitter self-accusations of *Clavigo*, it left deep wounds on the poet's sensitive soul.

To Strassburg we owe Goethe's first important drama, *Götz von Berlichingen*, or, as it was called in its earliest form, *Geschichte Gottfriedens von Berlichingen dramatisiert* (not published until 1831). Revised under the now familiar title, it appeared in 1773, after Goethe's return to Frankfort. In estimating this drama we must bear in mind Goethe's own Strassburg life, and the turbulent spirit of his own age, rather than the historical facts, which the poet found in the autobiography of his hero published in 1731. The latter supplied only the rough materials; the Götz von Berlichingen whom Goethe drew, with his lofty ideals of right and wrong, and his enthusiasm for freedom, is a very different personage from the unscrupulous robber-knight of the 16th century, the rough friend of Franz von Sickingen and of the revolting peasants. Still less historical justification is to be found for the vacillating Weisslingen in whom Goethe executed poetic justice on himself as the lover of Friederike, or in the women of the play, the gentle Maria, the heartless Adelheid. But there is genial, creative power in the very subjectivity of these characters, and a vigorous dramatic life, which is irresistible in its appeal. With *Götz von Berlichingen*, Shakespeare's art first triumphed on the German stage, and the literary movement known as *Sturm und Drang* was inaugurated.

Having received his degree in Strassburg, Goethe returned home in August 1771, and began his initiation into the routine of an advocate's profession. In the following year, in order to gain insight into another side of his calling, he spent four months at Wetzlar, where the imperial law-courts were established. But Goethe's professional duties had only a small share in the eventful years which lay between his return from Strassburg and that visit to Weimar at the end of 1775, which turned the whole course of his career, and resulted in his permanent attachment to the Weimar court. Goethe's life in Frankfort was a round of stimulating literary intercourse; in J. H. Merck (1741-1791), an army official in the neighbouring town of Darmstadt, he found a friend and mentor, whose irony and common-sense served as a corrective to his own exuberance of spirits. Wetzlar brought new friends and another passion, that for Charlotte Buff, the daughter of the *Amtmann* there—a love-story which has been immortalized in *Werthers Leiden*—and again the young poet's nature was obsessed by a love which was this time strong enough to bring him to the brink of that suicide with which the novel ends. A visit to the Rhine, where new interests and the attractions of Maximiliane von Laroche, a daughter of Wieland's friend, the novelist Sophie von Laroche, brought partial healing; his intense preoccupation with literary work on his return to Frankfort did the rest. In 1775 Goethe was attracted by still another type of woman, Lili Schönemann, whose mother was the widow of a wealthy Frankfort banker. A formal betrothal took place, and the beauty of the lyrics which Lili inspired leaves no room for doubt that here was a passion no less genuine than that for Friederike or Charlotte. But Goethe—more worldly wise than on former occasions—felt instinctively that the gay, social world in which Lili moved was not really congenial to him. A visit to Switzerland in the summer of 1775 may not have weakened his interest in her, but it at least allowed him to regard her objectively; and, without tragic consequences on either side, the passion was ultimately allowed to yield to the dictates of common-sense. Goethe's departure for Weimar in November made the final break less difficult.

The period from 1771 to 1775 was, in literary respects, the most productive of the poet's life. It had been inaugurated with *Götz von Berlichingen*, and a few months later this tragedy was followed by another, *Clavigo*, hardly less convincing in its character-drawing, and reflecting even more faithfully than the former the experiences Goethe had gone through in Strassburg. Again poetic justice is effected on the unfortunate hero who has chosen his own personal advancement in preference to his duty to the woman he loves; more pointedly than in *Götz* is the moral enforced by Clavigo's worldly friend Carlos, that the ground of Clavigo's tragic end lies not so much in the defiance of a moral law as in the hero's vacillation and want of character. With *Die Leiden des jungen Werthers* (1774), the literary precipitate of the author's own experiences in Wetzlar, Goethe succeeded in attracting, as no German had done before him, the attention of Europe. Once more it was the gospel that the world belongs to the strong, which lay beneath the surface of this romance. This, however, was not the lesson which was drawn from it by Goethe's contemporaries; they shed tears of sympathy over the lovelorn youth whose burden becomes too great for him to bear. While *Götz* inaugurated the manlier side of the *Sturm und Drang* literature, *Werther* was responsible for its sentimental excesses. And to the sentimental rather than to the heroic side belongs also *Stella*, "a drama for lovers," in which the poet again reproduced, if with less fidelity than in *Werther*, certain aspects of his own love troubles. A lighter vein is to be observed in various dramatic satires written at this time, such as *Götter, Helden und Wieland* (1774), *Hanswursts Hochzeit, Fastnachtsspiel vom Pater Brey, Satyros*, and in the *Singspiele, Erwin und Elmire*(1775) and *Claudine von Villa Bella* (1776); while in the *rankfurter Gelehrte Anzeiger* (1772-1773), Goethe drove home the principles of the new movement of *Sturm und Drang* in terse and pointed criticism. The exuberance of the young poet's genius is also to be seen in the many unfinished fragments of this period; at one time we find him occupied with dramas on *Caesar* and *Mahomet*, at another with an epic on *Der ewige Jude*, and again with a tragedy on *Prometheus*, of which a magnificent fragment has passed into his works. Greatest of all the torsos of this period, however, was the dramatization of *Faust*. Thanks to a manuscript copy of the play in its earliest form—discovered as recently as 1887—we are now able to distinguish how much of this tragedy was the immediate product of the *Sturm und Drang*, and to understand the intentions with which the young poet began his masterpiece. Goethe's hero changed with the author's riper experience and with his new conceptions of man's place and duties in the world, but the Gretchen tragedy was taken over into the finished poem, practically unaltered, from the earliest *Faust* of the *Sturm und Drang*. With these wonderful scenes, the most intensely tragic in all German literature, Goethe's poetry in this period reaches its climax. Still another important work, however, was conceived, and in large measure written at this time, the drama of *Egmont*, which was not published until 1788. This work may, to some extent, be regarded as supplementary to *Faust*; it presents the lighter, more cheerful and optimistic side of Goethe's philosophy in these years; Graf Egmont, the most winning and fascinating of the poet's heroes, is endowed with that "demonic" power over the sympathies of men and women, which Goethe himself possessed in so high a degree. But *Egmont* depends for its interest almost solely on two characters, Egmont himself and Klärchen, Gretchen's counterpart; regarded as a drama, it demonstrates the futility of that defiance of convention and rules with which the *Sturm und Drang* set out. It remained for Goethe, in the next period of his life, to construct on classic models a new vehicle for German dramatic poetry.

In December 1774 the young "hereditary prince" of Weimar, Charles Augustus, passing through Frankfort on his way to Paris, came into personal touch with Goethe, and invited the poet to visit Weimar when, in the following year, he took up the reins of government. In October 1775 the invitation was repeated, and on the 7th of November of that year Goethe arrived in the little Saxon capital which was to remain his home for the rest of his life. During the first few months in Weimar the poet gave himself up to the pleasures of the moment as unreservedly as his patron; indeed, the Weimar court even looked upon him for a time as a tempter who led the young duke astray. But the latter, although himself a mere stripling, had implicit faith in Goethe, and a firm conviction that his genius could be utilized in other fields besides literature. Goethe was not long in Weimar before he was entrusted with responsible state duties, and events soon justified the duke's confidence. Goethe proved the soul of the Weimar government, and a minister of state of energy and foresight. He interested himself in agriculture, horticulture and mining, which were of paramount importance to the welfare of the duchy, and out of these interests sprang his own love for the natural sciences, which took up so much of his time in later 184years. The inevitable love-interest was also not wanting. As Friederike had fitted into the background of Goethe's Strassburg life, Lotte into that of Wetzlar, and Lili into the gaieties of Frankfort, so now Charlotte von Stein, the wife of a Weimar official, was the personification of the more aristocratic ideals of Weimar society. We possess only the poet's share of his correspondence with Frau von Stein, but it is possible to infer from it that, of all Goethe's loves, this was intellectually the most worthy of him. Frau von Stein was a woman of refined literary taste and culture, seven years older than he and the mother of seven children. There was something more spiritual, something that partook rather of the passionate friendships of the 18th century than of love in Goethe's relations with her. Frau von Stein dominated the poet's life for twelve years, until his journey to Italy in 1786-1788. Of other events of this period the most notable were two winter journeys, the first in 1777, to the Harz Mountains, the second, two years later, to Switzerland—journeys which gave Goethe scope for that introspection and reflection for which his Weimar life left him little time. On the second of these journeys he revisited Friederike in Sesenheim, saw Lili, who had married and settled in Strassburg, and made the personal acquaintance of Lavater in Zürich.

The literary results of these years cannot be compared with those of the preceding period; they are virtually limited to a few wonderful lyrics, such as *Wanderers Nachtlied, An den Mond, Gesang der Geister über den Wassern*, or ballads, such as *Der Erlkönig*, a charming little drama, *Die Geschwister*(1776), in which the poet's relations to both Lili and Frau von Stein seem to be reflected, a dramatic satire, *Der Triumph der Empfindsamkeit* (1778), and a number of *Singspiele, Lila* (1777), *Die Fischerin, Scherz, List und Rache*, and *Jery und Bätely* (1780). But greater works were in preparation. A religious epic, *Die Geheimnisse*, and a tragedy *Elpenor*, did not, it is true, advance much further than plans; but in 1777, under the influence of the theatrical experiments at the Weimar court, Goethe conceived and in great measure wrote a novel of the theatre, which was to have borne the title *Wilhelm Meisters theatralische Sendung*; and in 1779 himself took part in a representation before the court at Ettersburg, of his drama *Iphigenie auf Tauris*. This *Iphigenie* was, however, in prose; in the following year Goethe remoulded it in iambics, but it was not until he went to Rome that the drama finally received the form in which we know it.

In September, 1786 Goethe set out from Karlsbad—secretly and stealthily, his plan known only to his servant—on that memorable journey to Italy, to which he had looked forward with such intense longing; he could not cross the Alps quickly enough, so impatient was he to set foot in Italy. He travelled by way of Munich, the Brenner and Lago di Garda to Verona and Venice, and from thence to Rome, where he arrived on the 29th of October 1786. Here he gave himself up unreservedly to the new impressions which crowded on him, and he was soon at home among the German artists in Rome, who welcomed him warmly. In the spring of 1787 he extended his journey as far as Naples and Sicily, returning to Rome in June 1787, where he remained until his final departure for Germany on the 2nd of April 1788. It is difficult to exaggerate the importance of Goethe's Italian journey. He himself regarded it as a kind of climax to his life; never before had he attained such complete understanding of his genius and mission in the world; it afforded him a vantage-ground from which he could renew the past and make plans for the future. In Weimar he had felt that he was no longer in sympathy with the *Sturm und Drang*, but it was Italy which first taught him clearly what might take the place of that movement in German poetry. To the modern reader, who may well be impressed by Goethe's extraordinary receptivity, it may seem strange that his interests in Italy were so limited; for, after all, he saw comparatively little of the art treasures of Italy. He went to Rome in Winckelmann's footsteps; it was the antique he sought, and his interest in the artists of the Renaissance was virtually restricted to their imitation of classic models. This search for the classic ideal is reflected in the works he completed or wrote under the Italian sky. The calm beauty of Greek tragedy is seen in the new iambic version of *Iphigenie auf Tauris* (1787); the classicism of the Renaissance gives the ground-tone to the wonderful drama of *Torquato Tasso* (1790), in which the conflict of poetic genius with the prosaic world is transmuted into imperishable poetry. Classic, too, in this sense, were the plans of a drama on *Iphigenie auf Delphos* and of an epic, *Nausikaa*. Most interesting of all, however, is the reflection of the classic spirit in works already begun in earlier days, such as *Egmont* and *Faust*. The former drama was finished in Italy and appeared in 1788, the latter was brought a step further forward, part of it being published as a *Fragment* in 1790.

Disappointment in more senses than one awaited Goethe on his return to Weimar. He came back from Italy with a new philosophy of life, a philosophy at once classic and pagan, and with very definite ideas of what constituted literary excellence. But Germany had not advanced; in 1788 his countrymen were still under the influence of that *Sturm und Drang* from which the poet had fled. The times seemed to him more out of joint than ever, and he withdrew into himself. Even his relations to the old friends were changed. Frau von Stein had not known of his flight to Italy until she received a letter from Rome; but he looked forward to her welcome on his return. The months of absence, however, the change he had undergone, and doubtless those lighter loves of which the *Römische Elegien* bear evidence, weakened the Weimar memories; if he left Weimar as Frau von Stein's lover he returned only as her friend; and she naturally resented the change. Goethe, meanwhile, satisfied to continue the freer customs to which he had adapted himself in Rome, found a new mistress in Christiane Vulpius (1765-1816), the least interesting of all the women who attracted him. But Christiane gradually filled up a gap in the poet's life; she gave him, quietly, unobtrusively, without making demands on him, the comforts of a home. She was not accepted by court society; it did not matter to her that even Goethe's intimate friends ignored her; and she, who had suited the poet's whim when he desired to shut himself off from all that might dim the recollection of Italy, became with the years an indispensable helpmate to him. On the birth in 1789 of his son, Goethe had some thought of legalizing his relations with Christiane, but this intention was not realized until 1806, when the invasion of Weimar by the French made him fear for both life and property.

The period of Goethe's life which succeeded his return from Italy was restless and unsettled; relieved of his state duties, he returned in 1790 to Venice, only to be disenchanted with the Italy he had loved so intensely a year or two before. A journey with the duke of Weimar to Breslau followed, and in 1792 he accompanied his master on that campaign against France which ended so ingloriously for the German arms at Valmy. In later years Goethe published his account both of this *Campagne in Frankreich* and of the *Belagerung von Mainz*, at which he was also present in 1793. His literary work naturally suffered under these distractions. *Tasso*, and the edition of the *Schriften* in which it was to appear, had still to be completed on his return from Italy; the *Römische Elegien*, perhaps the most Latin of all his works, were published in 1795, and the *Venetianische Epigramme*, the result of the second visit to Italy, in 1796. The French Revolution, in which all Europe was engrossed, was in Goethe's eyes only another proof that the passing of the old régime meant the abrogation of all law and order, and he gave voice to his antagonism to the new democratic principles in the dramas *Der Grosskophta* (1792), *Der Bürgergeneral* (1793), and in the unfinished fragments *Die Aufgeregten* and *Das Mädchen von Oberkirch*. The spirited translation of the epic of *Reinecke Fuchs* (1794) he took up as a relief and an antidote to the social disruption of the time. Two new interests, however, strengthened the ties between Goethe and Weimar,—ties which the Italian journey had threatened to sever: his appointment in 1791 as director of the ducal theatre, a post which he occupied for twenty-two years, and his absorption in scientific studies. In 1790 he published his important *Versuch, die Metamorphose der Pflanzen zu erklären*, which was an even more fundamental achievement for the new science of comparative morphology 185than his discovery some six years earlier of the existence of a formation in the human jaw-bone analogous to the intermaxillary bone in apes; and in 1791 and 1792 appeared two parts of his *Beiträge zur Optik*.

Meanwhile, however, Goethe had again taken up the novel of the theatre which he had begun years before, with a view to finishing it and including it in the edition of his *Neue Schriften* (1792-1800). *Wilhelm Meisters theatralische Sendung* became *Wilhelm Meisters Lehrjahre*; the novel of purely theatrical interests was widened out to embrace the history of a young man's apprenticeship to life. The change of plan explains, although it may not exculpate, the formlessness and loose construction of the work, its extremes of realistic detail and poetic allegory. A hero, who was probably originally intended to demonstrate the failure of the vacillating temperament when brought face to face with the problems of art, proved ill-adapted to demonstrate those precepts for the guidance of life with which the *Lehrjahre* closes; unstable of purpose, Wilhelm Meister is not so much an illustration of the author's life-philosophy as a lay-figure on which he demonstrates his views. *Wilhelm Meister* is a work of extraordinary variety, ranging from the commonplace realism of the troupe of strolling players to the poetic romanticism of Mignon and the harper; its flashes of intuitive criticism and its weighty apothegms add to its value as a *Bildungsroman* in the best sense of that word. Of all Goethe's works, this exerted the most immediate and lasting influence on German literature; it served as a model for the best fiction of the next thirty years.

In completing *Wilhelm Meister*, Goethe found a sympathetic and encouraging critic in Schiller, to whom he owed in great measure his renewed interest in poetry. After years of tentative approaches on Schiller's part, years in which that poet concealed even from himself his desire for a friendly understanding with Goethe, the favourable moment arrived; it was in June 1794, when Schiller was seeking collaborators for his new periodical *Die Horen*; and his invitation addressed to Goethe was the beginning of a friendship which continued unbroken until the younger poet's death. The friendship of Goethe and Schiller, of which their correspondence is a priceless record, had its limitations; it was purely intellectual in character, a certain barrier of personal reserve being maintained to the last. But for the literary life of both poets the gain was incommensurable. As far as actual work was concerned, Goethe went his own way as he had always been accustomed to do; but the mere fact that he devoted himself with increasing interest to literature was due to Schiller's stimulus. It was Schiller, too, who induced him to undertake those studies on the nature of epic and dramatic poetry which resulted in the epic of *Hermann und Dorothea* and the fragment of the *Achilleis*; without the friendship there would have been no *Xenien* and no ballads, and it was his younger friend's encouragement which induced Goethe to betake himself once more to the "misty path" of *Faust*, and bring the first part of that drama to a conclusion.

Goethe's share in the *Xenien* (1796) may be briefly dismissed. This collection of distichs, written in collaboration with Schiller, was prompted by the indifference and animosity of contemporary criticism, and its disregard for what the two poets regarded as the higher interests of German poetry. The *Xenien* succeeded as a retaliation on the critics, but the masterpieces which followed them proved in the long run much more effective weapons against the prevailing mediocrity. Prose works like the *Unterhaltungen deutscher Ausgewanderten* (1795) were unworthy of the poet's genius, and the translation of Benvenuto Cellini's *Life* (1796-1797) was only a translation. But in 1798 appeared *Hermann und Dorothea*, one of Goethe's most perfect poems. It is indeed remarkable—when we consider by how much reflection and theoretic discussion the composition of the poem was preceded and accompanied—that it should make upon the reader so simple and "naïve" an impression; in this respect it is the triumph of an art that conceals art. Goethe has here taken a simple story of village life, mirrored in it the most pregnant ideas of his time, and presented it with a skill which may well be called Homeric; but he has discriminated with the insight of genius between the Homeric method of reproducing the heroic life of primitive Greece and the same method as adapted to the commonplace happenings of 18th-century Germany. In this respect he was undoubtedly guided by a forerunner who has more right than he to the attribute "naïve," by J. H. Voss, the author of *Luise*. Hardly less imposing in their calm, placid perfection are the poems with which, in friendly rivalry, Goethe seconded the more popular ballads of his friend; *Der Zauberlehrling, Der Gott und die Bayadere, Die Braut von Korinth, Alexis und Dora, Der neue Pausias* and *Die schöne Müllerin*—a cycle of poems in the style of the *Volkslied*—are among the masterpieces of Goethe's poetry. On the other hand, even the friendship with Schiller did not help him to add to his reputation as a dramatist. *Die natürliche Tochter* (1803), in which he began to embody his ideas of the Revolution on a wide canvas, proved impossible on the stage, and the remaining dramas, which were to have formed a trilogy, were never written. Goethe's classic principles, when applied to the swift, direct art of the theatre, were doomed to failure, and *Die natürliche Tochter*, notwithstanding its good theoretic intention, remains the most lifeless and shadowy of all his dramas. Even less in touch with the living present were the various prologues and *Festspiele*, such as *Paläophron und Neoterpe* (1800), *Was wir bringen* (1802), which in these years he composed for the Weimar theatre.

Goethe's classicism brought him into inevitable antagonism with the new Romantic movement which had been inaugurated in 1798 by the *Athenaeum*, edited by the brothers Schlegel. The sharpness of the conflict was, however, blunted by the fact that, without exception, the young Romantic writers looked up to Goethe as its master; they modelled their fiction on *Wilhelm Meister*, they regarded his lyrics as the high-water mark of German poetry; Goethe, Novalis declared, was the "Statthalter of poetry on earth." With regard to painting and sculpture, however, Goethe felt that a protest was necessary, if the insidious ideas propounded in works like Wackenroder's *Herzensergiessungen* were not to do irreparable harm, by bringing back the confusion of the *Sturm und Drang*; and, as a rejoinder to the Romantic theories, Goethe, in conjunction with his friend Heinrich Meyer (1760-1832), published from 1798 to 1800 an art review, *Die Propyläen*. Again, in *Winckelmann und seine Zeit* (1805) Goethe vigorously defended the classical ideals of which Winckelmann had been the founder. But in the end he proved himself the greatest enemy to the strict classic doctrine by the publication in 1808 of the completed first part of *Faust*, a work which was accepted by contemporaries as a triumph of Romantic art. *Faust* is a patchwork of many colours. With the aid of the vast body of *Faust* literature which has sprung up in recent years, and the many new documents bearing on its history—above all, the so-called *Urfaust*, to which reference has already been made—we are able now to ascribe to their various periods the component parts of the work; it is possible to discriminate between the *Sturm und Drang* hero of the opening scenes and of the Gretchen tragedy—the contemporary of Götz and Clavigo—and the superimposed Faust of calmer moral and intellectual ideals—a Faust who corresponds to Hermann and Wilhelm Meister. In its original form the poem was the dramatization of a specific and individualized story; in the years of Goethe's friendship with Schiller it was extended to embody the higher strivings of 18th-century humanism; ultimately, as we shall see, it became, in the second part, a vast allegory of human life and activity. Thus the elements of which *Faust* is composed were even more difficult to blend than were those of *Wilhelm Meister*; but the very want of uniformity is one source of the perennial fascination of the tragedy, and has made it in a peculiar degree the national poem of the German people, the mirror which reflects the national life and poetry from the outburst of *Sturm und Drang* to the well-weighed and tranquil classicism of Goethe's old age.

The third and final period of Goethe's long life may be said to have begun after Schiller's death. He never again lost touch with literature as he had done in the years which preceded his 186friendship with Schiller; but he stood in no active or immediate connexion with the literary movement of his day. His life moved on comparatively uneventfully. Even the Napoleonic régime of 1806-1813 disturbed but little his equanimity. Goethe, the cosmopolitan*Weltbürger* of the 18th century, had himself no very intense feelings of patriotism, and, having seen Germany flourish as a group of small states under enlightened despotisms, he had little confidence in the dreamers of 1813 who hoped to see the glories of Barbarossa's empire revived. Napoleon, moreover, he regarded not as the scourge of Europe, but as the defender of civilization against the barbarism of the Slavs; and in the famous interview between the two men at Erfurt the poet's admiration was reciprocated by the French conqueror. Thus Goethe had no great sympathy for the war of liberation which kindled young hearts from one end of Germany to the other; and when the national enthusiasm rose to its highest pitch he buried himself in those optical and morphological studies, which, with increasing years, occupied more and more of his time and interest.

The works and events of the last twenty-five years of Goethe's life may be briefly summarized. In 1805, as we have seen, he suffered an irreparable loss in the death of Schiller; in 1806, Christiane became his legal wife, and to the same year belongs the magnificent tribute to his dead friend, the *Epilog zu Schillers Glocke*. Two new friendships about this time kindled in the poet something of the juvenile fire and passion of younger days. Bettina von Arnim came into personal touch with Goethe in 1807, and her *Briefwechsel Goethes mit einem Kinde* (published in 1835) is, in its mingling of truth and fiction, one of the most delightful products of the Romantic mind; but the episode was of less importance for Goethe's life than Bettina would have us believe. On the other hand, his interest in Minna Herzlieb, foster-daughter of the publisher Frommann in Jena, was of a warmer nature, and has left its traces on his sonnets.

In 1808, as we have seen, appeared the first part of *Faust*, and in 1809 it was followed by *Die Wahlverwandtschaften*. The novel, hardly less than the drama, effected a change in the public attitude towards the poet. Since the beginning of the century the conviction had been gaining ground that Goethe's mission was accomplished, that the day of his leadership was over; but here were two works which not merely re-established his ascendancy, but proved that the old poet was in sympathy with the movement of letters, and keenly alive to the change of ideas which the new century had brought in its train. The intimate psychological study of four minds, which forms the subject of the *Wahlverwandtschaften*, was an essay in a new type of fiction, and pointed out the way for developments of the German novel after the stimulus of *Wilhelm Meister* had exhausted itself. Less important than *Die Wahlverwandtschaften* was *Pandora* (1810), the final product of Goethe's classicism, and the most uncompromisingly classical and allegorical of all his works. And in 1810, too, appeared his treatise on *Farbenlehre*. In the following year the first volume of his autobiography was published under the title *Aus meinem Leben, Dichtung und Wahrheit*. The second and third volumes of this work followed in 1812 and 1814; the fourth, bringing the story of his life up to the close of the Frankfort period in 1833, after his death. Goethe felt, even late in life, too intimately bound up with Weimar to discuss in detail his early life there, and he shrank from carrying his biography beyond the year 1775. But a number of other publications—descriptions of travel, such as the *Italienische Reise* (1816-1817), the materials for a continuation of *Dichtung und Wahrheit* collected in *Tag- und Jahreshefte* (1830)—have also to be numbered among the writings which Goethe has left us as documents of his life. Meanwhile no less valuable biographical materials were accumulating in his diaries, his voluminous correspondence and his conversations, as recorded by J. P. Eckermann, the chancellor Müller and F. Soret. Several periodical publications, *Über Kunst und Altertum* (1816-1832), *Zur Naturwissenschaft überhaupt* (1817-1824). *Zur Morphologie* (1817-1824), bear witness to the extraordinary breadth of Goethe's interests in these years. Art, science, literature—little escaped his ken—and that not merely in Germany: English writers, Byron, Scott and Carlyle, Italians like Manzoni, French scientists and poets, could all depend on friendly words of appreciation and encouragement from Weimar.

In *West-östlicher Diwan* (1819), a collection of lyrics—matchless in form and even more concentrated in expression than those of earlier days—which were suggested by a German translation of Hafiz, Goethe had another surprise in store for his contemporaries. And, again, it was an actual passion—that for Marianne von Willemer, whom he met in 1814 and 1815—which rekindled in him the lyric fire. Meanwhile the years were thinning the ranks of Weimar society: Wieland, the last of Goethe's greater literary contemporaries, died in 1813, his wife in 1816, Charlotte von Stein in 1827 and Duke Charles Augustus in 1828. Goethe's retirement from the direction of the theatre in 1817 meant for him a break with the literary life of the day. In 1822 a passion for a young girl, Ulrike von Levetzow, whom he met at Marienbad, inspired the fine *Trilogie der Leidenschaft*, and between 1821 and 1829 appeared the long-expected and long-promised continuation of *Wilhelm Meister, Wilhelm Meisters Wanderjahre*. The latter work, however, was a disappointment: perhaps it could not have been otherwise. Goethe had lost the thread of his romance and it was difficult for him to resume it. Problems of the relation of the individual to society and industrial questions were to have formed the theme of the *Wanderjahre*; but since the French Revolution these problems had themselves entered on a new phase and demanded a method of treatment which it was not easy for the old poet to learn. Thus his intentions were only partially carried out, and the volumes were filled out by irrelevant stories, which had been written at widely different periods.

But the crowning achievement of Goethe's literary life was the completion of *Faust*. The poem had accompanied him from early manhood to the end and was the repository for the fullest "confession" of his life; it is the poetic epitome of his experience. The second part is, in form, far removed from the impressive realism of the *Urfaust*. It is a phantasmagory; a drama the actors in which are not creatures of flesh and blood, but the shadows of an unreal world of allegory. The lover of Gretchen had, as far as poetic continuity is concerned, disappeared with the close of the first part. In the second part it is virtually a new Faust who, at the hands of a new Mephistopheles, goes out into a world that is not ours. Yet behind these unconvincing shadows of an imperial court with its financial difficulties, of the classical *Walpurgisnacht*, of the fantastic creation of the Homunculus, the noble Helena episode and the impressive mystery-scene of the close, where the centenarian Faust finally triumphs over the powers of evil, there lies a philosophy of life, a ripe wisdom born of experience, such as no European poet had given to the world since the Renaissance. *Faust* has been well called the "divine comedy" of 18th-century humanism.

The second part of *Faust* forms a worthy close to the life of Germany's greatest man of letters, who died in Weimar on the 22nd of March 1832. He was the last of those universal minds which have been able to compass all domains of human activity and knowledge; for he stood on the brink of an era of rapidly expanding knowledge which has made for ever impossible the universality of interest and sympathy which distinguished him. As a poet, his fame has undergone many vicissitudes since his death, ranging from the indifference of the "Young German" school to the enthusiastic admiration of the closing decades of the 19th century—an enthusiasm to which we owe the Weimar *Goethe-Gesellschaft* (founded in 1885) and a vast literature dealing with the poet's life and work; but the fact of his being Germany's greatest poet and the master of her classical literature has never been seriously put in question. The intrinsic value of his poetic work, regarded apart from his personality, is smaller in proportion to its bulk than is the case with many lesser German poets and with the greatest poets of other literatures. But Goethe was a type of literary man hitherto unrepresented among the leading writers of the world's literature; he was a poet whose supreme greatness lay in his subjectivity. Only a small fraction 187of Goethe's work was written in an impersonal and objective spirit, and sprang from what might be called a conscious artistic impulse; by far the larger—and the better—part is the immediate reflex of his feelings and experiences.

It is as a lyric poet that Goethe's supremacy is least likely to be challenged; he has given his nation, whose highest literary expression has in all ages been essentially lyric, its greatest songs. No other German poet has succeeded in attuning feeling, sentiment and thought so perfectly to the music of words as he; none has expressed so fully that spirituality in which the quintessence of German lyrism lies. Goethe's dramas, on the other hand, have not, in the eyes of his nation, succeeded in holding their own beside Schiller's; but the reason is rather because Goethe, from what might be called a wilful obstinacy, refused to be bound by the conventions of the theatre, than because he was deficient in the cunning of the dramatist. For, as an interpreter of human character in the drama, Goethe is without a rival among modern poets, and there is not one of his plays that does not contain a few scenes or characters which bear indisputable testimony to his mastery. *Faust* is Germany's most national drama, and it remains perhaps for the theatre of the future to prove itself capable of popularizing psychological masterpieces like *Tasso* and *Iphigenie*. It is as a novelist that Goethe has suffered most by the lapse of time. The *Sorrows of Werther* no longer moves us to tears, and even *Wilhelm Meister* and *Die Wahlverwandtschaften* require more understanding for the conditions under which they were written than do *Faust* or *Egmont*. Goethe could fill his prose with rich wisdom, but he was only the perfect artist in verse.

Little attention is nowadays paid to Goethe's work in other fields, work which he himself in some cases prized more highly than his poetry. It is only as an illustration of his many-sidedness and his manifold activity that we now turn to his work as a statesman, as a theatre-director, as a practical political economist. His art-criticism is symptomatic of a phase of European taste which tried in vain to check the growing individualism of Romanticism. His scientific studies and discoveries awaken only an historical interest. We marvel at the obstinacy with which he, with inadequate mathematical knowledge, opposed the Newtonian theory of light and colour; and at his championship of "Neptunism," the theory of aqueous origin, as opposed to "Vulcanism," that of igneous origin of the earth's crust. Of far-reaching importance was, on the other hand, his foreshadowing of the Darwinian theory in his works on the metamorphosis of plants and on animal morphology. Indeed, the deduction to be drawn from Goethe's contributions to botany and anatomy is that he, as no other of his contemporaries, possessed that type of scientific mind which, in the 19th century, has made for progress; he was Darwin's predecessor by virtue of his enunciation of what has now become one of the commonplaces of natural science—organic evolution. Modern, too, was the outlook of the aging poet on the changing social conditions of the age, wonderfully sympathetic his attitude towards modern industry, which steam was just beginning to establish on a new basis, and towards modern democracy. The Europe of his later years was very different from the idyllic and enlightened autocracy of the 18th century, in which he had spent his best years and to which he had devoted his energies; yet Goethe was at home in it.

From the philosophic movement, in which Schiller and the Romanticists were so deeply involved, Goethe stood apart. Comparatively early in life he had found in Spinoza the philosopher who responded to his needs; Spinoza taught him to see in nature the "living garment of God," and more he did not seek or need to know. As a convinced realist he took his standpoint on nature and experience, and could afford to look on objectively at the controversies of the metaphysicians. Kant he by no means ignored, and under Schiller's guidance he learned much from him; but of the younger thinkers, only Schelling, whose mystic nature-philosophy was a development of Spinoza's ideas, touched a sympathetic chord in his nature. As a moralist and a guide to the conduct of life—an aspect of Goethe's work which Carlyle, viewing him through the coloured glasses of Fichtean idealism, emphasized and interpreted not always justly—Goethe was a powerful force on German life in years of political and intellectual depression. It is difficult even still to get beyond the maxims of practical wisdom he scattered so liberally through his writings, the lessons to be learned from *Meister* and *Faust*, or even that calm, optimistic fatalism which never deserted Goethe, and was so completely justified by the tenor of his life. If the philosophy of Spinoza provided the poet with a religion which made individual creeds and dogmas unnecessary and impossible, so Leibnitz's doctrine of predestinism supplied the foundations for his faith in the divine mission of human life.

This many-sided activity is a tribute to the greatness of Goethe's mind and personality; we may regard him merely as the embodiment of his particular age, or as a poet "for all time"; but with one opinion all who have felt the power of Goethe's genius are in agreement—the opinion which was condensed in Napoleon's often cited words, uttered after the meeting at Erfurt: *Voilà un homme!* Of all modern men, Goethe is the most universal type of genius. It is the full, rich humanity of his life and personality—not the art behind which the artist disappears, or the definite pronouncements of the thinker or the teacher—that constitutes his claim to a place in the front rank of men of letters. His life was his greatest work.

BIBLIOGRAPHY.—(*a*) *Collected Works, Diaries, Correspondence, Conversations.* The following authorized editions of Goethe's writings appeared in the poet's lifetime: *Schriften* (8 vols., Leipzig, 1787-1790); *Neue Schriften* (7 vols., Berlin, 1792-1800); *Werke* (13 vols., Stuttgart, 1806-1810); *Werke* (20 vols., Stuttgart, 1815-1819); to which six volumes were added in 1820-1822; Werke (Vollständige Ausgabe letzter Hand) (40 vols., Stuttgart, 1827-1830). Goethe's *Nachgelassene Werke* appeared as a continuation of this edition in 15 volumes (Stuttgart, 1832-1834), to which five volumes were added in 1842. These were followed by several editions of Goethe's *Sämtliche Werke*, mostly in forty volumes, published by Cotta of Stuttgart. The first critical edition with notes was published by Hempel, Berlin, in thirty-six volumes, 1868-1879; that in Kürschner's *Deutsche Nationalliteratur*, vols. 82-117 (1882-1897) is also important. In 1887 the monumental Weimar edition, which is now approaching completion, began to appear; it is divided into four sections: I. *Werke* (*c.* 56 vols.); II. *Naturwissenschaftliche Werke* (12 vols.); III.*Tagebücher* (13 vols.); IV. *Briefe* (*c.* 45 vols.). Of other recent editions the most noteworthy are: Sämtliche Werke (Jubiläums-Ausgabe), edited by E. von der Hellen (40 vols., Stuttgart, 1902 ff.); *Werke*, edited by K. Heinemann (30 vols., Leipzig, 1900 ff.), and the cheap edition of the*Sämtliche Werke*, edited by L. Geiger (44 vols., Leipzig, 1901). There are also innumerable editions of selected works; reference need only be made here to the useful collection of the early writings and letters published by S. Hirzel with an introduction by M. Bernays, *Der junge Goethe*(3 vols., Leipzig, 1875, 2nd ed., 1887). A French translation of Goethe's *Œuvres complètes*, by J. Porchat, appeared in 9 vols., at Paris, in 1860-1863. There is, as yet, no uniform English edition, but Goethe's chief works have all been frequently translated and a number of them will be found in Bohn's standard library.

The definitive edition of Goethe's diaries and letters is that forming Sections III. and IV. of the Weimar edition. Collections of selected letters based on the Weimar edition have been published by E. von der Hellen (6 vols., 1901 ff.), and by P. Stein (8 vols., 1902 ff.). Of the many separate collections of Goethe's correspondence mention may be made of the *Briefwechsel zwischen Schiller und Goethe*, edited by Goethe himself (1828-1829; 4th ed., 1881; also several cheap reprints. English translation by L. D. Schmitz, 1877-1879); *Briefwechsel zwischen Goethe und Zelter* (6 vols., 1833-1834; reprint in Reclam's *Universalbibliothek*, 1904; English translation by A. D. Coleridge, 1887); *Bettina von Arnim, Goethes Briefwechsel mit einem Kinde* (1835; 4th ed., 1890; English translation, 1838); *Briefe von und an Goethe*, edited by F. W. Riemer (1846);*Goethes Briefe an Frau von Stein*, edited by A. Schöll (1848-1851; 3rd ed. by J. Wahle, 1899-1900); *Briefwechsel zwischen Goethe und K. F. von Reinhard* (1850); *Briefwechsel zwischen Goethe und Knebel* (2 vols., 1851); *Briefwechsel zwischen Goethe und Staatsrat Schultz* (1853);*Briefwechsel des Herzogs Karl August mit Goethe* (2 vols., 1863); *Briefwechsel zwischen Goethe und Kaspar Graf von Sternberg* (1866); *Goethes naturwissenschaftliche Korrespondenz*, and *Goethes Briefwechsel mit den Gebrüdern von Humboldt*, edited by F. T. Bratranek (1874-1876);*Goethes und Carlyles Briefwechsel* (1887), also in English; *Goethe und die Romantik*, edited by C. Schüddekopf and O. Walzel (2 vols., 1898-1899); *Goethe und Lavater*, edited by H. Funck (1901); *Goethe und Österreich*, edited by A. Sauer (2 vols., 1902-1903). Besides the correspondence with Schiller and Zelter, Bonn's library contains a translation of *Early and Miscellaneous* 188*Letters*, by E. Bell (1884). The chief collections of Goethe's conversations are: J. P. Eckermann, *Gespräche mit Goethe* (1836; vol. iii., also containing conversations with Soret, 1848; 7th ed. by H. Düntzer, 1899; also new edition by L. Geiger, 1902; English translation by J. Oxenford, 1850). The complete conversations with Soret have been published in German translation by C. A. H. Burkhardt (1905); *Goethes Unterhaltungen mit dem Kanzler F. von Müller* (1870). Goethe's collected *Gespräche* were published by W. von Biedermann in 10 vols. (1889-1896).

(*b*) *Biography.*—Goethe's autobiography, *Aus meinem Leben: Dichtung und Wahrheit*, appeared in three parts between 1811 and 1814, a fourth part, bringing the history of his life as far as his departure for Weimar in 1775, in 1833 (English translation by J. Oxenford, 1846); it is supplemented by other biographical writings, as the *Italienische Reise, Aus einer Reise in die Schweiz im Jahre 1797; Aus einer Reise am Rhein, Main und Neckar in den Jahren 1814 und 1815, Tag- und Jahreshefte*, &c., and especially by his diaries and correspondence. The following are the more important biographies: H. Döring, *Goethes Leben* (1828; subsequent editions, 1833, 1849, 1856); H. Viehoff, *Goethes Leben* (4 vols., 1847-1854; 5th ed., 1887); J. W. Schäfer, *Goethes Leben* (2 vols.,

1851; 3rd ed., 1877); G. H. Lewes, *The Life and Works of Goethe* (2 vols., 1855; 2nd ed., 1864; 3rd ed., 1875; cheap reprint, 1906; the German translation by J. Frese is in its 18th edition, 1900; a shorter biography was published by Lewes in 1873 under the title *The Story of Goethe's Life)*; W. Mézières, *W. Goethe, les œuvres expliquées par la vie* (1872-1873); A. Bossert, *Goethe* (1872-1873); K. Goedeke, *Goethes Leben und Schriften* (1874; 2nd ed., 1877); H. Grimm, *Goethe: Vorlesungen* (1876; 8th ed., 1903; English translation, 1880); A. Hayward, *Goethe* (1878); H. H. Boyesen, *Goethe and Schiller, their Lives and Works* (1879); H. Düntzer,*Goethes Leben* (1880; 2nd ed., 1883; English translation, 1883); A. Baumgartner, *Goethe, sein Leben und seine Werke* (1885); J. Sime, *Life of Goethe* (1888); K. Heinemann, *Goethes Leben und Werke* (1889; 3rd ed., 1903); R. M. Meyer, *Goethe* (1894; 3rd ed., 1904); A. Bielschowsky,*Goethe, sein Leben und seine Werke* (vol. i., 1895; 5th ed., 1904; vol. ii., 1903; English translation by W. A. Cooper, 1905 ff.); G. Witkowsky, Goethe (1899); H. G. Atkins, *J. W. Goethe* (1904); P. Hansen and R. Meyer, *Goethe, hans Liv og Vaerker* (1906).

Of writings on special periods and aspects of Goethe's life the more important are as follows (the titles are arranged as far as possible in the chronological sequence of the poet's life): H. Düntzer, *Goethes Stammbaum* (1894); K. Heinemann, *Goethes Mutter* (1891; 6th ed., 1900); P. Bastier, *La Mère de Goethe* (1902); *Briefe der Frau Rat* (2 vols., 2nd ed., 1905); F. Ewart, *Goethes Vater* (1899); G. Witkowski, *Cornelia die Schwester Goethes* (1903); P. Besson, *Goethe, sa sœur et ses amies* (1898); H. Düntzer, *Frauenbilder aus Goethes Jugendzeit* (1852); W. von Biedermann, *Goethe und Leipzig* (1865); P. F. Lucius, *Friederike Brion* (1878; 3rd ed., 1904); A. Bielschowsky, *Friederike Brion* (1880); F. E. von Durckheim, *Lili's Bild geschichtlich entworfen* (1879; 2nd ed., 1894); W. Herbst, *Goethe in Wetzlar* (1881); A. Diezmann, *Goethe und die lustige Zeit in Weimar* (1857; 2nd ed., 1901); H. Düntzer, *Goethe und Karl August* (1859-1864; 2nd ed., 1888); also, by the same author, *Aus Goethes Freundeskreise* (1868) and *Charlotte von Stein* (2 vols., 1874); J. Haarhuus, *Auf Goethes Spuren in Italien* (1896-1898); O. Harnack, *Zur Nachgeschichte der italienischen Reise* (1890); H. Grimm, *Schiller und Goethe* (*Essays*, 1858; 3rd ed., 1884); G. Berlit, *Goethe und Schiller im persönlichen Verkehre, nach brieflichen Mitteilungen von H. Voss* (1895); E. Pasqué, *Goethes Theaterleitung in Weimar* (2 vols., 1863); C. A. H. Burkhards, *Das Repertoire des weimarischen Theaters unter Goethes Leitung* (1891); J. Wahle, *Das Weimarer Hoftheater unter Goethes Leitung*(1892); O. Harnack, *Goethe in der Epoche seiner Vollendung* (2nd ed., 1901); J. Barbey d'Aurevilly, *Goethe et Diderot* (1880); A Fischer,*Goethe und Napoleon* (1899; 2nd ed., 1900); R. Steig, *Goethe und die Gebrüder Grimm* (1892).

(*c*) *Criticism.*—H. G. Graef, *Goethe über seine Dichtungen* (1901 ff.); J. W. Braun, *Goethe im Urteile seiner Zeitgenossen* (3 vols., 1883-1885); T. Carlyle, *Essays on Goethe* (1828-1832); X. Marmier, *Études sur Goethe* (1835); W. von Biedermann, *Goethe-Forschungen* (1879, 1886); J. Minor and A. Sauer, *Studien zur Goethe-Philologie* (1880); H. Düntzer, *Abhandlungen zu Goethes Leben und Werken* (1881); A. Schöll, *Goethe in Hauptzügen seines Lebens und Wirkens* (1882); V. Hehn, *Gedanken über Goethe* (1884; 4th ed., 1900); W. Scherer, *Aufsätze über Goethe*(1886); J. R. Seeley, *Goethe reviewed after Sixty Years* (1894); E. Dowden, *New Studies in Literature* (1895); É. Rod, *Essai sur Goethe* (1898); A. Luther, *Goethe, sechs Vorträge* (1905); R. Saitschik, *Goethes Charakter* (1898); W. Bode, *Goethes Lebenskunst* (1900; 2nd ed., 1902); by the same, *Goethes Ästhetik* (1901); T. Vollbehr, *Goethe und die bildende Kunst* (1895); E. Lichtenberger, *Études sur les poésies lyriques de Goethe*(1878); T. Achelis, *Grundzüge der Lyrik Goethes* (1900); B. Litzmann, *Goethes Lyrik* (1903); R. Riemann, *Goethes Romantechnik* (1901); R. Virchow, *Goethe als Naturforscher* (1861); E. Caro, *La Philosophie de Goethe* (1866; 2nd ed., 1870); R. Steiner, *Goethes Weltanschauung*(1897); F. Siebeck, *Goethe als Denker* (1902); F. Baldensperger, Goethe en France (1904); S. Waetzoldt, *Goethe und die Romantik* (1888).

More special treatises dealing with individual works are the following: W. Scherer, *Aus Goethes Frühzeit* (1879); R. Weissenfels, *Goethe in Sturm und Drang*, vol. i. (1894); W. Wilmanns,*Quellenstudien zu Goethes Götz von Berlichingen* (1874); J. Baechtold, *Goethes Götz von Berlichingen in dreifacher Gestalt* (1882); J. W. Appell, *Werther und seine Zeit* (1855; 4th ed., 1896); E. Schmidt, *Richardson, Rousseau und Goethe* (1875); M. Herrmann, *Das Jahrmarktsfest zu Plundersweilen* (1900); E. Schmidt, Goethes Faust in ursprünglicher Gestalt (1887; 5th ed., 1901); J. Collin, *Goethes Faust in seiner ältesten Gestalt* (1896); H. Hettner, *Goethes Iphigenie in ihrem Verhältnis zur Bildungsgeschichte des Dichters* (1861; in *Kleine Schriften*, 1884); K. Fischer, *Goethes Iphigenie* (1888); F. T. Bratranek, *Goethes Egmont und Schillers Wallenstein*(1862); C. Schuchardt, *Goethes italienische Reise* (1862); H. Düntzer, *Iphigenie auf Tauris; die drei ältesten Bearbeitungen* (1854); F. Kern,*Goethes Tasso* (1890); J. Schubart, *Die philosophischen Grundgedanken in Goethes Wilhelm Meister* (1896); E. Boas, *Schiller und Goethe in Xenienkampf* (1851); E. Schmidt and B. Suphan, *Xenien 1796, nach den Handschriften* (1893); W. von Humboldt, *Ästhetische Versuche: Hermann und Dorothea* (1799); V. Hehn, *Über Goethes Hermann und Dorothea* (1893); A. Fries, *Quellen und Komposition der Achilleis* (1901); K. Alt, *Studien zur Entstehungsgeschichte von Dichtung und Wahrheit* (1898); A. Jung, *Goethes Wanderjahre und die wichtigsten Fragen des 19. Jahrhunderts* (1854); F. Kreyssig, *Vorlesungen über Goethes Faust* (1866); the editions of *Faust* by G. von Loeper (2 vols., 1879), and K. J. Schröer (2 vols., 3rd and 4th ed., 1898-1903); K. Fischer, *Goethes Faust* (3 vols., 1893, 1902, 1903); O. Pniower, *Goethes Faust, Zeugnisse und Excurse zu seiner Entstehungsgeschichte* (1899); J. Minor, *Goethes Faust, Entstehungsgeschichte und Erklärung* (2 vols., 1901).

(*d*) *Bibliographical Works, Goethe-Societies, &c.*—L. Unflad, *Die Goethe-Literatur in Deutschland* (1878); S. Hirzel, *Verzeichnis einer Goethe-Bibliothek* (1884), to which G. von Loeper and W. von Biedermann have supplied supplements. F. Strehlke, *Goethes Briefe: Verzeichnis unter Angabe der Quelle* (1882-1884); *British Museum Catalogue of Printed Books: Goethe* (1888); Goedeke's *Grundriss zur Geschichte der deutschen Dichtung* (2nd ed., vol. iv. 1891); and the bibliographies in the *Goethe-Jahrbuch* (since 1880). Also K. Hoyer, *Zur Einführung in die Goethe-Literatur* (1904). On Goethe in England see E. Oswald, *Goethe in England and America* (1899; 2nd ed., 1909); W. Heinemann, *A Bibliographical List of the English Translations and Annotated Editions of Goethe's Faust* (1886). Reference may also be made here to F. Zarncke's *Verzeichnis der Originalaufnahmen von Goethes Bildnissen* (1888).

A *Goethe-Gesellschaft* was founded at Weimar in 1885, and numbers over 2800 members; its publications include the annual *Goethe-Jahrbuch* (since 1880), and a series of *Goethe-Schriften*. A *Goethe-Verein* has existed in Vienna since 1887, and an English Goethe society, which has also issued several volumes of publications, since 1886.

(J. G. R.)

Goethe's Descendants.—Goethe's only son, AUGUST, born on the 25th of December 1789 at Weimar, married in 1817 Ottilie von Pogwisch (1796-1872), who had come as a child to Weimar with her mother (*née* Countess Henckel von Donnersmarck). The marriage was a very unhappy one, the husband having no qualities that could appeal to a woman who, whatever the censorious might say of her moral character, was distinguished to the last by a lively intellect and a singular charm. August von Goethe, whose sole distinction was his birth and his position as grand-ducal chamberlain, died in Italy, on the 27th of October 1830, leaving three children; WALTHER WOLFGANG, born on April 9, 1818, died on April 15, 1885; WOLFGANG MAXIMILIAN, born on September 18, 1820, died on January 20, 1883; ALMA, born on October 22, 1827, died on September 29, 1844.

Of Walther von Goethe little need be said. In youth he had musical ambitions, studied under Mendelssohn and Weinlig at Leipzig, under Loewe at Stettin, and afterwards at Vienna. He published a few songs of no great merit, and had at his death no more than the reputation among his friends of a kindly and accomplished man.

Wolfgang or, as he was familiarly called, Wolf von Goethe, was by far the more gifted of the two brothers, and his gloomy destiny by so much the more tragic. A sensitive and highly imaginative boy, he was the favourite of his grandfather, who made him his constant companion. This fact, instead of being to the boy's advantage, was to prove his bane. The exalted atmosphere of the great man's ideas was too rarefied for the child's intellectual health, and a brain well fitted to do excellent work in the world was ruined by the effort to live up to an impossible ideal. To maintain himself on the same height as his grandfather, and to make the name of Goethe illustrious in his descendants also, became Wolfgang's ambition; and his incapacity to realize this, very soon borne in upon him, paralyzed 189his efforts and plunged him at last into bitter revolt against his fate and gloomy isolation from a world that seemed to have no use for him but as a curiosity. From the first, too, he was hampered by wretched health; at the age of sixteen he was subjected to one of those terrible attacks of neuralgia which were to torment him to the last; physically and mentally alike he stood in tragic contrast with his grandfather, in whose gigantic personality the vigour of his race seems to have been exhausted.

From 1839 to 1845 Wolfgang studied law at Bonn, Jena, Heidelberg and Berlin, taking his degree of *doctor juris* at Heidelberg in 1845. During this period he had made his first literary efforts. His *Studenten-Briefe* (Jena, 1842), a medley of letters and lyrics, are wholly conventional. This was followed by *Der Mensch und die elementarische Natur* (Stuttgart and Tübingen, 1845), in three parts (*Beiträge*): (1) an historical and philosophical dissertation on the relations of mankind and the "soul of nature," largely influenced by Schelling, (2) a dissertation on the juridical side of the question, *De fragmento Vegoiae*, being the thesis presented for his degree, (3) a lyrical drama, *Erlinde*. In this last, as in his other poetic attempts, Wolfgang showed a considerable measure of inherited or acquired ability, in his wealth of language and his easy mastery of the difficulties of rhythm and rhyme. But this was all. The work was characteristic of his self-centred isolation: ultra-romantic at a time when Romanticism was already an outworn fashion, remote alike from the spirit of the age and from that of Goethe. The cold reception it met with shattered at a blow the dream of Wolfgang's life; henceforth he realized that to the world he was interesting mainly as "Goethe's grandson," that anything he might achieve would be measured by that terrible standard, and he hated the legacy of his name.

The next five years he spent in Italy and at Vienna, tormented by facial neuralgia. Returning to Weimar in 1850, he was made a chamberlain by the grand-duke, and in 1852, his health being now somewhat restored, he entered the Prussian diplomatic service and went as attaché to Rome. The fruit of his long years of illness was a slender volume of lyrics, *Gedichte* (Stuttgart and Tübingen, 1851), good in form, but seldom inspired, and showing occasionally the influence of a morbid sensuality. In 1854 he was appointed secretary of legation; but the aggressive ultramontanism of the Curia became increasingly intolerable to his overwrought nature, and in 1856 he was transferred, at his own request, as secretary of legation to Dresden. This post he resigned in 1859, in which year he was raised to the rank of *Freiherr* (baron). In 1866 he received the title of councillor of legation; but he never again occupied any diplomatic post.

The rest of his life he devoted to historical research, ultimately selecting as his special subject the Italian libraries up to the year 1500. The outcome of all his labours was, however, only the first part of *Studies and Researches in the Times and Life of Cardinal Bessarion*, embracing the period of the council of Florence (privately printed at Jena, 1871), a catalogue of the MSS. in the monastery of Sancta Justina at Padua (Jena, 1873), and a mass of undigested material, which he ultimately bequeathed to the university of Jena.

In 1870 Ottilie von Goethe, who had resided mainly at Vienna, returned to Weimar and took up her residence with her two sons in the Goethehaus. So long as she lived, her small salon in the attic storey of the great house was a centre of attraction for many of the most illustrious personages in Europe. But after her death in 1872 the two brothers lived in almost complete isolation. The few old friends, including the grand-duke Charles Alexander, who continued regularly to visit the house, were entertained with kindly hospitality by Baron Walther; Wolfgang refused to be drawn from his isolation even by the advent of royalty. "Tell the empress," he cried on one occasion, "that I am not a wild beast to be stared at!" In 1879, his increasing illness necessitating the constant presence of an attendant, he went to live at Leipzig, where he died.

Goethe's grandsons have been so repeatedly accused of having displayed a dog-in-the-manger temper in closing the Goethehaus to the public and the Goethe archives to research, that the charge has almost universally come to be regarded as proven. It is true that the house was closed and access to the archives only very sparingly allowed until Baron Walther's death in 1885. But the reason for this was not, as Herr Max Hecker rather absurdly suggests, Wolfgang's jealousy of his grandfather's oppressive fame, but one far more simple and natural. From one cause or another, principally Ottilie von Goethe's extravagance, the family was in very straitened circumstances; and the brothers, being thoroughly unbusinesslike, believed themselves to be poorer than they really were.1 They closed the Goethehaus and the archives, because to have opened them would have needed an army of attendants.2 If they deserve any blame it is for the pride, natural to their rank and their generation, which prevented them from charging an entrance fee, an expedient which would not only have made it possible for them to give access to the house and collections, but would have enabled them to save the fabric from falling into the lamentable state of disrepair in which it was found after their death. In any case, the accusation is ungenerous. With an almost exaggerated*Pietät* Goethe's descendants preserved his house untouched, at great inconvenience to themselves, and left it, with all its treasures intact, to the nation. Had they been the selfish misers they are sometimes painted, they could have realized a fortune by selling its contents.

Wolf Goethe (Weimar, 1889) is a sympathetic appreciation by Otto Mejer, formerly president of the Lutheran consistory in Hanover. See also Jenny v. Gerstenbergk, *Ottilie von Goethe und ihre Söhne Walther und Wolf* (Stuttgart, 1901), and the article on Maximilian Wolfgang von Goethe by Max F. Hecker in *Allgem. deutsche Biographie*, Bd. 49, *Nachträge* (Leipzig, 1904).

(W. A. P.)

1After Walther's death upwards of £10,000 in bonds, &c., were discovered put away and forgotten in escritoires and odd corners.
2This was the reason given by Baron Walther himself to the writer's mother, an old friend of Frau von Goethe, who lived with her family in the Goethehaus for some years after 1871.

GOETZ, HERMANN (1840-1876), German musical composer, was born at Königsberg in Prussia, on the 17th of December 1840, and began his regular musical studies at the comparatively advanced age of seventeen. He entered the music-school of Professor Stern at Berlin, and studied composition chiefly under Ulrich and Hans von Bülow. In 1863 he was appointed organist at Winterthur in Switzerland, where he lived in obscurity for a number of years, occupying himself with composition during his leisure hours. One of his works was an opera, *The Taming of the Shrew*, the libretto skilfully adapted from Shakespeare's play. After much delay it was produced at Mannheim (in October 1874), and its success was as instantaneous as it has up to the present proved lasting. It rapidly made the round of the great German theatres, and spread its composer's fame over all the land. But Goetz did not live to enjoy this happy result for long. In December 1876 he died at Zürich from overwork. A second opera, *Francesco da Rimini*, on which he was engaged, remained a fragment; but it was finished according to his directions, and was performed for the first time at Mannheim a few months after the composer's death on the 4th of December 1876. Besides his dramatic work, Goetz also wrote various compositions for chamber-music, of which a trio (Op. 1) and a quintet (Op. 16) have been given with great success at the London Monday Popular Concerts. Still more important is the *Symphony in F*. As a composer of comic opera Goetz lacks the sprightliness and artistic *savoir faire* so rarely found amongst Germanic nations. His was essentially a serious nature, and passion and pathos were to him more congenial than humour. The more serious sides of the subject are therefore insisted upon more successfully than Katherine's ravings and Petruchio's eccentricities. There are, however, very graceful passages, *e.g.* the singing lesson Bianca receives from her disguised lover. Goetz's style, although influenced by Wagner and other masters, shows signs of a distinct individuality. The design of his music is essentially of a polyphonic character, and the working out and interweaving of his themes betray the musician of high scholarship. But breadth and beautiful flow of melody also were his, as is seen in the symphony, and perhaps still more in the quintet for pianoforte and strings above referred to. The most important of Goetz's posthumous works are a setting of the 137th Psalm for soprano solo, chorus and orchestra, a "Spring" overture (Op. 15), and a pianoforte sonata for four hands (Op. 17).

GOFFE (or GOUGH), **WILLIAM** (fl. 1642-1660), English parliamentarian, son of Stephen Goffe, puritan rector of Stanmer in Essex, began life as an apprentice to a London salter, a zealous parliamentarian, but on the outbreak of the civil war he joined the army and became captain in Colonel Harley's regiment of the new model in 1645. He was imprisoned in 1642 for his share in the petition to give the control of the militia to the parliament. By his marriage with Frances, daughter of General Edward Whalley, he became connected with Oliver Cromwell's family and one of his most faithful followers. He was a member of the deputation which on the 6th of July 1647 brought up the charge against the eleven members. He was active in bringing the king to trial and signed the death warrant. In 1649 he received the honorary degree of M.A. at Oxford. He distinguished himself at Dunbar, commanding a regiment there and at Worcester. He assisted in the expulsion of Barebone's parliament in 1653, took an active part in the suppression of Penruddock's rising in July 1654, and in October 1655 was appointed major-general for Berkshire, Sussex and Hampshire. Meanwhile he had been elected member for Yarmouth in the parliament of 1654 and for Hampshire in that of 1656. He supported the proposal to bestow a royal title upon Cromwell, who greatly esteemed him, was included in the newly-constituted House of Lords, obtained Lambert's place as major-general of the Foot, and was even thought of as a fit successor to Cromwell. As a member of the committee of nine appointed in June 1658 on public affairs, he was witness to the protector's appointment of Richard Cromwell as his successor. He supported the latter during his brief tenure of power and his fall involved his own loss of influence. In November 1659 he took part in the futile mission sent by the army to Monk in Scotland, and at the Restoration escaped with his father-in-law General Edward Whalley to Massachusetts. Goffe's political aims appear not to have gone much beyond fighting "to pull down Charles and set up Oliver"; and he was no doubt a man of deep religious feeling, who acted throughout according to a strict sense of duty as he conceived it. He was destined to pass the rest of his life in exile, separated from his wife and children, dying, it is supposed, about 1679.

GOFFER, to give a fluted or crimped appearance to anything, particularly to linen or lace frills or trimmings by means of heated irons of a special shape, called goffering-irons or tongs. "Goffering," or the French term *gaufrage*, is also used of the wavey or crimped edging in certain forms of porcelain, and also of the stamped or embossed decorations on the edges of the binding of books. The French word *gaufre*, from which the English form is adapted, means a thin cake marked with a pattern like a honeycomb, a "wafer," which is etymologically the same word. *Waufre* appears in the phrase *un fer à waufres*, an iron for baking cakes on (quotation of 1433 in J. B. Roquefort's *Glossaire de la langue romane*). The word is Teutonic, cf. Dutch *wafel*, Ger. *Waffel*, a form seen in "waffle," the name given to the well-known batter-cakes of America. The "wafer" was so called from its likeness to a honeycomb, *Wabe*, ultimately derived from the root *wab-*, to weave, the cells of the comb appearing to be woven together.

GOG (possibly connected with the Gentilic *Gagaya*, "of the land of Gag," used in Amarna Letters i. 38, as a synonym for "barbarian," or with Ass.*Gagu*, a ruler of the land of *Sahi*, N. of Assyria, or with *Gyges*, Ass. *Gugu*, a king of Lydia), a Hebrew name found in Ezek. xxxviii.-xxxix. and in Rev. xx., and denoting an antitheocratic power that is to manifest itself in the world immediately before the final dispensation. In the later passage, Gog and Magog are spoken of as co-ordinate; in the earlier, Gog is given as the name of the person or people and Magog as that of the land of origin. Magog is perhaps a contracted form of Mat-gog, *mat* being the common Assyrian word for "land." The passages are, however, intimately related and both depend upon Gen. x. 2, though here Magog alone is mentioned. He is the second "son" of Japhet, and the order of the names here and in Ezekiel xxxviii. 2, indicates a locality between Cappadocia and Media, *i.e.* in Armenia. According to Josephus, who is followed by Jerome, the Scythians were primarily intended by this designation; and this plausible opinion has been generally followed. The name Σκύθαι, it is to be observed, however, is often but a vague word for any or all of the numerous and but partially known tribes of the north; and any attempt to assign a more definite locality to Magog can only be very hesitatingly made. According to some, the Maiotes about the Palus Maeotis are meant; according to others, the Massagetae; according to Kiepert, the inhabitants of the northern and eastern parts of Armenia. The imagery employed in Ezekiel's prophetic description was no doubt suggested by the Scythian invasion which about the time of Josiah, 630 B.C., had devastated Asia (Herodotus i. 104-106; Jer. iv. 3-vi. 30). Following on this description, Gog figures largely in Jewish and Mahommedan as well as in Christian eschatology. In the district of Astrakhan a legend is still to be met with, to the effect that Gog and Magog were two great races, which Alexander the Great subdued and banished to the inmost recesses of the Caucasus, where they are meanwhile kept in by the terror of twelve trumpets blown by the winds, but whence they are destined ultimately to make their escape and destroy the world.

The legends that attach themselves to the gigantic effigies (dating from 1708 and replacing those destroyed in the Great Fire) of Gog and Magog in Guildhall, London, are connected only remotely, if at all, with the biblical notices. According to the *Recuyell des histoires de Troye*, Gog and Magog were the survivors of a race of giants descended from the thirty-three wicked daughters of Diocletian; after their brethren had been slain by Brute and his companions, Gog and Magog were brought to London (Troy-novant) and compelled to officiate as porters at the gate of the royal palace. It is known that effigies similar to the present existed in London as early as the time of Henry V.; but when this legend began to attach to them is uncertain. They may be compared with the giant images formerly kept at Antwerp (Antigomes) and Douai (Gayant). According to Geoffrey of Monmouth (*Chronicles*, i. 16), Goëmot or Goëmagot (either corrupted from or corrupted into "Gog and Magog") was a giant who, along with his brother Corineus, tyrannized in the western horn of England until slain by foreign invaders.

GOGO, or GOGHA, a town of British India in Ahmedabad district, Bombay, 193 m. N.W. of Bombay. Pop. (1901) 4798. About ¾ m. east of the town is an excellent anchorage, in some measure sheltered by the island of Piram, which lies still farther east. The natives of this place are reckoned the best sailors in India; and ships touching here may procure water and supplies, or repair damages. The anchorage is a safe refuge during the south-west monsoon, the bottom being a bed of mud and the water always smooth. Gogo has lost its commercial importance and has steadily declined in population and trade since the time of the American Civil War, when it was an important cotton-mart.

GOGOL, NIKOLAI VASILIEVICH (1809-1852), Russian novelist, was born in the province of Poltava, in South Russia, on the 31st of March 1809. Educated at the Niezhin gymnasium, he there started a manuscript periodical, "The Star," and wrote several pieces including a tragedy, *The Brigands*. Having completed his course at Niezhin, he went in 1829 to St Petersburg, where he tried the stage but failed. Next year he obtained a clerkship in the department of appanages, but he soon gave it up. In literature, however, he found his true vocation. In 1829 he published anonymously a poem called *Italy*, and, under the pseudonym of V. Alof, an idyll, *Hans Kuchel Garten*, which he had written while still at Niezhin. The idyll was so ridiculed by a reviewer that its author bought up all the copies he could secure, and burnt them in a room which he hired for the purpose at an inn. Gogol then fell back upon South Russian popular literature, and especially the tales of Cossackdom on which his boyish fancy had been nursed, his father having occupied the 191post of "regimental secretary," one of the honorary officials in the Zaporogian Cossack forces.

In 1830 he published in a periodical the first of the stories which appeared next year under the title of *Evenings in a Farm near Dikanka: by Rudy Panko*. This work, containing a series of attractive pictures of that Little-Russian life which lends itself to romance more readily than does the monotony of "Great-Russian" existence, immediately obtained a great success—its light and colour, its freshness and originality being hailed with enthusiasm by the principal writers of the day in Russia. Whereupon Gogol planned, not only a history of Little-Russia, but also one of the middle ages, to be completed in eight or nine volumes. This plan he did not carry out, though it led to his being appointed to a professorship in the university of St Petersburg, a post in which he met with small success and which he resigned in 1835. Meanwhile he had published his *Arabesques*, a collection of essays and stories; his *Taras Bulba*, the chief of the *Cossack Tales* translated into English by George Tolstoy; and a number of novelettes, which mark his transition from the romantic to the realistic school of fiction, such as the admirable sketch of the tranquil life led in a quiet country house by two kindly specimens of *Old-world Gentlefolks*, or the description of the petty miseries endured by an ill-paid clerk in a government office, the great object of whose life is to secure the "cloak" from which his story takes its name. To the same period belongs his celebrated comedy, the *Revizor*, or government inspector. His aim in writing it was to drag into light "all that was bad in Russia," and to hold it up to contempt. And he succeeded in rendering contemptible and ludicrous the official life of Russia, the corruption universally prevailing throughout the civil service, the alternate arrogance and servility of men in office. The plot of the comedy is very simple. A traveller who arrives with an empty purse at a provincial town is taken for an inspector whose arrival is awaited with fear, and he receives all the attentions and bribes which are meant to propitiate the dreaded investigator of abuses. The play appeared on the stage in the spring of 1836, and achieved a full success, in spite of the opposition attempted by the official classes whose malpractices it exposed. The aim which Gogol had in view when writing the *Revizor* he afterwards fully attained in his great novel, *Mertvuiya Dushi*, or Dead Souls, the first part of which appeared in 1842. The hero of the story is an adventurer who goes about Russia making fictitious purchases of "dead souls," *i.e.* of serfs who have died since the last census, with the view of pledging his imaginary property to the government. But his adventures are merely an excuse for drawing a series of pictures, of an unfavourable kind, of Russian provincial life, and of introducing on the scene a number of types of Russian society. Of the force and truth with which these delineations are executed the universal consent of Russian critics in their favour may be taken as a measure. From the French version of the story a general idea of its merits may be formed, and some knowledge of its plot and its principal characters may be gathered from the English adaptation published in 1854, as an original work, under the title of *Home Life in Russia*. But no one can fully appreciate Gogol's merits as a humorist who is not intimate with the language in which he wrote as well as with the society which he depicted.

In 1836 Gogol for the first time went abroad. Subsequently he spent a considerable amount of time out of Russia, chiefly in Italy, where much of his *Dead Souls* was written. His residence there, especially at Rome, made a deep impression on his mind, which, during his later years, turned towards mysticism. The last works which he published, his *Confession* and *Correspondence with Friends*, offer a painful contrast to the light, bright, vigorous, realistic, humorous writings which had gained and have retained for him his immense popularity in his native land. Asceticism and mystical exaltation had told upon his nervous system, and its feeble condition showed itself in his literary compositions. In 1848 he made a pilgrimage to Jerusalem, and on his return settled down at Moscow, where he died on the 3rd of March 1852.

See *Materials for the Biography of Gogol* (in Russian) (1897), by Shenrok; "Illness and Death of Gogol," by N. Bazhenov, *Russkaya Muisl*, January 1902.

(W. R. S.-R.)

GOGRA, or GHAGRA, a river of northern India. It is an important tributary of the Ganges, bringing down to the plains more water than the Ganges itself. It rises in Tibet near Lake Manasarowar, not far from the sources of the Brahmaputra and the Sutlej, passes through Nepal where it is known as the Kauriala, and after entering British territory becomes the most important waterway in the United Provinces. It joins the Ganges at Chapra after a course of 600 m. Its tributary, the Rapti, also has considerable commercial importance. The Gogra has the alternative name of Sarju, and in its lower course is also known as the Deoha.

GOHIER, LOUIS JÉRÔME (1746-1830), French politician, was born at Semblançay (Indre-et-Loire) on the 27th of February 1746, the son of a notary. He was called to the bar at Rennes, and practised there until he was sent to represent the town in the states-general. In the Legislative Assembly he represented Ille-et-Vilaine. He took a prominent part in the deliberations; he protested against the exaction of a new oath from priests (Nov. 22, 1791), and demanded the sequestration of the emigrants' property (Feb. 7, 1792). He was minister of justice from March 1793 to April 1794, and in June 1799 he succeeded Treilhard in the Directory, where he represented the republican interest. His wife was intimate with Josephine Bonaparte, and when Bonaparte suddenly returned from Egypt in October 1799 he repeatedly protested his friendship for Gohier, who was then president of the Directory, and tried in vain to gain him over. After the *coup d'état* of the 18th Brumaire (Nov. 9, 1799), he refused to abdicate his functions, and sought out Bonaparte at the Tuileries "to save the republic," as he boldly expressed it. He was escorted to the Luxembourg, and on his release he retired to his estate at Eaubonne. In 1802 Napoleon made him consul-general at Amsterdam, and on the union of the Netherlands with France he was offered a similar post in the United States. His health did not permit of his taking up a new appointment, and he died at Eaubonne on the 29th of May 1830.

His *Mémoires d'un vétéran irréprochable de la Révolution* was published in 1824, his report on the papers of the civil list preparatory to the trial of Louis XVI. is printed in Le *Procès de Louis XVI* (Paris, an III) and elsewhere, while others appear in the *Moniteur*.

GÖHRDE, a forest of Germany, in the Prussian province of Hanover, immediately W. of the Elbe, between Wittenberg and Lüneburg. It has an area of about 85 sq. m. and is famous for its oaks, beeches and game preserves. It is memorable for the victory gained here, on the 16th of September 1813, by the allies, under Wallmoden, over the French forces commanded by Pecheur. The hunting-box situated in the forest was built in 1689 and was restored by Ernest Augustus, King of Hanover. It is known to history on account of the constitution of Göhrde, promulgated here in 1719.

GOITO, a village of Lombardy, Italy, in the province of Mantua, from which it is 11 m. N.W., on the road to Brescia. Pop. (village) 737; (commune) 5712. It is situated on the right bank of the Mincio near the bridge. Its position has given it a certain military importance in various campaigns and it has been repeatedly fortified as a bridge-head. The Piedmontese forces won two actions (8th of April and 30th of May 1848) over the Austrians here.

GOITRE (from Lat. *guttur*, the throat; synonyms, Bronchocele, Derbyshire Neck), a term applied to a swelling in the front of the neck caused by enlargement of the thyroid gland. This structure, which lies between the skin and the anterior surface of the windpipe, and in health is not large enough to give rise to any external prominence (except in the pictures of certain artists), is liable to variations in size, more especially in females, a temporary enlargement of the gland being not uncommon at the catamenial periods, as well as during pregnancy. In goitre the swelling is conspicuous and is not only unsightly but may occasion much discomfort from its pressure upon the windpipe and other important parts of the neck. J. L. Alibert recorded cases of 192goitre where the tumour hung down over the breast, or reached as low as the middle of the thigh.

Goitre usually appears in early life, often from the eighth to the twelfth year; its growth is at first slow, but after several years of comparative quiescence a sudden increase is apt to occur. In the earlier stages the condition of the gland is simply an enlargement of its constituent parts, which retain their normal soft consistence; but in the course of time other changes supervene, and it may become cystic, or acquire hardness from increase of fibrous tissue or from calcareous deposits. Occasionally the enlargement is uniform, but more commonly one of the lobes, generally the right, is the larger. In rare instances the disease is limited to the isthmus which connects the two lobes of the gland. The growth is unattended with pain, and is not inconsistent with good health.

Goitre is a marked example of an endemic disease. There are few parts of the world where it is not found prevailing in certain localities, these being for the most part valleys and elevated plains in mountainous districts (see CRETINISM). The malady is generally ascribed to the use of drinking water impregnated with the salts of lime and magnesia, in which ingredients the water of goitrous districts abounds. But in localities not far removed from those in which goitre prevails, and where the water is of the same chemical composition, the disease may be entirely unknown. The disease may be the result of a combination of causes, among which local telluric or malarial influences concur with those of the drinking water. Goitre is sometimes cured by removal of the individual from the district where it prevails, and it is apt to be acquired by previously healthy persons who settle in goitrous localities; and it is only in such places that the disease exhibits hereditary tendencies.

In the early stages, change of air, especially to the seaside, is desirable, and small doses of iron and of iodine should be given; if this fails small doses of thyroid extract should be tried. If palliative measures prove unsuccessful, operation must be undertaken for the removal of one lateral lobe and the isthmus of the tumour. This may be done under chloroform or after the subcutaneous injection of cocaine. If chloroform is used, it must be given very sparingly, as the breathing is apt to become seriously embarrassed during the operation. After the successful performance of the operation great improvement takes place, the remaining part of the gland slowly decreasing in size. The whole of the gland must not be removed during the operation, lest the strange disease known as Myxoedema should be produced (see METABOLIC DISEASES).

In *exophthalmic goitre* the bronchocele is but one of three phenomena, which together constitute the disease, viz. palpitation of the heart, enlargementof the thyroid gland, and protrusion of the eyeballs. This group of symptoms is known by the name of "Graves's disease" or "Von Basedow's disease"—the physicians by whom the malady was originally described. Although occasionally observed in men, this affection occurs chiefly in females, and in comparatively early life. It is generally preceded by impoverishment of blood, and by nervous or hysterical disorders, and it is occasionally seen in cases of organic heart disease. It has been suddenly developed as the effect of fright or of violent emotion. The first symptom is usually the palpitation of the heart, which is aggravated by slight exertion, and may be so severe as not only to shake the whole frame but even to be audible at some distance. A throbbing is felt throughout the body, and many of the larger blood-vessels are, like the heart, seen to pulsate strongly. The enlargement of the thyroid is gradual, and rarely increases to any great size, thus differing from the commoner form of goitre. The enlarged gland is of soft consistence, and communicates a thrill to the touch from its dilated and pulsating blood-vessels. Accompanying the goitre a remarkable change is observed in the eyes, which attract attention by their prominence, and by the startled expression thus given to the countenance. In extreme cases the eyes protrude from their sockets to such a degree that the eyelids cannot be closed, and injury may thus arise to the constantly exposed eyeballs. Apart from such risk, however, the vision is rarely affected. It occasionally happens that in undoubted cases of the disease one or other of the three above-named phenomena is absent, generally either the goitre or the exophthalmos. The palpitation of the heart is the most constant symptom. Sleeplessness, irritability, disorders of digestion, diarrhoea and uterine derangements, are frequent accompaniments. It is a serious disease and, if unchecked, may end fatally. Some cases are improved by general hygienic measures, others by electric treatment, or by the administration of animal extracts or of sera. Some cases, on the other hand, may be considered suitable for operative treatment.

(E. O.*)

GOKAK, a town of British India, in the Belgaum district of Bombay, 8 m. from a station on the Southern Mahratta railway. Pop. (1901) 9860. It contains old temples with inscriptions, and is known for a special industry of modelled toys. About 4 m. N.W. are the Gokak Falls, where the Ghatprabha throws itself over a precipice 170 ft. high. Close by, the water has been impounded for a large reservoir, which supplies not only irrigation but also motive power for a cotton-mill employing 2000 hands.

GOKCHA, (GÖK-CHAI; Armenian *Sevanga*; ancient *Haosravagha*), the largest lake of Russian Transcaucasia, in the government of Erivan, in 40° 9′ to 40° 38′ N. and 45° 1′ to 45° 40′ E. Its altitude is 6345 ft., it is of triangular shape, and measures from north-west to south-east 45 m., its greatest width being 25 m., and its maximum depth 67 fathoms. Its area is 540 sq. m. It is surrounded by barren mountains of volcanic origin, 12,000 ft. high. Its outflow is the Zanga, a left bank tributary of the Aras (*Araxes*); it never freezes, and its level undergoes periodical oscillations. It contains four species of *Salmonidae*, and two of *Cyprinidae*, which are only met with in the drainage area of this lake. A lava island in the middle is crowned by an Armenian monastery.

GOLCONDA, a fortress and ruined city of India, in the Nizām's Dominions, 5 m. W. of Hyderabad city. In former times Golconda was the capital of a large and powerful kingdom of the Deccan, ruled by the Kutb Shahi dynasty which was founded in 1512 by a Turkoman adventurer on the downfall of the Bahmani dynasty, but the city was subdued by Aurangzeb in 1687, and annexed to the Delhi empire. The fortress of Golconda, situated on a rocky ridge of granite, is extensive, and contains many enclosures. It is strong and in good repair, but is commanded by the summits of the enormous and massive mausolea of the ancient kings about 600 yds. distant. These buildings, which are now the chief characteristics of the place, form a vast group, situated in an arid, rocky desert. They have suffered considerably from the ravages of time, but more from the hand of man, and nothing but the great solidity of their walls has preserved them from utter ruin. These tombs were erected at a great expense, some of them being said to have cost as much as £150,000. Golconda fort is now used as the Nizām's treasury, and also as the state prison. Golconda has given its name in English literature to the diamonds which were found in other parts of the dominions of the Kutb Shahi dynasty, not near Golconda itself.

GOLD [symbol Au, atomic weight 195.7(H = 1), 197.2(O = 16)], a metallic chemical element, valued from the earliest ages on account of the permanency of its colour and lustre. Gold ornaments of great variety and elaborate workmanship have been discovered on sites belonging to the earliest known civilizations, Minoan, Egyptian, Assyrian, Etruscan (see JEWELRY, PLATE, EGYPT, CRETE, AEGEAN CIVILIZATION, NUMISMATICS), and in ancient literature gold is the universal symbol of the highest purity and value (cf. passages in the Old Testament, *e.g.* Ps. xix. 10 "More to be desired are they than gold, yea, than much fine gold"). With regard to the history of the metallurgy of gold, it may be mentioned that, according to Pliny, mercury was employed in his time both as a means of separating the precious metals and for the purposes of gilding. Vitruvius also gives a detailed account of the means of recovering gold, by amalgamation, from cloth into which it had been woven.

Physical Properties.—Gold has a characteristic yellow colour, which is, however, notably affected by small quantities of other metals; thus the tint is sensibly lowered by small quantities of silver, and heightened by copper. When the gold is finely 193divided, as in "purple of Cassius," or when it is precipitated from solutions, the colour is ruby-red, while in very thin leaves it transmits a greenish light. It is nearly as soft as lead and softer than silver. When pure, it is the most malleable of all metals (see GOLDBEATING). It is also extremely ductile; a single grain may be drawn into a wire 500 ft. in length, and an ounce of gold covering a silver wire is capable of being extended more than 1300 m. The presence of minute quantities of cadmium, lead, bismuth, antimony, arsenic, tin, tellurium and zinc renders gold brittle, 1/2000th part of one of the three metals first named being sufficient to produce that quality. Gold can be readily welded cold; the finely divided metal, in the state in which it is precipitated from solution, may be compressed between dies into disks or medals. The specific gravity of gold obtained by precipitation from solution by ferrous sulphate is from 19.55 to 20.72. The specific gravity of cast gold varies from 18.29 to 19.37, and by compression between dies the specific gravity may be raised from 19.37 to 19.41; by annealing, however, the previous density is to some extent recovered, as it is then found to be 19.40. The melting-point has been variously given, the early values ranging from 1425° C. to 1035° C. Using improved methods, C. T. Heycock and F. H. Neville determined it to be 1061.7° C.; Daniel Berthelot gives 1064° C., while Jaquerod and Perrot give 1066.1-1067.4° C. At still higher temperatures it volatilizes, forming a reddish vapour. Macquer and Lavoisier showed that when gold is strongly heated, fumes arise which gild a piece of silver held in them. Its volatility has also been studied by L. Eisner, and, in the presence of other metals, by Napier and others. The volatility is barely appreciable at 1075°; at 1250° it is four times as much as at 1100°. Copper and zinc increase the volatility far more than lead, while the greatest volatility is induced, according to T. Kirke Rose, by tellurium. It has also been shown that gold volatilizes when a gold-amalgam is distilled. Gold is dissipated by sending a powerful charge of electricity through it when in the form of leaf or thin wire. The electric conductivity is given by A. Matthiessen as 73 at 0° C., pure silver being 100; the value of this coefficient depends greatly on the purity of the metal, the presence of a few thousandths of silver lowering it by 10%. Its conductivity for heat has been variously given as 103 (C. M. Despretz), 98 (F. Crace-Calvert and R. Johnson), and 60 (G. H. Wiedemann and R. Franz), pure silver being 100. Its specific heat is between 0.0298 (Dulong and Petit) and 0.03244 (Regnault). Its coefficient of expansion for each degree between 0° and 100° C. is 0.000014661, or for gold which has been annealed 0.000015136 (Laplace and Lavoisier). The spark spectrum of gold has been mapped by A. Kirchhoff, R. Thalén, Sir William Huggins and H. Krüss; the brightest lines are 6277, 5960, 5955 and 5836 in the orange and yellow, and 5230 and 4792 in the green and blue.

Chemical Properties.—Gold is permanent in both dry and moist air at ordinary or high temperatures. It is insoluble in hydrochloric, nitric and sulphuric acids, but dissolves in *aqua regia*—a mixture of hydrochloric and nitric acids—and when very finely divided in a heated mixture of strong sulphuric acid and a little nitric acid; dilution with water, however, precipitates the metal as a violet or brown powder from this solution. The metal is soluble in solutions of chlorine, bromine, thiosulphates and cyanides; and also in solutions which generate chlorine, such as mixtures of hydrochloric acid with nitric acid, chromic acid, antimonious acid, peroxides and nitrates, and of nitric acid with a chloride. Gold is also attacked when strong sulphuric acid is submitted to electrolysis with a gold positive pole. W. Skey showed that in substances which contain small quantities of gold the precious metal may be removed by the solvent action of iodine or bromine in water. Filter paper soaked with the clear, solution is burnt, and the presence of gold is indicated by the purple colour of the ash. In solution minute quantities of gold may be detected by the formation of "purple of Cassius," a bluish-purple precipitate thrown down by a mixture of ferric and stannous chlorides.

The atomic weight of gold was first determined with accuracy by Berzelius, who deduced the value 195.7 (H = 1) from the amount of mercury necessary to precipitate it from the chloride, and 195.2 from the ratio between gold and potassium chloride in potassium aurichloride, KAuCl4. Later determinations were made by Sir T. E. Thorpe and A. P. Laurie, Krüss and J. W. Mallet. Thorpe and Laurie converted potassium auribromide into a mixture of metallic gold and potassium bromide by careful heating. The relation of the gold to the potassium bromide, as well as the amounts of silver and silver bromide which are equivalent to the potassium bromide, were determined. The mean value thus adduced was 195.86. Krüss worked with the same salt, and obtained the value 195.65; while Mallet, by analyses of gold chloride and bromide, and potassium auribromide, obtained the value 195.77.

Occlusion of Gas by Gold.—T. Graham showed that gold is capable of occluding by volume 0.48% of hydrogen, 0.20% of nitrogen, 0.29% of carbon monoxide, and 0.16% of carbon dioxide. Varrentrapp pointed out that "cornets" from the assay of gold may retain gas if they are not strongly heated.

Occurrence and Distribution.—Gold is found in nature chiefly in the metallic state, *i.e.* as "native gold," and less frequently in combination with tellurium, lead and silver. These are the only certain examples of natural combinations of the metal, the minute, though economically valuable, quantity often found in pyrites and other sulphides being probably only present in mechanical suspension. The native metal crystallizes in the cubic system, the octahedron being the commonest form, but other and complex combinations have been observed. Owing to the softness of the metal, large crystals are rarely well defined, the points being commonly rounded. In the irregular crystalline aggregates branching and moss-like forms are most common, and in Transylvania thin plates or sheets with diagonal structures are found. More characteristic, however, than the crystallized are the irregular forms, which, when large, are known as "nuggets" or "pepites," and when in pieces below ¼ to ½ oz. weight as gold dust, the larger sizes being distinguished as coarse or nuggety gold, and the smaller as gold dust proper. Except in the larger nuggets, which may be more or less angular, or at times even masses of crystals, with or without associated quartz or other rock, gold is generally found bean-shaped or in some other flattened form, the smallest particles being scales of scarcely appreciable thickness, which, from their small bulk as compared with their surface, subside very slowly when suspended in water, and are therefore readily carried away by a rapid current. These form the "float gold" of the miner. The physical properties of native gold are generally similar to that of the melted metal.

Of the minerals containing gold the most important are sylvanite or graphic tellurium (Ag, Au) Te2, with 24 to 26%; calaverite, AuTe2, with 42%; nagyagite or foliate tellurium (Pb, Au)16 Sb3(S, Te)24, with 5 to 9% of gold; petzite, (Ag, Au)2Te, and white tellurium. These are confined to a few localities, the oldest and best known being those of Nagyag and Offenbanya in Transylvania; they have also been found at Red Cloud, Colorado, in Calaveras county, California, and at Perth and Boulder, West Australia. The minerals of the second class, usually spoken of as "auriferous," are comparatively numerous. Prominent among these are galena and iron pyrites, the former being almost invariably gold-bearing. Iron pyrites, however, is of greater practical importance, being in some districts exceedingly rich, and, next to the native metal, is the most prolific source of gold. Magnetic pyrites, copper pyrites, zinc blende and arsenical pyrites are other and less important examples, the last constituting the gold ore formerly worked in Silesia. A native gold amalgam is found as a rarity in California, and bismuth from South America is sometimes rich in gold. Native arsenic and antimony are also very frequently found to contain gold and silver.

The association and distribution of gold may be considered under two different heads, namely, as it occurs in mineral veins—"reef gold," and in alluvial or other superficial deposits which are derived from the waste of the former—"alluvial gold." Four distinct types of reef gold deposits may be distinguished: (1) Gold may occur disseminated through metalliferous veins, generally with sulphides and more particularly with pyrites. These deposits seem to be the primary sources of native gold. (2) More common are the auriferous quartz-reefs—veins or masses of quartz containing gold in flakes visible to the naked eye, or so finely divided as to be invisible. (3) The "banket" formation, which characterizes the goldfields of South Africa, consists of a quartzite conglomerate throughout which gold is very finely disseminated. (4) The siliceous sinter at 194Mount Morgan, Queensland, which is obviously associated with hydrothermal action, is also gold-bearing. The genesis of the last three types of deposit is generally assigned to the simultaneous percolation of solutions of gold and silica, the auriferous solution being formed during the disintegration of the gold-bearing metalliferous veins. But there is much uncertainty as to the mechanism of the process; some authors hold that the soluble chloride is first formed, while others postulate the intervention of a soluble aurate.

116

In the alluvial deposits the associated minerals are chiefly those of great density and hardness, such as platinum, osmiridium and other metals of the platinum group, tinstone, chromic, magnetic and brown iron ores, diamond, ruby and sapphire, zircon, topaz, garnet, &c. which represent the more durable original constituents of the rocks whose distintegration has furnished the detritus.

Statistics of Gold Production.—The supply of gold, and also its relation to the supply of silver, has, among civilized nations, always been of paramount importance in the economic questions concerning money (see MONEY and BIMETALLISM); in this article a summary of the modern gold-producing areas will be given, and for further details reference should be made to the articles on the localities named. The chief sources of the European supply during the middle ages were the mines of Saxony and Austria, while Spain also contributed. The supplies from Mexico and Brazil were important during the 16th and 17th centuries. Russia became prominent in 1823, and for fourteen years contributed the bulk of the supply. The United States (California) after 1848, and Australia after 1851, were responsible for enormous increases in the total production, which has been subsequently enhanced by discoveries in Canada, South Africa, India, China and other countries.

TABLE I.

Per iod.	O z.	Per iod.	O z.
18 01-1810	59 0,750	18 56-1860	6, 350,180
18 11-1820	38 0,300	18 61-1865	5, 951,770
18 21-1830	47 2,400	18 66-1870	6, 169,660
18 31-1840	67 4,200	18 71-1875	5, 487,400
18 41-1850	1, 819,600	18 76-1880	5, 729,300
18 51-1855	6, 350,180	—	—

The average annual world's production for certain periods from 1801 to 1880 in ounces is given in Table I. The average production of the five years 1881-1885 was the smallest since the Australian and Californian mines began to be worked in 1848-1849; the minimum 4,614,588 oz., occurred in 1882. It was not until after 1885 that the annual output of the world began to expand. Of the total production in 1876, 5,016,488 oz., almost the whole was derived from the United States, Australasia and Russia. Since then the proportion furnished by these countries has been greatly lowered by the supplies from South Africa, Canada, India and China. The increase of production has not been uniform, the greater part having occurred most notably since 1895. Among the regions not previously important as gold-producers which now contribute to the annual output, the most remarkable are the goldfields of South Africa (Transvaal and Rhodesia, the former of which were discovered in 1885). India likewise has been added to the list, its active production having begun at about the same time as that of South Africa. The average annual product of India for the period 1886 to 1899 inclusive was £698,208, and its present annual product averages about 550,000 oz., or about £2,200,000, obtained almost wholly from the free-milling quartz veins of the Colar goldfields in Mysore, southern India. In 1900 the output was valued at £1,891,804, in 1905 at £2,450,536, and in 1908 at £2,270,000. Canada, too, assumed an important rank, having contributed in 1900 £5,583,300; but the output has since steadily declined to £1,973,000 in 1908. The great increase during the few years preceding 1899 was due to the development of the goldfields of the North-Western Territory, especially British Columbia. From the district of Yukon (Klondike, &c.) £2,800,000 was obtained in 1899, wholly from alluvial workings, but the progress made since has been slower than was expected by sanguine people. It is, however, probable that the North-Western Territory will continue to yield gold in important quantities for some time to come.

The output of the United States increased from £7,050,000 in 1881 to £16,085,567 in 1900, £17,916,000 in 1905, and to £20,065,000 in 1908. This increase was chiefly due to the exploitation of new goldfields. The fall in the price of silver stimulated the discovery and development of gold deposits, and many states formerly regarded as characteristically silver districts have become important as gold producers. Colorado is a case in point, its output having increased from about £600,000 in 1880 to £6,065,000 in 1900; it was £5,139,800 in 1905. Somewhat more than one-half of the Colorado gold is obtained from the Cripple Creek district.

117

Other states also showed a largely augmented product. On the other hand, the output of California, which was producing over £3,000,000 per annum in 1876, has fallen off, the average annual output from 1876 to 1900 being £2,800,000; in 1905 the yield was £3,839,000. This decrease was largely caused by the practical suspension for many years of the hydraulic mining operations, in preparation for which millions of dollars had been expended in deep tunnels, flumes, &c., and the active continuance of which might have been expected to yield some £2,000,000 of gold annually. This interruption, due to the practical prohibition of the industry by the United States courts, on the ground that it was injuring, through the deposit of tailings, agricultural lands and navigable streams, was lessened, though not entirely removed, by compromises and regulations which permit, under certain restrictions, the renewed exploitation of the ancient river-beds by the hydraulic method. On the other hand, the progressive reduction of mining and metallurgical costs effected by improved transportation and machinery, and the use of high explosives, compressed air, electric-power transmission, &c., resulted in California (as elsewhere) in a notable revival of deep mining. This was especially the case on the "Mother Lode," where highly promising results were obtained. Not only is vein-material formerly regarded as unremunerative now extracted at a profit, but in many instances increased gold-values have been encountered below zones of relative barrenness, and operators have been encouraged to make costly preparations for really deep mining—more than 3000 ft. below the surface. The gold product of California, therefore, may be fairly expected to maintain itself, and, indeed, to show an advance. Alaska appeared in the list of gold-producing countries in 1886, and gradually increased its annual output until 1897, when the country attracted much attention with a production valued at over £500,000; the opening up of new workings has increased this figure immensely, from about £1,400,000 in 1901 to £3,006,500 in 1905. The Alaska gold was derived almost wholly from the large low-grade quartz mines of Douglas Island prior to 1899, but in that year an important district was discovered at Cape Nome, on the north-western coast. The result of a few months' working during that year was more than £500,000 of gold, and a very much larger annual output may reasonably be anticipated in the future; in 1905 it was about £900,000. The gold occurs in alluvial deposits designated as gulch-, bar-, beach-, tundra- and bench-placers. The tundra is a coastal plain, swampy and covered with undergrowth and underlaid by gravel. The most interesting and, thus far, the most productive are the beach deposits, similar to those on the coast of Northern California. These occur in a strip of comparatively fine gravel and sand, 150 yds. wide, extending along the shore. The gold is found in stratified layers, with "ruby" and black sand. The "ruby" sand consists chiefly of fine garnets and magnetites, with a few rose-quartz grains. Further exploration of the interior will probably result in the discovery of additional gold districts.

Mexico, from a gold production of £200,000 in 1891, advanced to about £1,881,800 in 1900 and to about £3,221,000 in 1905. Of this increase, a considerable part was derived from gold-quartz mining, though much was also obtained as a by-product in the working of the ores of other metals. The product of Colombia, Venezuela, the Guianas, Brazil, Uruguay, Argentina, Chile, Bolivia, Peru and Ecuador amounted in 1900 to £2,481,000 and to £2,046,000 in 1905.

In 1876 Australasia produced £7,364,000, of which Victoria contributed £3,084,000. The annual output of Victoria declined 195until the year 1892, when it began to increase rapidly, but not to its former level, the values for 1900 and 1905 being £3,142,000 and £3,138,000. There has been an important increase in Queensland, which advanced from £1,696,000 in 1876 to £2,843,000 in 1900, and subsequently declined to £2,489,000 in 1905. There has been no increase, and, indeed, no large fluctuation until quite recently in the output of New Zealand, which averaged £1,054,000 per annum from 1876 to 1898, but the production of the two years 1900 and 1905 rose to £1,425,459 and £2,070,407 respectively. By far the most important addition to the Australasian product has come from West Australia, which began its production in 1887—about the time of the inception of mining at Witwatersrand ("the Rand") in South Africa—and by continuous increase, which assumed large proportions towards the close of the 19th century, was £6,426,000 in 1899, £6,179,000 in 1900, and £8,212,000 in 1905. The total Australasian production in 1908 was valued at £14,708,000.

Undoubtedly the greatest of the gold discoveries made in the latter half of the 19th century was that of the Witwatersrand district in the Transvaal. By reason of its unusual geological character and great economic importance this district deserves a more extended description. The gold occurs in conglomerate beds, locally known as "banket." There are several series of parallel beds, interstratified with quartzite and schist, the most important being the "main reef" series. The gold in this conglomerate reef is partly of detrital origin and partly of the genetic character of ordinary vein-gold. The formation is noted for its regularity as regards both the thickness and the gold-tenor of the ore-bearing reefs, in which respect it is unparalleled in the geology of the auriferous formations. The gold carries, on an average, £2 per ton, and is worked

118

by ordinary methods of gold-mining, stamp-milling and cyaniding. In 1899, 5762 stamps were in operation, crushing 7,331,446 tons of ore, and yielding £15,134,000, equivalent to 25.5% of the world's production. Of this, 80% came from within 12 m. of Johannesburg. After September 1899 operations were suspended, almost entirely owing to the Boer War, but on the 2nd of May 1901 they were started again. In 1905 the yield was valued at £20,802,074, and in 1909 at £30,925,788. So certain is the ore-bearing formation that engineers in estimating its auriferous contents feel justified in assuming, as a factor in their calculations, a vertical extension limited only by the lowest depths at which mining is feasible. On such a basis they arrived at more than £600,000,000 as the available gold contained in the Witwatersrand conglomerates. This was a conservative estimate, and was made before the full extent of the reefs was known; in 1904 Lionel Phillips stated that the main reef series had been proved for 61 m., and he estimated the gold remaining to be mined to be worth £2,500,000,000. Deposits similar to the Witwatersrand banket occur in Zululand, and also on the Gold Coast of Africa. In Rhodesia, the country lying north of the Transvaal, where gold occurs in well-defined quartz-veins, there is unquestionable evidence of extensive ancient workings. The economic importance of the region generally has been fully proved. Rhodesia produced £386,148 in 1900 and £722,656 in 1901, in spite of the South African War; the product for 1905 was valued at £1,480,449, and for 1908 at £2,526,000.

The gold production of Russia has been remarkably constant, averaging £4,899,262 per annum; the gold is derived chiefly from placer workings in Siberia.

The gold production of China was estimated for 1899 at £1,328,238 and for 1900 at £860,000; it increased in 1901 to about £1,700,000, to fall to £340,000 in 1905; in 1906 and 1907 it recovered to about £1,000,000.

TABLE II.—*Gold Production of Certain Countries, 1881-1908 (in oz.).*

Year.	Australasia.	Africa.	Canada.	India.	Mexico.	Russia.	United States.	Totals.
1881	1,475,161	.	52,483	.	41,545	1,181,853	1,678,612	4,976,980
1882	1,438,067	.	52,000	.	45,289	1,154,613	1,572,187	4,825,794
1883	1,333,849	.	46,150	.	46,229	1,132,219	1,451,250	4,614,588
1884	1,352,761	.	46,000	.	57,227	1,055,642	1,489,950	4,902,889
1885	1,309,804	.	53,987	.	46,941	1,225,738	1,538,325	5,002,584
1886	1,257,670	.	66,061	.	29,702	922,226	1,693,125	5,044,363
1887	1,290,202	28,754	59,884	15,403	39,861	971,656	1,596,375	5,061,490
1888	1,344,002	240,266	53,150	35,034	47,117	1,030,151	1,604,841	5,175,623
1889	1,540,607	366,023	62,658	78,649	33,862	1,154,076	1,587,000	5,611,245
1890	1,453,172	497,817	55,625	107,273	37,104	1,134,590	1,588,880	5,726,966
1891	1,518,690	729,268	45,022	131,776	48,375	1,168,764	1,604,840	6,287,591
	1,	1	4	1	5	1	1	7

892	638,238	,210,869	3,905	64,141	4,625	,199,809	,597,098	,102,172
893	1,711,892	1,478,477	44,853	207,152	63,144	1,345,224	1,739,323	7,772,585
894	2,020,180	2,024,164	50,411	210,412	217,688	1,167,455	1,910,813	8,813,848
895	2,170,505	2,277,640	92,440	257,830	290,250	1,397,767	2,254,760	9,814,505
896	2,185,872	2,280,892	136,274	323,501	314,437	1,041,794	2,568,132	9,950,861
897	2,547,704	2,832,776	294,582	350,585	362,812	1,124,511	2,774,935	11,420,068
898	3,137,644	3,876,216	669,445	376,431	411,187	1,231,791	3,118,398	13,877,806
899	3,837,181	3,532,488	1,031,563	418,869	411,187	1,072,333	3,437,210	14,837,775
900	3,555,506	419,503	1,348,720	456,444	435,375	974,537	3,829,897	12,315,135
901	3,719,080	439,704	1,167,216	454,527	497,527	1,105,412	3,805,500	12,698,089
902	3,946,374	1,887,773	1,003,355	463,824	491,156	1,090,053	3,870,000	14,313,660
903	4,315,538	3,289,409	911,118	552,873	516,524	1,191,582	3,560,000	15,852,620
904	4,245,744	4,156,084	793,350	556,097	609,781	1,199,857	3,892,480	16,790,351
905	4,159,220	5,477,841	700,863	576,889	779,181	1,063,883	4,265,742	18,360,945
906	3,984,538	6,449,749	581,709	525,527	896,615	1,087,056	4,565,333	19,620,272
907	3,659,693	7,270,464	399,844	495,965	903,672	1,282,635	4,374,827	19,988,144
908	3,557,705	7,983,348	462,467	504,309	1,182,445	1,497,076	4,659,360	21,529,300

Alloys.—Gold forms alloys with most metals, and of these many are of great importance in the arts. The alloy with mercury—gold amalgam—is so readily formed that mercury is one of the most powerful agents for extracting the precious metal. With 10% of gold present the amalgam is fluid, and with 12.5% pasty, while with 13% it consists of yellowish-white crystals. Gold readily alloys with silver and copper to form substances in use from remote times for money, jewelry and plate. Other metals which find application in the metallurgy of gold by virtue of their property of extracting the gold as an alloy are lead, which combines very readily when molten, and which can afterwards be separated by cupellation, and copper, which is separated from the gold by solution in acids or by electrolysis; molten lead also extracts gold from the copper-gold alloys. The relative amount of gold in an alloy is expressed in two ways: (1) as "fineness," *i.e.* the amount of gold in 1000 parts of alloy; (2) as "carats," *i.e.* the amount of gold in 24 parts of alloy. Thus, pure gold is 1000 "fine" or 24 carat. In England the following standards are used for plate and jewelry: 375, 500, 625, 750 and 916.6, corresponding to 9, 12, 15, 18 and 22 carats, the alloying metals being silver and copper in varying proportions. In France three alloys of the following standards are used for jewelry, 920, 840 and 750. A greenish alloy used by goldsmiths contains 70% of silver and 30% of gold. "Blue gold" is stated to contain 75% of gold and 25% of iron. The Japanese use for ornament an alloy of gold and silver, the standard of which varies from 350 to 500, the colour of the precious metal being developed by "pickling" in a mixture of plum-juice, vinegar and copper sulphate. They may be said to possess a series of bronzes, in which gold and silver replace tin and zinc, all these alloys being characterized by patina having a wonderful range of tint. The common alloy, Shi-ya-ku-Do, contains 70% of copper and 30% of gold; when exposed to air it becomes coated with a fine black patina, and is much used in Japan for sword ornaments. Gold wire may be drawn of any quality, but it is usual to add 5 to 9 dwts. of copper to the pound. The "solders" used for red gold contain 1 part of copper and 5 of gold; for light gold, 1 part of copper, 1 of silver and 4 of gold.

Gold and Silver.—Electrum is a natural alloy of gold and silver. Matthiessen observed that the density of alloys, the composition of which varies from AuAg6 to Au6Ag, is greater than that calculated from the densities of the constituent metals. These alloys are harder, more fusible and more sonorous than pure gold. The alloys of the formulae AuAg, AuAg2, AuAg4 and AuAg20 are perfectly homogeneous, and have been studied by Levol. Molten alloys containing more than 80% of silver deposit on cooling the alloy AuAg9, little gold remaining in the mother liquor.

Gold and Zinc.—When present in small quantities zinc renders gold brittle, but it may be added to gold in larger quantities without destroying the ductility of the precious metal; Péligot proved that a triple alloy of gold, copper and zinc, which contains 5.8% of the last-named, is perfectly ductile. The alloy of 11 parts gold and 1 part of zinc is, however, stated to be brittle.

Gold and Tin.—Alchorne showed that gold alloyed with 1/37th part of tin is sufficiently ductile to be rolled and stamped into coin, provided the metal is not annealed at a high temperature. The alloys of tin and gold are hard and brittle, and the combination of the metals is attended with contraction; thus the alloy SnAu has a density 14.243, instead of 14.828 indicated by calculation. Matthiessen and Bose obtained large crystals of the alloy Au2Sn5, having the colour of tin, which changed to a bronze tint by oxidation.

Gold and Iron.—Hatchett found that the alloy of 11 parts gold and 1 part of iron is easily rolled without annealing. In these proportions the density of the alloy is less than the mean of its constituent metals.

Gold and Palladium.—These metals are stated to alloy in all proportions. According to Chenevix, the alloy composed of equal parts of the two metals is grey, is less ductile than its constituent metals and has the specific gravity 11.08. The alloy of 4 parts of gold and 1 part of palladium is white, hard and ductile. Graham showed that a wire of palladium alloyed with from 24 to 25 parts of gold does not exhibit the remarkable retraction which, in pure palladium, attends its loss of occluded hydrogen.

Gold and Platinum.—Clarke states that the alloy of equal parts of the two metals is ductile, and has almost the colour of gold.

Gold and Rhodium.—Gold alloyed with 1/4th or 1/5th of rhodium is, according to Wollaston, very ductile, infusible and of the colour of gold.

Gold and Iridium.—Small quantities of iridium do not destroy the ductility of gold, but this is probably because the metal is only disseminated through the mass, and not alloyed, as it falls to the bottom of the crucible in which the gold is fused.

Gold and Nickel.—Eleven parts of gold and 1 of nickel yield an alloy resembling brass.

Gold and Cobalt.—Eleven parts of gold and 1 of cobalt form a brittle alloy of a dull yellow colour.

Compounds.—Aurous oxide, Au2O, is obtained by cautiously adding potash to a solution of aurous bromide, or by boiling mixed solutions of auric chloride and mercurous nitrate. It forms a dark-violet precipitate which dries to a greyish-violet powder. When freshly prepared it dissolves in cold water to form an indigo-coloured solution with a brownish fluorescence of colloidal aurous oxide; it is insoluble in hot water. This oxide is slightly basic. Auric oxide, Au2O3, is a brown powder, decomposed into its elements when heated to about 250° or on exposure to light. When a concentrated solution of auric chloride is treated with caustic potash, a brown precipitate of auric hydrate, Au(OH)3, is obtained, which, on heating, loses water to form auryl hydrate, AuO(OH), and auric oxide, Au2O3. It functions chiefly as an acidic oxide, being less basic than aluminium oxide, and forming no stable oxy-salts. It dissolves in alkalis to form well-defined crystalline salts; potassium aurate, KAuO2 ·3H2O, is very soluble in water, and is used in electro-gilding. With concentrated ammonia auric oxide forms a black, highly explosive compound of the composition AuN2H3 ·3H2O, named "fulminating gold"; this substance is generally considered to be Au(NH2)NH ·3H2O, but it may be an ammine of the formula [Au(NH3)2(OH)2]OH. Other oxides, e.g. Au2O2, have been described.

Aurous chloride, AuCl, is obtained as a lemon-yellow, amorphous powder, insoluble in water, by heating auric chloride to 185°. It begins to decompose into gold and chlorine at 185°, the decomposition being complete at 230°; water decomposes it into gold and auric chloride. Auric chloride, or gold trichloride, AuCl3, is a dark ruby-red or reddish-brown, crystalline, deliquescent powder obtained by dissolving the metal in aqua regia. It is also obtained by carefully evaporating a solution of the metal in chlorine water. The gold chloride of commerce, which is used in photography, is really a hydrochloride, chlorauric or aurichloric acid, HAuCl4 ·3H2O, and is obtained in long yellow needles by crystallizing the acid solution. Corresponding to this acid, a series of salts, named chloraurates or aurichlorides, are known. The potassium salt is obtained by crystallizing equivalent quantities of potassium and auric chlorides. Light-yellow monoclinic needles of 2KAuCl4 ·H2O are deposited from warm, strongly acid solutions, and transparent rhombic tables of KAuCl4 ·2H2O from neutral solutions. By crystallizing an aqueous solution, red crystals of AuCl3 ·2H2O are obtained. Auric chloride combines with the hydrochlorides of many organic bases—amines, alkaloids, &c.—to form characteristic compounds. Gold dichloride, probably Au2Cl4, = Au ·AuCl4, aurous chloraurate, is said to be obtained as a dark-red mass by heating finely divided gold to 140°-170° in chlorine. Water decomposes it into gold and auric chloride. The bromides and iodides resemble the chlorides. Aurous bromide, AuBr, is a yellowish-green powder obtained by heating the tribromide to 140°; auric bromide, AuBr3, forms reddish-black or scarlet-red leafy crystals, which dissolve in water to form a reddish-brown solution, and combines with bromides to form bromaurates corresponding to the chloraurates. Aurous iodide, AuI, is a light-yellow, sparingly soluble powder obtained, together with free iodine, by adding potassium iodide to auric chloride; auric iodide, AuI3, is formed as a dark-green powder at the same time, but it readily decomposes to aurous iodide and iodine. Aurous iodide is also obtained as a green solid by acting upon gold with iodine. The iodaurates correspond to the chlor- and bromaurates; the potassium salt, KAuI4, forms highly lustrous, intensely black, four-sided prisms.

Aurous cyanide, AuCN, forms yellow, microscopic, hexagonal tables, insoluble in water, and is obtained by the addition of hydrochloric acid to a solution of potassium aurocyanide, KAu(CN)2. This salt is prepared by precipitating a solution of gold in *aqua regia* by ammonia, and then introducing the well-washed precipitate into a boiling solution of potassium cyanide. The solution is filtered and allowed to cool, when colourless rhombic pyramids of the aurocyanide separate. It is also obtained in the action of potassium cyanide on gold in the presence of air, a reaction utilized in the MacArthur-Forrest process of gold extraction (see below). Auric cyanide, Au(CN)3, is not certainly known; its double salts, however, have been frequently described. Potassium auricyanide, 2KAu(CN)4 ·3H2O, is obtained as large, colourless, efflorescent tablets by crystallizing concentrated solutions of auric chloride and potassium cyanide. The acid, auricyanic acid, 2HAu(CN)4 ·3H2O, is obtained by treating the silver salt (obtained by precipitating the potassium salt with silver nitrate) with hydrochloric acid; it forms tabular crystals, readily soluble in water, alcohol and ether.

Gold forms three sulphides corresponding to the oxides; they readily decompose on heating. Aurous sulphide, Au2S, is a brownish-black powder formed by passing sulphuretted hydrogen into a solution of potassium aurocyanide and then acidifying. Sodium aurosulphide, NaAuS ·4H2O, is prepared by fusing gold with sodium sulphide and sulphur, the melt being extracted with water, filtered in an atmosphere of nitrogen, and evaporated in a vacuum over sulphuric acid. It forms colourless, monoclinic prisms, which turn brown on exposure to air. This method of bringing gold into solution is mentioned by Stahl in his *Observationes Chymico-Physico-Medicae*; he there remarks that Moses probably destroyed the golden calf by burning it with sulphur and alkali (Ex. xxxii. 20). Auric sulphide, Au2S3, is an amorphous powder formed when lithium aurichloride is treated with dry sulphuretted hydrogen at -10°. It is very unstable, decomposing into gold and sulphur at 200°.

Oxy-salts of gold are almost unknown, but the sulphite and thiosulphate form double salts. Thus by adding acid sodium sulphite to, or by passing sulphur dioxide at 50° into, a solution of sodium aurate, the salt, 3Na2SO3 ·Au2SO3 ·3H2O is obtained, which, when precipitated from its aqueous solution by alcohol, forms a purple powder, appearing yellow or green by reflected light. Sodium aurothiosulphate, 3Na2S2O3 ·Au2S2O3 ·4H2O, forms colourless needles; it is obtained in the direct action of sodium thiosulphate on gold in the presence of an oxidizing agent, or by the addition of a dilute solution of auric chloride to a sodium thiosulphate solution.

Mining and Metallurgy.

The various deposits of gold may be divided into two classes—"veins" and "placers." The vein mining of gold does not greatly differ from that of similar deposits of metals (see MINERAL DEPOSITS). In the placer or alluvial deposits, the precious metal is found usually in a water-worn condition imbedded in earthy matter, and the method of working all such deposits is based on the disintegration of the earthy matter by the action of a stream of water, which washes away the lighter portions and leaves the denser gold. In alluvial deposits the richest ground is usually found in contact with the "bed rock"; and, when the overlying cover of gravel is very thick, or, as sometimes happens, when the older gravel is covered with a flow of basalt, regular mining by shafts and levels, as in what are known as tunnel-claims, may be required to reach the auriferous ground.

The extraction of gold may be effected by several methods; we may distinguish the following leading types:

1. By simple washing, *i.e.* dressing auriferous sands, gravels, &c.;

2. By amalgamation, *i.e.* forming a gold amalgam, afterwards removing the mercury by distillation;

3. By chlorination, *i.e.* forming the soluble gold chloride and then precipitating the metal;

4. By the cyanide process, *i.e.* dissolving the gold in potassium cyanide solution, and then precipitating the metal;

5. Electrolytically, generally applied to the solutions obtained in processes (3) and (4).

1. *Extraction of Gold by Washing.*—In the early days of gold-washing in California and Australia, when rich alluvial deposits were common at the surface, the most simple appliances sufficed. The most characteristic is the "pan," a circular dish of sheet-iron or "tin," with sloping sides about 13 or 14 in. in diameter. The pan, about two-thirds filled with the "pay dirt" to be washed, is held in the stream or in a hole filled with water. The larger stones having been removed by hand, gyratory motion is given to the pan by a combination of shaking and twisting movements so as to keep its contents suspended in the stream of water, which carries away the bulk of the lighter material, leaving the heavy minerals, together with any gold which may have been present. The washing is repeated until enough of the enriched sand is collected, when the gold is finally recovered by careful washing or "panning out" in a smaller pan. In Mexico and South America, instead of the pan, a wooden dish or trough, known as "batea," is used.

The "cradle" is a simple appliance for treating somewhat larger quantities, and consists essentially of a box, mounted on rockers, and provided with a perforated bottom of sheet iron in which the "pay dirt" is placed. Water is poured on the dirt, and the rocking motion imparted to the cradle causes the finer particles to pass through the perforated bottom on to a canvas screen, and thence to the base of the cradle, where the auriferous particles accumulate on transverse bars of wood, called "riffles."

The "tom" is a sort of cradle with an extended sluice placed on an incline of about 1 in 12. The upper end contains a perforated riddle plate which is placed directly over the riffle box, and under certain circumstances mercury may be placed behind the riffles. Copper plates amalgamated with mercury are also used when the gold is very fine, and in some instances amalgamated silver coins have been used for the same purpose. Sometimes the stuff is disintegrated with water in a "puddling machine," which was used, especially in Australia, when the earthy matters are tenacious and water scarce. The machine frequently resembles a brickmaker's wash-mill, and is worked by horse or steam power.

In workings on a larger scale, where the supply of water is abundant, as in California, sluices were generally employed. They are shallow troughs about 12 ft. long, about 16 to 20 in. wide and 1 ft. in depth. The troughs taper slightly so that they can be joined in series, the total length often reaching several hundred feet. The incline of the sluice varies with the conformation of the ground and the tenacity of the stuff to be washed, from 1 in 16 to 1 in 8. A rectangular trough of boards, whose dimensions depend chiefly on the size of the planks available, is set up on the higher part of the ground at one side of the claim to be worked, upon trestles or piers of rough stone-work, at such an inclination that the stream may carry off all but the largest stones, which are kept back by a grating of boards about 2 in. apart. The gravel is dug by hand and thrown in at the upper end, the stones kept back being removed at intervals by two men with four-pronged steel forks. The floor of the sluice is laid with riffles made of strips of wood 2 in. square laid parallel to the direction of the current, and at other points with boards having transverse notches filled with mercury. These were known originally as Hungarian riffles.

In larger plant the upper ends of the sluices are often cut in rock or lined with stone blocks, the grating stopping the larger stones being known as a "grizzly." In order to save very fine and especially rusty particles of gold, so-called "under-current sluices" are used; these are shallow wooden tanks, 50 sq. yds. and upwards in area, which are placed somewhat below the main sluice, and communicate with it above and below, the entry being protected by a grating so that only the finer material is admitted. These are paved with stone blocks or lined with mercury riffles, so that from the greatly reduced velocity of flow, due to the sudden increase of surface, the finer particles of gold may collect. In order to save finely divided gold, amalgamated copper plates are sometimes placed in a nearly level position, at a considerable distance from the head of the sluice, the gold which is retained in it being removed from time to time. Sluices are often made double, and they are usually cleaned up—that is, the deposit rich in gold is removed from them—once a week.

The "pan" is now only used by prospectors, while the "cradle" and "tom" are practically confined to the Chinese; the sluice is considered to be the best contrivance for washing gold gravels.

2. *The Amalgamation Process.*—This method is employed to extract gold from both alluvial and reef deposits: in the first case it is combined with "hydraulic mining," *i.e.* disintegrating auriferous gravels by powerful jets of water, and the sluice system described above; in the second case the vein stuff is prepared by crushing and the amalgamation is carried out in mills.

Hydraulic mining has for the most part been confined to the country of its invention, California, and the western territories of America, where the conditions favourable for its use are more fully developed than elsewhere—notably the presence of thick banks of gravel that cannot be utilized by other methods, and abundance of water, even though considerable work may be required at times to make it available. The general conditions to be observed in such workings may be briefly stated as follows: (1) The whole of the auriferous gravel, down to the "bed rock," must be removed,—that is, no selection of rich or poor parts is possible; (2) this must be accomplished by the aid of water alone, or at times by water supplemented by blasting; (3) the conglomerate must be mechanically disintegrated without interrupting the whole system; (4) the gold must be saved without interrupting the continuous flow of water; and (5) arrangements must be made for disposing of the vast masses of impoverished gravel.

The water is brought from a ditch on the high ground, and through a line of pipes to the distributing box, whence the branch pipes supplying the jets diverge. The stream issues through a nozzle, termed a "monitor" or "giant," which is fitted with a ball and socket joint, so that the direction of the jet may be varied through considerable angles by simply moving a handle. The material of the bank being loosened by blasting and the cutting action of the water, crumbles into holes, and the superincumbent mass, often with large trees and stones, falls into the lower ground. The stream, laden with stones and gravel, passes into the sluices, where the gold is recovered in the manner already described. Under the most advantageous conditions the loss of gold may be estimated at 15 or 20%, the amount recovered representing a value of about two shillings per ton of gravel treated. The loss of mercury is about the same, from 5 to 6 cwt. being in constant use per mile of sluice.

In working auriferous river-beds, dredges have been used with considerable success in certain parts of New Zealand and on the Pacific slope in America. The dredges used in California are almost exclusively of the endless-chain bucket or steam-shovel pattern. Some dredges have a capacity under favourable conditions of over 2000 cub. yds. of gravel daily. The gravel is excavated as in the ordinary form of endless-chain bucket dredge and dumped on to the deck of the dredge. It then passes through screens and grizzlies to retain the coarse gravel, the finer material passing on to sluice boxes provided with riffles, supplied with mercury. There are belt conveyers for discharging the gravel and tailings at the end of the vessel remote from the buckets. The water necessary to the process is pumped from the river; as much as 2000 gallons per minute is used on the larger dredges.

The dressing or mechanical preparation of vein stuff containing gold is generally similar to that of other ores (see ORE-DRESSING), except that the precious metal should be removed from the waste substances as quickly as possible, even although other minerals of value that are subsequently recovered may be present. In all cases the quartz or other vein stuff must be reduced to a very fine powder as a preliminary to further operations. This may be done in several ways, *e.g.* either (1) by the Mexican crusher or *arrastra*, in which the grinding is effected upon a bed of stone, over which heavy blocks of stone attached to cross arms are dragged by the rotation of the arms about a central spindle, or (2) by the Chilean mill or *trapiche*, also known as the edge-runner, where the grinding stones roll upon the floor, at the same time turning about a central upright—contrivances which are mainly used for the preparation of silver ores; but by far the largest proportion of the gold quartz of California, Australia and Africa is reduced by (3) the stamp mill, which is similar in principle to that used in Europe for the preparation of tin and other ores.

The stamp mill was first used in California, and its use has since spread over the whole world. In the mills of the Californian type the stamp is a cylindrical iron pestle faced with a chilled cast iron shoe, removable so that it can be renewed when necessary, attached to a round iron rod or lifter, the whole weighing from 600 to 900 ℔; stamps weighing 1320 ℔ are in use in the Transvaal. The lift is effected by cams acting on the under surface of tappets, and formed by cylindrical boxes keyed on to the stems of the lifter about one-fourth of their length from the top. As, however, the cams, unlike those of European stamp mills, are placed to one side of the stamp, the latter is not only lifted but turned partly round on its own axis, whereby the shoes are worn down uniformly. The height of lift may be between 4 and 18 in., and the number of blows from 30 to over 100 per minute. The stamps are usually arranged in batteries of five; the order of working is usually 1, 4, 2, 5, 3, but other arrangements,*e.g.* 1, 3, 5, 2, 4, and 1, 5, 2, 4, 3, are common. The stuff, previously broken to about 2-in. lumps in a rock-breaker, is fed in through an aperture at the back of the "battery box," a constant supply of water is admitted from above, and mercury in a finely divided state is added at frequent intervals. The discharge of the comminuted material takes place through an aperture, which is covered by a thin steel plate perforated with numerous slits about 1/50th in. broad and ½ in. long, a certain volume being discharged at every blow and carried forward by the flushing water over an apron or table in front, covered by copper plates filled with mercury. Similar plates are often used to catch any particles of gold that may be thrown back, while the main operation is so conducted that the bulk of the gold may be reduced to the state of amalgam by bringing the two metals into intimate contact under the stamp head, and remain in the battery. The tables in front are laid at an incline of about 8° and are about 13 ft. long; they collect from 10 to 15% of the whole gold; a further quantity is recovered by leading the sands through a gutter about 16 in. broad and 120 ft. long, also lined with amalgamated copper plates, after the pyritic and other heavy minerals have been separated by depositing in catch pits and other similar contrivances.

When the ore does not contain any considerable amount of free gold mercury is not, as a rule, used during the crushing, but the amalgamation is carried out in a separate plant. Contrivances of the most diverse constructions have been employed. The most primitive is the rubbing together of the concentrated crushings with mercury in iron mortars. Barrel amalgamation, *i.e.* mixing the crushings with mercury in rotating barrels, is rarely used, the process being wasteful, since the mercury is specially apt to be "floured" (see below).

At Schemnitz, Kerpenyes, Kreuzberg and other localities in Hungary, quartz vein stuff containing a little gold, partly free and partly associated with pyrites and galena, is, after stamping in mills, similar to those described above, but without rotating stamps, passed through the so-called "Hungarian gold mill" or "quick-mill." This consists of a cast-iron pan having a shallow cylindrical bottom holding mercury, in which a wooden muller, nearly of the same shape as the inside of the pan, and armed below with several projecting blades, is made to revolve by gearing wheels. The stuff from the stamps is conveyed to the middle of the muller, and is distributed over the mercury, when the gold subsides, while the quartz and lighter materials are guided by the blades to the circumference and are discharged, usually into a second similar mill, and subsequently pass over blanket tables, *i.e.* boards covered with canvas or sacking, the gold and heavier particles becoming entangled in the fibres. The action of this mill is really more nearly analogous to that of a centrifugal pump, as no grinding action takes place in it. The amalgam is cleaned out periodically—fortnightly or monthly—and after filtering through linen bags to remove the excess of mercury, it is transferred to retorts for distillation (see below).

Many other forms of pan-amalgamators have been devised. The Laszlo is an improved Hungarian mill, while the Piccard is of the same type. In the Knox and Boss mills, which are also employed for the amalgamation of silver ores, the grinding is effected between flat horizontal surfaces instead of conical or curved surfaces as in the previously described forms.

One of the greatest difficulties in the treatment of gold by amalgamation, and more particularly in the treatment of pyrites, arises from the so-called "sickening" or "flouring" of the mercury; that is, the particles, losing their bright metallic surfaces, are no longer capable of coalescing with or taking up other metals. Of the numerous remedies proposed the most efficacious is perhaps sodium amalgam. It appears that amalgamation is often impeded by the tarnish found on the surface of the gold when it is associated with sulphur, arsenic, bismuth, antimony or tellurium. Henry Wurtz in America (1864) and Sir William Crookes in England (1865) made independently the discovery that, by the addition of a small quantity of sodium to the mercury, the operation is much facilitated. It is also stated that sodium prevents both the "sickening" and the "flouring" of the mercury which is produced by certain associated minerals. The addition of potassium cyanide has been suggested to assist the amalgamation and to prevent "flouring," but Skey has shown that its use is attended with loss of gold.

Separation of Gold from the Amalgam.—The amalgam is first pressed in wetted canvas or buckskin in order to remove excess of mercury. Lumps of the solid amalgam, about 2 in. in diameter, are introduced into an iron vessel provided with an iron tube that leads into a condenser containing water. The distillation is then effected by heating to dull redness. The amalgam yields about 30 to 40% of gold. Horizontal cylindrical retorts, holding from 200 to 1200 ℔ of amalgam, are used in the larger Californian mills, pot retorts being used in the smaller mills. The bullion left in the retorts is then melted in black-lead crucibles, with the addition of small quantities of suitable fluxes, *e.g.* nitre, sodium carbonate, &c.

The extraction of gold from auriferous minerals by fusion, except as an incident in their treatment for other metals, is very rarely practised. It was at one time proposed to treat the concentrated black iron obtained in the Ural gold washings, which consists chiefly of magnetite, as an iron ore, by smelting it with charcoal for auriferous pig-iron, the latter metal possessing the property of dissolving gold in considerable quantity. By subsequent treatment with sulphuric acid the gold could be recovered. Experiments on this point were made by Anossow in 1835, but they have never been followed in practice.

Gold in galena or other lead ores is invariably recovered in the refining or treatment of the lead and silver obtained. Pyritic ores containing copper are treated by methods analogous to those of the copper smelter. In Colorado the pyritic ores containing gold and silver in association with copper are smelted in reverberatory furnaces for regulus, which, when desilverized by Ziervogel's method, leaves a residue containing 20 or 30 oz. of gold per ton. This is smelted with rich gold ores, notably those containing tellurium, for white metal or regulus; and by a following process of partial reduction analogous to that of selecting in copper smelting, "bottoms" of impure copper are obtained in which practically all the gold is concentrated. By continuing the treatment of these in the ordinary way of refining, poling and granulating, all the foreign matters other than gold, copper and silver are removed, and, by exposing the granulated metal to a high oxidizing heat for a considerable time the copper may be completely oxidized while the precious metals are unaltered. Subsequent treatment with sulphuric acid renders the copper soluble in water as sulphate, and the final residue contains only gold and silver, which is parted or refined in the ordinary way. This method of separating gold from copper, by converting the latter into oxide and sulphate, is also used at Oker in the Harz.

Extraction by Means of Aqueous Solutions.—Many processes have been suggested in which the gold of auriferous deposits is converted into products soluble in water, from which solutions the gold may be precipitated. Of these processes, two only are of special importance, viz. the chlorination or Plattner process, in which the metal is converted into the chloride, and the cyanide or MacArthur-Forrest process, in which it is converted into potassium aurocyanide.

(3) *Chlorination or Plattner Process.*—In this process moistened gold ores are treated with chlorine gas, the resulting gold chloride dissolved out with water, and the gold precipitated with ferrous sulphate, charcoal, sulphuretted hydrogen or otherwise. The process originated in 1848 with C. F. Plattner, who suggested that the residues from certain mines at Reichenstein, in Silesia, should be treated with chlorine after the arsenical products had been extracted by roasting. It must be noticed, however, that Percy independently made the same discovery, and stated his results at the meeting of the British Association (at Swansea) in 1849, but the Report was not published until 1852. The process was introduced in 1858 by Deetken at Grass Valley, California, where the waste minerals, principally pyrites from tailings, had been worked for a considerable time by amalgamation. The process is rarely applied to ores direct; free-milling ores are generally amalgamated, and the tailings and slimes, after concentration, operated upon. Three stages in the process are to be distinguished: (i.) calcination, to convert all the metals, except gold and silver, into oxides, which are unacted upon by chlorine; (ii.) chlorinating the gold and lixiviating the product; (iii.) precipitating the gold.

The calcination, or roasting, is conducted at a low temperature in some form of reverberatory furnace. Salt is added in the roasting to convert any lime, magnesia or lead which may be present, into the corresponding chlorides. The auric chloride is, however, decomposed at the elevated temperature into finely divided metallic gold, which is then readily attacked by the chlorine gas. The high volatility of gold in the presence of certain metals must also be considered. According to Egleston the loss may be from 40 to 90% of the total gold present in cupriferous ores according to the temperature and duration of calcination. The roasted mineral, slightly moistened, is introduced into a vat made of stoneware or pitched planks, and furnished with a double bottom. Chlorine, generally prepared by the interaction of pyrolusite, salt and sulphuric acid, is led from a suitable generator beneath the false bottom, and rises through the moistened ore, which rests on a bed of broken quartz; the gold is thus converted into a soluble chloride, which is afterwards removed by washing with water. Both fixed and rotating vats are employed, the chlorination proceeding more rapidly in the latter case; rotating barrels are sometimes used.

There have also been introduced processes in which the chlorine is generated in the chloridizing vat, the reagents used being dilute solutions of bleaching powder and an acid. Munktell's process is of this type. In the Thies process, used in many districts in the United States, the vats are rotating barrels made, in the later forms, of iron lined with lead, and provided with a filter formed of a finely perforated leaden grating running from one end of the barrel to the other, and rigidly held in place by wooden frames. Chlorine is generated within the barrel from sulphuric acid and chloride of lime. After charging, the barrel is rotated, and when the chlorination is complete the contents are emptied on a filter of quartz or some similar material, and the filtrate led to settling tanks.

After settling the solution is run into the precipitating tanks. The precipitants in use are: ferrous sulphate, charcoal and sulphuretted hydrogen, either alone or mixed with sulphur dioxide; the use of copper and iron sulphides has been suggested, but apparently these substances have achieved no success.

In the case of ferrous sulphate, prepared by dissolving iron in dilute sulphuric acid, the reaction follows the equation $AuCl_3 + 3FeSO_4 = FeCl_3 + Fe_2(SO_4)_3 + Au$. At the same time any lead, calcium, barium and strontium present are precipitated as sulphates; it is therefore advantageous to remove these metals by the preliminary addition of sulphuric acid, which also serves to keep any basic iron salts in solution. The precipitation is carried out in tanks or vats made with wooden sides and a cement bottom. The solutions are well mixed by stirring with wooden poles, and the gold allowed to settle, the time allowed varying from 12 to 72 hours. The supernatant liquid is led into settling tanks, where a further amount of gold is deposited, and is then filtered through sawdust or sand, the sawdust being afterwards burnt and the gold separated from the ashes and the sand treated in the chloridizing vat. The precipitated gold is washed, treated with salt and sulphuric acid to remove iron salts, roughly dried by pressing in cloths or on filter paper, and then melted with salt, borax and nitre in graphite crucibles. Thus prepared it has a fineness of 800-960, the chief impurities usually being iron and lead.

Charcoal is used as the precipitant at Mount Morgan, Australia. Its use was proposed as early as 1818 and 1819 by Hare and Henry; Percy advocated it in 1869, and Davis adopted it on the large scale at a works in Carolina in 1880. The action is not properly understood; it may be due to the reducing gases (hydrogen, hydrocarbons, &c.) which are invariably present in wood charcoal. The process consists essentially in running the solution over layers of charcoal, the charcoal being afterwards burned. It has been found that the reaction proceeds faster when the solution is heated.

199

Precipitation with sulphur dioxide and sulphuretted hydrogen proceeds much more rapidly, and has been adopted at many works. Sulphur dioxide, generated by burning sulphur, is forced into the solution under pressure, where it interacts with any free chlorine present to form hydrochloric and sulphuric acids. Sulphuretted hydrogen, obtained by treating iron sulphide or a coarse matte with dilute sulphuric acid, is forced in similarly. The gold is precipitated as the sulphide, together with any arsenic, antimony, copper, silver and lead which may be present. The precipitate is collected in a filter-press, and then roasted in muffle furnaces with nitre, borax and sodium carbonate. The fineness of the gold so obtained is 900 to 950.

4. *Cyanide Process.*—This process depends upon the solubility of gold in a dilute solution of potassium cyanide in the presence of air (or some other oxidizing agent), and the subsequent precipitation of the gold by metallic zinc or by electrolysis. The solubility of gold in cyanide solutions was known to K. W. Scheele in 1782; and M. Faraday applied it to the preparation of extremely thin films of the metal. L. Eisner recognized, in 1846, the part played by the atmosphere, and in 1879 Dixon showed that bleaching powder, manganese dioxide, and other oxidizing agents, facilitated the solution. S. B. Christy (*Trans. A.I.M.E.*, 1896, vol. 26) has shown that the solution is hastened by many oxidizing agents, especially sodium and manganese dioxides and potassium ferricyanide. According to G. Bodländer (*Zeit. f. angew. Chem.*, 1896, vol. 19) the rate of solution in potassium cyanide depends upon the subdivision of the gold—the finer the subdivision the quicker the solution,—and on the concentration of the solution—the rate increasing until the solution contains 0.25% of cyanide, and remaining fairly stationary with increasing concentration. The action proceeds in two stages; in the first hydrogen peroxide and potassium aurocyanide are formed, and in the second the hydrogen peroxide oxidizes a further quantity of gold and potassium cyanide to aurocyanide, thus (1) $2Au + 4KCN + O_2 + 2H_2O = 2KAu(CN)_2 + 4KOH + H_2O_2$; (2) $2Au + 4KCN + 2H_2O_2 = 2KAu(CN)_2 + 4KOH$. The end reaction may be written $4Au + 8KCN + 2H_2O + O_2 = 4KAu(CN)_2 + 4KOH$.

The commercial process was patented in 1890 by MacArthur and Forrest, and is now in use all over the world. It is best adapted for free-milling ores, especially after the bulk of the gold has been removed by amalgamation. It has been especially successful in the Transvaal. In the

Witwatersrand the ore, which contains about 9 dwts. of gold to the metric ton (2000 ℔), is stamped and amalgamated, and the slimes and tailings, containing about 3½ dwts. per ton, are cyanided, about 2 dwts. more being thus extracted. The total cost per ton of ore treated is about 6s., of which the cyaniding costs from 2s. to 4s.

The process embraces three operations: (1) Solution of the gold; (2) precipitation of the gold; (3) treatment of the precipitate.

The ores, having been broken and ground, generally in tube mills, until they pass a 150 to 200-mesh sieve, are transferred to the leaching vats, which are constructed of wood, iron or masonry; steel vats, coated inside and out with pitch, of circular section and holding up to 1000 tons, have come into use. The diameter is generally 26 ft., but may be greater; the best depth is considered to be a quarter of the diameter. The vats are fitted with filters made of coco-nut matting and jute cloth supported on wooden frames. The leaching is generally carried out with a strong, medium, and with a weak liquor, in the order given; sometimes there is a preliminary leaching with a weak liquor. The strengths employed depend also upon the mode of precipitation adopted, stronger solutions (up to 0.25% KCN) being used when zinc is the precipitant. For electrolytic precipitation the solution may contain up to 0.1% KCN. The liquors are run off from the vats to the electrolysing baths or precipitating tanks, and the leached ores are removed by means of doors in the sides of the vats into wagons. In the Transvaal the operation occupies 3½ to 4 days for fine sands, and up to 14 days for coarse sands; the quantity of cyanide per ton of tailings varies from 0.26 to 0.28 ℔, for electrolytic precipitation, and 0.5 ℔ for zinc precipitation.

The precipitation is effected by zinc in the form of bright turnings, or coated with lead, or by electrolysis. According to Christy, the precipitation with zinc follows equations 1 or 2 according as potassium cyanide is present or not:

(1) $4KAu(CN)2 + 4Zn + 2H2O = 2Zn(CN)2 + K2Zn(CN)4 + Zn(OK)2 + 4H + 4Au$;

(2) $2KAu(CN)2 + 3Zn + 4KCN + 2H2O = 2K2Zn(CN)4 + Zn(OK)2 + 4H + 2Au$;

one part of zinc precipitating 3.1 parts of gold in the first case, and 2.06 in the second. It may be noticed that the potassium zinc cyanide is useless in gold extraction, for it neither dissolves gold nor can potassium cyanide be regenerated from it.

The precipitating boxes, generally made of wood but sometimes of steel, and set on an incline, are divided by partitions into alternately wide and narrow compartments, so that the liquor travels upwards in its passage through the wide divisions and downwards through the narrow divisions. In the wider compartments are placed sieves having sixteen holes to the square inch and bearing zinc turnings. The gold and other metals are precipitated on the under surfaces of the turnings and fall to the bottom of the compartment as a black slime. The slime is cleaned out fortnightly or monthly, the zinc turnings being cleaned by rubbing and the supernatant liquor allowed to settle in the precipitating boxes or in separate vessels. The slime so obtained consists of finely divided gold and silver (5-50%), zinc (30-60%), lead (10%), carbon (10%), together with tin, copper, antimony, arsenic and other impurities of the zinc and ores. After well washing with water, the slimes are roughly dried in bag-filters or filter-presses, and then treated with dilute sulphuric acid, the solution being heated by steam. This dissolves out the zinc. Lime is added to bring down the gold, and the sediment, after washing and drying, is fused in graphite crucibles.

5. *Electrolytic Processes.*—The electrolytic separation of the gold from cyanide solutions was first practised in the Transvaal. The process, as elaborated by Messrs. Siemens and Halske, essentially consists in the electrolysis of weak solutions with iron or steel plate anodes, and lead cathodes, the latter, when coated with gold, being fused and cupelled. Its advantages over the zinc process are that the deposited gold is purer and more readily extracted, and that weaker solutions can be employed, thereby effecting an economy in cyanide.

In the process employed at the Worcester Works in the Transvaal, the liquors, containing about 150 grains of gold per ton and from 0.08 to 0.01% of cyanide, are treated in rectangular vats in which is placed a series of iron and leaden plates at intervals of 1 in. The cathodes, which are sheets of thin lead foil weighing 1½ ℔ to the sq. yd., are removed monthly, their gold content being from 0.5 to 10%, and after folding are melted in reverberatory furnaces to ingots containing 2 to 4% of gold. Cupellation brings up the gold to about 900 fine. Many variations of the electrolytic process as above outlined have been suggested. S. Cowper Coles has suggested aluminium cathodes; Andreoli has recommended cathodes of iron and anodes of lead coated with lead peroxide, the gold being removed from the iron cathodes by a brief immersion in molten lead; in the Pelatan-Cerici process the gold is amalgamated at a mercury cathode (see also below).

Refining or Parting of Gold.—Gold is almost always silver-bearing, and it may be also noticed that silver generally contains some gold. Consequently the separation of these two metals Is one of the most important metallurgical processes. In addition to the separation of the silver the operation extends to the elimination of the last traces of lead, tin, arsenic, &c. which have resisted the preceding cupellation.

The "parting" of gold and silver is of considerable antiquity. Thus Strabo states that in his time a process was employed for refining and purifying gold in large quantities by cementing or burning it with an aluminous earth, which, by destroying the silver, left the gold in a state of purity. Pliny shows that for this purpose the gold was placed on the fire in an earthen vessel with treble its weight of salt, and that it was afterwards again exposed to the fire with two parts of salt and one of argillaceous rock, which, in the presence of moisture, effected the decomposition of the salt; by this means the silver became converted into chloride.

The methods of parting can be classified into "dry," "wet" and electrolytic methods. In the "dry" methods the silver is converted into sulphide or chloride, the gold remaining unaltered; in the "wet" methods the silver is dissolved by nitric acid or boiling sulphuric acid; and in the electrolytic processes advantage is taken of the fact that under certain current densities and other circumstances silver passes from an anode composed of a gold-silver alloy to the cathode more readily than gold. Of the dry methods only F. B. Miller's chlorine process is of any importance, this method, and the wet process of refining by sulphuric acid, together with the electrolytic process, being the only ones now practised.

The conversion of silver into the sulphide may be effected by heating with antimony sulphide, litharge and sulphur, pyrites, or with sulphur alone. The antimony, or *Guss und Fluss*, method was practised up till 1846 at the Dresden mint; it is only applicable to alloys containing more than 50% of gold. The fusion results in the formation of a gold-antimony alloy, from which the antimony is removed by an oxidizing fusion with nitre. The sulphur and litharge, or *Pfannenschmied*, process was used to concentrate the gold in an alloy in order to make it amenable to "quartation," or parting with nitric acid. Fusion with sulphur was used for the same purpose as the Pfannenschmied process. It was employed in 1797 at the St Petersburg mint.

The conversion of the silver into the chloride may be effected by means of salt—the "cementation" process—or other chlorides, or by free chlorine—Miller's process. The first process consists essentially in heating the alloy with salt and brickdust; the latter absorbs the chloride formed, while the gold is recovered by washing. It is no longer employed. The second process depends upon the fact that, if chlorine be led into the molten alloy, the base metals and the silver are converted into chlorides. It was proposed in 1838 by Lewis Thompson, but it was only applied commercially after Miller's improvements in 1867, when it was adopted at the Sydney mint. Sir W. C. Roberts-Austen introduced it at the London mint; and it has also been used at Pretoria. It is especially suitable to gold containing little silver and base metals—a character of Australian gold—but it yields to the sulphuric acid and electrolytic methods in point of economy.

200

The separation of gold from silver in the wet way may be effected by nitric acid, sulphuric acid or by a mixture of sulphuric acid and *aqua regia*.

Parting by nitric acid is of considerable antiquity, being mentioned by Albertus Magnus (13th cent.), Biringuccio (1540) and Agricola (1556). It is now rarely practised, although in some refineries both the nitric acid and the sulphuric acid processes are combined, the alloy being first treated with nitric acid. It used to be called "quartation" or "inquartation," from the fact that the alloy best suited for the operation of refining contained 3 parts of silver to 1 of gold. The operation may be conducted in vessels of glass or platinum, and each pound of granulated metal is treated with a pound and a quarter of nitric acid of specific gravity 1.32. The method is sometimes employed in the assay of gold.

Refining by sulphuric acid, the process usually adopted for separating gold from silver, was first employed on the large scale by d'Arcet in Paris in 1802, and was introduced into the Mint refinery, London, by Mathison in 1829. It is based upon the facts that concentrated hot sulphuric acid converts silver and copper into soluble sulphates without attacking the gold, the silver sulphate being subsequently reduced to the metallic state by copper plates with the formation of copper sulphate. It is applicable to any alloy, and is the best method for parting gold with the exception of the electrolytic method.

The process embraces four operations: (1) the preparation of an alloy suitable for parting; (2) the treatment with sulphuric acid; (3) the treatment of the residue for gold; (4) the treatment of the solution for silver.

It is necessary to remove as completely as possible any lead, tin, bismuth, antimony, arsenic and tellurium, impurities which impair the properties of gold and silver, by an oxidizing fusion, *e.g.* with nitre. Over 10% of copper makes the parting difficult; consequently in such alloys the percentage of copper is diminished by the addition of silver free from copper, or else the copper is removed by a chemical process. Other undesirable impurities are the platinum metals, special treatment being necessary when these substances are present. The alloy, after the preliminary refining, is granulated by being poured, while molten, in a thin stream into cold water which is kept well agitated.

The acid treatment is generally carried out in cast iron pots; platinum vessels used to be employed, while porcelain vessels are only used for small operations, e.g. for charges of 190 to 225 oz. as at Oker in the Harz. The pots, which are usually cylindrical with a hemispherical bottom, may hold as much as 13,000 to 16,000 oz. of alloy. They are provided with lids, made either of lead or of wood lined with lead, which have openings to serve for the introduction of the alloy and acid, and a vent tube to lead off the vapours evolved during the operation. The bullion with about twice its weight of sulphuric acid of 66° Bé is placed in the pot, and the whole gradually heated. Since the action is sometimes very violent, especially when the bullion is treated in the granulated form (it is steadier when thin plates are operated upon), it is found expedient to add the acid in several portions. The heating is continued for 4 to 12 hours according to the amount of silver present; the end of the reaction is known by the absence of any hissing. Generally the reaction mixture is allowed to cool, and the residue, which settles to the bottom of the pot, consists of gold together with copper, lead and iron sulphates, which are insoluble in strong sulphuric acid; silver sulphate may also separate if present in sufficient quantity and the solution is sufficiently cooled. The solution is removed by ladles or by siphons, and the residue is leached out with boiling water; this removes the sulphates. A certain amount of silver is still present and, according to M. Pettenkofer, it is impossible to remove all the silver by means of sulphuric acid. Several methods are in use for removing the silver. Fusion with an alkaline bisulphate converts the silver into the sulphate, which may be extracted by boiling with sulphuric acid and then with water. Another process consists in treating a mixture of the residue with one-quarter of its weight of calcined sodium sulphate with sulphuric acid, the residue being finally boiled with a large quantity of acid. Or the alloy is dissolved in *aqua regia*, the solution filtered from the insoluble silver chloride, and the gold precipitated by ferrous chloride.

The silver present in the solution obtained in the sulphuric acid boiling is recovered by a variety of processes. The solution may be directly precipitated with copper, the copper passing into solution as copper sulphate, and the silver separating as a mud, termed "cement silver." Or the silver sulphate may be separated from the solution by cooling and dilution, and then mixed with iron clippings, the interaction being accompanied with a considerable evolution of heat. Or Gutzkow's method of precipitating the metal with ferrous sulphate may be employed.

The electrolytic parting of gold and silver has been shown to be more economical and free from the objections—such as the poisonous fumes—of the sulphuric acid process. One process depends upon the fact that, with a suitable current density, if a very dilute solution of silver nitrate be electrolysed between an auriferous silver anode and a silver cathode, the silver of the anode is dissolved out and deposited at the cathode, the gold remaining at the anode. The silver is quite free from gold, and the gold after boiling with nitric acid has a fineness of over 999.

Gold is left in the anode slime when copper or silver are refined by the usual processes, but if the gold preponderate in the anode these processes are inapplicable. A cyanide bath, as used in electroplating, would dissolve the gold, but is not suitable for refining, because other metals (silver, copper, &c.) passing with gold into the solution would deposit with it. Bock, however, in 1880 (*Berg- und hüttenmännische Zeitung*, 1880, p. 411) described a process used at the North German Refinery in Hamburg for the refining of gold containing platinum with a small proportion of silver, lead or bismuth, and a subsequent patent specification (1896) and a paper by Wohlwill (*Zeits. f. Elektrochem.*, 1898, pp. 379, 402, 421) have thrown more light upon the process. The electrolyte is gold chloride (2.5-3 parts of pure gold per 100 of solution) mixed with from 2 to 6% of the strongest hydrochloric acid to render the gold anodes readily soluble, which they are not in the neutral chloride solution. The bath is used at 65° to 70° C. (150° to 158° F.), and if free chlorine be evolved, which is known at once by its pungent smell, the temperature is raised, or more acid is added, to promote the solubility of the gold. The bath is used with a current-density of 100 ampères per sq. ft. at 1 volt (or higher), with electrodes about 1.2 in. apart. In this process all the anode metals pass into solution except iridium and other refractory metals of that group, which remain as metals, and silver, which is converted into insoluble chloride; lead and bismuth form chloride and oxychloride respectively, and these dissolve until the bath is saturated with them, and then precipitate with the silver in the tank. But if the gold-strength of the bath be maintained, only gold is deposited at the cathode—in a loose powdery condition from pure solutions, but in a smooth detachable deposit from impure liquors. Under good conditions the gold should contain 99.98% of the pure metal. The tank is of porcelain or glazed earthenware, the electrodes for impure solutions are ½ in. apart (or more with pure solutions), and are on the multiple system, and the potential difference at the terminals of the bath is 1 volt. A high current-density being employed, the turn-over of gold is rapid—an essential factor of success when the costliness of the metal is taken into account. Platinum and palladium dissolved from the anode accumulate in the solution, and are removed at intervals of, say, a few months by chemical precipitation. It is essential that the bath should not contain more than 5% of palladium, or some of this metal will deposit with the gold. The slimes are treated chemically for the separation of the metals contained in them.

AUTHORITIES.—Standard works on the metallurgy of gold are the treatises of T. Kirke Rose and of M. Eissler. The cyanide process is especially treated by M. Eissler, *Cyanide Process for the Extraction of Gold*, which pays particular attention to the Witwatersrand methods; Alfred James,*Cyanide Practice*; H. Forbes Julian and Edgar Smart, *Cyaniding Gold and Silver Ores*. Gold milling is treated by Henry Louis, *A Handbook of Gold Milling*; C. G. Warnford Lock, *Gold Milling*; T. A. Rickard, *Stamp Milling of Gold Ores*. Gold dredging is treated by Captain C. C. Longridge in *Gold Dredging*, and hydraulic mining is discussed by the same author in his *Hydraulic Mining*. For operations in special districts see J. M. Maclaren, *Gold* (1908); J. H. Curle, *Gold Mines of the World*; Africa: F. H. Hatch and J. A. Chalmers, *Gold Mines of the Rand*; S. J. Truscott,*Witwatersrand Goldfields Banket and Mining Practice*; Australasia: D. Clark, *Australian Mining and Metallurgy*; Karl Schmeisser, *Goldfields of Australasia*; A. G. Charleton, *Gold Mining and Milling in Western Australia*; India: F. H. Hatch, *The Kolar Gold-Field*.

GOLD AND SILVER THREAD. Under this heading some general account may be given of gold and silver strips, threads and gimp used in connexion with varieties of weaving, embroidery and twisting and plaiting or lace work. To this day, in many oriental centres where it seems that early traditions of the knowledge and the use of fabrics wholly or partly woven, ornamented, and embroidered with gold and silver have been maintained, the passion for such brilliant and costly textiles is still strong and prevalent. One of the earliest mentions of the use of gold in a woven fabric occurs in the description of the ephod made for Aaron (Exod. xxxix. 2, 3), "And he made the ephod of gold, blue, and purple, and scarlet, and fine twined linen. And they did beat the gold into thin plates, and cut it into wires (strips), to work it in the blue, and in the purple, and in the scarlet, and in the fine linen, with cunning work." This is suggestive of early Syrian or Arabic in-darning or weaving with gold strips or tinsel. In both the *Iliad* and the *Odyssey* allusion is frequently made to inwoven and embroidered golden textiles. Assyrian sculpture gives an elaborately designed ornament upon the robe of King Assur-nasir-pal (884 B.C.) which was probably an interweaving of gold and coloured threads, and testifies to the consummate skill of Assyrian or Babylonian workers at that date. From Assyrian and Babylonian weavers the conquering Persians of the time of Darius derived their celebrity as weavers and users of splendid stuffs. Herodotus describes 201the corselet given by Amasis king of Egypt to the Minerva of Lindus and how it was inwoven or embroidered with gold. Darius, we are told, wore a war mantle on which were figured (probably inwoven) two golden hawks as if pecking at each other. Alexander the Great is said to have found Eastern kings and princes arrayed in robes of gold and purple. More than two hundred years later than Alexander the Great was the king of Pergamos (the third bearing the name Attalus) who gave much attention to working in metals and is mentioned by Pliny as having invented weaving with gold, hence the historic Attalic cloths. There are several references in Roman writings to costumes and stuffs woven and embroidered with gold threads and the Graeco-Roman *chryso-phrygium* and the Roman *auri-phrygium* are evidences not only of Roman work with gold threads but also of its indebtedness to Phrygian sources. The famous tunics of Agrippina and those of Heliogabalus are said to have been of tissues made entirely with gold threads, whereas the robes which Marcus Aurelius found in the treasury of Hadrian, as well as the costumes sold at the dispersal of the wardrobe of Commodus, were different in character, being of fine linen and possibly even of silken stuffs inwoven or embroidered with gold threads. The same description is perhaps correct of the reputedly splendid hangings with which King Dagobert decorated the early medieval oratory of St Denis. Reference to these and many such stuffs is made by the respectively contemporary or almost contemporary writers; and a very full and interesting work by Monsieur Francisque Michel (Paris, 1852) is still a standard book for consultation in respect of the history of silk, gold and silver stuffs.

From indications such as these, as well as those of later date, one sees broadly that the art of weaving and embroidering with gold and silver threads passed from one great city to another, travelling as a rule westward. Babylon, Tarsus, Bagdad, Damascus, the islands of Cyprus and Sicily, Constantinople, Venice and southern Spain appear successively in the process of time as famous centres of these much-prized manufactures. During the middle ages European royal personages and high ecclesiastical dignitaries used cloth and tissues of gold and silver for their state and ceremonial robes, as well as for costly hangings and decoration; and various names— ciclatoun, tartarium, naques or nac, baudekin or baldachin (Bagdad) and tissue—were applied to textiles in the making of which gold threads were almost always introduced in combination with others. The thin flimsy paper known as tissue paper is so called because it originally was placed between the folds of gold "tissue" (or weaving) to prevent the contiguous surfaces from fraying each other. Under the articles dealing with carpets, embroidery, lace and tapestry will be found notices of the occasional use in such productions of gold and silver threads. Of early date in the history of European weaving are rich stuffs produced in Southern Spain by Moors, as well as by Saracenic and Byzantine weavers at Palermo and Constantinople in the 12th century, in which metallic threads were freely used. Equally esteemed at about the same period were corresponding stuffs made in Cyprus, whilst for centuries later the merchants in such fabrics eagerly sought for and traded in Cyprus gold and silver threads. Later the actual manufacture of them was not confined to Cyprus, but was also carried on by Italian thread and trimming makers from the 14th century onwards. For the most part the gold threads referred to were of silver gilt. In rare instances of middle-age Moorish or Arabian fabrics the gold threads are made with strips of parchment or paper gilt and still rarer are instances of the use of real gold wire.

In India the preparation of varieties of gold and silver threads is an ancient and important art. The "gold wire" of the manufacturer has been and is as a rule silver wire gilt, the silver wire being, of course, composed of pure silver. The wire is drawn by means of simple draw-plates, with rude and simple appliances, from rounded bars of silver, or gold-plated silver, as the case may be. The wire is flattened into strip, tinsel or ribbon-like form, by passing fourteen or fifteen strands simultaneously, over a fine, smooth, round-topped anvil and beating each as it passes with a heavy hammer having a slightly convex surface. Such strips or tinsel of wire so flattened are woven into Indian *soniri*, tissue or cloth of gold, the web or warp being composed entirely of golden strips, and *ruperi*, similar tissue of silver. Other gold and silver threads suitable for use in embroidery, pillow and needlepoint lace making, &c., consist of fine strips of flattened wire wound round cores of orange (in the case of silver, white) silk thread so as to completely cover them. Wires flattened or partially flattened are also twisted into exceedingly fine spirals and much used for heavy embroideries. Spangles for embroideries, &c., are made from spirals of comparatively stout wire, by cutting them down ring by ring, laying each C-like ring on an anvil, and by a smart blow with a hammer flattening it out into a thin round disk with a slit extending from the centre to one edge. The demand for many kinds of loom-woven and embroidered gold and silver work in India is immense, and the variety of textiles so ornamented is also very great, chief amongst which are the golden or silvery tinsel fabrics known as kincobs.

Amongst Western communities the demand for gold and silver embroideries and braid lace now exists chiefly in connexion with naval, military and other uniforms, masonic insignia, court costumes, public and private liveries, ecclesiastical robes and draperies, theatrical dresses, &c.

The proportions of gold and silver in the gold thread for the woven braid lace or ribbon trade varies, but in all cases the proportion of gold is exceedingly small. An ordinary gold braid wire is drawn from a bar containing 90 parts of silver and 7 of copper, and plated with 3 of gold. On an average each ounce troy of a bar so plated is drawn into 1500 yds. of wire; and therefore about 16 grains of gold cover 1 m. of wire.

(A. S. C.)

GOLDAST AB HAIMINSFELD, MELCHIOR (1576-1635), Swiss writer, an industrious though uncritical collector of documents relating to the medieval history and Constitution of Germany, was born on the 6th of January 1576 (some say 1578), of poor Protestant parents, near Bischofszell, in the Swiss Canton of Thurgau. His university career, first at Ingolstadt (1585-1586), then at Altdorf near Nuremberg (1597-1598), was cut short by his poverty, from which he suffered all his life, and which was the main cause of his wanderings. In 1598 he found a rich protector in the person of Bartholomaeus Schobinger, of St Gall, by whose liberality he was enabled to study at St Gall (where he first became interested in medieval documents, which abound in the conventual library) and elsewhere in Switzerland. Before his patron's death (1604) he became (1603) secretary to Henry, duke of Bouillon, with whom he went to Heidelberg and Frankfort. But in 1604 he entered the service of the Baron von Hohensax, then the possessor of the precious MS. volume of old German poems, returned from Paris to Heidelberg in 1888, and, partially published by Goldast. Soon he was back in Switzerland, and by 1606 in Frankfort, earning his living by preparing and correcting books for the press. In 1611 he was appointed councillor at the court of Saxe-Weimar, and in 1615 he entered the service of the count of Schaumburg at Bückeburg. In 1624 he was forced by the war to retire to Bremen; there in 1625 he deposited his library in that of the town (his books were bought by the town in 1646, but many of his MSS. passed to Queen Christina of Sweden, and hence are now in the Vatican library), he himself returning to Frankfort. In 1627 he became councillor to the emperor and to the archbishop-elector of Trèves, and in 1633 passed to the service of the landgrave of Hesse-Darmstadt. He died at Giessen early in 1635.

His immense industry is shown by the fact that his biographer, Senckenburg, gives a list of 65 works published or written by him, some extending to several substantial volumes. Among the more important are his *Paraeneticorum veterum pars i.* (1604), which contained the old German tales of *Kunig Tyrol von Schotten*, the *Winsbeke* and the *Winsbekin; Suevicarum rerum scriptores* (Frankfort, 1605, new edition, 1727); *Rerum Alamannicarum scriptores* (Frankfort, 1606, new edition by Senckenburg, 1730); *Constitutiones imperiales* (Frankfort, 1607-1613, 4 vols.); *Monarchia s. Romani imperii*(Hanover and Frankfort, 1612-1614, 2023 vols.); *Commentarii de regni Bohemiae juribus* (Frankfort, 1627, new edition by Schmink, 1719). He also edited De Thou's *History* (1609-1610) and Willibald Pirckheimer's works (1610). In 1688 a volume of letters addressed to him by his learned friends was published.

Life by Senckenburg, prefixed to his 1730 work. See also R. von Raumer's *Geschichte d. germanischen Philologie* (Munich, 1870).

(W. A. B. C.)

GOLDBEATING.—The art of goldbeating is of great antiquity, being referred to by Homer; and Pliny (*N.H.* 33. 19) states that 1 oz. of gold was extended to 750 leaves, each leaf being four fingers (about 3 in.) square; such a leaf is three times as thick as the ordinary leaf gold of the present time. In all probability the art originated among the Eastern nations, where the working of gold and the use of gold ornaments have been distinguishing characteristics from the most remote periods. On Egyptian mummy cases specimens of original leaf-gilding are met with, where the gold is so thin that it resembles modern gilding (*q.v.*). The minimum thickness to which gold can be beaten is not known with certainty. According to Mersenne (1621) 1 oz. was spread out over 105 sq. ft.; Réaumur (1711) obtained 146½ sq. ft.; other values are 189 sq. ft. and 300 sq. ft. Its malleability is greatly diminished by the presence of other metals, even in very minute quantity. In practice the average degree of tenuity to which the gold is reduced is not nearly so great as the last example quoted above. A "book of gold" containing 25 leaves measuring each 3¼ in., equal to an area of 264 sq. in., generally weighs from 4 to 5 grains.

The gold used by the goldbeater is variously alloyed, according to the colour required. Fine gold is commonly supposed to be incapable of being reduced to thin leaves. This, however, is not the case, although its use for ordinary purposes is undesirable on account of its greater cost. It also adheres on one part of a leaf touching another, thus causing a waste of labour by the leaves being spoiled; but for work exposed to the weather it is much preferable, as it is more durable, and does not tarnish or change colour. The external gilding on many public buildings, *e.g.* the Albert Memorial in Kensington Gardens, London, is done with pure gold. The following is a list of the principal classes of leaf recognized and ordinarily prepared by British beaters, with the proportions of alloy per oz. they contain.

Name of leaf.		Pro portion of gold.	Pro portion of Silver.	Pro portion of Copper.
		Gra ins.	Gra ins.	Gra ins.
	Red	456 -460	..	20- 24
red	Pale	464	..	16
deep	Extra	456	12	12
	Deep	444	24	12
	Citron	440	30	10
w	Yello	408	72	..
yellow	Pale	384	96	..
n	Lemo	360	120	..
	Green	312	168	..

or pale White	240	240	..

The process of goldbeating is as follows: The gold, having been alloyed according to the colour desired, is melted in a crucible at a higher temperature than is simply necessary to fuse it, as its malleability is improved by exposure to a greater heat; sudden cooling does not interfere with its malleability, gold differing in this respect from some other metals. It is then cast into an ingot, and flattened, by rolling between a pair of powerful smooth steel rollers, into a ribbon of 1½ in. wide and 10 ft. in length to the oz. After being flattened it is annealed and cut into pieces of about 6½ grs. each, or about 75 per oz., and placed between the leaves of a "cutch," which is about ½ in. thick and 3½ in. square, containing about 180 leaves of a tough paper. Formerly fine vellum was used for this purpose, and generally still it is interleaved in the proportion of about one of vellum to six of paper. The cutch is beaten on for about 20 minutes with a 17-℔ hammer, which rebounds by the elasticity of the skin, and saves the labour of lifting, by which the gold is spread to the size of the cutch; each leaf is then taken out, and cut into four pieces, and put between the skins of a "shoder," 4½ in. square and ¾ in. thick, containing about 720 skins, which have been worn out in the finishing or "mould" process. The shoder requires about two hours' beating upon with a 9-℔ hammer. As the gold will spread unequally, the shoder is beaten upon after the larger leaves have reached the edges. The effect of this is that the margins of larger leaves come out of the edges in a state of dust. This allows time for the smaller leaves to reach the full size of the shoder, thus producing a general evenness of size in the leaves. Each leaf is again cut into four pieces, and placed between the leaves of a "mould," composed of about 950 of the finest gold-beaters' skins, 5 in. square and ¾ in. thick, containing the contents of one shoder filling three moulds. The material has now reached the last and most difficult stage of the process; and on the fineness of the skin and judgment of the workman the perfection and thinness of the leaf of gold depend. During the first hour the hammer is allowed to fall principally upon the centre of the mould. This causes gaping cracks upon the edges of the leaves, the sides of which readily coalesce and unite without leaving any trace of the union after being beaten upon. At the second hour, when the gold is about the 150,000th part of an inch in thickness, it for the first time permits the transmission of the rays of light. Pure gold, or gold but slightly alloyed, transmits green rays; gold highly alloyed with silver transmits pale violet rays. The mould requires in all about four hours' beating with a 7-℔ hammer, when the ordinary thinness for the gold leaf of commerce will be reached. A single ounce of gold will at this stage be extended to 75 × 4 × 4 = 1200 leaves, which will trim to squares of about 3¼ in. each. The finished leaf is then taken out of the mould, and the rough edges are trimmed off by slips of the ratan fixed in parallel grooves of an instrument called a waggon, the leaf being laid upon a leathern cushion. The leaves thus prepared are placed into "books" capable of holding 25 leaves each, which have been rubbed over with red ochre to prevent the gold clinging to the paper. Dentist gold is gold leaf carried no farther than the cutch stage, and should be perfectly pure gold.

By the above process also silver is beaten, but not so thin, the inferior value of the metal not rendering it commercially desirable to bestow so much labour upon it. Copper, tin, zinc, palladium, lead, cadmium, platinum and aluminium can be beaten into thin leaves, but not to the same extent as gold or silver.

The fine membrane called goldbeater's skin, used for making up the shoder and mould, is the outer coat of the caecum or blind gut of the ox. It is stripped off in lengths about 25 or 30 in., and freed from fat by dipping in a solution of caustic alkali and scraping with a blunt knife. It is afterwards stretched on a frame; two membranes are glued together, treated with a solution of aromatic substances or camphor in isinglass, and subsequently coated with white of egg. Finally they are cut into squares of 5 or 5½ in.; and to make up a mould of 950 pieces the gut of about 380 oxen is required, about 2½ skins being got from each animal. A skin will endure about 200 beatings in the mould, after which it is fit for use in the shoder alone.

The dryness of the cutch, shoder and mould is a matter of extreme delicacy. They require to be hot-pressed every time they are used, although they may be used daily, to remove the moisture which they acquire from the atmosphere, except in extremely frosty weather, when they acquire so little moisture that a difficulty arises from their over-dryness, whereby the brilliancy of the gold is diminished, and it spreads very slowly under the hammer. On the contrary, if the cutch or shoder be damp, the gold will become pierced with innumerable microscopic holes; and in the moulds in its more attenuated state it will become reduced to a pulverulent state. This condition is more readily produced in alloyed golds than in fine gold. It is necessary that each skin of the mould should be rubbed over with calcined gypsum each time the mould may be used, in order to prevent the adhesion of the gold to the surface of the skin in beating.

GOLDBERG, a town of Germany, in the Prussian province of Silesia,1 14 m. by rail
S.W. of Liegnitz, on the Katzbach, an affluent of the Oder. Pop. (1905) 6804. The principal
buildings are an old church dating from the beginning of the 13th century, the Schwabe-
Priesemuth institution, completed in 1876, for the board and education of orphans, and the
classical school or gymnasium (founded in 1524 by Duke Frederick II. of Liegnitz), which in the
17th century enjoyed great prosperity, and numbered Wallenstein among its pupils. The chief
manufactures are woollen cloth, flannel, gloves, stockings, leather and beer, and there is a
considerable trade in corn and fruit. Goldberg owes its origin and name to a gold mine in the
neighbourhood, which, however, has been wholly abandoned since the time of the Hussite wars.
The town obtained civic rights in 1211. It suffered heavily from the Tatars in 1241, from the
plague in 1334, from the Hussites in 1428, and from the Saxon, Imperial and Swedish forces
during the Thirty Years' War. On the 27th of May 1813 a battle took place near it between the
French and the 203Russians; and on the 23rd and the 27th of August of the same year fights
between the allies and the French.

See Sturm, *Geschichte der Stadt Goldberg in Schlesien* (1887).

1Goldberg is also the name of a small town in the grand-duchy of Mecklenburg-Schwerin.

GOLD COAST, that portion of the Guinea Coast (West Africa) which extends from
Assini upon the west to the river Volta on the east. It derives its name from the quantities of
grains of gold mixed with the sand of the rivers traversing the district. The term Gold Coast is
now generally identified with the British Gold Coast colony. This extends from 3° 7' W. to 1° 14'
E., the length of the coast-line being about 370 m. It is bounded W. by the Ivory Coast colony
(French), E. by Togoland (German). On the north the British possessions, including Ashanti
(*q.v.*) and the Northern Territories, extend to the 11th degree of north latitude. The frontier
separating the colony from Ashanti (fixed by order in council, 22nd of October 1906) is in
general 130 m. from the coast, but in the central portion of the colony the southern limits of
Ashanti project wedge-like to the confluence of the rivers Ofin and Prah, which point is but 60
m. from the sea at Cape Coast. The combined area of the Gold Coast, Ashanti and the Northern
Territories, is about 80,000 sq. m., with a total population officially estimated in 1908 at
2,700,000; the Gold Coast colony alone has an area of 24,200 sq. m., with a population of over a
million, of whom about 2000 are Europeans.

Physical features.—Though the lagoons common to the West African coast are found both
at the western and eastern extremities of the colony (Assini in the west and Kwitta in the east) the
greater part of the coast-line is of a different character. Cape Three Points (4° 44' 40" N. 2° 5'
45" W.) juts boldly into the sea, forming the most southerly point of the colony. Thence the coast
trends E. by N., and is but slightly indented. The usually low sandy beach is, however, diversified
by bold, rocky headlands. The flat belt of country does not extend inland any considerable
distance, the spurs of the great plateau which forms the major part of West Africa advancing in
the east, in the Akwapim district, near to the coast. Here the hills reach an altitude of over 2000
ft. Out of the level plain rise many isolated peaks, generally of conical formation. Numerous
rivers descend from the hills, but bars of sand block their mouths, and the Gold Coast possesses
no harbours. Great Atlantic rollers break unceasingly upon the shore. The chief rivers are the
Volta (*q.v.*), the Ankobra and the Prah. The Ankobra or Snake river traverses auriferous country,
and reaches the sea some 20 m. west of Cape Three Points. It has a course of about 150 m., and
is navigable in steam launches for about 80 m. The Prah ("Busum Prah," sacred river) is regarded
as a fetish stream by the Fanti and Ashanti. One of its sub-tributaries has its rise near Kumasi.
The Prah rises in the N.E. of the colony and flows S.W. Some 60 m. from its mouth it is joined
by the Ofin, which comes from the north-west. The united stream flows S. and reaches the sea in
1° 35' W. As a waterway the river, which has a course of 400 m., is almost useless, owing to the
many cataracts in its course. Another river is the Tano, which for some distance in its lower
course forms the boundary between the colony and the Ivory Coast.

Geology.—Cretaceous rocks occur at intervals along the coast belt, but are mostly hidden
under an extensive development of superficial deposits. Basalt occurs at Axim. Inland is a broad
belt of sandstone and marl with an occasional band of auriferous conglomerate, best known and
most extensively worked for gold in the Wasaw district. Though the conglomerates bear some
resemblance to the "Banket" of South Africa they are most probably of more recent date. The
alluvial silts and gravels also carry gold.

Climate.—The climate on the coast is hot, moist and unhealthy, especially for Europeans.
The mean temperature in the shade in the coast towns is 78° to 80° F. Fevers and dysentery are
the diseases most to be dreaded by the European. The native inhabitants, although they enjoy

tolerable health and live to an average age, are subject in the rainy season to numerous chest complaints. There are two wet seasons. From April to August are the greater rains, whilst in October and November occur the "smalls" or second rains. From the end of December to March the dry harmattan wind blows from the Sahara. In consequence of the prevalence of the sea-breeze from the south-west the western portion of the colony, up to the mouth of the Sekum river (a small stream to the west of Accra), is called the windward district, the eastward portion being known as the leeward. The rainfall at Accra, in the leeward district, averages 27 in. in the year, but at places in the windward district is much greater, averaging 79 in. at Axim.

Flora.—The greater part (probably three-fourths) of the colony is covered with primeval forest. Here the vegetation is so luxuriant that for great distances the sky is shut out from view. As a result of the struggle to reach the sunlight the forest growths are almost entirely vertical. The chief trees are silk cottons, especially the bombax, and gigantic hard-wood trees, such as the African mahogany, ebony, odum and camwood. The bombax rises for over 100 ft., a straight column-like shaft, 25 to 30 ft. in circumference, and then throws out horizontally a large number of branches. The lowest growth in the forest consists of ferns and herbaceous plants. Of the ferns some are climbers reaching 30 to 40 ft. up the stems of the trees they entwine. Flowering plants are comparatively rare; they include orchids and a beautiful white lily. The "bush" or intermediate growth is made up of smaller trees, the rubber vine and other creepers, some as thick as hawsers, bamboos and sensitive mimosa, and has a height of from 30 to 60 ft. The creepers are found not only in the bush, but on the ground and hanging from the branches of the highest trees. West of the Prah the forest comes down to the edge of the Atlantic. East of that river the coast land is covered with bushes 5 to 12 ft. high, occasional large trees and groves of oil palms. Still farther east, by Accra, are numerous arborescent Euphorbias, and immediately west of the lower Volta forests of oil palms and grassy plains with fan palms. Behind all these eastern regions is a belt of thin forest country before the denser forest is reached. In the north-east are stretches of orchard-like country with wild plum, shea-butter and kola trees, baobabs, dwarf date and fan palms. The cotton and tobacco plants grow wild. At the mouths of the rivers and along the lagoons the mangrove is the characteristic tree. There are numerous coco-nut palms along the coast. The fruit trees and plants also include the orange, pine-apple, mango, papaw, banana and avocado or alligator pear.

Fauna.—The fauna includes leopards, panthers, hyenas, Potto lemurs, jackals, antelopes, buffaloes, wild-hogs and many kinds of monkey, including the chimpanzee and the *Colobus vellerosus*, whose skin, with long black silky hair, is much prized in Europe. The elephant has been almost exterminated by ivory hunters. The snakes include pythons, cobras, horned and puff adders and the venomous water snake. Among the lesser denizens of the forest are the squirrel and porcupine. Crocodiles and in fewer numbers manatees and otters frequent the rivers and lagoons and hippopotami are found in the Volta. Lizards of brilliant hue, tortoises and great snails are common. Birds, which are not very numerous, include parrots and hornbills, kingfishers, ospreys, herons, crossbills, curlews, woodpeckers, doves, pigeons, storks, pelicans, swallows, vultures and the spur plover (the last-named rare). Shoals of herrings frequent the coast, and the other fish include mackerel, sole, skate, mullet, bonito, flying fish, fighting fish and shynose. Sharks abound at the mouths of all the rivers, edible turtle are fairly common, as are the sword fish, dolphin and sting ray (with poisonous caudal spine). Oysters are numerous on rocks running into the sea and on the 204exposed roots of mangrove trees. Insect life is multitudinous; beetles, spiders, ants, fireflies, butterflies and jiggers abound. The earthworm is rare. The mosquitos include the *Culex*or ordinary kind, the *Anopheles*, which carry malarial fever, and the *Stegomyia*, a striped white and black mosquito which carries yellow-fever.

Inhabitants.—The natives are all of the Negro race. The most important tribe is the Fanti (*q.v.*), and the Fanti language is generally understood throughout the colony. The Fanti and Ashanti are believed to have a common origin. It is certain that the Fanti came originally from the north and conquered many of the coast tribes, who anciently had owned the rule of the king of Benin. The districts in general are named after the tribes inhabiting them. Those in the western part of the colony are mainly of Fanti stock; the Accra and allied tribes inhabit the eastern portion and are believed to be the aboriginal inhabitants. The Akim (Akem), who occupy the north-east portion of the colony, have engaged in gold-digging from time immemorial. The capital of their country is Kibbi. The Akwapim (Aquapem), southern neighbours of the Akim, are extensively engaged in agriculture and in trade. The Accra, a clever race, are to be found in all the towns of the West African coast as artisans and sailors. They are employed by the interior tribes as middlemen and interpreters. On the right bank of the Volta occupying the low marshy land near the sea are the Adangme. The Krobos live in little villages in the midst of the palm tree woods which grow round about the Kroboberg, an eminence about 1000 ft. high. Their country lies between that of the Akim and the Adangme. In the west of the colony is the Ahanta country, formerly an independent kingdom. The inhabitants were noted for their skill in war. They are one of the finest and most intelligent of the tribes of Accra stock. The Apollonia, a kindred race, occupy the coast region nearest the Ivory Coast.

The Tshi, Tchwi or Chi language,1 which is that spoken on the Gold Coast, belongs to the great prefix-pronominal group. It comprises many dialects, which may, however, be reduced to two classes or types. Akan dialects are spoken in *Native Languages.* Assini, Amanahia (Apollonia), Awini, Ahanta, Wasaw, Tshuforo (Juffer or Tufel), and Denkyera in the west, and in Asen, Akim, and Akwapim in the east, as well as in the different parts of Ashanti. Fanti dialects are spoken, not only in Fanti proper, but in Afutu or the country round Cape Coast, in Abora, Agymako, Akomfi, Gomoa and Agona. The difference between the two types is not very great; a Fanti, for example, can converse without much difficulty with a native of Akwapim or Ashanti, his language being in fact a deteriorated form of the same original. Akim is considered the finest and purest of all the Akan dialects. The Akwapim, which is based on the Akim but has imbibed Fanti influences, has been made the book-language by the Basel missionaries. They had reduced it to writing before 1850. About a million people in all, it is estimated, speak dialects of the Tshi.

The south-eastern corner of the Gold Coast is occupied by another language known as the Ga or Accra, which comprises the Ga proper and the Adangme and Krobo dialects. Ga proper is spoken by about 40,000 people, including the inhabitants of Ga and Kinka (*i.e.* Accra, in Tshi, Nkran and Kankan), Osu (*i.e.* Christiansborg), La, Tessi, Ningua and numerous inland villages. It has been reduced to writing by the missionaries. The Adangme and Krobo dialects are spoken by about 80,000 people. They differ very considerably from Ga proper, but books printed in Ga can be used by both the Krobo and Adangme natives. Another language known as Guan is used in parts of Akwapim and in Anum beyond the Volta; but not much is known either about it or the Obutu tongue spoken in a few towns in Agona, Gomoa and Akomfi.

Fetishism (*q.v.*) is the prevailing religion of all the tribes. Belief in a God is universal, as also is a belief in a future state. Christianity and Mahommedanism are both making progress. The natives professing Christianity number about 40,000. *Religion and education.* A Moravian mission was started at Christiansborg about 1736; the Basel mission (Evangelical) was begun in 1828, the missionaries combining manual training and farm labour with purely religious work; the Wesleyans started a mission among the Fanti in 1835, and the Anglican and Roman Catholic Churches are also represented, as well as the Bremen Missionary Society. Elementary education is chiefly in the hands of the Wesleyan, Basel, Bremen and Roman Catholic missions, who have schools at many towns along the coast and in the interior. There are also government and Mahommedan schools. The natives generally are extremely intelligent. They obtain easily the means of subsistence, and are disinclined to unaccustomed labour, such as working in mines. They are keen traders. The native custom of burying the dead under the floors of the houses prevailed until 1874, when it was prohibited by the British authorities.

Towns.—Unlike the other British possessions on the west coast of Africa, the colony has many towns along the shore, this being due to the multiplicity of traders of rival nations who went thither in quest of gold. Beginning at the west, Newtown, on the Assini or Eyi lagoon, is just within the British frontier. The first place of importance reached is Axim (pop., 1901, 2189), the site of an old Dutch fort built near the mouth of the Axim river, and in the pre-railway days the port of the gold region. Rounding Cape Three Points, whose vicinity is marked by a line of breakers nearly 2½ m. long, Dixcove is reached. Twenty miles farther east is Sekondi (*q.v.*), (pop. about 5000), the starting-point of the railway to the goldfields and Kumasi. Elmina (*q.v.*), formerly one of the most important posts of European settlement, is reached some distance after passing the mouth of the Prah. Eight miles east of Elmina is Cape Coast (*q.v.*), pop. (1901) 28,948. Anamabo is 9 m. farther east. Here, in 1807, a handful of English soldiers made a heroic and successful defence of its fort against the whole Ashanti host. Saltpond, towards the end of the 19th century, diverted to itself the trade formerly done by Anamabo, from which it is distant 9 m. Saltpond is a well-built, flourishing town, and is singular in possessing no ancient fort. Between Anamabo and Saltpond is Kormantine (Cormantyne), noted as the place whence the English first exported slaves from this coast. Hence the general name Coromantynes given in the West Indies to slaves from the Gold Coast. Eighty miles from Cape Coast is Accra (*q.v.*) (pop. 17,892), capital of the colony. (Winnebah is passed 30 m. before Accra is reached. It is an old town noted for the manufacture of canoes.) There is no station of much importance in the 60 m. between Accra and the Volta, on the right bank of which river, near its mouth, is the town of Addah (pop. 13,240). Kwitta (pop. 3018) lies beyond the Volta not far from the German frontier. Of the inland towns Akropong, the residence of the king of Akwapim, is one of the best known. It is 39 m. N.E. of Accra, stands on a ridge 1400 ft. above sea-level, and is a healthy place for European residents. At Akropong are the headquarters of the Basel Missionary Society. Akuse is a large town on the banks of the Volta. Tarkwa is the centre of the gold mining industry in the

Wasaw district. Its importance dates from the beginning of the 20th century. Accra, Cape Coast and Sekondi possess municipal government.

Agriculture and Trade.—The soil is everywhere very fertile and the needs of the people being few there is little incentive to work. The forests alone supply an inexhaustible source of wealth, notably in the oil palm. Among vegetable products cultivated are cocoa, cotton, Indian corn, yams, cassava, peas, peppers, onions, tomatoes, groundnuts (*Arachis hypogaea*), Guinea corn (*Sorghum vulgare*) and Guinea grains (*Amomum grana-paradisi*). The most common article of cultivation is, however, the kola nut (*Sterculia acuminata*), the favourite substitute in West Africa for the betel nut. In 1890 efforts were made by the establishment of a government botanical station at Aburi in the Accra district to induce the natives to improve their methods of cultivation and to enlarge the number of their crops. This resulted in the formation of hundreds of cocoa plantations, chiefly in the district immediately north of Accra. Subsequently the cultivation of the plant extended to every district of the colony. The industry had been founded in 1879 by a native of Accra, but it was not until 1901, as the result of the government's fostering care, that the export became of importance. In that year the quantity exported slightly exceeded 2,000,000 ℔ and fetched £42,000. In 1907 the quantity exported was nearly 21,000,000 ℔ and in value exceeded £515,000. In 1904 efforts were begun by the government and the British Cotton Growing Association in co-operation to foster the growing of cotton for export and by 1907 the cotton industry had become firmly established. Tobacco and coffee are grown at some of the Basel missionary stations.

The chief exports are gold, palm oil and palm kernels, cocoa, rubber, timber (including mahogany) and kola nuts. Of these articles the gold and rubber are shipped chiefly to England, whilst Germany, France and America, take the palm products and groundnuts. The rubber comes chiefly from Ashanti. The imports consist of cotton goods, rum, gin and other spirits, rice, sugar, tobacco, beads, machinery, building materials and European goods generally.

The value of the trade increased from £1,628,309 in 1896 to £4,055,351 in 1906. In the last named year the imports were valued at £2,058,839 and the exports at £1,996,412. While the value of imports had remained nearly stationary since 1902 the value of exports had nearly trebled in that period. In the five years 1903-1907 the total trade increased from £3,063,486 to £5,007,869. Great Britain and British colonies take 66% of the exports and supply over 60% of the imports. In both import and export trade Germany is second, followed by France and the United States. Specie is included in these totals, over a quarter of a million being imported in 1904.

Fishing is carried on extensively along the coast, and salted and sun-dried fish from Addah and Kwitta districts find a ready sale inland. Cloths are woven by the natives from home-grown and imported yarn; the making of canoes, from the silk-cotton trees, is a flourishing industry, and salt from the lagoons near Addah is roughly prepared. There are also native artificers in gold and other metals, the workmanship in some cases being of conspicuous merit. Odum wood is largely used in building and for cabinet work.

Gold Mining.—Gold is found in almost every part of the colony, but only in a few districts in paying quantities. Although since the discovery of the coast gold had been continuously exported to Europe from its ports, it was not until the last twenty years of the 19th century that efforts were made to extract gold according to modern methods. The richness of the Tarkwa main reef was first 205discovered by a French trader, M. J. Bennat, about 1880. During the period 1880 to 1900 the value of the gold exported varied from a minimum of £32,000 to a maximum (1889) of £103,000 The increased interest shown in the industry led to the construction of a railway (see below) to the chief goldfields, whereby the difficulties of transport were largely overcome. Consequent upon the taking up of a number of concessions, a concessions ordinance was issued in August 1900. This was followed in 1901 by the grant of 2825 concessions, and a "boom" in the West African market on the London stock exchange. Many concessions were speedily abandoned, and in 1901 the export of gold dropped to its lowest point, 6162 oz., worth £22,186, but in 1902 a large company began crushing ore and the output of gold rose to 26,911 oz., valued at £96,880. In 1907 the export was 292,125 oz.,worth £1,164,676. It should be noted that one of the principal gold mines is not in the colony proper, but at Obuassi in Ashanti. Underground labour is performed mainly by Basas and Krumen from Liberia. Of native tribes the Apollonia have proved the best for underground work, as they have mining traditions dating from Portuguese times. A good deal of alluvial gold is obtained by dredging apparatus. The use of dredging apparatus is modern, but the natives have worked the alluvial soil and the sand of the seashore for generations to get the gold they contain.

Communications.—The colony possesses a railway, built and owned by the government, which serves the gold mines, and has its sea terminus at Sekondi. Work was begun in August 1898, but owing to the disturbance caused by the Ashanti rising of 1900 the rails only reached

Tarkwa (39 m.) in May 1901. Thence the line is carried to Kumasi, the distance to Obuassi (124 m.) being completed by December 1902, whilst the first train entered the Ashanti capital on the 1st of October 1903. The total length of the line is 168 m. The cost of construction was £1,820,000. The line has a gauge 3 ft. 6 in. There is a branch line, 20 m. long, from Tarkwa N.W. to Prestea on the Ankobra river. Another railway, built 1907-10, 35 m. in length, runs from Accra to Mangoase, in the centre of the chief cocoa plantations. An extension to Kumasi has been surveyed.

Tortuous bush tracks are the usual means of internal communication. These are kept in fair order in the neighbourhood of government stations. There is a well-constructed road 141 m. long from Cape Coast to Kumasi, and roads connecting neighbouring towns are maintained by the government. Systematic attempts to make use of the upper Volta as a means of conveying goods to the interior were first tried in 1900. The rapids about 60 m. from the mouth of the river effectually prevent boats of large size passing up the stream. Where railways or canoes are not available goods are generally carried on the heads of porters, 60 ℔ being a full load. Telegraphs, introduced in 1882, connect all the important towns in the colony, and a line starting at Cape Coast stretches far inland, via Kumasi to Wa in the Northern Territories. Accra and Sekondi are in telegraphic communication with Europe, the Ivory Coast, Lagos and the Cape of Good Hope. There is regular and frequent steamship communication with Europe by British, Belgian and German lines.

Administration, Revenue, &c.—The country is governed as a crown colony, the governor being assisted by a legislative council composed of officials and nominated unofficial members. Laws, called ordinances, are enacted by the governor with the advice and consent of this council. The law of the colony is the common law and statutes of general application in force in England in 1874, modified by local ordinances passed since that date. The governor is also governor of Ashanti and the Northern Territories, but in those dependencies the legislative council has no authority.

Native laws and customs—which are extremely elaborate and complicated—are not interfered with "except when repugnant to natural justice." Those relating to land tenure and succession may be thus summarized. Individual tenure is not unknown, but most land is held by the tribe or by the family in common, each member having the right to select a part of the common land for his own use. Permanent alienation can only take place with the unanimous consent of the family and is uncommon, but long leases are granted. Succession is through the female, *i.e.* when a man dies his property goes to his sister's children. The government of the tribes is by their own kings and chiefs under the supervision of district commissioners. Slavery has been abolished in the colony. In the Northern Territories the dealing in slaves is unlawful, neither can any person be put in pawn for debt; nor will any court give effect to the relations between master and slave except in so far as those relations may be in accordance with the English laws relating to master and servant.

For administrative purposes the colony is divided into three provinces under provincial commissioners, and each province is subdivided into districts presided over by commissioners, who exercise judicial as well as executive functions. The supreme court consists of a chief justice and three puisne judges. The defence of the colony is entrusted to the Gold Coast regiment of the West African Frontier Force, a force of natives controlled by the Colonial Office but officered from the British army. There is also a corps of volunteers (formed 1892).

The chief source of revenue is the customs and (since 1902) railway receipts, whilst the heaviest items of expenditure are transport (including railways) and mine surveys, medical and sanitary services, and maintenance of the military force. The revenue, which in the period 1894-1898 averaged £244,559 yearly, rose in 1898-1903 to an average of £556,316 a year. For the five years 1903-1907 the average annual revenue was £647,557 and the average annual expenditure £615,696. Save for municipal purposes there is no direct taxation in the colony and no poorhouses exist. There is a public debt of (December 1907) £2,206,964. It should be noted that the expenditure on Ashanti and the Northern Territories is included in the Gold Coast budget.

History.—It is a debated question whether the Gold Coast was discovered by French or by Portuguese sailors. The evidence available is insufficient to prove the assertion, of which there is no contemporary record, that a company of Norman merchants established themselves about 1364 at a place they named La Mina (Elmina), and that they traded with the natives for nearly fifty years, when the enterprise was abandoned. It is well established that a Portuguese expedition under Diogo d'Azambuja, accompanied probably by Christopher Columbus, took possession of (or founded) Elmina in 1481-1482. By the Portuguese it was called variously São Jorge da Mina or Ora del Mina—the mouth of the (gold) mines. That besides alluvial washings they also worked the gold mines was proved by discoveries in the latter part of the 19th century. The Portuguese remained undisturbed in their trade until the Reformation, when the papal bull which had given the country, with many others, to Portugal ceased to have a binding power. English ships in 1553 brought back from Guinea gold to the weight of 150 ℔. The fame of the Gold Coast thereafter attracted to it adventurers from almost every European nation. The English were followed by French, Danes, Brandenburgers, Dutch and Swedes. The most aggressive were the Dutch, who from the end of the 16th century sought to oust the Portuguese from the Gold Coast, and in whose favour the Portuguese did finally withdraw in 1642, in return for the withdrawal on the part of the Dutch of their claims to Brazil. The Dutch henceforth made Elmina their headquarters on the coast. Traces of the Portuguese occupation, which lasted 160 years, are still to be found, notably in the language of the natives. Such familiar words as palaver, fetish, caboceer and dash (*i.e.* a gift) have all a Portuguese origin.

An English company built a fort at Kormantine previously to 1651, and some ten years later Cape Coast Castle was built. The settlements made by the English provoked the hostility of the Dutch and led to war between England and *Appearance of the English.* Holland, during which Admiral de Ruyter destroyed (1664-1665) all the English forts save Cape Coast castle. The treaty of Breda in 1667 confirmed the Dutch in the possession of their conquests, but the English speedily opened other trading stations. Charles II. in 1672 granted a charter to the Royal African Company, which built forts at Dixcove, Sekondi, Accra, Whydah and other places, besides repairing Cape Coast Castle. At this time the trade both in slaves and gold was very great, and at the beginning of the 18th century the value of the gold exported annually was estimated by Willem Bosman, the chief Dutch factor at Elmina, to be over £200,000. The various European traders were constantly quarrelling among themselves and exercised scarcely any control over the natives. Piracy was rife along the coast, and was not indeed finally stamped out until the middle of the 19th century. The Royal African Company, which lost its monopoly of trade with England in 1700, was succeeded by another, the African Company of Merchants, which was constituted in 1750 by act of parliament and received an annual subsidy from government. The slave trade was then at its height and some 10,000 negroes were exported yearly. Many of the slaves were prisoners of war sold to the merchants by the Ashanti, who had become the chief native power. The abolition of the slave trade (1807) crippled the company, which was dissolved in 1821, when the crown took possession of the forts.

Since the beginning of the 19th century the British had begun to exercise territorial rights in the towns where they held forts, and in 1817 the right of the British to control the natives living in the coast towns was recognized by Ashanti. In 1824 the first step towards the extension of British authority beyond the coast region was taken by Governor Sir Charles M'Carthy, who incited the Fanti to rise against their oppressors, the Ashanti. (The Fanti's country had been conquered by the Ashanti in 1807.) 206Sir Charles and the Fanti army were defeated, the governor losing his life, but in 1826 the English gained a victory over the Ashanti at Dodowah. At this period, however, the home government, disgusted with the Gold Coast by reason of the perpetual disturbances in the protectorate and the trouble it occasioned, determined to abandon the settlements, and sent instructions for the forts to be destroyed and the Europeans brought home. The merchants, backed by Major Rickets, 2nd West India regiments, the administrator, protested, and as a compromise the forts were handed over to a committee of merchants (Sept. 1828), who were given a subsidy of £4000 a year. The merchants secured (1830) as their administrator Mr George Maclean—a gentleman with military experience on the Gold Coast and not engaged in trade. To Maclean is due the consolidation of British interests in the interior. He concluded, 1831, a treaty with the Ashanti advantageous to the Fanti, whilst with very inadequate means he contrived to extend British influence over the whole region of the present colony In the words of a Fanti trader Maclean understood the people, "he settled things quietly with them and the people also loved him."2 Complaints that Maclean encouraged slavery reached England, but these were completely disproved, the governor being highly commended on his administration by the House of Commons Committee. It was decided, nevertheless, that the Colonial Office should resume direct control of the forts, which was done in 1843, Maclean continuing to direct native affairs until his death in 1847. The jurisdiction of England on the Gold Coast was defined by the bond of the 6th of March 1844, *Danish and Dutch forts purchased.* an agreement with the native chiefs by which the crown received the right of trying criminals, repressing human sacrifice, &c. The limits of the protectorate inland were not defined. The purchase of the Danish forts in 1850, and of the Dutch forts and territory in 1871, led to the consolidation of the British power along the coast; and the Ashanti war of 1873-74 resulted in the extension of the area of British influence. Since that time the colony has been chiefly engaged in the development of its material resources, a development accompanied by a slow but substantial advance in civilization among the native population. (For further historical information see ASHANTI.)

For a time the Gold Coast formed officially a limb of the "West African Settlements" and was virtually a dependency of Sierra Leone. In 1874 the settlements on the Gold Coast and Lagos were created a separate crown colony, this arrangement lasting until 1886 when Lagos was cut off from the Gold Coast administration.

Northern Territories.

The Northern Territories of the Gold Coast form a British protectorate to the north of Ashanti. They are bounded W. and N.—where 11° N. is the frontier line except at the eastern extremity—by the French colonies of the Ivory Coast and Upper Senegal and Niger, E. by the German colony of Togoland. The southern frontier, separating the protectorate from Ashanti, is the Black Volta to a point a little above its junction with the White Volta. Thence the frontier turns south and afterwards east so as to include the Brumasi district in the protectorate, the frontier gaining the main Volta below Yeji. The Territories include nearly all the country from the meridian of Greenwich to 3° W. and between 8° and 11° N., and cover an area of about 33,000 sq. m.

Lying north of the great belt of primeval forest which extends parallel to the Guinea coast, the greater part of the protectorate consists of open country, well timbered, and much of it presenting a park-like appearance. There are also large stretches of grassy plains, and in the southeast an area of treeless steppe. The flora and fauna resemble those of Ashanti. The country is well watered, the Black Volta forming the west and southern frontier for some distance, while the White Volta traverses its central regions. Both rivers, and also the united stream, contain rapids which impede but do not prevent navigation (see VOLTA). The climate is much healthier than that of the coast districts, and the fever experienced is of a milder type. The rainfall is less than on the coast; the dry season lasts from November (when the harmattan begins to blow) to March. The mean temperature at Gambaga is 80° F., the mean annual rainfall 43 in. The inhabitants were officially estimated in 1907 to number "at least 1,000,000." The Dagomba, Dagarti, Grunshi, Kangarga, Moshi and Zebarima, Negro or Negroid tribes, constitute the bulk of the people, and Fula, Hausa and Yoruba have settled as traders or cattle raisers. A large number of the natives are Moslems, the rest are fetish worshippers. The tribal organization is maintained by the British authorities, who found comparatively little difficulty in putting an end to slave-raiding and gaining the confidence of the chiefs. Trained by British officers, the natives make excellent soldiers.

Agriculture and Trade.—The chief crops are maize, guinea-corn, millet, yams, rice, beans, groundnuts, tobacco and cotton. Cotton is grown in most parts of the protectorate, the soil and climate in many districts being very suitable for its cultivation. Rubber is found in the northwestern regions. When the protectorate was assumed by Great Britain the Territories were singularly destitute of fruit trees. The British have introduced the orange, citron, lime, guava, mango and soursop, and among plants the banana, pine-apple and papaw. A large number of vegetables and flowers have also been introduced by the administration.

Stock-raising is carried on extensively, and besides oxen and sheep there are large numbers of horses and donkeys in the Territories. The chief exports are cattle, *dawa-dawa* (a favourite flavouring matter for soup among the Ashanti and other tribes) and shea-butter—the latter used in cooking and as an illuminant. The principal imports are kola-nuts, salt and cotton goods. A large proportion of the European goods imported is German and comes through Togoland. The administration levies a tax on traders' caravans, and in return ensures the safety of the roads. This tax is the chief local source of revenue. The revenue and expenditure of the Territories, as well as statistics of trade, are included in those of the Gold Coast.

Gold exists in quartz formation, chiefly in the valley of the Black Volta, and is found equally on the British and French sides of the frontier.

Towns.—The headquarters of the administration are at Tamale (or Tamari), a town in the centre of the Dagomba country east of the White Volta and 200 m. N.E. of Kumasi. Its inhabitants are keen traders, and it forms a distributing centre for the whole protectorate. Gambaga, an important commercial centre and from 1897 to 1907 the seat of government, is in Mamprusi, the north-east corner of the protectorate and is 85 m. N.N.E. of Tamale. A hundred and forty miles due south of Gambaga is Salaga. This town is situated on the caravan route from the Hausa states to Ashanti, and has a considerable trade in kola-nuts, shea-butter and salt. On the White Volta, midway between Gambaga and Salaga, is the thriving town of Daboya. On the western frontier are Bole (Baule) and Wa. They carry on an extensive trade with Bontuku, the capital of Jaman, and other places in the Ivory Coast colony. In all the towns the population largely consists of aliens—Hausa, Ashanti, Mandingos, &c.

Communications.—Lack of easy communication with the sea hinders the development of the country. The ancient caravan routes have been, however, supplemented by roads built by the British, who have further organized a service of boats on the Volta. Large cargo boats, chiefly laden with salt, ascend that river from Addah to Yeji and Daboya. From Yeji, the port of Salaga, a good road, 150 m. long, has been made to Gambaga. There is also a river service from Yeji to Longoro on the Black Volta, the port of Kintampo, in northern Ashanti. There is a complete telegraphic system connecting the towns of the protectorate with Kumasi and the Gold Coast ports.

History.—It was not until the last quarter of the 19th century that the country immediately north of Ashanti became known to Europeans. The first step forward was made by Monsieur M. J. Bonnat (one of the Kumasi captives, see ASHANTI) who, ascending the Volta, reached Salaga (1875-1876). In 1882 Captain R. La Trobe Lonsdale, an officer in British colonial service, went farther, visiting Yendi in the north and Bontuku in the west. Two years later Captain Brandon Kirby made his way to Kintampo. In 1887-1889 Captain L. G. Binger, a French officer, traversed the country from north to south. Thereafter the whole region was visited by British, French and German political missions. Prominent among the British agents was Mr George E. Ferguson, a native of West Africa, who had previously explored northern Ashanti. Between 1892 and 1897 Ferguson concluded several treaties guarding British interests. In 1897 Lieutenant Henderson and Ferguson occupied Wa, where they were attacked by the *sofas* of Samory (see SENEGAL, § 3). 207Henderson, who had gone to the *sofa* camp to parley, was held prisoner for some time, while Ferguson was killed. Meantime negotiations were opened in Europe to settle the spheres of influence of the respective countries. (The Anglo-French agreement of 1889 had fixed the boundaries of the hinterlands of the French colony of the Ivory Coast and the British colony of the Gold Coast as far as 9° N. only.) A period of considerable tension, arising from the proximity of British and French troops in the disputed territory, was ended by the signature of a convention in Paris (14th of June 1898), in which the western and northern boundaries were defined. The British abandoned their claim to the important town and district of Wagadugu in the north. In the following year (14th of November 1899) an agreement defining the eastern frontier was concluded with Germany. Previously a square block of territory to the north of 8° N. had been regarded as neutral, both by Britain and Germany. This was in virtue of an arrangement made in 1888. By the 1899 convention the neutral zone was parcelled out between the two powers. The delimitation of the frontiers agreed upon took place during 1900-1904.

In 1897 the Northern Territories were constituted a separate district of the Gold Coast hinterland, and were placed in charge of a chief commissioner. Colonel H. P. Northcott (killed in the Boer War, 1899-1902) was the first commissioner and commandant of the troops. He was succeeded by Col. A. H. Morris. In 1901 the Territories were made a distinct administration, under the jurisdiction of the governor of the Gold Coast colony. The government was at first of a semi-military character, but in 1907 a civilian staff was appointed to carry on the administration, and a force of armed constabulary replaced the troops which had been stationed in the protectorate and which were then disbanded. The prosperity of the country under British administration has been marked.

BIBLIOGRAPHY.—A good summary of the condition and history of the colony to the close of the 19th century will be found in vol. 3, "West Africa," of the *Historical Geography of the British Empire* by C. P. Lucas (2nd ed., Oxford, 1900). For current information see the *Gold Coast Civil Service List* (London, yearly), the annual Blue Books published in the colony, and the annual *Report* issued by the Colonial Office, London. For fuller information consult the *Report from the Select Committee on Africa (Western Coast)* (London, 1865), a mine of valuable information;*The Gold Coast, Past and Present*, by G. Macdonald (London, 1898); *History of the Gold Coast and Ashanti*, by C. C. Reindorf, a native pastor (Basel, 1895); *A History of the Gold Coast*, by Col. A. B. Ellis (London, 1893); *Wanderings in West Africa* (London, 1863) and *To the Gold Coast for Gold* (London, 1883), both by Sir Richard Burton. Of the earlier books the most notable are *The Golden Coast or a Description of Guinney together with a relation of such persons as got wonderful estates by their trade thither* (London, 1665), and *A New and Accurate Description of the Coast of Guinea* written (in Dutch) by Willem Bosman, chief factor for the Dutch at Elmina (Eng. trans., 2nd ed., 1721). For a complete survey of the Gold Coast under Dutch control see "Die Niederländisch West-Indische Compagnie an der Gold-Küste" by J. G. Doorman in *Tijds Indische Taal-, Land- en Volkenk*, vol. 40 (1898). For ethnography, religion, law, &c., consult *The Land of Fetish* (London, 1883) and *The Tshi-speaking Peoples of the West Coast of Africa* (London, 1887), both by Col. A. B. Ellis; *Fanti Customary Law* (2nd ed., London, 1904) and *Fanti Law Report* (London, 1904), both by J. M. Sarbah. The *Sketch of the Forestry of West Africa* by Sir Alfred Moloney (London, 1887) contains a comprehensive list of economic plants. See also *Report on Economic Agriculture on the Gold Coast* (Colonial Office Reports, No. 110, 1890), and *Papers relating to the Construction of Railways in ... the Gold Coast* (London, 1904). The best map is that of Major F. G. Guggisberg, over 70 sheets, scale 1 : 125,000 (London, 1907-1909). There is a War Office map on the scale 1 : 1,000,000 in one sheet. See also the works quoted under ASHANTI.

For the Northern Territories see L. G. Binger, *Du Niger au Golfe de Guinée* (Paris, 1892), a standard authority; H. P. Northcott, *Report on the Northern Territories of the Gold Coast* (War Office, London, 1899), a valuable compilation summarizing the then available information. Annual*Reports* on the protectorate are issued by the British Colonial Office. A map on the scale of 1 : 1,000,000 is issued by the War Office.

(F. R. C.)

1This name appears in a great variety of forms—Kwi, Ekwi, Okwi, Oji, Odschi, Otsui, Tyi, Twi, Tschi, Chwee or Chee.

2Blue Book on *Africa (Western Coast)* (1865), p. 233.

GOLDEN, a city and the county-seat of Jefferson county, Colorado, U.S.A., on Clear Creek (formerly called the Vasquez fork of the South Platte), about 14 m. W. by N. of Denver. Pop. (1900) 2152; (1910) 2477. Golden is a residential suburb of Denver, served by the Colorado & Southern, the Denver & Intermountain (electric), and the Denver & North-Western Electric railways. It is about 5700 ft. above sea-level. About 600 ft. above the city is Castle Rock, with an amusement park, and W. of Golden is Lookout Mountain, a natural park of 3400 acres. About 1 m. S. of the city is a state industrial school for boys, and in Golden is the Colorado State School of Mines (opened 1874), which offers courses in mining engineering and metallurgical engineering. The Independent Pyritic Smelter is at Golden, and among the city's manufactures are pottery, firebrick and tile, made from clays found near by, and flour. There are deposits of coal, copper and gold in the vicinity. Truck-farming and the growing of fruit are important industries in the neighbourhood. The first settlement here was a gold mining camp, established in 1859, and named in honour of Tom Golden, one of the pioneer prospectors. The village was laid out in 1860, and Golden was incorporated as a town in 1865 and was chartered as a city in 1870. Golden was made the capital of Colorado Territory in 1862, and several sessions (or parts of sessions) of the Assembly were held here between 1864 and 1868, when the seat of government was formally established at Denver; the territorial offices of Colorado, however, were at Golden only in 1866-1867.

GOLDEN BULL (Lat. *Bulla Aurea*), the general designation of any charter decorated with a golden seal or *bulla*, either owing to the intrinsic importance of its contents, or to the rank and dignity of the bestower or the recipient. The custom of thus giving distinction to certain documents is said to be of Byzantine origin, though if this be the case it is somewhat strange that the word employed as an equivalent for golden bull in Byzantine Greek should be the hybrid χρυσόβουλλον (cf. Codinus Curopalates, ὁ μέγας λογοθέτης διατάττει τὰ παρὰ τοῦ βασιλέως ἀποστελλόμενα προστάγματα καὶ χρυσόβουλλα πρός τε Ῥήγας, Σούλτανας, καὶ τοπάρχους; and Anna Comnena, Alexiad, lib. iii. διὰ χρυσοβουλίου λόγου; lib. viii., χρυσόβουλον λόγον). In Germany a Golden Bull is mentioned under the reign of Henry I. the Fowler in Chronica Cassin. ii. 31, and the oldest German example, if it be genuine, dates from 983. At first the golden seal was formed after the type of a solid coin, but at a later date, while the golden surface presented to the eye was greatly increased, the seal was really composed of two thin metal plates filled in with wax. The number of golden bulls issued by the imperial chancery must have been very large; the city of Frankfort, for example, preserves no fewer than eight.

The name, however, has become practically restricted to a few documents of unusual political importance, the golden bull of the Empire, the golden bull of Brabant, the golden bull of Hungary and the golden bull of Milan—and of these the first is undoubtedly *the* Golden Bull *par excellence*. The main object of the Golden Bull was to provide a set of rules for the election of the German kings, or kings of the Romans, as they are called in this document. Since the informal establishment of the electoral college about a century before (see ELECTORS), various disputes had taken place about the right of certain princes to vote at the elections, these and other difficulties having arisen owing to the absence of any authoritative ruling. The spiritual electors, it is true, had exercised their votes without challenge, but far different was the case of the temporal electors. The families ruling in Saxony and in Bavaria had been divided into two main branches and, as the German states had not yet accepted the principles of primogeniture, it was uncertain which member of the divided family should vote. Thus, both the prince ruling in Saxe-Lauenburg and the prince ruling in Saxe-Wittenberg claimed the vote, and the two branches of the family of Wittelsbach, one settled in Bavaria and the other in the Rhenish palatinate, were similarly at variance, while the duke of Bavaria also claimed the vote at the expense of the king of Bohemia. Moreover, there had been several disputed and double elections to the German crown during the past century. In more than one instance a prince, chosen by a minority of the electors, had claimed to exercise the functions of king, and as often civil war had been the result. Under these circumstances the emperor Charles IV. determined by an [208]authoritative pronouncement to make such proceedings impossible in the future, and at the same time to add to his own power and prestige, especially in his capacity as king of Bohemia.

Having arranged various disputes in Germany, and having in April 1355 secured his coronation in Rome, Charles gave instructions for the bull to be drawn up. It is uncertain who is responsible for its actual composition. The honour has been assigned to Bartolo of Sassoferrato, professor of law at Pisa and Perugia, to the imperial secretary, Rudolph of Friedberg, and even to the emperor himself, but there is no valid authority for giving it to any one of the three in preference to the others. In its first form the bull was promulgated at the diet of Nuremberg on the 10th of January 1356, but it was not accepted by the princes until some modifications had been introduced, and in its final form it was issued at the diet of Metz on the 25th of December following.

The text of the Golden Bull consists of a prologue and of thirty-one chapters. Some lines of verse invoking the aid of Almighty God are followed by a rhetorical statement of the evils which arise from discord and division, illustrations being taken from Adam, who was divided from obedience and thus fell, and from Helen of Troy who was divided from her husband. The early chapters are mainly concerned with details of the elaborate ceremonies which are to be observed on the occasion of an election. The number of electors is fixed at seven, the duke of Saxe-Wittenberg, not the duke of Saxe-Lauenburg, receiving the Saxon vote, and the count palatine, not the duke of Bavaria, obtaining the vote of the Wittelsbachs. The electors were arranged in order of precedence thus: the archbishops of Mainz, of Trier and of Cologne, the king of Bohemia, *qui inter electores laicos ex regiae dignitatis fastigio jure et merito obtinet primatiam*, the count palatine of the Rhine, the duke of Saxony and the margrave of Brandenburg. The three archbishops were respectively arch-chancellors of the three principal divisions of the Empire, Germany, Arles and Italy, and the four secular electors each held an office in the imperial household, the functions of which they were expected to discharge on great occasions. The king of Bohemia was the arch-cupbearer, the count palatine was the arch-steward (*dapifer*), the duke of Saxony was arch-marshal, and the margrave of Brandenburg was arch-chamberlain. The work of summoning the electors and of presiding over their deliberations fell to the archbishop of Mainz, but if he failed to discharge this duty the electors were to assemble without summons within three months of the death of a king. Elections were to be held at Frankfort; they were to be decided by a majority of votes, and the subsequent coronation at Aix-la-Chapelle was to be performed by the archbishop of Cologne. During a vacancy in the Empire the work of administering the greater part of Germany was entrusted to the count palatine of the Rhine, the duke of Saxony being responsible, however, for the government of Saxony, or rather for the districts *ubi Saxonica jura servantur*.

The chief result of the bull was to add greatly to the power of the electors; for, to quote Bryce (*Holy Roman Empire*), it "confessed and legalized the independence of the electors and the powerlessness of the crown." To these princes were given sovereign rights in their dominions, which were declared indivisible and were to pass according to the rule of primogeniture. Except in extreme cases, there was to be no appeal from the sentences of their tribunals, and they were confirmed in the right of coining money, of taking tolls, and in other privileges, while conspirators against their lives were to suffer the penalties of treason. One clause gave special rights and immunities to the king of Bohemia, who, it must be remembered, at this time was Charles himself, and others enjoined the observance of the public peace. Provision was made for an annual meeting of the electors, to be held at Metz four weeks after Easter, when matters *pro bono et salute communi* were to be discussed. This arrangement, however, was not carried out, although the electors met occasionally. Another clause forbade the cities to receive *Pfahlbürger, i.e.* forbade them to take men dwelling outside their walls under their protection. It may be noted that there is no admission whatever that the election of a king needs confirmation from the pope.

The Golden Bull was thus a great victory for the electors, but it weakened the position of the German king and was a distinct humiliation for the other princes and for the cities. The status of those rulers who did not obtain the electoral privilege was lowered by this very fact, and the regulations about the *Pfahlbürger*, together with the prohibition of new leagues and associations, struck a severe blow at the cities. The German kings were elected according to the conditions laid down in the bull until the dissolution of the Empire in 1806. At first the document was known simply as the Lex Carolina; but gradually the name of the Book with the Golden Bull came into use, and the present elliptical title was sufficiently established by 1417 to be officially employed in a charter by King Sigismund. The original autograph was committed to the care of the elector of Mainz, and it was preserved in the archives at Mainz till 1789. Official transcripts were probably furnished to each of the seven electors at the time of the promulgation, and before long many of the other members of the Empire secured copies for themselves. The transcript which belonged to the elector of Trier is preserved in the state archives at Stuttgart, that of the elector of Cologne in the court library at Darmstadt, and that of the king of Bohemia in the imperial archives at Vienna. Berlin, Munich and Dresden also boast the possession of an electoral transcript; and the town of Kitzingen has a contemporary copy in its municipal archives. There appears, however, to be good reason to doubt the genuineness of most of these so-called original transcripts. But perhaps the best known example is that of Frankfort-on-Main, which was procured from the imperial chancery in 1366, and is adorned with a golden seal like the original. Not only was it regularly quoted as the indubitable authority in regard to the election of the emperors in Frankfort itself, but it was from time to time officially consulted by members of the Empire.

The manuscript consists of 43 leaves of parchment of medium quality, each measuring about 10⅛ in. in height by 7⅛ in breadth. The seal is of the plate and wax type. On the obverse appears a figure of the emperor seated on his throne, with the sceptre in his right hand and the globe in his left; a shield, with the crowned imperial eagle, occupies the space on the one side of the throne, and a corresponding shield, with the crowned Bohemian lion with two tails, occupies the space on the other side; and round the margin runs the legend, *Karolus quartus divina favente clementia, Romanorum imperator semper Augustus et Boëmiae rex*. On the reverse is a castle, with the words *Aurea Roma* on the gate, and the circumscription reads, *Roma caput mundi regit orbis frena rotundi*. The original Latin text of the bull was printed at Nuremberg by Friedrich Creussner in 1474, and a second edition by Anthonius Koburger (d. 1532) appeared at the same place in 1477. Since that time it has been frequently reprinted from various manuscripts and collections. M. Goldast gave the Palatine text, compared with those of Bohemia and Frankfort, in his *Collectio constitutionum et legum imperialium* (Frankfort, 1613). Another is to be found in *De comitiis imperii* of O. Panvinius, and a third, of unknown history, is prefixed to the *Codex recessuum Imperii* (Mainz, 1599, and again 1615). The Frankfort text appeared in 1742 as *Aurea Bulla secundum exemplar originale Frankfurtense*, edited by W. C. Multz, and the text is also found in J. J. Schmauss, Corpus juris publici, edited by R. von Hommel (Leipzig, 1794), and in the *Ausgewählte Urkunden zur Erläuterung der Verfassungsgeschichte Deutschlands im Mittelalter*, edited by W. Altmann and E. Bernheim (Berlin, 1891, and again 1895). German translations, none of which, however, had any official authority, were published at Nuremberg about 1474, at Venice in 1476, and at Strassburg in 1485. Among the earlier commentators on the document are H. Canisius and J. Limnaeus who wrote *In Auream Bullam* (Strassburg, 1662). The student will find a good account of the older literature on the subject in C. G. Biener's *Commentarii de origine et progressu legum juriumque Germaniae* (1787-1795). See also J. D. von Olenschläger, *Neue Erläuterungen der Guldenen Bulle* (Frankfort and Leipzig, 1766); H. G. von Thulemeyer, *De Bulla Aurea, Argentea*, &c. (Heidelberg, 1682); J. St Pütter, *Historische Entwickelung der heutigen Staatsverfassung des teutschen Reichs* (Göttingen, 1786-1787), and O. Stobbe, *Geschichte der deutschen Rechtsquellen* (Brunswick, 1860-1864). Among the more modern works may be mentioned: E. Nerger, *Die Goldne Bulle nach ihrem Ursprung* (Göttingen, 1877), O. Hahn, *Ursprung und Bedeutung der Goldnen Bulle* (Breslau, 1903); and M. G. Schmidt, *Die staatsrechtliche Anwendung der Goldnen Bulle* (Halle, 1894). There is a valuable contribution to the subject in the *Quellensammlung zur Geschichte der deutschen Reichsverfassung*, edited by K. Zeumer (Leipzig, 1904), and another by O. Harnack in his *Das Kurfürsten Kollegium bis zur Mitte des 14ten Jahrhunderts* (Giessen, 1883). There is an English translation of the bull in E. F. Henderson's *Select Historical Documents of the Middle Ages* (London, 1903).

(A. W. H.*)

GOLDEN-EYE, a name indiscriminately given in many parts of Britain to two very distinct species of ducks, from the rich yellow colour of their irides. The commonest of them—the *Anas fuligula* of Linnaeus and *Fuligula cristata* of most modern ornithologists—is, however, usually called by English writers the tufted duck, while "golden-eye" is reserved in books for the *A. clangula* and *A. glaucion* of Linnaeus, who did not know that the birds he so named were but examples of the same species, differing only in age or sex; and to this day many fowlers perpetuate a like mistake, deeming the "Morillon," which is the female or young male, distinct from the "Golden-eye" or "Rattle-wings" (as from its noisy flight they oftener call it), which is the adult male. This species belongs to the group known as diving ducks, and is the type of the very well-marked genus *Clangula* of later systematists, which, among other differences, has the posterior end of the sternum prolonged so as to extend considerably over, and, we may not unreasonably suppose, protect the belly—a character possessed in a still greater degree by the mergansers (*Merginae*), while the males also exhibit in the extraordinarily developed bony labyrinth of their trachea and its midway enlargement another resemblance to the members of the same subfamily. The golden-eye, *C. glaucion* of modern writers, has its home in the northern parts of both hemispheres, whence in winter it migrates southward; but as it is one of the ducks that constantly resorts to hollow trees for the purpose of breeding it hardly transcends the limit of the Arctic forests on either continent. So well known is this habit to the people of the northern districts of Scandinavia, that they very commonly devise artificial nest-boxes for its accommodation and their own profit. Hollow logs of wood are prepared, the top and bottom closed, and a hole cut in the side. These are affixed to the trunks of living trees in suitable places, at a convenient distance from the ground, and, being readily occupied by the birds in the breeding season, are regularly robbed, first of the numerous eggs, and finally of the down they contain, by those who have set them up.

The adult male golden-eye is a very beautiful bird, mostly black above, but with the head, which is slightly crested, reflecting rich green lights, a large oval white patch under each eye and elongated white scapulars; the lower parts are wholly white and the feet bright orange, except the webs, which are dusky. In the female and young male, dark brown replaces the black, the cheek-spots are indistinct and the elongated white scapulars wanting. The golden-eye of North America has been by some authors deemed to differ, and has been named *C. americana*, but apparently on insufficient grounds. North America, however, has, in common with Iceland, a very distinct species, *C. islandica*, often called Barrow's duck, which is but a rare straggler to the continent of Europe, and never, so far as known, to Britain. In Iceland and Greenland it is the only habitual representative of the genus, and it occurs from thence to the Rocky Mountains. In breeding-habits it differs from the commoner species, not placing its eggs in tree-holes; but how far this difference is voluntary may be doubted, for in the countries it frequents trees are wanting. It is a larger and stouter bird, and in the male the white cheek-patches take a more crescentic form, while the head is glossed with purple rather than green, and the white scapulars are not elongated. The New World also possesses a third and still more beautiful species of the genus in *C. albeola*, known in books as the buffel-headed duck, and to American fowlers as the "spirit-duck" and "butter-ball"—the former name being applied from its rapidity in diving, and the latter from its exceeding fatness in autumn. This is of small size, but the lustre of the feathers in the male is most brilliant, exhibiting a deep plum-coloured gloss on the head. It breeds in trees, and is supposed to have occurred more than once in Britain.

(A. N.)

GOLDEN FLEECE, in Greek mythology, the fleece of the ram on which Phrixus and Helle escaped, for which see ARGONAUTS. For the modern order of the Golden Fleece, see KNIGHTHOOD AND CHIVALRY, section *Orders of Knighthood*.

GOLDEN HORDE, the name of a body of Tatars who in the middle of the 13th century overran a great portion of eastern Europe and founded in Russia the Tatar empire of khanate known as the Empire of the Golden Horde or Western Kipchaks. They invaded Europe about 1237 under the leadership of Bātū Khan, a younger son of Juji, eldest son of Jenghiz Khan, passed over Russia with slaughter and destruction, and penetrated into Silesia, Poland and Hungary, finally defeating Henry II., duke of Silesia, at Liegnitz in the battle known as the Wahlstatt on the 9th of April 1241. So costly was this victory, however, that Bātū, finding he could not reduce Neustadt, retraced his steps and established himself in his magnificent tent (whence the name "golden") on the Volga. The new settlement was known as *Sir Orda* ("Golden Camp," whence "Golden *Horde*"). Very rapidly the powers of Bātū extended over the Russian princes, and so long as the khanate remained in the direct descent from Bātū nothing occurred to check the growth of the empire. The names of Bātū's successors are Sartak (1256), Bereke (Baraka) (1256-1266), Mangū-Timūr (1266-1280), Tūda Mangū (1280-1287). (?) Tūla Bughā (1287-1290), Tōktū (1290-1312), Ūzbeg (1312-1340), Tīn-Beg (1340), Jānī-Beg (1340-1357). The death of Jānī-Beg, however, threw the empire into confusion. Birdī-Beg (Berdi-Beg) only reigned for two years, after which two rulers, calling themselves sons of Jānī-Beg occupied the throne during one year. From that time (1359) till 1378 no single ruler held the whole empire under control, various members of the other branches of the old house of Jūjī assuming the title. At last in 1378 Tōktāmish, of the Eastern Kipchaks, succeeded in ousting all rivals, and establishing himself as ruler of eastern and western Kipchak. For a short time the glory of the Golden Horde was renewed, until it was finally crushed by Timur in 1395.

See further MONGOLS and RUSSIA; Sir Henry Howorth's *History of the Mongols*; S. Lane-Poole's *Mohammadan Dynasties* (1894), pp. 222-231; for the relations of the various descendants of Jenghiz, see Stockvis, *Manuel d'histoire*, vol. i. chap. ix. table 7.

GOLDEN ROD, in botany, the popular name for *Solidago virgaurea* (natural order Compositae), a native of Britain and widely distributed in the north temperate region. It is an old-fashioned border-plant flowering from July to September, with an erect, sparingly-branched stem and small bright-yellow clustered heads of flowers. It grows well in common soil and is readily propagated by division in the spring or autumn.

GOLDEN ROSE (*rosa aurea*), an ornament made of wrought gold and set with gems, generally sapphires, which is blessed by the pope on the fourth (*Laetare*) Sunday of Lent, and usually afterwards sent as a mark of special favour to some distinguished individual, to a church, or a civil community. Formerly it was a single rose of wrought gold, coloured red, but the form finally adopted is a thorny branch with leaves and flowers, the petals of which are decked with gems, surmounted by one principal rose. The origin of the custom is obscure. From very early times popes have given away a rose on the fourth Sunday of Lent, whence the name Dominica Rosa, sometimes given to this feast. The practice of blessing and sending some such symbol (*e.g. eulogiae*) goes back to the earliest Christian antiquity, but the use of the rose itself does not seem to go farther back than the 11th century. According to some authorities it was used by Leo IX. (1049-1054), but in any case Pope Urban II. sent one to Fulk of Anjou during the preparations for the first crusade. Pope Urban V., who sent a golden rose to Joanna of Naples in 1366, is alleged to have been the first to determine that one should be consecrated annually. Beginning with the 16th century there went regularly with the rose a letter relating the reasons why it was sent, and reciting the merits and virtues of the receiver. When the change was made from the form of the simple rose to the branch is uncertain. The rose sent by Innocent IV. in 1244 to Count Raymond Berengar IV. of Provence was a simple flower without any accessory ornamentation, while the one given by Benedict XI. in 1303 or 1304 to the 210church of St Stephen at Perugia consisted of a branch garnished with five open and two closed roses enriched with a sapphire, the whole having a value of seventy ducats. The value of the gift varied according to the character or rank of the recipient. John XXII. gave away some weighing 12 oz., and worth from £250 to £325. Among the recipients of this honour have been Henry VI. of England, 1446; James III. of Scotland, on whom the rose (made by Jacopo Magnolio) was conferred by Innocent VIII., James IV. of Scotland; Frederick the Wise, elector of Saxony, who received a rose from Leo X. in 1518; Henry VIII. of England, who received three, the last from Clement VII. in 1524 (each had nine branches, and rested on different forms of feet, one on oxen, the second on acorns, and the third on lions); Queen Mary, who received one in 1555 from Julius III.; the republic of Lucca, so favoured by Pius IV., in 1564; the Lateran Basilica by Pius V. three years later; the sanctuary of Loreto by Gregory XIII. in 1584; Maria Theresa, queen of France, who received it from Clement IX. in 1668; Mary Casimir, queen of Poland, from Innocent XI. in 1684 in recognition of the deliverance of Vienna by her husband, John Sobieski; Benedict XIII. (1726) presented one to the cathedral of Capua, and in 1833 it was sent by Gregory XVI. to the church of St Mark's, Venice. In more recent times it was sent to Napoleon III. of France, the empress Eugénie, and the queens Isabella II., Christina (1886) and Victoria (1906) of Spain. The gift of the golden rose used almost invariably to accompany the coronation of the king of the Romans. If in any particular year no one is considered worthy of the rose, it is laid up in the Vatican.

Some of the most famous Italian goldsmiths have been employed in making the earlier roses; and such intrinsically valuable objects have, in common with other priceless historical examples of the goldsmiths' art, found their way to the melting-pot. It is, therefore, not surprising that the number of existing historic specimens is very small. These include one of the 14th century in the Cluny Museum, Paris, believed to have been sent by Clement V. to the prince-bishop of Basel; another conferred in 1458 on his native city of Siena by Pope Pius II.; and the rose bestowed upon Siena by Alexander VII., a son of that city, which is depicted in a procession in a fresco in the Palazzo Pubblico at Siena. The surviving roses of more recent date include that presented by Benedict XIII. to Capua cathedral; the rose conferred on the empress Caroline by Pius VII., 1819, at Vienna; one of 1833 (Gregory XVI.) at St Mark's, Venice; and Pope Leo XIII.'s rose sent to Queen Christina of Spain, which is at Madrid.

AUTHORITIES.—Angelo Rocca, *Aurea Rosa*, &c. (1719); Busenelli, *De Rosa Aurea. Epistola* (1759); Girbal, *La Rosa de oro* (Madrid, 1820); C. Joret, *La Rose d'or dans l'antiquité et au moyen âge* (Paris, 1892), pp. 432-435; Eugène Muntz in *Revue d'art chrétien* (1901), series v. vol. 12 pp. 1-11; De F. Mely, *Le Trésor de Chartres* (1886); Marquis de Mac Swiney Mashanaglass, *Le Portugal et le Saint Siège: Les Roses d'or envoyées par les Papes aux rois de Portugal au XVIe siècle* (1904); Sir C. Young, *Ornaments and Gift consecrated by the Roman Pontiffs: the Golden Rose, the Cap and Swords presented to Sovereigns of England and Scotland* (1864).

(J. T. S.*; E. A. J.)

GOLDEN RULE, the term applied in all European languages to the rule of conduct laid down in the New Testament (Matthew vii. 12 and Luke vi. 31). "whatsoever ye would that men should do to you, do ye even so to them, for this is the law and the prophets." This principle has often been stated as the fundamental precept of social morality. It is sometimes put negatively or passively, "do not that to another which thou wouldst not have done to thyself" (cf. Hobbes, *Leviathan,* xv. 79, xvii. 85), but it should be observed that in this form it implies merely abstention from evil doing. In either form the precept in ordinary application is part of a hedonistic system of ethics, the criterion of action being strictly utilitarian in character.

See H. Sidgwick, *History of Ethics* (5th ed., 1902), p. 167; James Seth, *Ethical Principles,* p. 97 foll.

GOLDFIELD, a town and the county-seat of Esmeralda county, Nevada, U.S.A., about 170 m. S.E. of Carson City. Pop. (1910, U.S. census) 4838. It is served by the Tonopah & Groldfield, Las Vegas & Tonopah, and Tonopah & Tidewater railways. The town lies in the midst of a desert abounding in high-grade gold ores, and is essentially a mining camp. The discovery of gold at Tonopah, about 28 m. N. of Goldfield, in 1900 was followed by its discovery at Goldfield in 1902 and 1903; in 1904 the Goldfield district produced about 800 tons of ore, which yielded $2,300,000 worth of gold, or 30% of that of the State. This remarkable production caused Goldfield to grow rapidly, and it soon became the largest town in the state. In addition to the mines, there are large reduction works. In 1907 Goldfield became the county-seat. The gold output in 1907 was $8,408,396; in 1908, $4,880,251. Soon after mining on an extensive scale began, the miners organized themselves as a local branch of the Western Federation of Miners, and in this branch were included many labourers in Goldfield other than miners. Between this branch and the mine-owners there arose a series of more or less serious differences, and there were several set strikes—in December 1906 and January 1907, for higher wages; in March and April 1907, because the mine-owners refused to discharge carpenters who were members of the American Federation of Labour, but did not belong to the Western Federation of Miners or to the Industrial Workers of the World affiliated with it, this last organization being, as a result of the strike, forced out of Goldfield; in August and September 1907, because a rule was introduced at some of the mines requiring miners to change their clothing before entering and after leaving the mines,—a rule made necessary, according to the operators, by the wholesale stealing (in miners' parlance, "high-grading") of the very valuable ore (some of it valued at as high as $20 a pound); and in November and December 1907, because some of the mine-owners, avowedly on account of the hard times, adopted a system of paying in cashier's checks. Excepting occasional attacks upon non-union workmen, or upon persons supposed not to be in sympathy with the miners' union, there had been no serious disturbance in Goldfield; but in December 1907, Governor Sparks, at the instance of the mine-owners, appealed to President Roosevelt to send Federal troops to Goldfield, on the ground that the situation there was ominous, that destruction of life and property seemed probable, and that the state had no militia and would be powerless to maintain order. President Roosevelt thereupon (December 4th) ordered General Frederick Funston, commanding the Division of California, at San Francisco, to proceed with 300 Federal troops to Goldfield. The troops arrived in Goldfield on the 6th of December, and immediately afterwards the mine-owners reduced wages and announced that no members of the Western Federation of Miners would thereafter be employed in the mines. President Roosevelt, becoming convinced that conditions had not warranted Governor Sparks's appeal for Federal assistance, but that the immediate withdrawal of the troops might nevertheless lead to serious disorders, consented that they should remain for a short time on condition that the state should immediately organize an adequate militia or police force. Accordingly, a special meeting of the legislature was immediately called, a state police force was organized, and on the 7th of March 1908 the troops were withdrawn. Thereafter work was gradually resumed in the mines, the contest having been won by the mine-owners.

GOLDFINCH (Ger. *Goldfink*1), the *Fringilla carduelis* of Linnaeus and the *Carduelis elegans* of later authors, an extremely well-known bird found over the greater parts of Europe and North Africa, and eastwards to Persia and Turkestan. Its gay plumage is matched by its sprightly nature; and together they make it one of the most favourite cage-birds among all classes. As a songster it is indeed surpassed by many other species, but its docility and ready attachment to its master or mistress make up for any defect in its vocal powers. In some parts of England the trade in goldfinches is very considerable. In 1860 Mr Hussey reported (*Zool.,* p. 7144) the average annual captures near Worthing to exceed 11,000 dozens—nearly all being cock-birds; and a witness before a committee of the House of Commons in 1873 stated that, when a boy, he could take forty 211dozens in a morning near Brighton. In these districts and others the number has become much reduced, owing doubtless in part to the fatal practice of catching the birds just before or during the breeding-season; but perhaps the strongest cause of their growing scarcity is the constant breaking-up of waste lands, and the extirpation of weeds (particularly of the order *Compositae*) essential to the improved system of agriculture; for in many parts of Scotland, East Lothian for instance, where goldfinches were once as plentiful as sparrows, they are now only rare stragglers, and yet there they have not been thinned by netting. Though goldfinches may occasionally be observed in the coldest weather, incomparably the largest number leave Britain in autumn, returning in spring, and resorting to gardens and orchards to breed, when the lively song of the cock, and the bright yellow wings of both sexes, quickly attract notice. The nest is a beautifully neat structure, often placed at no great height from the ground, but generally so well hidden by the leafy bough on which it is built as not to be easily found, until, the young being hatched, the constant visits of the parents reveal its site. When the broods leave the nest they move into the more open country, and frequenting pastures, commons, heaths and downs, assemble in large flocks towards the end of summer. Eastward of the range of the present species its place is taken by its congener *C. caniceps*, which is easily recognized by wanting the black hood and white ear-coverts of the British bird. Its home seems to be in Central Asia, but it moves southward in winter, being common at that season in Cashmere, and is not unfrequently brought for sale to Calcutta. The position of the genus *Carduelis* in the family *Fringillidae* is not very clear. Structurally it would seem to have some relation to the siskins (*Chrysomitris*), though the members of the two groups have very different habits, and perhaps its nearest kinship lies with the hawfinches (*Coccothraustes*). See FINCH.

(A. N.)

1The more common German name, however, is *Distelfink* (Thistle-Finch) or *Stieglitz*.

GOLDFISH (*Cyprinus* or *Carassius auratus*), a small fish belonging to the Cyprinid family, a native of China but naturalized in other countries. In the wild state its colours do not differ from those of a Crucian carp, and like that fish it is tenacious of life and easily domesticated. Albinos seem to be rather common; and as in other fishes (for instance, the tench, carp, eel, flounder), the colour of most of these albinos is a bright orange or golden yellow; occasionally even this shade of colour is lost, the fish being more or less pure white or silvery. The Chinese have domesticated these albinos for a long time, and by careful selection have succeeded in propagating all those strange varieties, and even monstrosities, which appear in every domestic animal. In some individuals the dorsal fin is only half its normal length, in others entirely absent; in others the anal fin has a double spine; in others all the fins are of nearly double the usual length. The snout is frequently malformed, giving the head of the fish an appearance similar to that of a bull-dog. The variety most highly prized has an extremely short snout, eyes which almost wholly project beyond the orbit, no dorsal fin, and a very long three- or four-lobed caudal fin (Telescope-fish).

Telesco
pe-fish.

The domestication of the goldfish by the Chinese dates back from the highest antiquity, and they were introduced into Japan at the beginning of the 16th century; but the date of their importation into Europe is still uncertain. The great German ichthyologist, M. E. Bloch, thought he could trace it back in England to the reign of James I., whilst other authors fix the date at 1691. It appears certain that they were brought to France, only much later, as a present to Mme de Pompadour, although the de Goncourts, the historians of the mistresses of Louis XV., have failed to trace any records of this event. The fish has since spread over a considerable part of Europe, and in many places it has reverted to its wild condition. In many parts of south-eastern Asia, in Mauritius, in North and South Africa, in Madagascar, in the Azores, it has become thoroughly acclimatized, and successfully competes with the indigenous fresh-water fishes. It will not thrive in rivers; in large ponds it readily reverts to the coloration of the original wild stock. It flourishes best in small tanks and ponds, in which the water is constantly changing and does not freeze; in such localities, and with a full supply of food, which consists of weeds, crumbs of bread, bran, worms, small crustaceans and insects, it attains to a length of from 6 to 12 in., breeding readily, sometimes at different times of the same year.

GOLDFUSS, GEORG AUGUST (1782-1848), German palaeontologist, born at Thurnau near Bayreuth on the 18th of April 1782, was educated at Erlangen, where he graduated Ph.D. in 1804 and became professor of zoology in 1818. He was subsequently appointed professor of zoology and mineralogy in the university of Bonn. Aided by Count G. Münster he issued the important *Petrefacta Germaniae* (1826-1844), a work which was intended to illustrate the invertebrate fossils of Germany, but it was left incomplete after the sponges, corals, crinoids, echinids and part of the mollusca had been figured. Goldfuss died at Bonn on the 2nd of October 1848.

GOLDIE, SIR GEORGE DASHWOOD TAUBMAN (1846-   ), English administrator, the founder of Nigeria, was born on the 20th of May 1846 at the Nunnery in the Isle of Man, being the youngest son of Lieut.-Colonel John Taubman Goldie-Taubman, speaker of the House of Keys, by his second wife Caroline, daughter of John E. Hoveden of Hemingford, Cambridgeshire. Sir George resumed his paternal name, Goldie, by royal licence in 1887. He was educated at the Royal Military Academy, Woolwich, and for about two years held a commission in the Royal Engineers. He travelled in all parts of Africa, gaining an extensive knowledge of the continent, and first visited the country of the Niger in 1877. He conceived the idea of adding to the British empire the then little known regions of the lower and middle Niger, and for over twenty years his efforts were devoted to the realization of this conception. The method by which he determined to work was the revival of government by chartered companies within the empire—a method supposed to be buried with the East India Company. The first step was to combine all British commercial interests in the Niger, and this he accomplished in 1879 when the United African Company was formed. In 1881 Goldie sought a charter from the imperial government (the 2nd Gladstone ministry). Objections of various kinds were raised. To meet them the capital of the company (renamed the National African Company) was increased from £125,000 to £1,000,000, and great energy was displayed in founding stations on the Niger. At this time French traders, encouraged by Gambetta, established themselves on the lower river, thus rendering it difficult for the company to obtain territorial rights; but the Frenchmen were bought out in 1884, so that at the Berlin conference on West Africa in 1885 Mr Goldie, present as an expert on matters relating to the river, was able to announce that on the lower Niger the British flag alone flew. Meantime the Niger coast line had been placed under British protection. Through Joseph Thomson, David McIntosh, D. W. Sargent, J. Flint, William Wallace, E. Dangerfield and numerous other agents, over 400 political treaties—drawn up by Goldie—were made with the chiefs of the lower Niger and the Hausa states. The scruples of the British government being overcome, a charter was at length granted 212(July 1886), the National African Company becoming the Royal Niger Company, with Lord Aberdare as governor and Goldie as vice-governor. In 1895, on Lord Aberdare's death, Goldie became governor of the company, whose destinies he had guided throughout.

The building up of Nigeria as a British state had to be carried on in face of further difficulties raised by French travellers with political missions, and also in face of German opposition. From 1884 to 1890, Prince Bismarck was a persistent antagonist, and the strenuous efforts he made to secure for Germany the basin of the lower Niger and Lake Chad were even more dangerous to Goldie's schemes of empire than the ambitions of France. Herr E. R. Flegel, who had travelled in Nigeria during 1882-1884 under the auspices of the British company, was sent out in 1885 by the newly-formed German Colonial Society to secure treaties for Germany, which had established itself at Cameroon. After Flegel's death in 1886 his work was continued by his companion Dr Staudinger, while Herr Hoenigsberg was despatched to stir up trouble in the occupied portions of the Company's territory,—or, as he expressed it, "to burst up the charter." He was finally arrested at Onitsha, and, after trial by the company's supreme court at Asaba, was expelled the country. Prince Bismarck then sent out his nephew, Herr von Puttkamer, as German consul-general to Nigeria, with orders to report on this affair, and when this report was published in a White Book, Bismarck demanded heavy damages from the company. Meanwhile Bismarck maintained constant pressure on the British government to compel the Royal Niger Company to a division of spheres of influence, whereby Great Britain would have lost a third, and the most valuable part, of the company's territory. But he fell from power in March 1890, and in July following Lord Salisbury concluded the famous "Heligoland" agreement with Germany. After this event the aggressive action of Germany in Nigeria entirely ceased, and the door was opened for a final settlement of the Nigeria-Cameroon frontiers. These negotiations, which resulted in an agreement in 1893, were initiated by Goldie as a means of arresting the advance of France into Nigeria from the direction of the Congo. By conceding to Germany a long but narrow strip of territory between Adamawa and Lake Chad, to which she had no treaty claims, a barrier was raised against French expeditions, semi-military and semi-exploratory, which sought to enter

Nigeria from the east. Later French efforts at aggression were made from the western or Dahomeyan side, despite an agreement concluded with France in 1890 respecting the northern frontier.

The hostility of certain Fula princes led the company to despatch, in 1897, an expedition against the Mahommedan states of Nupé and Illorin. This expedition was organized and personally directed by Goldie and was completely successful. Internal peace was thus secured, but in the following year the differences with France in regard to the frontier line became acute, and compelled the intervention of the British government. In the negotiations which ensued Goldie was instrumental in preserving for Great Britain the whole of the navigable stretch of the lower Niger. It was, however, evidently impossible for a chartered company to hold its own against the state-supported protectorates of France and Germany, and in consequence, on the 1st of January 1900, the Royal Niger Company transferred its territories to the British government for the sum of £865,000. The ceded territory together with the small Niger Coast Protectorate, already under imperial control, was formed into the two protectorates of northern and southern Nigeria (see furtherNIGERIA).

In 1903-1904, at the request of the Chartered Company of South Africa, Goldie visited Rhodesia and examined the situation in connexion with the agitation for self-government by the Rhodesians. In 1902-1903 he was one of the royal commissioners who inquired into the military preparations for the war in South Africa (1899-1902) and into the operations up to the occupation of Pretoria, and in 1905-1906 was a member of the royal commission which investigated the methods of disposal of war stores after peace had been made. In 1905 he was elected president of the Royal Geographical Society and held that office for three years. In 1908 he was chosen an alderman of the London County Council. Goldie was created K.C.M.G. in 1887, and a privy councillor in 1898. He became an F.R.S., honorary D.C.L. of Oxford University (1897) and honorary LL.D. of Cambridge (1897). He married in 1870 Matilda Catherine (d. 1898), daughter of John William Elliott of Wakefield.

GOLDING, ARTHUR (*c.* 1536-*c.* 1605), English translator, son of John Golding of Belchamp St Paul and Halsted, Essex, one of the auditors of the exchequer, was born probably in London about 1536. His half-sister, Margaret, married John de Vere, 16th earl of Oxford. In 1549 he was already in the service of Protector Somerset, and the statement that he was educated at Queen's College, Cambridge, lacks corroboration. He seems to have resided for some time in the house of Sir William Cecil, in the Strand, with his nephew, the poet, the 17th earl of Oxford, whose receiver he was, for two of his dedications are dated from Cecil House. His chief work is his translation of Ovid. *The Fyrst Fower Bookes of P. Ovidius Nasos worke, entitled Metamorphosis, translated oute of Latin into Englishe meter* (1565), was supplemented in 1567 by a translation of the fifteen books. Strangely enough the translator of Ovid was a man of strong Puritan sympathies, and he translated many of the works of Calvin. To his version of the *Metamorphoses* he prefixed a long metrical explanation of his reasons for considering it a work of edification. He sets forth the moral which he supposes to underlie certain of the stories, and shows how the pagan machinery may be brought into line with Christian thought. It was from Golding's pages that many of the Elizabethans drew their knowledge of classical mythology, and there is little doubt that Shakespeare was well acquainted with the book. Golding translated also the *Commentaries* of Caesar (1565), Calvin's commentaries on the Psalms (1571), his sermons on the Galatians and Ephesians, on Deuteronomy and the book of Job, Theodore Beza's *Tragedie of Abrahams Sacrifice* (1577) and the *De Beneficiis* of Seneca (1578). He completed a translation begun by Sidney from Philippe de Mornay, *A Worke concerning the Trewnesse of the Christian Religion* (1604). His only original work is a prose *Discourse* on the earthquake of 1580, in which he saw a judgment of God on the wickedness of his time. He inherited three considerable estates in Essex, the greater part of which he sold in 1595. The last trace we have of Golding is contained in an order dated the 25th of July 1605, giving him licence to print certain of his works.

GOLDINGEN (Lettish, *Kuldiga*), a town of Russia, in the government of Courland, 55 m. by rail N.E. of Libau, and on Windau river, in 56° 58' N. and 22° E. Pop. (1897) 9733. It has woollen mills, needle and match factories, breweries and distilleries, a college for teachers, and ruins of a castle of the Teutonic Knights, built in 1248 and used in the 17th century as the residence of the dukes of Courland.

GOLDMARK, KARL (1832-   ), Hungarian composer, was born at Keszthely-am-Plattensee, in Hungary, on the 18th of May 1832. His father, a poor cantor in the local Jewish synagogue, was unable to assist to any extent financially in the development of his son's talents. Yet in the household much music was made, and on a cheap violin and home-made flute, constructed by Goldmark himself from reeds cut from the riverbank, the future composer gave rein to his musical ideas. His talent was fostered by the village schoolmaster, by whose aid he was able to enter the music-school of the Oedenburger Verein. Here he remained but a short time, his success at a school concert finally determining his parents to allow him to devote himself entirely to music. In 1844, then, he went to Vienna, where Jansa took up his cause and eventually obtained for him admission to the conservatorium. For two years Goldmark worked under Jansa at the violin, and on the outbreak of the revolution, after studying all the orchestral instruments he obtained an engagement in the orchestra at Raab. There, on the capitulation of Raab, he was to have been shot for a spy, and was only saved at the eleventh hour by the happy arrival of a former colleague. In 1850 Goldmark left Raab for Vienna, where from his friend Mittrich he obtained his first real knowledge of the classics. There, too, he devoted himself to composition. In 1857 Goldmark, 213who was then engaged in the Karl-theater band, gave a concert of his own works with such success that his first quartet attracted very general attention. Then followed the "Sakuntala" and "Penthesilea" overtures, which show how Wagner's influence had supervened upon his previous domination by Mendelssohn, and the delightful "Ländliche Hochzeit" symphony, which carried his fame abroad. Goldmark's reputation was now made, and very largely increased by the production at Vienna in 1875 of his first and best opera,*Die Königin von Saba*. Over this opera he spent seven years. Its popularity is still almost as great as ever. It was followed in November 1886, also at Vienna, by *Merlin*, much of which has been rewritten since then. A third opera, a version of Dickens's *Cricket on the Hearth*, was given by the Royal Carl Rosa Company in London in 1900. Goldmark's chamber music has not made much lasting impression, but the overtures "Im Frühling," "Prometheus Bound," and "Sapho" are fairly well known. A "programme" seems essential to him. In opera he is most certainly at his best, and as an orchestral colourist he ranks among the very highest.

GOLDONI, CARLO (1707-1793), Italian dramatist, the real founder of modern Italian comedy, was born at Venice, on the 25th of February 1707, in a fine house near St Thomas's church. His father Giulio was a native of Modena. The first playthings of the future writer were puppets which he made dance; the first books he read were plays,—among others, the comedies of the Florentine Cicognini. Later he received a still stronger impression from the*Mandragora* of Machiavelli. At eight years old he had tried to sketch a play. His father, meanwhile, had taken his degree in medicine at Rome and fixed himself at Perugia, where he made his son join him; but, having soon quarrelled with his colleagues in medicine, he departed for Chioggia, leaving his son to the care of a philosopher, Professor Caldini of Rimini. The young Goldoni soon grew tired of his life at Rimini, and ran away with a Venetian company of players. He began to study law at Venice, then went to continue the same pursuit at Pavia, but at that time he was studying the Greek and Latin comic poets much more and much better than books about law. "I have read over again," he writes in his own *Memoirs*, "the Greek and Latin poets, and I have told to myself that I should like to imitate them in their style, their plots, their precision; but I would not be satisfied unless I succeeded in giving more interest to my works, happier issues to my plots, better drawn characters and more genuine comedy." For a satire entitled *Il Colosso*, which attacked the honour of several families of Pavia, he was driven from that town, and went first to study with the jurisconsult Morelli at Udine, then to take his degree in law at Modena. After having worked some time as clerk in the chanceries of Chioggia and Feltre, his father being dead, he went to Venice, to exercise there his profession as a lawyer. But the wish to write for the stage was always strong in him, and he tried to do so; he made, however, a mistake in his choice, and began with a tragedy, *Amalasunta*, which was represented at Milan and proved a failure. In 1734 he wrote another tragedy, *Belisario*, which, though not much better, chanced nevertheless to please the public. This first success encouraged him to write other tragedies, some of which were well received; but the author himself saw clearly that he had not yet found his proper sphere, and that a radical dramatic reform was absolutely necessary for the stage. He wished to create a characteristic comedy in Italy, to follow the example of Molière, and to delineate the realities of social life in as natural a manner as possible. His first essay of this kind was *Momolo Cortesan* (Momolo the Courtier), written in the Venetian dialect, and based on his own experience. Other plays followed—some interesting from their subject, others from the characters; the best of that period are—*Le Trentadue Disgrazie d' Arlecchino*, *La Notte critica*, *La Bancarotta*, *La Donna di Garbo*. Having, while consul of Genoa at Venice, been cheated by a captain of Ragusa, he founded on this his play *L'Impostore*. At Leghorn he made the acquaintance of the comedian Medebac, and followed him to Venice, with his company, for which he began to write his best plays. Once he promised to write sixteen comedies in a year, and kept his word; among the sixteen are some of his very best, such as *Il Caffè*, *Il Bugiardo*, *La Pamela*. When he left the company of Medebac, he passed over to that maintained by the patrician Vendramin, continuing to write with the greatest facility. In 1761 he was called to Paris, and before leaving Venice he wrote *Una delle ultime sere di Carnevale* (One of the Last Nights of Carnival), an allegorical comedy in which he said good-bye to his country. At the end of the representation of this play, the theatre resounded with applause, and with shouts expressive of good wishes. Goldoni, at this proof of public sympathy, wept as a child. At Paris, during two years, he wrote comedies for the Italian actors; then he taught Italian to the royal princesses; and for the wedding of Louis XVI. and of Marie Antoinette he wrote in French one of his best comedies, *Le Bourru bienfaisant*, which was a great success. When he retired from Paris to Versailles, the king made him a gift of 6000 francs, and fixed on him an annual pension of 1200 francs. It was at Versailles he wrote his *Memoirs*, which occupied him till he reached his eightieth year. The Revolution deprived him all at once of his modest pension, and reduced him to extreme misery; he dragged on his unfortunate existence till 1793, and died on the 6th of February. The day after, on the proposal of André Chénier, the Convention agreed to give the pension back to the poet; and as he had already died, a reduced allowance was granted to his widow.

The best comedies of Goldoni are: *La Donna di Garbo, La Bottega di Caffè, Pamela nubile, Le Baruffe chiozzotte, I Rusteghi, Todero Brontolon, Gli Innamorati, Il Ventaglio, Il Bugiardo, La Casa nova, Il Burbero benefico, La Locandiera.* A collected edition (Venice, 1788) was republished at Florence in 1827. See P. G. Molmenti, *Carlo Goldoni* (Venice, 1875); Rabany, *Carlo Goldoni* (Paris, 1896). The *Memoirs* were translated into English by John Black (Boston, 1877). with preface by W. D. Howells.

GOLDS, a Mongolo-Tatar people, living on the Lower Amur in south-eastern Siberia. Their chief settlements are on the right bank of the Amur and along the Sungari and Usuri rivers. In physique they are typically Mongolic. Like the Chinese they wear a pigtail, and from them, too, have learnt the art of silk embroidery. The Golds live almost entirely on fish, and are excellent boatmen. They keep large herds of swine and dogs, which live, like themselves, on fish. Geese, wild duck, eagles, bears, wolves and foxes are also kept in menageries. There is much reverence paid to the eagles, and hence the Manchus call the Golds "Eaglets." Their religion is Shamanism.

See L. Schrenck, *Die Völker des Amurlandes* (St Petersburg, 1891); Laufer, "The Amoor Tribes," in *American Anthropologist* (New York, 1900); E. G. Ravenstein, *The Russians on the Amur* (1861).

GOLDSBORO, a city and the county-seat of Wayne county, North Carolina, U.S.A., on the Neuse river, about 50 m. S.E. of Raleigh. Pop. (1890) 4017; (1900) 5877 (2520 negroes); (1910) 6107. It is served by the Southern, the Atlantic Coast Line and the Norfolk & Southern railways. The surrounding country produces large quantities of tobacco, cotton and grain, and trucking is an important industry, the city being a distributing point for strawberries and various kinds of vegetables. The city's manufactures include cotton goods, knit goods, cotton-seed oil, agricultural implements, lumber and furniture. Goldsboro is the seat of the Eastern insane asylum (for negroes) and of an Odd Fellows' orphan home. The municipality owns and operates its water-works and electric-lighting plant. Goldsboro was settled in 1838, and was first incorporated in 1841. In the campaign of 1865 Goldsboro was the point of junction of the Union armies under generals Sherman and Schofield, previous to the final advance to Greensboro.

GOLDSCHMIDT, HERMANN (1802-1866), German painter and astronomer, was the son of a Jewish merchant, and was born at Frankfort on the 17th of June 1802. He for ten years assisted his father in his business; but, his love of art having been awakened while journeying in Holland, he in 1832 began the study of painting at Munich under Cornelius and Schnorr, and in 1836 established himself at Paris, where he painted a number of pictures of more than average merit, among which may be mentioned the "Cumaean Sibyl" (1844); an "Offering to Venus" (1845); a "View of Rome" (1849); the "Death of Romeo and Juliet" (1857); and several Alpine landscapes. In 1847 he began to devote his attention to astronomy; and from 1852 to 1861 he discovered fourteen asteroids between Mars and Jupiter, on which account he received the grand astronomical prize from the Academy of Sciences. His observations of the protuberances on the sun, made during the total eclipse on the 10th of July 1860, are included in the work of Mädler on the eclipse, published in 1861. Goldschmidt died at Fontainebleau on the 26th of August 1866.

GOLDSMID, the name of a family of Anglo-Jewish bankers sprung from Aaron Goldsmid (d. 1782), a Dutch merchant who settled in England about 1763. Two of his sons, Benjamin Goldsmid (*c.* 1753-1808) and Abraham Goldsmid (*c.* 1756-1810), began business together about 1777 as bill-brokers in London, and soon became great powers in the money market, during the Napoleonic war, through their dealings with the government. Abraham

153

Goldsmid was in 1810 joint contractor with the Barings for a government loan, but owing to a depreciation of the scrip he was forced into bankruptcy and committed suicide. His brother, in a fit of depression, had similarly taken his own life two years before. Both were noted for their public and private generosity, and Benjamin had a part in founding the Royal Naval Asylum. Benjamin left four sons, the youngest being Lionel Prager Goldsmid; Abraham a daughter, Isabel.

Their nephew, Sir Isaac Lyon Goldsmid, Bart. (1778-1859), was born in London, and began in business with a firm of bullion brokers to the Bank of England and the East India Company. He amassed a large fortune, and was made Baron da Palmeira by the Portuguese government in 1846 for services rendered In settling a monetary dispute between Portugal and Brazil, but he is chiefly known for his efforts to obtain the emancipation of the Jews in England and for his part in founding University College, London. The Jewish Disabilities Bill, first introduced in Parliament by Sir Robert Grant in 1830, owed its final passage to Goldsmid's energetic work. He helped to establish the University College hospital in 1834, serving as its treasurer for eighteen years, and also aided in the efforts to obtain reform in the English penal code. Moreover he assisted by his capital and his enterprise to build part of the English southern railways and also the London docks. In 1841 he became the first Jewish baronet, the honour being conferred upon him by Lord Melbourne. He had married his cousin Isabel (see above), and their second son was Sir Francis Henry Goldsmid, Bart. (1808-1878), born in London, and called to the bar at Lincoln's Inn in 1833 (the first Jew to become an English barrister; Q.C. 1858). After the passing of the Jewish Disabilities Bill, in which he had aided his father with a number of pamphlets that attracted great attention, he entered Parliament in 1860 (having succeeded to the baronetcy) as member for Reading, and represented that constituency until his death. He was strenuous on behalf of the Jewish religion, and the founder of the great Jews' Free School. He was a munificent contributor to charities and especially to the endowment of University College. He, like his father, married a cousin, and, dying without issue, was succeeded in the baronetcy by his nephew Sir Julian Goldsmid, Bart. (1838-1896), son of Frederick David Goldsmid (1812-1866), long M.P. for Honiton. Sir Julian was for many years in Parliament, and his wealth, ability and influence made him a personage of considerable importance. He was eventually made a privy councillor. He had eight daughters, but no son, and his entailed property passed to his relation, Mr d'Avigdor, his house in Piccadilly being converted into the Isthmian Club.

Another distinguished member of the same family, Sir Frederic John Goldsmid (1818-1908), son of Lionel Prager Goldsmid (see above), was educated at King's College, London, and entering the Madras army in 1839 served in the China War of 1840-41, with the Turkish troops in eastern Crimea in 1855-56, and was given political employment by the Indian government. He received the thanks of the commander-in-chief and of the war office for services during the Egyptian campaign, and was retired a major-general in 1875. Sir Frederic Goldsmid's name is, however, associated less with military service than with much valuable work in exploration and in surveying, for which he repeatedly received the thanks of government. From 1865 to 1870 he was director-general of the Indo-European telegraph, and carried through the telegraph convention with Persia; and between 1870 and 1872, as commissioner, he settled with Persia the difficult questions of the Perso-Baluch and Perso-Afghan boundaries. In the course of his work he had to travel extensively, and he followed this up by various responsible missions connected with emigration questions. In 1881-1882 he was in Egypt, as controller of the Daira Sanieh, and doing other miscellaneous military work; and in 1883 he went to the Congo, on behalf of the king of the Belgians, as one of the organizers of the new state, but had to return on account of illness. From his early years he had made studies of several Eastern languages, and he ranked among the foremost Orientalists of his day. In 1886 he was president of the geographical section of the British Association meeting held at Birmingham. He had married in 1849, and had two sons and four daughters. In 1871 he was made a K.C.S.I. Besides important contributions to the 9th edition of the*Encyclopaedia Britannica* and many periodicals, he wrote an excellent and authoritative biography of Sir James Outram (2 vols., 1880).

A sister of the last-named married Henry Edward Goldsmid (1812-1855), an eminent Indian civil servant, son of Edward Goldsmid; his reform of the revenue system in Bombay, and introduction of a new system, established after his death, through his reports in 1840-1847, and his devoted labour in land-surveys, were of the highest importance to western India, and established his memory there as a public benefactor.

GOLDSMITH, LEWIS (*c.* 1763-1846), Anglo-French publicist, of Portuguese-Jewish extraction, was born near London about 1763. Having published in 1801 *The Crimes of Cabinets, or a Review of the Plans and Aggressions for Annihilating the Liberties of France, and the Dismemberment of her Territories*, an attack on the military policy of Pitt, he moved, in 1802, from England to Paris. Talleyrand introduced him to Napoleon, who arranged for him to establish in Paris an English tri-weekly, the *Argus*, which was to review English affairs from the French point of view. According to his own account, he was in 1803 entrusted with a mission to obtain from the head of the French royal family, afterwards Louis XVIII., a renunciation of his claims to the throne of France, in return for the throne of Poland. The offer was declined, and Goldsmith says that he then received instructions to kidnap Louis and kill him if he resisted, but, instead of executing these orders, he revealed the plot. He was, nevertheless, employed by Napoleon on various other secret service missions till 1807, when his Republican sympathies began to wane. In 1809 he returned to England, where he was at first imprisoned but soon released; and he became a notary in London. In 1811, being now violently anti-republican, he founded a Sunday newspaper, the *Anti-Gallican Monitor* and *Anti-Corsican Chronicle*, subsequently known as the *British Monitor*, in which he denounced the French Revolution. In 1811 he proposed that a public subscription should be raised to put a price on Napoleon's head, but this suggestion was strongly reprobated by the British government. In the same year he published *Secret History of the Cabinet of Bonaparte and Recueil des manifestes, or a Collection of the Decrees of Napoleon Bonaparte*, and in 1812 *Secret History of Bonaparte's Diplomacy*. Goldsmith alleged that in the latter year he was offered £200,000 by Napoleon to discontinue his attacks. In 1815 he published *An Appeal to the Governments of Europe on the Necessity of bringing Napoleon Bonaparte to a Public Trial*. In 1825 he again settled down in Paris, and in 1832 published his *Statistics of France*. His only child, Georgiana, became, in 1837, the second wife of Lord Lyndhurst. He died in Paris on the 6th of January 1846.

GOLDSMITH, OLIVER (1728-1774), English poet, playwright, novelist and man of letters, came of a Protestant and Saxon family which had long been settled in Ireland. He is usually said to have been born at Pallas or Pallasmore, Co. Longford; but recent investigators have contended, with much 215show of probability, that his true birthplace was Smith-Hill House, Elphin, Roscommon, the residence of his mother's father, the Rev. Oliver Jones. His father, Charles Goldsmith, lived at Pallas, supporting with difficulty his wife and children on what he could earn, partly as a curate and partly as a farmer.

While Oliver was still a child his father was presented to the living of Kilkenny West, in the county of West Meath. This was worth about £200 a year. The family accordingly quitted their cottage at Pallas for a spacious house on a frequented road, near the village of Lissoy. Here the boy was taught his letters by a relative and dependent, Elizabeth Delap, and was sent in his seventh year to a village school kept by an old quartermaster on half-pay, who professed to teach nothing but reading, writing and arithmetic, but who had an inexhaustible fund of stories about ghosts, banshees and fairies, about the great Rapparee chiefs, Baldearg O'Donnell and galloping Hogan, and about the exploits of Peterborough and Stanhope, the surprise of Monjuich and the glorious disaster of Brihuega. This man must have been of the Protestant religion; but he was of the aboriginal race, and not only spoke the Irish language, but could pour forth unpremeditated Irish verses. Oliver early became, and through life continued to be, a passionate admirer of the Irish music, and especially of the compositions of Carolan, some of the last notes of whose harp he heard. It ought to be added that Oliver, though by birth one of the Englishry, and though connected by numerous ties with the Established Church, never showed the least sign of that contemptuous antipathy with which, in his days, the ruling minority in Ireland too generally regarded the subject majority. So far indeed was he from sharing in the opinions and feelings of the caste to which he belonged that he conceived an aversion to the Glorious and Immortal Memory, and, even when George III. was on the throne, maintained that nothing but the restoration of the banished dynasty could save the country.

From the humble academy kept by the old soldier Goldsmith was removed in his ninth year. He went to several grammar-schools, and acquired some knowledge of the ancient languages. His life at this time seems to have been far from happy. He had, as appears from the admirable portrait of him by Reynolds at Knole, features harsh even to ugliness. The small-pox had set its mark on him with more than usual severity. His stature was small, and his limbs ill put together. Among boys little tenderness is shown to personal defects; and the ridicule excited by poor Oliver's appearance was heightened by a peculiar simplicity and a disposition to blunder which he retained to the last. He became the common butt of boys and masters, was pointed at as a fright in the play-ground, and flogged as a dunce in the schoolroom. When he had risen to eminence, those who had once derided him ransacked their memory for the events of his early years, and recited repartees and couplets which had dropped from him, and which, though little noticed at the time, were supposed, a quarter of a century later, to indicate the powers which produced the *Vicar of Wakefield* and the *Deserted Village*.

On the 11th of June 1744, being then in his sixteenth year, Oliver went up to Trinity College, Dublin, as a sizar. The sizars paid nothing for food and tuition, and very little for lodging; but they had to perform some menial services from which they have long been relieved.

Goldsmith was quartered, not alone, in a garret of what was then No. 35 in a range of buildings which has long since disappeared. His name, scrawled by himself on one of its window-panes is still preserved in the college library. From such garrets many men of less parts than his have made their way to the woolsack or to the episcopal bench. But Goldsmith, while he suffered all the humiliations, threw away all the advantages of his situation. He neglected the studies of the place, stood low at the examinations, was turned down to the bottom of his class for playing the buffoon in the lecture-room, was severely reprimanded for pumping on a constable, and was caned by a brutal tutor for giving a ball in the attic storey of the college to some gay youths and damsels from the city.

While Oliver was leading at Dublin a life divided between squalid distress and squalid dissipation, his father died, leaving a mere pittance. In February 1749 the youth obtained his bachelor's degree, and left the university. During some time the humble dwelling to which his widowed mother had retired was his home. He was now in his twenty-first year; it was necessary that he should do something; and his education seemed to have fitted him to do nothing but to dress himself in gaudy colours, of which he was as fond as a magpie, to take a hand at cards, to sing Irish airs, to play the flute, to angle in summer and to tell ghost stories by the fire in winter. He tried five or six professions in turn without success. He applied for ordination; but, as he applied in scarlet clothes, he was speedily turned out of the episcopal palace. He then became tutor in an opulent family, but soon quitted his situation in consequence of a dispute about pay. Then he determined to emigrate to America. His relations, with much satisfaction, saw him set out for Cork on a good horse, with £30 in his pocket. But in six weeks he came back on a miserable hack, without a penny, and informed his mother that the ship in which he had taken his passage, having got a fair wind while he was at a party of pleasure, had sailed without him. Then he resolved to study the law. A generous uncle, Mr Contarine, advanced £50. With this sum Goldsmith went to Dublin, was enticed into a gaming-house and lost every shilling. He then thought of medicine. A small purse was made up; and in his twenty-fourth year he was sent to Edinburgh. At Edinburgh he passed eighteen months in nominal attendance on lectures, and picked up some superficial information about chemistry and natural history. Thence he went to Leiden, still pretending to study physic. He left that celebrated university, the third university at which he had resided, in his twenty-seventh year, without a degree, with the merest smattering of medical knowledge, and with no property but his clothes and his flute. His flute, however, proved a useful friend. He rambled on foot through Flanders, France and Switzerland, playing tunes which everywhere set the peasantry dancing, and which often procured for him a supper and a bed. He wandered as far as Italy. His musical performances, indeed, were not to the taste of the Italians; but he contrived to live on the alms which he obtained at the gates of convents. It should, however, be observed that the stories which he told about this part of his life ought to be received with great caution; for strict veracity was never one of his virtues; and a man who is ordinarily inaccurate in narration is likely to be more than ordinarily inaccurate when he talks about his own travels. Goldsmith, indeed, was so regardless of truth as to assert in print that he was present at a most interesting conversation between Voltaire and Fontenelle, and that this conversation took place at Paris. Now it is certain that Voltaire never was within a hundred leagues of Paris during the whole time which Goldsmith passed on the continent.

In February 1756 the wanderer landed at Dover, without a shilling, without a friend and without a calling. He had indeed, if his own unsupported evidence may be trusted, obtained a doctor's degree on the continent; but this dignity proved utterly useless to him. In England his flute was not in request; there were no convents; and he was forced to have recourse to a series of desperate expedients. There is a tradition that he turned strolling player. He pounded drugs and ran about London with phials for charitable chemists. He asserted, upon one occasion, that he had lived "among the beggars in Axe Lane." He was for a time usher of a school, and felt the miseries and humiliations of this situation so keenly that he thought it a promotion to be permitted to earn his bread as a bookseller's hack; but he soon found the new yoke more galling than the old one, and was glad to become an usher again. He obtained a medical appointment in the service of the East India Company; but the appointment was speedily revoked. Why it was revoked we are not told. The subject was one on which he never liked to talk. It is probable that he was incompetent to perform the duties of the place. Then he presented himself at Surgeons' Hall for examination, as "mate to an hospital." Even to so humble a post he was found unequal. Nothing remained but to return to the lowest drudgery of literature. Goldsmith took a room in a tiny square off Ludgate Hill, to which he had to climb 216from Sea-coal Lane by a dizzy ladder of flagstones called Breakneck Steps. Green Arbour Court and the ascent have long disappeared. Here, at thirty, the unlucky adventurer sat down to toil like a galley slave. Already, in 1758, during his first bondage to letters, he had translated Marteilhe's remarkable *Memoirs of a Protestant, Condemned to the Galleys of France for his Religion*. In the years that now succeeded he sent to the press some things which have survived, and many which have perished. He produced articles for reviews, magazines and newspapers; children's books, which, bound in gilt paper and adorned with hideous woodcuts, appeared in the window of Newbery's once far-famed shop at the corner of Saint Paul's churchyard; *An Inquiry into the State of Polite Learning in Europe*, which, though of little or no value, is still reprinted among his works; a volume of essays entitled *The Bee; a Life of Beau Nash*; a superficial and incorrect, but very readable, *History of England*, in a series of letters purporting to be addressed by a nobleman to his son; and some very lively and amusing sketches of London Society in another series of letters purporting to be addressed by a Chinese traveller to his friends. All these works were anonymous; but some of them were well known to be Goldsmith's; and he gradually rose in the estimation of the booksellers for whom he drudged. He was, indeed, emphatically a popular writer. For accurate research or grave disquisition he was not well qualified by nature or by education. He knew nothing accurately; his reading had been desultory; nor had he meditated deeply on what he had read. He had seen much of the world; but he had noticed and retained little more of what he had seen than some grotesque incidents and characters which had happened to strike his fancy. But, though his mind was very scantily stored with materials, he used what materials he had in such a way as to produce a wonderful effect. There have been many greater writers; but perhaps no writer was ever more uniformly agreeable. His style was always pure and easy, and, on proper occasions, pointed and energetic. His narratives were always amusing, his descriptions always picturesque, his humour rich and joyous, yet not without an occasional tinge of amiable sadness. About everything that he wrote, serious or sportive, there was a certain natural grace and decorum, hardly to be expected from a man a great part of whose life had been passed among thieves and beggars, street-walkers and merryandrews, in those squalid dens which are the reproach of great capitals.

As his name gradually became known, the circle of his acquaintance widened. He was introduced to Johnson, who was then considered as the first of living English writers; to Reynolds, the first of English painters; and to Burke, who had not yet entered parliament, but had distinguished himself greatly by his writings and by the eloquence of his conversation. With these eminent men Goldsmith became intimate. In 1763 he was one of the nine original members of that celebrated fraternity which has sometimes been called the Literary Club, but which has always disclaimed that epithet, and still glories in the simple name of the Club.

By this date Goldsmith had quitted his miserable dwelling at the top of Breakneck Steps, and, after living for some time at No. 6 Wine Office Court, Fleet Street, had moved into the Temple. But he was still often reduced to pitiable shifts, the most popular of which is connected with the sale of his solitary novel, the *Vicar of Wakefield*. Towards the close of 1764(?) his rent is alleged to have been so long in arrear that his landlady one morning called in the help of a sheriff's officer. The debtor, in great perplexity, despatched a messenger to Johnson; and Johnson, always friendly, though often surly, sent back the messenger with a guinea, and promised to follow speedily. He came, and found that Goldsmith had changed the guinea, and was railing at the landlady over a bottle of Madeira. Johnson put the cork into the bottle, and entreated his friend to consider calmly how money was to be procured. Goldsmith said that he had a novel ready for the press. Johnson glanced at the manuscript, saw that there were good things in it, took it to a bookseller, sold it for £60 and soon returned with the money. The rent was paid; and the sheriff's officer withdrew. (Unfortunately, however, for this time-honoured version of the circumstances, it has of late years been discovered that as early as October 1762 Goldsmith had already sold a third of the *Vicar* to one Benjamin Collins of Salisbury, a printer, by whom it was eventually printed for F. Newbery, and it is difficult to reconcile this fact with Johnson's narrative.)

But before the *Vicar of Wakefield* appeared in 1766, came the great crisis of Goldsmith's literary life. In Christmas week 1764 he published a poem, entitled the *Traveller*. It was the first work to which he had put his name, and it at once raised him to the rank of a legitimate English classic. The opinion of the most skilful critics was that nothing finer had appeared in verse since the fourth book of the *Dunciad*. In one respect the *Traveller* differs from all Goldsmith's other writings. In general his designs were bad, and his execution good. In the *Traveller* the execution, though deserving of much praise, is far inferior to the design. No philosophical poem, ancient or modern, has a plan so noble, and at the same time so simple. An English wanderer, seated on a crag among the Alps, near the point where three great countries meet, looks down on the boundless prospect, reviews his long pilgrimage, recalls the varieties of scenery, of climate, of government, of religion, of national character, which he has observed, and comes to the conclusion, just or unjust, that our happiness depends little on political institutions, and much on the temper and regulation of our own minds.

While the fourth edition of the *Traveller* was on the counters of the booksellers, the *Vicar of Wakefield* appeared, and rapidly obtained a popularity which has lasted down to our own time, and which is likely to last as long as our language. The fable is indeed one of the worst that ever was constructed. It wants, not merely that probability which ought to be found in a tale of common English life, but that consistency which ought to be found even in the wildest fiction about witches, giants and fairies. But the earlier chapters have all the sweetness of pastoral poetry, together with all the vivacity of comedy. Moses and his spectacles, the vicar and his monogamy, the sharper and his cosmogony, the squire proving from Aristotle that relatives are related, Olivia preparing herself for the arduous task of converting a rakish lover by studying the controversy between Robinson Crusoe and Friday, the great ladies with their scandal about Sir Tomkyn's amours and Dr Burdock's verses, and Mr Burchell with his "Fudge," have caused as much harmless mirth as has ever been caused by matter packed into so small a number of pages. The latter part of the tale is unworthy of the beginning. As we approach the catastrophe, the absurdities lie thicker and thicker, and the gleams of pleasantry become rarer and rarer.

The success which had attended Goldsmith as a novelist emboldened him to try his fortune as a dramatist. He wrote the *Good Natur'd Man*, a piece which had a worse fate than it deserved. Garrick refused to produce it at Drury Lane. It was acted at Covent Garden in January 1768, but was coldly received. The author, however, cleared by his benefit nights, and by the sale of the copyright, no less than £500, five times as much as he had made by the *Traveller* and the *Vicar of Wakefield* together. The plot of the *Good Natur'd Man* is, like almost all Goldsmith's plots, very ill constructed. But some passages are exquisitely ludicrous,—much more ludicrous indeed than suited the taste of the town at that time. A canting, mawkish play, entitled *False Delicacy*, had just been produced, and sentimentality was all the mode. During some years more tears were shed at comedies than at tragedies; and a pleasantry which moved the audience to anything more than a grave smile was reprobated as low. It is not strange, therefore, that the very best scene in the *Good Natur'd Man*, that in which Miss Richland finds her lover attended by the bailiff and the bailiff's follower in full court dresses, should have been mercilessly hissed, and should have been omitted after the first night, not to be restored for several years.

In May 1770 appeared the *Deserted Village*. In mere diction and versification this celebrated poem is fully equal, perhaps superior, to the *Traveller*; and it is generally preferred to the *Traveller* by that large class of readers who think, with Bayes in the *Rehearsal*, that the only use of a plot is to bring in fine things. More discerning judges, however, while they admire the beauty of the details, are shocked by one unpardonable fault which pervades the whole. The fault which we mean is not that theory about wealth and luxury which has so often been censured by political economists. The theory is indeed false; but the poem, considered merely as a poem, is not necessarily the worse on that account. The finest poem in the Latin language—indeed, the finest didactic poem in any language—was written in defence of the silliest and meanest of all systems of natural and moral philosophy. A poet may easily be pardoned for reasoning ill; but he cannot be pardoned for describing ill, for observing the world in which he lives so carelessly that his portraits bear no resemblance to the originals, for exhibiting as copies from real life monstrous combinations of things which never were and never could be found together. What would be thought of a painter who should mix August and January in one landscape, who should introduce a frozen river into a harvest scene? Would it be a sufficient defence of such a picture to say that every part was exquisitely coloured, that the green hedges, the apple-trees loaded with fruit, the waggons reeling under the yellow sheaves, and the sun-burned reapers wiping their foreheads were very fine, and that the ice and the boys sliding were also very fine? To such a picture the *Deserted Village* bears a great resemblance. It is made up of incongruous parts. The village in its happy days is a true English village. The village in its decay is an Irish village. The felicity and the misery which Goldsmith has brought close together belong to two different countries and to two different stages in the progress of society. He had assuredly never seen in his native island such a rural paradise, such a seat of plenty, content and tranquillity, as his Auburn. He had assuredly never seen in England all the inhabitants of such a paradise turned out of their homes in one day and forced to emigrate in a body to America. The hamlet he had probably seen in Kent; the ejectment he had probably seen in Münster; but by joining the two, he has produced something which never was and never will be seen in any part of the world.

In 1773 Goldsmith tried his chance at Covent Garden with a second play, *She Stoops to Conquer*. The manager was, not without great difficulty, induced to bring this piece out. The sentimental comedy still reigned, and Goldsmith's comedies were not sentimental. The *Good Natur'd Man* had been too funny to succeed; yet the mirth of the *Good Natur'd Man* was sober when compared with the rich drollery of *She Stoops to Conquer*, which is, in truth, an incomparable farce in five acts. On this occasion, however, genius triumphed. Pit, boxes and galleries were in a constant roar of laughter. If any bigoted admirer of Kelly and Cumberland ventured to hiss or groan, he was speedily silenced by a general cry of "turn him out," or "throw him over." Later generations have confirmed the verdict which was pronounced on that night.

While Goldsmith was writing the *Deserted Village* and *She Stoops to Conquer*, he was employed on works of a very different kind—works from which he derived little reputation but much profit. He compiled for the use of schools a *History of Rome*, by which he made £250; a *History of England*, by which he made £500; a *History of Greece*, for which he received £250; a *Natural History*, for which the booksellers covenanted to pay him 800 guineas. These works he produced without any elaborate research, by merely selecting, abridging and translating into his own clear, pure and flowing language, what he found in books well known to the world, but too bulky or too dry for boys and girls. He committed some strange blunders, for he knew nothing with accuracy. Thus, in his *History of England*, he tells us that Naseby is in Yorkshire; nor did he correct this mistake when the book was reprinted. He was very nearly hoaxed into putting into the *History of Greece* an account of a battle between Alexander the Great and Montezuma. In his *Animated Nature* he relates, with faith and with perfect gravity, all the most absurd lies which he could find in books of travels about gigantic Patagonians, monkeys that preach sermons, nightingales that repeat long conversations. "If he can tell a horse from a cow," said Johnson, "that is the extent of his knowledge of zoology." How little Goldsmith was qualified to write about the physical sciences is sufficiently proved by two anecdotes. He on one occasion denied that the sun is longer in the northern than in the southern signs. It was vain to cite the authority of Maupertuis. "Maupertuis!" he cried, "I understand those matters better than Maupertuis." On another occasion he, in defiance of the evidence of his own senses, maintained obstinately, and even angrily, that he chewed his dinner by moving his upper jaw.

Yet, ignorant as Goldsmith was, few writers have done more to make the first steps in the laborious road to knowledge easy and pleasant. His compilations are widely distinguished from the compilations of ordinary bookmakers. He was a great, perhaps an unequalled, master of the arts of selection and condensation. In these respects his histories of Rome and of England, and still more his own abridgments of these histories, well deserved to be studied. In general nothing is less attractive than an epitome; but the epitomes of Goldsmith, even when most concise, are always amusing; and to read them is considered by intelligent children not as a task but as a pleasure.

Goldsmith might now be considered as a prosperous man. He had the means of living in comfort, and even in what to one who had so often slept in barns and on bulks must have been luxury. His fame was great and was constantly rising. He lived in what was intellectually far the best society of the kingdom, in a society in which no talent or accomplishment was wanting, and in which the art of conversation was cultivated with splendid success. There probably were never four talkers more admirable in four different ways than Johnson, Burke, Beauclerk and Garrick; and Goldsmith was on terms of intimacy with all the four. He aspired to share in their colloquial renown, but never was ambition more unfortunate. It may seem strange that a man who wrote with so much perspicuity, vivacity and grace should have been, whenever he took a part in conversation, an empty, noisy, blundering rattle. But on this point the evidence is overwhelming. So extraordinary was the contrast between Goldsmith's published works and the silly things which he said, that Horace Walpole described him as an inspired idiot. "Noll," said Garrick, "wrote like an angel, and talked like poor Poll." Charnier declared that it was a hard exercise of faith to believe that so foolish a chatterer could have really written the *Traveller*. Even Boswell could say, with contemptuous compassion, that he liked very well to hear honest Goldsmith run on. "Yes, sir," said Johnson, "but he should not like to hear himself." Minds differ as rivers differ. There are transparent and sparkling rivers from which it is delightful to drink as they flow; to such rivers the minds of such men as Burke and Johnson may be compared. But there are rivers of which the water when first drawn is turbid and noisome, but becomes pellucid as crystal and delicious to the taste, if it be suffered to stand till it has deposited a sediment; and such a river is a type of the mind of Goldsmith. His first thoughts on every subject were confused even to absurdity, but they required only a little time to work themselves clear. When he wrote they had that time, and therefore his readers pronounced him a man of genius; but when he talked he talked nonsense and made himself the laughing-stock of his hearers. He was painfully sensible of his inferiority in conversation; he felt every failure keenly; yet he had not sufficient judgment and self-command to hold his tongue. His animal spirits and vanity were always impelling him to try to do the one thing which he could not do. After every attempt he felt that he had exposed himself, and writhed with shame and vexation; yet the next moment he began again.

His associates seem to have regarded him with kindness, which, in spite of their admiration of his writings, was not unmixed with contempt. In truth, there was in his character much to love, but very little to respect. His heart was soft even to weakness; 218he was so generous that he quite forgot to be just; he forgave injuries so readily that he might be said to invite them, and was so liberal to beggars that he had nothing left for his tailor and his butcher. He was vain, sensual, frivolous, profuse, improvident. One vice of a darker shade was imputed to

159

him, envy. But there is not the least reason to believe that this bad passion, though it sometimes made him wince and utter fretful exclamations, ever impelled him to injure by wicked arts the reputation of any of his rivals. The truth probably is that he was not more envious, but merely less prudent, than his neighbours. His heart was on his lips. All those small jealousies, which are but too common among men of letters, but which a man of letters who is also a man of the world does his best to conceal, Goldsmith avowed with the simplicity of a child. When he was envious, instead of affecting indifference, instead of damning with faint praise, instead of doing injuries slyly and in the dark, he told everybody that he was envious. "Do not, pray, do not, talk of Johnson in such terms," he said to Boswell; "you harrow up my very soul." George Steevens and Cumberland were men far too cunning to say such a thing. They would have echoed the praises of the man whom they envied, and then have sent to the newspapers anonymous libels upon him. Both what was good and what was bad in Goldsmith's character was to his associates a perfect security that he would never commit such villainy. He was neither ill-natured enough, nor long-headed enough, to be guilty of any malicious act which required contrivance and disguise.

Goldsmith has sometimes been represented as a man of genius, cruelly treated by the world, and doomed to struggle with difficulties, which at last broke his heart. But no representation can be more remote from the truth. He did, indeed, go through much sharp misery before he had done anything considerable in literature. But after his name had appeared on the title-page of the *Traveller*, he had none but himself to blame for his distresses. His average income, during the last seven years of his life, certainly exceeded £400 a year, and £400 a year ranked, among the incomes of that day, at least as high as £800 a year would rank at present. A single man living in the Temple, with £400 a year, might then be called opulent. Not one in ten of the young gentlemen of good families who were studying the law there had so much. But all the wealth which Lord Clive had brought from Bengal and Sir Lawrence Dundas from Germany, joined together, would not have sufficed for Goldsmith. He spent twice as much as he had. He wore fine clothes, gave dinners of several courses, paid court to venal beauties. He had also, it should be remembered, to the honour of his heart, though not of his head, a guinea, or five, or ten, according to the state of his purse, ready for any tale of distress, true or false. But it was not in dress or feasting, in promiscuous amours or promiscuous charities, that his chief expense lay. He had been from boyhood a gambler, and at once the most sanguine and the most unskilful of gamblers. For a time he put off the day of inevitable ruin by temporary expedients. He obtained advances from booksellers by promising to execute works which he never began. But at length this source of supply failed. He owed more than £2000; and he saw no hope of extrication from his embarrassments. His spirits and health gave way. He was attacked by a nervous fever, which he thought himself competent to treat. It would have been happy for him if his medical skill had been appreciated as justly by himself as by others. Notwithstanding the degree which he pretended to have received on the continent, he could procure no patients. "I do not practise," he once said; "I make it a rule to prescribe only for my friends." "Pray, dear Doctor," said Beauclerk, "alter your rule; and prescribe only for your enemies." Goldsmith, now, in spite of this excellent advice, prescribed for himself. The remedy aggravated the malady. The sick man was induced to call in real physicians; and they at one time imagined that they had cured the disease. Still his weakness and restlessness continued. He could get no sleep. He could take no food. "You are worse," said one of his medical attendants, "than you should be from the degree of fever which you have. Is your mind at ease?" "No; it is not," were the last recorded words of Oliver Goldsmith. He died on the 4th of April 1774, in his forty-sixth year. He was laid in the churchyard of the Temple; but the spot was not marked by any inscription and is now forgotten. The coffin was followed by Burke and Reynolds. Both these great men were sincere mourners. Burke, when he heard of Goldsmith's death, had burst into a flood of tears. Reynolds had been so much moved by the news that he had flung aside his brush and palette for the day.

A short time after Goldsmith's death, a little poem appeared, which will, as long as our language lasts, associate the names of his two illustrious friends with his own. It has already been mentioned that he sometimes felt keenly the sarcasm which his wild blundering talk brought upon him. He was, not long before his last illness, provoked into retaliating. He wisely betook himself to his pen; and at that weapon he proved himself a match for all his assailants together. Within a small compass he drew with a singularly easy and vigorous pencil the characters of nine or ten of his intimate associates. Though this little work did not receive his last touches, it must always be regarded as a masterpiece. It is impossible, however, not to wish that four or five likenesses which have no interest for posterity were wanting to that noble gallery, and that their places were supplied by sketches of Johnson and Gibbon, as happy and vivid as the sketches of Burke and Garrick.

160

Some of Goldsmith's friends and admirers honoured him with a cenotaph in Westminster Abbey. Nollekens was the sculptor, and Johnson wrote the inscription. It is much to be lamented that Johnson did not leave to posterity a more durable and a more valuable memorial of his friend. A life of Goldsmith would have been an inestimable addition to the Lives of the Poets. No man appreciated Goldsmith's writings more justly than Johnson; no man was better acquainted with Goldsmith's character and habits; and no man was more competent to delineate with truth and spirit the peculiarities of a mind in which great powers were found in company with great weaknesses. But the list of poets to whose works Johnson was requested by the booksellers to furnish prefaces ended with Lyttelton, who died in 1773. The line seems to have been drawn expressly for the purpose of excluding the person whose portrait would have most fitly closed the series. Goldsmith, however, has been fortunate in his biographers.

(M.)

Goldsmith's life has been written by Prior (1837), by Washington Irving (1844-1849), and by John Forster (1848, 2nd ed. 1854). The diligence of Prior deserves great praise; the style of Washington Irving is always pleasing; but the highest place must, in justice, be assigned to the eminently interesting work of Forster. Subsequent biographies are by William Black (1878), and Austin Dobson (1888, American ed. 1899). The above article by Lord Macaulay has been slightly revised for this edition by Mr Austin Dobson, as regards questions of fact for which there has been new evidence.

GOLDSTÜCKER, THEODOR (1821-1872), German Sanskrit scholar, was born of Jewish parents at Königsberg on the 18th of January 1821, and, after attending the gymnasium of that town, entered the university in 1836 as a student of Sanskrit. In 1838 he removed to Bonn, and, after graduating at Königsberg in 1840, proceeded to Paris; in 1842 he edited a German translation of the *Prabodha Chandrodaya*. From 1847 to 1850 he resided at Berlin, where his talents and scholarship were recognized by Alexander von Humboldt, but where his advanced political views caused the authorities to regard him with suspicion. In the latter year he removed to London, where in 1852 he was appointed professor of Sanskrit in University College. He now worked on a new Sanskrit dictionary, of which the first instalment appeared in 1856. In 1861 he published his chief work: *Pānini: his place in Sanskrit Literature*; and he was one of the founders and chief promoters of the Sanskrit Text Society; he was also an active member of the Philological Society, and of other learned bodies. He died in London on the 6th of March 1872.

As *Literary Remains* some of his writings were published in two volumes (London, 1879), but his papers were left to the India Office with the request that they were not to be published until 1920.

219

GOLDWELL, THOMAS (d. 1585), English ecclesiastic, began his career as vicar of Cheriton in 1531, after graduating M.A. at All Souls College, Oxford. He became chaplain to Cardinal Pole and lived with him at Rome, was attainted in 1539, but returned to England on Mary's accession, and in 1555 became bishop of St Asaph, a diocese which he did much to win back to the old faith. On the death of Mary, Goldwell escaped from England and in 1561 became superior of the Theatines at Naples. He was the only English bishop at the council of Trent, and in 1562 was again attainted. In the following year he was appointed vicar-general to Carlo Borromeo, archbishop of Milan. He died in Rome in 1585, the last of the English bishops who had refused to accept the Reformation.

GOLDZIHER, IGNAZ (1850-   ), Jewish Hungarian orientalist, was born in Stuhlweissenburg on the 22nd of June 1850. He was educated at the universities of Budapest, Berlin, Leipzig and Leiden, and became privat docent at Budapest in 1872. In the next year, under the auspices of the Hungarian government, he began a journey through Syria, Palestine and Egypt, and took the opportunity of attending lectures of Mahommedan sheiks in the mosque of el-Azhar in Cairo. He was the first Jewish scholar to become professor in the Budapest University (1894), and represented the Hungarian government and the Academy of Sciences at numerous international congresses. He received the large gold medal at the Stockholm Oriental Congress in 1889. He became a member of several Hungarian and other learned societies, was appointed secretary of the Jewish community in Budapest. He was made Litt. D. of Cambridge (1904) and LL.D. of Aberdeen (1906). His eminence in the sphere of scholarship is due primarily to his careful investigation of pre-Mahommedan and Mahommedan law, tradition, religion and poetry, in connexion with which he published a large number of treatises, review articles and essays contributed to the collections of the Hungarian Academy.

Among his chief works are: *Beiträge zur Literaturgeschichte der Schi'a* (1874); *Beiträge zur Geschichte der Sprachgelehrsamkeit bei den Arabern* (Vienna, 1871-1873); *Der Mythos bei den Hebräern und seine geschichtliche Entwickelung* (Leipzig, 1876; Eng. trans., R. Martineau, London, 1877); *Muhammedanische Studien* (Halle, 1889-1890, 2 vols.); *Abhandlungen zur arabischen Philologie* (Leiden, 1896-1899, 2 vols.);*Buch v. Wesen d. Seele* (ed. 1907).

GOLETTA [LA GOULETTE], a town on the Gulf of Tunis in 36° 50′ N. 10° 19′ E., a little south of the ruins of Carthage, and on the north side of the ship canal which traverses the shallow Lake of Tunis and leads to the city of that name. Built on the narrow strip of sand which separates the lake from the gulf, Goletta is defended by a fort and battery. The town contains a summer palace of the bey, the old seraglio, arsenal and customhouse, and many villas, gardens and pleasure resorts, Goletta being a favourite place for sea-bathing. A short canal, from which the name of the town is derived (Arab. *Halk-el-Wad*, "throat of the canal"), 40 ft. broad and 8½ ft. deep, divides the town and affords communication between the ship canal and a dock or basin, 1082 ft. long and 541 ft. broad. An electric tramway which runs along the north bank of the ship canal connects Goletta with the city of Tunis (*q.v.*). Pop. (1907) about 5000, mostly Jews and Italian fishermen.

Beyond Cape Carthage, 5 m. N. of Goletta, is La Marsa, a summer resort overlooking the sea. The bey has a palace here, and the French resident-general, the British consul, other officials, and many Tunisians have country-houses, surrounded by groves of olive trees.

Before the opening of the ship canal in 1893 Goletta, as the port of Tunis, was a place of considerable importance. The basin at the Goletta end of the canal now serves as a subsidiary harbour to that of Tunis. The most stirring events in the history of the town are connected with the Turkish conquest of the Barbary states. Khair-ed-Din Barbarossa having made himself master of Tunis and its port, Goletta was attacked in 1535 by the emperor Charles V., who seized the pirate's fleet, which was sheltered in the small canal, his arsenal, and 300 brass cannon. The Turks regained possession in 1574. (SeeTUNISIA: *History.*)

GOLF (in its older forms GOFF, GOUFF or GOWFF, the last of which gives the genuine old pronunciation), a game which probably derives its name from the Ger. *kolbe*, a club—in Dutch, *kolf*—which last is nearly in sound identical and might suggest a Dutch origin,1 which many pictures and other witnesses further support.

History.—One of the most ancient and most interesting of the pictures in which the game is portrayed is the tailpiece to an illuminated *Book of Hours*made at Bruges at the beginning of the 16th century. The original is in the British Museum. The players, three in number, have but one club apiece. The heads of the clubs are steel or steel covered. They play with a ball each. That which gives this picture a peculiar interest over the many pictures of Dutch schools that portray the game in progress is that most of them show it on the ice, the putting being at a stake. In this *Book of Hours* they are putting at a hole in the turf, as in our modern golf. It is scarcely to be doubted that the game is of Dutch origin, and that it has been in favour since very early days. Further than that our knowledge does not go. The early Dutchmen played golf, they painted golf, but they did not write it.

It is uncertain at what date golf was introduced into Scotland, but in 1457 the popularity of the game had already become so great as seriously to interfere with the more important pursuit of archery. In March of that year the Scottish parliament "decreted and ordained that *wapinshawingis* be halden be the lordis and baronis spirituale and temporale, four times in the zeir; and that the fute-ball and *golf be utterly cryit down, and nocht usit*; and that the bowe-merkis be maid at ilk paroche kirk a pair of buttis, and *schuttin be usit ilk Sunday.*" Fourteen years afterwards, in May 1471, it was judged necessary to pass another act "anent wapenshawings," and in 1491 a final and evidently angry fulmination was issued on the general subject, with pains and penalties annexed. It runs thus—"Futeball and Golfe forbidden. Item, it is statut and ordainit that in na place of the realme there be usit fute-ball, *golfe, or uther sik unprofitabill sportis,*" &c. This, be it noted, is an edict of James IV.; and it is not a little curious presently to find the monarch himself setting an ill example to his commons, by practice of this "unprofitabill sport," as is shown by various entries in the accounts of the lord high treasurer of Scotland (1503-1506).

About a century later, the game again appears on the surface of history, and it is quite as popular as before. In the year 1592 the town council of Edinburgh "ordanis proclamation to be made threw this burgh, that na inhabitants of the samyn be seen at ony pastymes within or without the toun, upoun the Sabboth day, sic as golfe, &c."2 The following year the edict was re-announced, but with the modification that the prohibition was "in tyme of sermons."

Golf has from old times been known in Scotland as "The *Royal and Ancient* Game of Goff." Though no doubt Scottish monarchs handled the club before him, James IV. is the first who figures formally in the golfing record. James V. was also very partial to the game distinctively known as "royal"; and there is some scrap of evidence to show that his daughter, the unhappy Mary Stuart, was a golfer. It was alleged by her enemies that, as showing her shameless indifference to the fate of her husband, a very few days after his murder, she "was seen playing *golf* and pallmall in the fields beside Seton."[3]That her son, James VI. (afterwards James I. of England), was a golfer, tradition confidently asserts, though the evidence which connects him with the personal practice of the game is slight. Of the interest he took in it we have evidence in his act—already alluded to—"anent *golfe ballis*," prohibiting their importation, except under certain 220restrictions. Charles I. (as his brother Prince Henry had been[4]) was devotedly attached to the game. Whilst engaged in it on the links of Leith, in 1642, the news reached him of the Irish rebellion of that year. He had not the equanimity to finish his match, but returned precipitately and in much agitation to Holyrood.[5] Afterwards, while prisoner to the Scots army at Newcastle, he found his favourite diversion in "the royal game." "The King was nowhere treated with more honour than at Newcastle, as he himself confessed, both he and his train having liberty to go abroad and play at goff in the Shield Field, without the walls."[6] Of his son, Charles II., as a golfer, nothing whatever is ascertained, but James II. was a known devotee.[7] After the Restoration, James, then duke of York, was sent to Edinburgh in 1681/2 as commissioner of the king to parliament, and an historical monument of his prowess as a golfer remains there to this day in the "Golfer's Land," as it is still called, 77 Canongate. The duke having been challenged by two English noblemen of his suite, to play a match against them, for a very large stake, along with any Scotch ally he might select, chose as his partner one "Johne Patersone," a shoemaker. The duke and the said Johne won easily, and half of the large stake the duke made over to his humble coadjutor, who therewith built himself the house mentioned above. In 1834 William IV. became patron of the St Andrews Golf Club (St Andrews being then, as now, the most famous seat of the game), and approved of its being styled "The *Royal and Ancient* Golf Club of St Andrews." In 1837, as further proof of royal favour, he presented to it a magnificent gold medal, which "should be challenged and played for annually"; and in 1838 the queen dowager, duchess of St Andrews, became patroness of the club, and presented to it a handsome gold medal—"The Royal Adelaide"—with a request that it should be worn by the captain, as president, on all public occasions. In June 1863 the prince of Wales (afterwards Edward VII.) signified his desire to become patron of the club, and in the following September was elected captain by acclamation. His engagements did not admit of his coming in person to undertake the duties of the office, but his brother Prince Leopold (the duke of Albany), having in 1876 done the club the honour to become its captain, twice visited the ancient city in that capacity.

In more recent days, golf has become increasingly popular in a much wider degree. In 1880 the man who travelled about England with a set of golf clubs was an object of some astonishment, almost of alarm, to his fellow-travellers. In those days the commonest of questions in regard to the game was, "You have to be a fine rider, do you not, to play golf?" so confounded was it in the popular mind with the game of polo. At Blackheath a few Scotsmen resident in London had long played golf. In 1864 the Royal North Devon Club was formed at Westward Ho, and this was the first of the seaside links discovered and laid out for golf in England. In 1869 the Royal Liverpool Club established itself in possession of the second English course of this quality at Hoylake, in Cheshire. A golf club was formed in connexion with the London Scottish Volunteers corps, which had its house on the Putney end of Wimbledon Common on Putney Heath; and, after making so much of a start, the progress of the game was slow, though steady, for many years. A few more clubs were formed; the numbers of golfers grew; but it could not be said that the game was yet in any sense popular in England. All at once, for no very obvious reason, the qualities of the ancient Scottish game seemed to strike home, and from that moment its popularity has been wonderfully and increasingly great. The English links that rose into most immediate favour was the fine course of the St George's Golf Club, near Sandwich, on the coast of Kent. To the London golfer it was the first course of the first class that was reasonably accessible, and the fact made something like an epoch in English golf. A very considerable increase, it is true, in the number of English golfers and English golf clubs had taken place before the discovery for golfing purposes of the links at Sandwich. Already there was a chain of links all round the coast, besides numerous inland courses; but since 1890 their increase has been extraordinary, and the number which has been formed in the colonies and abroad is very large also, so that in the *Golfer's Year Book* for 1906 a space of over 300 pages was allotted to the Club Directory alone, each page containing, on a rough average, six clubs. To compute the average membership of these clubs is very difficult. There is not a little overlapping, in the sense that a member of one club will often be a member of several others; but probably the average may be placed at something like 200 members for each club.

The immense amount of golf-playing that this denotes, the large industry in the making of clubs and balls, in the upkeep of links, in the actual work of club-carrying by the caddies, and in the instruction given by the professional class, is obvious. Golf has taken a strong hold on the affections of the people in many parts of Ireland, and the fashion for golf in England has reacted strongly on Scotland itself, the ancient home of the game, where since 1880 golfers have probably increased in the ratio of forty to one. Besides the industry that such a growth of the game denotes in the branches immediately connected with it, as mentioned above, there is to be taken into further account the visiting population that it brings to all lodging-houses and hotels within reach of a tolerable golf links, so that many a fishing village has risen into a moderate watering-place by virtue of no other attractions than those which are offered by its golf course. Therefore to the Briton, golf has developed from something of which he had a vague idea—as of "curling"—to something in the nature of an important business, a business that can make towns and has a considerable effect on the receipts of railway companies.

Moreover, ladies have learned to play golf. Although this is a crude and brief sentence, it does not state the fact too widely nor too forcibly, for though it is true that before 1885 many played on the short links of St Andrews, North Berwick, Westward Ho and elsewhere, still it was virtually unknown that they should play on the longer courses, which till then had been in the undisputed possession of the men. At many places women now have their separate links, at others they play on the same course as the men. But even where links are set apart for women, they are far different from the little courses that used to be assigned to them. They are links only a little less formidable in their bunkers, a little less varied in their features than those of men. The ladies have their annual championship, which they play on the long links of the men, sometimes on one, sometimes on another, but always on courses of the first quality, demanding the finest display of golfing skill.

The claim that England made to a golfing fellowship with Scotland was conceded very strikingly by the admission of three English greens, first those of Hoylake and of Sandwich, and in 1909 Deal, into the exclusive list of the links on which the open championship of the game is decided. Before England had so fully assimilated Scotland's game this great annual contest was waged at St Andrews, Musselburgh and Prestwick in successive years. Now the ancient green of Musselburgh, somewhat worn out with length of hard and gallant service, and moreover, as a nine-holes course inadequately accommodating the numbers who compete in the championships to-day, has been superseded by the course at Muirfield as a championship arena.

While golf had been making itself a force in the southern kingdom, the professional element—men who had learned the game from childhood, had become past-masters, were capable of giving instruction, and also of making clubs and balls and looking after the greens on which golf was played—had at first been taken from the northern side of the Border. But when golf had been started long enough in England for the little boys who were at first employed as "caddies"—in carrying the players' clubs—to grow to sufficient strength to drive the ball as far as their masters, it was inevitable that out of the number who thus began to play in their boyhood some few should develop an exceptional talent for the game. This, in fact, actually happened, and English golfers, both of the amateur 221and the professional classes, have proved themselves so adept at Scotland's game, that the championships in either the Open or the Amateur competitions have been won more often by English than by Scottish players of late years. Probably in the United Kingdom to-day there are as many English as Scottish professional golf players, and their relative number is increasing.

Golf also "caught on," to use the American expression, in the United States. To the American of 1890 golf was largely an unknown thing. Since then, however, golf has become perhaps a greater factor in the life of the upper and upper-middle classes in the United States than it ever has been in England or Scotland. Golf to the English and the Scots meant only one among several of the sports and pastimes that take the man and the woman of the upper and upper-middle classes into the country and the fresh air. To the American of like status golf came as the one thing to take him out of his towns and give him a reason for exercise in the country. To-day golf has become an interest all over North America, but it is in the Eastern States that it has made most difference in the life of the classes with whom it has become fashionable. Westerners and Southerners found more excuses before the coming of golf for being in the open country air. It is in the Eastern States more especially that it has had so much influence in making the people live and take exercise out of doors. In a truly democratic spirit the American woman golfer plays on a perfect equality with the American man. She does not compete in the men's championships; she has championships of her own; but she plays, without question, on the same links. There is no suggestion of relegating her, as a certain cynical writer in the Badminton volume on golf described it, to a waste corner, a kind of "Jews' Quarter," of the links. And the Americans have taken up golf in the spirit of a sumptuous and opulent people, spending money

164

on magnificent clubhouses beyond the finest dreams of the Englishman or the Scot. The greatest success achieved by any American golfer fell to the lot of Mr Walter Travis of the Garden City club, who in 1904 won the British amateur championship.

So much enthusiasm and so much golf in America have not failed to make their influence felt in the United Kingdom. Naturally and inevitably they have created a strong demand for professional instruction, both by example and by precept, and for professional advice and assistance in the laying-out and upkeep of the many new links that have been created in all parts of the States, sometimes out of the least promising material. By the offer of great prizes for exhibition matches, and of wages that are to the British rate on the scale of the dollar to the shilling, they have attracted many of the best Scottish and English professionals to pay them longer or shorter visits as the case may be, and thus a new opening has been created for the energies of the professional golfing class.

The Game.—The game of golf may be briefly defined as consisting in hitting the ball over a great extent of country, preferably of that sand-hill nature which is found by the seaside, and finally hitting or "putting" it into a little hole of some 4 in. diameter cut in the turf. The place of the hole is commonly marked by a flag. Eighteen is the recognized number of these holes on a full course, and they are at varying distances apart, from 100 yds. up to anything between a ¼ and ½ m. For the various strokes required to achieve the hitting of the ball over the great hills, and finally putting it into the small hole, a number of different "clubs" has been devised to suit the different positions in which the ball may be found and the different directions in which it is wished to propel it. At the start for each hole the ball may be placed on a favourable position (*e.g.* "tee'd" on a small mound of sand) for striking it, but after that it may not be touched, except with the club, until it is hit into the next hole. A "full drive," as the farthest distance that the ball can be hit is called, is about 200 yds. in length, of which some three-fourths will be traversed in the air, and the rest by bounding or running over the ground. It is easily to be understood that when the ball is lying on the turf behind a tall sand-hill, or in a bunker, a differently-shaped club is required for raising it over such an obstacle from that which is needed when it is placed on the tee to start with; and again, that another club is needed to strike the ball out of a cup or out of heavy grass. It is this variety that gives the game its charm. Each player plays with his own ball, with no interference from his opponent, and the object of each is to hit the ball from the starting-point into each successive hole in the fewest strokes. The player who at the end of the round (*i.e.* of the course of eighteen holes) has won the majority of the holes is the winner of the round; or the decision may be reached before the end of the round by one side gaining more holes than there remain to play. For instance, if one player be four holes to the good, and only three holes remain to be played, it is evident that the former must be the winner, for even if the latter win every remaining hole, he still must be one to the bad at the finish.

The British Amateur Championship is decided by a tournament in matches thus played, each defeated player retiring, and his opponent passing on into the next round. In the case of the Open Championship, and in most medal competitions, the scores are differently reckoned—each man's total score (irrespective of his relative merit at each hole) being reckoned at the finish against the total score of the other players in the competition. There is also a species of competition called "bogey" play, in which each man plays against a "bogey" score—a score fixed for each hole in the round before starting—and his position in the competition relatively to the other players is determined by the number of holes that he is to the good or to the bad of the "bogey" score at the end of the round. The player who is most holes to the good, or fewest holes to the bad, wins the competition. It may be mentioned incidentally that golf occupies the almost unique position of being the only sport in which even a single player can enjoy his game, his opponent in this event being "Colonel Bogey"—more often than not a redoubtable adversary.

The links which have been thought worthy, by reason of their geographical positions and their merits, of being the scenes on which the golf championships are fought out, are, as we have already said, three in Scotland—St Andrews, Prestwick and Muirfield—and three in England—Hoylake, Sandwich and Deal. This brief list is very far from being complete as regards links of first-class quality in Great Britain. Besides those named, there are in Scotland—Carnoustie, North Berwick, Cruden Bay, Nairn, Aberdeen, Dornoch, Troon, Machrihanish, South Uist, Islay, Gullane, Luffness and many more. In England there are—Westward Ho, Bembridge, Littlestone, Great Yarmouth, Brancaster, Seaton Carew, Formby, Lytham, Harlech, Burnham, among the seaside ones; while of the inland, some of them of very fine quality, we cannot even attempt a selection, so large is their number and so variously estimated their comparative merits. Ireland has Portrush, Newcastle, Portsalon, Dollymount and many more of the first class; and there are excellent courses in the Isle of Man. In America many fine courses have been constructed. There is not a British colony of any standing that is without its golf course—Australia, India, South Africa, all have their golf championships, which are keenly contested. Canada has had courses at

Quebec and Montreal for many years, and the Calcutta Golf Club, curiously enough, is the oldest established (next to the Blackheath Club), the next oldest being the club at Pau in the Basses-Pyrénées.

The Open Championship of golf was started in 1860 by the Prestwick Club giving a belt to be played for annually under the condition that it should become the property of any who could win it thrice in succession. The following is the list of the champions:—

860.	W. Park, Musselburgh	174—at Prestwick.
861.	Tom Morris, sen., Prestwick	163—at Prestwick.
862.	Tom Morris, sen., Prestwick	163—at Prestwick.
863.	W. Park, Musselburgh	168—at Prestwick.
864.	Tom Morris, sen., Prestwick	160—at Prestwick.
865.	A. Strath, St Andrews	162—at Prestwick.
866.	W. Park, Musselburgh	169—at Prestwick.
867.	Tom Morris, sen., St Andrews	170—at Prestwick.
868.	Tom Morris, jun., St Andrews	154—at Prestwick.
869.	Tom Morris, jun., St Andrews	157—at Prestwick.
870.	Tom Morris, jun., St Andrews	149—at Prestwick.

Tom Morris, junior, thus won the belt finally, according to the conditions. In 1871 there was no competition; but by 1872 the three clubs of St Andrews, Prestwick and Musselburgh had subscribed for a cup which should be played for over the course of each subscribing club successively, but should never become the property of the winner. In later years the course at Muirfield was substituted for that at Musselburgh, and Hoylake and Sandwich were admitted into the list of championship courses. Up to 1891, inclusive, the play of two rounds, or thirty-six holes, determined the championship, but from 1892 the result has been determined by the play of 72 holes.

222

After the interregnum of 1871, the following were the champions:—

872.	Tom Morris, jun., St Andrews	166—at Prestwick.
873.	Tom Kidd, St Andrews	179—at St Andrews.
874.	Mungo Park, Musselburgh	159—at Musselburgh.
875.	Willie Park, Musselburgh	166—at Prestwick.
876.	Bob Martin, St Andrews	176—at St Andrews.
877.	Jamie Anderson, St Andrews	160—at Musselburgh.
878.	Jamie Anderson, St Andrews	157—at Prestwick.
879.	Jamie Anderson, St Andrews	170—at St Andrews.
880.	Bob Fergusson, Musselburgh	162—at Musselburgh.
881.	Bob Fergusson, Musselburgh	170—at Prestwick.

882.	Bob Fergusson, Musselburgh	171—at St Andrews.
883.	W. Fernie, Dumfries	159—at Musselburgh.
884.	Jack Simpson, Carnoustie	160—at Prestwick.
885.	Bob Martin, St Andrews	171—at St Andrews.
886.	D. Brown, Musselburgh	157—at Musselburgh.
887.	Willie Park, jun., Musselburgh	161—at Prestwick.
888.	Jack Burns, Warwick	171—at St Andrews.
889.	Willie Park, jun., Musselburgh	155—at Musselburgh.
890.	Mr John Ball, jun., Hoylake	164—at Prestwick.
891.	Hugh Kirkaldy, St Andrews	166—at St Andrews.
892.	Mr H. H. Hilton, Hoylake	305—at Muirfield.
893.	W. Auchterlonie, St Andrews	322—at Prestwick.
894.	J. H. Taylor, Winchester	326—at Sandwich.
895.	J. H. Taylor, Winchester	322—at St Andrews.
896.	H. Vardon, Scarborough	316—at Muirfield.
897.	Mr H. H. Hilton, Hoylake	314—at Hoylake.
898.	H. Vardon, Scarborough	307—at Prestwick.
899.	H. Vardon, Scarborough	310—at Sandwich.
900.	J. H. Taylor, Richmond	309—at St Andrews.
901.	J. Braid, Romford	309—at Muirfield.
902.	A. Herd, Huddersfield	307—at Hoylake.
903.	H. Vardon, Ganton	300—at Prestwick.
904.	J. White, Sunningdale	296—at Sandwich.
905.	J. Braid, Walton Heath	318—at St Andrews.
906.	J. Braid, Walton Heath	300—at Muirfield.
907.	Arnaud Massey, La Boulie	312—at Hoylake.
908.	J. Braid, Walton Heath	291—at Prestwick.
909.	J. H. Taylor, Richmond	295—at Deal.
	J. Braid, Walton Heath	298—at St

The Amateur Championship is of far more recent institution.

886.	Mr Horace Hutchinson	at St Andrews.
887.	Mr Horace Hutchinson	at Hoylake.
888.	Mr John Ball	at Prestwick.
889.	Mr J. E. Laidlay	at St Andrews.
890.	Mr John Ball	at Hoylake.
891.	Mr J. E. Laidlay	at St Andrews.
892.	Mr John Ball	at Sandwich.
893.	Mr P. Anderson	at Prestwick.
894.	Mr John Ball	at Hoylake.
895.	Mr L. Balfour-Melville	at St Andrews.
896.	Mr F. G. Tait	at Sandwich.
897.	Mr J. T. Allan	at Muirfield.
898.	Mr John Ball	at Prestwick.
899.	Mr F. G. Tait	at Hoylake.
900.	Mr H. H. Hilton	at Sandwich.
901.	Mr H. H. Hilton	at St Andrews.
902.	Mr C. Hutchings	at Hoylake.
903.	Mr R. Maxwell	at Muirfield.
904.	Mr W. J. Travis	at Sandwich.
905.	Mr A. G. Barry	at St Andrews.
906.	Mr J. Robb	at Hoylake.
907.	Mr John Ball	at St Andrews.
908.	Mr E. A. Lassen	at Sandwich.
909.	Mr Robert Maxwell	at Muirfield.
910.	Mr John Ball	at Hoylake.

The Ladies' Championship was started in 1893.

893.	Lady M. Scott	at St Annes.
894.	Lady M. Scott	at Littlestone.

	Lady M.	at Portrush.
895.	Scott	
	Miss A. B.	at Hoylake.
896.	Pascoe	
	Miss E. C.	at Gullane.
897.	Orr	
	Miss L.	at Yarmouth.
898.	Thompson	
	Miss M.	at Newcastle.
899.	Hezlet	
	Miss R. K.	at Westward Ho.
900.	Adair	
	Miss M. A.	at Aberdovy.
901.	Graham	
	Miss M.	at Deal.
902.	Hezlet	
	Miss R. K.	at Portrush.
903.	Adair	
	Miss L. Dod	at Troon.
904.		
	Miss B.	at Cromer.
905.	Thompson	
	Mrs	at Burnham.
906.	Kennion	
	Miss M.	at Newcastle (Co.
907.	Hezlet	Down).
	Miss M.	at St Andrews.
908.	Titterton	
	Miss D.	at Birkdale.
909.	Campbell	
	Miss Grant	at Westward Ho.
910.	Suttie	

There have been some slight changes of detail and arrangement as time has gone on, in the rules of the game (the latest edition of the Rules should be consulted). A new class of golfer has arisen, requiring a code of rules framed rather more exactly than the older code. The Scottish golfer, who was "teethed" on a golf club, as Mr Andrew Lang has described it, imbibed all the traditions of the game with his natural sustenance. Very few rules sufficed for him. But when the Englishman, and still more the American (less in touch with the traditions), began to play golf as a new game, then they began to ask for a code of rules that should be lucid and illuminating on every point—an ideal perhaps impossible to realize. It was found, at least, that the code put forward by the Royal and Ancient Club of St Andrews did not realize it adequately. Nevertheless the new golfers were very loyal indeed to the club that had ever of old held, by tacit consent, the position of fount of golfing legislation. The Royal and Ancient Club was appealed to by English golfers to step into the place, analogous to that of the Marylebone Cricket Club in cricket, that they were both willing and anxious to give it. It was a place that the Club at St Andrews did not in the least wish to occupy, but the honour was thrust so insistently upon it, that there was no declining. The latest effort to meet the demands for some more satisfactory legislation on the thousand and one points that continually must arise for decision in course of playing a game of such variety as golf, consists of the appointment of a standing committee, called the "Rules of Golf Committee." Its members all belong to the Royal and Ancient Club; but since this club draws its membership from all parts of the United Kingdom, this restriction is quite consistent with a very general representation of the views of north, south, east and west—from Westward Ho and Sandwich to Dornoch, and all the many first-rate links of Ireland—on the committee. Ireland has, indeed, some of the best links in the kingdom, and yields to neither Scotland nor England in enthusiasm for the game. This committee, after a general revision of the rules into the form in which they now stand, consider every month, either by meeting or by correspondence, the questions that are sent up to it by clubs or by individuals; and the committee's answers to these questions have the force of law until they have come before the next general meeting of the Royal and Ancient Club at St Andrews, which may confirm or may reject them at will. The ladies of Great Britain manage otherwise. They have a Golfing Union which settles questions for them; but since this union itself accepts as binding the answers given by the Rules of Golf Committee, they really arrive at the same conclusions by a slightly different path. Nor does the American Union, governing the play of men and women alike in the States, really act differently. The Americans naturally reserve to themselves freedom to make their own rules, but in practice they conform to the legislation of Scotland, with the exception of a more drastic definition of the status of the amateur player, and certain differences as to the clubs used.

A considerable modification has been effected in the implements of the game. The tendency of the modern wooden clubs is to be short in the head as compared with the clubs of, say, 1880 or 1885. The advantage claimed (probably with justice) for this shape is that it masses the weight behind the point on which the ball is struck. Better material in the wood of the club is a consequence of the increased demand for these articles and the increased competition among their makers. Whereas under the old conditions a few workers at the few greens then in existence were enough to supply the golfing wants, now there is a very large industry in golf club and ball making, which not only employs workers in the local club-makers' shops all the kingdom over, but is an important branch of the commerce of the stores and of the big athletic outfitters, both in Great Britain and in the United States. By far the largest modification in the game since the change to gutta-percha balls from balls of leather-covering stuffed with feathers, is due to the American invention of the india-rubber cased balls. Practically it is as an American invention that it is still regarded, although the British law courts decided, after a lengthy trial (1905), that there had been "prior users" of the principle of the balls' manufacture, and therefore that the patent of Mr Haskell, by whose name the 223first balls of the kind were called, was not good. It is singular to remark that in the first introduction of the gutta-percha balls, superseding the leather and feather compositions, they also were called by the name of their first maker, "Gourlay." The general mode of manufacture of the rubber-cored ball, which is now everywhere in use, is interiorly, a hard core of gutta-percha or some other such substance; round this is wound, by machinery, india-rubber thread or strips at a high tension, and over all is an outer coat of gutta-percha. Some makers have tried to dispense with the kernel of hard substance, or to substitute for it kernels of some fluid or gelatinous substance, but in general the above is a sufficient, though rough, description of the mode of making all these balls. Their superiority over the solid gutta-percha lies in their superior resiliency. The effect is that they go much more lightly off the club. It is not so much in the tee-shots that this superiority is observed, as in the second shots, when the ball is lying badly; balls of the rubber-cored kind, with their greater liveliness, are more easy to raise in the air from a lie of this kind. They also go remarkably well off the iron clubs, and thus make the game easier by placing the player within an iron shot of the hole at a distance at which he would have to use a wooden club if he were playing with a solid gutta-percha ball. They also tend to make the game more easy by the fact that if they are at all mis-hit they go much better than a gutta-percha ball similarly inaccurately struck. As a slight set-off against these qualities, the ball, because of the greater liveliness, is not quite so good for the short game as the solid ball; but on the whole its advantages distinctly overbalance its disadvantages.

When these balls were first put on the market they were sold at two shillings each and even, when the supply was quite unequal to the demand, at a greater deal higher price, rising to as much as a guinea a ball. But the normal price, until about a year after the decision in the British courts of law affirming that there was no patent in the balls, was always two shillings for the best quality of ball. Subsequently there was a reduction down to one shilling for the balls made by many of the manufacturing companies, though in 1910 the rise in the price of rubber sent up the cost. The rubber-cored ball does not go out of shape so quickly as the gutta-percha solid ball and does not show other marks of ill-usage with the club so obviously. It has had the effect of making the game a good deal easier for the second- and third-class players, favouring especially those who were short drivers with the old gutta-percha ball. To the best players it has made the least difference, nevertheless those who were best with the old ball are also best with the new; its effect has merely been to bring the second, third and fourth best closer to each other and to the best.

Incidentally, the question of the expense of the game has been touched on in this notice of the new balls. There is no doubt that the balls themselves tend to a greater economy, not only because of their own superior durability but also because, as a consequence of their greater resiliency, they are not nearly so hard on the clubs, and the clubs themselves being perhaps made of better material than used to be given to their manufacture, the total effect is that a man's necessary annual expenditure on them is very small indeed even though he plays pretty constantly. Four or five rounds are not more than the average of golfers will make an india-rubber cored ball last them, so that the outlay on the weapons is very moderate. On the other hand the expenditure of the clubs on their courses has increased and tends to increase. Demands are more insistent than they used to be for a well kept course, for perfectly mown greens, renewed teeing grounds and so on, and probably the modern golfer is a good deal more luxurious in his clubhouse wants than his father used to be. This means a big staff of servants and workers on the green, and to meet this a rather heavy subscription is required. Such a subscription as five guineas added to a ten or fifteen guinea entrance fee is not uncommon, and even this is very moderate compared with the subscriptions to some of the clubs in the United States, where a hundred dollars a year, or twenty pounds of our money, is not unusual. But on the whole golf is a very economical pastime, as compared with almost any other sport or pastime which engages the attention of Britons, and it is a pastime for all the year round, and for all the life of a man or woman.

Glossary of Technical Terms used in the Game.

Addressing the Ball.—Putting oneself in position to strike the ball.

All Square.—Term used to express that the score stands level, neither side being a hole up.

Baff.—To strike the ground with the club when playing, and so loft the ball unduly.

Baffy.—A short wooden club, with laid-back face, for lofting shots.

Bogey.—The number of strokes which a good average player should take to each hole. This imaginary player is usually known as "Colonel Bogey," and plays a fine game.

Brassy.—A wooden club with a brass sole.

Bulger.—A driver in which the face "bulges" into a convex shape. The head is shorter than in the older-fashioned driver.

Bunker.—A sand-pit.

Bye.—The holes remaining after one side has become more holes up than remain for play.

Caddie.—The person who carries the clubs. Diminutive of "cad"; cf. laddie (from Fr. *cadet*).

Cleek.—The iron-headed club that is capable of the farthest drive of any of the clubs with iron heads.

Cup.—A depression in the ground causing the ball to lie badly.

Dead.—A ball is said to be "dead" when so near the hole that the putting it in in the next stroke is a "dead" certainty. A ball is said to "fall dead" when it pitches with hardly any run.

Divot.—A piece of turf cut out in the act of playing, which, be it noted, should always be replaced before the player moves on.

Dormy.—One side is said to be "dormy" when it is as many holes to the good as remain to be played—so that it cannot be beaten.

Driver.—The longest driving club, used when the ball lies very well and a long shot is needed.

Foozle.—Any very badly missed or bungled stroke.

"Fore!"—A cry of warning to people in front.

Foursome.—A match in which four persons engage, two on each side playing alternately with the same ball.

Green.—(*a*) The links as a whole; (*b*) the "putting-greens" around the holes.

Grip.—(*a*) The part of the club-shaft which is held in the hands while playing; (*b*) the grasp itself—*e.g.* "a firm grip," "a loose grip," are common expressions.

Half-Shot.—A shot played with something less than a full swing.

Halved.—A hole is "halved" when both sides have played it in the same number of strokes. A round is "halved" when each side has won and lost the same number of holes.

Handicap.—The strokes which a player receives either in match play or competition.

Hanging.—Said of a ball that lies on a slope inclining downwards in regard to the direction in which it is wished to drive.

Hazard.—A general term for bunker, whin, long grass, roads and all kinds of bad ground.

Heel.—To hit the ball on the "heel" of the club, *i.e.* the part of the face nearest the shaft, and so send the ball to the right, with the same result as from a slice.

Honour.—The privilege (which its holder is not at liberty to decline) of striking off first from the tee.

Iron.—An iron-headed club intermediate between the cleek and lofting mashie. There are driving irons and lofting irons according to the purposes for which they are intended.

Lie.—(*a*) The angle of the club-head with the shaft (*e.g.* a "flat lie," "an upright lie"); (*b*) the position of the ball on the ground (*e.g.* "a good lie," "a bad lie").

Like, The.—The stroke which makes the player's score equal to his opponent's in course of playing a hole.

Like-as-we-Lie.—Said when both sides have played the same number of strokes.

Line.—The direction in which the hole towards which the player is progressing lies with reference to the present position of his ball.

Mashie.—Ah iron club with a short head. The *lofting mashie* has the blade much laid back, for playing a short lofting shot. The *driving mashie* has the blade less laid back, and is used for longer, less lofted shots.

Match-Play.—Play in which the score is reckoned by holes won and lost.

Medal-Play.—Play in which the score is reckoned by the total of strokes taken on the round.

Niblick.—A short stiff club with a short, laid back, iron head, used for getting the ball out of a very bad lie.

Odd, The.—A stroke more than the opponent has played.

Press.—To strive to hit harder than you can hit with accuracy.

Pull.—To hit the ball with a pulling movement of the club, so as to make it curve to the left.

Putt.—To play the short strokes near the hole (pronounced as in "but").

Putter.—The club used for playing the short strokes near the hole. Some have a wooden head, some an iron head.

224

Rub-of-the-Green.—Any chance deflection that the ball receives as it goes along.

Run Up.—To send the ball low and close to the ground in approaching the hole—opposite to lofting it up.

Scratch Player.—Player who receives no odds in handicap competitions.

Slice.—To hit the ball with a cut across it, so that it flies curving to the right.

Stance.—(*a*) The place on which the player has to stand when playing—*e.g.* "a bad stance," "a good stance," are common expressions; (*b*) the position relative to each other of the player's feet.

Stymie.—When one ball lies in a straight line between another and the hole the first is said to "stymie," or "to be a stymie to" the other—from an old Scottish word given by Jamieson to mean "the faintest form of anything." The idea probably was, the "stymie" only left you the "faintest form" of the hole to aim at.

Tee.—The little mound of sand on which the ball is generally placed for the first drive to each hole.

Teeing-Ground.—The place marked as the limit, outside of which it is not permitted to drive the ball off. This marked-out ground is also sometimes called "the tee."

Top.—To hit the ball above the centre, so that it does not rise much from the ground.

Up.—A player is said to be "one up," "two up," &c., when he is so many holes to the good of his opponent.

Wrist-Shot.—A shot less in length than a half-shot, but longer than a putt.

BIBLIOGRAPHY.—The literature of the game has grown to some considerable bulk. For many years it was practically comprised in the fine work by Mr Robert Clark, *Golf: A Royal and Ancient Game*, together with two handbooks on the game by Mr Chambers and by Mr Forgan respectively, and the *Golfiana Miscellanea* of Mr Stewart. A small book by Mr Horace Hutchinson, named *Hints on Golf*, was very shortly followed by a much more important work by Sir Walter Simpson, Bart., called *The Art of Golf*, a title which sufficiently explains itself. The Badminton Library book on *Golf* attempted to collect into one volume the most interesting historical facts known about the game, with *obiter dicta* and advice to learners, and, on similar didactic lines, books have been written by Mr H. C. S. Everard, Mr Garden Smith and W. Park, the professional player. Mr H. J. Whigham, sometime amateur champion golfer of the United States, has given us a book about the game in that country. *The Book of Golf and Golfers*, compiled, with assistance, by Mr Horace Hutchinson, is in the first place a picture-gallery of famous golfers in their respective attitudes of play. Taylor, Vardon and Braid have each contributed a volume of instruction, and Mr G. W. Beldam has published a book with admirable photographs of players in action, called *Great Golfers: their Methods at a Glance*. A work intended for the use of green committees is among the volumes of the *Country Life* Library of Sport. Much interesting lore is contained in the *Golfing Annual*, in the *Golfer's Year Book* and in the pages of *Golf*, which has now become *Golf Illustrated*, a weekly paper devoted to the game. Among works that have primarily a local interest, but yet contain much of historical value about the game, may be cited the *Golf Book of East Lothian*, by the Rev. John Kerr, and the *Chronicle of Blackheath Golfers*, by Mr W. E. Hughes.

(H. G. H.)

1From an enactment of James VI. (then James I. of England), bearing date 1618, we find that a considerable importation of golf balls at that time took place from Holland, and as thereby "na small quantitie of gold and silver is transported zierly out of his Hienes' kingdome of Scoteland" (see letter of His Majesty from Salisbury, the 5th of August 1618), he issues a royal prohibition, at once as a wise economy of the national moneys, and a protection to native industry in the article. From this it might almost seem that the game was at that date still known and practised in Holland.

Records of the City of Edinburgh.
3*Inventories of Mary Queen of Scots*, preface, p. lxx. (1863).
4Anonymous author of MS. in the Harleian Library.
5See *History of Leith*, by A. Campbell (1827).
6*Local Records of Northumberland*, by John Sykes (Newcastle, 1833).
7Robertson's *Historical Notices of Leith.*

GOLIAD, an unincorporated village and the county-seat of Goliad county, Texas, U.S.A., on the N. bank of the San Antonio river, 85 m. S.E. of San Antonio. Pop. (1900) about 1700. It is served by the Galveston, Harrisburg & San Antonio railway (Southern Pacific System). Situated in the midst of a rich farming and stock-raising country, Goliad has flour mills, cotton gins and cotton-seed oil mills. Here are the interesting ruins of the old Spanish mission of La Bahia, which was removed to this point from the Guadaloupe river in 1747. During the struggle between Mexico and Spain the Mexican leader Bernardo Gutierrez (1778-1814) was besieged here. The name Goliad, probably an anagram of the name of the Mexican patriot Hidalgo (1753-1811), was first used about 1829. On the outbreak of the Texan War of Liberation Goliad was garrisoned by a small force of Mexicans, who surrendered to the Texans in October 1835, and on the 20th of December a preliminary "declaration of independence" was published here, antedating by several months the official Declaration issued at Old Washington, Texas, on the 2nd of March 1836. In 1836, when Santa Anna began his advance against the Texan posts, Goliad was occupied by a force of about 350 Americans under Colonel James W. Fannin (*c.* 1800-1836), who was overtaken on the Coletta Creek while attempting to carry out orders to withdraw from Goliad and to unite with General Houston; he surrendered after a sharp fight (March 19-20) in which he inflicted a heavy loss on the Mexicans, and was marched back with his force to Goliad, where on the morning of the 27th of March they were shot down by Santa Anna's orders. Goliad was nearly destroyed by a tornado on the 19th of May 1903.

GOLIARD, a name applied to those wandering students (*vagantes*) and clerks in England, France and Germany, during the 12th and 13th centuries, who were better known for their rioting, gambling and intemperance than for their scholarship. The derivation of the word is uncertain. It may come from the Lat. *gula*, gluttony (Wright), but was connected by them with a mythical "Bishop Golias," also called "*archipoëta*" and "*primas*"—especially in Germany—in whose name their satirical poems were mostly written. Many scholars have accepted Büdinger's suggestion (*Über einige Reste der Vagantenpoesie in Österreich*, Vienna, 1854) that the title of Golias goes back to the letter of St Bernard to Innocent II., in which he referred to Abelard as Goliath, thus connecting the goliards with the keen-witted student adherents of that great medieval critic. Giesebrecht and others, however, support the derivation of goliard from *gailliard*, a gay fellow, leaving "Golias" as the imaginary "patron" of their fraternity.

Spiegel has ingeniously disentangled something of a biography of an *archipoëta* who flourished mainly in Burgundy and at Salzburg from 1160 to beyond the middle of the 13th century; but the proof of the reality of this individual is not convincing. It is doubtful, too, if the jocular references to the rules of the "gild" of goliards should be taken too seriously, though their aping of the "orders" of the church, especially their contrasting them with the mendicants, was too bold for church synods. Their satires were almost uniformly directed against the church, attacking even the pope. In 1227 the council of Trèves forbade priests to permit the goliards to take part in chanting the service. In 1229 they played a conspicuous part in the disturbances at the university of Paris, in connexion with the intrigues of the papal legate. During the century which followed they formed a subject for the deliberations of several church councils, notably in 1289 when it was ordered that "no clerks shall be jongleurs, goliards or buffoons," and in 1300 (at Cologne) when they were forbidden to preach or engage in the indulgence traffic. This legislation was only effective when the "privileges of clergy" were withdrawn from the goliards. Those historians who regard the middle ages as completely dominated by ascetic ideals, regard the goliard movement as a protest against the spirit of the time. But it is rather indicative of the wide diversity in temperament among those who crowded to the universities in the 13th century, and who found in the privileges of the clerk some advantage and attraction in the student life. The goliard poems are as truly "medieval" as the monastic life which they despised; they merely voice another section of humanity. Yet their criticism was most keenly pointed, and marks a distinct step in the criticism of abuses in the church.

73

Along with these satires went many poems in praise of wine and riotous living. A remarkable collection of them, now at Munich, from the monastery at Benedictbeuren in Bavaria, was published by Schmeller (3rd ed., 1895) under the title *Carmina Burana*. Many of these, which form the main part of song-books of German students to-day, have been delicately translated by John Addington Symonds in a small volume, *Wine, Women and Song* (1884). As Symonds has said, they form a prelude to the Renaissance. The poems of "Bishop Golias" were later attributed to Walter Mapes, and have been published by Thomas Wright in *The Latin Poems commonly attributed to Walter Mapes* (London, 1841).

The word "goliard" itself outlived these turbulent bands which had given it birth, and passed over into French and English literature of the 14th century in the general meaning of jongleur or minstrel, quite apart from any clerical association. It is thus used in *Piers Plowman*, where, however, the *goliard* still rhymes in Latin, and in Chaucer.

See, besides the works quoted above, M. Haezner, *Goliardendichtung und die Satire im 13ten Jahrhundert in England* (Leipzig, 1905); Spiegel, *Die Vaganten und ihr "Orden"* (Spires, 1892); Hubatsch, *Die lateinischen Vagantenlieder des Mittelalters* (Görlitz, 1870); and the article in *La grande Encyclopédie*. All of these have bibliographical apparatus.

(J. T. S.*)

GOLIATH, the name of the giant by slaying whom David achieved renown (1 Sam. xvii.). The Philistines had come up to make war against Saul and, as the rival camps lay opposite each other, this warrior came forth day by day to challenge to single combat. Only David ventured to respond, and armed with a sling and pebbles he overcame Goliath. The Philistines, seeing their champion killed, lost heart and were easily put to flight. The giant's arms were placed in the sanctuary, and it was his famous sword which David took with him in his flight from Saul (1 Sam. xxi. 1-9). From another passage we learn that Goliath of Gath, "the shaft of whose spear was like a weaver's beam," was slain by a certain Elhanan of Bethlehem in one of David's conflicts with the Philistines (2 Sam. xxi. 18-22)—the parallel 1 Chron. xx. 5, avoids the contradiction by reading the "brother of Goliath." But this old popular story has probably preserved the more original tradition, and if Elhanan is the son of Dodo in the list of David's mighty men (2 Sam. xxiii. 9, 24), the resemblance between the two names may have led to the transference. The narratives of David's early life point to some exploit by means of which he gained the favour of Saul, Jonathan and Israel, but the absence of all reference to his achievement in the subsequent chapters (1 Sam. xxi. 11, xxix. 5) is evidence of the relatively late origin of a tradition which in course of time became one of the best-known incidents in David's life (Ps. cxliv., LXX. title, the apocryphal Ps. cli., Ecclus. xlvii. 4).

See DAVID; SAMUEL (BOOKS) and especially Cheyne, *Aids and Devout Study of Criticism*, pp. 80 sqq., 125 sqq. In the old Egyptian romance of *Sinuhit* (ascribed to about 2000 B.C.), the story of the slaying of the Bedouin hero has several points of resemblance with that of David and Goliath. See L. B. Paton, *Hist. of Syr. and Pal.*, p. 60; A. Jeremias, *Das A. T. im Lichte d. alten Orients*, 2nd ed. pp. 299, 491; A. R. S. Kennedy, *Century Bible: Samuel*, p. 122, argues that David's Philistine adversary was originally nameless, in 1 Sam. xvii. he is named only in v. 4.

GOLITSUIN, BORIS ALEKSYEEVICH (1654-1714), Russian statesman, came of a princely family, claiming descent from Prince Gedimin of Lithuania. Earlier members of the family were Mikhail (d. c. 1552), a famous soldier, and his great-grandson Vasily Vasilevich (d. 1619), who was sent as ambassador to Poland to offer the Russian crown to Prince Ladislaus. Boris became court chamberlain in 1676. He was the young tsar Peter's chief supporter when, in 1689, Peter resisted the usurpations of his elder sister Sophia, and the head of the loyal council which assembled at the Troitsa monastery during the crisis of the struggle. Golitsuin it was who suggested taking refuge in that strong fortress and won over the boyars of the opposite party. In 1690 he was created a boyar and shared with Lev Naruishkin, Peter's uncle, the conduct of home affairs. After the death of the tsaritsa Natalia, Peter's mother, in 1694, his influence increased still further. He accompanied Peter to the White Sea (1694-1695); took part in the Azov campaign (1695); and was one of the triumvirate who ruled Russia during Peter's first foreign tour (1697-1698). The Astrakhan rebellion (1706), which affected all the districts under his government, shook Peter's confidence in him, and seriously impaired his position. In 1707 he was superseded in the Volgan provinces by Andrei Matvyeev. A year before his death he entered a monastery. Golitsuin was a typical representative of Russian society of the end of the 17th century in its transition from barbarism to civilization. In many respects he was far in advance of his age. He was highly educated, spoke Latin with graceful fluency, frequented the society of scholars and had his children carefully educated according to the best European models. Yet this eminent, this superior personage was an habitual drunkard, an uncouth savage who intruded upon the hospitality of wealthy foreigners, and was not ashamed to seize upon any dish he took a fancy to, and send it home to his wife. It was his reckless drunkenness which ultimately ruined him in the estimation of Peter the Great, despite his previous inestimable services.

See S. Solovev, *History of Russia* (Rus.), vol. xiv. (Moscow, 1858); R. N. Bain, *The First Romanovs* (London, 1905).

(R. N. B.)

GOLITSUIN, DMITRY MIKHAILOVICH (1665-1737), Russian statesman, was sent in 1697 to Italy to learn "military affairs"; in 1704 he was appointed to the command of an auxiliary corps in Poland against Charles XII.; from 1711 to 1718 he was governor of Byelogorod. In 1718 he was appointed president of the newly erected *Kammer Kollegium* and a senator. In May 1723 he was implicated in the disgrace of the vice-chancellor Shafirov and was deprived of all his offices and dignities, which he only recovered through the mediation of the empress Catherine I. After the death of Peter the Great, Golitsuin became the recognized head of the old Conservative party which had never forgiven Peter for putting away Eudoxia and marrying the plebeian Martha Skavronskaya. But the reformers, as represented by Alexander Menshikov and Peter Tolstoi, prevailed; and Golitsuin remained in the background till the fall of Menshikov, 1727. During the last years of Peter II. (1728-1730), Golitsuin was the most prominent statesman in Russia and his high aristocratic theories had full play. On the death of Peter II. he conceived the idea of limiting the autocracy by subordinating it to the authority of the supreme privy council, of which he was president. He drew up a form of constitution which Anne of Courland, the newly elected Russian empress, was forced to sign at Mittau before being permitted to proceed to St Petersburg. Anne lost no time in repudiating this constitution, and never forgave its authors. Golitsuin was left in peace, however, and lived for the most part in retirement, till 1736, when he was arrested on suspicion of being concerned in the conspiracy of his son-in-law Prince Constantine Cantimir. This, however, was a mere pretext, it was for his anti-monarchical sentiments that he was really prosecuted. A court, largely composed of his antagonists, condemned him to death, but the empress reduced the sentence to lifelong imprisonment in Schlüsselburg and confiscation of all his estates. He died in his prison on the 14th of April 1737, after three months of confinement.

See R. N. Bain, *The Pupils of Peter the Great* (London, 1897).

(R. N. B.)

GOLITSUIN, VASILY VASILEVICH (1643-1714), Russian statesman, spent his early days at the court of Tsar Alexius where he gradually rose to the rank of boyar. In 1676 he was sent to the Ukraine to keep in order the Crimean Tatars and took part in the Chigirin campaign. Personal experience of the inconveniences and dangers of the prevailing system of preferment, the so-called *myestnichestvo*, or rank priority, which had paralysed the Russian armies for centuries, induced him to propose its abolition, which was accomplished by Tsar Theodore III. (1678). The May revolution of 1682 placed Golitsuin at the head of the *Posolsky Prikaz*, or ministry of foreign affairs, and during the regency of Sophia, sister of Peter the Great, whose lover he became, he was the principal minister of state (1682-1689) and "keeper of the great seal," a title bestowed upon only two Russians before him, Athonasy Orduin-Nashchokin and Artamon Matvyeev. In home affairs his influence was insignificant, but his foreign policy was distinguished by the peace with Poland in 1683, whereby Russia at last recovered Kiev. By the terms of the same treaty, he acceded to the grand league against the Porte, but his two expeditions against the Crimea (1687 and 1689), "the First Crimean War," were unsuccessful and made him extremely unpopular. Only with the utmost difficulty could Sophia get the young tsar Peter to decorate the defeated commander-in-chief as if he had returned a victor. In the civil war between Sophia and Peter (August-September 1689), Golitsuin half-heartedly supported his mistress and shared her ruin. His life was spared owing to the supplications of his cousin Boris, but he was deprived of his boyardom, his estates were confiscated and he was banished successively to Kargopol, Mezen and Kologora, where he died on the 21st of April 1714. Golitsuin was unusually well educated. He understood German and Greek as well as his mother-tongue, and could express himself fluently in Latin. He was a great friend of foreigners, who generally alluded to him as "the great Golitsuin."

His brother MIKHAIL (1674-1730) was a celebrated soldier, who is best known for his governorship of Finland (1714-1721), where his admirable qualities earned the remembrance of the people whom he had conquered. And Mikhail's son Alexander (1718-1783) 226was a diplomat and soldier, who rose to be field-marshal and governor of St Petersburg.

See R. N. Bain, *The First Romanovs* (London, 1905); A. Brückner, *Fürst Golizin* (Leipzig, 1887); S. Solovev, *History of Russia* (Rus.), vols. xiii.-xiv. (Moscow, 1858, &c.).

(R. N. B.)

GOLIUS or (GOHL), **JACOBUS** (1596-1667), Dutch Orientalist, was born at the Hague in 1596, and studied at the university of Leiden, where in Arabic and other Eastern languages he was the most distinguished pupil of Erpenius. In 1622 he accompanied the Dutch embassy to Morocco, and on his return he was chosen to succeed Erpenius (1624). In the following year he set out on a Syrian and Arabian tour from which he did not return until 1629. The remainder of his life was spent at Leiden where he held the chair of mathematics as well as that of Arabic. He died on the 28th of September 1667.

His most important work is the *Lexicon Arabico-Latinum*, fol., Leiden, 1653, which, based on the *Sihah* of Al-Jauhari, was only superseded by the corresponding work of Freytag. Among his earlier publications may be mentioned editions of various Arabic texts (*Proverbia quaedam Alis, imperatoris Muslemici, et Carmen Tograipoëtae doctissimi, necnon dissertatio quaedam Aben Synae*, 1629; and *Ahmedis Arabsiadae vitae et rerum gestarum Timuri, qui vulgo Tamer, lanes dicitur, historia*, 1636). In 1656 he published a new edition, with considerable additions, of the *Grammatica Arabica* of Erpenius. After his death, there was found among his papers a *Dictionarium Persico-Latinum* which was published, with additions, by Edmund Castell in his *Lexicon heptaglotton* (1669). Golius also edited, translated and annotated the astronomical treatise of Alfragan (*Muhammedis, filii Ketiri Ferganensis, qui vulgo Alfraganus dicitur, elementa astronomica Arabice et Latine*, 1669).

GOLLNOW, a town of Germany, in the Prussian province of Pomerania, on the right bank of the Ihna, 14 m. N.N.E. of Stettin, with which it has communication by rail and steamer. Pop. (1905) 8539. It possesses two Evangelical churches, a synagogue and some small manufactures. Gollnow was founded in 1190, and was raised to the rank of a town in 1268. It was for a time a Hanse town, and came into the possession of Prussia in 1720, having belonged to Sweden since 1648.

GOLOSH, or GALOSH (from the Fr. *galoche*, Low Lat. *calopedes*, a wooden shoe or clog; an adaptation of the Gr. καλοπόδιον, a diminutive formed of κᾱλον, wood, and ποῦς, foot), originally a wooden shoe or patten, or merely a wooden sole fastened to the foot by a strap or cord. In the middle ages "galosh" was a general term for a boot or shoe, particularly one with a wooden sole. In modern usage, it is an outer shoe worn in bad weather to protect the inner one, and keep the feet dry. Goloshes are now almost universally made of rubber, and in the United States they are known as "rubbers" simply, the word golosh being rarely if ever used. In the bootmakers' trade, a "golosh" is the piece of leather, of a make stronger than, or different from that of the "uppers," which runs around the bottom part of a boot or shoe, just above the sole.

GOLOVIN, FEDOR ALEKSYEEVICH, COUNT (d. 1706), Russian statesman, learnt, like so many of his countrymen in later times, the business of a ruler in the Far East. During the regency of Sophia, sister of Peter the Great, he was sent to the Amur to defend the new Muscovite fortress of Albazin against the Chinese. In 1689 he concluded with the Celestial empire the treaty of Nerchinsk, by which the line of the Amur, as far as its tributary the Gorbitsa, was retroceded to China because of the impossibility of seriously defending it. In Peter's grand embassy to the West in 1697 Golovin occupied the second place immediately after Lefort. It was his chief duty to hire foreign sailors and obtain everything necessary for the construction and complete equipment of a fleet. On Lefort's death, in March 1699, he succeeded him as admiral-general. The same year he was created the first Russian count, and was also the first to be decorated with the newly-instituted Russian order of St Andrew. The conduct of foreign affairs was at the same time entrusted to him, and from 1699 to his death he was "the premier minister of the tsar." Golovin's first achievement as foreign minister was to supplement the treaty of Carlowitz, by which peace with Turkey had only been secured for three years, by concluding with the Porte a new treaty at Constantinople (June 13, 1700), by which the term of the peace was extended to thirty years and, besides other concessions, the Azov district and a strip of territory extending thence to Kuban were ceded to Russia. He also controlled, with consummate ability, the operations of the brand-new Russian diplomatists at the various foreign courts. His superiority over all his Muscovite contemporaries was due to the fact that he was already a statesman, in the modern sense, while they were still learning the elements of statesmanship. His death was an irreparable loss to the tsar, who wrote upon the despatch announcing it, the words "Peter filled with grief."

See R. N. Bain, *The First Romanovs* (London, 1905).

GOLOVKIN, GAVRIIL IVANOVICH, COUNT (1660-1734), Russian statesman, was attached (1677), while still a lad, to the court of the tsarevitch Peter, afterwards Peter the Great, with whose mother Natalia he was connected, and vigilantly guarded him during the disquieting period of the regency of Sophia, sister of Peter the Great (1682-1689). He accompanied the young tsar abroad on his first foreign tour, and worked by his side in the dockyards of Saardam. In 1706 he succeeded Golovin in the direction of foreign affairs, and was created the first Russian grand-chancellor on the field of Poltava (1709). Golovkin held this office for twenty-five years. In the reign of Catherine I. he became a member of the supreme privy council which had the chief conduct of affairs during this and the succeeding reigns. The empress also entrusted him with her last will whereby she appointed the young Peter II. her successor and Golovkin one of his guardians. On the death of Peter II. in 1730 he declared openly in favour of Anne, duchess of Courland, in opposition to the aristocratic Dolgorukis and Golitsuins, and his determined attitude on behalf of autocracy was the chief cause of the failure of the proposed constitution, which would have converted Russia into a limited monarchy. Under Anne he was a member of the first cabinet formed in Russia, but had less influence in affairs than Ostermann and Münnich. In 1707 he was created a count of the Holy Roman empire, and in 1710 a count of the Russian empire. He was one of the wealthiest, and at the same time one of the stingiest, magnates of his day. His ignorance of any language but his own made his intercourse with foreign ministers very inconvenient.

See R. N. Bain, *The Pupils of Peter the Great* (London, 1897).

GOLOVNIN, VASILY MIKHAILOVICH (1776-1831), Russian vice-admiral, was born on the 20th of April 1776 in the village of Gulynki in the province of Ryazan, and received his education at the Cronstadt naval school. From 1801 to 1806 he served as a volunteer in the English navy. In 1807 he was commissioned by the Russian government to survey the coasts of Kamchatka and of Russian America, including also the Kurile Islands. Golovnin sailed round the Cape of Good Hope, and on the 5th of October 1809, arrived in Kamchatka. In 1810, whilst attempting to survey the coast of the island of Kunashiri, he was seized by the Japanese, and was retained by them as a prisoner, until the 13th of October 1813, when he was liberated, and in the following year he returned to St Petersburg. Soon after this the government planned another expedition, which had for its object the circumnavigation of the globe by a Russian ship, and Golovnin was appointed to the command. He started from St Petersburg on the 7th of September 1817, sailed round Cape Horn, and arrived in Kamchatka in the following May. He returned to Europe by way of the Cape of Good Hope, and landed at St Petersburg on the 17th of September 1819. He died on the 12th of July 1831.

Golovnin published several works, of which the following are the most important:— *Journey to Kamchatka* (2 vols., 1819); *Journey Round the World* (2 vols., 1822); and *Narrative of my Captivity in Japan, 1811-1813* (2 vols., 1816). The last has been translated into French, German and English, the English edition being in three volumes (1824). A complete edition of his works was published at St Petersburg in five volumes in 1864, with maps and charts, and a biography of the author by N. Grech.

GOLTZ, BOGUMIL (1801-1870), German humorist and satirist, was born at Warsaw on the 20th of March 1801. After attending the classical schools of Marienwerder and Königsberg, he learnt farming on an estate near Thorn, and in 1821 entered the university of Breslau as a student of philosophy. But he soon abandoned an academical career, and, after returning for a while to country life, retired to the small town of Gollub, where he devoted himself to literary studies. In 1847 he settled at Thorn, "the home of Copernicus," where he died on the 12th of November 1870. Goltz is best known to literary fame by his *Buch der Kindheit* (Frankfort, 1847; 4th ed., Berlin, 1877), in which, after the style of Jean Paul, and Adalbert Stifter, but with a more modern realism, he gives a charming and idyllic description of the impressions of his own childhood. Among his other works must be noted *Ein Jugendleben* (1852); *Der Mensch und die Leute* (1858); *Zur Charakteristik und Naturgeschichte der Frauen* (1859); *Zur Geschichte und Charakteristik des deutschen Genius* (1864), and *Die Weltklugheit und die Lebensweisheit* (1869).

Goltz's works have not been collected, but a selection will be found in Reclam's *Universalbibliothek* (ed. by P. Stein, 1901 and 1906). See O. Roquette, *Siebzig Jahre*, i. (1894).

GOLTZ, COLMAR, FREIHERR VON DER (1843-   ), Prussian soldier and military writer, was born at Bielkenfeld, East Prussia, on the 12th of August 1843, and entered the Prussian infantry in 1861. In 1864 he entered the Berlin Military Academy, but was temporarily withdrawn in 1866 to serve in the Austrian war, in which he was wounded at Trautenau. In 1867 he joined the topographical section of the general staff, and at the beginning of the Franco-German War of 1870-71 was attached to the staff of Prince Frederick Charles. He took part in the battles of Vionville and Gravelotte and in the siege of Metz. After its fall he served under the Red Prince in the campaign of the Loire, including the battles of Orleans and Le Mans. He was appointed in 1871 professor at the military school at Potsdam, and the same year was promoted captain and placed in the historical section of the general staff. It was then he wrote *Die Operationen der II. Armee bis zur Capitulation von Metz* and *Die Sieben Tage von Le Mans*, both published in 1873. In 1874 he was appointed to the staff of the 6th division, and while so employed wrote *Die Operationen der II. Armee an der Loire and Léon Gambetta und seine Armeen*, published in 1875 and 1877 respectively. The latter was translated into French the same year, and both are impartially written. The views expressed in the latter work led to his being sent back to regimental duty for a time, but it was not long before he returned to the military history section. In 1878 von der Goltz was appointed lecturer in military history at the military academy at Berlin, where he remained for five years and attained the rank of major. He published, in 1883, *Rossbach und Jena* (new and revised edition, *Von Rossbach bis Jena und Auerstädt*, 1906), *Das Volk in Waffen* (English translation *The Nation in Arms*), both of which quickly became military classics, and during his residence in Berlin contributed many articles to the military journals. In June 1883 his services were lent to Turkey to reorganize the military establishments of the country. He spent twelve years in this work, the result of which appeared in the Greco-Turkish War of 1897, and he was made a pasha and in 1895 a *mushir* or field-marshal. On his return to Germany in 1896 he became a lieutenant-general and commander of the 5th division, and in 1898, head of the Engineer and Pioneer Corps and inspector-general of fortifications. In 1900 he was made general of infantry and in 1902 commander of the I. army corps. In 1907 he was made inspector-general of the newly created sixth army inspection established at Berlin, and in 1908 was given the rank of colonel-general (*Generaloberst*).

In addition to the works already named and frequent contributions to military periodical literature, he wrote *Kriegführung* (1895, later edition *Krieg- und Heerführung*, 1901; Eng. trans. *The Conduct of War*); *Der thessalische Krieg* (Berlin, 1898); *Ein Ausflug nach Macedonien* (1894); *Anatolische Ausflüge* (1896); a map and description of the environs of Constantinople; *Von Jena bis Pr. Eylau* (1907), a most important historical work, carrying on the story of *Rossbach und Jena* to the peace of Tilsit, &c.

GOLTZIUS, HENDRIK (1558-1617), Dutch painter and engraver, was born in 1558 at Mülebrecht, in the duchy of Jülich. After studying painting on glass for some years under his father, he was taught the use of the burin by Dirk Volkertsz Coornhert, a Dutch engraver of mediocre attainment, whom he soon surpassed, but who retained his services for his own advantage. He was also employed by Philip Galle to engrave a set of prints of the history of Lucretia. At the age of twenty-one he married a widow somewhat advanced in years, whose money enabled him to establish at Haarlem an independent business; but his unpleasant relations with her so affected his health that he found it advisable in 1590 to make a tour through Germany to Italy, where he acquired an intense admiration for the works of Michelangelo, which led him to surpass that master in the grotesqueness and extravagance of his designs. He returned to Haarlem considerably improved in health, and laboured there at his art till his death, on the 1st of January 1617. Goltzius ought not to be judged chiefly by the works he valued most, his eccentric imitations of Michelangelo. His portraits, though mostly miniatures, are master-pieces of their kind, both on account of their exquisite finish, and as fine studies of individual character. Of his larger heads, the life-size portrait of himself is probably the most striking example. His "master-pieces," so called from their being attempts to imitate the style of the old masters, have perhaps been overpraised. In his command of the burin Goltzius is not surpassed even by Dürer; but his technical skill is often unequally aided by higher artistic qualities. Even, however, his eccentricities and extravagances are greatly counterbalanced by the beauty and freedom of his execution. He began painting at the age of forty-two, but none of his works in this branch of art—some of which are in the imperial collection at Vienna—display any special excellences. He also executed a few pieces in chiaroscuro.

His prints amount to more than 300 plates, and are fully described in Bartsch's *Peintre-graveur*, and Weigel's supplement to the same work.

GOLUCHOWSKI, AGENOR, COUNT (1849-   ), Austrian statesman, was born on the 25th of March 1849. His father, descended from an old and noble Polish family, was governor of Galicia. Entering the diplomatic service, the son was in 1872 appointed attaché to the Austrian embassy at Berlin, where he became secretary of legation, and thence he was transferred to Paris. After rising to the rank of counsellor of legation, he was in 1887 made minister at Bucharest, where he remained till 1893. In these positions he acquired a great reputation as a firm and skilful diplomatist, and on the retirement of Count Kalnoky in May 1895 was chosen to succeed him as Austro-Hungarian minister for foreign affairs. The appointment of a Pole caused some surprise in view of the importance of Austrian relations with Russia (then rather strained) and Germany, but the choice was justified by events. In his speech of that year to the delegations he declared the maintenance of the Triple Alliance, and in particular the closest intimacy with Germany, to be the keystone of Austrian policy; at the same time he dwelt on the traditional friendship between Austria and Great Britain, and expressed his desire for a good understanding with all the powers. In pursuance of this policy he effected an understanding with Russia, by which neither power was to exert any separate influence in the Balkan peninsula, and thus removed a long-standing cause of friction. This understanding was formally ratified during a visit to St Petersburg on which he accompanied the emperor in April 1897. He took the lead in establishing the European concert during the Armenian troubles of 1896, and again resisted isolated action on the part of any of the great powers during the Cretan troubles and the Greco-Turkish War. In November 1897, when the Austro-Hungarian flag was insulted at Mersina, he threatened to bombard the town if instant reparation were not made, and by his firm attitude greatly enhanced Austrian prestige in the East. In his speech to the delegations in 1898 he dwelt on the necessity of expanding Austria's mercantile marine, and of raising the fleet to a strength which, while not vying with the fleets of the great naval powers, would ensure respect for the Austrian flag wherever her interests needed protection. He also hinted at the necessity for European combination to resist American competition. The understanding with Russia in the matter of the Balkan States temporarily endangered friendly relations with Italy, 228who thought her interests threatened, until Goluchowski guaranteed in 1898 the existing order. He further encouraged a good understanding with Italy by personal conferences with the Italian foreign minister, Tittoni, in 1904 and 1905. Count Lamsdorff visited Vienna in December 1902, when arrangements were made for concerted action in imposing on the sultan reforms in the government of Macedonia. Further steps were taken after Goluchowski's interview with the tsar at Mürzsteg in 1903, and two civil agents representing the countries were appointed for two years to ensure the execution of the promised reforms. This period was extended in 1905, when Goluchowski was the chief mover in forcing the Porte, by an international naval demonstration at Mitylene, to accept financial control by the powers in Macedonia. At the conference assembled at Algeciras to settle the Morocco Question, Austria supported the German position, and after the close of the conferences the emperor William II. telegraphed to Goluchowski: "You have proved yourself a brilliant second on the duelling ground and you may feel certain of like services from me in similar circumstances." This pledge was redeemed in 1908, when Germany's support of Austria in the Balkan crisis proved conclusive. By the Hungarians, however, Goluchowski was hated; he was suspected of having inspired the emperor's opposition to the use of Magyar in the Hungarian army, and was made responsible for the slight offered to the Magyar deputation by Francis Joseph in September 1905. So long as he remained in office there was no hope of arriving at a settlement of a matter which threatened the disruption of the Dual monarchy, and on the 11th of October 1906 he was forced to resign.

GOMAL, or GUMAL, the name of a river of Afghanistan, and of a mountain pass on the Dera Ismail Khan border of the North-West Frontier Province of British India. The Gomal river, one of the most important rivers in Afghanistan, rises in the unexplored regions to the south-east of Ghazni. Its chief tributary is the Zhob. Within the limits of British territory the Gomal forms the boundary between the North-West Frontier Province and Baluchistan, and more or less between the Pathan and Baluch races. The Gomal pass is the most important pass on the Indian frontier between the Khyber and the Bolan. It connects Dera Ismail Khan with the Gomal valley in Afghanistan, and has formed for centuries the outlet for the povindah trade. Until the year 1889 this pass was almost unknown to the Anglo-Indian official; but in that year the government of India decided that, in order to maintain the safety of the railway as well as to perfect communication between Quetta and the Punjab, the Zhob valley should, like the Bori valley, be brought under British protection and control, and the Gomal pass should be opened. After the Waziristan expedition of 1894 Wana was occupied by British troops in order to dominate the Gomal and Waziristan; but on the formation of the North-West Frontier Province in 1901 it was decided to replace these troops by the South Waziristan militia, who now secure the safety of the pass.

GOMARUS, FRANZ (1563-1641), Dutch theologian, was born at Bruges on the 30th of January 1563. His parents, having embraced the principles of the Reformation, emigrated to the Palatinate in 1578, in order to enjoy freedom to profess their new faith, and they sent their son to be educated at Strassburg under Johann Sturm (1507-1589). He remained there three years, and then went in 1580 to Neustadt, whither the professors of Heidelberg had been driven by the elector-palatine because they were not Lutherans. Here his teachers in theology were Zacharius Ursinus (1534-1583), Hieronymus Zanchius (1560-1590), and Daniel Tossanus (1541-1602). Crossing to England towards the end of 1582, he attended the lectures of John Rainolds (1549-1607) at Oxford, and those of William Whitaker (1548-1595) at Cambridge. He graduated at Cambridge in 1584, and then went to Heidelberg, where the faculty had been by this time re-established. He was pastor of a Reformed Dutch church in Frankfort from 1587 till 1593, when the congregation was dispersed by persecution. In 1594 he was appointed professor of theology at Leiden, and before going thither received from the university of Heidelberg the degree of doctor. He taught quietly at Leiden till 1603, when Jakobus Arminius came to be one of his colleagues in the theological faculty, and began to teach Pelagian doctrines and to create a new party in the university. Gomarus immediately set himself earnestly to oppose these views in his classes at college, and was supported by Johann B. Bogermann (1570-1637), who afterwards became professor of theology at Franeker. Arminius "sought to make election dependent upon faith, whilst they sought to enforce absolute predestination as the rule of faith, according to which the whole Scriptures are to be interpreted" (J. A. Dorner, *History of Protestant Theology*, i. p. 417). Gomarus then became the leader of the opponents of Arminius, who from that circumstance came to be known as Gomarists. He engaged twice in personal disputation with Arminius in the assembly of the estates of Holland in 1608, and was one of five Gomarists who met five Arminians or Remonstrants in the same assembly of 1609. On the death of Arminius shortly after this time, Konrad Vorstius (1569-1622), who sympathized with his views, was appointed to succeed him, in spite of the keen opposition of Gomarus and his friends; and Gomarus took his defeat so ill that he resigned his post, and went to Middleburg in 1611, where he became preacher at the Reformed church, and taught theology and Hebrew in the newly founded *Illustre Schule*. From this place he was called in 1614 to a chair of theology at Saumur, where he remained four years, and then accepted a call as professor of theology and Hebrew to Groningen, where he stayed till his death on the 11th of January 1641. He took a leading part in the synod of Dort, assembled in 1618 to judge of the doctrines of Arminius. He was a man of ability, enthusiasm and learning, a considerable Oriental scholar, and also a keen controversialist. He took part in revising the Dutch translation of the Old Testament in 1633, and after his death a book by him, called the *Lyra Davidis*, was published, which sought to explain the principles of Hebrew metre, and which created some controversy at the time, having been opposed by Louis Cappel. His works were collected and published in one volume folio, in Amsterdam in 1645. He was succeeded at Groningen in 1643 by his pupil Samuel Maresius (1599-1673).

GOMBERVILLE, MARIN LE ROY, SIEUR DU PARC ET DE (1600-1674), French novelist and miscellaneous writer, was born at Paris in 1600. At fourteen years of age he wrote a volume of verse, at twenty a *Discours sur l'histoire* and at twenty-two a pastoral, *La Carithée*, which is really a novel. The persons in it, though still disguised as shepherds and shepherdesses, represent real persons for whose identification the author himself provides a key. This was followed by a more ambitious attempt, *Polexandre* (5 vols. 1632-1637). The hero wanders through the world in search of the island home of the princess Alcidiane. It contains much history and geography; the travels of Polexandre extending to such unexpected places as Benin, the Canary Islands, Mexico and the Antilles, and incidentally we learn all that was then known of Mexican history. *Cythérée* (4 vols.) appeared in 1630-1642, and in 1651 the *Jeune Alcidiane*, intended to undo any harm the earlier novels may have done, for Gomberville became a Jansenist and spent the last twenty-five years of his life in pious retirement. He was one of the earliest and most energetic members of the Academy. He died in Paris on the 14th of June 1674.

GOMER, the biblical name of a race appearing in the table of nations (Gen. x. 2), as the "eldest son" of Japheth and the "father" of Ashkenaz, Riphath and Togarmah; and in Ezek. xxxviii. 6 as a companion of "the house of Togarmah in the uttermost parts of the north," and an ally of Gog; both Gomer and Togarmah being credited with "hordes,"[1] E.V., *i.e.* "bands" or "armies." The "sons" of Gomer are probably tribes of north-east Asia Minor and Armenia, and Gomer is identified with the Cimmerians. These are referred to in cuneiform inscriptions under the Assyrian name *gimmirā* (*gimirrai*) as raiding Asia Minor from the north and north-east of the Black 229Sea, and overrunning Lydia in the 7th century B.C. (see CIMMERII, SCYTHIA, LYDIA). They do not seem to have made any permanent settlements, unless some such are indicated by the fact that the Armenians called Cappadocia *Gamir*. It is, however, suggested that this name is borrowed from the Old Testament.2

The name Gomer (Gomer bath Diblaim) was also borne by the unfaithful wife of Hosea, whom he pardoned and took back (Hosea i. 3). Hosea uses these incidents as symbolic of the sin, punishment and redemption of Israel, but there is no need to regard Gomer as a purely imaginary person.

(W. H. BE.)

1אגף *Āgaph*, a word peculiar to Ezekiel, Clarendon Press *Heb. Lex.*
2A. Jeremias, *Das A.T. im Lichte des alten Orients*, pp. 145 f.

GOMERA, an island in the Atlantic Ocean, forming part of the Spanish archipelago of the Canary Islands (*q.v.*). Pop. (1900) 15,358; area 144 sq. m. Gomera lies 20 m. W.S.W. of Teneriffe. Its greatest length is about 23 m. The coast is precipitous and the interior mountainous, but Gomera has the most wood and is the best watered of the group. The inhabitants are very poor. Dromedaries are bred on Gomera in large numbers. San Sebastian (3187) is the chief town and a port. It was visited by Columbus on his first voyage of discovery in 1492.

GOMEZ, DIOGO (DIEGO) (fl. 1440-1482), Portuguese seaman, explorer and writer. We first trace him as a *cavalleiro* of the royal household; in 1440 he was appointed receiver of the royal customs—in 1466 judge—at Cintra (*juiz das causas e feitorias contadas de Cintra*); on the 5th of March 1482 he was confirmed in the last-named office. He wrote, especially for the benefit of Martin Behaim, a Latin chronicle of great value, dealing with the life and discoveries of Prince Henry the Navigator, and divided into three parts: (1) *De prima inventione Guineae*; (2) *De insulis primo inventis in mare* (*sic*)*Occidentis*; (3) *De inventione insularum de Açores*. This chronicle contains the only contemporary account of the rediscovery of the Azores by the Portuguese in Prince Henry's service, and is also noteworthy for its clear ascription to the prince of deliberate scientific and commercial purpose in exploration. For, on the one hand, the infante sent out his caravels to search for new lands (*ad quaerendas terras*) from his wish to know the more distant parts of the western ocean, and in the hope of finding islands or *terra firma* beyond the limits laid down by Ptolemy (*ultra descriptionem Tolomei*); on the other hand, his information as to the native trade from Tunis to Timbuktu and the Gambia helped to inspire his persistent exploration of the West African coast—"to seek those lands by way of the sea." Chart and quadrant were used on the prince's vessels, as by Gomez himself on reaching the Cape Verde Islands; Henry, at the time of Diogo's first voyage, was in correspondence with an Oran merchant who kept him informed upon events even in the Gambia *hinterland*; and, before the discovery of the Senegal and Cape Verde in 1445, Gomez' royal patron had already gained reliable information of *some* route to Timbuktu. In the first part of his chronicle Gomez tells how, no long time after the disastrous expedition of the Danish nobleman "Vallarte" (Adalbert) in 1448, he was sent out in command of three vessels along the West African coast, accompanied by one Jacob, an Indian interpreter, to be employed in the event of reaching India. After passing the Rio Grande, beyond Cape Verde, strong currents checked his course; his officers and men feared that they were approaching the extremity of the ocean, and he put back to the Gambia. He ascended this river a considerable distance, to the negro town of "Cantor," whither natives came from "Kukia" and Timbuktu for trade; he gives elaborate descriptions of the negro world he had now penetrated, refers to the Sierra Leone ("Serra Lyoa") Mountains, sketches the course of this range, and says much of Kukia (in the upper Niger basin?), the centre of the West African gold trade, and the resort of merchants and caravans from Tunis, Fez, Cairo and "all the land of the Saracens." Mahommedanism was already dominant at the Cambria estuary, but Gomez seems to have won over at least one important chief, with his court, to Christianity and Portuguese allegiance. Another African voyage, apparently made in 1462, two years after Henry the Navigator's death (though assigned by some to 1460), resulted in a fresh discovery of the Cape Verde Islands, already found by Cadamosto (*q.v.*). To the island of Santiago Gomez, like his Venetian forerunner, claims to have given its present name. His narrative is a leading authority on the last illness and death of Prince Henry, as well as on the life, achievements and purposes of the latter; here alone is recorded what appears to have been the earliest of the navigator's exploring ventures, that which under João de Trasto reached Grand Canary in 1415.

Of Gomez' chronicle there is only one MS., viz. *Cod. Hisp.* 27, in the Hof- und Staats-Bibliothek, Munich; the original Latin text was printed by Schmeller "Über Valentim Fernandez Alemão" in the *Abhandlungen der philosoph.-philolog. Kl. der bayerisch. Akademie der Wissenschaften,* vol. iv., part iii. (Munich, 1847); see also Sophus Ruge, "Die Entdeckung der Azoren," pp. 149-180 (esp. 178-179) in the 27th*Jahresbericht des Vereins für Erdkunde* (Dresden, 1901); Jules Mees, *Histoire de la découverte des îles Açores,* pp. 44-45, 125-127 (Ghent, 1901); R. H. Major, *Life of Prince Henry the Navigator,* pp. xviii., xix., 64-65, 287-299, 303-305 (London, 1868); C. R. Beazley, *Prince Henry the Navigator,* 289-298, 304-305; and Introduction to Azurara's *Discovery and Conquest of Guinea,* ii., iv., xiv., xxv.-xxvii., xcii.-xcvi. (London, 1899).

(C. R. B.)

GOMEZ DE AVELLANEDA, GERTRUDIS (1814-1873), Spanish dramatist and poet, was born at Puerto Príncipe (Cuba) on the 23rd of March 1814, and removed to Spain in 1836. Her *Poesías líricas* (1841), issued with a laudatory preface by Gallego, made a most favourable impression and were republished with additional poems in 1850. In 1846 she married a diplomatist named Pedro Sabater, became a widow within a year, and in 1853 married Colonel Domingo Verdugo. Meanwhile she had published *Sab* (1839), *Guatimozín* (1846), and other novels of no great importance. She obtained, however, a series of successes on the stage with *Alfonso Munio* (1844), a tragedy in the new romantic manner; with *Saúl* (1849), a biblical drama indirectly suggested by Alfieri; and with *Baltasar* (1858), a piece which bears some resemblance to Byron's *Sardanapalus.* Her commerce with the world had not diminished her natural piety, and, on the death of her second husband, she found so much consolation in religion that she had thoughts of entering a convent. She died at Madrid on the 2nd of February 1873, full of mournful forebodings as to the future of her adopted country. It is impossible to agree with Villemain that "le génie de don Luis de Léon et de sainte Thérèse a reparu sous le voile funèbre de Gomez de Avellaneda," for she has neither the monk's mastery of poetic form nor the nun's sublime simplicity of soul. She has a grandiose tragical vision of life, a vigorous eloquence rooted in pietistic pessimism, a dramatic gift effective in isolated acts or scenes; but she is deficient in constructive power and in intellectual force, and her lyrics, though instinct with melancholy beauty, or the tenderness of resigned devotion, too often lack human passion and sympathy. The edition of her *Obras literarias* (5 vols., 1869-1871), still incomplete, shows a scrupulous care for minute revision uncommon in Spanish writers; but her emendations are seldom happy. But she is interesting as a link between the classic and romantic schools of poetry, and, whatever her artistic shortcomings, she has no rivals of her own sex in Spain during the 19th century.

GOMM, SIR WILLIAM MAYNARD (1784-1875), British soldier, was gazetted to the 9th Foot at the age of ten, in recognition of the services of his father, Lieut.-Colonel William Gomm, who was killed in the attack on Guadaloupe (1794). He joined his regiment as a lieutenant in 1799, and fought in Holland under the duke of York, and subsequently was with Pulteney's Ferrol expedition. In 1803 he became Captain, and shortly afterwards qualified as a staff officer at the High Wycombe military college. On the general staff he was with Cathcart at Copenhagen, with Wellington in the Peninsula, and on Moore's staff at Corunna. He was also on Chatham's staff in the disastrous Walcheren expedition of 1809. In 1810 he rejoined the Peninsular army as Leith's staff officer, and took part in all the battles of 1810, 1811 and 1812, winning his majority after Fuentes d'Onor and his lieutenant-colonelcy at Salamanca. His careful reconnaissances and skilful leading were invaluable to Wellington in the Vittoria campaign, and to the end of the war he was one of the 230most trusted men of his staff. His reward was a transfer to the Coldstream Guards and the K.C.B. In the Waterloo campaign he served on the staff of the 5th British Division. From the peace until 1839 he was employed on home service, becoming colonel in 1829 and major-general in 1837. From 1839 to 1842 he commanded the troops in Jamaica. He became lieutenant-general in 1846, and was sent out to be commander-in-chief in India, arriving only to find that his appointment had been cancelled in favour of Sir Charles Napier, whom, however, he eventually succeeded (1850-1855). In 1854 he became general and in 1868 field marshal. In 1872 he was appointed constable of the Tower, and he died in 1875. He was twice married, but had no children. His *Letters and Journals* were published by F. C. Carr-Gomm in 1881. Five "Field Marshal Gomm" scholarships were afterwards founded in his memory at Keble College, Oxford.

GOMPERS, SAMUEL (1850-   ), American labour leader, was born in London on the 27th of January 1850. He was put to work in a shoe-factory when ten years old, but soon became apprenticed to a cigar-maker, removed to New York in 1863, became a prominent member of the International Cigar-makers' Union, was its delegate at the convention of the Federation of

Organized Trade and Labor Unions of the United States and Canada, later known as the American Federation of Labor, of which he became first president in 1882. He was successively re-elected up to 1895, when the opposition of the Socialist Labor Party, then attempting to incorporate the Federation into itself, secured his defeat; he was re-elected in the following year. In 1894 he became editor of the Federation's organ, *The American Federationist*.

GOMPERZ, THEODOR (1832-   ), German philosopher and classical scholar, was born at Brünn on the 29th of March 1832. He studied at Brünn and at Vienna under Herman Bonitz. Graduating at Vienna in 1867 he became *Privatdozent*, and subsequently professor of classical philology (1873). In 1882 he was elected a member of the Academy of Science. He received the degree of Doctor of Philosophy *honoris causa* from the university of Königsberg, and Doctor of Literature from the universities of Dublin and Cambridge, and became correspondent for several learned societies. His principal works are: *Demosthenes der Staatsmann* (1864), *Philodemi de ira liber* (1864). *Traumdeutung und Zauberei* (1866), *Herkulanische Studien*(1865-1866), *Beiträge zur Kritik und Erklärung griech. Schriftsteller* (7 vols., 1875-1900), *Neue Bruchstücke Epikurs* (1876), *Die Bruchstücke der griech. Tragiker und Cobets neueste kritische Manier* (1878), *Herodoteische Studien* (1883), *Ein bisher unbekanntes griech. Schriftsystem* (1884), *Zu Philodems Büchern von der Musik* (1885), *Über den Abschluss des herodoteischen Geschichtswerkes* (1886), *Platonische Aufsätze* (3 vols., 1887-1905),*Zu Heraklits Lehre und den Überresten seines Werkes* (1887), *Zu Aristoteles' Poëtik* (2 parts, 1888-1896), *Über die Charaktere Theophrasts* (1888),*Nachlese zu den Bruchstücken der griech. Tragiker* (1888), *Die Apologie der Heilkunst* (1890), *Philodem und die ästhetischen Schriften der herculanischen Bibliothek* (1891), *Die Schrift vom Staatswesen der Athener* (1891), *Die jüngst entdeckten Überreste einer den Platonischen Phädon enthaltenden Papyrusrolle* (1892), *Aus der Hekale des Kallimachos* (1893), *Essays und Erinnerungen* (1905). He supervised a translation of J. S. Mill's complete works (12 vols., Leipzig, 1869-1880), and wrote a life (Vienna, 1889) of Mill. His *Griechische Denker: Geschichte der antiken Philosophie*(vols. i. and ii., Leipzig, 1893 and 1902) was translated into English by L. Magnus (vol. i., 1901).

GONAGUAS ("borderers"), descendants of a very old cross between the Hottentots and the Kaffirs, on the "ethnical divide" between the two races, apparently before the arrival of the whites in South Africa. They have been always a despised race and regarded as outcasts by the Bantu peoples. They were threatened with extermination during the Kaffir wars, but were protected by the British. At present they live in settled communities under civil magistrates without any tribal organization, and in some districts could be scarcely distinguished from the other natives but for their broken Hottentot-Dutch-English speech.

GONÇALVES DIAS, ANTONIO (1823-1864), Brazilian lyric poet, was born near the town of Caxias, in Maranhão. From the university of Coimbra, in Portugal, he returned in 1845 to his native province, well-equipped with legal lore, but the literary tendency which was strong within him led him to try his fortune as an author at Rio de Janeiro. Here he wrote for the newspaper press, ventured to appear as a dramatist, and in 1846 established his reputation by a volume of poems—*Primeiros Cantos*—which appealed to the national feelings of his Brazilian readers, were remarkable for their autobiographic impress, and by their beauty of expression and rhythm placed their author at the head of the lyric poets of his country. In 1848 he followed up his success by *Segundos Cantos e sextilhas de Frei Antão*, in which, as the title indicates, he puts a number of the pieces in the mouth of a simple old Dominican friar; and in the following year, in fulfilment of the duties of his new post as professor of Brazilian history in the Imperial College of Pedro II. at Rio de Janeiro, he published an edition of Berredo's *Annaes historicos do Maranhão* and added a sketch of the migrations of the Indian tribes. A third volume of poems, which appeared with the title of *Ultimos Cantos* in 1851, was practically the poet's farewell to the service of the muse, for he spent the next eight years engaged under government patronage in studying the state of public instruction in the north and the educational institutions of Europe. On his return to Brazil in 1860 he was appointed a member of an expedition for the exploration of the province of Ceará, was forced in 1862 by the state of his health to try the effects of another visit to Europe, and died in September 1864, the vessel that was carrying him being wrecked off his native shores. While in Germany he published at Leipzig a complete collection of his lyrical poems, which went through several editions, the four first cantos of an epic poem called *Os Tymbiras* (1857) and a *Diccionario da lingua Tupy* (1858).

A complete edition of the works of Dias has made its appearance at Rio de Janeiro. See Wolf, *Brésil littéraire* (Berlin, 1863); Innocencio da Silva, *Diccionario bibliographico portuguez*, viii. 157; Sotero dos Reis, *Curso de litteratura portugueza e brazileira*, iv. (Maranhão, 1868); José Verissimo, *Estudos de literatura brazileira, segunda serie* (Rio, 1901).

GONCHAROV, IVAN ALEXANDROVICH (1812-1891), Russian novelist, was born 6/18 July 1812, being the son of a rich merchant in the town of Simbirsk. At the age of ten he was placed in one of the gymnasiums at Moscow, from which he passed, though not without some difficulty on account of his ignorance of Greek, into the Moscow University. He read many French works of fiction, and published a translation of one of the novels of Eugène Sue. During his university career he devoted himself to study, taking no interest in the political and Socialistic agitation among his fellow-students. He was first employed as secretary to the governor of Simbirsk, and afterwards in the ministry of finance at St Petersburg. Being absorbed in bureaucratic work, Goncharov paid no attention to the social questions then ardently discussed by such men as Herzen, Aksakov and Bielinski. He began his literary career by publishing translations from Schiller, Goethe and English novelists. His first original work was *Obuiknovennaya Istoria*, "A Common Story" (1847). In 1856 he sailed to Japan as secretary to Admiral Putiatin for the purpose of negotiating a commercial treaty, and on his return to Russia he published a description of the voyage under the title of "The Frigate *Pallada*." His best work is *Oblomov* (1857), which exposed the laziness and apathy of the smaller landed gentry in Russia anterior to the reforms of Alexander II. Russian critics have pronounced this work to be a faithful characterization of Russia and the Russians. Dobrolubov said of it, "Oblomofka [the country-seat of the Oblomovs] is our fatherland: something of Oblomov is to be found in every one of us." Peesarev, another celebrated critic, declared that "Oblomovism," as Goncharov called the sum total of qualities with which he invested the hero of his story, "is an illness fostered by the nature of the Slavonic character and the life of Russian society." In 1858 Goncharov was appointed a censor, and in 1868 he published another novel called *Obreev*. He was not a voluminous writer, and during the latter part of his life produced nothing of any importance. His death occurred on 15/27 September 1891.

231

GONCOURT, DE, a name famous in French literary history. EDMOND LOUIS ANTOINE HUOT DE GONCOURT was born at Nancy on the 26th of May 1822, and died at Champrosay on the 16th of July 1896. JULES ALFRED HUOT DE GONCOURT, his brother, was born in Paris on the 17th of December 1830, and died in Paris on the 20th of June 1870.

Writing always in collaboration, until the death of the younger, it was their ambition to be not merely novelists, inventing a new kind of novel, but historians; not merely historians, but the historians of a particular century, and of what was intimate and what is unknown in it; to be also discriminating, indeed innovating, critics of art, but of a certain section of art, the 18th century, in France and Japan; and also to collect pictures and bibelots, always of the French and Japanese 18th century. Their histories (*Portraits intimes du XVIIIe siècle* (1857), *La Femme au XVIIIe siècle* (1862), *La du Barry* (1878), &c.) are made entirely out of documents, autograph letters, scraps of costume, engravings, songs, the unconscious self-revelations of the time; their three volumes on *L'Art du XVIIIe siècle* (1859-1875) deal with Watteau and his followers in the same scrupulous, minutely enlightening way, with all the detail of unpublished documents; and when they came to write novels, it was with a similar attempt to give the inner, undiscovered, minute truths of contemporary existence, the *inédit* of life. The same morbidly sensitive noting of the *inédit*, of whatever came to them from their own sensations of things and people around them, gives its curious quality to the nine volumes of the *Journal*, 1887-1896, which will remain, perhaps, the truest and most poignant chapter of human history that they have written. Their novels, *Sœur   Philomène* (1861), *Renée   Mauperin* (1864), *Germinie   Lacerteux* (1865), *Manette Salomon* (1865), *Madame Gervaisais* (1869), and, by Edmond alone, *La Fille Elisa* (1878), *Les Frères Zemganno* (1879), *La Faustin* (1882), *Chérie*(1884), are, however, the work by which they will live as artists. Learning something from Flaubert, and teaching almost everything to Zola, they invented a new kind of novel, and their novels are the result of a new vision of the world, in which the very element of sight is decomposed, as in a picture of Monet. Seen through the nerves, in this conscious abandonment to the tricks of the eyesight, the world becomes a thing of broken patterns and conflicting colours, and uneasy movement. A novel of the Goncourts is made up of an infinite number of details, set side by side, every detail equally prominent. While a novel of Flaubert, for all its detail, gives above all things an impression of unity, a novel of the Goncourts deliberately dispenses with unity in order to give the sense of the passing of life, the heat and form of its moments as they pass. It is written in little chapters, sometimes no longer than a page, and each chapter is a separate notation of some significant event, some emotion or sensation which seems to throw sudden light on the picture of a soul. To the Goncourts humanity is as pictorial a thing as the world it moves in; they do not search further than "the physical basis of life," and they find everything that can be known of that unknown force written visibly upon the sudden faces of little incidents, little expressive moments. The soul, to them, is a series of moods, which succeed one another, certainly without any of the too arbitrary logic of the novelist who has conceived of character as a solid or consistent thing. Their novels are hardly stories at all, but picture-galleries, hung with pictures of the momentary aspects of the world. French critics have complained that the language of the Goncourts is no longer French, no longer the French of the past; and this is true. It is their distinction—the finest of their inventions—that, in order to render new sensations, a new vision of things, they invented a new language.

(A. SY.)

In his will Edmond de Goncourt left his estate for the endowment of an academy, the formation of which was entrusted to MM. Alphonse Daudet and Léon Hennique. The society was to consist of ten members, each of whom was to receive an annuity of 6000 francs, and a yearly prize of 5000 francs was to be awarded to the author of some work of fiction. Eight of the members of the new academy were nominated in the will. They were: Alphonse Daudet, J. K. Huysmans, Léon Hennique, Octave Mirbeau, the two brothers J. H. Rosny, Gustave Geffroy and Paul Margueritte. On the 19th of January 1903, after much litigation, the academy was constituted, with Elémir Bourges, Lucien Descaves and Léon Daudet as members in addition to those mentioned in de Goncourt's will, the place of Alphonse Daudet having been left vacant by his death in 1897.

On the brothers de Goncourt see the *Journal des Goncourt* already cited; also M. A. Belloc (afterwards Lowndes) and M. L. Shedlock, *Edmond and Jules de Goncourt, with Letters and Leaves from their Journals* (1895); Alidor Delzant, *Les Goncourt* (1889) which contains a valuable bibliography; *Lettres de Jules de Goncourt* (1888), with preface by H. Céard; R. Doumic, *Portraits d'écrivains* (1892); Paul Bourget, *Nouveaux Essais de psychologie contemporaine* (1886); Émile Zola, *Les Romanciers naturalistes* (1881). &c.

GONDA, a town and district of British India, in the Fyzabad division of the United Provinces. The town is 28 m. N.W. of Fyzabad, and is an important junction on the Bengal & North-Western railway. The site on which it stands was originally a jungle, in the centre of which was a cattle-fold (*Gontha* or *Gothah*), where the cattle were enclosed at night as a protection against wild beasts, and from this the town derives its name. Pop. (1901) 15,811. The cantonments were abandoned in 1863.

The district of Gonda has an area of 2813 sq. m. It consists of a vast plain with very slight undulations, studded with groves of mango trees. The surface consists of a rich alluvial deposit which is naturally divided into three great belts known as the *tarai* or swampy tract, the *uparhar* or uplands, and the *tarhar* or wet lowlands, all three being marvellously fertile. Several rivers flow through the district, but only two, the Gogra and Rapti, are of any commercial importance, the first being navigable throughout the year, and the latter during the rainy season. The country is dotted with small lakes, the water of which is largely used for irrigation. On the outbreak of the Mutiny in 1857, the raja of Gonda, after honourably escorting the government treasure to Fyzabad, joined the rebels. His estates, along with those of the rani of Tulsipur, were confiscated, and conferred as rewards upon the maharajas of Balrampur and Ajodhya, who had remained loyal. In 1901 the population was 1,403,195, showing a decrease of 4% in one decade. The district is traversed by the main line and three branches of the Bengal & Northwestern railway.

GONDAL, a native state of India, in the Kathiawar political agency of Bombay, situated in the centre of the peninsula of Kathiawar. Its area is 1024 sq. m.; pop. (1901) 162,859. The estimated gross revenue is about £100,000, and the tribute £7000. Grain and cotton are the chief products. The chief, whose title is Thakur Sahib, is a Jadeja Rajput, of the same clan as the Rao of Cutch. The Thakur Sahib, Sir Bhagvat Sinhji (b. 1865), was educated at the Rajkot college, and afterwards graduated in arts and medicine at the university of Edinburgh. He published (in English) a *Journal of a Visit to England* and *A Short History of Aryan Medical Science*. In 1892 he received the honorary degree of D.C.L. of Oxford University. He was created K.C.I.E. in 1887 and G.C.I.E. in 1897. The state has long been conspicuous for its progressive administration. It is traversed by a railway connecting it with Bhaunagar, Rajkot and the sea-board. The town of Gondal is 23 m. by rail S. of Rajkot; pop. (1901) 19,592.

GONDAR, properly GUENDAR, a town of Abyssinia, formerly the capital of the Amharic kingdom, situated on a basaltic ridge some 7500 ft. above the sea, about 21 m. N.E. of Lake Tsana, a splendid view of which is obtained from the castle. Two streams, the Angreb on the east side and the Gaha or Kaha on the west, flow from the ridge, and meeting below the town, pass onwards to the lake. In the early years of the 20th century the town was much decayed, numerous ruins of castles, palaces and churches indicating its former importance. It was never a compact city, being divided into districts separated from each other by open spaces. The chief quarters were those of the Abun-Bed or bishop, the Etchege-Bed or chief of the monks, the Debra Berhan or Church of the Light, and the Gemp or castle. There was also a quarter for the Mahommedans. Gondar was a small village when at the beginning of the 16th century it was chosen by the Negus Sysenius (Seged I.) as the capital of his kingdom. His son Fasilidas, or A'lem-Seged (1633-1667), was the builder of the castle which bears his name. Later emperors built other castles and palaces, the latest in date being 232that of the Negus Yesu II. This was erected about 1736, at which time Gondar appears to have been at the height of its prosperity. Thereafter it suffered greatly from the civil wars which raged in Abyssinia, and was more than once sacked. In 1868 it was much injured by the emperor Theodore, who did not spare either the castle or the churches. After the defeat of the Abyssinians at Debra Sin in August 1887 Gondar was looted and fired by the dervishes under Abu Anga. Although they held the town but a short time they inflicted very great damage, destroying many churches, further damaging the castles and carrying off much treasure. The population, estimated by James Bruce in 1770 at 10,000 families, had dwindled in 1905 to about 7000. Since the pacification of the Sudan by the British (1886-1889) there has been some revival of trade between Gondar and the regions of the Blue Nile. Among the inhabitants are numbers of Mahommedans, and there is a settlement of Falashas. Cotton, cloth, gold and silver ornaments, copper wares, fancy articles in bone and ivory, excellent saddles and shoes are among the products of the local industry.

Unlike any other buildings in Abyssinia, the castles and palaces of Gondar resemble, with some modifications, the medieval fortresses of Europe, the style of architecture being the result of the presence in the country of numbers of Portuguese. The Portuguese were expelled by Fasilidas, but his castle was built, by Indian workmen, under the superintendence of Abyssinians who had learned something of architecture from the Portuguese adventurers, helped possibly by Portuguese still in the country. The castle has two storeys, is 90 ft. by 84 ft., has a square tower and circular domed towers at the corners. The most extensive ruins are a group of royal buildings enclosed in a wall. These ruins include the palace of Yesu II., which has several fine chambers. Christian Levantines were employed in its construction and it was decorated in part with Venetian mirrors, &c. In the same enclosure is a small castle attributed to Yesu I. The exterior walls of the castles and palaces named are little damaged and give to Gondar a unique character among African towns. Of the forty-four churches, all in the circular Abyssinian style, which are said to have formerly existed in Gondar or its immediate neighbourhood, Major Powell-Cotton found only one intact in 1900. This church contained some well-executed native paintings of St George and the Dragon, The Last Supper, &c. Among the religious observances of the Christians of Gondar is that of bathing in large crowds in the Gaha on the Feast of the Baptist, and again, though in more orderly fashion, on Christmas day.

See E. Rüppell, *Reise in Abyssinien* (Frankfort-on-the-Main, 1838-1840); T. von Heuglin, *Reise nach Abessinien* (Jena, 1868); G. Lejean,*Voyage en Abyssinie* (Paris, 1872); Achille Raffray, *Afrique orientale; Abyssinie* (Paris, 1876); P. H. G. Powell-Cotton, *A Sporting Trip through Abyssinia*, chaps. 27-30 (London, 1902); and *Boll. Soc. Geog. Italiana* for 1909. Views of the castle are given by Heuglin, Raffray and Powell-Cotton.

GONDOKORO, a government station and trading-place on the east bank of the upper Nile, in 4° 54′ N., 31° 43′ E. It is the headquarters of the Northern Province of the (British) Uganda protectorate, is 1070 m. by river S. of Khartum and 350 m. N.N.W. in a direct line of Entebbe on Victoria Nyanza. The station, which is very unhealthy, is at the top of a cliff 25 ft. above the river-level. Besides houses for the civil and military authorities and the lines for the troops, there are a few huts inhabited by Bari, the natives of this part of the Nile. The importance of Gondokoro lies in the fact that it is within a few miles of the limit of navigability of the Nile from Khartum up stream. From this point the journey to Uganda is continued overland.

Gondokoro was first visited by Europeans in 1841-1842, when expeditions sent out by Mehemet Ali, pasha of Egypt, ascended the Nile as far as the foot of the rapids above Gondokoro. It soon became an ivory and slave-trading centre. In 1851 an Austrian Roman Catholic mission was established here, but it was abandoned in 1859. It was at Gondokoro that J. H. Speke and J. A. Grant, descending the Nile after their discovery of its source, met, on the 15th of February 1863, Mr (afterwards Sir) Samuel Baker and his wife who were journeying up the river. In 1871 Baker, then governor-general of the equatorial provinces of Egypt, established a military post at Gondokoro which he named Ismailia, after the then khedive. Baker made this post his headquarters, but Colonel (afterwards General) C. G. Gordon, who succeeded him in 1874, abandoned the station on account of its unhealthy site, removing to Lado. Gondokoro, however, remained a trading-station. It fell into the hands of the Mahdists in 1885. After the destruction of the Mahdist power in 1898 Gondokoro was occupied by British troops and has since formed the northernmost post on the Nile of the Uganda protectorate (see SUDAN;NILE; and UGANDA).

GONDOMAR, DIEGO SARMIENTO DE ACUÑA, COUNT OF (1567-1626), Spanish diplomatist, was the son of Garcia Sarmiento de Sotomayor, corregidor of Granada, and governor of the Canary Islands, by his marriage with Juana de Acuña, an heiress. Diego Sarmiento, their eldest son, was born in the parish of Gondomar, in the bishopric of Tuy, Galicia, Spain, on the 1st of November 1567. He inherited wide estates both in Galicia and in Old Castile. In 1583 he was appointed by Philip II. to the military command of the Portuguese frontier and sea coast of Galicia. He is said to have taken an active part in the repulse of an English coast-raid in 1585, and in the defence of the country during the unsuccessful English attack on Corunna in 1589. In 1593 he was named corregidor of Toro. In 1603 he was sent from court to Vigo to superintend the distribution of the treasure brought from America by two galleons which were driven to take refuge at Vigo, and on his return was named a member of the board of finance. In 1609 he was again employed on the coast of Galicia, this time to repel a naval attack made by the Dutch. Although he held military commands, and administrative posts, his habitual residence was at Valladolid, where he owned the Casa del Sol and was already collecting his fine library. He was known as a courtier, and apparently as a friend of the favourite, the duke of Lerma. In 1612 he was chosen as ambassador in England, but did not leave to take up his appointment till May 1613.

His reputation as a diplomatist is based on his two periods of service in England from 1613 to 1618 and from 1619 to 1622. The excellence of his latinity pleased the literary tastes of James I., whose character he judged with remarkable insight. He flattered the king's love of books and of peace, and he made skilful use of his desire for a matrimonial alliance between the prince of Wales and a Spanish infanta. The ambassador's task was to keep James from aiding the Protestant states against Spain and the house of Austria, and to avert English attacks on Spanish possessions in America. His success made him odious to the anti-Spanish and puritan parties. The active part he took in promoting the execution of Sir Walter Raleigh aroused particular animosity. He was attacked in pamphlets, and the dramatist Thomas Middleton made him a principal person in the strange political play *A Game of Chess*, which was suppressed by order of the council. In 1617 Sarmiento was created count of Gondomar. In 1618 he obtained leave to come home for his health, but was ordered to return by way of Flanders and France with a diplomatic mission. In 1619 he returned to London, and remained till 1622, when he was allowed to retire. On his return he was named a member of the royal council and governor of one of the king's palaces, and was appointed to a complimentary mission to Vienna. Gondomar was in Madrid when the prince of Wales—afterwards Charles I.—made his journey there in search of a wife. He died at the house of the constable of Castile, near Haro in the Rioja, on the 2nd of October 1626.

Gondomar was twice married, first to his niece Beatrix Sarmiento, by whom he had no children, and then to his cousin Constanza de Acuña, by whom he had four sons and three daughters. The hatred he aroused in England, which was shown by constant jeers at the intestinal complaint from which he suffered for years, was the best tribute to the zeal with which he served his own master. Gondomar collected, both before he came to London and during his residence there, a very fine library of printed books and manuscripts. Orders for the arrangement, binding and storing of his books in his house at Valladolid take a prominent place in his voluminous correspondence. In 1785 the library was ceded by his descendant and representative the marquis of Malpica to King Charles III., and it is now in the Royal Library at Madrid. A portrait of Gondomar, attributed to Valazquez, was formerly at Stowe. It was mezzotinted by Robert Cooper.

AUTHORITIES.—Gondomar's missions to England are largely dealt with in S. R. Gardiner's *History of England* (London, 1883-1884). In Spanish, Don Pascual de Gayangos wrote a useful biographical introduction to a publication of a few of his letters—*Cinco Cartas político-literarias de Don Diego Sarmiento de Acuña, Conde de Gondomar,* issued at Madrid 1869 by the *Sociedad de Bibliófilos* of the Spanish Academy; and there is a life in English by F. H. Lyon (1910).

(D. H.)

GONDOPHARES, or GONDOPHERNES, an Indo-Parthian king who ruled over the Kabul valley and the Punjab. By means of his coins his accession may be dated with practical certainty at A.D. 21, and his reign lasted for some thirty years. He is notable for his association with St Thomas in early Christian tradition. The legend is that India fell to St Thomas, who showed unwillingness to start until Christ appeared in a vision and ordered him to serve King Gondophares and build him a palace. St Thomas accordingly went to India and suffered martyrdom there. This legend is not incompatible with what is known of the chronology of Gondophares' reign.

GONDWANA, the historical name for a large tract of hilly country in India which roughly corresponds with the greater part of the present Central Provinces. It is derived from the aboriginal tribe of Gonds, who still form the largest element in the population and who were at one time the ruling power. From the 12th to as late as the 18th century three or four Gond dynasties reigned over this region with a degree of civilization that seems surprising when compared with the existing condition of the people. They built large walled cities, and accumulated immense treasures of gold and silver and jewels. On the whole, they maintained their independence fairly well against the Mahommedans, being subject only to a nominal submission and occasional payment of tribute. But when the Mahratta invaders appeared, soon after the beginning of the 18th century, the Gond kingdoms offered but a feeble resistance and the aboriginal population fled for safety to the hills. Gondwana was thus included in the dominions of the Bhonsla raja of Nagpur, from whom it finally passed to the British in 1853.

The Gonds, who call themselves Koitur or "highlanders," are the most numerous tribe of Dravidian race in India. Their total number in 1901 was 2,286,913, of whom nearly two millions were enumerated in the Central Provinces, where they form 20% of the population. They have a language of their own, with many dialects, which is intermediate between the two great Dravidian languages, Tamil and Telugu. It is unwritten and has no literature, except a little provided by the missionaries. More than half the Gonds in the Central Provinces have now abandoned their own dialects, and have adopted Aryan forms of speech. This indicates the extent to which they have become Hinduized. The higher class among them, called Raj Gonds, have been definitely admitted into Hinduism as a pure cultivating caste; but the great majority still retain the animistic beliefs, ceremonial observances and impure customs of food which are common to most of the aboriginal tribes of India.

GONFALON (the late French and Italian form, also found in other Romanic languages, of *gonfanon,* which is derived from the O.H. Ger. *gundfano,gund,* war, and *fano,* flag, cf. Mod. Ger. *Fahne,* and English "vane"), a banner or standard of the middle ages. It took the form of a small pennon attached below the head of a knight's lance, or when used in religious processions and ceremonies, or as the banner of a city or state or military order, it became a many-streamered rectangular ensign, frequently swinging from a cross-bar attached to a pole. This is the most frequent use of the word. The title of "gonfalonier," the bearer of the gonfalon, was in the middle ages both military and civil. It was borne by the counts of Vexin, as leaders of the men of Saint Denis, and when the Vexin was incorporated in the kingdom of France the title of *Gonfalonier de Sant Denis* passed to the kings of France, who thus became the bearers of the "oriflamme," as the banner of St Denis was called. "Gonfalonier" was the title of civic magistrates of various degrees of authority in many of the city republics of Italy, notably of Florence, Sienna and Lucca. At Florence the functions of the office varied. At first the gonfaloniers were the leaders of the various military divisions of the inhabitants. In 1293 was created the office of gonfalonier of justice, who carried out the orders of the signiory. By the end of the 14th century the gonfalonier was the chief of the signiory. At Lucca he was the chief magistrate of the republic. At Rome two gonfaloniers must be distinguished, that of the church and that of the Roman people; both offices were conferred by the pope. The first was usually granted to sovereigns, who were bound to defend the church and lead her armies. The second bore a standard with the letters S.P.Q.R. on any enterprise undertaken in the name of the church and the people of Rome, and also at ceremonies, processions, &c. This was granted by the pope to distinguished families. Thus the Cesarini held the office till the end of the 17th century. The Pamphili held it from 1686 till 1764.

GONG (Chinese, *gong-gong* or *tam-tam*), a sonorous or musical instrument of Chinese origin and manufacture, made in the form of a broad thin disk with a deep rim. Gongs vary in diameter from about 20 to 40 in., and they are made of bronze containing a maximum of 22 parts of tin to 78 of copper; but in many cases the proportion of tin is considerably less. Such an alloy, when cast and allowed to cool slowly, is excessively brittle, but it can be tempered and annealed in a peculiar manner. If suddenly cooled from a cherry-red heat, the alloy becomes so soft that it can be hammered and worked on the lathe, and afterwards it may be hardened by re-heating and cooling it slowly. In these properties it will be observed, the alloy behaves in a manner exactly opposite to steel, and the Chinese avail themselves of the known peculiarities for preparing the thin sheets of which gongs are made. They cool their castings of bronze in water, and after hammering out the alloy in the soft state, harden the finished gongs by heating them to a cherry-red and allowing them to cool slowly. These properties of the alloy long remained a secret, said to have been first discovered in Europe by Jean Pierre Joseph d'Arcet at the beginning of the 19th century. Riche and Champion are said to have succeeded in producing tam-tams having all the qualities and timbre of the Chinese instruments. The composition of the alloy of bronze used for making gongs is stated to be as follows:1 Copper, 76.52; Tin, 22.43; Lead, 0.62; Zinc, 0.23; Iron, 0.18. The gong is beaten with a round, hard, leather-covered pad, fitted on a short stick or handle. It emits a peculiarly sonorous sound, its complex vibrations bursting into a wave-like succession of tones, sometimes shrill, sometimes deep. In China and Japan it is used in religious ceremonies, state processions, marriages and other festivals; and it is said that the Chinese can modify its tone variously by particular ways of striking the disk.

The gong has been effectively used in the orchestra to intensify the impression of fear and horror in melodramatic scenes. The tam-tam was first introduced into a western orchestra by François Joseph Gossec in the funeral march composed at the death of Mirabeau in 1791. Gaspard Spontini used it in *La Vestale* (1807), in the finale of act II., an impressive scene in which the high pontiff pronounces the anathema on the faithless vestal. It was also used in the funeral music played when the remains of Napoleon the Great were brought back to France in 1840. Meyerbeer made use of the instrument in the scene of the resurrection of the three nuns in *Robert le diable.* Four tam-tams are now used at Bayreuth in *Parsifal* to reinforce the bell instruments, although there is no indication given in the score (see PARSIFAL). The tam-tam has been treated from its ethnographical side by Franz Heger.2

(K. S.)

1See *La grande Encyclopédie*, vol. viii. (Paris), "Bronze," p. 146a.
2*Alte Metalltrommeln aus Südost-Asien* (Leipzig, 1902). Bd. i., Text; Bd. ii., Tafeln.

GÓNGORA Y ARGOTE, LUIS DE (1561-1627), Spanish lyric poet, was born at Cordova on the 11th of July 1561. His father, Francisco de Argote, was *corregidor* of that city; the poet early adopted the surname of his mother, Leonora de Góngora, who 234was descended from an ancient family. At the age of fifteen he entered as a student of civil and canon law at the university of Salamanca; but he obtained no academic distinctions and was content with an ordinary pass degree. He was already known as a poet in 1585 when Cervantes praised him in the *Galatea*; in this same year he took minor orders, and shortly afterwards was nominated to a canonry at Cordova. About 1605-1606 he was ordained priest, and thenceforth resided principally at Valladolid and Madrid, where, as a contemporary remarks, he "noted and stabbed at everything with his satirical pen." His circle of admirers was now greatly enlarged; but the acknowledgment accorded to his singular genius was both slight and tardy. Ultimately indeed, through the influence of the duke of Sandoval, he obtained an appointment as honorary chaplain to Philip III., but even this slight honour he was not permitted long to enjoy. In 1626 a severe illness, which seriously impaired his memory, compelled his retirement to Cordova, where he died on the 24th of May 1627. An edition of his poems was published almost immediately after his death by Juan Lopez de Vicuña; the frequently reprinted edition by Hozes did not appear till 1633. The collection consists of numerous sonnets, odes, ballads, songs for the guitar, and of certain larger poems, such as the *Soledades* and the *Polifemo.* Too many of them exhibit that tortuous elaboration of style (*estilo culto*) with which the name of Góngora is inseparably associated; but though Góngora has been justly censured for affected Latinisms, unnatural transpositions, strained metaphors and frequent obscurity, it must be admitted that he was a man of rare genius,—a fact cordially acknowledged by those of his contemporaries who were most capable of judging. It was only in the hands of those who imitated Góngora's style without inheriting his genius that *culteranismo* became absurd. Besides his lyrical poems Góngora is the author of a play entitled*Las Firmezas de Isabel* and of two incomplete dramas, the *Comedia venatoria* and *El Doctor Carlino.* The only satisfactory edition of his works is that published by R. Foulché-Delbose in the *Bibliotheca Hispanica.*

See Edward Churton, *Góngora* (London, 1862, 2 vols.); M. González y Francés, *Góngora racionero* (Córdoba, 1895); M. González y Francés,*Don Luis de Góngora vindicando su fama ante el propio obispo* (Córdoba, 1899); "Vingt-six Lettres de Góngora" in the *Revue hispanique*, vol. x. pp. 184-225 (Paris, 1903).

GONIOMETER (from Gr. γωνία, angle, and μέτρον, measure), an instrument for measuring the angles of crystals; there are two kinds—the contact goniometer and the reflecting goniometer. Nicolaus Stena in 1669 determined the interfacial angles of quartz crystals by cutting sections perpendicular to the edges, the plane angles of the sections being then the angles between the faces which are perpendicular to the sections. The earliest instrument was the contact goniometer devised by Carangeot in 1783.

FIG. 1.—Contact Goniometer.

The Contact Goniometer (or *Hand-Goniometer*).—This consists of two metal rules pivoted together at the centre of a graduated semicircle (fig. 1). The instrument is placed with its plane perpendicular to an edge between two faces of the crystal to be measured, and the rules are brought into contact with the faces; this is best done by holding the crystal up against the light with the edge in the line of sight. The angle between the rules, as read on the graduated semicircle, then gives the angle between the two faces. The rules are slotted, so that they may be shortened and their tips applied to a crystal partly embedded in its matrix. The instrument represented in fig. 1 is practically the same in all its details as that made for Carangeot, and it is employed at the present day for the approximate measurement of large crystals with dull and rough faces. S. L. Penfield (1900) has devised some cheap and simple forms of contact goniometer, consisting of jointed arms and protractors made of cardboard or celluloid.

FIG. 2.—Vertical-Circle Goniometer.

The Reflecting Goniometer.—This is an instrument of far greater precision, and is always used for the accurate measurement of the angles when small crystals with bright faces are available. As a rule, the smaller the crystal the more even are its faces, and when these are smooth and bright they reflect sharply defined images of a bright object. By turning the crystal about an axis parallel to the edge between two faces, the image reflected from a second face may be brought into the same position as that formerly occupied by the image reflected from the first face; the angle through which the crystal has been rotated, as determined by a graduated circle to which the crystal is fixed, is the angle between the normals to the two faces.

Several forms of instruments depending on this principle have been devised, the earliest being the vertical-circle goniometer of W. H. Wollaston, made in 1809. This consists of a circle m (fig. 2), graduated to degrees of arc and reading with the vernier b to minutes, which turns with the milled head t about a horizontal axis. The crystal is attached with wax (a mixture of beeswax and pitch) to the holder q, and by means of the pivoted arcs it may be adjusted so that the edge between two faces (a zone-axis) is parallel to, and coincident with, the axis of the instrument. The crystal-holder and adjustment-arcs, together with the milled head s, are carried on an axis which passes through the hollow axis of the graduated circle, and may thus be rotated independently of the circle. In use, the goniometer is placed directly opposite to a window, with its axis parallel to the horizontal window-bars, and as far distant as possible. The eye is placed quite close to the crystal, and the image of an upper window-bar (or better still a slit in a dark screen) as seen in the crystal-face is made to coincide with a lower window-bar (or chalk mark on the floor) as seen directly: this is done by turning the milled head s, the reading of the graduated circle having previously been observed. Without moving the eye, the milled head t, together with the crystal, is then rotated until the image from a second face is brought into the same position; the difference between the first and second readings of the graduated circle will then give the angle between the normals of the two faces.

FIG. 3.—Horizontal-Circle Goniometer.

Several improvements have been made on Wollaston's goniometer. The adjustment-arcs have been modified; a mirror of black glass fixed to the stand beneath the crystal gives a reflected image of the signal, with which the reflection from the crystal can be more conveniently made to coincide; a telescope provided with cross-wires gives greater precision to the direction of the reflected rays of light; and with the telescope a collimator has sometimes been used.

A still greater improvement was effected by placing the graduated circle in a horizontal position, as in the instruments of E. L. Malus (1810), F. C. von Riese (1829) and J. Babinet

(1839). Many forms of the *horizontal-circle goniometer* have been constructed; they are provided with a telescope and collimator, and in construction are essentially the same as a spectrometer, with the addition of arrangements for adjusting and centring the crystal. The instrument shown in fig. 3 is made by R. Fuess of Berlin. It has four concentric axes, which enable the crystal-holder A, together with the adjustment-arcs B and centring-slides D, to be raised or lowered, or to be rotated independently of the circle H; further, either the crystal-holder or the telescope T may be rotated with the circle, while the other 235remains fixed. The crystal is placed on the holder and adjusted so that the edge (zone-axis) between two faces is coincident with the axis of the instrument. Light from an incandescent gas-burner passes through the slit of the collimator C, and the image of the slit (signal) reflected from the crystal face is viewed in the telescope. The clamp a and slow-motion screw F enable the image to be brought exactly on the cross-wires of the telescope, and the position of the circle with respect to the vernier is read through the lens. The crystal and the circle are then rotated together until the image from a second face is brought on the cross-wires of the telescope, and the angle through which they have been turned is the angle between the normals to the two faces. While measuring the angles between the faces of crystals the telescope remains fixed by the clamp β, but when this is released the instrument may be used as a spectrometer or refractometer for determining, by the method of minimum deviation, the indices of refraction of an artificially cut prism or of a transparent crystal when the faces are suitably inclined to one another.

With a one-circle goniometer, such as is described above, it is necessary to mount and re-adjust the crystal afresh for the measurement of each zone of faces (*i.e.* each set of faces intersecting in parallel edges); with very small crystals this operation takes a considerable time, and the minute faces are not readily identified again. Further, in certain cases, it is not possible to measure the angles between zones, nor to determine the position of small faces which do not lie in prominent zones on the crystal. These difficulties have been overcome by the use of a two-circle goniometer or theodolite-goniometer, which as a combination of a vertical-circle goniometer and one with a horizontal-circle was first employed by W. H. Miller in 1874. Special forms have been designed by E. S. Fedorov (1889), V. Goldschmidt (1893). S. Czapski (1893) and F. Stoeber (1898), which differ mainly in the arrangement of the optical parts. In these instruments the crystal is set up and adjusted once for all, with the axis of a prominent zone parallel to the axis of either the horizontal or the vertical circle. As a rule, only in this zone can the angles between the faces be measured directly; the positions of all the other faces, which need be observed only once, are fixed by the simultaneous readings of the two circles. These readings, corresponding to the polar distance and azimuth, or latitude and longitude readings of astronomical telescopes, must be plotted on a projection before the symmetry of the crystal is apparent; and laborious calculations are necessary in order to determine the indices of the faces and the angles between them, and the other constants of the crystal, or to test whether any three faces are accurately in a zone.

These disadvantages are overcome by adding still another graduated circle to the instrument, with its axis perpendicular to the axis of the vertical circle, thus forming a three-circle goniometer. With such an instrument measurements may be made in any zone or between any two faces without re-adjusting the crystal; further the troublesome calculations are avoided, and, indeed, the instrument may be used for solving spherical triangles. Different forms of three-circle goniometers have been designed by G. F. H. Smith (1899 and 1904), E. S. Fedorov (1900) and J. F. C. Klein (1900). Besides being used as a one-, two-, or three-circle goniometer for the measurement of the interfacial angles of crystals, and as a refractometer for determining refractive indices by the prismatic method or by total reflection, Klein's instrument, which is called a polymeter, is fitted with accessory optical apparatus which enables it to be used for examining a crystal in parallel or convergent polarized light and for measuring the optic axial angle.

Goniometers of special construction have been devised for certain purposes; for instance, the inverted horizontal-circle goniometer of H. A. Miers (1903) for measuring crystals during their growth in the mother-liquid. A. E. Tutton (1894) has combined a goniometer with lapidaries' appliances for cutting section-plates and prisms from crystals accurately in any desired direction. The instrument commonly employed for measuring the optic axial angle of biaxial crystals is really a combination of a goniometer with a polariscope. For the optical investigation of minute crystals under the microscope, various forms of stage-goniometer with one, two or three graduated circles have been constructed. An ordinary microscope fitted with cross-wires and a rotating graduated stage serves the purpose of a goniometer for measuring the plane angles of a crystal face or section, being the same in principle as the contact goniometer.

For fuller descriptions of goniometers reference may be made to the text-books of Crystallography and Mineralogy, especially to P. H. Groth,*Physikalische Krystallographie* (4th ed.,

Leipzig, 1905). See also C. Leiss, *Die optischen Instrumente der Firma R. Fuess, deren Beschreibung, Justierung und Anwendung* (Leipzig, 1899).

(L. J. S.)

GONTAUT, MARIE JOSÉPHINE LOUISE, DUCHESSE DE (1773-1857). was born in Paris on the 3rd of August 1773, daughter of Augustin François, comte de Montaut-Navailles, who had been governor of Louis XVI. and his two brothers when children. The count of Provence (afterwards Louis XVIII.) and his wife stood sponsors to Joséphine de Montaut, and she shared the lessons given by Madame de Genlis to the Orleans family, with whom her mother broke off relations after the outbreak of the Revolution. Mother and daughter emigrated to Coblenz in 1792; thence they went to Rotterdam, and finally to England, where Joséphine married the marquis Charles Michel de Gontaut-Saint-Blacard. They returned to France at the Restoration, and resumed their place at court. Madame de Gontaut became lady-in-waiting to Caroline, duchess of Berry, and, on the birth of the princess Louise (Mlle d'Artois, afterwards duchess of Parma), governess to the children of France. Next year the birth of Henry, duke of Bordeaux (afterwards known as the comte de Chambord), added to her charge the heir of the Bourbons. She remained faithful to his cause all her life. Her husband died in 1822, and in 1827 she was created duchesse de Gontaut. She followed the exiled royal family in 1830 to Holyrood Palace, and then to Prague, but in 1834, owing to differences with Pierre Louis, duc de Blacas, who thought her comparatively liberal views dangerous for the prince and princess, she received a brusque congé from Charles X. Her twin daughters, Joséphine (1796-1844) and Charlotte (1796-1818), married respectively Ferdinand de Chabot, prince de Léon and afterwards duc de Rohan, and François, comte de Bourbon-Busset. She herself wrote in her old age some naïve memoirs, which throw an odd light on the pretensions of the "governess of the children of France." She died in Paris in 1857.

See her *Memoirs* (Eng. ed., 2 vols., 1894), and *Lettres inédites* (1895).

GONVILE, EDMUND (d. 1351), founder of Gonville Hall, now Gonville and Caius College, at Cambridge, England, is thought to have been the son of William de Gonvile, and the brother of Sir Nicholas Gonvile. In 1320 he was rector of Thelnetham, Suffolk, and steward there for William, earl Warren and the earl of Lancaster. Six years later he was rector of Rushworth, and in 1342 rector of Terrington St John and commissioner for the marshlands of Norfolk. In this year he founded and endowed a collegiate church at Rushworth, suppressed in 1541. The foundation of Gonville Hall at Cambridge was effected by a charter granted by Edward III. in 1348. It was called, officially, the Hall of the Annunciation of the Blessed Virgin, but was usually known as Gunnell or Gonville Hall. Its original site was in Free-school Lane, where Corpus Christi College now stands. Gonvile apparently wished it to be devoted to training for theological study, but after his death the foundation was completed by William Bateman, bishop of Norwich and founder of Trinity Hall, on a different site and with considerably altered statutes. (See also CAIUS, JOHN.)

GONZAGA, an Italian princely family named after the town where it probably had its origin. Its known history begins with the 13th century, when Luigi I. (1267-1360), after fierce struggles supplanted his brother-in-law Rinaldo (nicknamed Passerino) Bonacolsi as lord of Mantua in August 1328, with the title of captain-genera, and afterwards of vicar-general of the empire, adding the designation of count of Mirandola and Concordia, which fief the Gonzagas held from 1328 to 1354. In July 1335 his son Guido, with the help of Filippino and Feltrino Gonzaga, wrested Reggio from the Scaligeri and held it until 1371. Luigi was succeeded by Guido (d. 1369); the latter's son Luigi II. came next in succession (d. 1382), and then Giovan Francesco I. (d. 1407), who, although at one time allied with the treacherous Gian Galeazzo Visconti, incurred the latter's enmity and all but lost his estates and his life in consequence; eventually he joined the Florentines and Bolognese, enemies of Visconti. He promoted commerce and wisely developed the prosperity of his dominions. His son Giovan Francesco II. (d. 1444) succeeded him under the regency of his uncle Carlo Malatesta and the protection of the Venetians. He became a famous general, and was rewarded for his services to the emperor Sigismund with the title of marquess of Mantua for himself and his descendants (1432), an investiture which legitimatized the usurpations of the house of Gonzaga. His son Luigi III. "il Turco" (d. 1478) likewise became a celebrated soldier, and was also a learned and liberal prince, a patron of literature and the arts. His son Federigo I. (d. 1484) followed in his father's footsteps, and served under various foreign sovereigns, including Bona of Savoy and Lorenzo de' Medici; subsequently he upheld the rights of the house of 236Este against Pope Sixtus IV. and the Venetians, whose ambitious claims were a menace to his own dominions of Ferrara and Mantova. His son Giovan

192

Francesco III. (d. 1519) continued the military traditions of the family, and commanded the allied Italian forces against Charles VIII. at the battle of Fornovo; he afterwards fought in the kingdom of Naples and in Tuscany, until captured by the Venetians in 1509. On his liberation he adopted a more peaceful and conciliatory policy, and with the help of his wife, the famous Isabella d'Este, he promoted the fine arts and letters, collecting pictures, statues and other works of art with intelligent discrimination. He was succeeded by his son Federigo II. (d. 1540), captain-general of the papal forces. After the peace of Cambrai (1529) his ally and protector, the emperor Charles V., raised his title to that of duke of Mantua in 1530; in 1536 the emperor decided the controversy for the succession of Monferrato between Federigo and the house of Savoy in favour of the former. His son Francesco I. succeeded him, and, being a minor, was placed under the regency of his uncle Cardinal Ercole; he was accidentally drowned in 1550, leaving his possessions to his brother Guglielmo. The latter was an extravagant spendthrift, but having subdued a revolt in Monferrato was presented with that territory by the emperor Maximilian II. At his death in 1587 he was succeeded by his son Vincenzo I. (d. 1612), who was more addicted to amusements than to warfare. Then followed in succession his sons Francesco II. (d. 1612), Ferdinando (d. 1626), and Vincenzo II. (d. 1627), all three incapable and dissolute princes. The last named appointed as his successor Charles, the son of Henriette, the heiress of the French family of Nevers-Rethel, who was only able to take possession of the ducal throne after a bloody struggle; his dominions were laid waste by foreign invasions and he himself was reduced to the sorest straits. He died in 1637, leaving his possessions to his grandson Charles (Carlo) II. under the regency of the latter's mother Maria Gonzaga, which lasted until 1647. Charles died in consequence of his own profligacy and was succeeded by his son Ferdinand Charles (Ferdinando Carlo), who was likewise for some years under the regency of his mother Isabella of Austria. Ferdinand Charles, another extravagant and dissolute prince, acquired the county of Guastalla by marriage in 1678, but lost it soon afterwards; he involved his country in useless warfare, with the result that in 1708 Austria annexed the duchy. On the 5th of July of the same year he died in Venice, and with him the Gonzagas of Mantua came to an end.

Of the cadet branches of the house one received the lordship of Bozzolo, another the counties of Novellara and Bagnolo, a third, of which the founder was Ferrante I. (d. 1557), retained the county of Guastalla, raised to a duchy in 1621, and came to an end with the death of Giuseppe Maria on the 16th of August 1746.

BIBLIOGRAPHY.—S. Maffei, *Annali di Mantova* (Tortona, 1675); G. Veronesi, *Quadro storico della Mirandola* (Modena, 1847); T. Affò, *Storia di Guastalla* (Guastalla, 1875, 4 vols.); Alessandro Luzio, *I Precattori d'Isabella d'Este* (Ancona, 1887); A. Luzio and R. Renier, "Francesco Gonzaga alla battaglia di Fornovo (1495). secondo i documenti Mantovani" (in *Archivio storico italiano*, ser. v. vol. vi., 205-246); *id.*, *Mantova e Urbino, Isabella d'Este e Elisabeth Gonzaga nette relazioni famigliari e nelle vicende politiche* (Turin, 1893); L. G., Pélissier, "Les Relations de François de Gonzague, marquis de Mantoue, avec Ludovico Sforza et Louis XII" (in *Annales de la faculté de Lettres de Bordeaux*, 1893); Antonino Bertolotti, "Lettere del duca di Savoia Emanuele Filiberto a Guglielmo Gonzaga, duca di Mantova" (*Arch. stor. it.*, ser. v., vol. ix. pp. 250-283); Edmondo Solari, *Lettere inedite del card. Gasparo Contarini nel carteggio del card. Ercole Gonzaga* (Venice, 1904); Arturo Segrè, *Il Richiamo di Don Ferrante Gonzaga dal governo di Milano, e sue conseguenze* (Turin, 1904).

GONZAGA, THOMAZ ANTONIO (1744-1809), Portuguese poet, was a native of Oporto and the son of a Brazilian-born judge. He spent a part of his boyhood at Bahia, where his father was *disembargador* of the appeal court, and returning to Portugal he went to the university of Coimbra and took his law degree at the age of twenty-four. He remained on there for some years and compiled a treatise of natural law on regalist lines, dedicating it to Pombal, but the fall of the marquis led him to leave Coimbra and become a candidate for a magistracy, and in 1782 he obtained the posts of *ouvidor* and *provedor* of the goods of deceased and absent persons at Villa Rica in the province of Minas Geraes in Brazil. In 1786 he was named *disembargador* of the appeal court at Bahia, and three years later, as he was about to marry a young lady of position, D. Maria de Seixas Brandão, the *Marilia* of his verses, he suddenly found himself arrested on the charge of being the principal author of a Republican conspiracy in Minas. Conducted to Rio, he was imprisoned in a fortress and interrogated, but constantly asserted his innocence. However, his friendship with the conspirators compromised him in the eyes of his absolutist judges, who, on the ground that he had known of the plot and not denounced it, sentenced him in April 1792 to perpetual exile in Angola, with the confiscation of his property. Later, this penalty was commuted into one of ten years of exile to Mozambique, with a death sentence if he should return to America. After having spent three years in prison, Gonzaga sailed in May 1792 for Mozambique and shortly after his arrival a violent fever almost ended his life. A wealthy Portuguese gentleman, married to a lady of colour, charitably received him into his house, and when the poet recovered, he married their young daughter who had nursed him through the attack. He lived in exile until his death, practising advocacy at intervals, but his last years were embittered by fits of melancholia, deepening into madness, which were brought on by the remembrance of his misfortunes. His reputation as a poet rests on a little volume of bucolics entitled *Marilia*, which includes all his published verses and is divided into two parts, corresponding with those of his life. The first extends to his imprisonment and breathes only love and pleasure, while the main theme of the second part, written in prison, is his *saudade*for *Marilia* and past happiness. Gonzaga borrowed his forms from the best models, Anacreon and Theocritus, but the matter, except for an occasional imitation of Petrarch, the natural, elegant style and the harmonious metrification, are all his own. The booklet comprises the most celebrated collection of erotic poetry dedicated to a single person in the Portuguese tongue; indeed its popularity is so great as to exceed its intrinsic merit.

Twenty-nine editions had appeared up to 1854, but the Paris edition of 1862 in 2 vols, is in every way the best, although the authenticity of the verses in its 3rd part, which do not relate to *Marilia*, is doubtful. A popular edition of the first two parts was published in 1888 (Lisbon, Corazzi). A French version of *Marilia* by Monglave and Chalas appeared in Paris in 1825, an Italian by Vegezzi Ruscalla at Turin in 1844, a Latin by Dr Castro Lopes at Rio in 1868, and there is a Spanish one by Vedia.

See Innocencio da Silva, *Diccionario bibliographico portuguez*, vol. vii. p. 320, also Dr T. Braga, *Filinto Elysio e os Dissidentas da Arcadia*(Oporto, 1901).

(E. PR.)

GONZÁLEZ-CARVAJAL, TOMAS JOSÉ (1753-1834), Spanish, poet and statesman, was born at Seville in 1753. He studied at the university of Seville, and took the degree of LL.D. at Madrid. He obtained an office in the financial department of the government; and in 1795 was made intendant of the colonies which had just been founded in Sierra Morena and Andalusia. During 1809-1811 he held an intendancy in the patriot army. He became, in 1812, director of the university of San Isidro; but having offended the government by establishing a chair of international law, he was imprisoned for five years (1815-1820). The revolution of 1820 reinstated him, but the counter-revolution of three years later forced him into exile. After four years he was allowed to return, and he died, in 1834, a member of the supreme council of war. González-Carvajal enjoyed European fame as author of metrical translations of the poetical books of the Bible. To fit himself for this work he commenced the study of Hebrew at the age of fifty-four. He also wrote other works in verse and prose, avowedly taking Luis de Leon as his model.

See biographical notice in *Biblioteca de Rivadeneyra*, vol. lxvii., *Poetas del siglo 18*.

GONZALO DE BERCEO (*c.* 1180-*c.* 1246), the earliest Castilian poet whose name is known to us, was born at Berceo, a village in the neighbourhood of Calahorra in the province of Logroño. In 1221 he became a deacon and was attached, as a secular priest, to the Benedictine monastery of San Millan de la Cogolla, in the 237diocese of Calahorra. His name is to be met with in a number of documents between the years 1237 and 1246. He wrote upwards of 13,000 verses, all on devotional subjects. His best work is a life of St Oria; others treat of the life of St Millan, of St Dominic of Silos, of the Sacrifice of the Mass, the Martyrdom of St Laurence, the visible signs preceding the Last Judgment, the Praises of Our Lady, the Miracles of Our Lady and the Lamentations of the Virgin on the Passion of her Son. He writes in the common tongue, the *roman paladino*, and his claim to the name of poet rests on his use of the *cuaderna via* (single-rhymed quatrains, each verse being of fourteen syllables). Sometimes, however, he takes the more modest title of *juglar (jongleur)*, when claiming payment for his poems. His literary attainments are not great, and he lacks imagination and animation of style, but he has a certain eloquence, and in speaking of the Virgin and the saints a certain charm, while his verse bears at times the imprint of a passionate devotion, recalling the lyrical style of the great Spanish mystics. There is, however, a very strong popular element in his writings, which explains his long vogue. The great majority of his legends of the Virgin are obviously borrowed from the collection of a Frenchman, Gautier de Coinci; but he has succeeded in making this material entirely his own by reason of a certain conciseness and a realism in detail which make his work far superior to the tedious and colourless narrative of his model.

His *Poesías* are in the *Biblioteca de autores españoles* of Rivadeneyra, vol. lvii. (1864); *La Vida de San Domingo de Silos* has been edited by J. D. FitzGerald (Paris, 1904; see the *Bibliothèque de l'École des Hautes Études*, part 149); see also F. Fernandez y Gonzalez in the *Razón* (vol. i., Madrid, 1860); N. Hergueta, "Documentos referentes a Gonzalo de Berceo," in the *Revista de archivos*, (3rd series, Feb.-March, 1904, pp. 178-179).

(P. A.)

GOOCH, SIR DANIEL, Bart. (1816-1889), English mechanical engineer, was born at Bedlington, in Northumberland, on the 16th of August 1816. At the age of fifteen, having shown a taste for mechanics, he was put to work at the Tredegar Ironworks, Monmouthshire. In 1834 he went to Warrington, where, at the Vulcan foundry, under Robert Stephenson, he acquired the principles of locomotive design. Subsequently, after passing a year at Dundee, he was engaged by the Stephensons at their Gateshead works, where he seems to have conceived that predilection for the broad gauge for which he was afterwards distinguished, through having to design some engines for a 6-foot gauge in Russia and noticing the advantages it offered in allowing greater space for the machinery, &c., as compared with the standard gauge favoured by Stephenson. In 1837, on I. K. Brunel's recommendation, he was appointed locomotive superintendent to the Great Western railway at a time when the engines possessed by the railway were very poor and inefficient. He soon improved this state of affairs, and gradually provided his employers with locomotives which were unsurpassed for general excellence and economy of working. One of the most famous, the "Lord of the Isles," was awarded a gold medal at the Great Exhibition of 1851, and when, thirty years afterwards, it was withdrawn from active service it had run more than three-quarters of a million miles, all with its original boiler. In 1864 he left the Great Western and interested himself in the problem of laying a telegraph cable across the Atlantic. At this time the "Great Eastern" was in the hands of the bondholders, of whom he himself was one of the most important, and it occurred to him that she might advantageously be utilized in the enterprise. Accordingly, at his instance she was chartered by the Telegraph Construction Company, of which also he was a director, and in 1865 was employed in the attempt to lay a cable, Gooch himself superintending operations. The cable, however, broke in mid-ocean, and the attempt was a failure. Next year it was renewed with more success, for not only was a new cable safely put in place, but the older one was picked up and spliced, so that there were two complete lines between England and America. For this achievement Gooch was created a baronet. Meanwhile the Great Western railway had fallen on evil days, being indeed on the verge of bankruptcy, when in 1866 the directors appealed to him to accept the chairmanship of the board and undertake the rehabilitation of the company. He agreed to the proposal, and was so successful in restoring its prosperity that in 1889, at the last meeting over which he presided, a dividend was declared at the rate of 7½%. Under his administration the system was greatly enlarged and consolidated by the absorption of various smaller lines, such as the Bristol and Exeter and the Cornwall railways; and his appreciation of its strategic value caused him to be a strenuous supporter of the construction of the Severn Tunnel. His death occurred on the 15th of October 1889 at his residence, Clewer Park, near Windsor.

GOOD, JOHN MASON (1764-1827), English writer on medical, religious and classical subjects, was born on the 25th of May 1764 at Epping, Essex. After attending a school at Romsey kept by his father, the Rev. Peter Good, who was a Nonconformist minister, he was, at about the age of fifteen, apprenticed to a surgeon-apothecary at Gosport. In 1783 he went to London to prosecute his medical studies, and in the autumn of 1784 he began to practise as a surgeon at Sudbury in Suffolk. In 1793 he removed to London, where he entered into partnership with a surgeon and apothecary. But the partnership was soon dissolved, and to increase his income he began to devote attention to literary pursuits. Besides contributing both in prose and verse to the *Analytical* and *Critical Reviews* and the *British* and *Monthly Magazines*, and other periodicals, he wrote a large number of works relating chiefly to medical and religious subjects. In 1794 he became a member of the British Pharmaceutical Society, and in that connexion, and especially by the publication of his work, *A History of Medicine* (1795), he did much to effect a greatly needed reform in the profession of the apothecary. In 1820 he took the diploma of M.D. at Marischal College, Aberdeen. He died at Shepperton, Middlesex, on the 2nd of January 1827. Good was not only well versed in classical literature, but was acquainted with the principal European languages, and also with Persian, Arabic and Hebrew. His prose works display wide erudition; but their style is dull and tedious. His poetry never rises above pleasant and well-versified commonplace. His translation of Lucretius, *The Nature of Things* (1805-1807), contains elaborate philological and explanatory notes, together with parallel passages and quotations from European and Asiatic authors.

GOOD FRIDAY (probably "God's Friday"), the English name for the Friday before Easter, kept as the anniversary of the Crucifixion. In the Greek Church it has been or is known as πάσχα [σταυρώσιμον], παρασκευή, παρασκευὴ μεγάλη or ἁγία, σωτηρία or τὰ σωτήρια, ἡμέρα τοῦ σταυροῦ, while among the Latins the names of most frequent occurrence are Pascha Crucis, Dies Dominicae Passionis, Parasceve, Feria Sexta Paschae, Feria Sexta Major in

Hierusalem, Dies Absolutionis. It was called Long Friday by the Anglo-Saxons1 and Danes, possibly in allusion to the length of the services which marked the day. In Germany it is sometimes designated Stiller Freitag (compare Greek, ἑβδομὰς ἄπρακτος; Latin, *hebdomas inofficiosa, non laboriosa*), but more commonly Charfreitag. The etymology of this last name has been much disputed, but there seems now to be little doubt that it is derived from the Old High German *chara*, meaning suffering or mourning.

The origin of the custom of a yearly commemoration of the Crucifixion is somewhat obscure. It may be regarded as certain that among Jewish Christians it almost imperceptibly grew out of the old habit of annually celebrating the Passover on the 14th of Nisan, and of observing the "days of unleavened bread" from the 15th to the 21st of that month. In the Gentile churches, on the other hand, it seems to be well established that originally no yearly cycle of festivals was known at all. (See EASTER.)

From its earliest observance, the day was marked by a specially rigorous fast, and also, on the whole, by a tendency to greater simplicity in the services of the church. Prior to the 4th century there is no evidence of non-celebration of the eucharist on Good Friday; but after that date the prohibition of communion 238became common. In Spain, indeed, it became customary to close the churches altogether as a sign of mourning; but this practice was condemned by the council of Toledo (633). In the Roman Catholic Church the Good Friday ritual at present observed is marked by many special features, most of which can be traced back to a date at least prior to the close of the 8th century (see the Ordo Romanus in Muratori's *Liturg. Rom. Vet.*). The altar and officiating clergy are draped in black, this being the only day on which that colour is permitted. Instead of the epistle, sundry passages from Hosea, Habakkuk, Exodus and the Psalms are read. The gospel for the day consists of the history of the Passion as recorded by St John. This is often sung in plain-chaunt by three priests, one representing the "narrator," the other two the various characters of the story. The singing of this is followed by bidding prayers for the peace and unity of the church, for the pope, the clergy, all ranks and conditions of men, the sovereign, for catechumens, the sick and afflicted, heretics and schismatics, Jews and heathen. Then follows the "adoration of the cross" (a ceremony derived from the church of Jerusalem and said to date back to near the time of Helena's "invention of the cross"); the hymns *Pange lingua* and *Vexilla regis* are sung, and then follows the "Mass of the Presanctified." The name is derived from the fact that it is celebrated with elements consecrated the day before, the liturgy being omitted on this day. The priest merely places the Sacrament on the altar, censes it, elevates and breaks the host, and communicates, the prayers and responses interspersed being peculiar to the day. This again is followed by vespers, with a special anthem; after which the altar is stripped in silence. In many Roman Catholic countries—in Spain, for example—it is usual for the faithful to spend much time in the churches in meditation on the "seven last words" of the Saviour; no carriages are driven through the streets; the bells and organs are silent; and in every possible way it is sought to deepen the impression of a profound and universal grief. In the Greek Church also the Good Friday fast is excessively strict; as in the Roman Church, the Passion history is read and the cross adored; towards evening a dramatic representation of the entombment takes place, amid open demonstrations of contempt for Judas and the Jews. In Lutheran churches the organ is silent on this day, and altar, font and pulpit are draped in black, as indeed throughout Holy Week. In the Church of England the history of the Passion from the gospel according to John is also read; the collects for the day are based upon the bidding prayers which are found in the Ordo Romanus. The "three hours" service, borrowed from Roman Catholic usage and consisting of prayers, addresses on the "seven last words from the cross" and intervals for meditation and silent prayer, has become very popular in the Anglican Church, and the observance of the day is more marked than formerly among Nonconformist bodies, even in Scotland.

1See Johnson's *Collection of Ecclesiastical Laws* (vol. i., anno 957): "Housel ought not to be hallowed on Long Friday, because Christ suffered for us on that day."

GOODMAN, GODFREY (1583-1656), bishop of Gloucester, was born at Ruthin, Denbighshire, and educated at Westminster and Cambridge. He took orders in 1603, and in 1606 obtained the living of Stapleford Abbots, Essex, which he held together with several other livings. He was canon of Windsor from 1617 and dean of Rochester 1620-1621, and became bishop of Gloucester in 1625. From this time his tendencies towards Roman Catholicism constantly got him into trouble. He preached an unsatisfactory sermon at court in 1626, and in 1628 incurred charges of introducing popery at Windsor. In 1633 he secured the see of Hereford by bribery, but Archbishop Laud persuaded the king to refuse his consent. In 1638 he was said to be converted to Rome, and two years later he was imprisoned for refusing to sign the new canons denouncing popery and affirming the divine right of kings. He afterwards signed and was released on bail, but next year the bishops who had signed were all imprisoned in the Tower, by order of parliament, on the charge of treason. After eighteen weeks' imprisonment Goodman was allowed to return to his diocese. About 1650 he settled in London, where he died a confessed Roman Catholic. His best known book is *The Fall of Man* (London, 1616).

GOODRICH, SAMUEL GRISWOLD (1793-1860), American author, better known under the pseudonym of "Peter Parley," was born, the son of a Congregational minister, at Ridgefield, Connecticut, on the 19th of August 1793. He was largely self-educated, became an assistant in a country store at Danbury, Conn., in 1808, and at Hartford, Conn., in 1811, and from 1816 to 1822 was a bookseller and publisher at Hartford. He visited Europe in 1823-1824, and in 1826 removed to Boston, where he continued in the publishing business, and from 1828 to 1842 he published an illustrated annual, the *Token*, to which he was a frequent contributor both in prose and verse. A selection from these contributions was published in 1841 under the title *Sketches from a Student's Window*. The *Token* also contained some of the earliest work of Nathaniel Hawthorne, N. P. Willis, Henry W. Longfellow and Lydia Maria Child. In 1841 he established *Merry's Museum*, which he continued to edit till 1854. In 1827 he began, under the name of "Peter Parley," his series of books for the young, which embraced geography, biography, history, science and miscellaneous tales. Of these he was the sole author of only a few, but in 1857 he wrote that he was "the author and editor of about 170 volumes," and that about seven millions had been sold. In 1857 he published *Recollections of a Lifetime*, which contains a list both of the works of which he was the author or editor and of the spurious works published under his name. By his writings and publications he amassed a large fortune. He was chosen a member of the Massachusetts House of Representatives in 1836, and of the state Senate in 1837, his competitor in the last election being Alexander H. Everett, and in 1851-1853 he was consul at Paris, where he remained till 1855, taking advantage of his stay to have several of his works translated into French. After his return to America he published, in 1859, *Illustrated History of the Animal Kingdom*. He died, in New York, on the 9th of May 1860.

His brother, CHARLES AUGUSTUS GOODRICH (1790-1862), a Congregational clergyman, published various ephemeral books, and helped to compile some of the "Peter Parley" series.

GOODRICH, or GOODRICKE, THOMAS (d. 1554), English ecclesiastic, was a son of Edward Goodrich of East Kirkby, Lincolnshire, and was educated at Corpus Christi College, Cambridge, afterwards becoming a fellow of Jesus College in the same university. He was among the divines consulted about the legality of Henry VIII.'s marriage with Catherine of Aragon, became one of the royal chaplains about 1530, and was consecrated bishop of Ely in 1534. He was favourable to the Reformation, helped in 1537 to draw up the *Institution of a Christian Man* (known as the *Bishops' Book*), and translated the Gospel of St John for the revised New Testament. On the accession of Edward VI. in 1547 the bishop was made a privy councillor, and took a conspicuous part in public affairs during the reign. "A busy secular spirited man," as Burnet calls him, he was equally opposed to the zealots of the "old" and the "new religion." He assisted to compile the First Prayer Book of Edward VI., was one of the commissioners for the trial of Bishop Gardiner, and in January 1551-1552 succeeded Rich as lord high chancellor. This office he continued to hold during the nine days' reign of "Queen Jane" (Lady Jane Grey); but he continued to make his peace with Queen Mary, conformed to the restored religion, and, though deprived of the chancellorship, was allowed to keep his bishopric until his death on the 10th of May 1554.

See the *Dict. Nat. Biog.*, where further authorities are cited.

GOODSIR, JOHN (1814-1867), Scottish anatomist, born at Anstruther, Fife, on the 20th of March 1814, was the son of Dr John Goodsir, and grandson of Dr John Goodsir of Largo. He was educated at the burgh and grammar-schools of his native place and at the university of St Andrews. In 1830 he was apprenticed to a surgeon-dentist in Edinburgh, where he studied anatomy under Robert Knox, and in 1835 he joined his father in practice at Anstruther. Three years later he communicated to the British Association a paper on the pulps and sacs of the human teeth, his researches on the whole process of dentition 239being at this time distinguished by their completeness; and about the same date, on the nomination of Edward Forbes, he was elected to the famous coterie called the "Universal Brotherhood of the Friends of Truth," which comprised artists, scholars, naturalists and others, whose relationship became a potent influence in science. With Forbes he worked on marine zoology, but human anatomy, pathology and morphology formed his chief study. In 1840 he moved to Edinburgh, where in the following year he was appointed conservator of the museum of the College of Surgeons, in succession to William Macgillivray. Much of his reputation rested on his knowledge of the anatomy of tissues. In his lectures in the theatre of the college in 1842-1843 he evidenced the largeness of his observation of cell-life, both physiologically and pathologically, insisting on the importance of the cell as a centre of nutrition, and pointing out that the organism is subdivided into a number of departments. R. Virchow recognized his indebtedness to these discoveries by dedicating his *Cellular Pathologie* to Goodsir, as "one of the earliest and most acute observers of cell-life." In 1843 Goodsir obtained the post of curator in the university of Edinburgh; the following year he was appointed demonstrator of anatomy, and in 1845 curator of the entire museum. A year later he was elected to the chair of anatomy in the university, and devoted all his energies to anatomical research and teaching.

Human myology was his strong point; no one had laboured harder at the dissecting-table; and he strongly emphasized the necessity of practice as a means of research. He believed that anatomy, physiology and pathology could never be properly advanced without daily consideration and treatment of disease. In 1848 he became a fellow of the Royal College of Surgeons, and in the same year he joined the Highland and Agricultural Society, acting as chairman of the veterinary department, and advising on strictly agricultural matters. In 1847 he delivered a series of systematic lectures on the comparative anatomy of the invertebrata; and, about this period, as member of an aesthetic club, he wrote papers on the natural principles of beauty, the aesthetics of the ugly, of smell, the approbation or disapprobation of sounds, &c. Owing to the failing health of Professor Robert Jameson, Goodsir was induced to deliver the course of lectures on natural history during the summer of 1853.

The lectures were long remembered for their brilliancy, but the infinite amount of thought and exertion which they cost broke down the health of the lecturer. Goodsir, nevertheless, persevered in his labours, writing in 1855 on organic electricity, in 1856 on morphological subjects, and afterwards on the structure of organized forms. His speculations in the latter domain gave birth to his theory of a triangle as the mathematical figure upon which nature had built up both the organic and inorganic worlds, and he hoped to complete this triangle theory of formation and law as the greatest of his works. In his lectures on the skull and brain he held the doctrine that symmetry of brain had more to do with the higher faculties than bulk or form. He died at Wardie, near Edinburgh, on the 6th of March 1867, in the same cottage in which his friend Edward Forbes died. His anatomical lectures were remarkable for their solid basis of fact; and no one in Britain took so wide a field for survey or marshalled so many facts for anatomical tabulation and synthesis.

See *Anatomical Memoirs of John Goodsir, F.R.S., edited by W. Turner, with Memoir by H. Lonsdale* (2 vols., Edinburgh, 1868), in which Goodsir's lectures, addresses and writings are epitomized; *Proc. Roy. Soc.* vol. iv. (1868); *Trans. Bot. Soc. Edin.* vol. ix. (1868).

GOODWILL, in the law of property, a term of somewhat vague significance. It has been defined as every advantage which has been acquired in carrying on a business, whether connected with the premises in which the business has been carried on, or with the name of the firm by whom it has been conducted (*Churton* v. *Douglas*, 1859, Johns, 174). Goodwill may be either professional or trade. Professional goodwill usually takes the form of the recommendation by a retiring professional man, doctor, solicitor, &c., to his clients of the successor or purchaser coupled generally with an undertaking not to compete with him. Trade goodwill varies with the nature of the business with which it is connected, but there are two rights which, whatever the nature of the business may be, are invariably associated with it, viz. the right of the purchaser to represent himself as the owner of the business, and the right to restrain competition. For the purposes of the Stamp Act, the goodwill of a business is property, and the proper duty must be paid on the conveyance of such. (See also PARTNERSHIP; PATENTS.)

GOODWIN, JOHN (*c.* 1594-1665), English Nonconformist divine, was born in Norfolk and educated at Queens' College, Cambridge, where he was elected fellow in 1617. He was vicar of St Stephen's, Coleman Street, London, from 1633 to 1645, when he was ejected by parliament for his attacks on Presbyterianism, especially in his Θεομαχία(1644). He thereupon established an independent congregation, and put his literary gifts at Oliver Cromwell's service. In 1648 he justified the proceedings of the army against the parliament ("Pride's Purge") in a pamphlet *Might and Right Well Met*, and in 1649 defended the proceedings against Charles I. (to whom he had offered spiritual advice) in Ὑβριστοδίκαι. At the Restoration this tract, with some that Milton had written to Monk in favour of a republic, was publicly burnt, and Goodwin was ordered into custody, though finally indemnified. He died in 1665. Among his other writings are *Anti-Cavalierisme* (1642), a translation of the *Stratagemata Satanae* of Giacomo Aconcio, the Elizabethan advocate of toleration, tracts against Fifth-Monarchy Men, Cromwell's "Triers" and Baptists, and *Redemption Redeemed, containing a thorough discussion of ... election, reprobation and the perseverance of the* *saints* (1651, reprinted 1840). Goodwin's strongly Arminian tendencies brought him into conflict with Robert Baillie, professor of divinity of Glasgow, George Kendall, the Calvinist prebendary of Exeter, and John Owen (*q.v.*), who replied to *Redemption Redeemed* in *The Doctrine of the Saints' Perseverance*, paying a high tribute to his opponent's learning and controversial skill. Goodwin answered all three in the *Triumviri* (1658). John Wesley in later days held him in much esteem and published an abridged edition of his *Imputatio fidei*, a work on justification that had originally appeared in 1642.

Life by T. Jackson (London, 1839).

GOODWIN, NATHANIEL CARL (1857-   ), American actor, was born in Boston on the 25th of July 1857. While clerk in a large shop he studied for the stage, and made his first appearance in 1873 in Boston in Stuart Robson's company as the newsboy in Joseph Bradford's *Law*. He made an immediate success by his imitations of popular actors. A hit in the burlesque *Black-eyed Susan* led to his taking part in Rice and Goodwin's *Evangeline* company. It was at this time that he married Eliza Weathersby (d. 1887), an English actress with whom he played in B. E. Woolfl's *Hobbies*. It was not until 1889, however, that Nat Goodwin's talent as a comedian of the "legitimate" type began to be recognized. From that time he appeared in a number of plays designed to display his drily humorous method, such as Brander Matthews' and George H. Jessop's *A Gold Mine*, Henry Guy Carleton's *A Gilded Fool* and *Ambition*, Clyde Fitch's *Nathan Hale*, H. V. Esmond's *When we were Twenty-one*, &c. Till 1903 he was associated in his performances with his third wife, the actress Maxine Elliott (b. 1873), whom he married in 1898; this marriage was dissolved in 1908.

GOODWIN, THOMAS (1600-1680), English Nonconformist divine, was born at Rollesby, Norfolk, on the 5th of October 1600, and was educated at Christ's College, Cambridge, where in 1616 he graduated B.A. In 1619 he removed to Catharine Hall, where in 1620 he was elected fellow. In 1625 he was licensed a preacher of the university; and three years afterwards he became lecturer of Trinity Church, to the vicarage of which he was presented by the king in 1632. Worried by his bishop, who was a zealous adherent of Laud, he resigned all his preferments and left the university in 1634. He lived for some time in London, where in 1638 he married the daughter of an alderman; but in the following year he withdrew to Holland, and for some time was pastor of a small congregation of English merchants and refugees at Arnheim. Returning to London soon after Laud's impeachment by the Long Parliament, he ministered for some years to the 240Independent congregation meeting at Paved Alley Church, Lime Street, in the parish of St Dunstan's-in-the-East, and rapidly rose to considerable eminence as a preacher; in 1643 he was chosen a member of the Westminster Assembly, and at once identified himself with the Congregational party, generally referred to in contemporary documents as "the dissenting brethren." He frequently preached by appointment before the Commons, and in January 1650 his talents and learning were rewarded by the House with the presidentship of Magdalen College, Oxford, a post which he held until the Restoration. He rose into high favour with the protector, and was one of his intimate advisers, attending him on his death-bed. He was also a commissioner for the inventory of the Westminster Assembly, 1650, and for the approbation of preachers, 1653, and together with John Owen (*q.v.*) drew up an amended Westminster Confession in 1658. From 1660 until his death on the 23rd of February 1680 he lived in London, and devoted himself exclusively to theological study and to the pastoral charge of the Fetter Lane Independent Church.

The works published by Goodwin during his lifetime consist chiefly of sermons printed by order of the House of Commons; but he was also associated with Philip Nye and others in the preparation of the *Apologeticall Narration* (1643). His collected writings, which include expositions of the Epistle to the Ephesians and of the Apocalypse, were published in five folio volumes between 1681 and 1704, and were reprinted in twelve 8vo volumes (Edin., 1861-1866). Characterized by abundant yet one-sided reading, remarkable at once for the depth and for the narrowness of their observation and spiritual experience, often admirably thorough in their workmanship, yet in style intolerably prolix—they fairly exemplify both the merits and the defects of the special school of religious thought to which they belong. Calamy's estimate of Goodwin's qualities may be quoted as both friendly and just. "He was a considerable scholar and an eminent divine, and had a very happy faculty in descanting upon Scripture so as to bring forth surprising remarks, which yet generally tended to illustration." A memoir, derived from his own papers, by his son (Thomas Goodwin, "the younger," 1650?-1716?, Independent minister at London and Pinner, and author of the *History of the Reign of Henry V.*) is prefixed to the fifth volume of his collected works; as a "patriarch and Atlas of Independency" he is also noticed by

Anthony Wood in the*Athenae Oxonienses*. An amusing sketch, from Addison's point of view, of the austere and somewhat fanatical president of Magdalen is preserved in No. 494 of the *Spectator*.

GOODWIN, WILLIAM WATSON (1831-   ), American classical scholar, was born in Concord, Massachusetts, on the 9th of May 1831. He graduated at Harvard in 1851, studied in Germany, was tutor in Greek at Harvard in 1856-1860, and Eliot professor of Greek there from 1860 until his resignation in 1901. He became an overseer of Harvard in 1903. In 1882-1883 he was the first director of the American School for Classical Studies at Athens. Goodwin edited the *Panegyricus* of Isocrates (1864) and Demosthenes *On The Crown* (1901); and assisted in preparing the seventh edition of Liddell and Scott's *Greek-English Lexicon*. He revised an English version by several writers of *Plutarch's Morals* (5 vols., 1871; 6th ed., 1889), and published the Greek text with literal English version of Aeschylus' *Agamemnon* (1906) for the Harvard production of that play in June 1906. As a teacher he did much to raise the tone of classical reading from that of a mechanical exercise to literary study. But his most important work was his *Syntax of the Moods and Tenses of the Greek Verb* (1860), of which the seventh revised edition appeared in 1877 and another (enlarged) in 1890. This was "based in part on Madvig and Krüger," but, besides making accessible to American students the works of these continental grammarians, it presented original matter, including a "radical innovation in the classification of conditional sentences," notably the "distinction between particular and general suppositions." Goodwin's *Greek Grammar* (elementary edition, 1870; enlarged 1879; revised and enlarged 1892) gradually superseded in most American schools the*Grammar* of Hadley and Allen. Both the *Moods and Tenses* and the *Grammar* in later editions are largely dependent on the theories of Gildersleeve for additions and changes. Goodwin also wrote a few elaborate syntactical studies, to be found in *Harvard Studies in Classical Philology*, the twelfth volume of which was dedicated to him upon the completion of fifty years as an alumnus of Harvard and forty-one years as Eliot professor.

GOODWIN SANDS, a dangerous line of shoals at the entrance to the Strait of Dover from the North Sea, about 6 m. from the Kent coast of England, from which they are separated by the anchorage of the Downs. For this they form a shelter. They are partly exposed at low water, but the sands are shifting, and in spite of lights and bell-buoys the Goodwins are frequently the scene of wrecks, while attempts to erect a lighthouse or beacon have failed. Tradition finds in the Goodwins the remnant of an island called Lomea, which belonged to Earl Godwine in the first half of the 11th century, and was afterwards submerged, when the funds devoted to its protection were diverted to build the church steeple at Tenterden (*q.v.*). Four lightships mark the limits of the sands, and also signal by rockets to the lifeboat stations on the coast when any vessel is in distress on the sands. Perhaps the most terrible catastrophe recorded here was the wreck of thirteen ships of war during a great storm in November 1703.

GOODWOOD, a mansion in the parish of Boxgrove, in the Chichester parliamentary division of Sussex, England, 4 m. N.E. of Chichester. It was built from designs of Sir William Chambers with additions by Wyatt, after the purchase of the property by the first duke of Richmond in 1720. The park is in a hilly district, and is enriched with magnificent trees of many varieties, including some huge cedars. In it is a building containing a Roman slab recording the construction of a temple to Minerva and Neptune at Chichester. There is mention of a British tributary prince named Cogidubnus, who perhaps served also as a Roman official. A reference to early Christianity in Britain has been erroneously read into this inscription. On the racecourse a famous annual meeting, dating from 1802, is held in July. The parish church of SS. Mary and Blaize, Boxgrove, is almost entirely a rich specimen of Early English work.

GOODYEAR, CHARLES (1800-1860), American inventor, was born at New Haven, Connecticut, on the 29th of December 1800, the son of Amasa Goodyear, an inventor (especially of farming implements) and a pioneer in the manufacture of hardware in America. The family removed to Naugatuck, Conn., when Charles was a boy; he worked in his father's button factory and studied at home until 1816, when he apprenticed himself to a firm of hardware merchants in Philadelphia. In 1821 he returned to Connecticut and entered into a partnership with his father at Naugatuck, which continued till 1830, when it was terminated by business reverses. Already he was interested in an attempt to discover a method of treatment by which india-rubber could be made into merchandizable articles that would stand extremes of heat and cold. To the solution of this problem the next ten years of his life were devoted. With ceaseless energy and unwavering faith in the successful outcome of his labours, in the face of repeated failures and hampered by poverty, which several times led him to a debtor's prison, he persevered in his endeavours. For a time he seemed to have succeeded with a treatment (or "cure") of the rubber with *aqua fortis*. In

1836 he secured a contract for the manufacture by this process of mail bags for the U.S. government, but the rubber fabric was useless at high temperatures. In 1837 he met and worked with Nathaniel Hayward (1808-1865), who had been an employee of a rubber factory in Roxbury and had made experiments with sulphur mixed with rubber. Goodyear bought from Hayward the right to use this imperfect process. In 1839, by dropping on a hot stove some india-rubber mixed with sulphur, he discovered accidentally the process for the vulcanization of rubber. Two years more passed before he could find any one who had faith enough in his discovery to invest money in it. At last, in 1844, by which time he had perfected his process, his first patent was granted, and in the subsequent years more than sixty patents were granted to him for the application of his original process to various uses. Numerous infringements had to be fought in the courts, the decisive victory coming in 1852 in the case of *Goodyear* v. *Day*, in which his rights were defended by Daniel Webster and opposed by Rufus Choate. In 1852 he went to England, where articles made under his patents had been displayed at the International Exhibition of 1851, but he 241was unable to establish factories there. In France a company for the manufacture of vulcanized rubber by his process failed, and in December 1855 he was arrested and imprisoned for debt in Paris. Owing to the expense of the litigation in which he was engaged and to bad business management, he profited little from his inventions. He died in New York City on the 1st of July 1860. He wrote an account of his discovery entitled *Gum-Elastic and its Varieties* (2 vols., New Haven, 1853-1855).

See also B. K. Peirce, *Trials of an Inventor, Life and Discoveries of Charles Goodyear* (New York, 1866); James Parton, *Famous Americans of Recent Times* (Boston, 1867); and Herbert L. Terry, *India Rubber and its Manufacture* (New York, 1907).

GOOGE, BARNABE (1540-1594), English poet, son of Robert Googe, recorder of Lincoln, was born on the 11th of June 1540 at Alvingham, Lincolnshire. He studied at Christ's College, Cambridge, and at New College, Oxford, but does not seem to have taken a degree at either university. He afterwards removed to Staple's Inn, and was attached to the household of his kinsman, Sir William Cecil. In 1563 he became a gentleman pensioner to Queen Elizabeth. He was absent in Spain when his poems were sent to the printer by a friend, L. Blundeston. Googe then gave his consent, and they appeared in 1563 as *Eglogs, Epytaphes, and Sonettes.* There is extant a curious correspondence on the subject of his marriage with Mary Darrell, whose father refused Googe's suit on the ground that she was bound by a previous contract. The matter was decided by the intervention of Sir William Cecil with Archbishop Parker, and the marriage took place in 1564 or 1565. Googe was provost-marshal of the court of Connaught, and some twenty letters of his in this capacity are preserved in the record office. He died in February 1594. He was an ardent Protestant, and his poetry is coloured by his religious and political views. In the third "Eglog," for instance, he laments the decay of the old nobility and the rise of a new aristocracy of wealth, and he gives an indignant account of the sufferings of his co-religionists under Mary. The other eclogues deal with the sorrows of earthly love, leading up to a dialogue between Corydon and Cornix, in which the heavenly love is extolled. The volume includes epitaphs on Nicholas Grimald, John Bale and on Thomas Phaer, whose translation of Virgil Googe is uncritical enough to prefer to the versions of Surrey and of Gavin Douglas. A much more charming pastoral than any of those contained in this volume, "Phyllida was a fayer maid" (*Tottel's Miscellany*) has been ascribed to Barnabe Googe. He was one of the earliest English pastoral poets, and the first who was inspired by Spanish romance, being considerably indebted to the *Diana Enamorada* of Montemayor.

His other works include a translation from Marcellus Palingenius (said to be an anagram for Pietro Angelo Manzolli) of a satirical Latin poem, *Zodiacus vitae* (Venice, 1531?), in twelve books, under the title of *The Zodyake of Life* (1560); *The Popish Kingdome, or reign of Antichrist*(1570), translated from Thomas Kirchmayer or Naogeorgus; *The Spiritual Husbandrie* from the same author, printed with the last; *Foure Bookes of Husbandrie* (1577), collected by Conradus Heresbachius; and *The Proverbes of ... Lopes de Mendoza* (1579).

GOOLE, a market town and port in the Osgoldcross parliamentary division of the West Riding of Yorkshire, England, at the confluence of the Don and the Ouse, 24 m. W. by S. from Hull, served by the North Eastern, Lancashire & Yorkshire, Great Central and Asholme joint railways. Pop. of urban district (1901) 16,576. The town owes its existence to the construction of the Knottingley canal in 1826 by the Aire and Calder Navigation Company, after which, in 1829, Goole was made a bonding port. Previously it had been an obscure hamlet. The port was administratively combined with that of Hull in 1885. It is 47 m. from the North Sea (mouth of the Humber), and a wide system of inland navigation opens from it. There are eight docks supplied with timber ponds, quays, warehouses and other accommodation. The depth of water is

21 or 22 ft. at high water, spring tides. Chief exports are coal, stone, woollen goods and machinery; imports, butter, fruit, indigo, logwood, timber and wool. Industries include the manufacture of alum, sugar, rope and agricultural instruments, and iron-founding. Ship-building is also carried on, and there is a large dry dock and a patent slip for repairing vessels. Passenger steamship services are worked in connexion with the Lancashire & Yorkshire railway to Amsterdam, Antwerp, Bruges, Copenhagen, Rotterdam and other north European ports. The handsome church of St John the Evangelist, with a lofty tower and spire, dates from 1844.

GOOSE (a common Teut. word, O. Eng. *gós*, pl. *gés*, Ger. *Gans*, O. Norse *gás*, from Aryan root, *ghans*, whence Sans. *haṇsá*, Lat. *anser* (for *hanser*), Gr. χήν, &c.), the general English name for a considerable number of birds, belonging to the family *Anatidae* of modern ornithologists, which are mostly larger than ducks and less than swans. Technically the word goose is reserved for the female, the male being called gander (A.-S. *gandra*).

The most important species of goose, and the type of the genus *Anser*, is undoubtedly that which is the origin of the well-known domestic race (seePOULTRY), the *Anser ferus* or *A. cinereus* of most naturalists, commonly called in English the grey or grey lag1 goose, a bird of exceedingly wide range in the Old World, apparently breeding where suitable localities are to be found in most European countries from Lapland to Spain and Bulgaria. Eastwards it extends to China, but does not seem to be known in Japan. It is the only species indigenous to the British Islands, and in former days bred abundantly in the English Fen-country, where the young were caught in large numbers and kept in a more or less reclaimed condition with the vast flocks of tame-bred geese that at one time formed so valuable a property to the dwellers in and around the Fens. It is impossible to determine when the wild grey lag goose ceased from breeding in England, but it certainly did so towards the end of the 18th century, for Daniell mentions (*Rural Sports*, iii. 242) his having obtained two broods in one season. In Scotland this goose continues to breed sparingly in several parts of the Highlands and in certain of the Hebrides, the nests being generally placed in long heather, and the eggs seldom exceeding five or six in number. It is most likely the birds reared here that are from time to time obtained in England, for at the present day the grey lag goose, though once so numerous, is, and for many years has been, the rarest species of those that habitually resort to the British Islands. The domestication of this species, as Darwin remarks (*Animals and Plants under Domestication*, i. 287), is of very ancient date, and yet scarcely any other animal that has been tamed for so long a period, and bred so largely in captivity, has varied so little. It has increased greatly in size and fecundity, but almost the only change in plumage is that tame geese commonly lose the browner and darker tints of the wild bird, and are more or less marked with white—being often indeed wholly of that colour.2 The most generally recognized breeds of domestic geese are those to which the distinctive names of Emden and Toulouse are applied; but a singular breed, said to have come from Sevastopol, was introduced into western Europe about the year 1856. In this the upper plumage is elongated, curled and spirally twisted, having their shaft transparent, and so thin that it often splits into fine filaments, which, remaining free for an inch or more, often coalesce again;3 while the quills are aborted, so that the birds cannot fly.

242

The other British species of typical geese are the bean-goose (*A. segetum*), the pink-footed (*A. brachyrhynchus*) and the white-fronted (*A. albifrons*). On the continent of Europe, but not yet recognized as occurring in Britain, is a small form of the last (*A. erythropus*) which is known to breed in Lapland. All these, for the sake of discrimination, may be divided into *two* groups—(1) those having the "nail" at the tip of the bill white, or of a very pale flesh colour, and (2) those in which this "nail" is black. To the former belong the grey lag goose, as well as *A. albifrons* and *A. erythropus*, and to the latter the other two. *A. albifrons* and *A. erythropus*, which differ little but in size,—the last being not much bigger than a mallard (*Anas boschas*),—may be readily distinguished from the grey lag goose by their bright orange legs and their mouse-coloured upper wing-coverts, to say nothing of their very conspicuous white face and the broad black bars which cross the belly, though the last two characters are occasionally observable to some extent in the grey lag goose, which has the bill and legs flesh-coloured, and the upper wing-coverts of a bluish-grey. Of the second group, with the black "nail," *A. segetum* has the bill long, black at the base and orange in the middle; the feet are also orange, and the upper wing-coverts mouse-coloured, as in *A. albifrons* and *A. erythropus*, while *A. brachyrhynchus* has the bill short, bright pink in the middle, and the feet also pink, the upper wing-coverts being nearly of the same bluish-grey as in the grey lag goose. Eastern Asia possesses in *A. grandis* a third species of this group, which chiefly differs from *A. segetum* in its larger size. In North America there is only one species of typical goose, and that belongs to the white-"nailed" group. It very nearly resembles *A. albifrons*, but is larger, and has been described as distinct under the name of *A. gambeli*. Central Asia and India possess in the bar-headed goose (*A. indicus*) a bird easily distinguished from any of the foregoing by the character implied by its English name; but it is certainly somewhat abnormal, and, indeed, under the name of *Eulabia*, has been separated from the genus *Anser*, which has no other member indigenous to the Indian Region, nor any at all to the Ethiopian, Australian or Neotropical Regions.

America possesses by far the greatest wealth of Anserine forms. Beside others, presently to be mentioned, its northern portions are the home of all the species of snow-geese belonging to the genus *Chen*. The first of these is *C. hyperboreus*, the snow-goose proper, a bird of large size, and when adult of a pure white, except the primaries, which are black. This has long been deemed a visitor to the Old World, and sometimes in considerable numbers, but the later discovery of a smaller form, *C. albatus*, scarcely differing except in size, throws some doubt on the older records, especially since examples which have been obtained in the British Islands undoubtedly belong to this lesser bird, and it would be satisfactory to have the occurrence in the Old World of the true *C. hyperboreus* placed on a surer footing. So nearly allied to the species last named as to have been often confounded with it, is the blue-winged goose, *C. coerulescens*, which is said never to attain a snowy plumage. Then we have a very small species, long ago described as distinct by Samuel Hearne, the Arctic traveller, but until 1861 discredited by ornithologists. Its distinctness has now been fully recognized, and it has received, somewhat unjustly, the name of *C. rossi*. Its face is adorned with numerous papillae, whence it has been removed by Elliot to a separate genus, *Exanthemops*, and for the same reason it has long been known to the European residents in the fur countries as the "horned wavey"—the last word being a rendering of a native name, *Wawa*, which signifies goose. Finally, there appears to belong to this section, though it has been frequently referred to another (*Chloephaga*), and has also been made the type of a distinct genus (*Philacte*), the beautiful emperor goose, *P. canagica*, which is almost peculiar to the Aleutian Islands, though straying to the continent in winter, and may be recognized by the white edging of its remiges.

The southern portions of the New World are inhabited by about half a dozen species of geese not nearly akin to the foregoing, and separated as the genus *Chloephaga*. The most noticeable of them are the rock or kelp goose, *C. antarctica*, and the upland goose, *C. magellanica*. In both of these the sexes are totally unlike in colour, but in others a greater similarity obtains.4 Formerly erroneously associated with the birds of this group comes one which belongs to the northern hemisphere, and is common to the Old World as well as the New. It contains the geese which have received the common names of bernacles or brents,5 and the scientific appellations of *Bernicla* and *Branta*—for the use of either of which much may be said by nomenclaturists. All the species of this section are distinguished by their general dark sooty colour, relieved in some by white of greater or less purity, and by way of distinction from the members of the genus *Anser*, which are known as grey geese, are frequently called by fowlers black geese. Of these, the best known both in Europe and North America is the brent-goose—the *Anas bernicla* of Linnaeus, and the *B. torquata* of many modern writers—a truly marine bird, seldom (in Europe at least) quitting salt-water, and coming southwards in vast flocks towards autumn, frequenting bays and estuaries on the British coasts, where it lives chiefly on sea-grass (*Zostera maritima*). It is known to breed in Spitsbergen and in Greenland. A form which is by some ornithologists deemed a good species, and called by them *B. nigricans*, occurs chiefly on the Pacific coast of North America. In it the black of the neck, which in the common brent terminates just above the breast, extends over most of the lower parts. The true bernacle-goose,6 the *B. leucopsis* of most authors, is but a casual visitor to North America, but is said to breed in Iceland, and occasionally in Norway. Its usual *incunabula*, however, still form one of the puzzles of the ornithologist, and the difficulty is not lessened by the fact that it will breed freely in semi-captivity, while the brent-goose will not. From the latter the bernacle-goose is easily distinguished by its larger size and white cheeks. Hutchins's goose (*B. Hutchinsi*) seems to be its true representative in the New World. In this the face is dark, but a white crescentic or triangular patch extends from the throat on either side upwards behind the eye. Almost exactly similar in coloration to the last, but greatly superior in size, and possessing 18 rectrices, while all the foregoing have but 16, is the common wild goose of America, *B. canadensis*, which, for more than two centuries has been introduced into Europe, where it propagates so freely that it has been included by nearly all the ornithologists of this quarter of the globe as a member of its fauna. An allied form, by some deemed a species, is *B. leucopareia*, which ranges over the western part of North America, and, though having 18 rectrices, is distinguished by a white collar round the lower part of the neck. The most diverse species of this group of geese are the beautiful *B. ruficollis*, a native of north-eastern Asia, which occasionally strays to western Europe, and has been obtained more than once in Britain, and that which is peculiar to the Hawaian archipelago, *B. sandvicensis*.

The largest living goose is that called the Chinese, Guinea or swan-goose, *Cygnopsis cygnoides*, and this is the stock whence the domestic geese of several eastern countries have sprung. It may often be seen in English parks, and it is found to cross readily with the common tame goose, the offspring being fertile, 243and Blyth has said that these crosses are very abundant in India. The true home of the species is in eastern Siberia or Mongolia. It is distinguished by its long smooth neck, marked dorsally by a chocolate streak. The reclaimed form is usually distinguished by the knob at the base of the bill, but the evidence of many observers shows that this is not found in the wild race. Of this bird there is a perfectly white breed.

We have next to mention a very curious form, *Cereopsis novae-hollandiae*, which is peculiar to Australia, and is a more terrestrial type of goose than any other now existing. Its short, decurved bill and green cere give it a very peculiar expression, and its almost uniform grey plumage, bearing rounded black spots, is also remarkable. It bears captivity well, breeding in confinement, but is now seldom seen. It appears to have been formerly very abundant in many parts of Australia, from which it has of late been exterminated. Some of its peculiarities seem to have been still more exaggerated in a bird that is wholly extinct, the *Cnemiornis calcitrans* of New Zealand, the remains of which were described in full by Sir R. Owen in 1873 (*Trans. Zool. Society*, ix. 253). Among the first portions of this singular bird that were found were the *tibiae*, presenting an extraordinary development of the *patella*, which, united with the shank-bone, gave rise to the generic name applied. For some time the affinity of the owner of this wonderful structure was in doubt, but all hesitation was dispelled by the discovery of a nearly perfect skeleton, now in the British Museum, which proved the bird to be a goose, of great size, and unable, from the shortness of its wings, to fly. In correlation with this loss of power may also be noted the dwindling of the keel of the sternum. Generally, however, its osteological characters point to an affinity to *Cereopsis*, as was noticed by Dr Hector (*Trans. New Zeal. Institute*, vi. 76-84), who first determined its Anserine character.

Birds of the genera *Chenalopex* (the Egyptian and Orinoco geese), *Plectropterus*, *Sarcidiornis*, *Chlamydochen* and some others, are commonly called geese. It seems uncertain whether they should be grouped with the *Anserinae*. The males of all, like those of the above-mentioned genus *Chloëphaga*, appear to have that curious enlargement at the junction of the bronchial tubes and the trachea which is so characteristic of the ducks or *Anatinae*.

(A. N.)

1The meaning and derivation of this word *lag* had long been a puzzle until Skeat suggested (*Ibis*, 1870, p. 301) that it signified late, last, or slow, as in *laggard*, a loiterer, *lagman*, the last man, *lagteeth*, the posterior molar or "wisdom" teeth (as the last to appear), and *lagclock*, a clock that is behind time. Thus the grey lag goose is the grey goose which in England when the name was given was not migratory but *lagged* behind the other wild species at the season when they betook themselves to their northern breeding-quarters. In connexion with this word, however, must be noticed the curious fact mentioned by Rowley (*Orn. Miscell.*, iii. 213), that the flocks of tame geese in Lincolnshire are urged on by their drivers with the cry of "lag'em, lag'em."

2From the times of the Romans white geese have been held in great estimation, and hence, doubtless, they have been preferred as breeding stock, but the practice of plucking geese alive, continued for so many centuries, has not improbably also helped to perpetuate this variation, for it is well known to many bird-keepers that a white feather is often produced in place of one of the natural colour that has been pulled out.

3In some English counties, especially Norfolk and Lincoln, it was no uncommon thing formerly for a man to keep a stock of a thousand geese, each of which might be reckoned to rear on an average seven goslings. The flocks were regularly taken to pasture and water, just as sheep are, and the man who tended them was called the gooseherd, corrupted into gozzerd. The birds were plucked five times in the year, and in autumn the flocks were driven to London or other large markets. They travelled at the rate of about a mile an hour, and would get over nearly 10 m. in the day. For further particulars the reader may be referred to Pennant's *British Zoology*; Montagu's *Ornithological Dictionary*; Latham's *General History of Birds*; and Rowley's *Ornithological Miscellany* (iii. 206-215), where some account also may be found of the goose-fatting at Strassburg.

4See Sclater and Salvin, Proc. Zool. Society (1876), pp. 361-369.

5The etymology of these two words is exceedingly obscure. The ordinary spelling bernicle seems to be wrong, if we may judge from the analogy of the French*Bernache*. In both words the *e* should be sounded as *a*.

6The old fable, perhaps still believed by the uneducated in some parts of the world, was that bernacle-geese were produced from the barnacles (*Lepadidae*) that grow on timber exposed to salt-water.

GOOSE (GAME OF), an ancient French game, said to have been derived from the Greeks, very popular at the close of the middle ages. It was played on a piece of card-board upon which was drawn a fantastic scroll, called the *jardin de l'Oie* (goose-garden), divided into 63 spaces marked with certain emblems, such as dice, an inn, a bridge, a labyrinth, &c. The emblem inscribed on 1 and 63, as well as every ninth space between, was a goose. The object was to land one's counter in number 63, the number of spaces moved through being determined by throwing two dice. The counter was advanced or retired according to the space on which it was placed. For instance if it rested on the inn it must remain there until each adversary, of which there might be several, had played twice; if it rested on the *death's head* the player must begin over again; if it went beyond 63 it must be retired a certain number of spaces. The game was usually played for a stake, and special fines were exacted for resting on certain spaces. At the end of the 18th century a variation of the game was called the *jeu de la Révolution Française*.

GOOSEBERRY, *Ribes Grossularia*, a well-known fruit-bush of northern and central Europe, placed in the same genus of the natural order to which it gives name (Ribesiaceae) as the closely allied currants. It forms a distinct section *Grossularia*, the members of which differ from the true currants chiefly in their spinous stems, and in their flowers growing on short footstalks, solitary, or two or three together, instead of in racemes.

The wild gooseberry is a small, straggling bush, nearly resembling the cultivated plant,— the branches being thickly set with sharp spines, standing out singly or in diverging tufts of two or three from the bases of the short spurs or lateral leaf shoots, on which the bell-shaped flowers are produced, singly or in pairs, from the groups of rounded, deeply-crenated 3- or 5-lobed leaves. The fruit is smaller than in the garden kinds, but is often of good flavour; it is generally hairy, but in one variety smooth, constituting the *R. Uva-crispa* of writers; the colour is usually green, but plants are occasionally met with having deep purple berries. The gooseberry is indigenous in Europe and western Asia, growing naturally in alpine thickets and rocky woods in the lower country, from France eastward, perhaps as far as the Himalaya. In Britain it is often found in copses and hedgerows and about old ruins, but has been so long a plant of cultivation that it is difficult to decide upon its claim to a place in the native flora of the island. Common as it is now on some of the lower slopes of the Alps of Piedmont and Savoy, it is uncertain whether the Romans were acquainted with the gooseberry, though it may possibly be alluded to in a vague passage of Pliny: the hot summers of Italy, in ancient times as at present, would be unfavourable to its cultivation. Abundant in Germany and France, it does not appear to have been much grown there in the middle ages, though the wild fruit was held in some esteem medicinally for the cooling properties of its acid juice in fevers; while the old English name, *Fea-berry*, still surviving in some provincial dialects, indicates that it was similarly valued in Britain, where it was planted in gardens at a comparatively early period. William Turner describes the gooseberry in his *Herball*, written about the middle of the 16th century, and a few years later it is mentioned in one of Thomas Tusser's quaint rhymes as an ordinary object of garden culture. Improved varieties were probably first raised by the skilful gardeners of Holland, whose name for the fruit, *Kruisbezie*, may have been easily corrupted into the present English vernacular word.1 Towards the end of the 18th century the gooseberry became a favourite object of cottage-horticulture, especially in Lancashire, where the working cotton-spinners have raised numerous varieties from seed, their efforts having been chiefly directed to increasing the size of the fruit. Of the many hundred sorts enumerated in recent horticultural works, few perhaps equal in flavour some of the older denizens of the fruit-garden, such as the "old rough red" and "hairy amber." The climate of the British Islands seems peculiarly adapted to bring the gooseberry to perfection, and it may be grown successfully even in the most northern parts of Scotland; indeed, the flavour of the fruit is said to improve with increasing latitude. In Norway even, the bush flourishes in gardens on the west coast nearly up to the Arctic circle, and it is found wild as far north as 63°. The dry summers of the French and German plains are less suited to it, though it is grown in some hilly districts with tolerable success. The gooseberry in the south of England will grow well in cool situations, and may be sometimes seen in gardens near London flourishing under the partial shade of apple trees; but in the north it needs full exposure to the sun to bring the fruit to perfection. It will succeed in almost any soil, but prefers a rich loam or black alluvium, and, though naturally a plant of rather dry places, will do well in moist land, if drained.

The varieties are most easily propagated by cuttings planted in the autumn, which root rapidly, and in a few years form good fruit-bearing bushes. Much difference of opinion prevails regarding the mode of pruning this valuable shrub; it is probable that in different situations it may require varying treatment. The fruit being borne on the lateral spurs, and on the shoots of the last year, it is the usual practice to shorten the side branches in the winter, before the buds begin to expand; some reduce the longer leading shoots at the same time, while others prefer to nip off the ends of these in the summer while they are still 244succulent. When large fruit is desired, plenty of manure should be supplied to the roots, and the greater portion of the berries picked off while still small. If standards are desired, the gooseberry may be with advantage grafted or budded on stocks of some other species of *Ribes*, R. *aureum*, the ornamental golden currant of the flower garden, answering well for the purpose. The giant gooseberries of the Lancashire "fanciers" are obtained by the careful culture of varieties specially raised with this object, the growth being encouraged by abundant manuring, and the removal of all but a very few berries from each plant. Single gooseberries of nearly 2 oz. in weight have been occasionally exhibited; but the produce of such fanciful horticulture is generally insipid. The bushes at times suffer much from the ravages of the caterpillars of the gooseberry or magpie moth, *Abraxas grossulariata*, which often strip the branches of leaves in the early summer, if not destroyed before the mischief is accomplished. The most effectual way of getting rid of this pretty but destructive insect is to look over each bush carefully, and pick off the larvae by hand; when larger they may be shaken off by striking the branches, but by that time the harm is generally done—the eggs are laid on the leaves of the previous season. Equally annoying in some years is the smaller larva of the V-moth, *Halias vanaria*, which often appears in great numbers, and is not so readily removed. The gooseberry is sometimes attacked by the grub of the gooseberry sawfly, *Nematus ribesii*, of which several broods appear in the course of the spring and summer, and are very destructive. The grubs bury themselves in the ground to pass into the pupal state; the first brood of flies, hatched just as the bushes are coming into leaf in the spring, lay their eggs on the lower side of the leaves, where the small greenish larvae soon after emerge. For the destruction of the first broods it has been recommended to syringe the bushes with tar-water; perhaps a very weak solution of carbolic acid might prove more effective. The powdered root of white hellebore is said to destroy both this grub and the caterpillars of the gooseberry moth and V-moth; infusion of foxglove, and tobacco-water, are likewise tried by some growers. If the fallen leaves are carefully removed from the ground in the autumn and burnt, and the surface of the soil turned over with the fork or spade, most eggs and chrysalids will be destroyed.

FIG. 1.—A Fungal Disease of the Gooseberry (*Aecidium Grossulariae*.)

1, Leaf showing patches of cluster-cups on surface; 2, Fruit, showing same; 3, Cluster-cups much enlarged.

The gooseberry was introduced into the United States by the early settlers, and in some parts of New England large quantities of the green fruit are produced and sold for culinary use in the towns; but the excessive heat of the American summer is not adapted for the healthy maturation of the berries, especially of the English varieties. Perhaps if some of these, or those raised in the country, could be crossed with one of the indigenous species, kinds might be obtained better fitted for American conditions of culture, although the gooseberry does not readily hybridize. The attacks of the American gooseberry mildew have largely contributed to the failure of the crop in America.

Occasionally the gooseberry is attacked by the fungus till recently called *Aecidium Grossulariae*, which forms little cups with white torn edges clustered together on reddish spots on the leaves or fruits (fig. 1). It has recently been discovered that the spores contained in these cups will not reproduce the disease on the gooseberry, but infect species of *Carex* (sedges) on which they produce a fungus of a totally different appearance. This stage in the life-history of the parasite gives its name to the whole fungus, so that it is now known as *Puccinia Pringsheimiana*. Both *uredospores* and *teleutospores* are formed on the sedge, and the latter live through the winter and produce the disease on the gooseberry in the succeeding year. In cases where the disease proves troublesome the sedges in the neighbourhood should be destroyed.

From George Massee's *Text-Book of Plant Diseases*, by permission of Duckworth & Co.

FIG. 2.—Gooseberry Mildew (Microsphaeria Grossulariae.)

1, Leaf attacked by the fungus; 2, Fructification or *perithecium*, the end of one of its numerous appendages is shown more highly magnified in 3, 4, 5, spore sacs (*asci*) from the *perithecium*, containing spores.

A much more prevalent disease is that caused by *Microsphaeria Grossulariae*. This is a mildew growing on the surface of the leaf and sending suckers into the epidermis. The white mycelium gives the leaves of the plant the appearance of having been whitewashed (fig. 2). Numerous white spores are produced in the summer which are able to germinate immediately, and later small blackish fruits (*perithecia*) are produced that pass uninjured through the winter liberating the spores they contain in the spring, which infect the young developing leaves of the bush. In bad cases the plants are greatly injured but frequently little harm is done. Attacked plants should be sprayed with potassium sulphide.

An allied fungus, *Sphaerotheca mors-uvae*, of much greater virulence, has recently appeared in England, causing the disease known as "American gooseberry mildew" (fig. 3A). In the main the mode of attack is similar to that of the last-mentioned, but not only are the leaves attacked, but the tips of the young shoots and the fruits become covered by the cobweb-like mycelium, the attack frequently resulting in the death of the shoots and the destruction of the fruits. After a 245time the mycelium becomes rusty brown and produces the winter form of the fungus. Through the winter the shoots are covered thickly with the brown mycelium and in the spring the spores contained in the perithecia germinate and start the infection anew, as in the case of the European mildew. This fungus has recently been the subject of legislation, and when it appears in a district strong repressive measures are called for. In bad cases the attacked bushes should be destroyed, while in milder attacks frequent spraying with potassium sulphide and the pruning off and immediate destruction by fire of all the young shoots showing the mildew should be resorted to.

From the *Journal of the Board of Agriculture* (May 1907), by permission of the Dept. of Agriculture and Technical Instruction for Ireland.

FIG. 3A.—American Gooseberry Mildew (*Sphaerotheca mors-uvae*). Plant with leaves and fruit attacked by the fungus.

The gooseberry, when ripe, yields a fine wine by the fermentation of the juice with water and sugar, the resulting sparkling liquor retaining much of the flavour of the fruit. By similarly treating the juice of the green fruit, picked just before it ripens, an effervescing wine is produced, nearly resembling some kinds of champagne, and, when skilfully prepared, far superior to much of the liquor sold under that name. Brandy has been made from ripe gooseberries by distillation; by exposing the juice with sugar to the acetous fermentation a good vinegar may be obtained. The gooseberry, when perfectly ripe, contains a large quantity of sugar, most abundant in the red and amber varieties; in the former it amounts to from 6 to upwards of 8%. The acidity of the fruit is chiefly due to malic acid.

FIG. 3B.—1, Fructification (*perithecium*) bursting, ascus containing spores protruding; 2, Ascus with spores more highly magnified.

Several other species of the sub-genus produce edible fruit, though none have as yet been brought under economic culture. Among them may be noticed *R. oxyacanthoides* and *R. Cynosbati*, abundant in Canada and the northern parts of the United States, and *R. gracile*, common along the Alleghany range. The group is a widely distributed one in the north temperate zone,—one species is found in Europe extending to the Caucasus and North Africa (Atlas Mountains), five occur in Asia and nineteen in North America, the range extending southwards to Mexico and Guatemala.

1The first part of the word has been usually treated as an etymological corruption either of this Dutch word or the allied Ger. *Krausbeere*, or of the earlier forms of the Fr. *groseille*. The *New English Dictionary* takes the obvious derivation from "goose" and "berry" as probable; "the grounds on which plants and fruits have received names associating them with animals are so commonly inexplicable, that the want of appropriateness in the meaning affords no sufficient ground for assuming that the word is an etymologizing corruption." Skeat (*Etym. Dict.*, 1898) connects the French, Dutch and German words, and finds the origin in the M.H.G. *krus*, curling, crisped, applied here to the hairs on the fruit. The French word was latinized as *grossularia* and confused with *groseus*, thick, fat.

GOOTY, a town and hill fortress in southern India, in the Anantapur district of Madras, 48 m. E. of Bellary. Pop. (1901) 9682. The town is surrounded by a circle of rocky hills, connected by a wall. On the highest of these stands the citadel, 2100 ft. above sea-level and 1000 ft. above the surrounding country. Here was the stronghold of Morari Rao Ghorpade, a famous Mahratta warrior and ally of the English, who was ultimately starved into surrender by Hayder Ali in 1775.

GOPHER (*Testudo polyphemus*), the only living representative on the North American continent of the genus *Testudo* of the family *Testudinidae* or land tortoises; it occurs in the south-eastern parts of the United States, from Florida in the south to the river Savannah in the north. Its carapace, which is oblong and remarkably compressed, measures from 12-18 in. in extreme length, the shields which cover it being grooved, and of a yellow-brown colour. It is characterized by the shape of the front lobe of the plastron, which is bent upwards and extends beyond the carapace. The gopher abounds chiefly in the forests, but occasionally visits the open plains, where it does great damage, especially to the potato crops, on which it feeds. It is a nocturnal animal, remaining concealed by day in its deep burrow, and coming forth at night to feed. The eggs, five in number, almost round and 1½ in. in diameter, are laid in a separate cavity near the entrance. The flesh of the gopher or mungofa, as it is also called, is considered excellent eating.

The name "gopher" is more commonly applied to certain small rodent mammals, particularly the pocket-gopher.

GÖPPINGEN, a town of Germany, in the kingdom of Württemberg, on the right bank of the Fils, 22 m. E.S.E. of Stuttgart on the railway to Friedrichshafen. Pop. (1905) 20,870. It possesses a castle built, partly with stones from the ruined castle of Hohenstaufen, by Duke Christopher of Württemberg in the 16th century and now used as public offices, two Evangelical churches, a Roman Catholic church, a synagogue, a classical school, and a modern school. The manufactures are considerable and include linen and woollen cloth, leather, glue, paper and toys. There are machine shops and tanneries in the town. Three m. N. of the town are the ruins of the castle of Hohenstaufen. Göppingen originally belonged to the house of Hohenstaufen, and in 1270 came into possession of the counts of Württemberg. It was surrounded by walls in 1129, and was almost entirely rebuilt after a fire in 1782.

See Pfeiffer, *Beschreibung und Geschichte der Stadt Göppingen* (1885).

GORAKHPUR, a city, district and division of the United Provinces of British India. The city is situated on the left bank of the river Rapti. Pop. (1901) 64,148. It is believed to have been founded about 1400 A.D. It is the civil headquarters of the district and was formerly a military cantonment. It consists of a number of adjacent village sites, sometimes separated by cultivated land, and most of the inhabitants are agriculturists.

The DISTRICT OF GORAKHPUR has an area of 4535 sq. m. It lies immediately south of the lower Himalayan slopes, but itself forms a portion of the great alluvial plain. Only a few sandhills break the monotony of its level surface, which is, however, intersected by numerous rivers studded with lakes and marshes. In the north and centre dense forests abound, and the whole country has a verdant appearance. The principal rivers are the Rapti, the Gogra, the Gandak and Little Gandak, the Kuana, the Rohin, the Ami and the Gunghi. Tigers are found in the north, and many other wild animals abound throughout the district. The lakes are well stocked with fish. The district is not subject to very intense heat, from which it is secured by its vicinity to the hills and the moisture of its soil. Dust-storms are rare, and cool breezes from the north, rushing down the gorges of the Himalayas, succeed each short interval of warm weather. The climate is, however, relaxing. The southern and eastern portions are as healthy as most parts of the province, but the *tarai* and forest-tracts are still subject to malaria.

Gautama Buddha, the founder of the religion bearing his name, was born, and died near the boundaries of the district. From the beginning of the 6th century the country was the scene of a continuous struggle between the Bhars and their Aryan antagonists, the Rathors. About 900 the Domhatars or military Brahmans appeared, and expelled the Rathors from the town of Gorakhpur, but they also were soon driven back by other invaders. During the 15th and 16th centuries, after the district had been desolated by incessant war, the descendants of the various conquerors held parts of the territory, and each seems to have lived quite isolated, as no bridges or roads attest any intercourse with each other. Towards the end of the 16th century Mussulmans occupied Gorakhpur town, but they interfered very little with the district, and allowed it to be controlled by the native rajas. In the middle of the 18th century a formidable foe, the Banjaras from the west, so weakened the power of the rajas that they could not resist the fiscal exactions of the Oudh officials, who plundered the country to a great extent. The district formed part of the territory ceded by Oudh to the British under the treaty of 1801. During the Mutiny it was lost for a short time, but under the friendly Gurkhas the rebels were driven out. The population in 1901 was 2,957,074, showing a decrease of 3% in the decade. The district is traversed by the main line and several branches of the Bengal & North-Western railway, and the Gandak, the Gogra and the Rapti are navigable.

246

The DIVISION has an area of 9534 sq. m. The population in 1901 was 6,333,012, giving an average density of 664 persons per sq. m., being more than one to every acre, and the highest for any large tract in India.

GORAL, the native name of a small Himalayan rough-haired and cylindrical-horned ruminant classed in the same group as the chamois. Scientifically this animal is known as *Urotragus* (or *Cemas*) *goral*, and the native name is now employed as the designation of all the other members of the same genus. In addition to certain peculiarities in the form of the skull, gorals are chiefly distinguished from serows (*q.v.*) by not possessing a gland below the eye, nor a corresponding depression in the skull. Several species are known, ranging from the Himalaya to Burma, Tibet and North China. Of these, the two Himalayan gorals (*U. goral* and *U. bedfordi*) are usually found in small parties, but less commonly in pairs. They generally frequent grassy hills, or rocky ground clothed with forest; in fine weather feeding only in the mornings and evenings, but when the sky is cloudy grazing throughout the day.

GORAMY, or GOURAMY (*Osphromenus olfax*), reputed to be one of the best-flavoured freshwater fishes in the East Indian archipelago. Its original home is Java, Sumatra, Borneo and several other East Indian islands, but thence it has been transported to and acclimatized in Penang, Malacca, Mauritius and even Cayenne. Being an almost omnivorous fish and tenacious of life, it seems to recommend itself particularly for acclimatization in other tropical countries; and specimens kept in captivity become as tame as carps. It attains the size of a large turbot. Its shape is flat and short, the body covered with large scales; the dorsal and anal fins are provided with numerous spines, and the ventral fins produced into long filaments. Like *Anabas*, the climbing perch, it possesses a suprabranchial accessory respiratory organ.

G

oramy.

GÖRBERSDORF, a village and climatic health resort of Germany, in the Prussian province of Silesia, romantically situated in a deep and well-wooded valley of the Waldenburg range, 1900 ft. above the sea, 60 m. S.W. of Breslau by the railway to Friedland and 3 m. from the Austrian frontier. Pop. 700. It has four large sanatoria for consumptives, the earliest of which was founded in 1854 by Hermann Brehmer (1826-1889).

GORBODUC, a mythical king of Britain. He gave his kingdom away during his lifetime to his two sons, Ferrex and Porrex. The two quarrelled and the younger stabbed the elder. Their mother, loving the latter most, avenged his death by murdering her son, and the people, horrified at her act, revolted and murdered both her and King Gorboduc. This legend was the subject of the earliest regular English tragedy which in 1561 was played before Queen Elizabeth in the Inner Temple hall. It was written by Thomas Sackville, Lord Buckhurst and Thomas Norton in collaboration. Under the title of *Gorboduc* it was published first very corruptly in 1565, and in better form as *The Tragedy of Ferrex and Porrex* in 1570.

GORCHAKOV, or GORTCHAKOFF, a noble Russian family, descended from Michael Vsevolodovich, prince of Chernigov, who, in 1246, was assassinated by the Mongols. PRINCE ANDREY IVANOVICH (1768-1855), general in the Russian army, took a conspicuous part in the final campaigns against Napoleon. ALEXANDER IVANOVICH (1769-1825) served with distinction under his relative Suvarov in the Turkish Wars, and took part as a general officer in the Italian and Swiss operations of 1799, and in the war against Napoleon in Poland in 1806-1807 (battle of Heilsberg). PETR DMITRIEVICH (1790-1868) served under Kamenski and Kutusov in the campaign against Turkey, and afterwards against France in 1813-1814. In 1820 he suppressed an insurrection in the Caucasus, for which service he was raised to the rank of major-general. In 1828-1829 he fought under Wittgenstein against the Turks, won an action at Aidos, and signed the treaty of peace at Adrianople. In 1839 he was made governor of Eastern Siberia, and in 1851 retired into private life. When the Crimean War broke out he offered his services to the emperor Nicholas, by whom he was appointed general of the VI. army corps in the Crimea. He commanded the corps in the battles of Alma and Inkerman. He retired in 1855 and died at Moscow, on the 18th of March 1868.

PRINCE MIKHAIL DMITRIEVICH (1795-1861), brother of the last named, entered the Russian army in 1807 and took part in the campaigns against Persia in 1810, and in 1812-1815 against France. During the Russo-Turkish War of 1828-1829 he was present at the sieges of Silistria and Shumla. After being appointed, in 1830, a general officer, he was present in the campaign in Poland, and was wounded at the battle of Grochow, on the 25th of February 1831. He also distinguished himself at the battle of Ostrolenka and at the taking of Warsaw. For these services he was promoted to the rank of lieutenant-general. In 1846 he was nominated military governor of Warsaw. In 1849 he commanded the Russian artillery in the war against the Hungarians, and in 1852 he visited London as a representative of the Russian army at the funeral of the duke of Wellington. At this time he was chief of the staff of the Russian army and adjutant-general to the tsar. Upon Russia declaring war against Turkey in 1853, he was appointed commander-in-chief of the troops which occupied Moldavia and Wallachia. In 1854 he crossed the Danube and besieged Silistria, but was superseded in April by Prince Paskevich, who, however, resigned on the 8th of June, when Gorchakov resumed the command. In July the siege of Silistria was raised, and the Russian armies recrossed the Danube; in August they withdrew to Russia. In 1855 he was appointed commander-in-chief of the Russian forces in the Crimea in place of Prince Menshikov. Gorchakov's defence of Sevastopol, and final retreat to the northern part of the town, which he continued to defend till peace was signed in Paris, were conducted with skill and energy. In 1856 he was appointed governor-general of Poland in succession to Prince Paskevich. He died at Warsaw on the 30th of May 1861, and was buried, in accordance with his own wish, at Sevastopol.

PRINCE GORCHAKOV, ALEXANDER MIKHAILOVICH (1798-1883). Russian statesman, cousin of Princes Petr and Mikhail Gorchakov, was born on the 16th of July 1798, and was educated at the lyceum of Tsarskoye Selo, where he had the poet Pushkin as a school-fellow. He became a good classical scholar, and learnt to speak and write in French with facility and elegance. Pushkin in one of his poems described young Gorchakov as "Fortune's favoured son," and predicted his success. On leaving the lyceum Gorchakov entered the foreign office under Count Nesselrode. His first diplomatic work of importance was the negotiation of a marriage between the grand duchess Olga and the crown prince Charles of Württemberg. He remained at Stuttgart for some years as Russian minister and confidential adviser of the crown princess. He foretold the outbreak of the revolutionary spirit in Germany and Austria, and was credited with counselling the abdication of Ferdinand in favour of Francis Joseph. When the German confederation was re-established in 1850 in place of the parliament of Frankfort, Gorchakov was appointed Russian minister to the diet. It was here that he first met Prince Bismarck, with whom he formed a friendship which was afterwards renewed at St Petersburg. The emperor Nicholas found that his ambassador at Vienna, Baron Meyendorff, was not a sympathetic instrument for carrying out his schemes in the East. He therefore transferred Gorchakov to Vienna, where the latter remained through the critical period of the Crimean War. 247Gorchakov perceived that Russian designs against Turkey, supported by Great Britain and France, were impracticable, and he counselled Russia to make no more useless sacrifices, but to accept the bases of a pacification. At the same time, although he attended the Paris conference of 1856, he purposely abstained from affixing his signature to the treaty of peace after that of Count Orlov, Russia's chief representative. For the time, however, he made a virtue of necessity, and Alexander II., recognizing the wisdom and courage which Gorchakov had exhibited, appointed him minister of foreign affairs in place of Count Nesselrode. Not long after his accession to office Gorchakov issued a circular to the foreign powers, in which he announced that Russia proposed, for internal reasons, to keep herself as free as possible from complications abroad, and he added the now historic phrase, "*La Russie ne boude pas; elle se recueille.*" During the Polish insurrection Gorchakov rebuffed the suggestions of Great Britain, Austria and France for assuaging the severities employed in quelling it, and he was especially acrid in his replies to Earl Russell's despatches. In

July 1863 Gorchakov was appointed chancellor of the Russian empire expressly in reward for his bold diplomatic attitude towards an indignant Europe. The appointment was hailed with enthusiasm in Russia, and at that juncture Prince Chancellor Gorchakov was unquestionably the most powerful minister in Europe.

An *approchement* now began between the courts of Russia and Prussia; and in 1863 Gorchakov smoothed the way for the occupation of Holstein by the Federal troops. This seemed equally favourable to Austria and Prussia, but it was the latter power which gained all the substantial advantages; and when the conflict arose between Austria and Prussia in 1866, Russia remained neutral and permitted Prussia to reap the fruits and establish her supremacy in Germany. When the Franco-German War of 1870-71 broke out Russia answered for the neutrality of Austria. An attempt was made to form an anti-Prussian coalition, but it failed in consequence of the cordial understanding between the German and Russian chancellors. In return for Russia's service in preventing the aid of Austria from being given to France, Gorchakov looked to Bismarck for diplomatic support in the Eastern Question, and he received an instalment of the expected support when he successfully denounced the Black Sea clauses of the treaty of Paris. This was justly regarded by him as an important service to his country and one of the triumphs of his career, and he hoped to obtain further successes with the assistance of Germany, but the cordial relations between the cabinets of St Petersburg and Berlin did not subsist much longer. In 1875 Bismarck was suspected of a design of again attacking France, and Gorchakov gave him to understand, in a way which was not meant to be offensive, but which roused the German chancellor's indignation, that Russia would oppose any such scheme. The tension thus produced between the two statesmen was increased by the political complications of 1875-1878 in south-eastern Europe, which began with the Herzegovinian insurrection and culminated at the Berlin congress. Gorchakov hoped to utilize the complications in such a way as to recover, without war, the portion of Bessarabia ceded by the treaty of Paris, but he soon lost control of events, and the Slavophil agitation produced the Russo-Turkish campaign of 1877-78. By the preliminary peace of San Stefano the Slavophil aspirations seemed to be realized, but the stipulations of that peace were considerably modified by the congress of Berlin (13th June to 13th July 1878), at which the aged chancellor held nominally the post of first plenipotentiary, but left to the second plenipotentiary, Count Shuvalov, not only the task of defending Russian interests, but also the responsibility and odium for the concessions which Russia had to make to Great Britain and Austria. He had the satisfaction of seeing the lost portion of Bessarabia restored to his country by the Berlin treaty, but at the cost of greater sacrifices than he anticipated. After the congress he continued to hold the post of minister for foreign affairs, but lived chiefly abroad, and resigned formally in 1882, when he was succeeded by M. de Giers. He died at Baden-Baden on the 11th of March 1883. Prince Gorchakov devoted himself entirely to foreign affairs, and took no part in the great internal reforms of Alexander II.'s reign. As a diplomatist he displayed many brilliant qualities—adroitness in negotiation, incisiveness in argument and elegance in style. His statesmanship, though marred occasionally by personal vanity and love of popular applause, was far-seeing and prudent. In the latter part of his career his main object was to raise the prestige of Russia by undoing the results of the Crimean War, and it may fairly be said that he in great measure succeeded.

(D. M. W.)

GORDIAN, or GORDIANUS, the name of three Roman emperors. The first, Marcus Antonius Gordianus Sempronianus Romanus Africanus (A.D. 159-238), an extremely wealthy man, was descended from the Gracchi and Trajan, while his wife was the great-granddaughter of Antoninus Pius. While he gained unbounded popularity by his magnificent games and shows, his prudent and retired life did not excite the suspicion of Caracalla, in whose honour he wrote a long epic called *Antoninias.* Alexander Severus called him to the dangerous honours of government in Africa, and during his proconsulship occurred the usurpation of Maximin. The universal discontent roused by the oppressive rule of Maximin culminated in a revolt in Africa in 238, and Gordian reluctantly yielded to the popular clamour and assumed the purple. His son, Marcus Antonius Gordianus (192-238), was associated with him in the dignity. The senate confirmed the choice of the Africans, and most of the provinces gladly sided with the new emperors; but, even while their cause was so successful abroad, they had fallen before the sudden inroad of Cappellianus, legatus of Numidia and a supporter of Maximin. They had reigned only thirty-six days. Both the Gordians had deserved by their amiable character their high reputation; they were men of great accomplishments, fond of literature, and voluminous authors; but they were rather intellectual voluptuaries than able statesmen or powerful rulers. Having embraced the cause of Gordian, the senate was obliged to continue the revolt against Maximin, and appointed Pupienus Maximus and Caelius Balbinus, two of its noblest and most esteemed members, as joint emperors. At their inauguration a sedition arose, and the popular outcry for a Gordian was appeased by the association with them of M. Antonius Gordianus Pius (224-244), grandson of the elder Gordian, then a boy of thirteen. Maximin forthwith invaded Italy, but was murdered by his own troops while besieging Aquileia, and a revolt of the praetorian guards, to which Pupienus and Balbinus fell victims, left Gordian sole emperor. For some time he was under the control of his mother's eunuchs, till Timesitheus,[1] his father-in-law and praefect of the praetorian guard, persuaded him to assert his independence. When the Persians under Shapur (Sapor) I. invaded Mesopotamia, the young emperor opened the temple of Janus for the last time recorded in history, and marched in person to the East. The Persians were driven back over the Euphrates and defeated in the battle of Resaena (243), and only the death of Timesitheus (under suspicious circumstances) prevented an advance into the enemy's territory. Philip the Arabian, who succeeded Timesitheus, stirred up discontent in the army, and Gordian was murdered by the mutinous soldiers in Mesopotamia.

See lives of the Gordians by Capitolinus in the *Scriptores historiae Augustae*; Herodian vii. viii.; Zosimus i. 16, 18; Ammianus Marcellinus, xxiii. 5; Eutropius ix. 2; Aurelius Victor, *Caesares*, 27; article SHAPUR (I.); Pauly-Wissowa, *Realencyclopädie*, i. 2619 f. (von Rohden).

1For this name see footnote to SHAPUR.

GORDIUM, an ancient city of Phrygia situated on the Persian "Royal road" from Pessinus to Ancyra, and not far from the Sangarius. It lies opposite the village Pebi, a little north of the point where the Constantinople-Angora railway crosses the Sangarius. It is not to be confused with Gordiou-kome, refounded as Juliopolis, a Bithynian town on a small tributary of the Sangarius, about 47 m. in an air-line N.W. of Gordium. According to the legend, Gordium was founded by Gordius, a Phrygian peasant who had been called to the throne by his countrymen in obedience to an oracle of Zeus commanding them to select the first person that rode up to the temple of the god in a wagon. The king afterwards dedicated his car to the god, and another 248oracle declared that whoever succeeded in untying the strangely entwined knot of cornel bark which bound the yoke to the pole should reign over all Asia. Alexander the Great, according to the story, cut the knot by a stroke of his sword. Gordium was captured and destroyed by the Gauls soon after 189B.C. and disappeared from history. In imperial times only a small village existed on the site. Excavations made in 1900 by two German scholars, G. and A. Koerte, revealed practically no remains later than the middle of the 6th century B.C. (when Phrygia fell under Persian power).

See *Jahrbuch des Instituts*, Ergänzungsheft v. (1904).

(J. G. C. A.)

GORDON, the name of a Scottish family, no fewer than 157 main branches of which are traced by the family historians. A laird of Gorden, in Berwickshire, near the English border, is said to have fallen in the battle of the Standard (1138). The families of the two sons ascribed to him by tradition, Richard Gordon of Gordon and Adam Gordon of Huntly, were united by the marriage of their great-grandchildren Alicia and Sir Adam, whose grandson Sir Adam (killed at Halidon Hill, 1333) at first took the English side in the Scottish struggle for independence, and is the first member of the family definitely to emerge into history. He was justiciar of Scotland in 1310, but after Bannockburn he attached himself to Robert Bruce, who granted him in 1318 the lordship of Strathbogie in Aberdeenshire, to which Gordon gave the name of Huntly from a village on the Gordon estate in Berwickshire. He had two sons, Adam and William. The younger son, laird of Stitchel in Roxburghshire, was the ancestor of William de Gordon of Stitchel and Lochinvar, founder of the Galloway branch of the family represented in the Scottish peerage by the dormant viscounty of Kenmure (*q.v.*), created in 1633; most of the Irish and Virginian Gordons are offshoots of this stock. The elder son, Adam, inherited the Gordon-Huntly estates. He had two grandsons, Sir John (d. 1394) and Sir Adam (slain at Homildon Hill, 1403). Sir John had two illegitimate sons, Jock of Scurdargue, the ancestor of the earls of Aberdeen, and Tam of Ruthven. From these two stocks most of the northern Gordon families are derived. Sir Adam's daughter and heiress, Elizabeth, married Sir Alexander Seton, and with her husband was confirmed in 1408 in the possession of the barony of Gordon and Huntly in Berwickshire and of the Gordon lands in Aberdeen. The Seton-Gordons are their descendants. Their son Alexander was created earl of Huntly (see HUNTLY, EARLS AND MARQUESSES OF), probably in 1445; and his heirs became dukes of Gordon, George Gordon (c. 1650-1716), 4th marquess of Huntly, being created duke of Gordon in 1684. He had been educated in a French Catholic seminary, and served in the French army in the campaigns of 1673 to 1675. Under James II. he was made keeper of Edinburgh Castle on account of his religion, but he refused to support James's efforts to impose Roman Catholicism on his subjects. He offered little active resistance when the castle was besieged by William III.'s forces. After his submission he was more than once imprisoned on suspicion of Jacobite leanings, and was ordered by George I. to reside on parole in Edinburgh. For some time before his death he was separated from his wife Elizabeth Howard, daughter of the 6th duke of Norfolk. His son Alexander, 2nd duke of Gordon (c. 1678-1728), joined the Old Pretender, but gained the royal pardon after the surrender of Gordon Castle in 1716. Of his children by his wife Henrietta Mordaunt, second daughter of Charles Mordaunt, earl of Peterborough, Cosmo George (c. 1720-1752) succeeded as 3rd duke; Lord Lewis Gordon (d. 1754) took an active part in the Jacobite rising of 1745; and General Lord Adam Gordon (c. 1726-1801) became commander of the forces in Scotland in 1782, and governor of Edinburgh Castle in 1786. Lord George Gordon (q.v.) was a younger son of the 3rd duke.

The title, with the earldom of Norwich and the barony of Gordon Huntly, became extinct on the death of George, 5th duke (1770-1836), a distinguished soldier who raised the corps now known as the 2nd battalion of the Gordon Highlanders. The marquessate of Huntly passed to his cousin and heir-male, George, 5th earl of Aboyne. Lady Charlotte Gordon, sister of and co-heiress with the 5th duke, married Charles Lennox, 4th duke of Richmond, whose son took the name of Gordon-Lennox. The dukedom of Gordon was revived in 1876 in favour of the 6th duke of Richmond, who thenceforward was styled duke of Richmond and Gordon. Adam Gordon of Aboyne (d. 1537) took the courtesy title of earl of Sutherland in right of his wife Elizabeth, countess of Sutherland in her own right, sister of the 9th earl. The lawless and turbulent Gordons of Gight were the maternal ancestors of Lord Byron.

Among the many soldiers of fortune bearing the name of Gordon was Colonel John Gordon, one of the murderers of Wallenstein. Patrick Gordon (1635-1699) was born at Auchleuchries in Aberdeenshire, entered the service of Charles X. of Sweden in 1651 and served against the Poles. He changed sides more than once before he found his way to Moscow in 1661 and took service under the tsar Alexis. He became general in 1687; in 1688 he helped to secure Peter the Great's ascendancy; and later he crushed the revolt of the Streltzi. His diary was published in German (3 vols., 1849-1853, Moscow and St Petersburg), and selections from the English original by the Spalding Club (Aberdeen, 1859).

The Gordons fill a considerable place in Scottish legend and ballad. "Captain Car," or "Edom (Adam) of Gordon" describes an incident in the struggle between the Forbeses and Gordons in Aberdeenshire in 1571; "The Duke of Gordon's Daughter" has apparently no foundation in fact, though "Geordie" of the ballad is sometimes said to have been George, 4th earl of Huntly; "The Fire of Frendraught" goes back to a feud (1630) between James Crichton of Frendraught and William Gordon of Rothiemay; the "Gallant Gordons Gay" figure in "Chevy Chase"; William Gordon of Earlston, the Covenanter, appears in "Bothwell Bridge" &c.

See William Gordon (of old Aberdeen), *The History of the Ancient, Noble, and Illustrious House of Gordon* (2 vols., Edinburgh, 1726-1727), of which *A Concise History of the ... House of Gordon*, by C. A. Gordon (Aberdeen, 1754) is little more than an abridgment; *The Records of Aboyne, 1230-1681*, edited by Charles, 11th marquess of Huntly, &c. (New Spalding Club, Aberdeen, 1894); *The Gordon Book*, ed. J. M. Bulloch (1902); *The House of Gordon*, ed. J. M. Bulloch (Aberdeen, vol. i., 1903); and Mr Bulloch's *The First Duke of Gordon* (1909).

GORDON, ADAM LINDSAY (1833-1870), Australian poet, was born at Fayal, in the Azores, in 1833, the son of a retired Indian officer who taught Hindustani at Cheltenham College. Young Gordon was educated there and at Merton College, Oxford, but a youthful indiscretion led to his being sent in 1853 to South Australia, where he joined the mounted police. He then became a horsebreaker, but on his father's death he inherited a fortune and obtained a seat in the House of Assembly. At this time he had the reputation of being the best non-professional steeplechase rider in the colony. In 1867 he moved to Victoria and set up a livery stable at Ballarat. Two volumes of poems, *Sea Spray and Smoke Drift* and *Ashtaroth*, were published in this year, and two years later he gave up his business and settled at New Brighton, near Melbourne. A third volume of poetry, *Bush Ballads and Galloping Rhymes*, appeared in 1870. It brought him more praise than emolument, and, thoroughly discouraged by his failure to make good his claim to some property in Scotland to which he believed himself entitled, he committed suicide on the 24th of June 1870. His reputation rose after his death, and he became the best known and most widely popular of Australian poets. Much of Gordon's poetry might have been written in England; when, however, it is really local, it is vividly so; his genuine feeling frequently kindles into passion; his versification is always elastic and sonorous, but sometimes too reminiscent of Swinburne. His compositions are almost entirely lyrical, and their merit is usually in proportion to the degree in which they partake of the character of the ballad.

Gordon's poems were collected and published in 1880 with a biographical introduction by Marcus Clarke.

GORDON, ALEXANDER (*c.* 1692-*c.* 1754), Scottish antiquary, is believed to have been born in Aberdeen in 1692. He is the "Sandy Gordon" of Scott's *Antiquary*. Of his parentage and early history nothing is known. He appears to have 249distinguished himself in classics at Aberdeen University, and to have made a living at first by teaching languages and music. When still young he travelled abroad, probably in the capacity of tutor. He returned to Scotland previous to 1726, and devoted himself to antiquarian work. In 1726 appeared the *Itinerarium Septentrionale*, his greatest and best-known work. He was already the friend of Sir John Clerk, of Penicuik, better known as Baron Clerk (a baron of the exchequer); and the baron and Roger Gale (vice-president of the Society of Antiquaries) are the "two gentlemen, the honour of their age and country," whose letters were published, without their consent it appears, as an appendix to the *Itinerarium*. Subsequently Gordon was appointed secretary to the Society for the Encouragement of Learning, with an annual salary of £50. Resigning this post, or, as there seems reason for believing, being dismissed for carelessness in his accounts, he succeeded Dr Stukeley as secretary to the Society of Antiquaries, and also acted for a short time as secretary to the Egyptian Club, an association composed of gentlemen who had visited Egypt. In 1741 he accompanied James Glen (afterwards governor), to South Carolina. Through his influence Gordon, besides receiving a grant of land in South Carolina, became registrar of the province and justice of the peace, and filled several other offices. From his will, dated the 22nd of August 1754, it appears he had a son Alexander and a daughter Frances, to whom he bequeathed most of his property, among which were portraits of himself and of friends painted by his own hand.

See Sir Daniel Wilson, *Alexander Gordon, the Antiquary*; and his Papers in the *Proceedings of the Society of Antiquaries of Scotland*, with Additional Notes and an Appendix of Original Letters by Dr David Laing (*Proc. Soc. of Antiq. of Scot.* x. 363-382).

GORDON, CHARLES GEORGE (1833-1885), British soldier and administrator, fourth son of General H. W. Gordon, Royal Artillery, was born at Woolwich on the 28th of January 1833. He received his early education at Taunton school, and was given a cadetship in the Royal Military Academy, Woolwich, in 1848. He was commissioned as second lieutenant in the corps of Royal Engineers on the 23rd of June 1852. After passing through a course of instruction at the Royal Engineers' establishment, Chatham, he was promoted lieutenant in 1854, and was sent to Pembroke dock to assist in the construction of the fortifications then being erected for the defence of Milford Haven. The Crimean War broke out shortly afterwards, and Gordon was ordered on active service, and landed at Balaklava on the 1st of January 1855. The siege of Sevastopol was in progress, and he had his full share of the arduous work in the trenches. He was attached to one of the British columns which assaulted the Redan on the 18th of June, and was also present at the capture of that work on the 8th of September. He took part in the expedition to Kinburn, and then returned to Sevastopol to superintend a portion of the demolition of the Russian dockyard. After peace with Russia had been concluded, Gordon was attached to an international commission appointed to delimit the new boundary, as fixed by treaty, between Russia and Turkey in Bessarabia; and on the conclusion of this work he was ordered to Asia Minor on similar duty, with reference to the eastern boundary between the two countries. While so employed Gordon took the opportunity to make himself well acquainted with the geography and people of Armenia, and the knowledge of dealing with eastern nations then gained was of great use to him in after life.

He returned to England towards the end of 1858, and was then selected for the appointment of adjutant and field-works instructor at the Royal Engineers' establishment, and took up his new duties at Chatham after promotion *In China*. to the rank of captain in April 1859. But his stay in England was brief, for in 1860 war was declared against China, and Gordon was ordered out there, arriving at Tientsin in September. He was too late for the attack on the Taku forts, but was present at the occupation of Peking and destruction of the Summer Palace. He remained with the British force of occupation in northern China until April 1862, when the British troops, under the command of General Staveley, proceeded to Shanghai, in order to protect the European settlement at that place from the Taiping rebels. The Taiping revolt, which had some remarkable points of similarity with the Mahdist rebellion in the Sudan, had commenced in 1850 in the province of Kwangsi. The leader, Hung Sin Tsuan, a semi-political, semi-religious enthusiast, assumed the title of Tien Wang, or Heavenly King, and by playing on the feelings of the lower class of people gradually collected a considerable force. The Chinese authorities endeavoured to arrest him, but the imperialist troops were defeated. The area of revolt extended northwards through the provinces of Hunan and Hupeh, and down the valley of the

Yangtsze-kiang as far as the great city of Nanking, which was captured by the rebels in 1853. Here the Tien Wang established his court, and while spending his own time in heavenly contemplation and earthly pleasures, sent the assistant Wangs on warlike expeditions through the adjacent provinces. For some years a constant struggle was maintained between the Chinese imperialist troops and the Taipings, with varying success on both sides. The latter gradually advanced eastwards, and approaching the important city of Shanghai, alarmed the European inhabitants, who subscribed to raise a mixed force of Europeans and Manila men for the defence of the town. This force, which was placed under the command of an American, Frederick Townsend Ward (1831-1862), took up a position in the country west of Shanghai to check the advance of the rebels. Fighting continued round Shanghai for about two years, but Ward's force was not altogether successful, and when General Staveley arrived from Tientsin affairs were in a somewhat critical condition. He decided to clear the district of rebels within a radius of 30 m. from Shanghai, and Gordon was attached to his staff as engineer officer. A French force, under the command of Admiral Prôtet, co-operated with Staveley and Ward, with his little army, also assisted. Kahding, Singpo and other towns were occupied, and the country was fairly cleared of rebels by the end of 1862. Ward was, unfortunately, killed in the assault of Tseki, and his successor, Burgevine, having had a quarrel with the Chinese authorities, Li Hung Chang, the governor of the Kiang-su province, requested General Staveley to appoint a British officer to command the contingent. Staveley selected Gordon, who had been made a brevet-major in December 1862 for his previous services, and the nomination was approved by the British government. The choice was judicious as further events proved. In March 1863 Gordon proceeded to Sungkiang to take command of the force, which had received the name of "The Ever-Victorious Army," an encouraging though somewhat exaggerated title, considering its previous history. Without waiting to reorganize his troops he marched at once to the relief of Chansu, a town 40 m. north-west of Shanghai, which was invested by the rebels. The relief was successfully accomplished, and the operation established Gordon in the confidence of his troops. He then reorganized his force, a matter of no small difficulty, and advanced against Quinsan, which was captured, though with considerable loss. Gordon then marched through the country, seizing town after town from the rebels until at length the great city of Suchow was invested by his army and a body of Chinese imperialist troops. The city was taken on the 29th of November, and after its capture Gordon had a serious dispute with Li Hung Chang, as the latter had beheaded certain of the rebel leaders whose lives the former had promised to spare if they surrendered. This action, though not opposed to Chinese ethics, was so opposed to Gordon's ideas of honour that he withdrew his force from Suchow and remained inactive at Quinsan until February 1864. He then came to the conclusion that the subjugation of the rebels was more important than his dispute with Li, and visited the latter in order to arrange for further operations. By mutual consent no allusion was made to the death of the Wangs. This was a good example of one of Gordon's marked characteristics, that, though a man of strong personal feelings, he was always prepared to subdue them for the public benefit. He declined, however, to take any decoration or reward from the emperor for his services at the capture of Suchow. After 250 the meeting with Li Hung Chang the "Ever-Victorious Army" again advanced and took a number of towns from the rebels, ending with Chanchufu, the principal military position of the Taipings. This fell in May, when Gordon returned to Quinsan and disbanded his force. In June the Tien Wang, seeing his cause was hopeless, committed suicide, and the capture of Nanking by the imperialist troops shortly afterwards brought the Taiping revolt to a conclusion. The suppression of this serious movement was undoubtedly due in great part to the skill and energy of Gordon, who had shown remarkable qualities as a leader of men. The emperor promoted him to the rank of Titu, the highest grade in the Chinese army, and also gave him the Yellow Jacket, the most important decoration in China. He wished to give him a large sum of money, but this Gordon refused. He was promoted lieutenant-colonel for his Chinese services, and made a Companion of the Bath. Henceforth he was often familiarly spoken of as "Chinese" Gordon.

Gordon was appointed on his return to England Commanding Royal Engineer at Gravesend, where he was employed in superintending the erection of forts for the defence of the Thames. He devoted himself with energy to his official duties, and his leisure hours to practical philanthropy. All the acts of kindness which he did for the poor during the six years he was stationed at Gravesend will never be fully known. In October 1871 he was appointed British representative on the international commission which had been constituted after the Crimean War to maintain the navigation of the mouth of the river Danube, with headquarters at Galatz. During 1872 Gordon was sent to inspect the British military cemeteries in the Crimea, and when passing through Constantinople on his return to Galatz he made the acquaintance of Nubar Pasha, prime minister of Egypt, who sounded him as to whether he would take service under the khedive. Nothing further was settled at the time, but the following year he received a definite offer from the khedive, which he accepted with the consent of the British government, and proceeded to Egypt early in 1874. He was then a colonel in the army, though still only a captain in the corps of Royal Engineers.

To understand the object of the appointment which Gordon accepted in Egypt, it is necessary to give a few facts with reference to the Sudan. In 1820-22 Nubia, Sennar and Kordofan had been conquered by Egypt, and the authority of the Egyptians was subsequently extended southward, eastward to the Red Sea and westward over Darfur (conquered by Zobeir Pasha in 1874). One result of the Egyptian occupation of the country was that the slave trade was largely developed, especially in the White Nile and Bahr-el-Ghazal districts. Captains Speke and Grant, who had travelled through Uganda and came down the White Nile in 1863, and Sir Samuel Baker, who went up the same river as far as Albert Nyanza, brought back harrowing tales of the misery caused by the slave-hunters. Public opinion was considerably moved, and in 1869 the khedive Ismail decided to send an expedition up the White Nile, with the double object of limiting the evils of the slave trade and opening up the district to commerce. The command of the expedition was given to Sir Samuel Baker, who reached Khartum in February 1870, but, owing to the obstruction of the river by the sudd or grass barrier, did not reach Gondokoro, the centre of his province, for fourteen months. He met with great difficulties, and when his four years' service came to an end little had been effected beyond establishing a few posts along the Nile and placing some steamers on the river. It was to succeed Baker as governor of the equatorial regions that the khedive asked for Gordon's services, having come to the conclusion that the latter was the most likely person to bring the affair to a satisfactory conclusion. After a short stay in Cairo, Gordon proceeded to Khartum by way of Suakin and Berber, a route which he ever afterwards regarded as the best mode of access to the Sudan. From Khartum he proceeded up the White Nile to Gondokoro, where he arrived in twenty-four days, the sudd, which had proved such an obstacle to Baker, having been removed since the departure of the latter by the Egyptian governor-general. Gordon remained in the equatorial provinces until October 1876, and then returned to Cairo. The two years and a half thus spent in Central Africa was a time of incessant toil. A line of stations was established from the Sobat confluence on the White Nile to the frontier of Uganda—to which country he proposed to open a route from Mombasa—and considerable progress was made in the suppression of the slave trade. The river and Lake Albert were mapped by Gordon and his staff, and he devoted himself with wonted energy to improving the condition of the people. Greater results might have been obtained but for the fact that Khartum and the whole of the Sudan north of the Sobat were in the hands of an Egyptian governor, independent of Gordon, and not too well disposed towards his proposals for diminishing the slave trade. On arriving in Cairo Gordon informed the khedive of his reasons for not wishing to return to the Sudan, but did not definitely resign the appointment of governor of the equatorial provinces. But on reaching London he telegraphed to the British consul-general in Cairo, asking him to let the khedive know that he would not go back to Egypt. Ismail Pasha, feeling, no doubt, that Gordon's resignation would injure his prestige, wrote to him saying that he had promised to return, and that he expected him to keep his word. Upon this Gordon, to whom the keeping of a promise was a sacred duty, decided to return to Cairo, but gave an assurance to some friends that he would not go back to the Sudan unless he was appointed governor-general of the entire country. After some discussion the khedive agreed, and made him governor-general of the Sudan, inclusive of Darfur and the equatorial provinces.

One of the most important questions which Gordon had to take up on his appointment was the state of the political relations between Egypt and Abyssinia, which had been in an unsatisfactory condition for some years. The dispute *Governor General* centred round the district of Bogos, lying not far inland from Massawa, which both the khedive and King John of Abyssinia claimed as belonging to their respective dominions. War broke out in 1875, when an Egyptian expedition was despatched to Abyssinia, and was completely defeated by King John near Gundet. A second and larger expedition, under Prince Hassan, the son of the khedive, was sent the following year from Massawa. The force was routed by the Abyssinians at Gura, but Prince Hassan and his staff got back to Massawa. Matters then remained quiet until March 1877, when Gordon proceeded to Massawa to endeavour to make peace with King John. He went up to Bogos, and had an interview with Walad Michael, an Abyssinian chief and the hereditary ruler of Bogos, who had joined the Egyptians with a view to raiding on his own account. Gordon, with his usual powers of diplomacy, persuaded Michael to remain quiet, and wrote to the king proposing terms of peace. But he received no reply at that time, as John, feeling pretty secure on the Egyptian frontier after his two successful actions against the khedive's troops, had gone southwards to fight with Menelek, king of Shoa. Gordon, seeing that the Abyssinian difficulty could wait for a few months, proceeded to Khartum. Here he took up the slavery question, and proposed to issue regulations making the registration of slaves compulsory, but his proposals were not approved by the Cairo government. In the meantime an insurrection had broken out in Darfur, and Gordon proceeded to that province to relieve the Egyptian garrisons, which were considerably stronger than the force he had available, the insurgents also being far more numerous than his little army. On coming up with the main body of rebels he saw that diplomacy gave a better chance of success than fighting, and, accompanied only by an interpreter, rode into the enemy's camp to discuss the situation. This bold move, which probably no one but Gordon would have attempted, proved quite successful, as part of the insurgents joined him, and the remainder retreated to the south. The relief of the Egyptian garrisons was successfully accomplished, and Gordon visited the provinces of Berber and Dongola, whence he had again to return to the Abyssinian frontier to treat with King John. But no satisfactory settlement was arrived at, and Gordon came back to Khartum in January 1878. There he had scarcely a week's rest when the 251khedive summoned him to Cairo to assist in settling the financial affairs of Egypt. He reached Cairo in March, and was at once appointed by Ismail as president of a commission of inquiry into the finances, on the understanding that the European commissioners of the debt, who were the representatives of the bondholders, and whom Ismail regarded as interested parties, should not be members of the commission. Gordon accepted the post on these terms, but the consuls-general of the different powers refused to agree to the constitution of the commission, and it fell to the ground, as the khedive was not strong enough to carry his point. The attempt of the latter to utilize Gordon as a counterpoise to the European financiers having failed, Ismail fell into the hands of his creditors, and was deposed by the sultan in the following year in favour of his son Tewfik. After the conclusion of the financial episode, Gordon proceeded to the province of Harrar, south of Abyssinia, and, finding the administration in a bad condition, dismissed Raouf Pasha, the governor. He then returned to Khartum, and in 1879 went again into Darfur to pursue the slave traders, while his subordinate, Gessi Pasha, fought them with great success in the Bahr-el-Ghazal district and killed Suleiman, their leader and a son of Zobeir. This put an end to the revolt, and Gordon went back to Khartum. Shortly afterwards he went down to Cairo, and when there was requested by the new khedive to pay a visit to King John and make a definite treaty of peace with Abyssinia. Gordon had an interesting interview with the king, but was not able to do much, as the king wanted great concessions from Egypt, and the khedive's instructions were that nothing material was to be conceded. The matter ended by Gordon being made a prisoner and sent back to Massawa. Thence he returned to Cairo and resigned his Sudan appointment. He was considerably exhausted by the three years' incessant work, during which he had ridden no fewer than 8500 m. on camels and mules, and was constantly engaged in the task of trying to reform a vicious system of administration.

In March 1880 Gordon visited the king of the Belgians at Brussels, and King Leopold suggested that he should at some future date take charge of the Congo Free State. In April the government of the Cape Colony telegraphed *1880-1884.*to him offering the position of commandant of the Cape local forces, but he declined the appointment. In May the marquess of Ripon, who had been given the post of governor-general of India, asked Gordon to go with him as private secretary. This he agreed to do, but a few days later, feeling that he was not suitable for the position, asked Lord Ripon to release him. The latter refused to do so, and Gordon accompanied him to India, but definitely resigned his post on Lord Ripon's staff shortly afterwards. Hardly had he resigned when he received a telegram from Sir Robert Hart, inspector-general of customs in China, inviting him to go to Peking. He started at once and arrived at Tientsin in July, where he met Li Hung Chang, and learnt that affairs were in a critical condition, and that there was risk of war with Russia. Gordon proceeded to Peking and used all his influence in favour of peace. His arguments, which were given with much plainness of speech, appear to have convinced the Chinese government, and war was avoided. Gordon returned to England, and in April 1881 exchanged with a brother officer, who had been ordered to Mauritius as Commanding Royal Engineer, but who for family reasons was unable to accept the appointment. He remained in Mauritius until the March following, when, on promotion to the rank of major-general, he had to vacate the position of Commanding Royal Engineer. Just at the same time the Cape ministry telegraphed to him to ask if he would go to the Cape to consult with the government as regards settling affairs in Basutoland. The telegram stated that the position of matters was grave, and that it was of the utmost importance that the colony should secure the services of someone of proved ability, firmness and energy. Gordon sailed at once for the Cape, and saw the governor, Sir Hercules Robinson, Mr Thos. Scanlen, the premier, and Mr. J. X. Merriman, a member of the ministry, who, for political reasons, asked him not to go to Basutoland, but to take the appointment of commandant of the colonial forces at King William's Town. After a few months, which were spent in reorganizing the colonial forces, Gordon was requested to go up to Basutoland to try to arrange a settlement with the chief Masupha, one of the most powerful of the Basuto leaders. Greatly to his surprise, at the very time he was with

217

Masupha, Mr. J. W. Sauer, a member of the Cape government, was taking steps to induce Lerethodi, another chief, to advance against Masupha. This not only placed Gordon in a position of danger, but was regarded by him as an act of treachery. He advised Masupha not to deal with the Cape government until the hostile force was withdrawn, and resigned his appointment. He considered that the Basuto difficulty was due to the bad system of administration by the Cape government. That Gordon's views were correct is proved by the fact that a few years later Basutoland was separated from Cape Colony and placed directly under the imperial government. After his return to England from the Cape, being unemployed, Gordon decided to go to Palestine, a country he had long desired to visit. Here he remained for a year, and devoted his time to the study of Biblical history and of the antiquities of Jerusalem. The king of the Belgians then asked him to take charge of the Congo Free State, and he accepted the mission and returned to London to make the necessary preparations. But a few days after his arrival he was requested by the British government to proceed immediately to the Sudan. To understand the reasons for this, it is necessary briefly to recapitulate the course of events in that country since Gordon had left it in 1879.

After his resignation of the post of governor-general, Raouf Pasha, an official of the ordinary type, who, as already mentioned, had been dismissed by Gordon for misgovernment in 1878, was appointed to succeed him. As Raouf was instructed to increase the receipts and diminish the expenditure, the system of government naturally reverted to the old methods, which Gordon had endeavoured to improve. The fact that justice and firmness were succeeded by injustice and weakness tended naturally to the outbreak of revolt, and unfortunately there was a leader ready to head a rebellion—one Mahommed Ahmed, already known for some years as a holy man, who was insulted by an Egyptian official, and retiring with some followers to the island of Abba on the White Nile, proclaimed himself as the mahdi, a successor of the prophet. Raouf endeavoured to take him prisoner but without success, and the revolt spread rapidly. Raouf was recalled, and succeeded by Abdel Kader Pasha, a much stronger governor, who had some success, but whose forces were quite insufficient to cope with the rebels. The Egyptian government was too busily engaged in suppressing Arabi's revolt to be able to send any help to Abdel Kader, and in September 1882, when the British troops entered Cairo, the position in the Sudan was very perilous. Had the British government listened to the representations then made to them, that, having conquered Egypt, it was imperative at once to suppress the revolt in the Sudan, the rebellion could have been crushed, but unfortunately Great Britain would do nothing herself, while the steps she allowed Egypt to take ended in the disaster to Hicks Pasha's expedition. Then, in December 1883, the British government saw that something must be done, and ordered Egypt to abandon the Sudan. But abandonment was a policy most difficult to carry out, as it involved the withdrawal of thousands of Egyptian soldiers, civilian employés and their families. Abdel Kader Pasha was asked to undertake the work, and he agreed on the understanding that he would be supported, and that the policy of abandonment was not to be announced. But the latter condition was refused, and he declined the task. The British government then asked General Gordon to proceed to Khartum to report on the best method of carrying out the evacuation. The mission was highly popular in England. Sir Evelyn Baring (Lord Cromer) was, however, at first opposed to Gordon's appointment. His objections were overcome, and Gordon received his instructions in London on the 18th of January 1884, and started at once for Cairo, accompanied by Lieut.-Colonel J. D. H. Stewart.

At Cairo he received further instructions from Sir Evelyn Baring, and was appointed by the khedive as governor-general, with executive powers. Travelling by Korosko and Berber, he arrived at Khartum on the 18th of February, *At Khartum.* and was well received by the inhabitants, who believed that he had come to save the country from the rebels. Gordon at once commenced the task of sending the women and children and the sick and wounded to Egypt, and about two thousand five hundred had been removed before the mahdi's forces closed upon Khartum. At the same time he was impressed with the necessity of making some arrangement for the future government of the country, and asked for the help of Zobeir (*q.v.*), who had great influence in the Sudan, and had been detained in Cairo for some years. This request was made on the very day Gordon reached Khartum, and was in accordance with a similar proposal he had made when at Cairo. But, after delays which involved the loss of much precious time, the British government refused (13th of March) to sanction the appointment, because Zobeir had been a notorious slave-hunter. With this refusal vanished all hope of a peaceful retreat of the Egyptian garrisons. Wavering tribes went over to the mahdi. The advance of the rebels against Khartum was combined with a revolt in the eastern Sudan, and the Egyptian troops in the vicinity of Suakin met with constant defeat. At length a British force was sent to Suakin under the command of General Sir Gerald Graham, and routed the rebels in several hard-fought actions. Gordon telegraphed to Sir Evelyn Baring urging that the road from Suakin to Berber should be opened by a small force. But this request, though strongly supported by Baring and the British military authorities in Cairo, was refused by the government in London. In April General Graham and his forces were withdrawn from Suakin, and Gordon and the Sudan were seemingly abandoned to their fate. The garrison of Berber, seeing that there was no chance of relief, surrendered a month later and Khartum was completely isolated. Had it not been for the presence of Gordon the city would also soon have fallen, but with an energy and skill that were almost miraculous, he so organized the defence that Khartum held out until January 1885. When it is remembered that Gordon was of a different nationality and religion to the garrison and population, that he had only one British officer to assist him, and that the town was badly fortified and insufficiently provided with food, it is just to say that the defence of Khartum is one of the most remarkable episodes in military history. The siege commenced on the 18th of March, but it was not until August that the British government under the pressure of public opinion decided to take steps to relieve Gordon. General Stephenson, who was in command of the British troops in Egypt, wished to send a brigade at once to Dongola, but he was overruled, and it was not until the beginning of November that the British relief force was ready to start from Wadi Haifa under the command of Lord Wolseley. The force reached Korti towards the end of December, and from that place a column was despatched across the Bayuda desert to Metemma on the Nile. After some severe fighting in which the leader of the column, Sir Herbert Stewart, was mortally wounded, the force reached the river on the 20th of January, and the following day four steamers, which had been sent down by Gordon to meet the British advance, and which had been waiting for them for four months, reported to Sir Charles Wilson, who had taken command after Sir Herbert Stewart was wounded.*Death.*On the 24th Wilson started with two of the steamers for Khartum, but on arriving there on the 28th he found that the place had been captured by the rebels and Gordon killed two days before. A belief has been entertained that Wilson might have started earlier and saved the town, but this is quite groundless. In the first place, Wilson could not have started sooner than he did; and in the second, even if he had been able to do so, it would have made no difference, as the rebels could have taken Khartum any time they pleased after the 5th of January, when the provisions were exhausted. Another popular notion, that the capture of the place was due to treachery on the part of the garrison, is equally without foundation. The attack was made at a point in the fortifications where the rampart and ditch had been destroyed by the rising of the Nile, and when the mahdi's troops entered the soldiers were too weak to make any effectual resistance. Gordon himself expected the town to fall before the end of December, and it is really difficult to understand how he succeeded in holding out until the 26th of January. Writing on the 14th of December he said, "Now, mark this, if the expeditionary force—and I ask for no more than two hundred men—does not come in ten days, the town may fall, and I have done my best for the honour of my country." He had indeed done his best, and far more than could have been regarded as possible. To understand what he went through during the latter months of the siege, it is only necessary to read his own journal, a portion of which, dating from 10th September to 14th December 1884, was fortunately preserved and published.

Gordon was not an author, but he wrote many short memoranda on subjects that interested him, and a considerable number of these have been utilized, especially in the work by his brother, Sir Henry Gordon, entitled *Events in the Life of Charles George Gordon, from its Beginning to its End.* He was a voluminous letter-writer, and much of his correspondence has been published. His character was remarkable, and the influence he had over those with whom he came in contact was very striking. His power to command men of non-European races was probably unique. He had no fear of death, and cared but little for the opinion of others, adhering tenaciously to the course he believed to be right in the face of all opposition. Though not holding to outward forms of religion, he was a truly religious man in the highest sense of the word, and was a constant student of the Bible. To serve God and to do his duty were the great objects of his life, and he died as he had lived, carrying out the work that lay before him to the best of his ability. The last words of his last letter to his sister, written when he knew that death was very near, sum up his character: "I am quite happy, thank God, and, like Lawrence, I have *tried* to do my duty."[1]

253

AUTHORITIES.—*The Journals of Major-General Gordon at Khartoum* (1885); Lord Cromer, *Modern Egypt* (2 vols., 1908); F. R. Wingate,*Mahdiism and the Egyptian Sudan* (1891); the *British Parliamentary Paper on Egypt* (1884-1885); C. G. Gordon, *Reflections in Palestine* (1884); edited by D. C. Boulger, *General Gordon's Letters from the Crimea, the Danube, and Armenia* (1884); edited by G. B. Hill, *Colonel Gordon in Central Africa* (1881); *Letters of General C. G. Gordon to his Sister* (1888); H. W. Gordon, *Events in the Life of C. G. Gordon* (1886); Commander L. Brine, *The*

Taeping Rebellion in China (1862); A. Wilson, *Gordon's Campaigns and the Taeping Rebellion* (1868); D. C. Boulger,*Life of Gordon* (1896); A. Egmont Hake, *The Story of Chinese Gordon* (1st vol. 1884, 2nd vol. 1885); Colonel Sir W. F. Butler, *Charles George Gordon* (1889); Archibald Forbes, *Chinese Gordon* (1884); edited by A. Egmont Hake, *Events in the Taeping Rebellion* (1891); S. Mossman,*General Gordon's Diary in China* (1885); Lieutenant T. Lister, R.E., *With Gordon in the Crimea* (1891); Lieutenant-General Sir G. Graham, *Last Words with Gordon* (1887); "War Correspondent," *Why Gordon Perished* (1896).

(C. M. W.)

1With this estimate of Gordon's character may be contrasted those of Lord Cromer (the most severe of Gordon's critics), and of Lord Morley of Blackburn; in their strictures as in their praise they help to explain both the causes of the extraordinary influence wielded by Gordon over all sorts and conditions of men and also his difficulties. Lord Cromer's criticism, it should be remembered, does not deal with Gordon's career as a whole but solely with his last mission to the Sudan; Lord Morley's is a more general judgment.

Lord Cromer (*Modern Egypt*, vol. i., ch. xxvii., p. 565-571) says: "We may admire, and for my own part I do very much admire General Gordon's personal courage, his disinterestedness and his chivalrous feeling in favour of the beleaguered garrisons, but admiration of these qualities is no sufficient plea against a condemnation of his conduct on the ground that it was quixotic. In his last letter to his sister, dated December 14, 1884, he wrote: 'I am quite happy, thank God, and, like Lawrence, I have tried to do my duty' ... I am not now dealing with General Gordon's character, which was in many respects noble, or with his military defence of Khartoum, which was heroic, but with the political conduct of his mission, and from this point of view I have no hesitation in saying that General Gordon cannot be considered to have tried to do his duty unless a very strained and mistaken view be taken of what his duty was.... As a matter of public morality I cannot think that General Gordon's process of reasoning is defensible.... I do not think that it can be held that General Gordon made any serious effort to carry out the main ends of British and Egyptian policy in the Sudan. He thought more of his personal opinions than of the interests of the state.... In fact, except personal courage, great fertility in military resource, a lively though sometimes ill-directed repugnance to injustice, oppression and meanness of every description, and a considerable power of acquiring influence over those, necessarily limited in numbers, with whom he was brought into personal contact, General Gordon does not appear to have possessed any of the qualities which would have fitted him to undertake the difficult task he had in hand."

Lord Morley (*Life of Gladstone*, vol. iii., 1st ed., 1903, ch. 9, p. 151) says: "Gordon, as Mr Gladstone said, was a hero of heroes. He was a soldier of infinite personal courage and daring, of striking military energy, initiative and resource; a high, pure and single character, dwelling much in the region of the unseen. But as all who knew him admit, and as his own records testify, notwithstanding an undercurrent of shrewd common sense, he was the creature, almost the sport, of impulse; his impressions and purposes changed with the speed of lightning; anger often mastered him; he went very often by intuitions and inspirations rather than by cool inference from carefully surveyed fact; with many variations of mood he mixed, as we often see in people less famous, an invincible faith in his own rapid prepossessions while they lasted. Everybody now discerns that to despatch a soldier of this temperament on a piece of business [the mission to the Sudan in 1884] that was not only difficult and dangerous, as Sir E. Baring said, but profoundly obscure, and needing vigilant sanity and self-control, was little better than to call in a wizard with his magic. Mr Gladstone always professed perplexity in understanding why the violent end of the gallant Cavagnari in Afghanistan stirred the world so little in comparison with the fate of Gordon. The answer is that Gordon seized the imagination of England, and seized it on its higher side. His religion was eccentric, but it was religion; the Bible was the rock on which he founded himself, both old dispensation and new; he was known to hate forms, ceremonies and all the 'solemn plausibilities'; his speech was sharp, pithy, rapid and ironic; above all, he knew the ways of war and would not bear the sword for nought."